On Evil

On Evil

Thomas Aquinas

Translated by
RICHARD REGAN

Edited with an Introduction and Notes by
BRIAN DAVIES

OXFORD
UNIVERSITY PRESS

2003

OXFORD
UNIVERSITY PRESS

Oxford University Press, Inc., publishes works that further
Oxford University's objective of excellence
in research, scholarship, and education.

Oxford   New York
Auckland   Cape Town   Dar es Salaam   Hong Kong   Karachi
Kuala Lumpur   Madrid   Melbourne   Mexico City   Nairobi
New Delhi   Shanghai   Taipei   Toronto

With offices in
Argentina   Austria   Brazil   Chile   Czech Republic   France   Greece
Guatemala   Hungary   Italy   Japan   Poland   Portugal   Singapore
South Korea   Switzerland   Thailand   Turkey   Ukraine   Vietnam

Copyright © 2003 by Brian Davies and Richard Regan

Published by Oxford University Press, Inc.
198 Madison Avenue, New York, New York 10016

www.oup-usa.org

Oxford is a registered trademark of Oxford University Press

Library of Congress Cataloging-in-Publication Data
Thomas, Aquinas, Saint, 1225?-1274.
[Quaestiones disputatae de malo. English]
On evil / Thomas Aquinas ; translated by Richard Regan ; edited with
an introduction and notes by Brian Davies.
p.   cm.
Includes bibliographical references and index.
ISBN-13 978-0-19-515853-3; 978-0-19-509183-0 (pbk.)
ISBN 0-19-515853-9; 0-19-509183-3 (pbk.)
1. Good and evil. 2. Sin. I. Regan, Richard J.
II. Davies, Brian, 1951-   III. Title.
BJ225.T2 Q3413 2003
111'.84—dc21
2002155694

3 5 7 9 8 6 4 2
Printed in the United States of America
on acid-free paper

In memory of Vincent Potter S.J.

and with gratitude to Sara Penella

Preface

Is anything objectively evil? Is anything objectively good? How does what is evil differ from what is good? Can there be evil without good? Does evil have a cause? Does goodness have a cause? Do people have freedom of choice? Or is what they do always outside their control? If people can act freely, under what conditions can they be rightly thought to be responsible for what they do? And how is their behavior to be evaluated and explained? Is there such a thing as sin? If so, what is it? And how does it arise? Does it admit of degrees? Does it come from what is not human? Or does its source lie wholly in us?

These are questions that Aquinas discussed at various times in his life. But he was especially concerned with them when completing his Disputed Question *De malo* (*On Evil*). Probably prepared for publication in the early to mid-1270s, this work represents some of Aquinas's most mature thinking on goodness, badness, and human agency. Together with the Second Part of the *Summa theologiae*, it is one of his most sustained contributions to moral philosophy and theology and ranks among his major writings.

In the present work readers will find a new translation of the *De malo* based on the authoritative 1982 edition provided by the Leonine Commission. They will also find a detailed introduction designed to place the *De malo* in the context of Aquinas's life and thought. At the end of the work there are notes on certain terms used in the *De Malo,* notes on auhtors cited in it, and a list of texts referred to by Aquinas.

Some years ago I suggested to Father Vincent Potter S.J. that there was need for a new English edition of the *De malo*. Even though he was suffering from severe medical disabilities, Father Potter managed to complete a first-draft translation of the text just before he died in 1994. This draft, however, was very much a preliminary one. Richard Regan S.J. subsequently agreed to translate the *De malo* afresh, and it is his translation that appears below.

In my editorial work for this volume I owe a huge debt to Sara Penella. She has assisted me in all sort of ways, especially in the compilation of notes on authors and texts referred to in the *De malo*.

Quotations from the *Summa theologiae,* which appear in my introduction, come from the Blackfriars edition (London, 1964–80). In quoting from other works of Aquinas I have aimed, as far as possible, to use conveniently available translations of them and to give references accordingly.

Brian Davies OP

Contents

Translator's Note

Translations should be faithful and felicitous. The two objectives are often difficult to reconcile. Fidelity to the text has been my priority, but I am confident that the reader will find my translation of the *De malo* to be clear and idiomatic. Translation of some key words inevitably involves interpretation. For example, I have generally translated the word *culpa* as *moral wrong*, rather than as *fault* or *guilt*, in order better to convey the objective defect of morally evil acts with which St. Thomas was typically concerned. The notes in the translation are an abbreviated and simplified version of those that appear in the edition of the *De malo* published by the Leonine Commission. But they are sufficient to provide the reader with information about the source of citations or quotations and about cross-references. The Psalms are numbered according to the numbering in the Hebrew Bible, and all biblical references conform to the conventions of the RSV translation of the Bible. I have translated Aquinas's scriptural quotations as he phrases them, not as they appear in the Vulgate. I have cited Aristotle according to the Bekker divisions, but I have retained St. Thomas's divisions into books and chapters of works of Aristotle (except the *Ethics*) on which he wrote commentaries. For patristic citations or quotations, I have referred the reader to the Migne edition.

Richard J. Regan S.J.

Abbreviations

Abbreviations for Works of Aquinas Cited

ST	*Summa theologiae* [*Summa of Theology*]
SG	*Summa contra gentiles* [*Summa Against the Pagans*]
Comp	*Compendium theologiae* [*Compendium of Theology*]
De ver	*De veritate* [*On Truth*]
In Eth	*Sententia libri Ethicorum* [*Commentary on Aristotle's Nichomachean Ethics*]
In Meta	*In Metaphysicam Aristotelis commentaria* [*Commentary on Aristotle's Metaphysics*]
De pot	*Quaestiones Disputatae De potentia Dei* [*Disputed Questions on the Power of God*]

Biblical Abbreviations

Am.	Amos	Lam.	Lamentations
Chr.	Chronicles	Lev.	Leviticus
Cor.	Corinthians	Lk.	Luke
Dan.	Daniel	Mal.	Malachi
Dt.	Deuteronomy	Mk.	Mark
Eccl.	Ecclesiastes	Mt.	Matthew
Eph.	Ephesians	Num.	Numbers
Ex.	Exodus	Pet.	Peter
Ez.	Ezekiel	Phil.	Philippians
Gal.	Galatians	Prov.	Proverbs
Gen.	Genesis	Ps.	Psalms
Hab.	Habakkuk	Rev.	Revelation
Heb.	Hebrews	Rom.	Romans
Hos.	Hosea	Sam.	Samuel
Is.	Isaiah	Sir.	Sirach
Jas.	James	Thes.	Thessalonians
Jer.	Jeremiah	Tim.	Timothy
Jn.	John	Tob.	Tobit
Kgs.	Kings	Wis.	Wisdom of Solomon

Other Abbreviations

A., a.	article
ad	reply to objection
c.	cause
chap.	chapter
comm.	comment
d.	distinction
hom.	homily
n.	number or paragraph
PG	J. P. Migne et al., *Patrologia Graeca* (Paris, 1842–1905)
PL	J. P. Migne et al., *Patrologia Latina* (Paris, 1842–1905)
prop.	proposition
Q., q.	question
tr.	treatise
v.	verse

Ascriptions

The Apostle	St. Paul
The Commentator	Averroes
The Master	Peter Lombard
The Philosopher	Aristotle

Compendia of Minor Works Cited by Aquinas

Emil Friedberg (ed.), *Corpus Iuris Canonici*, 2 vols. (Leipzig, 1879).

R. Heinze (ed.), *Themistii in libros Aristotelis De anima Paraphrasis* (Berlin, 1899).

G. Heylbut (ed.), *Eustrati et Michaelis et anonyma in Ethcs Nochomachea Commentaria* (Berlin, 1892).

Angelo Mai (ed.), *Nova Patrum Biblioteca*, 9 vols. (Rome, 1852–1888).

L. Minio-Paluello (ed.), *Averroes. Explanation of the Poetics* (Brussells and Paris, 1968).

L. Minio-Paluello (ed.), *Porphyry. Isagoge. Translation of Boethius* (Bruges and Paris, 1966).

X. Ochoa and A. Diez (eds.), *Raymond of Penafort. Summa de poenitentia* (Rome, 1976).

A. Pattin (ed.), *Simplicius: Commentaire sur les Categories d'Aristote*, trans. of William of Moeerbeke, 2 vols. (Louvain-Paris, 1971–1975).

J. H. Waszink (ed.), *Plato, Timaeus, a Calcidio translatus commentarioque instructus* (London and Leiden, 1962).

On Evil

Introduction

Aquinas's Life and Works

We have three main sources for our knowledge of Aquinas's life. The first is the text of his canonization process (Naples 1319). Then there are two early biographies. One is by William Tocco, who knew Aquinas personally. The other is by Bernard Gui, whose account depends partly on that of Tocco, but may also incorporate independent and reliable information.[1] Putting these documents together allows us to form a generally credible outline of Aquinas's career. But they also leave us with many unanswered, and probably unanswerable, questions. Hence we find that the three most recent biographies of Aquinas differ significantly on a number of issues.[2] They do so, for example, even when it comes to the year of Aquinas's birth, which can arguably be placed anywhere from 1224 to 1226.

Aquinas was born in the kingdom of Naples, then ruled by the Emperor Frederick II. His family were local gentry, and his birthplace was probably the castle of Roccasecca. His father was known as "Lord Landulph d'Aquino." His mother, of noble Neapolitan background, was called Theodora. It was customary at the time for wealthy families to present their younger boys as oblates of monasteries, so Aquinas, who was the youngest of four brothers, was in 1230 or 1231 dispatched to the abbey of Monte Cassino, where he lived and studied for some eight years.

It is possible that Aquinas's family had hopes of him succeeding to high office in the abbey. But military conflict between Frederick II and Pope Gregory IX made Monte

---

1. All of these sources can be found in D. Prümmer and M. H. Laurent (eds.), *Fontes Vitae Sancti Thomae Aquinatis*, to be found in *Revue Thomiste* (1911–1937). See also A. Ferrua (ed.), *Thomae Aquinatis vitae fontes praecipuae* (Alba, 1968). For English translations of source material for Aquinas's life, see Kenelm Foster (ed.), *The Life of Thomas Aquinas* (London and Baltimore, 1959).

2. The attempts in question are (1) Jean-Pierre Torrell, *Saint Thomas Aquinas: The Person and His Work* (Washington, D.C., 1996), (2) Simon Tugwell (ed.), *Albert and Thomas—Selected Writings* (New York, Mahwah, and London, 1988), pp. 201–267, and (3) James A. Weisheipl O.P., *Friar Thomas D'Aquino* (Oxford, 1974; republished with Corrigenda and Addenda, Washington, 1983).

Cassino a center of imperial-papal rivalry. Frederick's troops occupied the abbey early in 1239, and, by July of that year, Thomas's parents (then supporting the imperial cause) removed him from Monte Cassino and sent him to study at the recently founded university (or *studium generale*) founded by Frederick in Naples.[3] Here he was almost certainly introduced to the study of Aristotle (384–322 B.C.). Most probably, he will also have become familiar with the writings of thinkers such as the Arabic author Averroes (1126–1198) and the Jewish author Maimonides (1135–1204). Early accounts of Aquinas's life mention two people in particular under whom he worked. Of one, a certain "Master Martin," we know nothing. But research has recently uncovered some information concerning the other, known as "Master Peter of Ireland."[4]

Though Aquinas was not a professed Benedictine when he went to study in Naples, we have no reason to suppose that he or his family were not at that time still expecting him to have a Benedictine future. In Naples, however, Aquinas encountered the Dominican Order of friars founded by St. Dominic Guzman (c. 1170–1221), and he entered that order sometime between 1242 and 1244.[5] We have no special historical evidence to explain why he chose to become a Dominican, but his writings testify to a deep commitment to the order's ideals of poverty, mendicancy, and teaching.[6] And he evidently entered it with a strong personal resolve, for he firmly resisted his family's attempts to remove him from it. In an effort to dissuade him from remaining with the Dominicans, his mother tried to track him down first in Naples and then in Rome. Having failed to catch up with him, she arranged for him to be detained by his brothers and subsequently held for around two years in the family homes at Montesangiovanni and Roccasecca. But Aquinas refused to leave the Dominicans, and by the middle of 1246 he was with them again.[7] To begin with, he probably studied for a short time in Paris, where he transcribed the lectures of Albert on the anonymous author known as Denys (or Dionysius) the

---

3. In 1245, following the excommunication of Frederick by the First Council of Lyons, Aquinas's family changed their allegiance and defended the papal cause. As Torrell observes (*Aquinas: The Person*, pp. 14f.), there is reason to think that Thomas's time with the Benedictines had a lasting effect on his thinking.

4. See Michael Bertram Crowe, "Peter of Ireland: Aquinas's Teacher of the ARTES LIBERALES," in *Arts Liberaux et Philosophie au Moyen Age* (Paris, 1969).

5. For a defense of the view that Aquinas received the Dominican habit in 1242 or 1243, see Tugwell, *Albert and Thomas*, p. 204. For a different verdict, see Torrell, *Aquinas: The Person*, pp. 8ff. Not surprisingly, Tugwell and Torrell are in notable disagreement when it comes to the chronology of Aquinas's life in the period immediately following his becoming a Dominican. The Dominican priory in Naples was founded in 1231. By 1239 only two Dominicans were in residence there: John of San Giuliano and Thomas of Lentini, from whom Thomas received the habit and who later became patriarch of Jerusalem.

6. Cf. Weisheipl, *Friar Thomas D'Aquino*, p. 25, Tugwell, *Albert and Thomas*, pp. 203f., and Torrell, *Aquinas: The Person*, pp. 14ff.

7. Note that Thomas enjoyed a fair degree of liberty while detained by his family. He had access to books and to members of the Dominican Order. And he acted as a tutor to his sisters. His family eventually abandoned their resistence to his choice of the Dominicans, and he subsequently remained on very good terms with them.

Areopagite.[8] He then moved to Cologne, where he continued to work under Albert and was probably ordained to the priesthood. Aquinas clearly showed himself to be a gifted student, and by 1256 he was back again in Paris.[9] Now, however, his role was that of teacher rather than student.

First of all, he lectured on the *Sentences* of Peter Lombard (c. 1095–1160). In 1256 he became a master in theology lecturing on the Bible and presiding over a series of class-room debates covering a range of theological questions.[10] During this time also (commonly known as his "first Parisian regency"), Aquinas produced the earliest of the works for which he is best known today. Even before arriving in Paris he may have completed his commentary on the Book of Isaiah and his short treatise *De principiis naturae*.[11] From the time he first taught in Paris, however, we can date his commentary on the *Sentences* of Lombard, his disputed question *De veritate*, the work known as *De ente et essentia*, a commentary on Boethius's *De trinitate*, and a defense of the mendicant orders—*Contra impugnantes Dei cultum et religionem*.[12] During his first Parisian regency Aquinas also started work on his lengthy *Summa contra Gentiles*.[13]

A *summa* ("summary") was an extended treatment of doctrinal matters set out in an orderly and comprehensive manner.[14] It was a standard literary genre for medieval writ-

---

8. Cf. Tugwell, *Albert and Thomas*, p. 208. For introductions to Denys, see Andrew Louth, *Denys the Areopagite* (London, 1989). Paul Rorem, *Pseudo-Dionysius: A Commentary on the Texts and an Introduction to Their Influence* (New York and Oxford, 1993). Also see "Albert and the Dionysian Tradition" in Simon Tugwell, *Albert and Thomas*, pp. 39ff. The relation between Denys and Aquinas is explored in Fran O'Rourke, *Pseudo-Dionysius and the Metaphysics of Aquinas* (Leiden, New York, and Köln, 1992).

9. Aquinas may have returned to Paris as early as 1251. He received a license to teach in the university there in 1256.

10. Aquinas's inaugural lecture (or *principium*) as master is a short commentary on Psalm 103:13. In it he explores the role of the Christian teacher and the way in which Christian truth is received and delivered. For an English translation of the text, see Tugwell, *Albert and Thomas*, pp. 355–360.

11. For the dating of the commentary on Isaiah, see Torrell, *Aquinas: The Person*, pp. 27f. For the dating of *De principiis naturae*, see Tugwell, *Albert and Thomas*, p. 210.

12. Aquinas's work on disputed questions is discussed in the next section of this introduction. The *De ente et essentia*, as its name implies, is an essay on the relation between existence and essence. It has proved to be one of Aquinas's most popular works. The *Contra impugnantes* was written in the wake of polemical charges from opponents of the ecclesiastical status and lifestyle of the orders of friars—opponents such as William of Saint-Amour (c.1200–1272). Hostility to the friars was a force they had much to reckon with around the time of Aquinas's first Parisian regency and later. Among other things, it led some to boycott Aquinas's inaugural lecture as master. It also resulted in the fact that Aquinas was not formally admitted to the body of Parisian university masters until 1257.

13. Manuscript evidence suggests that Aquinas wrote the first fifty-three chapters of Book I of the *Summa contra gentiles* before the end of the summer of 1259. The final text was finished around or before 1265. The title *Summa contra gentiles* is not Aquinas's. We do not know what title, if any, he gave it. In some medieval manuscripts it is called *Liber de veritate catholicae fidei contra errores infidelium* (*A Book about the Truth of the Catholic Faith, Directed against Mistakes Made by Unbelievers*). The title *Summa contra gentiles* (*Summa against the Pagans*) derives from around 1272.

14. Hence, from the twelfth century on we find *summae* dealing not only with theological matters, but also with, for example, law and medicine.

ers from around the early twelfth century. Discussing the purpose of the *Summa contra Gentiles*, early in the text Aquinas says that he aims "by the way of reason to pursue those things about God which human reason is able to investigate."[15] And that is very much what he does both in the *Summa contra Gentiles* and in its famous sequel, the *Summa theologiae*, which he began around 1265–1268 and which remained unfinished at the time of his death.[16] This work, commonly deemed to be Aquinas's greatest achievement, contains three long treatises (or "parts") divided into subsections called "Questions" and "Articles." It ranges over topics such as God, creation, angels, human nature and happiness, grace, virtues, Christ, and sacraments. But, despite its impressiveness, its purpose seems to have been pretty down to earth. For, as has been plausibly argued by Leonard Boyle, there is reason to think that, in writing the *Summa theologiae*, Aquinas "had young and run-of-the-mill Dominicans primarily in mind and not a more sophisticated, perhaps university audience." The work, we may say, was "his own very personal contribution to a lopsided system of theological education in the Order to which he belonged."[17] Considered from this viewpoint, the *Summa theologiae* is original for more than its teaching. As Boyle puts it:

> All Dominican writers of *summae* previous to Thomas had valiantly covered various aspects of learning for their confrères in the pastoral care. . . . Now Thomas went further than anything hitherto attempted. He provided a *summa* of general theology, a manual which dealt with God and Trinity and Creation and Incarnation as well as with man, his strengths and weaknesses.[18]

In other words, with the *Summa theologiae* Aquinas was filling a gap. He was putting practical theology in a full theological context.

Aquinas's medieval biographers seem little interested in sorting out the details of his career from around 1256. Instead, they tend to focus on his character and status as saint, teacher, and author. We can, however, be sure that he vacated his teaching position at Paris before 1260, that he lived and taught for a time at Orvieto, that in 1265 he was assigned by the Dominicans to establish a house of studies for the order in Rome, and that he was reassigned to teach at Paris in 1268 and by 1269 had resumed his posi-

---

15. *Summa contra gentiles* I, 9, 4. I quote from the translation by Anton C. Pegis (Notre Dame and London, 1975). The intention of Aquinas in writing the *Summa contra gentiles* has been a subject of much dispute among commentators. For an introduction to the discussion, see, for example, *Summa contra gentiles*, I, text and French translation with an introduction by A. Gauthier (Paris, 1961), A. Patfoort, *Thomas d'Aquin: Les Clés d'une théologie* (Paris, 1983), and Norman Kretzmann, *The Metaphysics of Theism: Aquinas's Natural Theology in Summa Contra Gentiles I* (Oxford, 1997).

16. Again, the title is not Aquinas's. It emerges in thirteenth-century manuscripts. Printed editions often call it the *Summa theologica*.

17. Leonard E. Boyle, *The Setting of the Summa Theologiae of Saint Thomas* (The Etienne Gilson Series, 5, Toronto, 1982), pp. 17 and 30.

18. Boyle, *Setting of the Summa Theologiae*, pp. 15 f. Boyle's account of the *Summa theologiae* has been severely criticized by John Jenkins. See John Jenkins, *Knowledge and Faith in Thomas Aquinas* (Cambridge, 1997). Jenkins's critique of Boyle (and of others taking a broadly similar approach to the *Summa theologiae*) is arguably open to serious criticism. See my review of Jenkins's book in *Journal of Theological Studies* 49 (1998): 876–879.

tion there. And still the writing continued. At Orvieto, for instance, Aquinas worked on the *Catena aurea* (*Golden Chain*, a continuous commentary on the four Gospels composed of quotations from the church fathers), the *Contra errores graecorum* (*Against the Errors of the Greeks*, a set of opinions on certain Greek Orthodox theologians), an edition of a liturgy for the newly created feast of Corpus Christi, and a commentary on the book of Job.[19] In Rome he began the *Summa theologiae*. Among other things, he also worked on the disputed question *De potentia*, the theological synthesis known as the *Compendium theologiae*, the political treatise *De regno*, and a commentary on Aristotle's *De anima*.[20] Having returned to Paris in or around 1268, Aquinas's output included more of the *Summa theologiae*, notably the second half of its large second part (the *Secunda secundae*), the disputed question *De virtutibus*, the *De aeternitati mundi* (on the question "Did the world have a beginning?"), and the *De unitate intellectus* (a critique of what Averroës taught on the nature of intellect).[21] Also during his second Parisian regency, Aquinas began commenting on the gospels of Matthew and John, and on Aristotle's *Physics*, *Nichomachaean Ethics*, and *Metaphysics*.[22]

19. Aquinas lived in the Dominican convent in Orvieto, where he was assigned as a teacher (*lector*) of Dominicans in residence there—Dominicans preparing for pastoral work. During this time, he also attended various Dominican Provincial chapters at a variety of Italian locations. He began the *Catena aurea* at the request of Pope Urban IV, who was living at Orvieto when Aquinas was there. The commentary on Job is something of a novelty since in it Aquinas, unlike most previous commentators, provides a detailed literal reading of the text and a full-scale treatment of divine providence. Also composed at the request of Urban IV, the *Contra errores Graecorum* is a discussion of a collection of texts from the Greek fathers probably compiled by one Nicholas de Durazzo. While in Orvieto, Aquinas may also have written *De rationibus fidei*, a remarkable little work very reminiscent of the *Summa contra gentiles* in its treatment of faith and reason. Doubt has been cast on Aquinas's authorship of the Office for the feast of Corpus Christi, but the evidence now seems to suggest that he did, indeed, compose it. Cf. Torrell, *Aquinas: The Person*, pp. 129–132.

20. In Rome Aquinas was in charge of a new Dominican study house (*studium*) the organization of which was left to him. Probably located at the priory of Santa Sabina, it must, as Tugwell observes (*Albert and Thomas*, p. 224) have been "one of the most remarkable study houses the Order had ever possessed." The *Compendium theologiae* holds a special place in Aquinas's work since, though it ranges over many of the same topics we find covered in the *Summa theologiae*, its treatment of them is remarkably concise and straightforward.

21. Why was Aquinas sent back to Paris? Our sources permit us only to conjecture, but it may partly have been because he was thought of as someone well able to deal with what some theologians then perceived to be a dangerous use of Aristotle in the Parisian Faculty of Arts. His *Aeternitate mundi* and *De unitate intellectus* certainly deal directly with questions much at issue in the Faculty of Arts at the time.

22. As we shall see below, Aquinas may also have worked on the *De malo* during his second Parisian regency. The reader should appreciate that we suffer from a high degree of uncertainty when it comes to dating Aquinas's writings. Much that we now find published under his name (especially the biblical commentaries and the commentaries on Aristotle) may well represent work he did at different periods. And some of it may come to us by means of people reporting what he said in lectures rather than from the hand of Aquinas himself. For detailed discussions of problems concerning the dating of Aquinas's works, see Tugwell, *Albert and Thomas*, pp. 244–258, and Torrell, *Aquinas: The Person*, especially pp. 332–359.

Sometime in 1272 Aquinas left Paris once again. The Dominican Roman Provincial Chapter of that year deputed him to establish a theological study house in a place of his choosing and with staff selected by him. Aquinas opted for Naples, where he was present by the autumn of the year.[23] Here, again, he taught and wrote. He carried on, for instance, with the *Summa theologiae* (now into its third part). He also probably lectured on St. Paul's Letter to the Romans, and he may have lectured on the Psalter. By now, however, Aquinas was reaching the end of his life. In December 1273 he abandoned his usual routine and neither wrote nor dictated anything else. Exactly what had happened is uncertain, though an explanation commonly given nowadays is that Aquinas suffered a stroke or a physical and emotional breakdown caused by overwork.[24] Whatever the truth of the matter is, the crisis of 1273 was clearly the beginning of the end for him.

Late in 1273 he was instructed to attend the second Council of Lyons. He set out for Lyons, but became seriously ill and lodged for a while with his niece at the castle of Maenza. He is reported to have said here: "If the Lord is coming for me, I had better be found in a religious house than in a castle."[25] So he was carried to Fossanova, south of Rome, where he died in a Cistercian guest room a week or two later. The cause of his death is unknown. One account tells us that, on the journey to Lyons, Aquinas struck his head against a tree that had fallen across the road and that this left him half stunned and hardly able to stand.[26] On the basis of this report it has been suggested that he died of a brain hemorrhage.[27] In any event, by the afternoon of March 7, 1274, he was dead.

Disputed Questions

Aquinas's many writings contain works of different types. There are, for example, commentaries (on Scripture and on authors such as Aristotle). There are also self-contained treatises (like *De ente et essentia*) and full-scale essays dealing with almost all the major articles of the Christian creed (like the *Compendium theologiae* and the *Summa theologiae*). As we have also seen, however, some of Aquinas's works fall under the heading of "disputed questions" (*quaestiones disputatae*), and it is to this group that the *De malo* belongs. But what, precisely, is a disputed question? And what sort of text is the *De malo*? The short answer is that Aquinas's disputed questions, including the *De malo*, are solid discussions of a limited range of topics written with a special eye on arguments for and against the positions on them which Aquinas wishes to uphold. But this brief description needs to be somewhat fleshed out with an eye on the place of disputed questions in the history of the teaching of theology.

---

23. As Torrell observes (*Aquinas: The Person*, pp. 248f.), though the Roman Provincial chapter formally left the choice of the study house's location to Thomas, there are reasons for supposing that he had little choice but to place it in Naples.

24. Cf. Weisheipl, *Friar Thomas D'Aquino*, pp. 322f.

25. Cf. A. Ferrua, *Thomae Aquinatis*, p. 213.

26. Cf. Ferrua, *Thomae Aquinatis*, p. 317.

27. Cf. Weisheipl, *Friar Thomas D'Aquino*, p. 329. For other discussions of Aquinas's final days, see Tugwell, *Albert and Thomas*, pp. 233–234 and pp. 265–267, and Torrell, *Aquinas: The Person*, pp. 289–295.

Before his inception as a master in theology in 1256, Aquinas's first task was that of a *cursor biblicus*, which meant that he had to lecture on the Bible. This, in turn, meant that he was obliged to read and expound biblical texts considered as works of authority. And this systematic exposition of texts deemed to be authoritative (or the *lectio* as it was called) formed a major part of the way in which theology was taught both in universities and in other establishments long before the thirteenth century.[28] In the writings of Aquinas, its fruits can be seen in works like his commentaries on the gospels of Matthew and John. The product of classroom expositions, each of these is a reading (*lectura*) of a text the purpose of which is chiefly to note what it says and to bring out its meaning.

But, of course, texts, especially ones dealing with difficult subjects, raise questions. Not surprisingly, therefore, from at least as far back as the twelfth century, teachers of theology also taught in a different way: by means of the question (*quaestio*). That is to say, they also taught by formally isolating and answering problems which they found posed by the subject matter dealt with by the authorities they were trying to elucidate— as, for example, Aquinas does in his commentary on the *Sentences* of Peter Lombard. This work is no mere exposition of the *Sentences*. In it Aquinas uses Lombard's writings as an opportunity to discuss topics touched on in them. And, in doing so, he moves from question (*questio*) to question. Along the way he mentions arguments that might be advanced in favor of different answers (often arguments based on the Bible or on the teaching of the church fathers), and he proceeds (often with appeal to theological authority) to offer some answers of his own. And it is this style of teaching, focused on discussion of questions, that emerges in the so-called disputed question (*quaestio disputata*) or the disputation (*disputatio*) considered as a formal teaching genre.

By the time of Aquinas, this was very much a feature of university life, though it was also employed in study houses distinct from the context of a university.[29] It can basically be thought of as an exercise in rigorous thinking. At its core was a question or a series of questions, often ranging widely in subject matter and raised without special reference to any one text or author. The aim of the exercise was to arrive at a solution to these questions in the light of a detailed discussion chiefly consisting of objections to a given thesis and of replies to these objections. In universities such as Paris, disputations were organized and presided over by a master, whose job was to provide the sought-for conclusion in the light of the objections and replies that surfaced in the course of the discussion. And the disputations themselves were of two main kinds.[30]

---

28. It was also standardly employed as a method of teaching in disciplines other than theology, such as grammar, philosophy, and law. Those presenting a reading (*lectura*) of biblical texts either simply went through them rapidly (as a *cursor biblicus* normally did) or proceeded with more attention to detail and speaking as experts (as masters usually did).

29. In 1259 the Dominicans decreed that it should be employed as a basic teaching method in all their centers of learning.

30. I should stress that it is difficult to be certain about the ways in which disputations were conducted in thirteenth-century universities since we lack official texts legislating for their occurrence and procedure. In what follows I am drawing on what seems to be the current scholarly consensus based on available information. For the most recent study of the nature and history of medieval disputed questions, see Bernardo C. Bazàn, John W. Wippel, Gérard Fransen, and Danielle Jacquart, *Les Questions Disputées et les Questions Quodlibétiques dans les Facultés de Théologie, de Droit et de Médecine* (Turnhout, 1985).

To begin with, there was the public disputation (*disputatio publica*), which masters were able (though not obliged) to hold at regular intervals during the academic year. Public disputations took place in the master's own school, and he decided on the question or questions to be discussed.[31] He then appointed people officially to take part in the disputation, and he arranged for it to be advertised in advance. The dispute ran over two days. On the first day, visitors from other schools (possibly including other masters) raised points from the floor (usually in opposition to the position ultimately defended by the master). These were replied to by someone appointed by the master (normally his apprentice professor, or "bachelor"), and notes on the proceedings were made. On the following day the master determined the issues previously debated. And, normally, he eventually worked over the material of the dispute and prepared it for publication. Some of these public disputations (the so-called Quodlibets, held twice a year in Paris during Lent and Advent) were very formal occasions interrupting the regular course of teaching throughout the university. They differed from the other kind of disputation in that the subjects discussed in them were not chosen by the master but by participants in the discussion. And the master had to determine them on the spot.[32]

But there were also disputations of a less public kind. These so called "private disputations" (*disputatio privata*) took place only between the master and his own students and bachelors. And they seem to have been much more frequent than the public disputations. They took basically the same form as the public ones, however: a question was chosen; arguments were advanced in defense of conflicting positions; and the master determined. In many ways the private disputation resembled the modern university seminar in which students are required to contribute to a discussion in the presence of a teacher whose aim is to inform students as well as to listen to them. And it may well be that many of Aquinas's disputed questions in the form we have them now originated as private disputations. His quodlibetal questions as published certainly reflect public disputations. But that may not always be true in the case of his nonquodlibetal ones.

One reason for thinking so derives from a plausible way of answering the question "What was the basic unit of the disputed question?" In their final, written form, Aquinas's disputed questions are broken down into questions and articles. Each question comprises several articles, each consisting of a single question. Hence, for example, the *De veritate* consists of twenty-nine questions, the second of which contains fifteen articles dealing with problems concerning God's knowledge (e.g., "Is there knowledge in God?", "Does God know things other than himself?", and "Does God's knowledge change?"). But when Aquinas conducted disputations, was it a whole question or merely an article that occupied participants in a single session of discussion?

31. In Paris, Aquinas functioned as a master of theology teaching in the Dominican house of St Jacques.

32. Our text of the *De malo* does not reflect a quodlibetal disputation. But Aquinas frequently held quodlibets dealing with more than two hundred questions. The fruits of these can be found in volume 25 of the Leonine edition of the works of Aquinas. Few of Aquinas's quodlibets have been translated into English, but see *Thomas Aquinas, Quodlibetal Questions 1 and 2*, translated and introduced by S. Edwards (Toronto, 1983).

Some scholars have held that it was an article.[33] But that suggestion would leave Aquinas conducting disputations much more frequently than it seems plausible to suppose him to have done given the length of the Parisian terms and given the other teaching which took place in the university.

So perhaps we should conclude that the disputation's basic unit was the question.[34] But that suggestion also poses problems. As James Weisheipl comments, "it does not, for example, explain how a question of twenty articles compares with a question of two articles in an afternoon session."[35]

In trying to settle the matter, Bernardo Bazán has suggested that, at least in the case of the *De veritate*, Aquinas disputed privately and frequently with the article as the business for a single meeting. And this reconstruction seems perfectly plausible. In that case, however, disputed questions of Aquinas other than the *De veritate* may also have been privately disputed, article by article. And, as Jean-Pierre Torrell observes, this may well have been the case with the *De malo*.[36] That work may reflect a series of discussions at which people other than Aquinas and his own students were present. But it may equally well derive from something more of a family affair.

Either way, the *De malo*'s structure certainly conforms to that of standard thirteenth-century disputations. First we have a question raised. There then follows a series of arguments designed to favor a particular answer to the question. These are followed by a series of counterarguments and a sustained discussion of the question intended to resolve it. This in turn is followed by a blow-by-blow reply to the arguments advanced at the outset. Hence, for example, article 3 of *De malo*'s Question I first asks whether good is the cause of evil. We then find nineteen arguments offered in defense of the conclusion that it is and two arguments favoring the opposite conclusion. These are followed by a discussion in which Aquinas explains why we should deny that good causes evil, and the article winds up with responses to the first nineteen arguments. And this pattern can also be found in works of Aquinas other than his disputed questions. It is there, for example, in the commentary on the *Sentences*. It is even more clearly present in the *Summa theologiae*, each article of which reads like an abbreviated article of texts like the *De malo*.

We know, of course, that the *Summa theologiae* is a work written entirely by Aquinas. It is very much his own. But are his disputed questions to be thought of in the same way? The answer is basically "Yes," though with certain qualifications.

As we have seen, it was left to the master to prepare a publishable version of disputations at which he presided and determined. And this version, especially its determinations (i.e., its resolutions of individual questions), can be thought of as the work of the

---

33. Cf. P. Mandonnet's introduction to his edition of Aquinas's *Quaestiones disputatae*, Vol. 1 (Paris, 1925), and P. Glorieux, "Les Questions Disputés de Saint Thomas et leur Suite Chronologique," *Récherches de Théologie Ancienne et Médiévale* 4 (1932).

34. This is the view advanced by A. Dondaine, *Secrétaires de saint Thomas* (Rome, 1956), pp. 209–216.

35. Weisheipl, *Friar Thomas D'Aquino*, p. 124.

36. Torrell rightly notes, however, that there are grounds for doubting that all of Aquinas's disputed questions, apart from his Quodlibets, were privately debated.

master. But masters did not script all the counterarguments offered in the course of a disputation. So their disputations as published almost certainly incorporate ideas brought up by others. These, however, were evidently worked into the finished text by the master, who must therefore be regarded as essentially its author. And texts like Aquinas's disputed questions most likely include more than was said in the course of the discussions they reflect. For, as Torrell puts it, speaking of Aquinas's private disputations:

> It appears probable that the final result does not resemble, except in a very general way, the real unfolding of these private discussions between the master and the students. It suffices to read the text of the *De veritate* or the *De potentia* to understand that these texts are very much above the level of what a discussion could be for average students. The students of Paris . . . could doubtless follow the most difficult expositions, but even with them the discussion could not have taken the exact form of long, complex, and probing research; by necessity it was briefer and simpler. We, therefore, must admit that what has come down to us bears witness to considerable editing.[37]

In other words, though Aquinas's disputed questions as published certainly put us in touch with a live and relatively spontaneous debate, they are also very much the work of Aquinas and should be read as such.[38]

Dating the *De malo*

The *De malo* contains sixteen questions. The earliest manuscripts of the text stop at the end of Question XV, though there is evidence that the complete work was available to read by 1275–1280. But when was it actually written? And can we date the time of the discussions it represents? The short answer to these questions is that we cannot be sure, though we can make some reasonable conjectures.

The primitive catalog submitted by Bartholomew of Capua for Aquinas's canonization process deals with the chronology of his disputed questions by saying: "In three parts: one part disputed at Paris, namely *De veritate*; the second in Italy, namely *De potentia Dei*, and the rest (*et ultra*); the third at the second time in Paris, namely *De virtutibus* and the rest."[39] But this is hardly a helpful guide to chronology since Batholomew does not explain what he means by "the rest." The *De malo* clearly falls under this heading, but are we to suppose that it derives from Aquinas's time in Italy or from the time of his second Parisian regency?

The original disputation may well have taken place during the time that Aquinas worked at Santa Sabina in Rome. Tolomeo of Lucca, a contemporary of Aquinas, places the *De malo* in Italy in the time of Pope Clement IV (1265–1268), and there is nothing in the general drift of the text that prevents us from accepting this dating, especially since it fits with what we can surmise to be interests of Aquinas around the time he was living

---

37. Torrell, *Aquinas: The Person*, p. 62.

38. Some of them (for example, the *Quaestiones de anima*) may even be nothing but literary creations of Aquinas derived from no conducted disputation. Cf. Torrell, *Aquinas: The Person*, p. 63.

39. Cf. Ferrua, *Thomas Aquinatis*, p. 330. "De questionibus disputatis partes tres: unam disputavit Parisius, scilicet de veritate; aliam in Italia, scilicet de potentia Dei et ultra; aliam secunda vice Parisius, scilicet de virtutibus et ultra."

in Rome. Hard on his return to Paris around 1268, he started work on the second part of the *Summa theologiae*, in which he discusses topics which also get treated in the *De malo*. So he may well have been reflecting systematically on them in the period leading up to 1268. In Question I of the *De malo* Aquinas cites a commentary on Aristotle's *Categories* by the sixth-century author Simplicius, and in Question XVI he cites thoughts on Aristotle's *De anima* coming from Themistius (fourth century). He could not have had access to the Simplicius text until around the middle of 1266. And he could not have had access to the thinking of Themistius until late 1267. So it seems fairly certain that the final edition of the *De malo* was produced later than 1267.[40] But this does not mean that it was disputed later than 1267. It only means that its first and sixteenth questions were written up for publication after that year.

On the other hand, however, the manuscript tradition of the *De malo* springs from a single Parisian copy. And *De malo*'s Question VI (on whether people act freely or from necessity) might possibly have been designed as an attempt to defend the position adopted by Stephen Tempier, bishop of Paris, who in 1270 condemned a number of propositions thought to be assented to by certain Parisian Aristotelians. Tempier denied that people act of necessity, and most of *De malo*'s Question VI is devoted to arguing at length that people do, indeed, act freely and not from necessity. And the question has often been thought to contain material which seems to have been written later than Aquinas's *Quodlibet* I and earlier than Questions 9 and 10 of the *Summa theologiae*'s *Prima secundae*. *Quodlibet* I is now commonly dated to 1269, so it looks as though Question VI of the *De malo*, at least, was not written until 1269–1270. For these reasons, one might therefore surmise that, as prepared for publication by Aquinas, the *De malo* belongs to his second stay in Paris.[41]

Yet we need to distinguish between the *De malo* as an historical dispute and the *De malo* as a text written by Aquinas and subsequently published. So, even if there are elements in it which seem to reflect a date during Aquinas's second Parisian regency, it does not follow that the discussions on which its final form is based actually took place in that period of his life. They may have. But we just cannot be sure.[42] The most we can say with

40. Aquinas used Latin translations when reading authors who wrote in Greek. And we can date the translations available to him of Simplicius on the *Categories* and Themistius on the *De anima* with some confidence. Cf. A. Pattin (ed.), *Simplicius, Commentaire sur les Catégories d'Aristote, Traduction de Guillaume de Moerbeke* (Louvain-Paris, 1971), pp. xi–xii, and G. Verbeke (ed.), *Thémistius, Commentaire sur le traité de l'âme d'Aristote, Traduction de Guillaume de Moerbeke* (Louvain-Paris, 1957), p. lxiii.

41. Note, however, that Aquinas argues in favor of human freedom in works produced before 1270. And there is nothing in *Quodlibet* 1 or *Summa theologiae* Ia2ae, 9–10 which proves that Aquinas disputed or wrote up Question VI of the *De malo* after the former and before the latter. I should add that some scholars have argued that Aquinas began writing *Summa theologiae* Ia,2ae sometime before his assignation to Paris in 1268.

42. Scholars have significantly differed with respect to the dating of the *De malo*. Some have argued that it was disputed in Italy. Thus: P. Mandonnet, "Chronologie des questions disputées de saint Thomas d'Aquin," *Revue Thomiste* 23 (1918), and R.-A. Gauthier, "La Date du Commentaire de Saint Thomas sur L'Ethique à Nicomaque," *Recherches de Théologie Ancienne et Médiévale* 18 (1951). Others, however, place it during Aquinas's second Parisian regency. Thus, for example, O. Lottin, "La date de la question disputée *De Malo* de saint Thomas d'Aquin," *Revue d'Histoire Ecclésiastique* 24 (1928). In the Leonine edition of the *De malo* (Rome and Paris, 1982), Louis Bataillon suggests that, though we cannot be sure when Aquinas actively disputed the questions discussed in it, the final version was completed around 1270–1272.

confidence, perhaps, is that the final form of the *De malo* is to be roughly dated around the time that Aquinas was working on the *Prima secundae*. And on this count alone, the work is important for those with an interest in Aquinas's thinking. For it derives from a time when he was brooding on its subject matter in a particularly sustained way. And it stands in its own right as a major and characteristic example of his approach to the topics with which it deals.

The Subject and Approach of the *De malo*

The English noun "evil" (Latin: *malum*) is most frequently used today to refer to what is truly and horrendously undesirable, especially in the field of human behavior. And "evil" is nowadays normally applied as an adjective when people are describing disasters and moral monsters. Hence, for example, we speak naturally enough about the evil of genocide and drug dealing, but not about the evil of dandruff. And though we typically describe famine and brutal dictators as evil, we use a weaker term when talking of inclement weather or of those who tell lies merely to avoid an awkward business appointment.

For Aquinas, however, *malum* (sometimes used as a noun and sometimes used as an adjective) bears a more inclusive sense than "evil" does for us. In writing the *De malo*, he is not concerned only with amazingly wicked deeds. He is concerned with what we might call "badness across the board" or "the undesirable in general." And he thinks of this as present in more than human behavior. He also regards it as something that admits of degrees. So the topic at stake in the *De malo* is a broad one. The Latin word *malum* can be translated by nouns such as "damage," "harm," "hurt," "injury," "misfortune," and "misdeed." And the *De malo* is concerned with all these things as well as with what might more naturally be referred to as "evil' by contemporary speakers of English. It is especially concerned with human wrongdoing, but its scope also extends to other things—such as pain and suffering. Hence we find Aquinas starting the work with a general analysis of what it means to say that anything at all is *malum*, where *malum* signifies any kind of failure or shortcoming, anything we might think of as less than good (Latin: *bonum*). For Aquinas, we are dealing with evil whenever we are faced by whatever can be thought of as a case of *falling short*. For him, there is evil wherever goodness is lacking. And his task in the *De malo* is to explore and to understand such a lack, to see what it amounts to, and to grasp what it implies.

But how does Aquinas pursue this task? In seeking to make sense of evil, one could adopt a scientific approach. In other words, one could take instances of evil and then try to explain them in terms of natural causes—as doctors, for instance, do. In the *De malo*, however, Aquinas's chief concern is a different one. For him, the world is created and governed by a perfectly good God who is also omnipotent and omniscient. And he writes about evil in the light of this belief. In the *De malo* he is not concerned with scientific descriptions and scientific accounts of the causes of particular instances of evil (though he has things to say about them). Rather, he is out to focus on badness or evil in general. And he seeks to understand it as part of a world made by God. Hence, for example, he asks if God can be thought of as causing evil. And his account of human wrongdoing treats it chiefly as sin and as falling short with respect to God. Hence, too, he touches on specifically Christian notions such as the doctrine of original sin.

In other words, the *De malo* is very much a work of Christian theology. Its readers, however, should also note that Aquinas sees theology as a discipline which must draw on the best human thinking available. For this reason, even his most explicitly theological discussions (for example, his expositions of Scripture) are shot through with arguments or considerations which are not just the property of theologians. For the most part, he is concerned to expound what he calls "holy teaching" (*sacra doctrina*), which he basically thinks of as what you can find in the Bible.[43] And, in doing so, he defers to authority, both scriptural and patristic. But he also examines what his Christian sources present him with, and he sees himself as a teacher who must reflect and engage with his authorities, using all relevant available resources. Hence, in his inaugural lecture of 1256, we find him explaining the role of the professor of "holy teaching" in these terms:

> All the teachers of sacred scripture ought to be "high" because of the high quality of their lives, so that they will be capable of preaching effectively. As Gregory says in the *Pastoral Rule*, "If your life is despised then unavoidably your preaching will also be despised." "The words of the wise are like goads and like nails deeply fixed" (Eccles. 12:11). Hearts cannot be goaded on or fixed in the fear of God unless they are fixed in an elevated way of life.
>
> They need to be enlightened, so that they can suitably teach by lecturing. "To me, the least of all the saints, the grace has been given to enlighten everyone" (Eph. 3:8–9).
>
> And they need to be well-armed so that they can refute errors by arguing against them. "I will give you a wisdom they will not be able to resist" (Luke 21:15).
>
> These three functions, preaching, teaching and disputing, are mentioned in Titus 1:9, "So that he will be capable of exhorting people" (this refers to preaching) 'in sound teaching' (this refers to lecturing) "and defeating those who contradict" (this refers to disputing).[44]

Preaching, teaching, and disputing were the three tasks of a master in theology as laid down by the statutes of the University of Paris when Aquinas taught there—"disputing" clearly being understood to involve engaging with ideas and arguments coming even from non-Christian quarters. And "disputing," in this sense, as well as teaching (in the sense implied by the quotation above) is very much a feature of Aquinas's writings in general, and of his disputed questions in particular. In approaching the *De malo*, therefore, we should also bear in mind that in it Aquinas is not simply handing out doctrinal conclusions. Nor is he simply invoking authorities for them. In the true spirit of the

---

43. Cf. Victor White O.P., *Holy Teaching: The Idea of Theology according to St. Thomas Aquinas* (The Aquinas Society of London Aquinas Paper No. 33, London, 1958). Aquinas discusses the nature of *sacra doctrina* directly and at some length in *Summa theologiae* Ia, 1.

44. I quote from the translation of the inaugural lecture provided in Tugwell, *Albert and Thomas*, pp. 355–360.

medieval disputation, he is seeking to explore, support, and to fathom them in a number of different ways. For this reason, therefore, the *De malo* is of more than merely theological interest.[45]

Aquinas, God, and Being

In the pages of the *De malo* Aquinas deals with a number of specific questions to which he offers a range of specific answers. Fully to appreciate what he is saying, however, we need more than the text of the *De malo* before us. We need to know something of how he thinks generally about matters that he directly discusses only in other works. And perhaps the first thing worth noting is that, according to him, creatures have being (*esse*) the source of which is God, who can consequently be referred to as "Being Itself" or "Subsisting Being Itself" (*Ipsum esse subsistens*).[46]

One of Aquinas's most frequently repeated teachings is that the knowledge we have of God in this life is derived from what we know of creatures. On his account, we have no direct knowledge of God ("knowledge by acquaintance," as we might call it).[47] On his account too, we cannot know God by inference which depends on some prior under-

---

45. It is manifestly of great philosophical import, for example, since much of it deals with questions and arguments that philosophers today would regard as relevant to their discipline. The extent to which Aquinas may be thought of as a philosopher (as opposed to a theologian) has been a topic of some debate in recent years. For a range of opinions, see: James Anderson, "Was St. Thomas a Philosopher?" *New Scholasticism* 38 (1964); Mark Jordan, *The Alleged Aristotelianism of Thomas Aquinas* (Toronto, 1992), and "Theology and Philosophy," in Norman Kretzmann and Eleonore Stump (eds.), *The Cambridge Companion to Aquinas* (Cambridge, 1993). To a large extent it is, perhaps, misleading to ask whether Aquinas was a theologian or a philosopher. As I have said elsewhere (*The Thought of Thomas Aquinas*, Oxford, 1992, p. 14): "Much of what he says can be read either as philosophy or as theology. It is, perhaps, most accurate of all simply to call him a Christian thinker, though this should not be taken to mean that his thought can be divided into two: a system of philosophy, founded solely on reason, and—based on and completing this—a system of revealed theology. He thinks as a Christian, and he uses his ability to think in a way which, in his view, does all that it can to show that the revelation given in Christianity is not just a creed for those who cannot think and give reasons for what they believe."

46. As Aquinas often uses it, the word *esse* is best translated as if it were a kind of noun, literally as "the to be." Normally, though, when Aquinas uses *esse* in this sense, translators report him as talking about "being," which is also a perfectly respectable way of translating him. But we should not suppose that Aquinas thinks of *esse* as if it were an individual of some kind (as Mary is an individual woman, or Paul an individual man). Nor does Aquinas think that *esse* is a distinguishing property or quality of anything—like redness or triangularity. *Esse*, for him, is no independently existing thing. Nor is it anything that can enter into a description of what a thing is (in the language of Aquinas, it is not the name of a "form"). Yet it is, so he thinks, very much to be reckoned with.

47. There is, for Aquinas, nothing even in the life to come which could rightly be called "knowledge by acquaintance" in modern English. He teaches that the blessed in heaven enjoy the vision of God, but he does not conceive of this "vision" as like looking at an object or encountering something by means of sensory experience. In heaven, so he thinks, the blessed know God because God imparts to them a share in his own way of being. And even this, so Aquinas thinks, does not leave the blessed with a comprehensive knowledge of what God is. Cf. *Summa theologiae* Ia, 12.

standing of what God is ("knowledge based on the concept of God," as we might call it).[48] According to Aquinas:

> The knowledge that is natural to us has its source in the senses and extends just so far as it can be led by sensible things; from these, however, our understanding cannot reach to the divine essence. . . . In the present life our intellect has a natural relation to the natures of material things; thus it understands nothing except by turning to sense images. . . . In this sense it is obvious that we cannot, primarily and essentially, in the mode of knowing that we experience, understand immaterial substances since they are not subject to the senses and imagination. . . . What is understood first by us in the present life is the whatness of material things . . . [hence] . . . we arrive at a knowledge of God by way of creatures.[49]

As Herbert McCabe nicely puts it, Aquinas's view is that "when we speak of God, although we know how to use our words, there is an important sense in which we do not know what they mean. . . . We know how to talk about God, not because of any understanding of God, but because of what we know about his creatures."[50] So to understand Aquinas on *esse* as had by creatures, and to understand what he means in speaking of God as *ipsum esse subsistens*, we shall need to start by looking at what he thinks of creatures. And the point we need most especially to note is that creatures, for Aquinas, are more than the meanings of words.

Suppose I am talking about unicorns and suppose I observe that a unicorn has no horn on its forehead. Any sensible child will rightly correct me. And rightly so. Of course unicorns have horns on their foreheads. The fact can be quickly verified. Just consult a decent dictionary. So I need to be careful to get things right as I tell my tale of unicorns. For I can make mistakes as I speak of them.

On the other hand, however, these same dictionaries which confirm that unicorns have horns also tell us that unicorns are mythical animals. And, so we might say, mythical animals do not exist. In that case, however, how can one make mistakes about them? The answer, of course, is that I can make mistakes about unicorns since I can offend against what people rightly take to be the meaning of the word "unicorn." This term is not a piece of gibberish. It is there in the dictionaries. And it is with reference to dictionaries that one can make mistakes when talking of unicorns, albeit that unicorns do not exist.

Now suppose we ask what a unicorn is. Our answer will have to be based on some literary detective work. We shall start, perhaps, with a standard dictionary. Then we shall move from there to other writings in which "unicorn" occurs. And, if we are very per-

---

48. These theses are defended by Aquinas in many places. They are most succinctly defended in *Summa theologiae* Ia,2,1. For an account of them in the writings of Aquinas see my *The Thought of Thomas Aquinas*, chapters 2 and 3.

49. *Summa theologiae* Ia, 12, 12; Ia, 88, 1; Ia, 88, 3.

50. Herbert McCabe O.P., appendix 3 to Volume 3 of the Blackfriars edition of the *Summa theologiae* (London, 1964). See also Brian Davies, "Aquinas on What God Is Not," *Revue Internationale de Philosophie* 52 (1998).

sistent, we shall, from our reading, have lots to say about unicorns. Yet there are, of course, no unicorns. And there never have been any unicorns. That is why I say that our answer to the question "What is a unicorn?" will have to be settled on literary grounds. In trying to answer the question, we are seeking to learn what people mean by the word "unicorn." We are seeking a kind of nominal definition. We are looking for the meaning of a word. Knowing what a unicorn is simply amounts to knowing what a particular word means.

Aquinas, we should note, is perfectly aware of this fact. He even appeals to it as a reason for rejecting a famous argument for God's existence based on the meaning of the word "God."[51] For him, however, we might know what something is in a way that goes beyond learning what a dictionary tells us that a word (e.g., "unicorn") means. For, in his opinion, we might actually develop a *scientific* understanding of things and in this way be able to say what they are. There are no unicorns. But there are lots of cats. And, though we shall never be able to study any unicorns, we can certainly get our hands on a number of cats. And (as in fact has happened), on this basis we can develop an understanding of them, a grasp of what they are, a science of cats. As Aquinas would say, we can begin to explain *what it is to be* a cat. We can begin to explain what cats actually are—something we cannot do with respect to unicorns and the like since they are not actually anything (since there can be no science of unicorns).

For Aquinas, then, there is a difference between "A unicorn has a horn on its forehead" and anything that a scientist might come up with as an account of what cats are. And it is this difference which Aquinas has chiefly in mind when he says that creatures have *esse*. His idea is that, in truly knowing what, for example, a cat (as opposed to a unicorn) is, we are latching onto the fact that cats have *esse*. And the best way of expressing this fact is to say, as Herbert McCabe again usefully puts it, that, according to Aquinas: "It is not simply in our capacity to use signs, our ability for example, to understand words, but in our actual use of them to say what is the case that we have need of and lay hold on the *esse* of things."[52]

Given what I have been saying, Aquinas's teaching on *esse* is decidedly matter of fact and even pedestrian. For him, we lay hold on the *esse* of things by living in the world and by truly saying what things are. We lay hold on *esse* by being natural scientists exploring our environment and talking about it as we try to understand it. In Aquinas's view, however, our environment itself is a puzzling thing. For how come the world in which we try to say what things are? At the end of his *Tractatus Logico Philosophicus*, Ludwig Wittgenstein says: "Not *how* the world is, is the mystical, but *that* it is."[53] For Wittgenstein, *how the world is* is a scientific matter with scientific answers. But, so he insists, even when the scientific answers are in, we are still left with the *thatness* of the world, the fact *that* it is. As Wittgenstein himself puts it: "We feel that even if *all possible*

51. Cf. *Summa theologiae* Ia, 2, 1. The argument in question is sometimes called "the Ontological Argument."

52. Herbert McCabe O.P., "The Logic of Mysticism—I," in Martin Warner (ed.), *Religion and Philosophy* (Cambridge, 1992), p. 45.

53. Ludwig Wittgenstein, *Tractatus Logico-Philosophicus*, trans. D. F. Pears and B. F. McGuinness (London, 1961), 6.44.

scientific questions be answered, the problems of life have still not been touched at all."[54] And Aquinas is of the same mind. We can, he thinks, explore the world and develop an account of what things in it are. But we are still left with a decidedly nonscientific question. And he thinks of this question as causal. Or, as we may also put it, Aquinas's view is that, as well as asking "What *in the world* accounts for this, that, or the other?" we can also ask "Why *any world at all?*" or "How come the whole familiar business of asking and answering 'How come?'" And it is here that Aquinas thinks in terms of God. For him, the question "How come any universe?" is a serious one to which there must be an answer. And he gives the name "God" to whatever the answer is. God, for Aquinas, is the reason why there is any universe at all. God, he says, is the source of the *esse* of things— the fact that they are more than the meanings of words.[55] And, he adds, considered as such God is *ipsum esse subsistens*. Why? Because, so Aquinas thinks, God cannot be something the existence of which is derived from another. If God exists at all, so Aquinas reasons, then we cannot think of his nature or essence except as existing. And, for this reason Aquinas finds it appropriate to say that *what* God is and *that* God is amount to the same thing—that God's essence (his "whatness") is to be.[56] He also maintains that, insofar as something exists, it is caused to do so by God.

In other words, Aquinas holds that reflecting on the fact that things exist ought to lead us to see that there is something which is making them to be. And, with this thought in mind, he repeatedly insists that creatures depend intimately on God for as long as they continue to exist. Or, as he puts it in the *Summa theologiae*:

> God exists in everything; not indeed as part of their substance or as an accident, but as an agent is present to that in which its action is taking place. . . . Since it is God's nature to exist, he it must be who properly causes existence in creatures, just as it is fire itself which sets other things on fire. And God is causing this effect in things not just when they begin to exist, but all the time they are maintained in existence. . . . Now existence is more intimately and profoundly interior to things than anything else, for everything as we said is potential when compared to existence. So God must exist and exist intimately in everything.[57]

In other words, insofar as something can be said to be, God is making it to be or producing all that is real in it. Or, as Timothy McDermott nicely puts it, God, for Aquinas, is

54. *Tractatus*, 6.52.

55. Aquinas clearly sees this teaching as a way of bringing out what the Bible teaches concerning God as the maker of the world. But he also takes it to be philosophically cogent in its own right (as thinking which ought to be acceptable to any reasonable person with or without the benefit of biblical revelation). For representative texts in which he defends himself on this score, see: *De ente et essentia*, 4–5; *Summa contra gentiles* I, 13, 22; II, 6–10, 15–21; *Summa theologiae* Ia, 2–3, 8, 44–46; *De potentia* VII, 2.

56. Aquinas also thinks that this is the way to understand the Old Testament story of God revealing his name to Moses (Exodus 3:13–14). Reading the story in the text of the Latin Vulgate, he takes Moses to have been taught that God is "He who is" (*Qui est*). He interprets this as meaning that God is "existence itself" and that "the existence of God is his essence." Cf. *Summa theologiae* Ia, 13, 11.

57. *Summa theologiae* Ia, 8, 1. Cf. *De potentia* III, 7.

"the doing of all being."[58] For Aquinas, God is not an agent who gets things going and subsequently stands back as they enjoy an existence which does not depend on him. For Aquinas, God directly causes the being of everything at all times. Or, as Aquinas himself observes:

> There are two ways in which one thing may be kept in being by another. The first is indirect and incidental, as when one who removes a destructive force is said to preserve a thing in existence; for example, one who watches over a child lest it fall into a fire is said to preserve the child's life. The second is a *per se* and direct way of preserving a thing in existence, insofar, namely, as the thing preserved is so dependent that without the preserver it could not exist. This is the way that all creatures need God to keep them in existence.[59]

Aquinas, God, and Evil

In that case, however, what about evil? Does this need God to keep it in existence? Is it caused to be by God? Aquinas's way of dealing with this question (to be found in the *De malo*, though also throughout his writings) is to argue that evil cannot be caused by God since there is a serious sense in which it can be thought of as lacking in being. But what does he mean by arguing in this way?

Following Aristotle, Aquinas distinguishes between the use of "is" in sentences like "John is blind" and "John is" (i.e., exists). He takes the first use to signify that a predicate (e.g., "is blind") can be attached to a name (e.g., "John") so as to result in a true statement. He takes the second use to signify that "John" is a genuine name (i.e., a word which labels something in the real world, something which has what Aquinas calls *esse*). In the light of these considerations, Aquinas goes on to maintain that, since God is the source of there being what has *esse*, God cannot be thought of as causing evil to be. For evil is not anything actual (whether a substance or a property). It is what we may talk of things as "being" only in the sense that we may speak of people as "being blind."[60] Or, as Aquinas typically puts it, it is the absence of a good that ought to be present. There are holes in walls, but holes have no independent existence. There are holes in walls only because there are walls with something missing. There are blind people. But blindness has no independent existence. There are blind people only because there are people who can-

---

58. Timothy McDermott (ed.), *St. Thomas Aquinas, Summa Theologiae: A Concise Translation* (London, 1989), p. 105.

59. *Summa theologiae* Ia, 104, 1.

60. Cf. *De ente et essentia* 1: "There are two proper uses of the term 'being': firstly, generally for whatever falls into one of Aristotle's ten basic categories of thing, and secondly, for whatever makes a proposition true. These differ: in the second sense anything we can express in an affirmative proposition, however unreal, is said to be: in this sense lacks and absences are, since we say that absences are opposed to presences, and blindness exists in an eye. But in the first sense only what is real is, so that in this sense blindness and such are not beings." (I quote from Timothy McDermott (ed.), *Aquinas: Selected Philosophical Writings*, Oxford, 1993, pp. 91f.) Aquinas draws attention to the distinction he makes here in several other places. See, for example: his commentary on Aristotle's *Metaphysics*, Book V, lectio 9; *Summa theologiae* Ia, 3, 4 ad 2; *Summa theologiae* Ia, 48, 2 ad 2.

not see. In a similar way, so Aquinas holds, evil has no independent existence. It "is there" only in the sense that something "is missing." And, so Aquinas thinks, what is *not there* cannot be thought of as made to be by the source of the being of things. It cannot be thought to be made to be by God.

In other words (and as we can especially see in *De malo* I), Aquinas's view is that evil is not an individual with a life or character of its own. He also thinks that it is not a positive quality, like being square or being plastic.[61] In the *De malo* and elsewhere Aquinas distinguishes between what he calls *malum poenae* (literally: "evil of penalty") and *malum culpae* (literally: "evil of fault"). By the first expression he is referring to what later writers sometimes call "natural" or "physical" evil—pain, sickness, injury, and the like. We might translate *malum poenae* by the phrase "evil suffered." By the second expression he is referring to moral evil, or evil in human action (we might call it "evil done").[62] And he is perfectly clear both that there are victims of evil suffered and that there are people who are morally bad. According to him, however, what renders them bad is the gap between what they are and what they should be but are not. On his account, human sickness would not worry us if it did not amount to there being people deprived of some thriving, prospering, or flourishing. He also thinks that acting people would not strike us as morally bad unless we recognized that, in acting as they do, they fail to do what they ought or need to do (or they fail to be what they ought or need to be). His final conclusion, therefore, is that, though evil is parasitic on good, it is not part of the fabric of the universe. For it is not, itself, something which has being. Or as we read in the *Summa theologiae*:

> Like night from day, you learn about one opposite from the other. So you take good in order to grasp what evil means. Now we have accepted the definition that good is everything that is desirable. Well, then, since each real thing tends to its own existence and completion, we have to say that this fulfils the meaning of good in every case. Therefore evil cannot signify a certain existing being, or a real shaping or positive kind of thing. Consequently, we are left to infer that it signifies a certain absence of a good.[63]

---

61. The same conclusion is famously drawn by St. Augustine. Cf. *Enchiridion*, chapter 11: "For what is that which we call evil but the absence of good? In the bodies of animals, disease and wounds mean nothing but the absence of health; for when a cure is effected, that does not mean that the evils which were present—namely, the disease and wounds—go away from the body and dwell elsewhere: they altogether cease to exist; for the wound or disease is not a substance, but a defect in the fleshly substance, the flesh itself being a substance, and therefore something good, of which those evils—that is privations of the good which we call health—are accidents." The notion of evil as privation of good can also be found in various Neoplatonic writings. See, for instance, Plotinus, *Enneads* I, 8,3. Notice, however, that it also makes sense on Aristotelian grounds, for, according to Aristotle, badness always involves the absence of what is desirable. In *Summa theologiae* Ia, 5, 1 Aquinas picks up on Aristotle's account in order to defend the view that goodness and being have a kind of equivalence.

62. The expression *malum poenae* reflects the fact that Aquinas, like many Christian writers, understands pain, sickness, and the like (sometimes people call these "naturally occurring evils") to be ultimately due to the sin of Adam, whose wrongdoing led to punishment that deprived him and his offspring of paradise. But one can understand Aquinas's use of the expression even without reference to the notion of a primeval fall.

63. *Summa theologiae* Ia, 48, 1.

On the other hand, however, there is evil suffered (e.g., there are ill human beings), and there is evil done (e.g., there are people who act unjustly). So what does Aquinas think to be going on when these come to pass? Here, again, his notion of God as the source of *esse* is relevant. For his answer is that God is producing all that is required for things to fall short.

Notice that, confronted by evil suffered, we naturally look for a natural explanation. If Mary is sick, we try to discover what (in the world) accounts for her state. If we come across the corpse of a zebra, we assume that something (in the world) was responsible for the zebra's death. In other words, we never assume that evil suffered is *naturally inexplicable*. We assume, in fact, that there is something (even if we do not, as yet, know what exactly that is) which, by being *good in its way*, is causing something else to be *bad in its way*. We assume, in effect, that nothing ever suffers evil except at the hands of some other being which is gaining some good (even though, in the case of a free creature, it may be, in a deeper sense, damaging itself by practicing evil done).[64]

What does this tell us about God and evil suffered? Aquinas thinks it tells us that evil suffered is a necessary concomitant of certain goods, and that God can be said to have brought it about only in the sense that he brought about those goods.[65] Critics of belief in God have sometimes suggested that there is *too much* evil suffered in God's world (the implication being that God is either bad or nonexistent).[66] According to Aquinas, however, in the case of evil suffered, there can never be more evil than there need be. He thinks that any evil suffered that is *more than there need be* would be *lacking a natural cause*. It would be scientifically inexplicable. He therefore suggests that the evil suffered in the world is neither *more* nor *less* than what we can expect in a material world in which scientific explanations can be given for what happens. According to Aquinas, God has created a material world in which there is evil suffered. And, in making this world to be, God is making what is good. Indeed, Aquinas thinks, God is making nothing but what is good. And he thinks this not because he views evil as an illusion of some kind, but because he sees goodness as what we have when things succeed in being what they need to be considered as the things that they are by nature. For him, "good" signifies some kind of success or achievement. It may be bad for me that a lion should eat me. But, Aquinas maintains, even as an injured man (the victim of evil suffered) I still succeed in being human. And the lion that eats me (the cause of the evil I suffer) is doing just what we expect a lion to do. According to Herbert McCabe:

> You can't have badness unless there is some goodness, whereas you can have goodness without any badness. The two are not symmetrical, so to say. I mean that if a washing machine is to be a bad one it must be at least good enough at being a washing machine for us to call it one. If I produce a cup and saucer and complain that it is a useless washing machine because it never gets the clothes clean, you will gently correct me

64. Cf. Herbert McCabe O.P., *God Matters* (London, 1987), pp. 31–32.
65. In the *De malo*, Aquinas does not dwell on what we might call "the metaphysics of evil suffered," though his views on this are clearly not far below the surface of the text. For a direct treatment, see *Summa theologiae* Ia, 19, 9 and Ia, 48 and 49.
66. See, for example, William Rowe, "The Problem of Evil and Some Varieties of Atheism," *American Philosophical Quarterly* 16 (1979).

and explain that what I have is not a washing machine at all. So even the worst washing machine must be a little good, otherwise it is not even a washing machine and cannot therefore be a bad one.[67]

This is exactly how Aquinas thinks when it comes to evil suffered and the sense in which even what is bad is also somehow good. And his suggestion that evil suffered is explicable in terms of goodness is also well expressed by McCabe. He writes:

> There is no mystery about my headache. Similarly with my cancer or my influenza— always there is a natural explanation and always the explanation is in terms of some things, cells or germs or whatever, doing what comes naturally, being good. Sometimes, of course, and rather more often than he admits, the doctor is baffled. But he puts this down to his own ignorance; he says: "Well eventually we may hope to find out what is causing this, what things are bringing it about simply by being their good selves, but for the moment we don't know." What he does *not* say is this: there is no explanation in nature for this, it is an anti-miracle worked by a malignant God.[68]

These comments also nicely capture what Aquinas thinks when it comes to evil suffered. But what about "evil done"? Unlike evil suffered, Aquinas thinks that this can hardly be thought of as *benefiting* something. He holds that those who wrong others harm their victims and in doing so harm (are bad in) themselves. For Aquinas, there is no concomitant good in the case of evil done. There is nothing but failure. Aquinas concedes that evil done often involves a kind of success, that, for example, even the murderer may be getting things right in all sorts of ways—as a killer, a strategist, and so on. In Aquinas's view, however, agents of evil done are fundamentally failing to be good and nothing is benefiting from this (except accidentally). The evil in their actions is nothing but such failure. And from this Aquinas concludes that it cannot be made by God, that it represents no action of God. Why? Because, says Aquinas, for God to act is for God to make things to be. And the evil in evil done is, for Aquinas, no more possessed of being (*esse*) than is the evil in evil suffered. It is part of God's world only in the sense that there are agents who somehow fall short, as Aquinas directly argues in *De malo* I–III, and as he assumes throughout the rest of the text.

Aquinas and Human Action

But what now of these agents who fall short? How does Aquinas view them? A point worth noting is that he takes them to be rather more numerous than many people would since he believes in the existence of fallen angels. Hence the references to the devil in *De malo* III. Hence, also, the discussion of demons in *De malo* VIII. In the *De malo* as a whole, however, and his writings in general, Aquinas is chiefly concerned with evil done insofar as its agents are people. And he takes it to be ascribable to them since, in his view, they can (at least sometimes) act freely and can therefore be held accountable for their

---

67. McCabe, *God Matters*, p. 30.
68. McCabe, *God Matters*, p. 32.

actions. According to Aquinas, freedom is required for *malum culpae*. And, as he argues in *De malo* VI, human beings have freedom. But what does Aquinas mean by saying so? And how does his approach to human action in the *De malo* fit with his general account of human agency as developed in other texts?

(a) Knowledge, Ends, and Action

To understand what Aquinas says about human action in the *De malo*, it helps, for a start, to be aware of what he argues elsewhere when considering what he takes to be the difference between people and other things in the world. In particular, it is useful to bear in mind that people, for Aquinas, are things with the ability to transcend their individuality. For, on his account (especially as found in the *Summa theologiae* and the commentary on Aristotle's *De anima*) people can act because they can understand. According to him, people, unlike other animals, can pursue ends or goals. And they can do so purposefully, consciously, or intelligently. Or, to put it another way, people, in Aquinas's view, are the highest form of life short of the angels and God.

For Aquinas, living things are, quite literally, automobiles—subjects that can move on their own (unlike, say, stones). "To live," he says, "is attributed to some beings because they are seen to move themselves, but not to be moved by another."[69] But why do living things move as they do? Here Aquinas draws some distinctions. For, he says, some things (e.g., plants and non-human animals) move insofar as their physical makeup dictates. All things being equal, plants will stretch out roots and turn toward the sun, while cats will not only grow but also, for instance, breathe, yawn, and defecate. Thinking them more complicated than plants, Aquinas also thinks that nonhuman animals have abilities to respond to the world at a sensual level. They can find it agreeable or disagreeable, nice or nasty, painful or pleasant. And on that basis they can move in ways different from plants. Hence, for example, cats can chase mice and shun rain.[70] But people, Aquinas argues, are even more complicated than nonhuman animals. Like plants and other animals, he says, they grow and function physically. They move in ways recorded by biologists. But they can also, Aquinas thinks, move as knowers, not simply as physical entities or reactors. As Aquinas sees it, though nonhuman animals can react to their environment in a variety of ways, they do not understand it. They can respond to it. But they do so instinctively, as their bodies (through which they can sense things) make contact with the world beyond themselves. With people, however, things can be different. Or so Aquinas maintains. For people, so he argues, are not purely physical.

It is important to stress that in taking this line Aquinas is not embracing what we might call a "dualistic" account of the human person. He does not mean that people are composed of two distinct things, as, for example, Descartes thought. According to

---

69. *Summa contra gentiles* I, 97. Cf. *Summa theologiae* Ia, 18, 1–3 and *Commentary on Aristotle's De anima* I, 135–157 and II, 163–181. In various places (e.g., *Summa contra gentiles* I, 13), Aquinas teaches that nothing, apart from God, is *wholly* self-moving. But he does not think that this truth entails that we cannot distinguish between, say, stones and cats so as to find in the latter a source of movement that can intelligibly be thought of as internal.

70. Cf. *Summa theologiae* Ia, 83, 1 and *Disputed Questions on the Soul* (*Quaestiones de anima*) XIII.

Descartes: "I have a clear and distinct idea of myself, in so far as I am simply a thinking, non-extended thing; and on the other I have a clear and distinct idea of body, in so far as this is simply an extended non-thinking thing. And accordingly, it is certain that I am really distinct from my body and can exist without it."[71] But this is not how Aquinas reasons. For him, people are essentially bodily. "For as it belongs to the very conception of 'this human being' that there should be this soul, flesh and bone," he writes, "so it belongs to the very conception of 'human being' that there be soul, flesh and bone."[72] Hence it is that, when speaking of life after death, Aquinas looks forward to the resurrection of the body.[73] Yet Aquinas also insists that, bodily though they are, people are more than wholly material entities. And he does so because he thinks that, unlike other animals, people rise beyond the level of sensation.

According to Aquinas, sensations are particular physical occurrences going on in particular physical organisms. And for this reason he takes them to be what we might call the ultimate in private property. He does not, of course, deny that two people can share a sensation in that, for example, you and I can both feel heat when sitting before a fire. But, he thinks, the occurrence of the sensation of heat in me is different from its occurrence in you— just, for example, as my breathing is *my* breathing and not *your* breathing. In other words, Aquinas views sensations as local or confined, as, so to speak, "trapped" in the bodies of those who have them. Echoing Aristotle, however, he also maintains that people enjoy more than sensations. For, on his account, people can have knowledge, which he takes to be universal and unconfined—the ultimate in public property. And it is as knowers, Aquinas thinks, that people are more than merely bodies in motion. For, he holds, though I cannot have your very own sensations, I can have the very same thoughts as you, from which it follows, he concludes, that knowing is not a physical process since physical processes are events which occur in and to different individuals.

One way of putting all this is to say that meanings, for Aquinas, can never be particular physical objects. His view of understanding is that it should never be confused with encountering a thing at the sensory level and should never be identified with any individual physical process. Aquinas thinks that we cannot understand material individuals. We can confront them at a sensory level, but that, so he argues, is different from understanding them. For him, understanding is expressible in judgments or statements, and it can be shared by human beings (though not with other animals) in a way that sensations cannot. And, Aquinas argues, since statements can be either true or false, knowledge or understanding can lead people to recognize alternatives. To understand a state-

71. *The Philosophical Writings of Descartes*, trans. John Cottingham, Robert Stoothhoff, and Dugald Murdoch (Cambridge, 1984), Volume II, p. 54. For modern defenses of Descartes's position, see H. D. Lewis, *The Elusive Self* (London, 1982), and Richard Swinburne, *The Evolution of the Soul* (Oxford, 1986). That people are really non-material is also the view defended by Plato in dialogues such as the *Phaedo*.

72. *Summa theologiae* Ia, 75, 4.

73. Aquinas often refers to the thesis that people are essentially substances different from bodies on which they act (a view which he ascribes to Plato). But he rejects it quite strongly, as, for example, at *Summa contra gentiles* II, 57, where he observes: "Plato and his followers asserted that the intellectual soul is not united to the body as form to matter, but only as mover to movable, for Plato said that the soul is in the body 'as a sailor in a ship.' Thus the union of soul and body would only be by contact of power. . . . But this doctrine seems not to fit the facts."

ment, Aquinas thinks, is also to understand its negation. It is to be able to view the world as containing possibilities, as possibly being other than it is in fact now. And, for this reason, Aquinas also holds that with the ability to understand comes the ability to *act* and not simply to *react*. Why? Because, he thinks, action involves more than being affected by external stimuli and responding accordingly. It depends on understanding how things are and how they could be. And it consists in seeking that they should be one way as opposed to some other way.

According to Aquinas, nonhuman animals can also be said to seek. For he thinks that they have tendencies to behave in accordance with their natures, that they have "appetites."[74] We speak of water naturally "seeking" its own level, and Aquinas, in a similar way, speaks of animals "seeking" to be what they naturally are and to have what they naturally need. Left to themselves, he thinks, they just are what they are by nature. They may be interfered with, and may, therefore, become thwarted or defective. And how they behave in particular circumstances may be impossible for us to predict with a high degree of accuracy. According to Aquinas, however, in the absence of interference, they simply realize their natures. They "seek" to be themselves. But not, so Aquinas holds, in a conscious sense. Their seeking is not based on knowing how things might be and moving accordingly. It is not a matter of planning that a possibly attainable end should come to pass. Rather, it is a combination of instinct affected by circumstances. It is a product of complex and given structures. It is lived out rather than chosen. And, Aquinas thinks, it therefore falls short of action—or, at any rate, of what he takes to be involved in genuine human action. For, in his view, this is irreducibly and consciously end directed, and it depends on understanding since it is only by understanding the world that we can consciously seek to affect it. Aquinas does not want to say that we cannot act unless we have a complete understanding of the world and of how things are within it. Indeed, he thinks, we often act in ignorance. But he also holds that we cannot truly act without some conception of how things are and of how they might be. And it is thus that he views human action as end or goal directed (i.e., intentional). In Aquinas's view, human action differs from the behavior of nonhuman animals since it is done with reasons. It always invites the question "With a view to what are you doing that?" And, Aquinas also thinks, acting for reasons is always a matter of seeking what one takes to be good.

(b) Goodness, Action, and Will

Yet how are we to understand the word *good* in this context? As we have seen, Aquinas associates goodness with success or achievement. And he certainly wants to say that when seeking what we take to be good we are trying to succeed or achieve in some way. Further to fathom Aquinas on this matter, however, it is useful to remember that, when he explains what goodness is, he typically says that to be good is, quite generally (and not

---

74. Aquinas also ascribes natural tendencies or appetites to non-organic things and to creatures (e.g., angels) who are wholly immaterial. And he ascribes them to people considered as merely physical organisms.

only with respect to people), the same as being *desirable*. As he writes, for example, in the *Summa theologiae*: "The goodness of a thing consists in its being desirable. . . . Now clearly desirability is consequent upon perfection, for things always desire their perfection."[75] Aquinas frequently observes that anything can be called good (though not perfect) insofar as its natural tendencies or appetites remain in operation. His view is that something can be called good if it has features that are desirable for it. So he thinks of goodness as something to which everything naturally tends, as something which everything seeks. And it is with this thought in mind that he argues that, when people act with reasons, they always aim at what they take to be good. In his view, all things always tend to what is good for them. But, so he thinks, people do not always do simply as their nature dictates (as is the case with nonhuman animals). They can understand what they are able to do, and they can perceive alternatives. Their tending can be governed by understanding, in which case, so Aquinas says, it will always be influenced not just by the draw of goodness in general but also by what is *thought* to be good. According to Aquinas, we do not just seek what is naturally good for us. We also seek what we believe to be so. In this sense, he thinks, acting people can never consciously fail to aim at what attracts them. Their actions will always reflect what they find desirable.

Another way of making the point is to say that Aquinas sees human actions as always expressing the *will* of those who perform them. But it is important to recognize that "will," for him, does not signify some kind of entity which is radically to be distinguished from anything we might call "knowledge" or "understanding." For him, human action is a matter of will inasmuch as acting people are doing what they find it desirable to do. But he also thinks that what we find desirable depends on how we view things—that is, that willing and understanding go together. According to Aquinas, there is no operation of the will which is not also an operation of the reason, and vice versa. There is an interweaving of being attracted and understanding that cannot be unraveled in practice. We think of what we are *attracted* to thinking of, and we are attracted to what we *think* of. Insofar as we consciously aim at what we are attracted to, we act voluntarily or with will. This, of course, means that, for Aquinas, there is no place for the notion of willing as something we have to do *after* we have cleared our minds and decided what it is good for us to do. On some accounts of human agency, people first decide what is good and then (maybe with difficulty) choose to will it.[76] But this is not how it is on Aquinas's account. For him, our perception and wanting of what is good are of a piece. We naturally want what we take to be good. And what we take to be good depends on what we

---

75. *Summa theologiae* Ia, 5, 1. Cf. *De veritate* I, 21, 1; *Summa contra gentiles* I, 37. In *Summa theologiae* Ia, 5, 1 Aquinas goes on to say: "The perfection of a thing depends on how far it has achieved actuality. It is clear then that a thing is good inasmuch as it exists, for . . . it is by existing that everything achieves actuality." Here we can see him thinking of goodness in terms of being. Aquinas does not think that "good" and "existing" are synonymous. For he concedes that something can exist without being wholly perfect. But he also argues that, even if something is not good without qualification (even if it is not wholly actual), it must be actual, and therefore good, simply by virtue of existing. In this sense, he concludes, everything that exists is good.

76. Hence we have the notion that people need willpower—the idea being that one can have a clear view of what needs to be done or of what ought to be done without the will to do it.

want. Aquinas does not doubt that we might often be mistaken about what is good for us. For him, however, our actions (as opposed to our mechanical reactions or bits of behavior in which we engage unthinkingly) are always directed to what we take to be good for us. They always express our desires (our will) and, in this sense, are voluntary. "A good understood," says Aquinas, "is will's object and moves it by being something to aim for."[77]

Does this, however, mean that we can only act in one way at any given time? Is Aquinas saying that people inevitably follow their desires? At one level he is, for he is committed to the view that there is a sense in which people can aim only for what they desire. For he thinks that, whether they realize it or not, what people ultimately desire (their ultimate and true good) is God, to whom they cannot but be attracted.[78] At the same time, however, he is equally clear that God is not an immediate object of knowledge for people in this life. If we enjoyed a clear understanding of God, then, so he thinks, we would simply aim at God. Instead, however, we find ourselves presented with a variety of competing goods. And for this reason Aquinas holds that we do not of necessity desire as we do. "The will of one who sees God's essence," he writes, "necessarily clings to God, because then we cannot help willing to be happy." Yet, so he also says, "there are individual good things that have no necessary connection with happiness because a man can be happy without them, and the will does not have to cling to these."[79] In general, Aquinas thinks, we cannot but aim at what we desire. But our desires, he thinks, depend on what we know in particular and different circumstances. "The will can tend towards nothing that is not conceived to be good," he explains, "but because there are many kinds of good thing it is not by any necessity determined to any particular one."[80]

(c) Acting in Practice

For Aquinas, then, acting persons intend (aim at) what attracts them. But what is going on as they act in specific circumstances? Aquinas's answer is that they live out or engage in examples of what he calls "practical reasoning." On his account, human action is always a reasonable business since it always involves seeking what one takes (even if mistakenly) to be somehow desirable. And, in this sense, he conceives of it as always conforming to a certain pattern of reasonableness comparable to what is involved when we reason not about what to do (practical reasoning) but about what is the case (theoretical reasoning). We may, so he thinks, reason to the *truth* of some matter. We might work

---

77. *Summa theologiae* Ia, 82, 4. As Daniel Westberg observes (*Right Practical Reason*, Oxford, 1994, p. 37), when it comes to Aquinas: "The key is to understand human choice and action not as a process of reasoning followed by an 'act of will' to carry it out, but as an operation combining both belief and desire."

78. Cf. *Summa theologiae* Ia2ae, 2, 8: "The object of the will, that is the human appetite, is the Good without reserve, just as the object of the mind is the True without reserve. Clearly, then, nothing can satisfy our will except such goodness, which is found, not in anything created, but in God alone.' Cf. also *Summa theologiae* Ia, 82, 1: "It is most necessary that the will of necessity cleave to its final fulfilment, happiness, just as the understanding must of necessity cleave to first principles."

79. *Summa theologiae* Ia, 82, 2.

80. *Summa theologiae* Ia, 82, 2 ad 1.

out how things *are*. But we can also, he says, reason as to *what is to be done*. We might work out *how to behave*. And this, he thinks, is what we are doing as we settle down to action in practice.

On Aquinas's account, essential to human action is what he calls "choice" or "decision" (*electio*). Or, to put it another way, Aquinas takes human action as a *doing in the light of alternatives*.[81] In saying so, however, he does not mean that action is something which follows choice or decision—as if acting people first make choices or decisions and then subsequently act on them. For Aquinas, actual human actions are human choices or decisions, and to describe them is to state how we have chosen or decided (what our choices or decisions have amounted to). Yet Aquinas does not think that our actions come out of the blue, as it were. For him, particular choices or decisions reflect the way in which people think. They also reflect the character of the people in question. Or, as Aquinas puts it, choice (*electio*) springs from *deliberation* (*consilium*), and both choice and deliberation arise from *dispositions* of various kinds.

When he refers to deliberation (*consilium*) Aquinas has in mind a reasoning process having to do with how to obtain what we want. Action, he thinks, starts with desire for something one finds attractive (something one takes to be good). But how is that something to be achieved? Here, he says, reason comes in as suggesting the recipe for success. Before choosing what to do (before actually acting), we may have to consider how best to get what we are looking for at the outset.[82] We may be clear as to what we want to achieve. But we might have to think about how to achieve it. Or, as Aquinas puts it:

> The field of practice is attended with much uncertainty, for our acts are engaged with contingent individual cases, which offer no fixed and certain points because they are so variable. The reason does not pronounce a verdict in matters doubtful and open to question without having conducted an investigation. Such an inquiry is necessary before coming to a decision on what is to be chosen; it is called deliberation.[83]

The end to be achieved is not, one should notice, the business of what Aquinas means by deliberation. He does not conceive of this as helping us to determine what we want or should want. In his view, we deliberate in the light of desire. We do not desire in the

---

81. So he denies that nonhuman animals exercise choice as they respond to external stimuli. Cf. *Summa theologiae* Ia2ae, 13, 2. Choice, for Aquinas, can only belong to beings who can consciously opt in the light of reasons for one way of proceeding rather than another.

82. I say "we may have to consider" since Aquinas does not think that action always proceeds from a process of inquiry or reasoning. Rather, he thinks that it is proceeds when we are initially uncertain as to how to get what we want. Where such uncertainty is lacking, then so is deliberation. Cf. *Summa theologiae* Ia2ae, 14, 4: "Deliberation is a kind of inquiry. Now we are wont to inquire into matters we are doubtful about, and conduct a reasoned investigation, called the argument, in order to find a reason that attests to a fact previously open to doubt. There are two factors in a situation which put elements of human activity beyond doubt. First, when determinate ends are reached along determinate ways, as happens in the arts which are governed by fixed rules, thus a calligrapher does not question the shape of the letters of the alphabet; his art takes this for granted. Second, when it is a matter of little moment whether a thing is done in this way or in that, as happens in petty decisions which scarcely help or hinder the accomplishment of an end and can be treated lightly."

83. *Summa theologiae* Ia2ae, 14, 1.

light of deliberation. For Aquinas, deliberation presupposes goals, ends, or intentions.[84] But not all courses of action lead to the same goal. And some courses of action can be better at getting us what we want than others. For Aquinas, therefore, deliberation has to do with means. It is a way of helping our will to have its full rein. It is rational reflection on how to obtain what we want.[85]

Yet what about our wants? How does Aquinas see these as entering into the occurrence of genuine human actions? This is where the notion of dispositions comes in. For, to put it as simply as possible, Aquinas views the wants reflected in particular human actions as deriving from what we are (or, rather, from what we have become), considered not just as doing this or that, but as being people *of a certain kind*—people who find it desirable to act in certain kinds of ways, people with certain tastes, likes, and dislikes. For him, concrete actions reflect our characters or settled personalities. He thinks that there are patterns of action to which we tend as individuals, and that our tendencies can be affected or influenced by our past and by choices we make. We do not, he holds, act in an historical vacuum. We act on the basis of dispositions.

What I am calling a "disposition" Aquinas calls a *habitus*,[86] and, though *habitus* can be translated "habit," it is better rendered by "disposition."[87] For Aquinas's *habitus* is not a "habit' in the modern sense. When we speak today of people having a habit, we normally imply that they would find it hard not to act in certain ways. Hence, for example, we speak of someone having the habit of smoking. A habit, for us, is a kind of addiction. For Aquinas, however, a *habitus* puts one's activity more under one's control than it might otherwise be. In this sense, to have a *habitus* is to be disposed to some activity or other— not because one tends to that activity on every possible occasion, but because one finds it natural, readily coped with, an obvious activity to engage in, and so on. In Aquinas's thinking, for example, fluency in a foreign language is a *habitus*. Someone who possesses it may refrain from displaying it for one reason or another. But, when speaking the language, such a person will do so easily and with a proficiency which many lack entirely. Or, again, people who are naturally or instinctively generous would, for Aquinas, have a *habitus*. They would be generous without effort. There would be little or no question of "going against the grain." As Anthony Kenny explains, a *habitus*, for Aquinas is, "halfway between a capacity and an action, between pure potentiality and full actuality."[88] Suppose you say that you can speak French. Your statement could be true even though you are not speaking French. But it will not be true just because it is possible for you to speak French in some abstract sense. "I can speak French" does not entail that I am speaking French at the time the statement is made. On the other hand, however, it entails more than the suggestion that it is logically possible for me to speak French. It entails that I

84. Cf. *Summa theologiae* Ia2ae, 14, 2.

85. Of course, Aquinas does not mean that deliberation cannot lead us to want to act in certain ways which we might not have thought about before deliberating. Hence, for example, he can speak of it as involving advice from others (cf. *Summa theologiae* Ia2ae, 14, 3). His point, however, is that the purpose of deliberation is to work out effective ways of getting what we want to start with.

86. There is an extended treatment of *habitus* in *Summa theologiae* Ia2ae, 49–54.

87. For a defense of this translation, see the introduction to Volume 22 of the Blackfriars edition of the *Summa theologiae*.

88. Ibid., p. xxi.

have a genuine ability that not everyone has. In this sense, "I can speak French" ascribes to me an ability or skill that endures over time and can, as things are, be exercised in actual definite bits of behavior. In the thinking of Aquinas, it ascribes to me a *habitus* or disposition.

We may put it by saying that, in Aquinas's view, people can acquire settled ways of acting. And, for him, this means that they can acquire a settled range of aims, tastes, or wants which play a vital role when it comes to concrete decisions. For, he holds, these express our wants—even insofar as they spring from deliberation. In choosing, he thinks, we aim for what attracts us, and we ignore or avoid what does not. And we pay attention to what attracts us even as we consider how to obtain what we want—since how we choose to achieve our purposes depends on what we are prepared to take seriously and on what we are prepared to disregard.[89] Or, as Aquinas frequently explains, human actions reflect the virtues and vices of people. For, on his account, virtues and vices are dispositions to act in certain ways—the difference between them being that virtues help us to act well as human beings while vices help us to act badly.[90] Hence, for example, with an eye on what he calls the virtue of temperateness (the disposition to act so as not to be overcome by certain, mostly physical, desires), Aquinas in the *De malo* writes:

> Since sinful and virtuous acts are done by choice, and choice is the desire for something about which one has deliberated beforehand, and deliberation is an inquiry, there needs to be a quasi-syllogistic deduction regarding every virtuous or sinful act. And yet a temperate person syllogizes in one way, an intemperate person in another way, and a continent person in one way, an incontinent person in another way. For only the judgment of reason moves the temperate person. And so the temperate person employs a syllogism with three propositions and deduces like this: no fornication should be committed; this act would be fornication; therefore, I should not do it. And the intemperate person completely follows his desires, and so even such a person employs a syllogism with three propositions and quasi-deduces like this: everything pleasurable should be enjoyed; this act would be pleasurable; therefore, I should do it. But both the continent person and the incontinent person are moved in two ways: indeed by reason to avoid sin, and by concupiscence to commit it. And the judgment of reason prevails in the case of the continent person, while the movement of concupiscence prevails in the case of the incontinent person. And so both employ a syllogism with four propositions but reach contrary conclusions. For the continent person syllogizes as follows. No sin should be committed. And although the judgment of reason proposes this, the movement of concupiscence causes the person to reflect that everything pleasurable should be pursued. But because the judgment of reason prevails in the

89. In other words, and as noted above, according to Aquinas we think of what we are attracted to thinking of, and we are attracted to what we think of—which is not to be confused with believing what we want to believe. Aquinas's point is that decisions to act depend on the fact that we pay attention to what we want to attend to and that we are attracted to what we present to ourselves as good.

90. Notice, therefore, that Aquinas, unlike some moralists, does not think of and evaluate human actions simply with respect to whether or not they count as obeying or disobeying rules. He is concerned with human action as something to which education is relevant. He is concerned with the acquiring of character which enables people instinctively to act well.

person, the person subsumes under the first proposition and draws a conclusion as follows: no sin should be committed; this is a sin; therefore, this should not be done. And the incontinent person, in whom the movement of concupiscence prevails, subsumes under the second proposition and draws a conclusion as follows: everything pleasurable should be pursued; this is pleasurable; therefore, this should be pursued. And properly speaking, such a person is one who sins out of weakness. And so it is evident that such a person, although knowing regarding the universal, nonetheless does not know regarding the particular, since the person subsumes according to concupiscence and not according to reason.[91]

Aquinas is not here asserting that people go through a complicated piece of reasoning every time they decide to act. His point is that the intellectual structure of decisions (their "logic," if you like) can be exhibited in a rational form. And in making the point he is anxious to stress that the ways in which we act can be profoundly affected by the characters we have developed—whether virtuous or vicious.[92]

Sin

Notice now, however, that in the passage just cited Aquinas contrasts virtuous activity not with what is vicious but with what is sinful. Why so? The reason lies in the fact that he thinks of people not just as able to act well or badly in general but also as able to act well or badly when considered as creatures of God.

According to Aquinas, one can give a sensible account of how people come to act as they do even if one has no particular theological commitment. He also thinks that, even from a non-theological perspective, one can give some account of the difference between acting well or badly—the difference between succeeding as a human being (being a good human being) and failing as such (being a bad human being). In other words, he thinks that it is possible to offer a sound philosophical account of human action. He also thinks it possible to give good philosophical reasons for acting in some ways rather than others. So he says, for example, that, though "there is a true bliss located after this life," it is also true that "a certain imitation of bliss is possible in this life if human beings perfect them-

---

91. *De malo* III, 9 ad 7. For a detailed discussion of temperance by Aquinas, see *Summa theologiae* 2a2ae, 141–154.

92. For Aquinas on virtues in general, see *Summa theologiae* Ia2ae, 55–67. Philosophers sometimes ask how people can do what they know to be bad—a topic that Aquinas touches on in *De malo* III, 9. Some thinkers have held that we do what we know to be bad out of ignorance. Others have held that we do what we know to be bad because our actions spring from will, not knowledge, so that we can know what is good but fail to aim for it. For Aquinas, however, the will is our being attracted by the good as it appears to our minds. So, though he concedes that bad actions sometimes spring from ignorance, he also thinks that will depends on understanding and that understanding depends on will. He therefore argues that we do what we know to be bad because of a sidelining of reason through weakness of temperateness or through strength of uncontrolled passion. For this reason, his account of what is sometimes called "weakness of will" depends on his notion of a *habitus*. We can do what we know to be wrong because we have become the sort of people who instinctively act in certain ways. And, so he thinks, we can be held responsible for ending up like this.

selves in the goods firstly of contemplative and secondly of practical reason" and that "this is the happiness Aristotle discusses in his *Ethics* without either advocating or rejecting another bliss after this life."[93] As we have seen, however, Aquinas takes God to be the ultimate (even if unrecognized) object of human desire. And his approach to human conduct is infected by this conviction. For it leads him to see human actions as having more than what we might call a merely human significance. It leads him to see them as significant before God and as affecting our standing considered as God's creatures.[94]

More precisely, it leads him to see them as being in or out of tune with what he calls "Eternal Law." According to Aquinas, "Law is nothing but a dictate of practical reason issued by a sovereign who governs a complete community."[95] And, he adds, "The whole community of the universe is governed by God's mind."[96] "Through his wisdom," says Aquinas, "God is the founder of the universe of things, and . . . in relation to them he is like an artist with regard the things he makes. . . . And so, as being the principle through which the universe is created, divine wisdom means art, or exemplar, or idea, and likewise it also means law, as moving all things to their due ends. Accordingly the Eternal Law is nothing other than the exemplar of divine wisdom as directing the motions and actions of everything."[97]

Since Aquinas takes God to be noncomposite, since he believes that all that is *in* God *is* God, he thinks that God and the Eternal Law are one and the same reality.[98] For him,

93. *Commentary on the Sentences of Peter Lombard*, Book 4, Distinction 49, Question 1, Article 1. I quote from McDermott, *Aquinas: Selected Philosophical Writings*, pp. 325f.

94. As I have noted, much literature on Aquinas has been devoted to the question "Should Aquinas be thought of as a philosopher or a theologian?" Some have insisted that it is quite wrong to think of him as a philosopher since his interests were chiefly theological. Others have suggested that the theology of Aquinas cannot be properly understood if one does not see it as resting on indisputably philosophical foundations. In reflecting on this debate, we need to remember the following facts: (1) Aquinas never suggests that theology (i.e., *sacra doctrina*) is to be grounded in purely philosophical argument (i.e., argument which takes no theological teaching for granted); (2) When Aquinas uses the word "philosophers" he is always thinking of pagans (i.e., people whom he takes not to believe in what he most firmly believes in—the content of *sacra doctrina*); (3) When reflecting on Christian teaching, Aquinas frequently draws on arguments that he clearly thinks of as ones which any sensible person (whether Christian or not) should accept. In view of these facts it seems fair to say that Aquinas can be viewed both as a philosopher and as a theologian. He is a philosopher since much that he says is presented by him as reflection which does not begin by assuming theological beliefs. He is a theologian since much of his thinking is influenced by what he takes to be true apart from philosophical considerations. And this is how we must view him when he writes about human action. At one level, he takes them to be understandable without reference to theological doctrines. But he also thinks that theology can help us to understand them better.

95. *Summa theologiae* Ia2ae, 91, 1.

96. *Summa theologiae* Ia2ae, 91, 1.

97. *Summa theologiae* Ia2ae, 93,1.

98. For Aquinas, God cannot be thought of as an individual with properties really distinct from himself. We speak of God as if he were just this, and, so Aquinas thinks, it is proper that we should do so (cf. *Summa theologiae* Ia, 13, 1). However, so he argues in various places, properties that we truly attribute to God (e.g., knowledge, power, goodness, or whatever) are not (as they are in us) distinct realities. Nor are they distinct from the subject God is. As we may put it, Aquinas's view is that there is no real difference between *who* God is and *what* God is. This is part of what is commonly referred

therefore, human actions must ultimately be viewed as conforming, or as failing to conform, to the goodness that God is essentially. On his account, God, who is perfectly good, is the standard by which creatures can be thought of as good or as failing to be good. So, when people succeed or fail in goodness, they succeed or fail with respect to God. Insofar as they succeed, then, Aquinas thinks, they reflect the goodness that is God. Insofar as they fail, they stray from this goodness. Or, as Aquinas says, they sin. Drawing on St. Augustine of Hippo, Aquinas defines sin as "nothing else than to neglect eternal things, and to seek after temporal things." All human wickedness, he adds, "consists in making means of ends and ends of means."[99]

In other words, Aquinas takes bad human actions to be actions the nature of which can only be properly grasped if we see them as leaving us short of what God is all about. Or, as he puts it in the *Summa theologiae*:

> A human act is human because it is voluntary. . . . A human act is evil because it does not meet the standard for human behavior. Standards are nothing other than rules. The human will is subject to a twofold rule: one is proximate and on his own level, i.e., human reason; the other is the first rule beyond man's own level, i.e., the eternal law which is the mind of God.[100]

On this account, there is no conflict between rational human action and action which conforms to the goodness that is God. But the former is seen as an instance of the latter—the idea being that sound moral philosophy is, in the end, also sound from the viewpoint of theology. This is not to say that Aquinas thinks of moral philosophers (even the best of them) as our most trustworthy advisers when it comes to matters theological (when it comes to conforming to the mind of God). Nor is it to say that he thinks of rational reflection as able, by itself, to lead us to ultimate happiness. It is, however, to say that Aquinas finds no difficulty with the suggestion that genuine moral failure (something which he thinks can be understood at a philosophical level) can also be viewed as failure with respect to God—as a matter of people failing to rise to the goodness which God is.

And it is on this basis that Aquinas reasons throughout the *De malo*. In this work, much that he calls "sin" is something that he thinks can be analyzed and reflected on in the light of what he thinks about goodness and badness in general and with no explicit reliance on the teachings of theologians. He also thinks of it as something which can be

---

to as Aquinas's "doctrine of divine simplicity" (which also holds that God's nature is *esse*, that God is *ipsum esse subsistens*), and it has been subject to much philosophical and theological criticism. For an exposition of it, see Brian Davies, *The Thought of Thomas Aquinas* (Oxford, 1992), chapter 3. For brief defenses of it, see Brian Davies, "Aquinas and the Doctrine of Divine Simplicity," in Brian Davies (ed.), *Language, Meaning and God* (London, 1987), and Eleonore Stump and Norman Kretzmann, "Absolute Simplicity", *Faith and Philosophy* 2 (1985). For a recent book that defends the notion of divine simplicity, see Barry Miller, *A Most Unlikely God* (Notre Dame and London, 1996). For a book which offers a full-scale attack on the notion, see Christopher Hughes, *On a Complex Theory of a Simple God* (Ithaca, 1980). For another detailed attack on the notion, see Alvin Plantinga, *Does God Have a Nature?* (Marquette, 1980).

99. *Summa theologiae* Ia2ae, 71, 6.
100. *Ibid.*

analyzed and reflected on in the light of what (without depending on uniquely theological premises) he takes to be the nature and aim of human action. Or, to put it another way, much that Aquinas calls "sin" in the *De malo* is something which he believes to be understandable in terms of his approach to human action as I have described it above—an approach which is therefore of philosophical and not just theological relevance. For, though it is mainly presented by Aquinas in writings which are primarily intended by him to be contributions to Christian theology (notably the *Summa theologiae*), it is also presented by him as something which ought to seem acceptable to any clear-thinking person. In the words of a notable interpreter of Aquinas, it is "not just exegesis of the Bible or the Fathers but the asking of radical questions and the application of critical intelligence to the formulation of our belief."[101]

Freedom of Choice

Yet if Aquinas is right in his analysis of human action, how much place is left for the notion of human freedom? We have already seen something of Aquinas's view of freedom, but now we need to focus on it in more detail. For the topic of human freedom is a major one in the *De malo*. And it is one to which Aquinas turns in a number of other writings, some of which throw considerable light on what he says about it there.

(a) Free Will or Free Choice?

Question VI of the *De malo* is devoted to what Aquinas calls "human choice" (*electio*). But what is Aquinas talking about as he deals with this theme? He is clearly defending belief in human freedom somehow. But how should we represent his line on this? In particular, should we say that he is out to defend belief in *free will*?

Commentators on Aquinas have sometimes suggested that he is. For, so they argue, he is, in general, a defender of the view that people have free will. In fact, however, the notion that people have free will is not one supported by Aquinas. And one should bear this in mind both when reading the *De malo* and when reading what Aquinas says about freedom in other texts. What he believes in is not free will. What he believes in is freedom of choice.[102]

When Aquinas attributes freedom to people, he frequently says that they have what he calls *liberum arbitrium*. And, though translators of Aquinas often render this phrase by the English expression "free will," its significance is different.[103] For the thesis that people have free will is commonly taken to mean that freedom is something which belongs only to the will, that it is, if you like, the prerogative of will or a peculiar property of it. And Aquinas does not share this assumption. For, as we have seen, he believes that

---

101. McCabe, *God Matters*, p. 55.

102. Emphasis on the freedom of the will, though it has often been attributed to Aquinas, is something that really only arises in thinkers later than him. For a discussion of the matter, see Westberg, *Right Practical Reason*.

103. Aquinas uses no Latin expression which corresponds exactly to the English "free will." He speaks of will (*voluntas*) but not of free will (*libera voluntas*) or freedom of the will (*libertas voluntatis*).

will and understanding are intimately comingled when it comes to human action. On his account, intellect and will are at no point separated in the exercise of practical reason. There is no act of practical intelligence that is not also one of will, and vice versa.

Yet Aquinas is prepared to ask whether or not the choices people make on the basis of what they think and are attracted to can be genuinely attributed to *them* and are not, in fact, the action of something else working in them in a way that always renders them nonresponsible for what they do. And this is the question he has in mind when he asks in the *De malo* "Do human beings have free choice in their acts or do they choose necessarily?" and when he asks, in other works, "Do people have *liberum arbitrium?*"[104]

(b) Why Believe that People Have Freedom?

The operative word in the question "Do human beings have free choice in their acts or do they choose necessarily?" is "necessarily." And, in this context, "necessarily" means something like inevitably, unavoidably. If you pour acid on a human hand, the skin will immediately corrode. And it does so inevitably, unavoidably, or, as we might say, necessarily. If you drop a ton weight on a mouse, the mouse will become an ex-mouse. And it will do so inevitably, unavoidably, or, as we might say, necessarily. But what about the actions of people? Are these what they are inevitably, unavoidably, or necessarily? Is everything we do to be thought of as coming to pass as skin reacts to acid and as mice get squashed by weights? Aquinas's answer, as one might expect, is "No." But why does he think that this answer is true?

To begin with, he has theological reasons. For, so he says (both in the *De malo* and elsewhere), Scripture teaches that people have freedom. In the book of Sirach, we read: "God from the beginning constituted and left human beings in the hands of their own deliberation." Aquinas takes this passage as ascribing to people the freedom to decide.[105] And, so he thinks, if people lacked such freedom, there could be nothing we could recognize as moral philosophy. Just as various natural sciences rest on the assumption that things undergo change, so, in Aquinas's view, thinking about morality rests on the assumption that people act with freedom. Or, as he puts it in the *Summa theologiae*: "Man is free to make decisions. Otherwise counsels, precepts, prohibitions, rewards and punishment would all be pointless."[106] If you believe there is no change, then you cannot consistently be a research chemist. By the same token, Aquinas suggests, you cannot seriously engage in ethical thinking if you deny human freedom.

But Aquinas's most developed defense of human freedom is neither biblical nor of an *ad hominem* nature. Rather, it springs from his conviction that human actions are done for reasons and that they cannot therefore be assimilated to processes which come about inevitably, unavoidably, or necessarily. Why not? Because, so he says, it belongs to the very nature of reason to deliberate with an eye on alternatives. Some of the changes that things undergo happen, so he thinks, because things are doing what they cannot, in the

---

104. For Aquinas discussing *liberum arbitrium*, see, for example, Question XXIV of the *De veritate* 24 and *Summa theologiae* Ia, 83.

105. This is Aquinas's biblical "proof text" in *De malo* VI. He also invokes it in *Summa theologiae* Ia, 83, 1.

106. *Summa theologiae* Ia, 83, 1.

circumstances, avoid doing. But, he insists, this is not the case when people act for reasons. Why not? Basically, so he argues, because acting for reasons means thinking and because reasons for action can never compel assent.

Here, once again, it is important to note how, in Aquinas's view, human animals differ from nonhuman ones. In fact, he thinks that they have a great deal in common, for he takes both to be living things with the ability to undergo sensations. He also takes both to have various inbuilt desires, tendencies, or instincts that greatly affect the ways in which they behave. For Aquinas, however, people can understand how things are and respond (rather than merely react) to them on this basis. They do not just behave. They can describe what is around them, and they can behave as they do for reasons which are different from what might be mentioned when accounting for the behavior of nonhuman animals. One might well speak of the reason why the cat chased the mouse. But "reason" here has nothing to do with framed intentions. There may be reasons why the cat chased the mouse. But they are not the cat's reasons. In Aquinas's opinion, however, human action is precisely a matter of things acting with reasons of their own. And, he thinks, with the ability to act with reasons of one's own comes an understanding of the world under many different descriptions. Or, rather, as Aquinas sees it, the ability to understand the world under many different descriptions is why people have the ability to act with reasons of their own.

It might help here if we focus on the notion of interpreting the world. For Aquinas, this is something which both human and nonhuman animals do. For both of them have senses in terms of which the world becomes significant for them. According to Aquinas, however, people can interpret the world not just as sensed but also as understood. So they can speak about it. They can, for example, not just sense wetness. They can talk about it raining. And they can ask what rain is and why it is raining now though it was not raining yesterday. For Aquinas, people can interpret the world by describing it. And, he thinks, this opens out for them possibilities of interpretation which are just not available to nonhuman animals. For, as he sees it, to be aware of things not just in terms of their sensible appearance but also under a description is to be aware of things under an indefinite number of descriptions.

Suppose that I and a mouse smell a piece of cheese. On Aquinas's account, the cheese is significant for the mouse and, all things being equal, it will be drawn to it. According to Aquinas, however, I can perceive the cheese as more than something to eat without thinking. I can see it, for example, as somebody else's cheese, or as bad for me if I want to lose weight, or as what I promised to give up for Lent, or as more expensive than I can decently afford, and so on. And, Aquinas thinks, my ability to think of the cheese in these ways is the root of my human freedom. For, he argues, there is a big difference between how we might think of something like a piece of cheese and how we inevitably think about certain other matters.

Take, for example, the way in which we think when reasoning as follows:

If all human beings are mortal
and all Australians are human beings
then all Australians are mortal.

Here we cannot but accept the conclusion given the premises supplied. And no additional information can leave us with any alternative but to accept it. We accept the conclusion of necessity.

But now consider this argument:

I want to get to Paris
If I catch this flight it will get me to Paris
So I should catch this flight.

Might additional information leave me unable but to conclude that I should catch the flight? Well hardly. What about "If I catch this flight I shall be boarding an aeroplane with terrorists on it"? If I consider the flight under that description, then I will not conclude that I should catch it. And yet, Aquinas thinks, when reflecting on the world we can always view it under different descriptions. So he also thinks that we can engage with it not because we are forced to think about it only in one way. We can engage with it as able to think about it in different ways. And we can act accordingly. Or, as Anthony Kenny helpfully explains:

> If the will is a rational appetite, an ability to have reasons for acting and to act for reasons, then the nature of the will must depend on the nature of practical reasoning. In practical reasoning the relationship between premises and conclusion is not as tight or as easy to regiment as that between premises and conclusion in theoretical reasoning. When we look at a piece of practical reasoning—reasoning about what to do—we often appear to find, where the analogy of theoretical reasoning would lead us to expect necessitation, merely contingent and defeasible connections between one step and another. Aquinas believed that the peculiar contingency of practical reasoning was an essential feature of the human will as we know it. . . . He states this contingency as being the fundamental ground of human freedom.[107]

For Aquinas, people have freedom of choice since, unlike nonhuman animals, they can interpret the world in different ways (under different descriptions) and act in the light of the ways in which they interpret it. In this sense, so he thinks, their actions are governed by reasons that are fully their own.[108] As we have seen, his view is that we are drawn to what we take to be good. But, so he also thinks, we are not compelled to act in any particular way simply because of our tastes. On his account, we aim for what we want in a world in which we (as thinkers) can recognize different things as likely to satisfy us in different ways. And on this basis we deliberate with an eye on means and ends. And, so he concludes, we cannot but agree that the choices we make are not necessary as, for example, the scorching of skin is a necessary consequence of acid being poured on it, or

107. Anthony Kenny, *Aquinas on Mind* (London and New York, 1993), pp. 76f.

108. One might suggest that our thinking is identical with processes in our brains over which we have no control. And one might therefore suggest that our actions have irreducibly physical causes over which we have no control. For Aquinas, however, thinking cannot be identified with any physical process. On his account, we depend on our bodies in order to interpret the world. Indeed, so he thinks, all our knowledge depends on the ways in which we function as bodily things. But, so he suggests, our interpreting the world cannot be identified with a particular physical process. If it were, so he thinks, then meanings would be the same as physical objects, which, in his view, they are not. In this respect Aquinas's thinking can be usefully compared with that presented by Ludwig Wittgenstein. See Ludwig Wittgenstein, *Philosophical Investigations*, trans. G. E. M. Anscombe (Oxford, 1958).

as the eating of a piece of cheese might be inevitable for a mouse. Our choices, he thinks, are actions which flow from what we, as individuals, are. They reflect our desires and our view of things.[109] And they might have been otherwise. In place of a particular repertoire of particular instincts, people, Aquinas thinks, have a general capacity to reason. And, since particular matters like what to do in this or that situation are not subject to conclusive argument, people are not determined to any one course.

(c) Freedom and God

Yet Aquinas does not think that our actions come about as wholly uncaused. Some philosophers have argued that people can only be free if their actions have absolutely no cause outside themselves. But this is not Aquinas's view. For, he argues, though people can act freely, it must still be the case that their actions are caused by God. Aquinas finds it unthinkable that any created event, including whatever we take to be there when human choosing occurs, should come to pass without God making it to be.

Why? Because of what we have already seen him teaching about God as the creator of things. For him, God is the cause of the existence of everything, the reason why there is something rather than nothing, the source of *esse*. And since he takes human free actions to be perfectly real, he concludes that they must, like anything else, be caused to exist by God. Or, as he writes in the *De potentia*: "We must unequivocally concede that God is at work in all activity, whether of nature or of will." For Aquinas, God "causes everything's activity inasmuch as he gives the power to act, maintains it in existence, applies it to its activity, and inasmuch as it is by his power that every other power acts."[110]

One may, of course, say that, if my actions are ultimately caused by God, then I do not act freely at all. Aquinas, however, would reply that my actions are free if nothing *in the world* is acting on me so as to make me perform them, not if God is not acting in me. According to him, what is incompatible with freedom is "necessity of coercion" or the effect of violence, as when something acts on one and "applies force to the point where one cannot act otherwise."[111] But, he explains, it is not against will that one should be drawn to what one's nature needs for its fulfilment. This kind of necessity is, he thinks, essential to will, just as the being drawn of necessity to truth is needed for the intellect to be itself.

To quote Herbert McCabe again, Aquinas's position is that "to be free means not to be under the influence of some other *creature*, it is to be independent of other *bits of*

109. Aquinas, I should stress, does not deny that people may often behave without exercising freedom of choice. For he takes them to be part of a material world in which all sorts of things can interfere with their ability to act with reasons of their own. As he indicates in the *De malo*, however, he does not conclude that behaving under the influence of something else automatically exonerates people from responsibility. We would normally agree that drivers under the influence of alcohol might well not have chosen to kill those knocked down by their cars. But we would normally regard them as responsible for what they brought about if we thought that they chose to drive while drunk. In the same way, Aquinas thinks that responsibility can be ascribed to people when they bring things about even if they do not directly intend to so so.

110. *De potentia* III, 7. I quote from McDermott, *Aquinas: Selected Philosophical Writings*, pp. 299ff.

111. *Summa theologiae* Ia, 82, 1.

the universe; it is not and could not mean to be independent of God."[112] For him, God does not interfere with created free agents to push them into action in a way that infringes their freedom. He does not act *on* them (as Aquinas thinks created things do when they cause others to act as determined by them). He makes them to be what they are—freely acting agents. And, with these points in mind, Aquinas argues in the *De malo* and elsewhere that human freedom is not something to be thought of as threatened by God's causality. On the contrary: his position is that we are free not *in spite of* God but *because of* God.[113] Or, as he writes in his commentary on Aristotle's *De Interpretatione*:

> God's will is to be thought of as existing outside the realm of existents, as a cause from which pours forth everything that exists in all its variant forms. Now what can be and what must be are variants of being, so that it is from God's will itself that things derive whether they must be or may or may not be and the distinction of the two according to the nature of their immediate causes. For he prepares causes that must cause for those effects that he wills must be, and causes that might cause but might fail to cause for those effects that he wills might or might not be. And it is because of the nature of these causes that these effects are said to be effects that must be and those effects that need not be, although all depend on God's will as primary cause, a cause which transcends this distinction between must and might not. But the same cannot be said of human will or of any other cause, since every other cause exists within the realm of must and might not. So of every other cause it must be said either that it can fail to cause, or that its effect must be and cannot not be; God's will however cannot fail, and yet not all his effects must be, but some can be or not be.[114]

In terms of this account, God is not to be thought of as an external agent able to interfere with human freedom by acting on it coercively from outside. Rather, God is the cause of all that is real as both free created agents and nonfree created agents exist and operate. According to James F. Ross:

> The being of the cosmos is like *a song on the breath of a singer*. It has endless internal universal laws, and structures nested within structures, properties that are of *the song* and *not* of the singer or the voice or the singer's thought, though produced by them and attributively predicated of them. . . . The universe is continuously depending, like a song or a light show . . . ; its being is its own, yet it is from a cause, everywhere, and at no *including* time. . . . God produces, for each individual being, the one that does such and such (whatever it does) throughout its whole time in being . . . God does not make the person act; he makes the so acting person *be*. . . . The whole physical uni-

112. McCabe, *God Matters*, p. 14.

113. For a recent defense of a similar line of reasoning, see William E. Mann, "God's Freedom, Human Freedom, and God's Responsibility for Sin," in Thomas V. Morris (ed.), *Divine and Human Action* (Ithaca and London, 1988). See also Brian Davies, "The Problem of Evil," in Brian Davies (ed.), *Philosophy of Religion: A Guide to the Subject* (London, 1998).

114. *Commentary on Aristotle's De Interpretatione* Book I, Lectio 14. I quote from McDermott, *Aquinas: Selected Philosophical Writings*, pp. 282f. Cf. *De malo* XV, 7 ad 15.

verse, all of it, is actively caused to be. Still, to say that freedom or human agency is thereby impeded is absurd. Nothing can be or come about unless caused to be by the creator. So the fact that God's causing is necessary for whatever happens cannot impede liberty; it is a condition for it. Similarly, in no way is our liberty impeded by the fact that God's causing is sufficient for the being of the very things that do the very things that we do. Nothing possible can be impeded by its necessary conditions. . . . God did not make Adam to be the first man to defy God; God made Adam, who was the first man to defy God, to be. God made Adam, who undertook to sin. . . . God makes all the free things that do *as* they do, instead of doing otherwise as is in their power, by their *own* undertaking. So God does not make Adam sin. But God makes the sinning Adam, the person who, *able* not to sin, does sin. It follows logically that if Adam had not sinned, God would have made a person who, though able to sin, did not. And, surely, God *might* have made a person who, though able to sin, did not. . . . It is the whole being, doing as it does, whether a free being or not, that is entirely produced and sustained for its time by God.[115]

And this is precisely what Aquinas thinks. In this sense, so he holds, human free actions are caused by God. Or, as he writes in the *Summa theologiae*:

Free decision spells self-determination because man by his free decision moves himself into action. Freedom does not require that a thing is its own first cause, just as in order to be the cause of something else a thing does not have to be its first cause. God is the first cause on which both natural and free agents depend. And just as his initiative does not prevent natural causes from being natural, so it does not prevent voluntary action from being voluntary but rather makes it be precisely this. For God works in each according to its nature.[116]

(d)   The Cause of Sin?

Yet if God is the source of my freely chosen actions, does it not follow that God is also the cause of sin? Aquinas turns directly to the question in *De malo* III. By now, though, the reader may have already anticipated his approach to the question. We can summarize it, however, as follows:

115. James F. Ross, "Creation II" in Alfred J. Freddoso (ed.), *The Existence and Nature of God* (Notre Dame and London, 1983), pp. 128–134.
116. *Summa theologiae* Ia, 83, 1 ad 3. Commenting on this passage, Anthony Kenny describes it as teaching that "self-determination is . . . compatible with divine determination," so that Aquinas "appears to believe that freedom is compatible with some sorts of determinism" (*Aquinas on Mind*, London and New York, 1993, p. 77). But this is a very misleading way of representing Aquinas since he strongly denies that God should be understood as what would normally be thought to be a determining agent. Normally, such an agent is taken to be something in the world that acts on something else so as to render the second thing's behavior or processes inevitable. For Aquinas, however, God does not act *on* things. He makes things to be (from nothing). When seeking to understand what Aquinas says about God and human freedom one must, as so often when reading Aquinas, keep firmly in mind how strongly he wishes to distinguish between God the Creator and creatures. For more on this, see my *The Thought of Thomas Aquinas* (Oxford, 1992), chapters 3–9.

1. God is the cause of all that is real in creation.
2. So everything that can be thought to be real when sin occurs is part of what God brings about.
3. At the same time, God cannot make evil to be. So when people sin, there is no question of God causing the evil of sin to have some kind of real existence. Like all evil, the evil of sin consists in absence or a failure of some kind.
4. Yet the absence involved in sin is still open to causal explanation. For it "comes about" insofar as people aim for what is not good. So sin has a cause. It is caused by the choices people make.
5. And in acting as they do, people are good (insofar as they exist). They are also always aiming at what (however mistakenly) they take to be desirable.
6. Insofar as sin can be spoken of as having a cause, therefore, the cause lies in people who aim wrongly.

In other words, Aquinas's view is that God can be said to cause sin only insofar as he is the creative source of human activity, an activity which often fails or falls short with respect to goodness. And, since he takes such failure to derive from what people decide, he concludes that responsibility for it is rightly to be ascribed to them. So his final position is that God can be said to cause the actions we refer to when we speak of people sinning, though he cannot be said to be the cause of sin. That, so he reasons, can only be thought of as caused by a freely acting agent who chooses to settle for a goodness which is less than the goodness of God himself. Or, as he writes in the *Summa theologiae*:

> A man causes sin in himself or another person either directly, i.e., by willing to sin or by persuading another to sin; or indirectly, i.e., not dissuading somebody from sinning. . . . However, it is not right to say that God causes sin in himself or another directly or even indirectly. Sin is by definition a withdrawal from the order of things which has God as its purpose. For his part, God inclines all things and draws them to himself. . . . Hence, he cannot withdraw either himself or another from an order of things which has himself as its center. So he cannot directly cause sin. Nor can God indirectly cause sin [though] it can happen that God withholds his help, and that without this help one falls into sin. . . . The act of sin not only belongs to the realm of being but it is also an act. And from both of these points of view it somehow comes from God. . . . But sin can be called a being and an action only in the sense that something is missing. And this missing element comes from a created cause, i.e., the free will in its departure from order to the First Agent who is God. Accordingly, this defect is not ascribed to God as its cause, but to the free will, just as the limp in a cripple comes from his deformity and not from his power to move even though this power enables him to limp.[117]

Notice that Aquinas is here allowing that God could have made a world in which nobody sins, for he says that people might be given help so as not to fall into sin. So he is not suggesting that, as we might put it, sin is wholly, totally, and finally explicable simply

---

117. *Summa theologiae* Ia2ae, 79, 1 and 2.

with reference to people. He is, however, saying that God can never be intelligibly thought of as causing sin to be.[118]

Original Sin

Even though they might not agree with him, readers of the *De malo* will have little difficulty in understanding what Aquinas is talking about as he turns, in detail, to sins of particular kinds (the "capital" sins, as he calls them). And his discussion of them, together with his attempts to distinguish between degrees of sin, should be fairly intelligible in the light of my comments above and in the light of the glossary of terms to be found at the end of this volume. In *De malo* IV and V, however, Aquinas writes about a sin which not everyone will find readily comprehensible. For here he addresses the topic of original sin. And one might wonder what he is trying to say about it.

Given some ways in which belief in original sin has been expressed, it might initially help to note what he does *not* want to say about it. So, for example, he does not believe that the reality of original sin is something empirically verifiable. Some theologians have suggested that the doctrine of original sin can be quickly seen to be true by simple observation of the ways in which people behave (i.e., nasty ways). But this is not Aquinas's view. For him, belief in original sin can be based only on divine revelation. It is not something the truth of which can be proved by sensory investigation or even by rational argument.[119] Nor does he take the doctrine of original sin as teaching that people are now fundamentally corrupt or depraved (so that sin belongs to people essentially, as Martin Luther seemed to think), or that those who die without Christian baptism (which Aquinas regards as a remedy for original sin) are automatically doomed to hell (as Augustine of Hippo seemed to think).[120] In a serious sense, Aquinas does not think that original sin is really sin at all. For, except with respect to Adam, he does not conceive of it as something for which people can be thought to be responsible when considered as individuals. It is not, for him, an action. On his account, it is sin because it amounts to a

---

118. To understand Aquinas on divine causation and human action, it is worth noting how, in *De malo* III, he speaks of how the devil might be thought to cause sin. For Aquinas, the devil is a created agent who cannot therefore act creatively in people and cannot be thought of as the source of their freedom. He can merely make suggestions to them.

119. Throughout his writings Aquinas sharply distinguishes between (a) what can be known on the basis of sensory experience and rational reflection, and (b) what can be held to be true on the basis of divine revelation. And he thinks of those beliefs that define Christianity (the "articles of faith," as he calls them) as revealed, and not as discovered by natural human resources. For an introduction to Aquinas on these matters, see Davies, *The Thought of Thomas Aquinas*, chapters 10–15.

120. For Aquinas on baptism, see *Summa theologiae* 3a, 66–69. For Luther on original sin, see his *Lectures on Genesis* 2 and 3 (for an English translation, see Martin Luther, *Commentary on Genesis*, trans. J. Theodore Mueller [Grand Rapids, Michigan, 1958]). For Augustine on the fate of children who die without baptism, see, for example, his *The Punishment and Forgiveness of Sins and the Baptism of Little Ones* (*De peccatorum meritis et remissione et de baptismo parvulorum*) I, 24, 34 and I, 24, 35. (For an English translation of this work, see Part I, Volume 23 (*Answer to the Pelagians*, trans. Roland J. Teske, New York, 1997) of *The Works of Saint Augustine: A Translation for the 21st Century* (New York, 1990).

falling short with respect to God. But (except in the case of Adam) it is not something chosen by anyone.[121]

To appreciate what Aquinas takes original sin to be, however, we need first to stand back from what he says about it directly and to note how he thinks in general about people as creatures of God. And one point worth stressing is that he takes them to be limited in various ways.

As we have seen, Aquinas has a high regard for people considered as things in nature. For he views them as living agents able to think and to reason. And he takes them to be good (because existing) and as firmly grounded in a desire for what is good (because of their will). But he also regards them as decidedly restricted. For one thing, so he holds, they are parts of a material world. So they are limited by their bodies and by material objects around them (they cannot, for example, be everywhere at once, and they cannot move mountains).

They are also, he thinks, limited when it comes to their understanding. For he holds that what we might call their "mental life' hugely depends on the ways in which they encounter and interiorize things at a physical level. "The knowledge that is natural to us," he argues, "has its source in the senses and extends just so far as it can be led by sensible things. . . . In the present life our intellect has a natural relation to the natures of material things; thus it understands nothing except by turning to sense images."[122] For Aquinas, the model for human understanding is talking (not having sensations, as some philosophers have thought).[123] And talking, for him, is the deployment of symbols which have significance for us as creatures that belong to a material world. He does not think that understanding is the operation of any physical organ (e.g., the brain). He argues, in fact, that it is nonmaterial, that understanding occurs as material limitations are transcended.[124] But he also takes human understanding to depend on our bodies and our sensual awareness. And from this he concludes that, though we far surpass objects like

---

121. In accordance with the theological tradition he inherits, Aquinas takes original sin to derive from the sin of Adam as reported in chapter 3 of the Old Testament book of Genesis. He discusses this, and the state of Adam before his fall, in *Summa theologiae* Ia, 90–102. He clearly regards Adam as a single historical individual, but most of what he says about original sin can be restated without supposing the literal historicity of the Genesis account. Karl Rahner has suggested that contemporary Roman Catholics can subscribe to the doctrine of original sin without taking the Genesis account literally ("The Sin of Adam," in Karl Rahner, *Theological Investigations*, Volume XI, London and New York, 1974). For much the same reasons as those given by Rahner, it seems to me that Aquinas's fundamental teaching on original sin does not depend on a literal reading of the Genesis account. It does, however seem to depend on the view that sin had an origin by which the original sinner or sinners were deprived of something (a state of grace) present before sin. So it is not obviously independent of what we might call historical beliefs, though, arguably, it might be restated even without recourse to these.

122. *Summa theologiae* Ia, 12, 1 and 88, 1.

123. An example is David Hume, who, at the opening of his *Treatise Concerning Human Nature*, takes thinking to depend on ideas that are "faint images" of strong sensory "impressions." For Hume, the difference between feeling (having sensations) and thinking seems to be like the difference between hearing a shout and hearing a whisper. For Aquinas, it is to be contrasted with, say, the difference between feeling hot and the activity of saying, "It's a warm day."

124. Cf. *Summa theologiae* Ia, 14, 1; 75, 1; 75, 5.

stones since we can *understand* things and not just *be* them, we are also intellectually limited. For what of things that are wholly immaterial? Can we understand them? According to Aquinas, we cannot. And he takes one implication of this fact to be that we cannot, in the present life, understand what God is. We can, he is sure, talk sensibly and truly about God.[125] We can even demonstrate God's existence by raising questions about the source of the world and the ways in which it works.[126] But we cannot understand what the reality of God amounts to in itself. In the sense that we can know what, for example, it takes to be a hyena or a zebra, we cannot, Aquinas thinks, know what it takes to be God.[127] We can know *that* God is, but not *what* God is. Or, as Aquinas also puts it: "The Divine substance surpasses every form that our intellect reaches."[128]

So how are we to engage with "the divine substance"? Here, Aquinas thinks, we must simply recognize the difference between creatures and their Creator. So, if we are to learn more of God than we can as the creatures we are, then God will have to inform us about himself somehow. And, if we are to live with God as anything more than creatures who do not know what God is, then God is going to have to do something to give us a way of living that goes beyond what we can manage on our own. On Aquinas's account, we have, simply as human animals, all the resources we need to discern that there is something which accounts for the being of the world. And we have the resources to make something of the world and of ourselves as we engage in the business of practical reasoning. But is there anything more to be said about what accounts for the world other than that it accounts for the world and that it has to be whatever is needed to do so? And is there any reason to think that people are of any special significance to it? If there is, Aquinas thinks, then we have to be told so by God himself. And if we are to accomplish anything more than we are naturally able to, then, Aquinas adds, God must help us to do it.

But how? The question effectively brings us to the heart of Aquinas's theological thinking: his account of the work of Christ and the way in which this matters and can become effective in the lives of human beings. The account is a long one, and it is developed in detail by Aquinas in works like the second and third parts of the *Summa theologiae*. But its basic teaching is that God, in Christ, has done what people are unable to do naturally (by being merely human) since (and as cannot be anticipated by any philosophical theory) he has united himself with the human race and freely offered it a share in what God is by nature from all eternity—a perfect life of love shared by Father, Son, and Holy Spirit. There is, says Aquinas, "a special love" by which God "draws the rational creature above its natural condition to have a part in the divine goodness. And it is by this love that he is said to love someone simply speaking; because by this love God simply

---

125. Cf. *Summa theologiae* Ia, 13.

126. Cf. *Summa theologiae* Ia, 2, 3 and *Summa contra gentiles* I, 13.

127. Cf. *Summa theologiae* Ia, 2,1–6; 12, 4; 12, 7; 12, 11. I discuss this aspect of Aquinas's thinking in "Aquinas on What God Is Not," *Revue Internationale de Philosophie* 52 (1998).

128. *Summa contra gentiles* I, 14. According to Aquinas: "The most perfect state to which we can achieve in this life in our knowledge of God is that he transcends all that can be conceived by us, and that the naming of God through remotion (*per remotionem*) is most proper. . . . The primary mode of naming God is through the negation of all things, since he is beyond all, and whatever is signified by any name whatsoever is less than that which God is" (*Commentary on Dionysius's Divine Names* I, iii, 83–84.

speaking wills for the creature that eternal good which is himself."[129] According to Aquinas, this "special love" is incarnate in Jesus Christ. Also according to Aquinas, God goes out in love to people not just by virtue of the Incarnation but also by enabling them to appropriate for themselves the love which God, in Christ, is about (by enabling them to reflect what God is more than they do simply by being God's creatures).[130] Or, as Aquinas typically puts it, people can share in what God is about because God is prepared to empower them to do so. How? By what Aquinas calls "grace." Or, more specifically, by what he calls the "New Law," which he takes to be the working of God in people, lifting them up not only to be objects of God's love but also to be things which live in the world what that love is from eternity. "The New Law," he says, "consists chiefly in the grace of the Holy Spirit, which is shown forth by faith working through love. . . . People become receivers of this grace through God's Son made human whose humanity grace filled first, and thence flowed forth to us."[131] On Aquinas's account, God is not simply one who can be discerned by philosophy to be the maker of the world. God is the lover of people who has shown himself such by the Incarnation and by consequently sending his Spirit upon them. The New Law, says Aquinas, "is instilled in our hearts," and it has its effect "not only by indicating to us what we should do, but also by helping us to accomplish it."[132]

In all that Aquinas says on this matter, he continually emphasizes that what he is talking about is the work of grace and not what people can naturally achieve for themselves. He thinks that we can do many things by exercising our natural human abilities. But he does not think that we can by these make God achieve what the Incarnation is about. "The gift of grace," he observes, "surpasses every capacity of created nature, since it is nothing other than a certain participation in the divine nature, which surpasses every other nature."[133] "A person is perfected by virtue towards those actions by which he or she is directed towards happiness," he says. But:

> Our happiness or felicity is twofold. . . . One is proportionate to human nature, and this we can reach through our own resources. The other, a happiness surpassing our nature, we can attain only by the power of God, by a kind of participation of the Godhead; thus it is written that by Christ we are made *partakers of the divine nature*. Because such happiness goes beyond the reach of human nature, the inborn resources by which we are able to act well according to our capacity are not adequate to direct us to it. And so, to be sent to this supernatural happiness, we have to be divinely endowed with some additional sources of activity; their role is like that of our native

129. *Summa theologiae* Ia2ae, 110, 1.

130. Working on the principle that what causes bring about (i.e., their effects) must somehow reflect their nature (i.e., the nature of their causes), Aquinas argues philosophically that all creatures must somehow show forth what God essentially is. Or, as he puts it: "What an agent does reflects what it is" (*omne agens agit sibi simile*). See, for example, *Summa contra gentiles* I, 29; I, 73; II, 6; II, 20. But, so he thinks, there is a way in which some creatures—people—can reflect what God is more precisely: by being literally loved by God in the way that the persons of the Trinity are loved by each other, and by loving as they do.

131. *Summa theologiae* Ia2ae, 108, 1.

132. *Summa theologiae* Ia2ae, 106, 1 and Ia2ae, 106, 1 ad 2.

133. *Summa theologiae* Ia2ae, 112, 1.

capabilities which direct us, not, of course, without God's help, to our connatural end.[134]

And it is with this teaching in mind that we need to approach what Aquinas says about original sin, both in the *De malo* and elsewhere.[135] For what he chiefly wants to say about this is that it amounts to falling short of what God offers in Christ. For Aquinas, to be in original sin is to be deprived of what we can think of as the fullness of grace when reflecting on the life and meaning of Christ, and on what is brought about as people come to be caught up in this by the work of God in them. Hence, for example, Aquinas denies, as we have seen, that the human successors of Adam are (at birth) in a state of original sin because they are personally guilty of any particular wrongdoing. He is very clear on this. For him, there is no sense at all in the suggestion that original sin is something which we have chosen to commit. To his way of thinking, to be born in original sin is to be in need of the grace which comes through the life, death, and resurrection of Christ. It is not to have done anything. Rather, it is to be in need of what anybody needs in order to be more than merely human. Or, in Aquinas's terminology, it is to be in need of what Adam once enjoyed because of God's grace.

When Aquinas writes of Adam, he always sees him as being everything that all of us are by nature (as the typical human being). But he also sees him as what human beings are ultimately able to be in God's scheme of things. On his account, Adam knew and loved God, and everything in his life contributed to his doing this in peace and harmony with the whole created order. Adam, says Aquinas, did not see God's essence. He did not enjoy the beatific vision.[136] But he was physically and intellectually mature, as befits the father of the human race, and his reason and actions were graced.[137] Furthermore, he was immortal "by virtue of a supernatural force given by God to the soul, whereby it was enabled to preserve the body from all corruption so long as it remained itself subject to God."[138] In this sense, Adam lived the life of God, "his reason being subject to God, the lower powers to reason, and the body to the soul."[139] The Bible teaches that Adam was created in Paradise. Aquinas interprets this to mean that he lived in a state where God "might himself work in people and keep them by sanctifying them."[140] In Paradise, he says, Adam, in a sense, possessed all the virtues, for "the virtues are nothing but those perfections whereby reason is directed to God and the inferior powers regulated according to the dictate of reason."[141] And, to understand what Aquinas says of Adam here, we need to remember what we saw him above to be saying when it comes to

---

134. *Summa theologiae* Ia2ae, 62, 1. The reference to Scripture here is to 2 Peter 1:4, where Aquinas's notion that the end for people is to become like God finds its clearest biblical statement.

135. Apart from that of the *De malo*, Aquinas's most sustained treatment of original sin comes in *Summa theologiae* Ia2ae, 81–85, in which he takes pretty much the same line as he does in the *De malo*.

136. *Summa theologiae* Ia, 94, 1.

137. *Summa theologiae* Ia, 95, 1–3.

138. *Summa theologiae* Ia, 97, 1.

139. *Summa theologiae* Ia, 95, 1.

140. *Summa theologiae* Ia, 102, 3.

141. *Summa theologiae* Ia, 95, 3.

human freedom. For, as Aquinas understands Adam, he was a human actor and therefore not a divine puppet. He veered toward the things of God as a human being. And he did so with the assistance of God, as (so Aquinas thinks) do all human beings when they act as they do. But he did what he did as a free human agent (as, Aquinas thinks, are all human actors). And he chose to fall. Or, to put it another way, Aquinas sees Adam as a human being who freely decided to aim at less than what is ultimately desirable for people.

But Aquinas also sees Adam as more than a typical human being. He takes him to be literally the father of the whole human race. And on that basis he takes the fall of Adam as having consequences for others than him. Indeed, so he says, we need to be baptized since we share in Adam's sin. But in what way? Could it be because all of us were literally part of Adam when he sinned and can therefore be thought of as guilty with respect to his sin? St. Augustine seems to have thought so.[142] But Aquinas does not. Rather, he thinks, we share in Adam's sin because we fall short of what he enjoyed before he indulged in it, and because he passed to us what he was as a result of his fall. We are, says Aquinas, born in original sin because we are born in need of grace.

How so? Because, Aquinas thinks, we are descended from Adam and therefore inherit what he had to pass on as fallen: human nature lacking the grace which Adam once enjoyed. We cannot, says Aquinas, take Adam's descendants to be responsible for what he did. So we cannot think of them as committing his sin or as sharing in his guilt. But we can, Aquinas argues, reasonably think of them as sharing his lot as fallen. For they get from Adam what he has causally to give as father of the human race. Or, as we read in the *Summa theologiae*: "The very fact of acquiring a defect by way of origin rules out culpability, since by definition fault must be voluntary. . . . All who are born of Adam can be considered as one man by reason of sharing the one nature inherited from the first parent."[143] We cannot, says Aquinas, take a human limb to be a responsible acting agent. But the way in which it behaves can sometimes be causally explained in terms of the choices of the agent to which it belongs. In a similar way, Aquinas suggests, the state of Adam's descendants can be causally understood with respect to Adam's decision to sin.[144] Or, as Aquinas puts it in *De malo* IV, we can "consider the whole population of human beings receiving their nature from our first parent as one community, or rather as the one body of one human being." And original sin is consequently to be viewed as a privation that can only be thought of as having the nature of moral fault since its source is someone's actual sin. Or, as Aquinas puts it: "Original sin regarding particular human beings consists only of what accrues to them from the sin of our first parent by reason of their physical descent from him."[145] It is a way of being (not a particular sin) which we

---

142. For a thoughtful and provocative critique of Augustine on original sin (with which one can imagine Aquinas agreeing on various philosophical grounds, though not, perhaps, with the author's exposition of Augustine), see Christopher Kirwan, *Augustine* (London and New York, 1989), chapter VII.

143. *Summa theologiae* Ia2ae, 81, 1.

144. For the limb analogy, see *De malo* IV, 1, and *Summa theologiae* Ia2ae, 81, 1.

145. *De malo* IV, 2.

inherit just as we inherit bodily qualities. Or, to repeat, Aquinas takes people born in original sin simply to be people in need of grace—a need shared by their physical ancestor and consequently passed on from him to them.[146] For this reason Aquinas suggests that we would have no reason to ascribe original sin to a new human being miraculously created without human parents.[147] And he takes disbelief in original sin to be expressible in the claim that people can happily do without what God offers to them in Christ.[148] He also maintains that there can be no question of there being pain and suffering due to original sin on the part of those who inherit it and who die before making any choices. In writing on original sin, St. Augustine insists that babies who die before baptism suffer accordingly in hell—a view that St. Anselm also accepts.[149] According to Aquinas, however, the fate of babies who die before baptism can only be assumed to be whatever counts as less than what is gained by those who choose to accept what God offers to people in Christ. And this, so he argues, need be anything but unpleasant. Quite the contrary.[150]

For Aquinas, therefore, to be in original sin is essentially to be in need of what God is about in Christ.[151] And that is how readers should understand what he says of it in the *De malo*.

146. Cf. G. Vandervelde, *Original Sin: Two Major Trends in Contemporary Roman Catholic Reinterpretation* (Amsterdam, 1975), pp. 30f.: "In applying the body-analogy to the reality of original sin . . . [Aquinas] elaborates the image in a very specific direction. Just as murder is not solely an act of the will but also an act of the hand, so the disorder which exists in man is due to the will of the first parents who by motion of generation moves all who derive their origin from him. Although Thomas begins by viewing mankind as an organic moral unity, the image shifts towards the idea of a 'first mover' who causes a *disorder* in (human) nature. Accordingly, Thomas calls original sin a sin of *nature* which a *person* receives. This elaboration of the body-analogy indicates that the unity of mankind is seen, not in terms of our involvement in Adam's sin, but in terms of the derivation of our defective, disordered nature from Adam."

147. Cf. *Summa theologiae* Ia2ae, 81, 4.

148. Cf. *Summa theologiae* Ia2ae, 81, 3: "That all men descended from Adam, Christ alone excepted, contract original sin from him must be firmly held according to the Catholic Faith. The denial of this truth implies the error that not all would be in need of redemption through Christ."

149. For Anselm on the fate of unbaptized children, see *On the Virgin Conception and Original Sin (De conceptu virginali et de originali peccato)*, p. 28. For a good and concise indication of the different ways in which Augustine, Anselm, and Aquinas deal with the topic of original sin, see G. Vandervelde, *Original Sin*, pp. 14–21 and pp. 26–32. For a survey of Augustine on original sin see the article on original sin in Allan D. Fitzgerald (ed.), *Augustine Through the Ages: An Encyclopaedia* (Grand Rapids, and Cambridge, U.K., 1999).

150. Cf. *De malo* V, 2 and 3. Also cf. Aquinas's commentary on Book II of Peter Lombard's *Sentences*, 33, 2, 1.

151. Hence, perhaps, it may indeed be possible (as I suggested in note 122) to represent Aquinas's teaching on original sin without reference to historical considerations concerning the genesis of the human race. For suppose you do not believe that Adam ever existed as an historical individual with the grace to which Aquinas ascribes him. Suppose, indeed, you believe that there is no reason to believe in anything we might call "the first human sin" (albeit that there must have been a time before which nobody freely did wrong and a time after which somebody freely did wrong). If Aquinas is right in his general thinking on the New Law and grace, it would still be the case that all people need what God offers in Christ. That all people need this seems to be what Aquinas wants most to emphasize as he writes on original sin.

The *De malo* and "the Problem of Evil"

Prospective readers of the *De malo* may expect to find in it an extended discussion of what is nowadays commonly called "the problem of evil." That is to say, they might expect to find Aquinas dealing directly in it with questions like "Does evil show that there is no God?" or "How can belief in the reality of evil be reconciled with belief in the existence of a good, omniscient, and omnipotent God?" But should the *De malo* be read as an essay on "the problem of evil' in this sense? The most accurate and short answer to this question is "No." For Aquinas in the *De malo* never attempts to defend belief in the existence of God. Throughout the text he takes it for granted that God certainly exists. And he never tries to show that we can consistently believe both that there is evil and that God exists. His discussion proceeds on the assumption that evil and God are both somehow there to be talked about.[152] But his treatment of evil in the *De malo*, and what he says about it in other works, can still be read as engaging with what I am calling "the problem of evil." And we need to be clear as to how this is so.

(a) Moves that Aquinas Does Not Make

To begin with, we need to note that there are some popular ways of approaching the problem of evil of which Aquinas does not avail himself. In particular, so I need to stress, he makes no attempt to show that the evil we encounter is something permitted by God for a morally sufficient reason. Also, so I must emphasize, Aquinas never tries to argue that evil arises by virtue of causes over which God has no control. Those who believe in God's existence despite evils occurring often suggest that these evils can always be viewed as necessary means to a good end and that God is morally justified in allowing them or in bringing them about. They often also argue that much occurring evil consists in or derives from the bad moral choices of creatures and that God is therefore not to be blamed for it.[153] But this is not how Aquinas thinks. Why not? Partly because he does not think that the goodness of God is that of someone always acting with morally sufficient reasons. But also because he does not think that the choices of creatures derive from them as opposed to God. Or, to put things another way: God, for Aquinas, is not a good moral agent; and, for Aquinas, the choices of creatures always show forth the action of God, not his permission of actions that somehow arise only from agents other than himself.

---

152. Aquinas's discussion also proceeds on this basis in his commentary on the book of Job—as Eleonore Stump emphasizes in "Biblical Commentary and Philosophy," in Kretzmann and Stump, *The Cambridge Companion to Aquinas*.

153. These two lines of thinking are commonly run together, for it is often suggested that God permits moral evil because he (legitimately) wishes to bring about an end with respect to which his permission of moral evil can be viewed as a necessary means. For an example of someone who advocates a means-ends approach to the topic of God and evil (one which incorporates the claim that God's permission of moral evil can be thought of as part of this approach), see Richard Swinburne, *The Existence of God*, revised edition (Oxford, 1991), chapter 11, and Richard Swinburne, *Providence and the Problem of Evil* (Oxford, 1998). For a comparable study see John Hick, *Evil and the God of Love*, 2nd ed. (London, 1975).

With respect to God's goodness, Aquinas's point is not, of course, that God is immoral or submoral. Rather, it is that God cannot be the sort of thing we have in mind when we allude to agents acting (or failing to act) with morally sufficient reasons (i.e., for the most part, people). As we have seen, Aquinas has a lot to say on moral agency. But he does not take what we have seen him to think about this as applicable to God. For him, God is good not because God, like a virtuous human being, is well behaved, but because God is the source of all creaturely goodness which, in turn, reflects (in all its diversity) what God is by essence eternally.[154] Or, in Aquinas's words:

> Goodness should be associated above all with God. For goodness is consequent upon desirability. Now things desire their perfection; and an effect's perfection and form consists in resembling its cause, since what a thing does reflects what it is. So the cause itself is desirable and can be called "good," what is desired from it being a share in resembling it. Clearly, then, since God is the primary operative cause of everything, goodness and desirability belong to him.[155]

For Aquinas, created things are made by God, and they all seek to be themselves (they seek their good) by acting in accordance with what God intends (has in mind) for them. For this reason Aquinas suggests that, in seeking (tending to) their good, creatures are manifesting a kind of blueprint in the divine mind, that "all things are said to be good by divine goodness, which is the pattern, source and goal of all goodness."[156] As he sees it, this means that they are seeking God. For their goal is something that lies in God as their maker. God is that by virtue of which there is something instead of nothing. So he is the ultimate maker, the ultimately desirable, the ultimate good. He is the *omega* because he is the *alpha*. He is the end (what is desirable) because he is the beginning.

So what does God's goodness therefore amount to in detail? Aquinas does not claim to know. For, as we have seen, he takes God to be fundamentally incomprehensible to us. It is clear, however, that he does not take God's goodness to be that of something like a human being acting in the light of moral considerations. He certainly thinks that terms signifying human moral perfections can be predicated of God. He is clear that we can speak of God as just, truthful, or loving, for instance. But words that designate moral perfections in human beings do not, for him, signify God's moral integrity. They signify what flows from God and what must be somehow in God if God is the source of the being of things. But they do not signify moral attributes had by God as some of his creatures can be said to have such attributes. For Aquinas, therefore, questions like "Does God act with an eye on morally sufficient reasons?" or "Is God well behaved?" are irrelevant when

---

154. For Aquinas, to say that something is good is to say something about it which is objectively true. Yet Aquinas also takes goodness to be relative since he thinks of it as taking different forms in things of different kinds. In general, as we have seen, he identifies goodness and being. He also says that the good is what is desirable. However, so he adds, there are different ways in which something might be. And what is desirable in a thing of one kind might be very different from what is desirable in something of another kind. On his account, therefore, "___ is good" in statements of the form "X is good" may vary in its sense depending on what "X" stands for.

155. *Summa theologiae* Ia, 6, 1. Cf. *Summa contra gentiles* I, 28, 29, and I, 37–41.

156. *Summa theologiae* Ia, 6, 4.

it comes to thinking about God and evil (they are effectively like asking whether God always takes care to keep himself fit, or whether he does enough to provide for his retirement).[157] They spring from confusing the Creator with his creatures.[158]

As for Aquinas on choices independent of God, we have already seen how Aquinas thinks on the matter. For, as I noted above, even free human actions are, for Aquinas, caused by God. A popular line of reasoning frequently advanced in discussions of God and evil runs thus:

1. Much evil is the result of what people freely choose to do.
2. It is good that there should be a world with agents able to act freely, and a world containing such agents would be better than a world of puppets controlled by God.
3. Even an omnipotent God cannot ensure that free people act well (for, if they are free and not puppets controlled by God, what they do is up to them).
4. Therefore, much evil is explicable in terms of God allowing for the possible consequences of his willing a great good.

But this "free will defense," as it is usually called, is simply unavailable to Aquinas, given his account of God as the source of the beings of things and given how he applies it with respect to the actions of reasoning, creaturely agents. For him, there is no such thing as a real creaturely choice that is not caused by God.

(b) Aquinas, God, and Evil

How, then, does Aquinas view evil in the light of God's existence? What, positively speaking, does he say about the problem of evil? If we take what we find him maintaining in the *De malo*, and if we read it together with his other writings, the main points he makes are these:

1. God cannot be thought of as a creative cause of evil since evil always consists of absence or a failure to be.
2. All things created by God are good (considered as real or actual). Indeed, they are nothing but good since God (as Creator) makes things to be and since something is good insofar as it exists (is real or actual).

---

157. Aquinas, I should note, never puts matters precisely like this because it seems never to occur to him directly to ask questions like "Is God a good moral agent?"—meaning, "Does God act with morally sufficient reasons?" and the like. In expounding Aquinas here I am indicating how his thinking bears on such questions (I am drawing attention to what in his thinking allows one to say how he would have replied to them had he asked them). Notice, however, that Aquinas does ask whether God can sin. He replies that the ability to sin cannot be attributed to an omnipotent God, that "to be able to sin is to be able to fail in doing, which cannot be reconciled with omnipotence" (*Summa theologiae* Ia, 25, 3 ad.2).

158. One might ask whether Aquinas on God's goodness makes sense in itself. One might also ask if it can be reconciled with what those who believe in the existence of God commonly take God to be. I discuss these questions a little in "How Is God Love?' (in Luke Gormally, ed., *Moral Truth and Moral Tradition: Essays in Honour of Peter Geach and Elizabeth Anscombe*, Dublin and Portland, 1994) and in "The Problem of Evil" (in Davies, *Philosophy of Religion*).

3. Things are bad insofar as they fail in some respect. The failure in bad things cannot be thought of as creatively caused by God, though things may sometimes fail because God is bringing it about that other things do well (because God is bringing some good about).

4. Moral evil occurs as free, rational agents turn from what is actually good in order to pursue other goals. As with all evil, its "reality" is that of failure. And it is not something creatively made by God.

5. All that is real when evil comes about is caused to be by God, who is the source of all good.

What Aquinas means by these theses should be relatively clear from what I have written above.[159] Here, therefore, the point most worth stressing, perhaps, is that Aquinas's contribution to discussions of the "the problem of evil" is essentially a negative one. For it is mostly concerned to stress that God does not creatively make evil to be.

At the same time, however (and bearing in mind what he does *not* want to say on the matter), Aquinas's approach to the topic of God and evil is a rounded and distinctive one. And it is grounded in a whole way of thinking about a variety of questions, not just those that might naturally occur to someone reflecting on what is nowadays often meant by "the problem of evil." Aquinas turns directly to some of these questions in the *De malo*. And, though it is only in other writings that he deals more directly with the rest, his discussions in the *De malo* frequently hark back to or presuppose what he says elsewhere. For this reason, as for others, the *De malo* is one of the works of Aquinas to which readers might most profitably be directed as they seek to understand him in general.

159. I should add that Aquinas sometimes declares that evil has an educative purpose in that it may sometimes be thought of as helping us to understand something about ourselves as creatures of God. See, for example, his commentary on Job, chapter 9, 11–21, and his commentary on John, chapter XII, 1478.

QUESTION I

On Evil

First Article

Is Evil an Entity?

It seems that evil is such, for the following reasons:

1. Every created thing is an entity. But evil is something created, as Is. 45:6–7 says: "I am the Lord, who causes peace and creates evil." Therefore, evil is an entity.

2. Contrary things are things in nature, since we posit them in the same genus. But evil is contrary to good, as Sir. 33:15 says: "Evil is opposed to good." Therefore, evil is an entity.

3. People have said that evil, considered abstractly, is a privation rather than a contrary, while an evil, considered concretely, is a contrary and an entity. But nothing is contrary to something else in what it has in common with the other. For example, black is not contrary to white insofar as both have color. And evil, in what underlies it, is like good. Therefore, evil is not contrary to good by reason of what evil and good have in common but by reason of the very aspect that is evil.

4. There is even contrariety of form and privation in things of nature. But we do not speak of good and evil as contraries in such things; rather, we only speak of good and evil as contraries in moral matters, since good and evil as contraries comprise virtue and vice. Therefore, we do not understand the contrariety of good and evil by the contrariety of possession and privation of a form.

5. Dionysius[1] and John Damascene[2] say that evil is like darkness. But darkness is contrary to light, as the *De anima* says.[3] Therefore, evil is both contrary to good and not only the privation of good.

6. Augustine says that what once exists never completely ceases to exist.[4] Therefore, if the sun illumines air, the light produced in the air does not completely cease to

---

1. *On the Divine Names* 4, n. 32 (PG 3:732D).
2. *On Orthodox Faith* II, 4 (PG 94:876A).
3. Aristotle, *De anima* II, 7 (418b18).
4. *On Church Customs* II, 7 (PL 32:1349).

exist, nor can we say that the light is returned to its source. Therefore, part of it remains in the subject and is like an incomplete disposition, and we call the invisibility of light darkness. Therefore, darkness is an entity contrary to light and not only a privation. And the argument is the same regarding good and evil. Therefore, evil is not only the privation but the contrary of good.

7. There is nothing between possessing and lacking a form in things capable of receiving the form. But there is something between good and evil, and some things are neither good nor evil, as the *Categories* says.[5] Therefore, good and evil are not contrary to one another as possession of a form is to its privation, but as contraries between which there can be something intermediate. And so evil is an entity.

8. Everything that corrupts acts. But evil as such corrupts, as Dionysius says in his work *On the Divine Names*.[6] Therefore, evil as such acts. But nothing acts except insofar as it is an entity. Therefore, evil as such is an entity.

9. People have said that corruption is due to lack of activity rather than activity. But corruption involves movement or change. Therefore, corruption causes change. But causing change is activity. Therefore, corruption is activity.

10. There is passing away and coming to be in the things of nature, as the Philosopher says in the *Physics*.[7] But every natural change involves something that the cause of change intrinsically strives for. Therefore, there is in the passing away of things something that the cause of passing away intrinsically strives for. But corruption belongs to evil, as Dionysius says.[8] Therefore, evil has a nature that strives for an end.

11. A genus cannot be a nonentity, since species belong to being, as the Philosopher says.[9] But evil is a genus, for he says in the *Categories* that good and evil are the genera of other things and do not belong to a genus.[10] Therefore, evil is an entity.

12. A nonentity cannot be the constitutive difference of anything, since every such difference is one thing and real, as the *Metaphysics* says.[11] But good and evil are the constitutive differences of virtue and vice. Therefore, evil is an entity.

13. A nonentity cannot be greater or lesser. But evil is greater or lesser; for example, murder is a greater evil than adultery. Nor can we call an evil greater insofar as it corrupts more good, since the corruption of good is the effect of evil, and a cause is not greater or lesser because of its effect. Rather, the converse is true: an effect is greater or lesser because of its cause. Therefore, evil is an entity.

14. Everything existing in a place is an entity. But evil exists in a place, for Augustine says that "evil in its place more excellently commends good."[12] Nor can we say that we should understand this about evil regarding the good in which it exists, since evil commends good by the contrast that it has to goodness itself, for contraries when juxtaposed are illumined more clearly. Therefore, evil as such is an entity.

5. Aristotle, *Categories* 10 (12a16–17).
6. *On the Divine Names* 4, n. 20 (PG 3:717B).
7. *Physics* V, 1 (225a12–20).
8. *On the Divine Names* 4, n. 20 (PG 3:717B).
9. *Topics* IV, 6 (128b9).
10. *Categories* 11 (14a23–25).
11. Aristotle, *Metaphysics* III, 3 (998b26).
12. *Enchiridion* II (PL 40:236).

15. The Philosopher says in the *Physics* that changes are from subject to subject or from subject to nonsubject or from nonsubject to subject, and he calls a subject the thing that an affirmation points to.[13] But if a person goes from good to evil, the person is not changed from a subject to a nonsubject, nor from a nonsubject to a subject, since such changes are passing away and coming to be. Therefore, the person is changed from subject to subject. And so evil is evidently something that positively exists.

16. The Philosopher says in his work *On Generation and Corruption* that the passing away of one thing is the coming to be of another.[14] But evil as such corrupts, as Dionysius says in his work *On the Divine Names*.[15] Therefore, evil as such causes something to come to be. And so evil is necessarily an entity, since something else causes everything that comes to be to come to be.

17. Good has the character of being desirable, since good is what everything desires, as the *Ethics* says,[16] and by the same reasoning, evil has the character of being something to be avoided. But something negatively designated may be naturally desired, and something affirmatively designated may be naturally avoided. For example, sheep naturally flee from the presence of wolves and desire their absence. Therefore, good is no more an entity than evil is.

18. Punishment as such is just, and what is just is good. Therefore, punishment as such is a good. But punishment as such is an evil, for we distinguish the evil of punishment from the evil of moral wrong. Therefore, an evil as such is good. But every good is an entity. Therefore, evil as such is an entity.

19. If goodness were not an entity, nothing would be good. Therefore, likewise, if malice is not an entity, nothing is evil. But there are evidently many evils. Therefore, malice is an entity.

20. People have said that evil is a conceptual being, not a natural being or a moral entity. But the Philosopher says in the *Metaphysics* that good and evil are in things, and true and false in the intellect.[17] Therefore, evil is not only a conceptual being but a thing among the things of nature.

On the Contrary:

1. Augustine says in the *City of God* that evil is not a nature, but that the lack of good took on this ascription.[18]

2. Jn. 1:3 says: "All things were made by him." But the Word did not cause evil, as Augustine says.[19] Therefore, evil is not an entity.

3. Jn. 1:3 adds: "Without him was made nothing," that is, sin, "since sin is nothing, and human beings become nothing when they sin," as a gloss says.[20] And any other evil is nothing by the same reasoning. Therefore, evil is not an entity.

---

13. *Physics* V, 1 (225a3–7).
14. *On Generation and Corruption* I, 3 (318a23–25).
15. *On the Divine Names* 4, n. 20 (PG 3:717B).
16. Aristotle, *Ethics* I, 1 (1094a2–3).
17. *Metaphysics* VI, 4 (1027b25–27).
18. *City of God* XI, 9 (PL 41:325).
19. *On the Gospel of John*, tr. I, 1, n. 13 (PL 35:1385).
20. Ibid.

Answer:

We speak of evil in two ways, just as we do of white. For when we speak of white in one way, we can understand the subject that is white. In the second way, we call white what is white as such, namely, the very accidental quality. And we can similarly understand evil in one way as the subject that is evil, and this subject is an entity. In the second way, we can understand evil itself, and evil so understood is the very privation of a particular good, not an entity.

And to prove this, we need to note that good is, properly speaking, something real insofar as it is desirable, for the Philosopher in the *Ethics* says those who said that good is what all things desire defined it best.[21] But we call what is contrary to good evil. And so evil is necessarily what is contrary to the desirable as such. And what is contrary to the desirable as such cannot be an entity. And this is evident for three reasons.

First, it is evident because the desirable has the nature of an end, and the order of ends is just like the order of efficient causes. For the higher and more universal an efficient cause is, the more universal is also the end for the sake of which the efficient cause acts, since every efficient cause acts for the sake of an end and some good. And this is clearly evident in human affairs; for example, the administrator of a city strives for a particular good that is the welfare of the city, and the king, who is superior to the city administrator, strives for the universal good, namely, the security of the whole kingdom. But it is impossible to regress endlessly in a series of efficient causes, and we need to arrive at one first efficient cause that is the universal cause of being. Therefore, there also needs to be a universal good to which we trace back all goods. And this universal good can only be the very thing that is the first and universal efficient cause. This is so because, since the desirable moves desire, and the first cause of movement is necessarily itself unmoved, the first and universal efficient cause is necessarily itself the first and universal desirable thing, that is, the first and universal good, which produces all things because of the love of its very self. Therefore, as every real thing needs to come from the first and universal cause, so every reality in things needs to come from the first and universal good. And since what the first and universal cause of being causes is a particular being, what the first and universal good causes can only be a particular good. Therefore, everything that is a real thing needs to be a particular good and so, by reason of what exists, cannot be contrary to good. And so we conclude that evil as such is the privation of a particular good, a privation that is associated with a particular good, and not an entity.

Second, the same conclusion is evident from the fact that every real thing has an inclination and desire for something that befits itself. But everything that has the nature of being desirable has the nature of good. Therefore, every real thing has a conformity with some good, and evil as such is not in harmony with good but contrary to it. Therefore, evil is not an entity. And if evil were a real thing, it would neither desire anything nor be desired by anything, and so have no activity or movement, since nothing acts or moves except because of the desire of an end.

Third, the same conclusion is evident from the fact that existing itself chiefly has the nature of being desirable, and so we perceive that everything by nature desires to

21. *Ethics* I, 1 (1094a2–3).

conserve its existing and avoids things destructive of its existing and resists them as far as possible. Therefore, existing itself, insofar as it is desirable, is good. Therefore, evil, which is universally contrary to good, is necessarily also contrary to existing. And what is contrary to existing cannot be an entity.

And so I say that evil is not an entity, but the subject that evil befalls is, since evil is only the privation of a particular good. For example, blindness itself is not an entity, but the subject that blindness befalls is.

Replies to the Objections:

1. We call something evil in two ways: in one way, absolutely; in the second way, in a particular respect. And we call what is evil as such evil absolutely, and this consists of something being deprived of a particular good that is required for its perfection. For example, sickness is evil for an animal because it deprives the animal of the balance of fluids that is required for the perfection of the animal's existing. And we call evil in a particular respect what is not evil as such; rather, we call evil in a particular respect what befalls something because it is deprived of a good that is required for the perfection of something else, not one that is required for its own perfection. For example, fire is deprived of the form of water, which is required for the perfection of water, not of a form that is required for the perfection of fire. And so fire is evil for water, not evil as such. And the order of justice likewise has a connected privation of the particular good of one who sins, since the order of justice requires that the person who sins should be deprived of a good that the person desires. Therefore, the punishment itself is, absolutely speaking, good, although it is evil for the person. And Scripture says that God creates this evil and makes peace, since the will of the sinner does not cooperate in punishment, nor does the will of the recipient of peace cooperate in peace-making. And to create is to make something without presupposing the existence of anything. And so it is evident that Scripture says that God created evil, not because it is evil, but because it is good, absolutely speaking, and evil in a particular respect.

2. Properly speaking, good and evil are contraries like the possession and privation of a quality, since, as Simplicius says in his *Commentary on the Categories*,[22] we properly call things contraries if both of them are in accord with nature (e.g., hot and cold, white and black). But things of which one is in accord with nature, and the other a departure from nature, are opposed as possession and privation of a quality, not, properly speaking, as contraries. And there are two kinds of privation: one, indeed, that consists in the privation of existing (e.g., death and blindness), and one that consists in the process inducing privation (e.g., sickness, which is a process inducing death, and ophthalmia, which is a process inducing blindness). And we sometimes call the latter kind of privations contraries, since they still retain part of that of which they are being deprived, and it is in this way that we call evil a contrary, since it remains partially good and is not deprived of all good.

3. Unless black were partially to retain the nature of color, black could not be the contrary of white, since contraries necessarily belong to the same genus. Therefore, although what white has in common with black is inadequate to explain their contrariety, there could be no contrariety without white and black having something in common. And likewise,

---

22. *Commentary on the Categories of Aristotle*, on chap. 11 (Pattin II:572).

although what evil has in common with good is inadequate to explain their contrariety, there could be no contrariety without evil and good having something in common.

4. We say that evil is contrary to good as regards moral matters but not as regards things of nature, since moral matters depend on the will, and the object of the will is good or evil. And we name and specify every act by its object. Therefore, acts of the will, when borne to evil, take on the nature and name of evil, and such evil is in the proper sense contrary to good. And this contrariety passes from acts to habits, since acts and habits are similar.

5. Darkness is the privation, not the contrary, of light. But Aristotle often employs the term *contrary* to describe privation, since he himself says that privation is a contrary in one respect, and that the primary contrariety is between privation and possession of forms.

6. At the advent of darkness, no light remains; there remains only potentiality for light, which potentiality is not a part of darkness but its subject. For example, air has only potentiality for light before it is illumined. Nor, properly speaking, does light either exist or come into existence or pass out of existence. Rather, we say that light either has illumined or is illumining or ceases to illumine the air.

7. As Simplicius says in his *Commentary on the Categories*,[23] there is something intermediate between good and evil as employed regarding moral matters. For example, morally indifferent acts lie in between virtuous and vicious acts.

8. We do not say that evil, considered abstractly, that is, the very evil, is the efficient cause of corruption. We say that evil so considered is the formal cause of corruption in that it is the very corruption of good. For example, we say that blindness corrupts sight in that blindness is the very corruption or privation of sight. And the evil, if it is, indeed, absolutely evil (i.e., evil in itself as such), indeed corrupts (i.e., brings something corrupt into actuality and as an effect) by nonactivity (i.e., by deficiency of active power), not by activity. For example, disordered semen is deficient in the power to beget and begets a monster, which is a corruption of the natural order. But what is not evil absolutely and as such, causes complete corruption by its active power, not absolutely but of something.

9. Corruption in the formal sense signifies being corrupted, neither causing movement nor acting. And corruption in the active sense signifies causing movement and acting, yet in such a way that everything therein regarding action and movement belongs to the power of good, and everything therein regarding deficiency belongs to evil in whatever way the latter is understood. For example, everything regarding movement when one is lame is due to the power of walking, and the lack of straightness in the limb is due to the limb's curvature. And fire produces fire insofar as it has such a form, but fire causes water to cease to be insofar as such a privation is connected with the form of fire.

10. The corruption that results from something evil absolutely and in its very self cannot be natural and is rather an accident of nature. And the corruption that results from something evil for something else can be by nature, as, for example, fire causes water to cease to be. And so fire strives for something good absolutely, namely, the form of fire, and fire aims chiefly that the fire produced exist, and secondarily that water not exist, since the nonexistence of water is required in order that fire exist.

11. The cited statement of the Philosopher poses a problem, since, if good and evil are genera and not in a genus, the classification of the ten categories is useless. And so, as

23. Ibid., on chap. 10 (Pattin II:527).

Simplicius notes in his *Commentary on the Categories*,[24] some said by way of solving the problem that we should understand the Philosopher's statement in such a way that good and evil are the genera of contraries, namely, virtue and vice, but belong to the genus of quality rather than to a genus that is composed of contraries. But this explanation does not seem appropriate, since this third kind of contrary in Aristotle's classification does not differ from the first kind that he posits, namely, that there are some contraries in one and the same genus.[25] And so Porphyry said that some contraries are univocal.[26] And such contraries are in one proximate genus, as, for example, white and black are in the genus of color, and contraries in one proximate genus belong to the first kind of contrary that Aristotle posits. Or univocal contraries are in proximate contrary genera, as, for example, purity and sexual lust are in the genera of virtue and vice, respectively, and contraries in proximate contrary genera belong to the second kind of contrary that Aristotle posits. And some contraries, such as good, which like being encompasses every genus, and evil, are equivocal. And so Porphyry said that good and evil are neither in one genus nor in several but are themselves genera, since we can call things themselves that transcend genera, like being and one, genera.[27] And Iamblicus offers two other solutions.[28] One of these is that we call good and evil genera of contraries insofar as one of the contraries is deficient with respect to the other, as, for example, black is deficient with respect to white, and bitter is deficient with respect to sweet. And so we in some way trace all contraries to good and evil, since every deficiency belongs to the nature of evil. And so the *Physics* says that contraries are always related to one another as better or worse.[29] Iamblicus's second solution is that Aristotle said that good and evil are genera in the opinion of Pythagoras, who posited two orders of things, one of which is included under good, and the other under evil. (Aristotle in the course of argument often makes use of supplementary examples that others think probable, but that he holds not to be true). And so the above make clear that we do not need to hold that evil is an entity.

12. Good and evil are differences only in moral matters, regarding which we positively affirm something to be evil, since we call the very act of the will evil by reason of what is willed, although we could only will the evil itself under the aspect of good.

13. We do not call one thing more evil than another by approximation to an entity that is the maximum evil or by their diverse sharing in a form, as, for example, we call things more or less white by their diverse sharing in whiteness. Rather, we say that things are more or less evil insofar as they are more or less deprived of good, not indeed efficaciously but formally. For example, we call murder a greater sin than adultery because it to a greater degree takes away the goodness of the very act, not because it to a greater degree corrupts the natural good of the soul. For murder is to a greater degree than adultery contrary to the good of charity, by which good virtuous acts ought to be informed.

24. Ibid., on chap. 11 (Pattin II:569).
25. On Aristotle's classification, see *Categories* 11 (14a19–25).
26. According to Simplicius, *On the Categories of Aristotle*, on chap. 11 (Pattin II:569).
27. Ibid.
28. Ibid. (Pattin II:570).
29. Aristotle, *Physics* I, 5 (189a3–4).

14. Nothing prevents evil from being situated in a place by reason of what is retained in it of good, and it, insofar as it is evil, commends good by its contrariety.

15. An affirmatively designated subject may not only be a contrary but may also be a privation; for example, the Philosopher says in the cited text that privations like nakedness are affirmatively designated. And besides, nothing prevents us from saying that a change from good to evil is a sort of passing away, so that we can call it a change from a subject to a nonsubject. Nonetheless, when human beings go from the goodness of virtue to malice, there is a change from one quality to another, as things set forth in the objection make clear.

16. As Dionysius explains in the cited text, evil as evil corrupts, but it causes something to come to be insofar as it retains some good in it, not insofar as it is evil.

17. Nothing ever desires nonexisting except insofar as some nonexisting preserves the thing's own existing; for example, sheep desire the absence of wolves in order to preserve their own lives, and avoid the presence of wolves only because wolves can destroy their lives. And so it is evident that being is itself intrinsically desired and shunned incidentally, and nonbeing is intrinsically shunned and desired incidentally. And so good as such is an entity, and evil as such is a privation.

18. Punishment as such is an evil for someone; punishment as just is good absolutely. And nothing prevents something absolutely good from being an evil for something else, as, for example, the form of fire is a good absolutely and an evil for water.

19. We speak of being in two ways. We speak of being in one way as it signifies the natures of the ten genera, and then neither evil nor any privation is a being or an entity. We speak of being in the second way as a response to the question "Does evil exist?" and then evil, just like blindness, exists. Nonetheless, evil is not an entity, since being an entity signifies both the response to the question "Does it exist?" and the response to the question "What is it?"

20. Evil is indeed in things, although as a privation and not as an entity, and in concept as something understood, and so we can say that evil is a conceptual being and not a real being, since evil is something in the intellect and not an entity. And insofar as we call some things conceptual beings, the very beings that the intellect understands are good, since it is good to understand things.

Second Article

Is There Evil in Good?

It seems that evil is not, for the following reasons:

1. Dionysius says in his work *On the Divine Names* that evil is neither an existing thing nor in existing things.[30] And he proves this as follows: every existing thing is good; there is no evil in good; therefore, there is no evil in existing things. And so it plainly seems as if there is no evil in good.

2. People have said that evil is in an existing thing or good insofar as the thing is deficient, not insofar as it is existing or good. But every deficiency belongs to the nature

---

30. *On the Divine Names* 4, n. 20 (PG 3:720B–D).

of evil. Therefore, if evil is in an existing thing insofar as the thing is deficient, there is evil in the existing thing insofar as the existing thing is evil. Therefore, evil is presupposed in an existing thing in order that the thing can be the subject of evil, and the question about the evil that is its subject will come up again. And if the existing thing, insofar as it is deficient, is the subject of this evil, it will be necessary to presuppose another evil, and so on endlessly. Therefore, we need to take the opposite position, namely, that evil, if it is in an existing thing, is in it insofar as it is existing, not insofar as it is deficient. And this is contrary to Dionysius.[31]

3. Good and evil are contraries. But one contrary is not in the other; for example, there is nothing cold in fire. Therefore, there is no evil in good.

4. People have said that there is no evil in the good contrary to itself, but there is in something else. But everything common to many things is common to them by the same nature. And good is common to many things, and so is evil. Therefore, good is common to all good things by a single common nature, and evil is common to all bad things by a single nature. But evil is commonly taken to be the contrary of good. Therefore, anything evil is contrary to anything good. And so, if something evil is in something good, it follows that a contrary is in its contrary.

5. Augustine says in his *Enchiridion* that if there be evil in good, the rule of logic that states that contraries cannot coexist breaks down.[32] But the rule would not break down unless the evil were to be in the good contrary to the evil. Therefore, because there is evil in good, it follows that a contrary is in a contrary. And this cannot at all be so, since all contraries involve contradiction, and contradictories cannot at all coexist. Therefore, there is no evil in good.

6. Everything in something is caused either as a natural accident by the subject, as, for example, fire causes heat, or by an external cause, as, for example, fire causes water to become hot, and the water's heat is an accident that does not emanate from the water's nature. Therefore, if there is evil in good, the evil is caused by the good or something else. And evil is not caused by good, since good cannot cause evil, as Mt. 7:18 says: "A good tree cannot bear bad fruit." Nor, on the other hand, is evil caused by anything else, since the other is also either evil or a common source of good and evil. And evil uncaused by good cannot be the cause of evil that is in good, since it would then follow that it would not always be the case that each of two combined elements have a prior unity. Nor, again, can it be that there would be a common source of good and evil, since one and the same thing as such does not produce different and contrary things. Therefore, there can in no way be evil in good.

7. No accident lessens or destroys the subject in which it inheres. But evil lessens or destroys good. Therefore, there is no evil in good.

8. As good concerns actuality, so evil contrarily concerns potentiality. And so there is no evil except in things that have potentiality, as the *Metaphysics* says.[33] But evil has potentiality, just as any privation does. Therefore, evil is in evil, not in good.

---

31. Ibid.
32. *Enchiridion* 14 (PL 40:238).
33. Aristotle, *Metaphysics* IX, 9 (1051a19–21).

9. Good is the same as end, as the *Metaphysics*[34] and the *Physics*[35] say. And form and end coincide, as the *Physics* says.[36] But the privation of substantial form bars form from matter. Therefore, no good remains. Therefore, since the privation of substantial form is in matter and has the nature of evil, it seems that not every evil is in good.

10. The more perfect a subject, the more its accidents belong to it. For example, the more perfect a fire, the hotter it is. Therefore, if good is a subject in which there is evil, it will follow that the more perfect the good is, the more evil it has. And this is impossible.

11. Every subject seeks to preserve its accidents. But good destroys rather than preserves evil. Therefore, evil is not in good as an accident in a subject.

12. Every accident gives its name to its subject. Therefore, if there is evil in good, evil will give its name to good, and so it will follow that good is evil. And this is contrary to what Is. 5:20 says: "Woe to those who call good evil."

13. Nonbeings are not in anything. But evil is a nonbeing. Therefore, evil is not in good.

14. As deficiency belongs to the nature of evil, so perfection belongs to the nature of good. But evil, since it is corruption, is not in anything perfect. Therefore, evil is not in anything good.

15. Good is what all things desire. But what is subject to evil is not desirable; for example, no one desires to live in misery, as the *Ethics* says.[37] Therefore, the subject of evil is not good.

16. Nothing harms anything but its contrary. Therefore, evil, if it is in another good rather than in the good contrary to the very evil, will not harm the other good. And so it will not have the nature of evil, since it is evil inasmuch as it injures good, as Augustine says in his *Enchiridion* and his work *On the Nature of Good*.[38] And good cannot be in the evil contrary to itself. Therefore, evil is not in any good.

On the Contrary:

1. Augustine says in his *Enchiridion* that there cannot be evil except in good.[39]

2. Evil is the privation of good, as Augustine says.[40] But privation limits its subject, for it is the negation of a form in a substance, as the *Metaphysics* says.[41] Therefore, evil limits its subject. But every subject, as an existing thing, is good, since being and good are convertible terms. Therefore, evil is in good.

Answer:

Evil can only be in good. To prove this, we should note that we may speak of good in two ways: in one way of good absolutely; in the second way as we call a particular thing good, as, for example, we speak of a good man or a good eye. Therefore, when we speak

34. Ibid., V, 2 (1013b25–26).
35. Aristotle, *Physics* II, 3 (195a23–24).
36. Ibid., II, 7 (198a25–26).
37. Aristotle, *Ethics* IX, 9 (1170a22–23).
38. *Enchiridion* 12 (PL 40:237); *On the Nature of Good* 6 (PL 42:554).
39. *Enchiridion* 14 (PL 40:238).
40. Ibid., 11 (PL 40:236).
41. Aristotle, *Metaphysics* IV, 2 (1004a15–16).

of good absolutely, good has the greatest extension, even greater than being, as the Platonists held.[42] For as good is something desirable, what is as such desirable is as such good and an end. And because we desire an end, we desire the means ordained for the end. Consequently, the means ordained for the end, from the very fact that they are ordained for the end or good, gain the nature of good. And so the useful is included within the classification of good. And everything that has potentiality for good, from the very fact that it has such potentiality, has an ordination to good, since having potentiality is simply being ordained for actuality. Therefore, whatever has potentiality, from the very fact that it does, evidently has the nature of good. Therefore, every subject, even prime matter, insofar as it has potentiality regarding any perfection, by that very fact has the nature of good. And the Platonists, since they failed to distinguish between matter and privation and classified matter with nonbeing,[43] said that good has a greater extension than being.

And Dionysius seems to have followed the same path in his work *On the Divine Names*, ranking good before being.[44] And although matter is distinguished from privation and is nonbeing only incidentally, Dionysius's ranking of good before being is to some extent true, since we call prime matter only a potential being, and prime matter has existing absolutely through a form and has potentiality in and of itself. And since potentiality belongs to the nature of good, as I have just said, it follows that good belongs to potentiality in and of itself.

And although we can call any being, whether actual or potential, good absolutely, nothing is by this very fact a particular good. For example, although human beings are good absolutely, it does not follow that they are good zither players; rather, they are good zither players when they have perfected the skill of zither-playing. Therefore, although human beings, by the very fact that they are human beings, are one kind of good, still they are not by that very fact good human beings; rather, it is the proper virtue of each thing that makes it good. For virtue makes its possessor good, as the Philosopher says in the *Ethics*.[45] And virtue is a thing's highest potentiality, as the *On Heaven and Earth* says.[46] Therefore, we evidently call things particular goods when they have their proper perfection. For example, we call human beings good when they have the perfection proper to human beings, and eyes good when they have the perfection proper to eyes.

Therefore, it is evident from the foregoing that we speak of good in three ways. For we in one way call the very perfection of a thing good, as, for example, we call accurate vision the eyes' good, and virtue the good of human beings. In the second way, we call good the thing that has its proper perfection, as, for example, we call good human beings who are virtuous, and eyes that see accurately. In the third way, we call good the very subject as it has potentiality for perfection, as, for example, we call good the soul that has potentiality for virtue, and eyes that have potentiality for accurate vision. And as I have said before,[47] evil is only the privation of a due perfection, and privation is only a poten-

---

42. Cf. ST I, q. 5, a. 2.
43. Cf. Aristotle, *Physics* I, 8–9 (191b35–192a1).
44. *On the Divine Names* 4, n. 3 (PG 3:697A).
45. *Ethics* II, 6 (1106a15 and 22).
46. Aristotle, *On Heaven and Earth* I, 11 (281a14).
47. A. 1.

tial being, since we say that things that nature designs to possess a perfection that they do not have are deprived. Therefore, it follows that there is evil in good, since we call potential beings good.

But evil deprives things of the good that is perfection. And so there cannot be evil in such a good. And evil lessens the good composed of a subject and its proper perfection insofar as the perfection is removed and the subject remains. For example, blindness takes away sight and lessens the eyes' power of sight and belongs to the substance of the eyes and even to the very animal as the deprived subject.

And so if there is a good that is pure actuality, an actuality that has no mixture of potentiality—and God is such—there cannot in any way be evil in such a good.

Replies to the Objections:
1. Dionysius means that as evil is nothing intrinsically existing, so evil is nothing positively existing in a subject, not that there is nothing evil in existing things as privations in subjects.

2. When people say that there is evil in an existing thing insofar as the thing is deficient, we can understand their statement in two ways. We can understand it in one way so that the words *insofar as* signify a concomitance, and then the statement is true, just as we could say that there is white in a material substance insofar as the material substance is white. We can understand the statement in a second way so that the words *insofar as* signify a consideration that pre-exists in a subject, and the argument of the objection adopts this sense.

3. Evil is not contrary to the good in which it is, since it is in a good that has potentiality. And evil is a privation, and potentiality is contrary neither to privation nor to perfection but rather underlies both. Nonetheless, Dionysius uses this argument in his work *On the Divine Names* to show that evil is not in good as a really existing thing.[48]

4. The argument of this objection is defective in several respects. For the first statement, that what is common to several things is common to them by one and the same common nature, is true about what is univocally predicated of several things. But good is not univocally predicated of all good things, nor is being predicated univocally of all beings, since both predicates encompass all genera. And Aristotle in the *Ethics* demonstrates by this argument that there is no single common idea of good.[49] Second, granted that we were to predicate good as well as evil univocally, we do not predicate evil of many things by a single common nature, since evil is a privation. Third, granted that both good and evil were univocal, and that both were to signify a nature, we would indeed be able to say that the common nature of evil would be contrary to the common nature of good. Still, this would not necessitate that every evil is contrary to every good, since vice in general is contrary to virtue in general, but not every vice is contrary to every virtue. For example, intemperance is not contrary to generosity.

5. The rule of logic does not truly break down if there is evil in good, since there is no evil in the good contrary to the evil, as I have said.[50] But the rule of logic appears to break down inasmuch as evil, absolutely speaking, and good seem to be contraries.

---

48. *On the Divine Names* 4, n. 21 (PG 3:721C).
49. *Ethics* I, 6 (1096a17–34).
50. In the answer.

6. A subject does not cause evil, since evil is not in a subject as a natural accident, just as potentiality does not cause privation. And again, evil has an external cause by accident, not intrinsically, as I will make clear when I treat of the cause of evil.[51]

7. Evil is in the good that it lessens or corrupts, as in a subject, insofar as we call potential beings good.

8. Although actuality as such is good, it does not follow that potentiality as such is evil; rather, the privation contrary to actuality is. And potentiality, by the very fact that it has an ordination to actuality, has the nature of good, as I have said.[52]

9. There are many defects in the argument of the objection. First, assuming that an end as such is good, not only is the end good, but the means ordained for the end, by reason of that very ordination, have the nature of good, as I have said.[53] Second, assuming that some ends are the same as forms, still it does not follow that every end is a form, since the very activity or use of a thing is also in some cases an end, as the *Ethics* says.[54] And besides, since a product is in some way the end of the producer, the disposition for a form is the end in the case of skills that prepare matter to receive the form. And matter itself as the product of God's skill is for that reason good and an end, since the act of creation terminates in it.

10. The argument of the objection is valid regarding accidents that result from the nature of a subject; for example, heat results from the nature of fire. But it is otherwise regarding accidents like sickness that are departures from nature. For if sickness is an animal's accident, it does not follow that the stronger the animal, the sicker it is; rather, the converse is true. And the reasoning is the same regarding any evil. Nonetheless, we can say that the greater the potentiality a thing has, and the more disposed it is for good, the worse it is for that thing to be deprived of good. And the good that is the subject of evil is a potentiality. And so, in a way, the greater the good that is the subject of evil, the greater the evil.

11. A subject preserves accidents that by nature inhere in it, and so evil is not in good as if by nature inhering in it. And yet there could not be evil if good were to be completely lacking.

12. As Augustine says in his *Enchiridion*,[55] the prophet's judgment is directed against those who say that good as such is evil, and not against those who say that something good in one respect is evil in another.

13. We say that evil is in good as a privation, not as if in an entity in the positive sense.

14. Both perfect things and those with potentiality for perfection have the nature of good. And there is evil in the latter kind of good.

15. The subject of privation, although undesirable by reason of being subject to privation, is still desirable by reason of having potentiality for perfection. And the subject is good in this respect.

---

51. A. 3.
52. In the answer.
53. Ibid.
54. Aristotle, *Ethics* I, 1 (1094a3–5).
55. *Enchiridion* 13 (PL 40:237).

16. Evil harms a good composed of potentiality and actuality insofar as evil takes away from such a good its perfection. It also harms the very good that has potentiality, not as if it takes anything away from that good, but insofar as it is the very removal or privation of the contrary perfection.

Third Article

Is Good the Cause of Evil?

It seems that good does not cause evil, for the following reasons:

1. Mt. 7:18 says: "A good tree cannot bear bad fruit." But we call the effects of a cause the fruit. Therefore, good cannot cause evil.

2. Effects are like their cause, since every efficient cause produces something like itself. But no likeness of evil pre-exists in good. Therefore, good does not cause evil.

3. The properties of effects substantially pre-exist in the effects' causes. Therefore, if good causes evil, evil substantially pre-exists in good. And this is impossible.

4. One contrary does not cause the other. But evil is the contrary of good. Therefore, good does not cause evil.

5. Dionysius says in *On the Divine Names* that "evil does not come from good, and whatever comes from good is not evil."[56]

6. People have said that good insofar as it is deficient causes evil. But every deficiency has the nature of evil. Therefore, if good insofar as it is deficient causes evil, it follows that good causes evil insofar as good already has within itself some evil. And then the question will recur about that evil. Therefore, either there is an infinite regression, or we will need to trace the cause of evil to a first evil, or we will need to say that good as such causes evil.

7. People have said that the deficiency that pre-exists in good insofar as good causes evil is the capacity or potentiality for being deficient, not actual evil. But the Philosopher says in the *Physics* that causes as potential are related to effects as potential, and causes as actual are related to effects as actual.[57] Therefore, nothing by reason of its being potentially deficient causes actual deficiency, which is actual evil.

8. Given a sufficient cause, we presuppose its effect, since it belongs to the nature of a cause to bring about its due effect. But a creature does not have actual evil whenever it has the capacity to be deficient. Therefore, let us assume that there is something defectible but not yet deficient in instance A, and actually deficient in instance B. Therefore, either something not in A came about in B, or nothing did. If nothing, there will be no deficiency in B, just as there was and continues to be no deficiency in A. And if something has been added, it is either good or evil. If evil, there will be an infinite regress just like the one in the previous objection. If good, then good as such causes evil, and so it follows that a greater good causes a greater evil, and the greatest good causes the greatest evil. Therefore, good insofar as it is deficient does not cause evil.

---

56. *On the Divine Names* 4, n. 19 (PG 3:716B).
57. *Physics* II, 3 (195b27–28).

9. Every created good insofar as it is such a good is capable of being deficient. Therefore, if good insofar as it is capable of being deficient causes evil, it follows that good insofar as it is created causes evil. But created good always remains something created. Therefore, created good will always be the cause of evil. And this is improper.

10. If good, insofar as it is actually or potentially deficient, causes evil, it follows that what is in no way deficient, neither actually nor potentially, cannot cause evil. And this is contrary to what Is. 45:7 says, "I, the Lord, who create evil," and to what Am. 3:6 says, "There is no evil in the city that God does not make." Therefore, good insofar as it is deficient does not cause evil.

11. Deficiency is related to evil as perfection is to good. Therefore, conversely, perfection is related to evil as deficiency is to good. But some deficiencies as such cause good; for example, faith as obscure vision, which belongs to deficient vision, causes merit. Therefore, good insofar as it is perfect and not insofar as it is deficient can cause evil.

12. Three things are required for human activity: reason, which directs; will, which commands; and the powers that execute the commands. But deficiency in reason, which is ignorance, excuses from evil, that is, from moral wrong, and so does not cause evil. And likewise, the deficiency of powers, which is weakness, also excuses. Therefore, the will insofar as it is a deficient good does not cause evil.

13. If the will as deficient causes evil, then this is so inasmuch as the will lacks a good that ought to be in it, and this is punishment, and so punishment would precede moral wrong. Or else the will lacks a good that need not be in it, and no evil results from such a deficiency. For example, no evil results in a stone from the fact that it does not have the power of sight. Therefore, good insofar as it is deficient in no way causes evil.

14. People have said that good as such can cause evil but only accidentally. But the activity of an efficient cause accidentally attains an effect; for example, the activity of a gravedigger leads to the discovery of treasure. Therefore, if good accidentally causes evil, it follows that the activity of the good extends to evil itself. And this conclusion seems improper.

15. A person who unintentionally does something illicit does not sin, as, for example, if one should intend to strike an enemy but strike one's father. But to cause something by accident is not to intend the thing itself. Therefore, if evil has a cause only by accident, it follows that no one who does evil sins. And this conclusion is improper.

16. We trace every cause that causes by accident to a cause that causes intrinsically. Therefore, if evil should have an accidental cause, it seems to follow that evil would have an intrinsic cause.

17. What happens by accident, happens in very few cases. But evil happens in most cases, since, as Eccl. 1:15 says, "The number of fools is infinite." Therefore, evil has an intrinsic cause and not an accidental cause.

18. Nature is the intrinsic cause of the things that come about by nature, as the *Physics* says.[58] But some evils come about by nature, as, for example, dying and growing old do, as the *Physics* says.[59] Therefore, we should not say that good causes evil by accident.

---

58. Ibid., II, 1 (192b20–23).
59. Ibid., V, 10 (230a26–28).

19. Good includes both actuality and potentiality. But neither causes evil, since form, which is actuality, is taken away by evil, and the good that is potentiality is related to both, namely, to good and evil. Therefore, nothing good causes evil.

On the Contrary:

1. Augustine says in the *Enchiridion* that evil can only originate from good.[60]

2. Dionysius says in his work *On the Divine Names* that the source and end of all evils is good.[61]

Answer:

The cause of evil is good in the way in which evil can have a cause. For we should note that evil cannot have an intrinsic cause. And this is indeed evident for three reasons. First, effects that have an intrinsic cause are effects that their cause aims to bring about, since everything that results in addition to what the cause aims to bring about is an accidental, not an intrinsic, effect. For example, the digging of a grave is by accident the cause of finding treasure if the discovery is beyond the intention of the gravedigger. And evil as such cannot be intended, nor in any way willed or desired, since being desirable has the nature of good, to which evil as such is contrary. And so we see that no person does any evil except intending something that seems good to the person. For example, it seems good to the adulterer that he enjoy sense pleasure, and he commits adultery for that reason. And so we conclude that evil does not have an intrinsic cause.

Second, the same is evident from the fact that every intrinsic effect resembles its cause in some way, either by reason of having the same nature, as in the case of what univocal efficient causes effect, or by reason of having a lesser nature, as in the case of what equivocal efficient causes effect. For every efficient cause causes insofar as it is actual, and this belongs to the nature of good. And so evil as such is not like its efficient cause in what the cause positively causes. We conclude, therefore, that evil does not have an intrinsic cause.

Third, the same is evident from the fact that every intrinsic cause has a sure and fixed ordination to its effect. But what results by ordination is not evil; rather, evil results when ordination is neglected. And so evil as such does not have an intrinsic cause.

But evil necessarily has a cause in some way. For it is evident that, since evil is not an intrinsically existing thing but is present in something as a privation (which indeed is a deficiency of what is by nature designed to be present and is not), being evil is outside the ordination of nature in the thing in which it is. For if there are deficiencies in aspects of things of nature, we cannot say that the deficiencies are evils for them. For example, it is not evil for human beings not to have wings, nor for stones not to have the power of sight, since these deficiencies are according to nature. And everything that is in something outside the ordination of nature needs to have a cause. For example, water is not hot unless it is made hot by a cause. And so we conclude that every evil has a cause, but only by accident, since evil cannot have an intrinsic cause. And we trace everything that is by accident to what exists intrinsically. And if evil does not have an intrinsic cause, as

60. *Enchiridion* 14 (PL 40:238).
61. *On the Divine Names* 4, n. 31 (PG 3:732B).

I have just shown, then only good has an intrinsic cause. Nor can the intrinsic cause of good be anything but good, since intrinsic causes produce things like themselves. Therefore, we conclude that good is the accidental cause of every evil. And an evil that is a deficient good may be the cause of evil, although we need to come back to the fact that the first cause of evil is good, not evil.

Therefore, there are two ways in which good causes evil. In one way, good as deficient causes evil; in the second way, good as an accidental cause causes evil. And this is indeed easily evidenced in the things of nature. For example, the cause of the evil that is the destruction of water is the causal power of fire. And this power indeed does not chiefly and intrinsically strive to destroy water but chiefly strives to induce the form of fire in the matter, which end necessarily involves the destruction of water. And so it is by accident that fire causes water not to exist. And the cause of the evil of giving birth to a monster is the deficient power in the semen. And if we seek the cause of the deficiency that is the evil in the semen, we will come to a good that causes the evil by accident and not insofar as the good is deficient. For the cause of the deficiency in the semen is a source of mutation, which induces a quality contrary to the quality required for the right disposition of the semen. And the more perfect the power of this source of mutation, the more it induces the contrary quality and so the resulting deficiency of the semen. And so the evil in the semen is caused by good insofar as it is perfect, not by good insofar as it is deficient.

And voluntary things are somewhat the same but not in every respect. For it is evident that sense pleasure moves the will to adultery and influences it to delight in such pleasure contrary to the ordination of reason and God's law. And this is moral evil. Therefore, if the will were necessarily to receive the imprint of something enticingly pleasurable in the same way that natural material substances necessarily receive the imprint of efficient causes, the situation would be completely the same regarding voluntary things and the things of nature. But this is not so, since, however much the exterior object of the senses attracts, it still is in the power of the will to acquiesce or not acquiesce. And so the cause of the evil that results from acquiescence is the will itself rather than the pleasurable thing that entices.

And the will is indeed the cause of evil in both of the aforementioned ways, namely, both by accident and insofar as good is deficient. The will indeed causes evil by accident when the will is borne to something that is good in some respect but is linked to something that is unqualifiedly evil. And the will as a deficient good causes evil because the will necessarily considers a deficiency before making the very choice that is deficient, the choice wherein the will chooses something good in some respect but evil in an absolute sense.

And so this is clear. For in all things of which one ought to be the rule and measure of another, good results in what is regulated and measured from the fact that it is regulated and conformed to the rule and measure, while evil results from the fact that it is not being ruled or measured. Therefore, suppose there is a carpenter who ought to cut a piece of wood straight by using a ruler; if he does not cut straight, which is to make a bad cut, the bad cutting will be due to his failure to use the ruler or measuring bar. Likewise, pleasure and everything else in human affairs should be measured and regulated by the rule of reason and God's law. And so the nonuse of the rule of reason and God's law is presupposed in the will before the will made its disordered choice.

And there is no need to seek a cause of this nonuse of the aforementioned rule, since the very freedom of the will, by which it can act or not act, is enough to explain the nonuse. And absolutely considered, not actually attending to such a rule is itself not evil, neither moral wrong nor punishment, since the soul is not held, nor is it able, always actually to attend to such a rule. But not attending to the rule first takes on the aspect of evil because the soul proceeds to make a moral choice without considering the rule. Just so, the carpenter errs because he proceeds to cut the piece of wood without using the measuring bar, not because he does not always use the bar. And likewise, the moral fault of the will consists in the fact that the will proceeds to choose without using the rule of reason or God's law, not simply in the fact that the will does not actually attend to the rule. And it is for this reason that Augustine says in the *City of God* that the will causes sin insofar as the will is deficient, but he compares that deficiency to silence or darkness, since the deficiency is just a negation.[62]

Replies to the Objections:

1. As Augustine explains in his *Enchiridion*,[63] tree signifies the will, and its fruit external deeds. Therefore, we should understand that a good tree cannot bear bad fruit because bad deeds do not proceed from a bad will, just as good deeds do not proceed from a bad will. But still, even the bad will itself proceeds from something good, just as the bad tree itself is the product of good soil. For if a bad effect is produced by a bad cause that is a deficient good, it still ought to come down to this, that the evil is caused by accident by a good that is not deficient, as I have said before.[64]

2. The argument of this objection is valid regarding intrinsic causes, since a likeness of the effects pre-exists in such causes. But good does not cause evil in this way, as I have said before; rather, good causes evil by accident.

3. The argument of this objection is also valid regarding intrinsic causes and effects, since causes that substantially precontain what is brought about in their effects are intrinsic causes.

4. A contrary is not the intrinsic cause of its contrary, although nothing prevents a contrary from being the accidental cause of its contrary. For example, cold, when its direction has been changed "in some way and so as to encompass heat," as the *Physics* says,[65] causes heat.

5. Dionysius in the cited text understands that evil does not proceed from good as the intrinsic cause of evil, and he later in the same chapter shows that evil proceeds from good by accident.

6. Some good causes evil insofar as such good is deficient, but this is not the only way that good causes evil. Good also causes evil in another way incidentally, not insofar as good is deficient. But in voluntary things, the cause of the evil that is sin is a deficient will, and that deficiency, as conceived prior to sin, does not have the aspect either of moral wrong or of punishment, as I have explained.[66] Nor do we need to look for another cause of this deficiency, and so we do not need to make an infinite regression. Therefore, when

---

62. *City of God* XII, 7 (PL 41:355).
63. *Enchiridion* 15 (PL 40:238).
64. In the answer.
65. Aristotle, *Physics* VIII, 1 (251a32).
66. In the answer.

one says that good insofar as it is deficient causes evil, if the words *insofar as* should signify something pre-existing, then the statement is not universally true. And if the words signify something concomitant, then the statement is universally true, since everything that causes evil is deficient, that is, causing deficiency. This is like saying that everything that heats heats insofar as it is heating.

7. Good insofar as it is inclined to be deficient is not the sufficient cause of actual evil. But good insofar as it has an actual deficiency is the sufficient cause, as I have also explained in the case of the will.[67] And yet it is not even necessary that good have any kind of defect in order to cause evil, since good, even if it is not deficient, can cause evil by accident.

8. The reply to this objection is likewise evident from the previous reply.

9. Good because it is created can in some way be deficient by the sort of deficiency by which voluntary evil comes about, since it follows from the very fact that it is created that it itself is subject to another as its rule or measure. And if its very self were its rule or measure, it could not proceed to act apart from the rule. Therefore, God, who is his own rule, cannot err, just as a carpenter could not err in cutting wood were he to use his hand as a ruler for the cutting.

10. The good that causes evil by accident does not need to be a deficient good, as I have already said.[68] And God thus causes the evil of punishment, since God in inflicting punishment does not intend evil for those he punishes but intends to imprint the ordination of his justice on things. And to achieve this end, evil results for those punished, just as water's privation of its form results from the presence of fire's form.

11. Faith is not meritorious because it is obscure knowledge, but because the will uses such knowledge well, to wit, by assenting to unseen things because God says that they are true. And nothing prevents a person from earning merit by making good use of evil, just as, conversely, nothing prevents a person from earning demerit by making bad use of good.

12. The very deficiency of the will consists of moral wrong, just as the deficiency of the intellect consists of ignorance, and the deficiency of a power that executes what the will wills consists of weakness. Therefore, the deficiency of the will does not excuse one from wrongdoing, just as the deficiency of the intellect does not prevent ignorance, and the deficiency of a power of execution does not prevent weakness.

13. The deficiency presupposed in the will before sin is a simple negation, not a moral fault or a punishment. But the will incurs the nature of moral wrong because it undertakes the evil deed in the state of such negation, since in undertaking the very deed, the good that is lacking becomes requisite, namely, actually attending to the rule of reason and God's law.

14. We say that something accidentally causes something else in two ways. In one way, something regarding the cause accidentally causes, as, for example, when the intrinsic cause of building a house is its builder, who happens to be a musician. So here we call being a musician, which is accidental to the intrinsic cause, the accidental cause of the house. In the second way, something accidentally causes something regarding the

---

67. Ibid.
68. In the reply to objection 6.

effect. This would be like saying that the builder intrinsically causes the house he builds and accidentally causes something that befalls the house, for example, that the house be lucky or unlucky, that is, that something good or evil befall someone dwelling in the house that was built. Therefore, when we say that good causes evil accidentally, we should understand that it is by accident that the evil happens to the effect, namely, insofar as the good causes something good that a privation we call evil befalls. And although causal action sometimes extends to the very effect that is accidental (as, for example, when a gravedigger in the course of his digging discovers treasure), this is nonetheless not always the case; for example, the activity of the builder does not extend to the good or ill that befalls one who dwells in the house. And so I say that the action of the good does not extend to an evil result. And it is for this reason that Dionysius says in his work *On the Divine Names* that evil is not only outside one's intention but also outside the course of the action, since movement does not intrinsically result in evil.[69]

15. Sometimes an accidental product of an effect is in very few cases and rarely associated with the effect, and then the cause, in intending the intrinsic effect, need not in any way intend the accidental effect. And sometimes such an accident always or in most cases accompanies the effect chiefly intended, and then the accident is not dissociated from the intention of the cause. Therefore, if an evil is in very few cases associated with the good that the will intends, the will can be excused from sin; for example, a falling branch may kill someone when a woodsman is cutting trees in a forest through which people rarely travel. But if evil is always or in most cases associated with the good intrinsically intended, the will is not excused from sin, although the will does not intrinsically intend the evil. And an evil, namely, the privation of the order of justice, is always associated with the pleasure involved in adultery. And so the will is not excused from sin, since the will, in choosing the good with which the evil is always associated, although not willing the evil itself as such, still prefers to fall into the evil than to be without such a good.

16. As we trace something accidental regarding a cause to a cause acting intrinsically, so we trace something accidental regarding an effect to an intrinsic effect. And we trace evil, since it is an accidental effect, to the good with which it is associated, which good is an intrinsic effect.

17. Accidental things sometimes happen occasionally but other times always or generally. For example, one who goes to the market to buy something either always or generally finds a crowd of people, although the buyer does not intend this. In like manner, the adulterer who intends the good with which the evil is always associated, always falls into the evil. And the fact that very few people are virtuous, and most people wicked, comes about because there are more ways to deviate from the mean than there are ways to adhere to it, as the *Ethics* says,[70] and because most people are more aware of sensual goods than rational goods.

18. We call passing away a natural change by reason of nature as a whole, which causes things to come to be and pass away, not by reason of the particular nature of what passes away. Nature as a whole indeed causes things to come to be for that very reason,

69. *On the Divine Names* 4, n. 32 (PG 3:732C).
70. Aristotle, *Ethics* II, 9 (1109a24–25).

and things to pass away because things cannot come to be without other things passing away. And so nature intrinsically and chiefly strives only for things to come to be, not that things pass away.

19. The accidental cause of evil is not the good that evil takes away, nor the good that underlies evil, but the good that is causing, which brings in one form and takes away another.

Fourth Article

Is Evil Suitably Divided into the Evil of Moral Wrong and the Evil of Punishment?

It seems that evil is not suitably so divided, for the following reasons:

1. Every good division is by contraries. But punishment and moral wrong are not contraries, since some sin is punishment for sin, as Gregory says in a homily on Ezekiel.[71] Therefore, evil is not suitably divided by punishment and moral wrong.

2. People have said that sin as such is not punishment; rather, sin is punishment because there is a concomitance of the two. But acts as disordered are evil, and acts as disordered are punishment. For Augustine says in his *Confessions*: "You have commanded, O Lord, and so it is that every disordered soul is its own punishment."[72] Therefore, sin as such is punishment.

3. Secondary perfection (i.e., activity) is better than primary perfection (i.e., form or habit). And so also the Philosopher proves in the *Ethics* that the highest human good, namely, happiness, consists of activity, not habits.[73] Therefore, if being deprived of primary perfection is punishment, much more is sin, which takes away secondary perfection, namely, morally correct activity.

4. Every emotion that induces anxiety seems to contain punishment. But many sins are accompanied by emotions that induce anxiety (such emotions as envy, apathy, anger, and the like), and many sins involve difficulty in their activity. And so Wis. 5:9 says in the mouth of the wicked: "We have trod difficult paths." Therefore, it seems that sin as such is punishment.

5. If punishment accompanies sin, every sin accompanied by punishment will be punishment. But punishment accompanies the first sin. Therefore, it follows that the first sin is punishment. And this conclusion is contrary to the teaching of Augustine, who says that only the sins in between the first sin of apostasy and the final punishment of hell are punishments.[74]

6. As Augustine says in his work *On the Nature of the Good*,[75] evil corrupts the measure, form, and order of nature, and he is speaking about evil in general. But he says

71. *Commentary on Ezekiel* I, hom. 1, n. 24 (PL 76:915A).
72. *Confessions* I, 12 (PL 32:670).
73. *Ethics* I, 7 (1097b22ff.).
74. *Expositions on the Psalms*, Ps. 58:9, n. 18 (PL 36:687).
75. *On the Nature of the Good* 4 (PL 42:553).

subsequently that being contrary to nature belongs to the nature of punishment. Therefore, it seems that every evil is punishment. Therefore, we ought not divide evil into the evil of moral wrong and the evil of punishment.

7. Without grace, some may sin. But every moral wrong, since it is evil, takes away some good, and it does not take away the good that is grace, since we are supposing that such individuals do not possess grace. Therefore, it takes away a natural good. Therefore, it is punishment, since it belongs to the nature of punishment to be contrary to the nature of good, as Augustine says.[76]

8. The very sinful act, since it is an act, is both good and from God. Therefore, as the act has some corruption, so it has the evil of moral wrong. But every corruption has the nature of punishment. Therefore, the evil of moral wrong, as evil, is punishment. And so we ought not contradistinguish the evil of moral wrong from the evil of punishment.

9. We ought not posit what is of its very self good as a subdivision of evil. But punishment as such is good, since it is just. And so we praise even those satisfying justice by punishment in that they want to undergo punishment for their sins. Therefore, we ought not to posit punishment as a subdivision of evil.

10. There is an evil that consists neither of punishment nor of moral wrong, namely, natural evil. Therefore, the division of evil into the evil of punishment and the evil of moral wrong does not suffice.

11. It belongs to the nature of punishment to be against the will of the one suffering punishment, and it belongs to the nature of moral wrong to be voluntary. But human beings suffer some evils that they do not will, and that are contrary to their will; for example, owners suffer evil when their property is plundered in their absence and without their knowledge. Therefore, the division of evil into the evil of punishment and the evil of moral wrong does not suffice.

12. When we speak of one contrary, we speak of the other, as the Philosopher says.[77] But we speak of good being of three kinds, namely, the worthy, the useful, and the pleasurable. Therefore, evil ought also to be divided into three rather than two kinds.

13. According to the Philosopher in the *Ethics*,[78] there are more kinds of evil than there are of good. But there are three kinds of good, namely, those of nature, those of grace, and those of glory. Therefore, it seems that there ought to be more kinds of evil. And so it seems that we inappropriately divide evil into just two kinds.

On the Contrary:
Augustine says in his work *On Faith, to Peter*:[79] "Rational creatures can suffer two evils: one whereby they voluntarily defect from the highest good; the other whereby they are punished against their will." And these two evils describe punishment and moral wrong. Therefore, we divide evil into the evil of punishment and the evil of moral wrong.

76. Ibid., 7 (PL 42:554).
77. *Topics* I, 15 (106b14–15).
78. *Ethics* II, 6 (1106b28–33), and 9 (1109a24–25).
79. Actually, Fulgentius (PL 65:700A). Cf. Augustine (Pseudo) (PL 40:773).

Answer:

A rational or intellectual nature, in contrast to the nature of other creatures, is related to good and evil in a special way, since nature ordains every other creature for a particular good, and only an intellectual nature by its intellect apprehends the very universal nature of good, and by its appetite of will is moved to seek good in general. And so we in a special way divide the evil proper to rational creatures into the evil of moral wrong and the evil of punishment, since this division belongs to evil only as found in a rational nature, as the cited authority of Augustine makes clear.[80] And we can on his authority understand an argument for this division, namely, that it belongs to the nature of moral wrong to be willed, and it belongs to the nature of punishment to be unwilled, and only an intellectual nature has a will.

We can understand the distinction between these two kinds of evil in the following way. For we need to divide evil as we divide good, since evil is the contrary of good. And good signifies a perfection. And there are two kinds of perfection, namely, one that consists of forms or dispositions, and one that consists of activities. And we can trace everything that we employ in activities to the first kind of perfection, the employment of which is activity. And so, conversely, there are two kinds of evil: one, indeed, in the active cause itself, insofar as the cause is deprived of a form or disposition or any prerequisite of activity (e.g., blindness or crookedness of the leg is such an evil), and there is another kind of evil in the deficient act itself (e.g., if we should say that lameness is an evil). And as other things may have these two kinds of evil, so also may an intellectual nature, which acts voluntarily. And in such a nature, it is clear that disordered acts of the will have the character of moral wrong, since one is blamed and rendered culpable by voluntarily engaging in disordered acts. And intellectual creatures also suffer evil when they are deprived of forms or dispositions or anything else potentially necessary for good activity, whether the things belong to the soul or the body or external things. And such evil, in the judgment of the Catholic faith, needs to be called punishment.

For three things belong to the nature of punishment. The first is that it should have a relation to moral fault; for example, we say that someone is properly punished if the person suffers evil for something the person did. And the tradition of faith holds that rational creatures would be unable to incur any harm, whether regarding the soul or the body or external things, except because of a previous moral fault, whether in the person or at least in human nature. And so it follows that we call every privation of a good that human beings can employ for good activity a punishment. And a like argument applies to angels. And so every evil befalling a rational creature is included either in the evil of moral wrong or in the evil of punishment. The second characteristic of the nature of punishment is that it is contrary to the will of the one suffering punishment. For everyone's will inclines to seek the person's own good, and so it is contrary to one's will to be deprived of one's own good. Still, we should note that punishment is contrary to one's will in three ways. Punishment is indeed sometimes contrary to one's actual will, as when one knowingly receives a punishment. And punishment is sometimes only contrary to one's habitual will, as when a piece of property is stolen from someone unaware of the theft, over which the person would grieve were the person to know about it. And

---

80. In the section *On the Contrary*.

sometimes punishment is only contrary to the natural inclination of the will, as when a person is deprived of a virtuous habit that the person does not want, although the will by nature inclines toward the good of virtue. The third characteristic of the nature of punishment seems to consist of being acted upon, since things that come about contrary to one's will are caused by an external cause, whose effect we call being acted upon, and not by an internal cause, that is, the will.

Therefore, punishment and fault differ in three ways. First, indeed, they differ in that fault is an evil of the very action, while punishment is an evil befalling the cause of the action. But these two kinds of evil are ordained differently in natural and voluntary actions. For in natural actions, the action's evil results from the cause's evil, as, for example, limping results from a crooked leg. But in voluntary actions, the converse is true; the cause's evil, that is, punishment, results from the action's evil, that is, moral fault, with divine providence rectifying moral fault by punishment. Second, punishment differs from moral fault in that the latter is voluntary, while the former is contrary to the will of the one suffering punishment, as the previously cited authority of Augustine makes clear.[81] And third, punishment differs from moral fault in that the latter consists of acting, and the former in being acted upon, as Augustine makes clear in his work *On Free Choice*,[82] where he calls moral fault the evil that we do, and punishment the evil that we undergo.

Replies to the Objections:

1. As it belongs to the nature of moral wrong to be voluntary, and it belongs to the nature of punishment to be contrary to one's will, as I have said,[83] the same thing as such cannot be both punishment and moral wrong, since the same thing as such cannot be voluntary and contrary to one's will. But nothing prevents the same thing being voluntary and against one's will in different respects, for something contrary to our will can be associated with something that we do will, and by seeking what we will, we incur what we would not will. And this happens when sinners sin. For when they are inordinately attracted to a created good, they incur separation from the uncreated good and other such things that they would not will. And so the same thing can in different respects, not the same respect, be moral wrong and punishment.

2. The very act is not willed insofar as it is disordered but is willed regarding something else, and the will when seeking this incurs the aforementioned deordination that it would not will. And so the act has the aspect of moral wrong because it is willed, and it involves the aspect of punishment because a person in one respect suffers deordination unwillingly.

3. The disordered activity itself, insofar as it derives from the will, has the character of moral wrong, and insofar as the one who acts incurs thereby an obstacle to proper activity, the result has the character of punishment. And so the same thing can be moral wrong and punishment, although not in the same respect.

4. Even such emotional anxieties result in the sinner apart from the sinner's will. For example, angry persons would choose to rouse themselves to punish others in such a

81. Ibid.
82. *On Free Choice* I, 1 (PL 32:1221–22).
83. In the answer.

way that they themselves would thereby suffer no anxiety or distress. And so when angry persons incur these things without willing them, the result belongs to the nature of punishment.

5. Things receive their names from the things on which they depend rather than from the things that depend on them. And sin has an associated punishment in two ways. Punishment is indeed associated with sin in one way as one thing somehow depends on another, as, for example, when a person's very sinning results from the fact that the person is deprived of grace because of previous moral wrong, and so we call the very sin a punishment by reason of the deprivation of grace on which the sin depends. And so, although the first sin cannot be called a punishment, subsequent sins can. And punishment is associated with sin in a second way as a result of the very sin, for example, separation from God or privation of grace or deordination of the one who acts, or emotional or distressful anxiety. And so we do not properly call sin punishment by reason of the punishment so associated, although we can even in this way call sin punishment by reason of what sin causes, as Augustine says that a disordered soul is its own punishment.[84]

6. Evil taken generally is a natural corruption of measure, form, and order taken generally. But the evil of punishment befalls the very one who acts, and the evil of moral wrong as such befalls the very action.

7. Moral wrong deprives one without grace of the disposition to receive grace by lessening the disposition, not by completely taking it away. And such a deprivation is not formally the evil of moral wrong; rather, the deprivation is an effect of moral wrong that is a punishment. And the evil of moral wrong is formally the deprivation of measure, form, and order in the will's very act.

8. The corruption of the good in an action, as such, is not strictly speaking punishment of the one who acts, but it would be a punishment belonging to the action if the punishment were to coincide with the action. And a corruption or privation in the one who acts, which has the nature of punishment, results from the corruption or privation in the action.

9. Punishment as related to the subject punished is evil insofar as the punishment in some way deprives the subject of something. But punishment as related to the cause that inflicts punishment sometimes then has the nature of good, if the one punishing does so for the sake of justice.

10. As I have said,[85] the division of evil into the evil of moral wrong and the evil of punishment is not a division of evil taken generally but of the evil in rational creatures. And in this division, there cannot be any evil that would not consist of moral wrong or punishment, as I have said.[86] Still, we should understand that only the deficiency of a good that nature has designed for something to possess, not every sort of deficiency, has the character of evil. And so there is no deficiency in the inability of human beings to fly, and hence neither moral wrong nor punishment.

84. *Confessions* I, 12 (PL 32: 670).
85. In the answer.
86. Ibid.

11. The inconveniences and harms that one suffers unwittingly, although they are not contrary to one's actual will, are still contrary to one's habitual or natural will, as I have said.[87]

12. The useful good is ordained for pleasurable and worthy goods as ends. And so there are two chief goods, namely, the worthy and pleasurable goods. And there are two evils contrary to these goods: moral wrong, which is an evil contrary to worthy good, and punishment, which is an evil contrary to pleasurable good.

13. Regarding each of the three goods, namely, those of nature, those of grace, and those of glory, we need to consider form and act, by whose difference we distinguish the evil of moral wrong from the evil of punishment, as I have said.[88]

Fifth Article

Does Punishment or Moral Wrong Have More of the Nature of Evil?

It seems that punishment does, for the following reasons:

1. Moral wrong is related to punishment as merit is to reward. But reward is a greater good than merit. Therefore, punishment is a greater evil than moral wrong.

2. What is contrary to a greater good is a greater evil. But punishment is contrary to the good of the one who acts, and moral wrong is contrary to the good of the action. Therefore, since the one who acts is a greater good than the action, it seems that punishment is a worse evil than moral wrong.

3. People have said that moral wrong, since it separates one from the highest good, is a worse evil than punishment. But nothing separates one from the highest good more than that very separation. And that very separation is a punishment. Therefore, punishment remains more evil than moral wrong.

4. Our end is a greater good than our ordination to the end. But the very privation of the end is the punishment that we call being deprived of the vision of God, and the evil of moral wrong results from the privation of being ordained to the end. Therefore, punishment is a greater evil than moral wrong.

5. Being deprived of the possibility of acting is a greater evil than being deprived only of an act; for example, the blindness that deprives one of the power of sight is a greater evil than the darkness that prevents vision itself. But moral wrong is contrary to merit itself, and privation of the grace that makes it possible to merit is punishment. Therefore, punishment is a greater evil than moral wrong.

6. People have said that moral wrong is a greater evil than its punishment, since moral wrong is also the reason for the punishment. But although intrinsic causes are more powerful than their effect, the same is not necessary regarding accidental causes, for an accidental cause may be less good than its effect. For example, grave digging accidentally causes treasure to be discovered. And likewise, an accidental cause may be less evil

87. Ibid.
88. Ibid.

than its effect; for example, tripping over a stone is less evil than falling into the hands of a pursuing enemy, which accidentally results from tripping over the stone. But punishment is the accidental effect of moral wrong, for the sinner does not intend to incur punishment. Therefore, the fact that moral wrong causes punishment does not suffice to prove that moral wrong is a greater evil than punishment.

7. If moral wrong has the nature of evil because it causes punishment, then the malice of moral wrong is because of the malice of punishment. But causes are greater than their effects. Therefore, punishment will be a greater evil than moral wrong.

8. What we predicate of something by reason of a form it possesses befits it more truly than what we predicate of something by reason of what it causes. For example, we more truly predicate "healthy" of animals than of medicine. Therefore, if we note the malice of moral wrong by reason of the fact that moral wrong causes punishment, then punishment is a greater evil than moral wrong, since we predicate evil of moral wrong because moral wrong causes punishment, while we predicate evil of punishment because punishment is formally such.

9. People have said that we also predicate evil of moral wrong formally. But we formally call something evil insofar as it has a privation of good. And the good taken away by the very privation that is punishment, namely, the end itself, is greater than the good that the evil in moral wrong takes away, that is, the ordination to the end. Therefore, punishment will still be a greater evil than wrongdoing.

10. As Dionysius says in his work *On the Divine Names*,[89] no one acts looking for evil, and he also says that evil is contrary to what one wills.[90] Therefore, what is more contrary to what one wills is a greater evil. But punishment is more contrary to what one wills than moral wrong is, since it belongs to the nature of punishment to be contrary to one's will, as I have said.[91] Therefore, punishment is a greater evil than moral wrong.

11. As it belongs to the nature of good to be desirable, so it belongs to the nature of evil to be avoided. Therefore, what is more to be avoided is a greater evil. But moral wrong is avoided because of the threat of punishment, and so punishment is more avoided than moral wrong, since causes are greater than their effects. Therefore, punishment is a greater evil than moral wrong.

12. A subsequent privation is more harmful than the first; for example, a second wound is more harmful than the first. But punishment is subsequent to moral wrong. Therefore, punishment is more harmful than moral wrong. Therefore, punishment is a greater evil than moral wrong, since we call things evil inasmuch as they cause harm, as Augustine says in his *Enchiridion*.[92]

13. Since death is a punishment, punishment can destroy the subject punished. But moral wrong, which only defiles the subject, does not. Therefore, punishment does more harm than moral wrong. Therefore, punishment is a greater evil.

14. We presume that a just person prefers the lesser evil. But Lot, because just, preferred moral wrong to punishment, namely, by offering his daughters to the lust of

89. *On the Divine Names* 4, nn. 19 and 31 (PG 3:716C and 732B).

90. Ibid., 4, n. 32 (PG 3:732D).

91. In the answer of a. 4.

92. *Enchiridion* 12 (PL 40:237).

the men of Sodom, which was moral wrong, to avoid allowing injustice in his home by violence inflicted on his guests, which is punishment.[93] Therefore, punishment is a greater evil than moral wrong.

15. God inflicts eternal punishment for temporal sin, since, as Gregory says,[94] the eternal is what torments, the temporal what pleases. But eternal evil is worse than temporal evil, just as eternal good is better than temporal good. Therefore, punishment is a greater evil than moral wrong.

16. According to the Philosopher in the *Topics*,[95] evil is more prevalent than good. But punishment is more prevalent than moral wrong, since many who are faultless are punished, and every moral wrong has at least the punishment connected with it. Therefore, punishment is a greater evil than moral wrong.

17. As in the case of good things, ends are better than means to the ends, so in the case of evil things, ends are worse than means. But punishment is the end of moral wrong. Therefore, punishment is a greater evil than moral wrong.

18. Regarding any moral wrong, human beings can be released. And so Cain is rebuked for saying: "My iniquity is too great for me to deserve pardon."[96] But there is a punishment from which human beings cannot be released, namely, the punishment of hell. Therefore, punishment is a greater evil than moral wrong.

19. When we analogously predicate something of many things, it seems to be predicated primarily of what is more known to be such. But punishment is more known to be evil than moral wrong is, since more people think that punishment is evil than think moral wrong is. Therefore, we predicate evil primarily of punishment rather than moral wrong.

20. Concupiscence is the font of every sin, and so it is worse than any sin. But concupiscence is a punishment. Therefore, punishment is a greater evil than moral wrong.

On the Contrary:

1. What the good hate more is a greater evil than what the wicked hate more. But the wicked hate more the evils of punishment, and the good hate more the evils of moral wrong, as Augustine says in the *City of God*.[97] Therefore, moral wrong is a greater evil than punishment.

2. According to Augustine in his work *On the Nature of the Good*,[98] evil is the privation of right order. But moral wrong is further removed from right order than punishment is, since moral wrong as such is disordered, and punishment rectifies it. Therefore, moral wrong is a greater evil than punishment.

3. The evil of moral wrong is contrary to a worthy good, and the evil of punishment contrary to a pleasurable good. But worthy goods are better than pleasurable goods. Therefore, the evil of moral wrong is worse than the evil of punishment.

---

93. Gen. 19:8.
94. *Morals* XIV, 10, n. 12 (PL 75:1046A).
95. Actually, *Ethics* II, 6 (1106b28–33), and 9 (1109a24–25).
96. Gen. 4:13.
97. *City of God* III, 1 (PL 41:79).
98. *On the Nature of the Good* 4 (PL 42:553).

Answer:

This question indeed seems superficially easy to answer, since most people understand punishment only as corporal or painful to the senses, and such punishments undoubtedly have less of the nature of evil than does moral wrong, which is contrary to grace and glory. But the privations of grace and glory, since they are also kinds of punishment, seem equally to have the nature of evil if we were to consider the good to which each evil is contrary. This is because the privation of the final end itself, which is the greatest good, also has the nature of punishment.

But convincing arguments can demonstrate that moral wrong, absolutely speaking, has more of the character of evil than punishment has. First, this is indeed the case because whatever causes a subject to be such is much more such than what cannot do so. For example, if something is not white enough for us to call a subject white, the thing has less whiteness than if whiteness were to make the subject white. For things that do not affect or designate a subject seem to belong to it in a qualified way, while things that affect and designate a subject seem to belong to it in an absolute sense. And it is obvious that we call a person in whom the evil of moral wrong is present evil for that reason, and we do not call a person who suffers the evil of punishment evil for that reason as such. And so Dionysius says in his work *On the Divine Names* that "suffering punishment is not evil, but being worthy of punishment is."[99] And so it follows that the evil of moral wrong has more of the nature of evil than the evil of punishment does. And we should understand why we call people evil because of the evil of moral wrong and not because of the evil of punishment. We do so because we call actual things good or evil without qualification, and potential things good or evil in some respect, for the potentiality for good or evil is good or evil in a qualified way but not absolutely. And there are two kinds of actuality, to wit: a first actuality, which consists of a disposition or form, and a second actuality, which consists of activity (e.g., knowing and contemplating). And if the first kind of actuality inheres in a subject, the subject thus far has only the potentiality for the second kind of actuality. For example, a knowing subject may not yet be contemplating but can do so. Therefore, we note things as good or evil absolutely because of the second kind of actuality, which is activity, and things as good or evil relatively in some respect because of the first kind of actuality.

And in beings having wills, acts of the will bring every power and habit to good acts, since the object of the will is good in general, and all the particular goods for the sake of which every power and habit acts are included therein. And the power that aims at the chief end, by its commands, moves a power that aims at a secondary end, as the art of piloting governs the art of shipbuilding, and the art of war the art of cavalry. For it does not follow from the fact that one has habitual knowledge of grammar that the person speaks grammatically or well, since the person with such habitual knowledge may not use it or may act contrary to it, as when a grammarian intentionally makes a solecism and acts correctly regarding his art when he wishes to do so. And so we call human beings who have a good will good human beings absolutely, as if they by acts of a good will use well everything they possess, and we call human beings good grammarians rather than good human beings if they have habitual knowledge of grammar. And it is like-

---

99. *On the Divine Names* 4, n. 22 (PG 3:724B).

wise in the case of evil. Therefore, since the evil of moral wrong is an evil in the act of the will, and the evil of punishment is a privation of something that the will can use in some way for good activity, the evil of moral wrong makes a human being evil absolutely, and the evil of punishment does not.

And the second argument is as follows. Since God is the very essence of goodness, the more something is foreign to God, the more it has the nature of evil. But moral wrong is more foreign to God than punishment is, since God is the cause of punishment and not the cause of moral wrong. Therefore, it is clear from this that moral wrong is a greater evil than punishment. And we understand from this why God is the cause of punishment and not the cause of moral wrong. For the evil of moral wrong, which is in the act of the will, is directly contrary to the act of charity, which is the primary and chief perfection of the will. And charity directs the act of the will to God, and does so not only that human beings may enjoy the divine good (for this belongs to the love we call the love of desire) but also as the divine good is in God himself (which belongs to the love of friendship). And so it cannot be from God that anyone would not will the divine good as it is in God himself, since, conversely, God inclines every will to will what he himself wills, and he wills his good as it is in himself. And so the evil of moral wrong cannot be from God. And God can will that the divine good itself or any other good included in it be taken away from someone unfit for it, since the good of right order demands that nothing should have something of which it is unworthy. And the very taking away of the uncreated good or any other good from one who is unworthy has the nature of punishment. Therefore, God is the cause of punishment but cannot be the cause of moral wrong.

The third argument is that the evil that an expert artisan introduces to avoid another evil has less of the nature of evil than the evil that the introduced evil would avoid. For example, if an expert doctor amputates a hand in order that the body not perish, amputating the hand is clearly a lesser evil than destruction of the body. And it is clear that the wisdom of God introduces punishment in order that moral wrong should be avoided either by the one who is punished, or at least by others, as Job 19:29 says: "Flee from the face of iniquity, since the sword punishes iniquity." Therefore, moral wrong, for the avoidance of which punishment is introduced, is a greater evil than the punishment itself.

The fourth argument is that the evil of moral wrong consists of acting, and the evil of punishment of being acted upon, as I have said before.[100] And what acts evilly manifests itself to be already evil, while what suffers an evil does not thereby manifest itself to be evil but to be on the way to evil, as it were, since what undergoes something is changed into that. For example, limping itself shows that a leg is already subject to evil, and the fact that a leg suffers pain shows that the leg is not yet subject to defect but is becoming defective. For as the activity of an actually existing thing is better than the movement toward actuality and perfection, so also the evil of activity, considered in itself, has more of the nature of evil than the evil of undergoing suffering. And so moral wrong has more of the nature of evil than punishment does.

Replies to the Objections:
1. With regard to the end results, if we relate reward to merit, and punishment to moral wrong, then there is a like relationship in both cases, since moral wrong results in pun-

---

100. In the answer of a. 4.

ishment, just as merit results in reward. But with regard to intention, if we compare the two cases, there is no like relationship; rather, the reverse is true, since one inflicts punishment to avoid moral wrong, while one acts meritoriously to receive a reward. And so as reward is better than merit, moral wrong is worse than punishment.

2. The good of the one who acts is both a primary perfection, the privation of which is a punishment, and a secondary perfection, that is, an activity, the contrary of which is moral wrong. But secondary perfection itself is better than primary perfection. And so the moral wrong contrary to secondary perfection has more of the nature of evil than the punishment contrary to primary perfection.

3. Moral wrong separates human beings from God in a way contrary to the union of charity whereby they will the good of God himself as he is in himself. But punishment separates human beings from God in a way contrary to their enjoying the divine good. And so the separation involved in moral wrong is worse than the separation involved in punishment.

4. We can understand separation from ordination to the end in two ways. We can understand the separation in one way regarding the very human being, in which case privation of ordination to the end, just like privation of the end, is punishment. We can understand the separation in a second way regarding an action, in which case privation of ordination to the end is moral wrong, since human beings are culpable because they perform an action not proper for their end. And so there is no relationship between the evil of moral wrong and the evil of punishment like the one between our end and ordination to it, since each of the evils in some respect deprives human beings of both their end and their ordination to the end.

5. The privation of habitual grace itself is punishment, but the privation of an act that ought to proceed from grace is the evil of moral wrong. And so the evil of moral wrong is clearly contrary to the more perfect good, since acts perfect habits.

6. Although moral wrong causes punishment accidentally with respect to the one who suffers punishment, moral wrong is nonetheless the intrinsic cause of punishment with respect to the one who inflicts punishment, since the one who inflicts punishment intends to inflict it to punish moral wrong.

7. Moral wrong is not evil because punishment is inflicted to punish it, but rather the converse: the evil of punishment is inflicted to restrain and rectify the wickedness of moral wrong. And so it is clear that we predicate evil of moral wrong formally as well as causally, and more significantly than we predicate evil of punishment, as is evident from what I have said.[101]

8–9. And the foregoing response makes clear the answers to the eighth and ninth objections.

10. We should judge things by the estimation of the virtuous, not by the estimation of the wicked, just as we should judge the taste of things by the estimation of the healthy, not by the estimation of the sick. And so we should not judge punishment to be worse because the wicked flee from it more willingly; rather, we should judge moral wrong to be worse because the virtuous flee from it more willingly.

101. In the answer.

11. It is characteristic of the virtuous to flee from moral wrong because of its very nature and not because of threatened punishment. But it is characteristic of the wicked to flee from moral wrong because of threatened punishment, as Horace says: "The wicked hate sinning because of fear of punishment, the virtuous hate sinning because of love of virtue."[102] And moreover, God inflicts punishment only because of moral wrong, as I have said.[103]

12. A subsequent privation is worse than a previous privation when the second includes the first, and so we seem to be able to say that punishment in addition to moral wrong is worse than moral wrong alone. And this is indeed true regarding the one who is punished. But regarding the one who inflicts punishment, punishment has the nature of justice and right order, and so moral wrong is made less evil by the connection of good, as Boethius demonstrates in his work *On Consolation*.[104]

13. Moral wrong and punishment belong to rational nature, which in what is rational cannot pass away. And so punishment, although it takes away the life of the body, does not take away the subject with a rational nature. And so we should concede that, strictly speaking, punishment is worse for the body than moral wrong is.

14. Lot did not prefer moral wrong to punishment but showed that we should observe right order in fleeing from moral wrongs, since it is more tolerable for a person to commit a lesser fault than a greater.

15. Although moral wrong is temporal as regards the act, it is nonetheless eternal as regards the state of the guilty person and the person's guilt, unless repentance should wipe out the moral fault. And the eternity of the moral fault is the reason why the punishment is eternal.

16. Most human beings have some evil, namely, the evil in their moral acts, because most follow their sensual nature rather than reason. And so it is not necessarily true that the more things generally happen, the more evil they are, since then venial sins, which are committed frequently, would be worse than mortal sins.

17. Punishment is the end of moral wrong regarding end result but not regarding intention, as I have said before.[105]

18. A person cannot return to life from the punishment of hell because the moral fault of those in hell cannot be expiated. And so the impossibility of returning to life from the punishment of hell does not demonstrate that punishment is a greater evil than moral wrong.

19. We predicate a name primarily of one thing rather than another in two ways: in one way regarding how the things are given the name; in the other way regarding the nature of the things. For example, regarding the imposition of names, we predicate names predicated of God and creatures primarily of creatures, but as regards the nature of things, we predicate the names primarily of God, from whom every perfection in creatures is

---

102. *Epistles* I, 16, ll. 50–53, as cited by the anonymous author of *Moral Philosophy*, q. 5, n. 68 (PL 171:1053D).

103. In the answer.

104. *On Consolation*, prose 4 (PL 63:805B).

105. Reply to objection 1.

derived. And likewise, nothing prevents us from predicating evil primarily of punishment as regards the imposition of the name, and secondarily of punishment as regards the nature of things.

20. Concupiscence is potentially the source of moral wrongs, but actual evil is worse than potential evil, as the Philosopher says in the *Metaphysics*.[106] And so concupiscence is not a greater evil than moral wrong.

---

106. Aristotle, *Metaphysics* IX, 9 (1051a15–16).

QUESTION II

On Sins

First Article

Is an Act Involved in Every Sin?

It seems that an act is, for the following reasons:

1. Augustine says that "sin is a word or deed or desire contrary to the law of God."[1] But an act is implied in each of those three things. Therefore, an act is involved in every sin.

2. Augustine says that sin is so voluntary that there is no sin unless it is voluntary.[2] But nothing can be voluntary unless by an act of the will. Therefore, there needs to be at least an act of the will in any sin.

3. Contraries belong to the same genus. But merit and demerit are contraries, and merit belongs to the genus of action, since we merit by our acts. Therefore, it seems that demerit or sin belongs to the genus of action by the same reasoning.

4. Sin is a privation, since sin is nothing, as Augustine says.[3] But sin is grounded in something. Therefore, there needs to be an act to ground sin.

5. Augustine says in his *Enchiridion* that there can be evil only in good.[4] But the good in which the malice of sin is grounded is an act. Therefore, there needs to be an act in any sin.

6. Augustine says in his work *Book of the 83 Questions* that "we cannot justly impute any sin or good deed to anyone who has done nothing by his or her own will."[5] But one cannot do anything by one's own will without an act. Therefore, we cannot impute to a person anything as a sin unless there be an act in sinning.

---

1. *Against Faustus* XXII, 27 (PL 42:418).
2. Cf. *On True Religion* 14, n. 27 (PL 34:133).
3. Cf. *On the Gospel of John* I, l, n. 13 (PL 35:1385).
4. *Enchiridion* 14 (PL 40:238).
5. *Book of the 83 Questions*, q. 24 (PL 40:17).

7. John Damascene says that praise and blame result from acts.[6] But every sin should be blamed. Therefore, every sin consists of an act.

8. A gloss says every sin is the product of concupiscence.[7] But the product of concupiscence involves an act. Therefore, every sin involves an act.

9. If there is any sin without an act, such a sin seems especially to regard a sin of omission. But omission is not without an act, since omission is a negation, and every negation is grounded in an affirmation. And so a sin of omission needs to be grounded in an act. Therefore, much more does any other sin.

10. Omission is a sin only insofar as the omission is contrary to the law of God. But this is done with contempt, and contempt is done by an act. Therefore, a sin of omission is grounded in an act, and much more are other sins.

11. If a sin of omission consists solely of not acting, it would follow that one sins as long as one does not act. And so the danger of sinning by omission would be greater than the danger of sinning by transgression, which passes, although the state of guilt remains. But this is not true, since a sin of transgression, other things being equal, is greater. For example, it is a greater sin to steal than not to give alms. Therefore, a sin of omission does not consist solely of not acting.

12. According to the Philosopher in the *Physics*,[8] there can be sin in the means to an end. But action ordains things for ends. Therefore, every sin consists of an act.

On the Contrary:

1. Jas. 4:17 says: "One who knows what is right and does not do it is guilty of sin." Therefore, the very failure to act in such a case is a sin.

2. Punishment is justly inflicted only to punish sin. But punishment is inflicted to punish the simple failure to act, without regard to any associated act. Therefore, sin can consist solely in the failure to act.

3. According to the Philosopher in the *Physics*,[9] there may be fault in things that come to be by human skill and in things that come to be by nature. Therefore, as being contrary to nature is a fault in things that come to be by nature, so being contrary to the rules of skills is a fault in things that come to be by human skills. And likewise in moral matters, being contrary to reason is a sin. But both motions and states of rest can be contrary to nature, as the *Physics* says.[10] Therefore, in moral matters, both acts and desistance from acting, if they are contrary to reason, are sins.

4. The will may be borne to neither of two contradictories. For example, it is not true to say that God wills that evil be done, since he would be the cause of the evil, and it is also not true to say that he wills evil not to be done, since then his will would not be efficacious in fulfilling everything that he wills. Therefore, suppose that someone is presently bound to give alms and yet neither wills to do so nor wills not to do so because the person does not think about it at all. Therefore, there can be a sin even without an act of the will.

---

6. Cf. *On Orthodox Faith* II, 24 (PG 94:953A).
7. Peter Lombard, *Gloss*, on Rom. 7:20 (PL 191:1424C).
8. *Physics* II, 8 (199b1–2).
9. Ibid., II, 8 (199a33–b4).
10. Ibid., V, 6 (231a9–10).

5.   People have said that although the act of the will is not borne either to give alms or not to give alms, the will is still borne to something else whereby it is prevented from giving. But the other thing to which the will is accidentally borne is related to the sin of omission, for the other thing is not contrary to the affirmative precept of the law by reason of which contrariety the sin of omission results. And we should not judge anything by what is accidental; rather, we should judge things by what is intrinsic. Therefore, we should not say that a sin of omission consists of an act because of an associated act.

6.   Even in the case of a sin of transgression, there may be an associated act that does not belong to the sin, since the associated act is only accidentally related to the sin itself. For example, a thief while stealing may say or see something. Therefore, neither does an act associated with an omission belong to the sin of omission.

7.   As there are some acts that cannot be good deeds, such as fornicating and lying, so there are some acts that cannot be bad deeds, such as loving and praising God. But someone omitting something may be occupied in praising God. For example, if persons at the time when they are obliged to honor their parents should persist in praising God and fail to honor their parents, such persons evidently sin by omission, and yet the act of divine praise cannot belong to the sin of omission, since praising God cannot be a bad deed. Therefore, the whole sin consists solely of the omission of the requisite act. Therefore, an act is not required for there to be sin.

8.   We contract original sin apart from any act of ours. Therefore, not every sin consists of an act.

9.   Augustine says in his work *Book of the 83 Questions*: "Some sins are sins of weakness, some sins of ignorance, some sins of malice."[11] Weakness is contrary to virtue, ignorance to wisdom, and wickedness to goodness, and contraries belong to the same genus. Therefore, since virtue, wisdom, and goodness are habitual dispositions, it seems that sins are also. But there can be habitual dispositions apart from acts. Therefore, there can be sin without an act.

Answer:

There are two opinions about this matter. For some have said that there is an act in every sin, even one of omission. The act is an interior act of the will, as when one sins in not giving alms, one wills not to give alms. Or else the act is an associated exterior act whereby the one who sins is drawn away from the requisite act. And the associated act may be simultaneous with the omission, as when one wanting to play fails to go to church. Or the act may precede the omission, as when a monk is prevented from rising for matins because he, by reason of some preoccupation, stayed up too late the evening before. And this opinion reflects the words of Augustine, who said that "sin is a word or deed or desire contrary to the law of God."[12]

And others have said that the sin of omission does not have any act, but that the very failure to act is the sin of omission. And they explain the statement of Augustine that sin is a word or deed or desire to mean that he understands desiring and not desiring, saying and not saying, doing and not doing to be the same as far as the nature of sin is concerned.

---

11. *Book of the 83 Questions*, q. 26 (PL 40:17).
12. *Against Faustus* XXII, 27 (PL 42:418).

And so the *Gloss* says that "I do" and "I do not" are different kinds of doing.[13] And this seems to be a reasonable statement, since affirmation and negation are related to the same genus. And so also Augustine says in his work *On the Trinity* that unbegotten and begotten belong to the genus of relation.[14]

And each opinion is true in some respect. For if we should consider what is required for there to be sin, as belonging to the essence of sin, then an act is not required for a sin of omission; rather, absolutely speaking, the sin of omission consists of the very desistance from action. And this is evident if we attend to the nature of sin, for as the Philosopher says in the *Physics*,[15] there may be fault both in things that come to be by nature and in things that come to be by human skill when nature or skill does not attain the end for which it acts. And what acts by skill or nature may not attain its end because it deviates from the measure or rule of requisite activity. And the measure or rule in the things of nature is indeed the very inclination of nature that results from a form, and the measure or rule in artifacts is the very rule governing the skills. Therefore, we can note two things in faults, namely, departure from the rule or measure and departure from the end.

And sometimes there may be both in nature and human skill a departure from the end without a departure from the rule or measure whereby one acts for the sake of the end. For example, there may indeed be a defect of digestion without a fault of nature if someone swallows something indigestible like iron or stone. Likewise, if a doctor should administer medicine according to the rules of medical practice, and the sick person should fail to be cured, whether because the sick person has an incurable disease, or because the sick person does something adverse to the person's health, the doctor is indeed not at fault even though he fails to achieve the end. And conversely, if the doctor were to achieve the end but were to deviate from the rules of medical practice, we would nonetheless say that the doctor erred. And it is evident from this that it belongs more to the nature of fault to disregard a rule of action than even to fail to attain the end of the action. Therefore, it belongs intrinsically to the nature of fault, whether in nature or human skills or moral matters, to be contrary to a rule of action.

And a rule of action, since it establishes a mean between too much and too little, needs to proscribe certain things and prescribe others. And so also particular negative and affirmative precepts are contained in the natural power of reason and in the divine law, which ought to govern our actions. And as affirmation is contrary to negation, so negation is contrary to affirmation. And so as we impute acting as sin in that action is contrary to a negative precept of the law, so also we impute nonacting itself as sin in that nonaction is contrary to an affirmative precept of the law. Therefore, absolutely speaking, there can be a sin for which an act belonging to the essence of sin is not required. And the second opinion is true in this respect.

And if we should consider what is required for sin regarding the cause of sin, then an act needs to be required for any sin, even one of omission. And this is evidenced as follows. For as the Philosopher says in the *Physics*,[16] if something sometimes is in motion

---

13. Peter Lombard, *Gloss*, on Rom. 7:15 (PL 191:1422D).
14. *On the Trinity* V, 7 (PL 42:916).
15. *Physics* II, 8 (199a33–b4).
16. Ibid., VIII, 1 (251a23ff.).

and sometimes is not, we need to assign a cause for its state of rest, since we perceive that as a thing capable of motion and the cause of its motion are disposed in the same way, a thing is in like manner in motion or not in motion. And by the same argument, there needs to be a cause for a person not doing what the person should do. And if the cause was totally extrinsic, such an omission does not have the nature of sin, as, for example, would be the case if a falling rock prevents an injured person from going to church, or if a theft prevents someone from giving alms. Therefore, we only impute omission as sin when it has an intrinsic voluntary cause, not an intrinsic cause of any kind. For if an intrinsic involuntary cause, for example, fever, were to prevent a person from doing what the person should do, the argument would be the same as in the case of an extrinsic cause doing so. Therefore, for the omission of a duty to be a sin, it is required that a voluntary act cause the omission.

But the will indeed sometimes causes something intrinsically and sometimes accidentally. The will indeed causes intrinsically when it intentionally acts to produce such an effect (e.g., if one seeking to find treasure, should find some in the course of digging). The will causes accidentally when the effect is outside one's intention (e.g., if one wanting to dig a grave should find treasure). Therefore, a voluntary act is sometimes the intrinsic cause of omitting a duty but not in such a way that the will is directly borne to the omission. This is because nonbeing and evil are outside one's intention and one's power to will, as Dionysius says in his work *On the Divine Names*,[17] and the object of the will is being and good. Rather, the will is indirectly borne to something positive when one foresees the resulting omission. For example, one wills to play games, knowing that doing so means not going to church, and we say that a thief, not shrinking from the deformity of injustice, wants money. And a voluntary act is sometimes the accidental cause of omitting a duty, as when a person occupied in some activity does not recall something that the person is obliged to do. And it makes no difference in this regard whether the voluntary act that intrinsically or accidentally causes the omission is simultaneous with the omission itself or even precedes it. (Regarding a voluntary act preceding an omission, I have spoken above about the monk who, too busy about something, goes to bed late and thereby prevents himself from rising on time for matins). Therefore, the first opinion is true in this respect, that a voluntary act needs to cause the omission of a duty for the omission to be sinful.

Therefore, since each opinion is in some respect true, we need to reply to the arguments for each.

Replies to the Objections:

1. In the definition of sin, we should understand as the same a word expressed or one unexpressed, a deed done or one not done, as I have said before.[18]

2. We call something voluntary both because it falls within an act of the will, and because it falls within the power of the will. For in the latter case, we call even nonwilling itself voluntary, since it is within the power of the will to will or not to will, and likewise to do or not to do, something.

---

17. *On the Divine Names* 4, n. 32 (PG 3:732C–D).
18. In the answer.

3. More things are required for good than for evil, since good is the product of a cause that is one and integral, and evil results from any deficiency, as Dionysius says in his work *On the Divine Names*.[19] Therefore, an act of the will is required for merit, but it is only required for demerit that the will not will good when it should, nor need it always will evil to incur demerit.

4. It is not true to say that a sin of transgression is a privation; rather, the sin is an act deprived of due order, as, for example, theft or adultery is a disordered act. For sin is "nothing" in the way in which human beings in sinning become nothing, not indeed in such a way that they become nothing itself, but that they, as sinners, are deprived of a good, and the privation itself is a nonbeing in the subject. And likewise, sin is an act deprived of due order, and we call sin nothing by reason of that very privation. But in a sin of omission, it is true, absolutely speaking, that the sin is only a privation, and the subject of the privation is not a habit but a power, as the subject of blindness is not vision but what nature ordains for vision. Therefore, the subject of the omission of a duty is the power of the will, not indeed any act.

5. And the foregoing makes clear the solution to the fifth objection.

6. In the cited authority, even deeds not done are included in deeds, as I have said.[20]

7. Praise and blame are proper both for voluntary acts and failures to act.

8. The argument comes to the valid conclusion that an act is required for a culpable omission as the cause of the omission, although we could say that the concupiscence about which the gloss in the cited text speaks is habitual rather than actual.

9. Not every negation is grounded on a real affirmation, since, as the Philosopher says in the *Categories*,[21] we can predicate "not sitting" truthfully of one who exists and one who does not. And yet every negation is grounded on an understood or imaginary affirmation, since we need to understand that of which something is denied. Therefore, omission does not need to be grounded in a really existing act. But if every negation were to be grounded on a real affirmation, so that the negation would be posited as a privation, it would be necessary that omission, which is nonaction, be grounded on the power of the will rather than an act.

10. It is not always necessary that there be actual contempt in omissions or even in transgressions, although it is necessary that there be at least habitual or even implicit contempt, since, to wit, we infer that someone is contemptuous if the person does not do what is commanded or does what is prohibited.

11. Omission is contrary to an affirmative precept, and affirmative precepts, although always obligations, nevertheless do not oblige in all circumstances. For example, human beings are not obliged to be always engaged in honoring their parents, although they are always obliged to honor their parents when they ought to. Therefore, the sin of omission actually perdures as long as the time when the affirmative precept obliges perdures. And when that time ceases, the sin ceases to be actual and abides in the state of the guilt, and when such a time returns, the sin of omission is repeated.

12. As persons fall away from their end by evil deeds, so do they by omitting obligatory acts.

19. *On the Divine Names* 4, n. 30 (PG 3:729C).
20. In the answer.
21. *Categories* 10 (12b12–15).

Replies to the Arguments in the Section On the Contrary:

1. The cited authority holds that the very nondoing of good is a sin but does not deny that the cause of such nondoing of good is an act.

2. Punishment is administered for the moral wrong of omitting an act, and yet the moral wrong of omission may be caused by an act, which is sometimes morally wrong, as when sin causes another sin, and sometimes not.

3. Even a state of rest contrary to nature is caused by a previous act.

4. God neither wills that evil be done nor that evil not be done, and yet he wills the very fact that he neither wills that evil be done nor wills that evil not be done.

5. The act required for a sin of omission is not always accidentally related to the very sin but is sometimes the intrinsic cause of the sin, as I have said.[22]

6. A similar qualification is to be made to the sixth argument.

7. Reason should govern every act, and so any act can be an evil deed if it is not properly governed, namely, that it is done when it ought to be done, and for the reason that it ought to be done, and so forth regarding the other things that ought to be observed in human acts. And so even the very act of loving God can be an evil deed, as, for example, if one loves God for the sake of temporal benefits. And the very act of praising God orally can be an evil deed if it is done when it ought not to be done, namely, when one is obliged to do other things. And if we should understand an act governed by reason, as we signify when we speak of acting moderately or acting justly, then there cannot be an evil deed. But if we were to grant that an act could not be an evil deed, it would not be improper for it to be an accidental cause of a sinful omission, since good can cause evil accidentally.

8. An act, namely, the actual sin of our first parent, also causes us to contract original sin.

9. As there are acts and habits regarding virtues, so there are such regarding vices. Still, we call only acts meritorious or sinful, although we can call habits virtuous or vicious.

Second Article

Does Sin Consist Solely of the Will's Act?

It seems that sin does, for the following reasons:

1. Augustine says in his work *Retractions* that sin is only in the will.[23] Therefore, sin consists only of the will's act.

2. Augustine says in his work *On Two Souls*: "Sin consists of the will to retain or acquire what justice forbids."[24] But he here understands will to mean the will's act. Therefore, sin consists solely of the will's act.

3. Augustine says that continence is a habit of the soul, and that external acts manifest the habit.[25] Therefore, conversely, incontinence and every sin also consist solely of the will, and external acts only manifest sin.

---

22. In the answer.
23. *Retractions* I, 15, n. 2 (PL 32:609).
24. *On Two Souls* 11 (PL 42:105).
25. *On Marital Good* 21, n. 25 (PL 40:390).

4. Chrysostom says in his *Unfinished Work on Matthew*: "The will is either rewarded for good or condemned for evil, and deeds bear witness to the will. Therefore, God does not seek deeds for his own sake, that he know how to judge, but for the sake of others, that all understand that he is just."[26] But only that for which God punishes is sin. Therefore, sin consists solely of the will's act.

5. Things connected with sin are accidentally related to it if there is sin whether or not the things are posited. But whether or not an external act is posited, there is still sin in the will alone. Therefore, external acts are accidentally related to sin. Therefore, sin does not consist of external acts but only of the will's interior act.

6. We do not impute to anyone as sin any act that is in no way in the person's power. And so if a person should take hold of another person's hand against the latter's will and use it to kill someone, we do not impute the sin of murder to the person whose hand struck the blow but to the person who used the hand. But the external members of the body can in no way resist the commands of the will. Therefore, sin does not consist of the members' external acts; rather, sin consists of the will's internal acts that make use of the body's members.

7. Augustine says in his work *On True Religion* that if one should perceive an oar to be bent at the waterline, this is not a fault of the person's vision, which reports what it received to report, but this is a fault of the power whose function is to judge.[27] But the body's external members received from God their ordination to do what the will commands. Therefore, fault or sin is in the will's acts, not those of the body's members.

8. If sin consists of the will's acts and also of external acts, it will be a greater sin to sin both by an act of the will and by an external act than to sin only by an internal act, since as a quantity added to a quantity results in a greater quantity, so sin added to sin seems to result in greater sin. But this is not true, for a gloss says, "You do as much as you intend to do."[28] And so the sin of the internal will and the external act is not greater than the sin of the internal act alone. Therefore, sin consists only of internal acts and not of external acts.

9. Suppose that two persons have the same intention to commit the same kind of sin (e.g., fornication), and one has an opportunity and carries out his intention, and the other has no opportunity but would like to. There is evidently no difference between the two regarding what is in their power. But we do not consider sin, nor consequently an increase of sin, by something not in one's power. Therefore, one does not sin more than the other, and so sin seems to consist only of the will's act.

10. Sin destroys the good of grace, which is in the will, not in any lower power, as the subject of grace. But contraries concern the same thing. Therefore, sin consists solely of the will.

11. Internal acts cause external acts. But the very same thing does not cause itself. Therefore, since sin is one and the same thing, it seems that sin could not consist of an external act if it consists of an act of the will.

12. The same accident cannot be in two subjects. But deformity is related to a deformed act as an accident is to a subject. Therefore, since one sin has one deformity, one

26. John Chrysostom (Pseudo.), *Unfinished Work on Matthew*, hom. 46 (PG 56:891).
27. *On True Religion* 33, n. 62 (PL 34: 149).
28. *Interlinear Gloss*, on Mt. 12:35.

sin cannot consist of two acts, namely, an internal act and an external act. But sin is evidently in the will's internal act. Therefore, sin is in no way in an external act.

13. Anselm, speaking of external acts, says in his work *On the Virgin Conception*: "Justice does not consist of any kind of these."[29] Therefore, by the same argument, neither does injustice, and so sin does not consist of an external act.

14. Augustine says that sin ceases actually and abides in the condition of the guilty.[30] But this would not be so if an external act itself were to be a sin. Therefore, an external act is not itself a sin.

On the Contrary:

Everything that the law of God forbids is a sin, since "sin is a word or a deed or a desire contrary to the law of God."[31] But the law of God forbids external acts when Ex. 20:13–15 says: "Thou shalt not kill, thou shalt not commit adultery, thou shalt not steal." And the law of God separately forbids internal acts when Ex. 20:17 says: "Thou shalt not covet." Therefore, both external acts and acts of the will are sins.

Answer:

There have been three opinions about this matter. For some have said that no act as such, whether internal or external, is a sin; rather, privation alone has the nature of sin, since Augustine says that sin is nothing.[32] And others have said that sin consists solely of an internal act of the will. And still others have said that sin consists both of an internal act of the will and of an external act. And although the latter opinion is more true, still all are in some measure true.

And we should note that the three things—evil, sin, and moral wrong—are related to one another as more and less general. For evil is the most general, since the privation of form or right order or due measure in anything, whether subject or act, has the nature of evil. But we call sins acts lacking due order or form or measure. And so we can say that a crooked leg is a bad leg, but we cannot say that it is a sin, except perhaps in the manner of speaking whereby we call the effects of sin sin. And we call limping itself a sin, since we can call any disordered act a sin, whether of nature or human skill or morals. But sin has the nature of moral wrong only because it is voluntary, since we do not impute any disordered act to anyone as moral wrong unless the act is within the person's power. And so sin is evidently more general than moral wrong, although the common usage of theologians takes sin and moral wrong to be the same.

Therefore, those who in the matter of sin considered only the nature of evil said that the deformity of an act rather than the substance of the act is sin. And those who in the matter of sin considered only that whereby sin has the nature of moral wrong said that sin consists solely of the will. But we need in the matter of sin to consider both the deformity itself and the act underlying the deformity, since sin consists of the deformed act, not the deformity. And the act is deformed because it is at variance with the requisite rule of reason or of God's law. And there can be such deformity in both internal and

---

29. *On the Virgin Conception* 4 (PL 158:437B).
30. Cf. *On Marriage and Concupiscence* I, 26, n. 29 (PL 44:430).
31. Augustine, *Against Faustus* XXII, 27 (PL 42:418).
32. Cf. *On the Gospel of John* I, 1, n. 13 (PL 35:1385).

external acts, although it is because of the will that we impute external deformed acts to human beings as moral wrongs. And so if we want to consider everything involved in sin, it is evident that sin consists not only of privation, nor only of internal acts, but also of external acts. And we should also understand about the absence of acts in sins of omission, as considered in the previous article, what we are here saying about acts in sins of transgression.

Replies to the Objections:

1. The will produces both the internal acts that it elicits and the external acts that it commands. And so the very sin committed by external acts is sin committed by the will.

2. Augustine says that sin is the will because all of sin consists of the will being the source of sin, not that the whole substance of sin belongs to the will's act.

3. The will causes acts to be praiseworthy (i.e., meritorious and virtuous) or blameworthy (i.e., demeritorious and vicious). And so we call every virtue and vice a habit of the soul and the will because there are virtuous and vicious acts only insofar as the soul's will commands them, not without external acts belonging to such acts.

4. Chrysostom says that only the will is rewarded or condemned because nothing is condemned or rewarded except because the will causes it.

5. In acts of the soul, that in connection with which, whether or not posited, there still remains something else is sometimes materially and not accidentally related to the other. For the reason for the other is always related to the associated thing as something formal is to something material. For example, in acts of vision, we see color by means of light, and color is something material in relation to light, which can be seen even apart from color, although color cannot be seen apart from light. And similarly in acts of the will, ends are the reason why one wills means. And so ends are desirable even apart from means, and yet means are materially, not accidentally, related to desirable ends. And it is likewise in understanding principles and conclusions, since we can understand principles apart from conclusions but not the converse. Therefore, since acts of the will are the reason why external acts are culpable, acts of the will are, with respect to there being culpable sins, something formal in relation to external acts, and external acts are something material, not accidental, in relation to such sins.

6. The act of the person whose hand someone were to use to kill would indeed be a disordered act, but it would only have the nature of moral wrong in relation to the one who uses the hand of the other. And likewise, the external action of the bodily member is deformed, but it does not have the nature of moral wrong unless it proceeds from the will. And so if the will and the hand were two persons, the hand would not sin, but the will would both by its own act, which is to will, and by the act of the hand that it uses. And in the instant case, there is one person who is the author of, and punished for, both acts.

7. The foregoing makes clear the answer to the seventh objection.

8. If we should ask whether one who sins only by the will sins as much as one who sins by the will and an external act, we should say that this happens in two ways: in one way such that there is an equality regarding the will in the two cases; in the second way such that there is not. But there may be inequality of the will in three ways. There may be inequality of the will in one way by number. For example, a person may by one movement of the will will to sin, and that movement of the will may cease because the person does not have an opportunity to sin, and the act of the will may be repeated in a second movement of the same person's will when an opportunity to sin arises. And then the

person has a twice evil will, one unaccompanied and the other accompanied by an external act. We can consider inequality of the will in a second way regarding the will's movement. For example, one person having the will to sin and knowing that the opportunity to do so is lacking may desist from such movement of the will, and another person having the will to sin and knowing that the opportunity to sin is present may persist in the will's movement until the external act is consummated. There may be inequality of the will in a third way regarding the will's intensity. For example, there are some pleasurable sinful acts in which the will becomes more intense when, as it were, the restraint of reason that was in some measure demurring before the acts were committed has been removed. And there is inequality of sin in whatever measure there is inequality of the will.

And if there is complete equality regarding the will, then it seems that we should distinguish regarding sin just as we do regarding merit. For example, a person who has the will to give alms and does not do so for lack of opportunity, merits in relation to the essential reward, that is, joy in God, just as much as if the person were to give alms, since this reward corresponds to charity, which belongs to the will. But in relation to the accidental reward, that is, joy in any created good, persons who both will to give and do give merit more, since such persons will rejoice both because they willed to give, and because they gave, and because of all the benefits that resulted from the giving. And similarly, if we were to consider the quantity of demerit in relation to the essential punishment, which consists of separation from God and of the suffering resulting therefrom, the person who sins only by the will incurs no less demerit than the person who sins by the will and an external act. This is because such punishment is rejection by God, who regards the will. But regarding the secondary punishment, which consists of suffering in any other evil, then the person who sins by the will and by an external act incurs more demerit, since the person will suffer both for having willed evil and for having done evil and for all the evils that result from the person's evil deeds. And so also penitents, who by repenting forestall future punishment, grieve for all such evils.

Therefore, we should understand the statement that a quantity added to a quantity results in a greater quantity to be about the case where we call both things quantities in the same respect. But where one thing is the reason for the quantity of the other, the statement is not necessarily true. For example, if a piece of word has a certain length, there will be a line of a certain length, but the wood together with the line need not be longer than the line, which is the measure of the length of the wood. So also, I have said that external acts derive their character of moral wrong from acts of the will.[33] And the statement that "you do as much as you intend to do" holds true in the case of evil deeds, since if a person should intend to commit a mortal sin, although the person should actually commit a sin that is of its nature venial or no sin, the person commits a mortal sin, since an erroneous conscience obliges. But if a person, intending to do a meritorious deed, should do something that is of its nature a mortal sin, the person does not merit, since an erroneous conscience does not excuse. Still, if we should understand by intention both the end intended and the deed willed, then it is true regarding good and evil that one does as much as one intends to do. For example, one who wants to kill saints in order to

---

33. In the answer.

render obedience to God, or one who wants to steal in order to be able to give alms, seems indeed to intend good and will evil. And therefore, if we should also understand the will by intention, so that we call the whole, both the end intended and the deed willed, the intention, the intention also will be evil.

9. One earns merit for acts, and no one incurs demerit for habits. And so persons may be so weak that they would sin if temptation were to overcome them, and yet they would not sin if temptation should not overcome them. Nor would they incur demerit on that account, since one is punished for what one does, not for what one would do, as Augustine says.[34] Therefore, although having or not having an opportunity to sin is not in the power of the sinner, using or not using the opportunity when it is at hand is in the power of the sinner, and the sinner thereby sins, and his sin is increased.

10. Since there is sin in other acts only insofar as they proceed from the will, sin takes away what is in the will, namely, grace.

11. Everything related to something else as the cause of it being such is related to it as form to matter. And so two things, as matter and form, make one thing. And so color and light are one visible thing, since color is visible because of light. And likewise, since external acts have the nature of sin from acts of the will, the same sin is an act of the will and an accompanying external act. But if a person should at first only will to commit a sinful act and later deliberately do it, there are two sins, since there are two acts of the will. And when one thing arises out of two things, nothing prevents one of the two being the cause of the other. And acts of the will are in this way the causes of external acts, just as acts of higher powers are the causes of acts of lower powers, and acts of the will are always related to external acts as form to matter.

12. The deformity of sin consists of both acts, namely, the internal act and the external act, and yet there is one and the same deformity of both. And this is so because one causes the deformity in the other.

13. Anselm says that no justice consists essentially of external acts because external acts belong to the genus of morals only insofar as they are voluntary.

14. The condition of the sinner, that is, the liability of the sinner for punishment, is an effect resulting from sin. And so when Augustine says that the sin ceases as to the act and abides in the condition of the sinner, this is the same as if he were to say that sin ceases as to its essence but abides in its effect.

Third Article

Does Sin Consist Chiefly of Acts of the Will?

It seems that sin does not, for the following reasons:

1. We name things by what is chief in them, as the De anima says.[35] But sin is named by external acts, as, for example, when we call theft or murder a sin. Therefore, sin does not consist chiefly of acts of the will.

---

34. Cf. On Predestination of the Saints 12, n. 24 (PL 44:977); On the Gift of Perseverance 10 (PL 45:1007).

35. Aristotle, De anima II, 4 (416b23–24).

2. An act of the will cannot be evil, since the very power of the will is good, and a good tree cannot produce bad fruit, as Mt. 7:18 says. Therefore, sin does not consist chiefly of acts of the will.

3. Anselm says in his work *On the Fall of the Devil*: "The will or the cause of the will's movement, not the movement of the will, is evil."[36] But the will's movement is the will's act. Therefore, sin does not consist chiefly of acts of the will.

4. The will does not cause what necessity causes. But Augustine says that some things done out of necessity are to be disapproved,[37] and so they are sins. Therefore, sin does not consist chiefly of the will.

5. A gloss says every sin results from concupiscence,[38] and concupiscence belongs to the concupiscible power, not to the will. Therefore, sin does not consist chiefly of the will.

6. Only sin taints the powers of the soul. But people say that of all the powers of the soul, the concupiscible power is the most tainted. Therefore, sin consists chiefly of that power, not of the will.

7. Appetitive powers are related to cognitive powers as consequences. But intellectual cognitive powers depend on sensory cognitive powers. Therefore, higher appetitive powers likewise depend on lower appetitive powers. And so sin seems to consist of acts of lower appetitive powers, that is, the irascible and concupiscible powers, rather than acts of the will.

8. "Causes are greater than their effects," as the *Posterior Analytics* says.[39] But an act of the will is evil because an external act is evil. For example, willing to steal is evil because stealing is evil. Therefore, sin is not primarily in acts of the will.

9. The will tends toward good as its object, and so the will always wills either a real good, and then there is no sin, or something that seems good but is not really so, and then there is sin. But a defect of the intellect or another cognitive power causes something to seem good that is not really so. Therefore, sin does not consist chiefly of the will.

On the Contrary:
Augustine says in his work *On Free Choice*:[40] "It is certain that inordinate desire prevails in every evil deed." But inordinate desire belongs to the will. Therefore, sin consists chiefly of the will.

Answer:
Some sins involve external acts that are not intrinsically evil but evil insofar as they proceed from a perverted intention or will, as, for example, when one wills to give alms for the sake of vainglory. And it is evident in the case of such sins that the sin chiefly consists of the will in every respect. And some sins involve external acts that are intrinsically evil, as is obvious in the case of theft, adultery, murder, and the like. And in the case of such

36. *On the Fall of the Devil* 20 (PL 158:352A).
37. Cf. *On Free Choice* III, 18, n. 51 (PL 32:1295).
38. Peter Lombard, *Gloss*, on Rom. 7:20 (PL 191:1424C).
39. *Posterior Analytics* I, 6 (72a29).
40. *On Free Choice* I, 3, n. 8 (PL 32:1225).

sins, we seem to need to make two distinctions. The first distinction is that we speak of "chiefly" in two ways, namely, to mean fundamentally and to mean completely. The second distinction is that we can consider external acts in two ways: in one way as understood regarding their nature; in the other way as executed. Therefore, if we should consider an intrinsically evil act (e.g., theft or murder) as understood regarding its nature, then the nature of evil is fundamentally in the very act, since it is bereft of the requisite circumstances. And because it is an evil act, that is, lacks due measure, form, and order, it has the nature of sin, for then it, considered in itself, is related to the will as the will's object as the act is willed. And as acts have priority over powers, so also objects have priority over acts. And so the nature of evil and sin is fundamentally in external acts so considered rather than in acts of the will, but the nature of moral wrong and moral evil is completed as acts of the will assent to the deeds. But if we should understand the sinful acts as regards carrying out the deeds, then moral wrong is primarily and fundamentally in the will. And so we have said that evil is primarily in external acts rather than the will if we should consider external acts as understood regarding their nature, and conversely if we should consider external acts as they are carried out. This is because external acts are related to acts of the will as objects that have the nature of ends, and ends, although prior in intention, are posterior in existence.

Replies to Objections:

1. Acts take their species from their object, and so we name sins by external acts as the sins are related to them as the sins' objects.

2. The will by its nature is good, and so also the will's natural act is good. And I say "the will's natural act" to mean that human beings by their nature will to exist, to live, and to enjoy happiness. But if we should speak of moral good, then the will, absolutely considered, is potentially, not actually, good or evil.

3. Anselm is talking about when an external act is intrinsically evil, for then the movement of the will takes on the nature of evil from the cause of the movement, that is, from the very external act as the will's object.

4. The necessity resulting from coercion is absolutely contrary to the voluntary, and such necessity altogether excludes moral fault. But there is a kind of necessity that is compatible with the voluntary, for example when a sailor is compelled to jettison cargo in order to keep the ship from sinking. And things done out of such necessity can have the nature of moral wrong insofar as they are partially voluntary. For such deeds are more voluntary than involuntary, as the Philosopher says in the *Ethics*.[41]

5. We sometimes also include the disordered will as part of concupiscence. But even if we understand concupiscence as it belongs to the concupiscible power, we say that sin arises from concupiscence because concupiscence incites to sin, not in such a way that sin consists chiefly of concupiscence itself. And sin is chiefly in the will insofar as the will consents wrongly to concupiscence.

6. We say that the concupiscible power is the most tainted power regarding the transmission of original sin from parents to offspring, but this very tainting came from the disordered will of our first parent.

41. *Ethics* III, 1 (1110a8–19).

7. In us who get knowledge from things, the movement from things to the soul causes cognitive acts. But the senses are closer to sensibly perceptible things than the intellect is, and so the intellect receives from the senses as the senses receive from sensibly perceptible things. And acts of appetitive powers are produced by the movement from the soul to things, and so, conversely, the movement proceeds by nature from the higher appetite to the lower, as the *De anima* says.[42]

8. We call internal acts evil because of the external acts that are their object, but the nature of moral wrong is completed in the internal acts.

9. What is not really good seems to be good for two reasons. It sometimes seems to be good because of a defect of the intellect, as when one has a false opinion about a prospective action, as is evident in the case of a person who thinks that fornication is not a sin, or even of a person without the use of reason, and such a defect regarding the intellect lessens or totally excuses moral fault. And sometimes there is a defect regarding the will rather than the intellect itself. For "an end seems to a person as the person is disposed," as the *Ethics* says,[43] since we know by experience that things seem good to us regarding things we love and bad to us regarding things we hate. And so when a person is inordinately disposed toward something, the inordinate disposition hinders the intellect's judgment regarding a particular object of choice. And so the defect is chiefly in the disposition, not the cognition. And so we say that the sinner sins in ignorance, as the *Ethics* says,[44] and not because of ignorance.

Fourth Article

Is Every Act Morally Indifferent?

It seems that every act is, for the following reasons:

1. Anselm says in his work *On the Virgin Conception*: "There is no justice in the essence of these [i.e., acts], nor, by the same reasoning, any injustice."[45] But we call an act in which there is neither justice nor injustice morally indifferent. Therefore, all acts are morally indifferent.

2. What is intrinsically good cannot be evil, since what is intrinsically in something is necessarily in it. But there is no act that could not be done wrongly, even the very act of loving God, as is evidently the case in one who loves God for the sake of temporal benefits. Therefore, no act is intrinsically good, and by like reasoning, neither is any act intrinsically evil. Therefore, every act is intrinsically morally indifferent.

3. Since good and being are convertible terms, a thing will have from the same source that it is good, and that it is a being. But acts have their moral being from the will, for there is no moral act if the act is not voluntary. Therefore, acts have both moral goodness and wickedness from the will. Therefore, acts are intrinsically morally indifferent, neither good nor evil.

---

42. *De anima* III, 11 (434a12–15).
43. Aristotle, *Ethics* III, 5 (1114a32–b1).
44. Ibid., III, 1 (1110b28).
45. *On the Virgin Conception* 4 (PL 158:437B).

4. People say that although acts insofar as they are voluntary are moral, which is something general, they as such nonetheless have the particular character of being good or evil. But good and evil are the specific differences of moral acts. And specific differences intrinsically divide a genus. And so specific differences need not be related to anything but the genus. Therefore, if acts have from the will the general element of being moral, they will also have from the same will the particular character of being good or evil. And so they are as such morally indifferent.

5. We call a moral act good insofar as it is adorned by the requisite circumstances, and evil insofar as it is adorned by improper circumstances. But circumstances, since they are the accidents of an act, are not part of the species of the act. Therefore, since we say that what belongs to something by its species belongs to it intrinsically, it seems that an act as such is morally indifferent, neither good nor bad.

6. As white and black belong to the same species of human being, so good and evil belong to the same species of act. For example, there is no specific difference between having sexual intercourse with one's wife and having sexual intercourse with a woman who is not one's wife. And this is evident in the effect, since a human offspring is begotten in both cases, although one deed is good, and the other evil. But white and black do not intrinsically belong to being human. Therefore, neither good nor evil belong intrinsically to acts. And so every act, absolutely considered, is morally indifferent.

7. Things that inhere intrinsically do not vary regarding the numerically same subject. For example, the same number is not even and odd. But an act numerically one and same may be good and evil, since a continuous act is numerically one and the same, and there may be first good and later evil in the act, or the converse order. For example, such would be the case if a person should start out for church with a bad intention, and the person's intention be converted to good. Therefore, good and evil do not intrinsically belong to acts, and so every act of itself is morally indifferent.

8. Evil as such is nonbeing. But nonbeing cannot be part of the substance of any being. Therefore, an act, since it is a being, cannot as such be evil, nor consequently as such good, since a good act is the contrary of an evil act, and contraries belong to the same genus. Therefore, the same conclusion follows as before.

9. We call an act good or bad by its ordination to an end. But acts do not take their species from their ends, for then all kinds of acts might belong to the same species, since different kinds of acts may be ordained for the same end. Therefore, good and evil do not belong to the species of the act. And so acts, absolutely considered, are morally indifferent, neither good nor evil.

10. Other things besides acts have good and evil. But good and evil do not distinguish the species of other things. Therefore, neither do good and evil distinguish the species of acts. And so acts as such are neither good nor bad.

11. We call good moral acts virtuous acts, and evil moral acts vicious acts. But virtue and vice belong to the genus of habit. Therefore, the character of being good or evil belongs to acts by reason of another genus and not to the acts by reason of their very selves.

12. Something prior does not depend on the properties of something posterior. But being an act is by nature prior to being a moral act, since every moral act is an act, but the converse is not true. Therefore, good and evil, since they are the properties of moral acts, do not belong intrinsically to the acts as acts.

13. What is by nature such is always and everywhere such. But things are not always and everywhere just and good, since it is just to do things in one place and time and unjust to do them in another place or time. Therefore, nothing is by nature just and good, and so by nature neither unjust nor evil. Therefore, every act as such is morally indifferent.

On the Contrary:
Augustine says in his work *On the Lord's Sermon on the Mount* that there are some things "that cannot be done with a good will, for example, debauchery, blasphemy, and the like, and we are permitted so to judge about them."[46] Therefore, some acts are not morally indifferent.

Answer:
Ancient teachers held different opinions about this matter. For some said that every act of itself is morally indifferent, and others denied this, saying that some acts are intrinsically good, and others intrinsically evil.

To investigate the truth regarding this matter, we need to consider that good implies a perfection, and that the privation of such perfection is evil, so that we use the term "perfection" in a broad sense to include in it proper measure and form and order. And so Augustine in his work *On the Nature of the Good* constituted the nature of good in measure, form, and order, and the nature of evil in the privation of these.[47] And it is evidently not true that all things have the same proper perfection. Rather, different kinds of things have different kinds of perfection. This is true whether we understand the diversity to be between different species, as between horses and oxes, whose perfections are different, or we understand the diversity to be between genus and species, as between animal and human being, for something belongs to the perfection of human being that does not belong to the perfection of animal. And so we need to understand in different ways the good proper to animals and the good proper to human beings and the good of horses and the good of oxen, and we need to say the same about the contrary evils. For it is obvious that for a human being not to have hands is an evil but for a horse or an ox or even an animal as such not to have hands is not an evil. And we need to say likewise about the good and evil in acts. For the consideration of good and evil in acts as such is one thing, and the consideration of the good and evil in different kinds of acts is another, since if we should consider acts as such, their goodness consists of the acts being emanations from the powers of their causes. And so we understand the good and evil in acts in different ways according to the different kinds of causes. And in things of nature, acts are good if they are in keeping with the nature of the cause, and acts are evil if they are not. And so we may judge in different ways about one and the same act in relation to different causes. For example, upward movement regarding fire is a good act, since the movement is natural for fire, and upward movement regarding the earth is an evil act, since the movement is contrary to the earth's nature, and upward movement regarding moveable material substances in general does not have the nature either of good or of evil. But we are currently speaking about human acts. And so we should understand the

---

46. *On the Lord's Sermon on the Mount* II, 18, n. 59 (PL 34:1296).
47. *On the Nature of the Good* 3 and 4 (PL 42:553).

good and evil in the acts currently discussed by what is proper to human beings as such, and what is proper to human beings is reason. And so we consider the good and evil in human acts as they are in accord with reason informed by the divine law, whether by nature or by instruction or by infusion. And so also Dionysius says in his work *On the Divine Names* that it is evil for the soul to act contrary to reason, and for the body to act contrary to nature.[48]

Therefore, if being in accord with reason and being contrary to reason belong to the species of human acts, we should say that some acts are intrinsically good, and some acts intrinsically evil. For we say that both what belongs to something by the nature of its genus, and what belongs to it by the nature of its species, belong to it intrinsically. For example, rational and irrational intrinsically belong to animals by the nature of their species but not by the nature of their genus (i.e., animal), since animals as such are neither rational nor irrational. But if being in accord with reason or being contrary to reason does not belong to the species of a human act, the human act is consequently morally indifferent, intrinsically neither good nor evil. For example, human beings are intrinsically neither white nor black. Therefore, it is this on which the true answer to this question depends.

And to prove this, we should consider that, since acts are specified by their objects, an aspect of the object will specify the act in relation to one cause and not to another. For example, seeing color and hearing sound are specifically different acts in relation to sense powers, since such things are intrinsically perceptible by specific senses. And they are not specifically different acts in relation to the intellect, since the intellect understands them in a common aspect of the object, namely, being or truth. And likewise perceiving white and perceiving black differ specifically in relation to vision, not in relation to taste. And we can thereby understand that what intrinsically and not only accidentally belongs to any power specifies the acts of the power. Therefore, if we should consider the objects of human acts that differ by something intrinsically belonging to reason, the acts will be specifically different as acts of reason, although not as the acts of a power. For example, having intercourse with one's wife and having intercourse with a woman who is not have objects that differ by something belonging to reason, since a rule of reason determines what is one's own, and what is not, and yet the differences are accidentally related to the power of generation or even to the concupiscible power. And so having intercourse with one's wife and having intercourse with a woman who is not differ specifically as acts of reason and not as acts of the generative or concupiscible power. But the acts are human acts insofar as they are acts of reason. Therefore, the acts as human evidently differ specifically. Therefore, human acts are evidently good or evil by reason of their species.

And so we should say absolutely that some acts are intrinsically good or evil, and that not every act is morally indifferent, unless per chance we consider them only generically. For as we say that animal as such is neither rational nor irrational, so we can say that human acts as such do not yet have the character of good or evil unless they have something added that contracts them to a species. But even by reason of the very fact that the acts are human acts, and further even by reason of the fact that they are acts, and further by reason of the fact that they are beings, they have an aspect of good but not of the moral good of being in accord with reason, and it is of this that we are now treating.

---

48. *On the Divine Names* 4, n. 32 (PG 3:733A).

Replies to the Objections:

1. Anselm is speaking about acts according to their generic rather than their specific nature.

2. What results from a thing's species always belongs to it. Therefore, since human acts gain their species from the nature of their objects, by which they are good or evil, the acts so specified as good can never be evil, nor acts specified as evil ever be good. But there may be associated with an intrinsically good act another act that is evil by some disorder, and we say that the good act becomes evil by reason of the associated evil act, not that the good act in itself is evil. For example, giving alms to the poor or loving God is an intrinsically good act. But relating such an act to a disordered end, such as cupidity or vainglory, is another act, which is evil, and yet the two acts are rendered one by an ordination of one act to the other. And good results from the whole and integral cause, and evil from individual defects, as Dionysius says.[49] And so whichever one of the two, whether the act or the ordination of the act to the end, is evil, we judge the whole to be evil, and we do not judge the whole to be good unless both be good. Just so, we do not judge a human being to be handsome unless all the person's bodily members are comely, and we judge a human being to be ugly even if only one bodily member is deformed. And that is why an evil act cannot be a good deed, since there cannot be an integral good out of which there is an evil act; on the other hand, a good act can become an evil deed, since being evil in some respect is enough for the deed to be evil, and it is not required that the deed be an integral evil.

3. Being voluntary belongs to the nature of human acts as such. And so what belongs to the acts as voluntary, whether generically or by specific difference, belongs to the acts intrinsically, not accidentally.

4. The foregoing makes clear the answer to the fourth objection.

5. Circumstances are related to moral acts like accidents that are extraneous to the notion of species regarding things of nature. And as I have said,[50] moral acts take their species from their objects as the latter are related to reason. And so we commonly say that some acts are generically good or evil, and that generically good acts concern proper matter, such as feeding the hungry, and generically evil acts concern improper matter, such as stealing what belongs to another, for we call the matter of acts their object. And to this goodness or wickedness, there can be an additional goodness or wickedness from something external that we call a circumstance, such as the circumstance of place or time or condition of the cause or the like, as, for example, if a person takes what does not belong to the person from a sacred place or apart from need or anything else of the sort. And such goodness or wickedness belongs, although not intrinsically, to the moral act specifically considered, since there are different aspects of goodness by reason of different perfections, as I have said before.[51]

6. Moral acts of the same species can by reason of circumstances be good or evil, just as human beings, who belong to the same species, can be white or black. And yet intrinsically good acts differ specifically from intrinsically evil acts as moral acts, although

---

49. *On the Divine Names* 4, n. 30 (PG 3:729C).

50. In the answer.

51. Ibid.

per chance they do not differ specifically as natural acts, as is evidently the case regarding the two acts, one of having intercourse with one's wife and the other of having intercourse with a woman who is not.

7. Nothing prevents something being numerically the same with respect to one genus and yet both numerically and specifically diverse with respect to another genus. For example, if a continuous material substance is partially white and partially black, it is numerically one insofar as it is continuous but both numerically and specifically diverse insofar as it is colored. And likewise if the will's intention in one continuous act is first borne to good and later to evil, then the act is numerically one regarding its nature and yet specifically diverse as it belongs to the genus of morals. Still, we could say that the act always retains either the goodness or the wickedness that it has from its species even though different ends could change the actual intention regarding the same act.

8. As in things of nature, privation results from the presence of a form (e.g., privation of fire's form results from the presence of water's form), so in moral acts, privation of due measure or form or order results from the positing of another measure or form or order. And so acts take their species from what is in the acts positively, and we call them evil from the resulting privation. And as it intrinsically belongs to water not to be fire, so it intrinsically belongs to such moral acts to be evil even regarding their species.

9. There are two kinds of ends, the proximate and the remote. The proximate end of acts is the same as the object of the acts, and acts take their species from the object. And acts do not take their species from the remote end; rather, the ordination to such an end is a circumstance of the acts.

10. Good has the nature of end, and so an end as such is the object of the will. And since moral matters depend on the will, it follows that good and evil in moral matters are specifically different. And this is not so in the case of other things.

11. We call some acts virtuous and some acts vicious both because they proceed from virtuous or vicious habits, and because they are like acts that proceed from such habits. And so also a person performs a virtuous act in one way before the person has the virtue, and in another way after the person has the virtue. For a person indeed does just things before the person has the virtue of justice, but the person does not do them from the virtue of justice, and a person does chaste things before the person has the virtue of chastity, but the person does not do them from the virtue of chastity, as the Philosopher in the *Ethics* makes clear.[52] Therefore, there are evidently three grades of goodness and wickedness in moral acts: first, indeed, generically or specifically in relation to the object or matter; second, according to the circumstances; and third, by reason of the habit that informs the act.

12. The argument of this objection is valid regarding acts as to their generic nature, and acts do not thereby have moral goodness or wickedness. But acts by their species have moral goodness or wickedness, as I have said.[53]

13. We can consider just and good things in two ways: in one way formally, and then they are always and everywhere the same, since the principles of justice in the natural power of reason do not change; in the second way materially, and then just and good

---

52. *Ethics* II, 4 (1105a26).
53. In the answer.

things are not everywhere and among all peoples the same, and such things need to be determined by law. And the latter happens because of the mutability of human nature and because of the different conditions of human beings and things at different times and in different places. For example, justice always requires that there be an equal exchange in buying and selling, but justice requires that so much be given for a measure of grain in a certain place or at a certain time, and that more or less be given in another place or at another time.

Fifth Article

Are Some Acts Morally Indifferent?

It seems that no acts are, for the following reasons:

1. Being as such is good, and nonbeing is the contrary of being, and evil the contrary of good. But there is nothing in between being and nonbeing. Therefore, neither is there anything in between good and evil. Therefore, every act needs to be good or evil, and no act can be morally indifferent.

2. People have said that being and good are convertible terms in the genus of nature but not in the genus of morals, and so it is not necessary that good and evil in the genus of morals preclude something in between. But moral good is a greater good than natural good. Therefore, moral good has a greater opposition to evil. Therefore, if natural good is so contrary to evil as to preclude anything in between, much more is this the case regarding moral evil.

3. Evil is not opposed to good as a contrary of good, since evil posits nothing; rather, evil is opposed to good as a privation of good. But things opposed by way of privation do not have anything in between regarding their proper subject, and the proper subject of moral good and evil is a human act. Therefore, every human act is good or evil, and no human act is morally indifferent.

4. Human acts proceed from a deliberate will, and a deliberate will always acts to achieve an end. Therefore, every human act is for an end. And every end is either good or evil, and an act for a good end is good, and an act for an evil end is evil. Therefore, every human act is either good or evil, and no human act is morally indifferent.

5. Every human activity involves either using or enjoying something. But everyone who uses something uses it either rightly or wrongly (i.e., abusively). And likewise, everyone who enjoys something either takes enjoyment in God, which is good, or takes enjoyment in a creature, which is evil. Therefore, every human act is either good or evil.

6. As Augustine says in his work *Book of the 83 Questions*,[54] no act in nature is by chance, since every act has hidden causes, although the causes are unknown to us. But as there is nothing in nature by chance, so there seems to be nothing morally indifferent, that is, nothing without an intention to do good or evil. Therefore, no moral act is indifferent.

7. Every act proceeding from a will informed by charity is meritorious, and every act proceeding from a will not informed by charity is demeritorious. This is because all

---

54. *Book of the 83 Questions*, q. 24 (PL 40:17).

are bound to conform their will to the divine will, especially regarding the way they will, so that one wills out of charity what one wills, just as God does, and a person who does not have charity cannot observe this mandate. Therefore, every act is meritorious or demeritorious, and no act is morally indifferent.

8. One is condemned only for moral wrong. But one is condemned for not having charity, as Mt. 22:12–13 makes clear about the man excluded from the wedding feast because he was not dressed in a wedding garment, by which charity is meant. Therefore, not having charity is a sin, and everything done by a person who lacks charity is demeritorious. And so the same conclusion follows as before.

9. The Philosopher says in the *Ethics* that actions in moral matters are like conclusions in matters of deduction, in which there are truth and falsehood just as there are goodness and wickedness in moral matters.[55] But every conclusion is true or false. Therefore, every moral act is either true or false, and no moral act is indifferent.

10. Gregory says in his work *Morals* that the wicked accomplish the will of God in the very thing in which they are striving to go contrary to his will.[56] Therefore, much more do those who are not striving to go contrary to the will of God accomplish his will. But accomplishing the will of God is good. Therefore, it follows that every act is good, and no act is morally indifferent.

11. In order that an act be meritorious in one having charity, the act need not be related to God, but it suffices that the act be actually related to a suitable end that is habitually related to God. For example, if a person wishing to make a pilgrimage to honor God should buy a horse without actually thinking about God but only of the journey that the person has already ordained to God, this is indeed meritorious. But those who have charity have evidently ordained themselves and everything they possess to God, to whom they cling as their final end. Therefore, whatever they ordain regarding themselves or anything else of theirs, they do meritoriously even if they do not actually think about God, unless they are prevented from meriting by the disorder of an act that cannot be related to God. But the latter cannot happen without at least a venial sin. Therefore, every act by a person who has charity is either meritorious or a sin, and no act by such a person is morally indifferent. And the same reasoning seems to apply to other things.

12. People have said that acts cannot be meritorious or proper simply because persons negligently and out of surprise do not relate the acts at once to suitable ends. But negligence itself is a mortal or a venial sin, and even some venial sins occur when a person is taken by surprise, as is especially evident in the case of the first movements of concupiscence. Therefore, negligence and being taken by surprise do not preclude there being venial sin.

13. A gloss of Augustine says that those who adhere to permissible things more than they ought build with firewood, hay, and straw.[57] But those who build with firewood, hay, or straw sin; otherwise, they would not be punished by fire. Therefore, those who adhere to permissible things more than they ought, sin. But everyone who does some-

---

55. *Ethics* VII, 8 (1151a16–17).
56. *Morals* VI, 18, n. 28 (PL 75:745B).
57. Actually, Peter Lombard, *Gloss*, on 1 Cor. 3:12 (PL 191:1557D).

thing adheres either to permissible things or to impermissible things. If persons adhere to impermissible things, they sin; if to permissible things more than they ought, they likewise sin; if to permissible things as they ought, they act rightly. Therefore, every human act is either good or bad, and no human act is morally indifferent.

On the Contrary:

1. Augustine says in his work *On the Lord's Sermon on the Mount* that "there are some deeds in between good and evil, deeds that can be done with a good or evil intention, and it is rash to pass judgment on them."[58]

2. The Philosopher says that good and evil are contraries, with some things in between.[59] Therefore, there is something in between good and evil, something morally indifferent.

Answer:

As I have said before,[60] moral acts, in addition to the goodness or wickedness they have from their species, can have another goodness or wickedness from their circumstances, which are related to the acts as accidents. But as we consider genera in their nature apart from specific differences, without which there can be no species, so we consider species in their nature apart from accidents, but without which there can be no individual. For example, being white or black or the like does not belong to the nature of human being, but it is impossible to be an individual human being without being white or black or the like. Therefore, if we speak of moral acts as considered in their species, we can call the acts generically good or evil. But goodness or wickedness from circumstances does not belong to moral acts generically or specifically; rather, such goodness or wickedness can belong to individual moral acts.

Therefore, if we should speak of moral acts regarding their species, then some moral acts are morally indifferent rather than good or evil, since moral acts take their species from their object by the object's ordination to reason, as I have said before.[61] And there is one kind of object that introduces something in accord with reason and makes an act generically good (e.g., clothing the naked). And there is another kind of object that introduces something in discord with reason and makes an act generically evil (e.g., taking what belongs to another). And there is another kind of object that introduces something neither in accord nor in discord with reason and leaves an act morally indifferent (e.g., picking up straw from the ground, or the like). And in this respect, those who divided acts into three kinds, saying that some are good, some evil, some morally indifferent, spoke the truth.

But if we should speak of moral acts as individual acts, then every particular moral act needs to be good or evil by reason of some circumstance. For an individual act cannot happen without circumstances that make the very act right or wrong. For if any act is done when, where, and as it ought to be, and so forth, the act is rightly ordered and good,

---

58. *On the Lord's Sermon on the Mount* II, 18, n. 60 (PL 34:1297).
59. *Categories* 10 (12a16–17).
60. A. 4.
61. Ibid.

and if any of these things is lacking, the act is disordered and evil. And we can especially consider this in the circumstance of end. For example, things done because of just necessity or pious utility are laudably done, and the acts are good, but things lacking just necessity or pious utility are considered idle, as Gregory says.[62] And an idle word is a sin, and much more so is an idle deed, for Mt. 12:36 says: "Human beings shall render account of every idle word spoken." Therefore, good and evil acts are generically contrary to one another but with some acts in between, and some acts considered in their species are morally indifferent. But good and evil by reason of circumstances do not allow anything in between, since we distinguish such good and evil by an opposition of contradiction, namely, by the fact that the act is or is not as it ought to be, not as it ought to be in every circumstance. And such good and evil belong to individual acts, and so no individual human act can be morally indifferent. And I call a human act one that proceeds from a deliberate will. For if an act is indeliberate and proceeds only from the power of imagination (e.g., rubbing one's beard or the like), it is outside the genus of morals and so does not partake of moral goodness or wickedness.

Replies to the Objections:

1. Although being as such is good, still not every nonbeing is evil; for example, not having eyes is not evil for a stone. And so it is not necessary that good and evil be without things in between if there is nothing in between being and nonbeing.

2. Being and good are convertible terms absolutely and in every genus, and so the Philosopher in the *Ethics* distinguishes good by the genera of beings.[63] But it is true that being is not absolutely convertible with moral good, just as being is not absolutely convertible with natural good. And moral good is in one respect a greater good than natural good, namely, insofar as the moral good is an actuality and perfection of the natural good, although the natural good is also in one respect better, as substances are better than their accidents. And it is evident that not even natural good and evil are contraries without anything in between, since not every nonbeing is evil in the way every being is good. And so the argument fails.

3. The good and evil in moral matters are opposed as contraries and not as privation and possession of a form, since evil imposes something inasmuch as it attains an order or measure or form, as I have said before,[64] and so nothing prevents moral good and evil being contraries with something in between, as the Philosopher holds.[65] But natural evil results absolutely from privation. And so natural good and evil, although they are not absolutely without something in between, as I have said,[66] are yet, as privation and possession of a form, without anything in between regarding their proper subject.

4–5. We concede the fourth and fifth objections, for they are valid regarding individual acts as they proceed from the will and not specific kinds of acts.

6. Nothing in nature is related to the first cause by chance, since God provides for everything. But some things are related to proximate causes by chance, for having a cause

---

62. *Book of the Pastoral Rules*, part 3, chap. 14 (PL 77:74A).
63. *Ethics* I, 6 (1096a23–27).
64. A. 4.
65. *Categories* 10 (12a16–17).
66. In the answer.

does not preclude effects being by chance, although having an intrinsic cause does, since effects happen by chance if they are caused accidentally. And there are indeed some acts of human beings that are done for the sake of an imaginary rather than a rationally deliberate end, such as rubbing one's beard or the like. And we consider such acts in the moral genus somewhat as we consider chance events in nature, since the acts do not proceed from reason, which is the intrinsic cause of moral acts.

7. If we should understand the will to mean the power, not every act proceeding from a will informed by charity is meritorious; otherwise, the venial sins that even persons having charity sometimes commit would be meritorious. But it is true that every act done out of charity is meritorious. And it is absolutely false that every act that does not proceed from a will informed by charity is demeritorious. Otherwise, those in a state of mortal sin would sin in every one of their acts, nor ought they to be advised to do whatever good they could while in that state, nor would the generically good deeds they do dispose them to receive grace. And all of the latter things are false. And all are bound to conform their will to the divine will as to willing whatever God wills them to will, insofar as God's prohibitions and precepts make his will known, and not as to willing out of charity, except according to those who say that the mode of charity is prescribed. And the latter opinion is partially true; otherwise, one without charity could fulfill the law, which belongs to the impiety of Pelagius. And yet the opinion is not completely true, since then persons lacking charity would by that mode's omission sin mortally when they honor their parents, and this is false. And so the mode of charity falls under the necessity of precept as precepts are ordained in order that human beings obtain happiness, and not in order that they avoid the condition of being liable for punishment. And so those who honor their parents apart from charity do not merit eternal life, and yet they do not incur demerit. And it is evident from this that not every act, even considered individually, is meritorious or demeritorious, although every act is good or evil. And I say this in behalf of those without charity, of those who cannot merit. But for those with charity, every act is meritorious or demeritorious, as the argument of the objection proves.

8. Not having charity does not merit punishment, since as we merit by acts, not by habits, so neither do we incur demerit by the very lack of habits. And a person incurs demerit because the person does something that blocks charity, whether by omission or commission. And we say that the person mentioned in the Gospel is punished because the person had entered the wedding feast without a wedding garment, not simply because the person was not clothed in a wedding garment. For Mt. 22:12 says of him: "How did you come to be here without a wedding garment?"

9. Truth and falsity are contraries regarding being and nonbeing. For there is truth when we say that what exists exists, or what does not exist does not exist, and there is falsity when we say that what does not exist exists, or what exists does not exist. And so as there is nothing in between existing and nonexisting, so there is nothing in between truth and falsity. And the argument is different regarding good and evil, as is evident from what I have said before.[67]

10. Those who strive contrary to the will of God fulfill his very will apart from their intention, as, for example, the Jews who put Jesus to death fulfilled the will of God re-

67. Ibid.

garding the redemption of the human race apart from their intention. And this is one of the examples that Gregory uses.[68] And fulfilling the will of God in this way is neither good nor praiseworthy.

11–13. We concede all three objections, since they are valid regarding the execution of individual acts. We also admit the arguments advanced in the section *On the contrary*, since they are valid regarding good and evil generically.

Sixth Article

Do Circumstances Specify Sins or Alter the Species of Sin By Transferring Them into Different Kinds of Sin?

It seems that circumstances do not, for the following reasons:

1. The sources of species are intrinsic, and circumstances, as the very name reflects, are extrinsic. Therefore, circumstances do not specify sins.

2. People have said that the circumstances of acts considered in the acts' natural species give species to acts as moral. But as objects are related to acts in general, so moral objects are related to moral acts. And objects give acts their species. Therefore, moral objects specify moral acts. Therefore, circumstances do not.

3. The same sinful act has many circumstances. Therefore, if circumstances specify sins, it follows that the same sin belongs to different species. And the latter is impossible.

4. What is constituted under one species does not take on a new species from something else unless the previous species has been eliminated. But theft is already constituted in a species of sin, and an additional circumstance such as stealing from a sacred place or stealing a sacred object does not take away the original species, since such stealing is still stealing. Therefore, the aforementioned circumstance does not give the sin involved a species. And by like argument, neither does any other circumstance.

5. Sins seem to be distinguished from one another by excess and defect; for example, lack of suitable generosity is contrasted with extravagant generosity. But excess and defect seem to belong to only one circumstance, namely, quantity. Therefore, other circumstances do not distinguish the species of sins.

6. Every sin is voluntary, as Augustine says.[69] But the will does not focus on circumstances; for example, a person who steals a consecrated golden chalice is concerned with the fact that the chalice is made of gold, not the fact that it is consecrated. Therefore, that circumstance does not specify that sin, and by like reasoning, neither do other circumstances specify sins.

7. What does not abide and immediately expires cannot be altered by a species that it previously possessed. But sinful acts do not abide and immediately expire. Therefore, circumstances cannot alter the species of sins.

8. As there may be defects in moral matters with respect to some circumstances, so also in things of nature. For example, monstrosities happen in nature, sometimes indeed

---

68. *Morals* VI, 18, n. 32 (PL 75:746D).
69. Cf. *On True Religion* 14, n. 27 (PL 34:133).

because of spatial constriction, and sometimes because of too much or even too little matter, and because of other like causes, and yet what is generated is always specifically the same. Therefore, neither does the corrupting influence of diverse circumstances in moral matters distinguish the species of sins.

9. Ends specify acts in moral matters, since we judge moral acts to be good or evil from the intention of the agent. But circumstances are not ends. Therefore, circumstances do not specify sins.

10. Sin is contrary to virtue. But circumstances do not alter the species of virtues. For example, it belongs to the same virtue, namely, generosity or mercy, to benefit a cleric or a lay person. Therefore, circumstances do not alter the species of sins.

11. If a circumstance alters the species of a sin, the circumstance necessarily makes the sin more serious. But sometimes a circumstance, namely, the one that seems to alter the species, does not make the sin worse (e.g., if the circumstance be unknown). For example, if a man should have sexual intercourse with a married woman whom he does not know to be a married woman, he commits adultery, and yet the circumstance does not seem to make the sin more serious, since what has less voluntariness has less nature of sin. Therefore, no such circumstance alters the species of sins.

12. If the circumstance that consists of something being sacred specifies a sin, then there is in the theft of something sacred both a sacrilege and a theft, since there remains theft in theft, and so the circumstance causes there to be two sins in one act. And this seems improper.

13. According to the Philosopher in the *Ethics*,[70] actions in moral matters are like conclusions in theoretical matters. But circumstances do not alter the species of conclusions. Therefore, neither do circumstances change the species of moral acts. And so circumstances do not specify sins.

14. Moral acts are like the acts proper to skills. But circumstances do not alter the acts of a blacksmith's skill, since, regarding the skill, it does not matter where or when or for what reason the blacksmith makes a knife. Therefore, neither do circumstances alter the species of moral acts.

15. We usually contradistinguish evil by genus from evil by circumstance. But sin by genus belongs to the very species of sin. Therefore, the circumstances of sin do not belong to the species of sin. Therefore, circumstances do not specify sins.

16. Circumstances, since they make sins more serious, cause evils to be greater. But more and less do not distinguish species. Therefore, circumstances making sins more serious do not alter the species of sins.

On the Contrary:
1. Place is a circumstance. But place specifies a sin, for we say that it is a sacrilege to steal from a sacred place. Therefore, circumstances can specify sins.

2. If a man should have sexual intercourse with a married woman, he commits adultery, and adultery is a species of sin. But being a married or unmarried woman is a circumstance of the act. Therefore, circumstances can specify sins.

---

70. *Ethics* VII, 8 (1151a16–17).

Answer:

In order to analyze this question, we need to consider three things: first, from what sins take their species; second, what circumstances are; and then, third, we shall be able to show how circumstances specify sins.

Therefore, as to the first point, we need to consider that moral acts, since they are voluntary acts that proceed from reason, necessarily take their species from some aspect of an act's object considered in relation to reason. And so I have said in the preceding question that moral acts will be specifically good acts if they are in accord with reason, and moral acts will be specifically bad acts if they are in discord with reason.[71] And what is in discord with reason in the object under consideration can distinguish the species of sins in two ways: indeed, in one way materially; in the second way formally. We can indeed distinguish the species of sins materially by what is contrary to virtue, since virtues differ specifically as reason finds the mean in different subject matters. For example, justice consists in reason establishing the mean in exchanges and distributions and like actions, moderation in reason establishing the mean in desires, and fortitude in reason establishing the mean in fears and acts of boldness, and so forth regarding other subject matters. Nor should anyone think it improper if we distinguish virtues by diverse subject matters although diversity of matter usually causes diversity of individuals rather than diversity of species. This is so because diversity of matter even in things of nature causes diversity in species if different matter requires different forms. And so also there needs to be in moral matters specifically different virtues regarding the different subject matters in which reason finds the mean. For example, reason finds the mean in desires by restraint, and so also the virtue established in their regard is closer to defect than to excess, as the very term "moderation" manifests. And reason finds the mean in fear and acts of boldness by pushing forward rather than by restraint, and so the virtue established in these matters is closer to excess than to defect, as the very term "fortitude" manifests. And we see the like in the subject matters of other virtues.

Therefore, sins involving different subject matters (e.g., murder, adultery, and theft) differ specifically by reason of what is contrary to virtues. Nor should we say that sins differ specifically because the precepts are different; rather, the converse is true: we distinguish precepts because virtues and vices are different, since the purpose of precepts is that we act virtuously and avoid sins. (But if some sins were to be sins only because they are prohibited, it would be in accord with reason that they differ specifically because they are contrary to different precepts.)

But there may be specifically different sins regarding one and the same subject matter, as there is one and the same virtue. Therefore, we need next to consider formally the specific difference in sins, namely, as the sins are committed either by excess or by defect, as timidity differs from temerity, and stinginess from extravagance, or by different circumstances, as we distinguish species of gluttony by the things described in this verse: "Hastily, sumptuously, excessively, greedily, zealously."[72]

Therefore, having considered how sins differ specifically, we need to consider what the circumstances of acts are. And we call things surrounding acts, things considered as

---

71. A. 4.
72. Cf. Alexander of Hales, *Summa of Theology* II–II, n. 579.

if extrinsic to the substance of the acts, circumstances. And this is indeed the case in one way regarding the act's cause, whether the final cause (when we consider why someone has done something), or the chief efficient cause (when we consider who has done something), or the instrumental efficient cause (when we consider with what instrument or means someone has done something). Something surrounds an act in a second way regarding the act's spatial or temporal limits (when we consider where or when someone does something). Something surrounds an act in a third way regarding the act itself. This is so whether we should consider the way of acting (e.g., whether one has struck lightly or vigorously, once or many times), or we should consider the object or matter of the act (e.g., whether one has struck one's father or a stranger) or even the effect caused by the action (e.g., whether one in striking the blow has wounded or even killed someone). And all these things are included in the verse: "Who, what, where, by what means, why, how, where."[73] But the things are included in such a way as to include in "what" both the effect and the object of the act, so that we understand in "what" both "what" and "regarding what."

Therefore, having considered the above, we need to consider that in other things, something intrinsic to a species is extrinsic to a genus (e.g., rational is outside the nature of animal and yet belongs to the nature of human being). Just so, something that we cannot call a circumstance in relation to an act considered in greater particularity is a circumstance in relation to the nature of the act more generally considered. For example, if we should consider the act that consists of taking money, it does not belong to the nature of money to belong to another, and so belonging to another is related as a circumstance to the act of taking so considered. But it belongs to the nature of theft that the money taken belong to another, and so the belonging of the money to another is not a circumstance of theft. Still, something outside the nature of a genus need not belong to the nature of a species. For example, white does not belong to the nature of human being any more than it belongs to the genus of animal, and so it is related accidentally to both. And it is likewise not necessary that everything that is a circumstance of a more general act constitute a species of acts; only something intrinsically belonging to acts does so. And I have already said that something intrinsically belongs to moral acts insofar as it is related to reason as concordant or discordant.[74] Therefore, if a circumstance added to an act introduces no special repugnance to reason, it does not specify the act. For example, using something white adds nothing belonging to the nature of an act, and so white does not constitute the species of a moral act, but using something that belongs to another adds something to the nature of an act and so constitutes the species of the moral act.

And we should consider further that an added circumstance belonging to the nature of an act can constitute a new species of sin in two ways. Such a circumstance can do so in one way so that the species constituted by the circumstance is a species of the sin that was previously considered in a more general act, whether the new species of sin is constituted materially or formally. Such will indeed be the case materially, for example, if "wife" is added to my statement about using what belongs to another, and adultery is thereby constituted. And such will be the case formally, for example, if I should take

---

73. Cicero, *On Invention* I, 24–27.
74. A. 5.

something belonging to another from a sacred place, for the theft will become a sacrilege, which is a species of theft. And sometimes a circumstance constitutes an altogether disparate species, one that does not belong to the previous genus of sin. For example, if I should steal something that belongs to another in order to be able to commit murder or simony, the theft is drawn into an altogether disparate species of sin. And we also find such like in other things. For example, if we should consider that something is white in addition to considering that it is colored, the species of quality subsequently considered is the same as what was first considered. But if we should understand that something is sweet over and above understanding that it is colored, another, altogether disparate species of quality is constituted. And the reason for this difference is because when something added intrinsically distinguishes the thing to which it is added, it constitutes a species of the latter, and when it is accidentally related to the thing to which it is added, it indeed has its own species. But this species is not a species of that to which it is added, since what comes accidentally to something does not become intrinsically one with that thing.

Therefore, it is evident how circumstances can constitute species of sin.

Replies to the Objections:

1. What we consider as a circumstance and extrinsic regarding an act considered in one way we can also consider as intrinsic regarding the act considered in another way, and the circumstance then specifies the act.

2. As acts in general take their species from their object, so moral acts take their species from their moral object. But moral acts are not precluded on that account from taking on species from circumstances, since we can consider the object of an act to have a new condition by reason of a circumstance, and the circumstance specifies the act because of the object's new condition. For example, if I should say "taking another's property presently in a sacred place," I here consider the condition of the object by reason of the circumstance of place, and then the species of theft that is sacrilege is constituted by the circumstance of place and yet by the object's condition. And this is likewise necessarily the case whenever the species of a sin constituted by a circumstance is related to a previously understood sin as species to genus, as, for example, sacrilege is to theft, or adultery to fornication. And when the species of sin deriving from a circumstance is not the species of a previously understood sin but another, disparate species, then we can understand that the circumstance specifies as we consider it the object of another, encompassing act, not as a condition regarding the object that results from it. For example, if one commits adultery in order to steal, another species of sin is added because the intended act aims to achieve the evil end that is the intended object. And likewise if one should do something improper at a sacred time, we can consider the sacred time understood as a circumstance regarding the improper act done at that time as the object regarding another, encompassing act, which consists of showing contempt for a sacred time. And we can say the like in other cases.

3. When a circumstance constitutes a species of sin in relation to a previously understood sin as a species in relation to an included genus, it does not follow that the same sin is included in different species. For example, being human and being animal does not mean being included in two species, since human beings are truly animals, and the like is true regarding sacrilege and theft. But if a circumstance should constitute another,

disparate species of sin, then the same act is included in different species of sin. And this is not inappropriate, since species of sin are species of acts regarding their moral dimension, not their nature, as I have said before.[75] And the moral dimension of sins is related to the nature of acts as quality to substance, or rather as the deformity of quality to the subject. Therefore, as it is not inappropriate that the same material substance be white and sweet, which are different species of quality, and that the same human being be blind and deaf, which are specifically different deficiencies, so it is not inappropriate that the same act belong to different species of sin.

4. And the foregoing makes clear the reply to the fourth objection.

5. Not every difference of sins is by reason of excess and defect, but some differences of sins are due to different subject matters and to excess and defect in different circumstances. And yet we consider excess and defect both by quantity and by every kind of circumstance, since there will be excess if one should act where or when one should not, and so forth, and there will be defect if there is deficiency in any of the foregoing aspects.

6. Although the will of the thief is chiefly directed to the gold, not to the sacred object, the thief's will is still directed to the sacred object by implication, since the thief prefers to steal the sacred object than to lack the gold.

7. When we say that a circumstance alters the species of a sin or transfers the sin into another genus, we do not understand that an act previously existing in one species is repeated and becomes the act of another species. Rather, we understand that an act that would not belong to such a species of sin unless we consider a particular circumstance has that species of sin when the circumstance is added.

8. The deficiency of a circumstance found in nature does not alter the natural species of a substance, but it does alter the species of deformity. For example, spatial constriction and abundance of matter cause different kinds of monstrous things. And it is likewise in the matter under discussion, as I have said.[76]

9. Moral acts take their species from the proximate end that is their object, not from the acts' remote end. And I have said that circumstances specify insofar as they are the object of acts, or a condition regarding the object results from them.[77]

10. Even in the case of virtues, circumstances, although not all circumstances, transfer acts to other species. For example, making great public expenditures is an act of the virtue of magnificence, and making great public expenditures to construct a place of worship is an act of the virtue of religion.

11. Every circumstance constituting a species of sin necessarily makes the sin more serious, since such a circumstance makes a sin of what is not a sin if there was no sin apart from the circumstance, and such a circumstance causes there to be several deformities of sin if there was sin apart from the circumstance. And if such a circumstance is completely unknown, it will, because such ignorance involves no moral wrong, constitute a species of sin only in a material, not a formal, sense. For example, if a man has sexual intercourse with a married woman whom he does know to be married, he indeed commits what is

---

75. Ibid.
76. In the answer.
77. Ibid.

adultery, yet not as an adulterer, since the form of a moral act proceeds from reason and the will. But what is unknown is not voluntary. And so if a man were to have sexual intercourse with the wife of another whom he thinks to be his own wife, he would be without sin, as when Jacob was brought to lie with Leah instead of Rachel.[78]

12. If a circumstance should constitute a species of sin that is related to a previously understood sin as a species of the latter, as, for example, adultery is to fornication, there is only one sin, not two, just as Socrates is not two substances because he is a human being and an animal. But if a circumstance should constitute a disparate species of sin, there will indeed be one sin because of the essential unity of the act, and multiple sins because of the different deformities of the sin, just as an apple is one of a certain kind because of the unity of the subject but of many kinds because of the difference between color and taste.

13. Aristotle notes the likeness of conclusions in theoretical matters to actions in moral matters regarding the fact that as acts of deduction end in conclusions, so processes of reasoning in moral matters end in acts,[79] but there is not likeness in every respect. For moral actions deal with singulars, in the case of which we consider different circumstances, while we reach conclusions in theoretical matters by abstracting from singulars. And yet even conclusions vary regarding circumstances that belong to the nature of deduction. For example, there are different kinds of conclusions in necessary and hypothetical subject matters, and there are different ways of deduction in different sciences.

14. Even the actions proper to a skill vary according to different circumstances belonging to the nature of the skill. For example, a builder constructs a house in one way with mortar and in another way with clay, even differently in one country than in another. But we should consider that some circumstances belong to the nature of moral acts that do not belong to the nature of skills, and vice versa.

15. When we contradistinguish evil by circumstance from evil by genus, we are talking about evil by circumstance as the latter makes a sin more serious but does not transfer the sin to another genus.

16. More and less sometimes result from different forms, and then they distinguish species, as, for example, if we should say that red has more color than yellow. But more or less sometimes results from different sharing in one and the same form, and then they do not distinguish species, as, for example, if we should call one thing whiter than another.

Seventh Article

Do Circumstances Make Sins More Serious without Imputing Species to Sins?

It seems that circumstances do not, for the following reasons:

1. Sin has malice in relation to turning away from God. But circumstances are understood in relation to turning toward creatures. Therefore, circumstances do not make the malice of sins more serious.

---

78. Gen. 29:23ff.
79. *Ethics* III, 1 (1110b6 and 1111a23).

2. If circumstances should in themselves have malice, they constitute species of sin. And if they should not in themselves have any malice, there is no reason why they should make the sins more serious. Therefore, there is no circumstance that makes a sin more serious that does not impute species to sin.

3. Dionysius says that good results from a cause that is one and integral, and that evil results from any single defect.[80] But we consider a single defect regarding any circumstance. Therefore, there is a species of evil and sin regarding any circumstance that makes the evil and sin more serious.

4. Every circumstance that makes a sin more serious causes a difference in malice, which is in a way the substance of a sin as such. But what causes a difference in substance changes the species of sin. Therefore, circumstances that make sins more serious change the species of sin.

5. We grow and are constituted by the same things by which we are nourished, and we are nourished by the things by which we are constituted, as the work *On Generation and Corruption* says.[81] Therefore, if the circumstances that make sins more serious increase the malice of sin, the malice of sin seems to have species of sin by the same circumstances.

6. Virtue and vice are contraries. But circumstances constitute every virtue in a species. For example, confronting fearsome things as, where, and when one ought, and so forth regarding other circumstances, belongs to the virtue of fortitude. Therefore, sin also takes its species from every kind of circumstance.

7. Sin takes its species from its object. But at least any circumstance that makes a sin more serious alters the goodness or wickedness of the object of sin. Therefore, every circumstance that makes a sin more serious specifies the sin.

8. We judge the same about like things. But some circumstances, such as the object that we call "what," and the end that we signify by what we call "why," in the aforementioned verse,[82] always specify sins. Therefore, by like reasoning, every other circumstance making a sin more serious specifies the sin.

On the Contrary:
Stealing a large amount of money is more serious than stealing a little amount but is not a different species of sin. Therefore, not every circumstance that makes a sin more serious alters the species of sin.

Answer:
Circumstances are related to sinful acts in three ways. For circumstances sometimes neither alter the species of sin nor make sins more serious, as, for example, striking a human being wearing a white or red garment. And circumstances sometimes constitute species of sin. The act to which a circumstance is added may belong to a morally indifferent genus (as when a person picks up straw from the ground to show contempt of another). Or the act to which a circumstance is added may be generically good (as when

---

80. *On the Divine Names* 4, n. 30 (PG 3:729C).
81. *On Generation and Corruption* II, 8 (335a10–11).
82. In the answer, a. 6.

a person gives alms to gain human praise). Or the act to which a circumstance is added maybe generically evil, and the circumstance adds a species of malice to the act (as when a person steals a sacred object). And added circumstances sometimes indeed make sins more serious but do not constitute species of sin (as when a person steals a large amount of money).

And the reason for this diversity is because if the circumstance added to an act is morally indifferent in relation to reason, such a circumstance neither specifies a sin nor makes it more serious. For example, it is irrelevant in relation to reason whether the one who strikes a blow is clothed in this or that garment. But if a circumstance added to an act makes a moral difference in relation to reason, the circumstance either does or does not introduce something primarily and intrinsically contrary to reason. If the circumstance does, then it specifies a sin, for example, taking what belongs to another. If the circumstance does not, it is contrary to reason because of its relation to what is primarily and intrinsically contrary to reason. For example, taking a great amount of something describes nothing contrary to reason. But taking a great amount of someone else's property describes something more contrary to reason than taking a small amount, and so the circumstance of quantity makes the sin of theft more serious inasmuch as quantity determines the extent of the circumstance that specifies the sin. And the fourth category, that a circumstance specify a sin but not make it more serious, is impossible, as I have said before.[83]

Replies to the Objections:

1. Inordinate turning toward a transient good causes sinners to turn away from God, and so circumstances that are understood in relation to turning toward creatures can add to the malice that regards turning away from God.

2. A circumstance that makes a sin more serious and does not specify the sin does not of itself contain any malice but determines the extent of another circumstance containing malice.

3. The defect of any circumstance can cause a species of sin, but there is not always a defect in every circumstance as such. Rather, a circumstance sometimes has a defect in relation to another defect.

4. Circumstances that make sins more serious do not always alter the species of malice. Rather, such circumstances sometimes alter only the amount of malice.

5. As the things whereby we are nourished and grow do not always constitute a new substance but sometimes preserve and enlarge one that already exists, so circumstances do not always necessarily cause new species of sin but sometimes enlarge one that already exists.

6. As virtue sometimes takes its species from requisite circumstances, so also sin sometimes takes its species from the deficiency of a requisite circumstance. And yet not every circumstance causes the defect of sin, since some are morally indifferent, and some determine the extent of other circumstances.

7. Circumstances that make sins more serious indeed cause an altered malice regarding the object but not always an altered species of sin. Rather, such circumstances sometimes cause only an altered quantity.

8. An object has many conditions, and nothing prevents us from considering as a circumstance regarding one condition what we consider as an object regarding another

83. Reply to objection 11, a. 6.

condition. And circumstances sometimes specify sins, sometimes not. For example, the property of another is the particular object of theft, the object that specifies theft. The property of another can also be of great worth, and this circumstance only makes the theft more serious without introducing a new species of sin. The property of another can also be sacred, and this circumstance will constitute a new species of sin. The property of another can also be white or black, and this circumstance will be morally indifferent regarding the object, neither making the sin more serious nor constituting a species of sin. And we likewise need to say about the end that the proximate end is the same as the object, and that we need to speak about the proximate end and the object in the same way. And we hold the remote end to be a circumstance.

Eighth Article

Do Circumstances Make Sins Infinitely More Serious, Namely, so as to Make Venial Sins Mortal?

It seems that circumstances do, for the following reasons:

1. Adam in the state of innocence could not sin venially. Therefore, every sin of his would have been mortal. But not every sin of his after the fall was mortal, and this difference is only by reason of a circumstance of the person. Therefore, circumstances make sins infinitely more serious.

2. Making a nonsin a sin is greater than making a venial sin mortal. But circumstances make nonsins sins. For example, engaging in business, as such, is not a sin, but it is a sin for clerics because of a circumstance of the persons. Therefore, much more do circumstances make venial sins mortal.

3. Getting inebriated once is a venial sin. And people say that getting inebriated repeatedly is a mortal sin. Therefore, the circumstance "how often" makes venial sins mortal.

4. We call sins committed out of pure malice unpardonable and not venial. Therefore, circumstances make sins infinitely more serious.

5. Jerome says that trifles from the mouth of lay persons are trifles, but from the mouth of priests blasphemies.[84] But blasphemy is by its genus a mortal sin. Therefore, the circumstance of person makes venial sins mortal.

On the Contrary:

Circumstances are related to sins as accidents are to their subjects. But infinite accidents cannot belong to finite subjects. Therefore, circumstances cannot give to sins the infinite gravity of mortal sin.

Answer:

Circumstances making sins more serious sometimes constitute new species of sin and sometimes do not, as I have said.[85] But mortal and venial sin evidently belong to different species. For as some acts are by their genus good, and some by their genus evil, so

---

84. Actually, Bernard, *On Reflection* II, 13 (PL 182:756B).
85. A. 7.

some sins are by their genus venial, and some by their genus mortal. Therefore, circumstances that so make sins more serious that the circumstances constitute new species of sin can constitute species of mortal sin and so make sins infinitely more serious. For example, such would be the case if a person should say something facetious in order to provoke someone to lust or hatred. But if circumstances so make sins more serious that the circumstances do not constitute new species of sin, such circumstances cannot make sins infinitely more serious by making venial sins mortal. This is because the gravity by reason of a sin's species is always greater than the gravity by reason of a sin's circumstance that does not constitute a species.

Replies to the Objections:

1. We say that Adam in the state of innocence could not sin venially, not because the sins that are venial for us would be mortal for him, but because he could not before he sinned mortally commit sins that are venial for us. For unless he were to turn away from God by mortal sin, he could have no defect in him, whether of the soul or the body.

2. Circumstances that make nonsin sin constitute species of sin, and such circumstances can also make venial sins mortal.

3. The frequency of inebriation is not a circumstance constituting a species of sin. And so, absolutely speaking, getting inebriated frequently is as much a venial sin as getting inebriated once. And getting inebriated frequently can be a mortal sin accidentally and dispositively. For example, such would be the case if a person were by habit to be brought to so great a state of complacency in inebriation that the person would deliberately get inebriated in contempt of the divine precept.

4. Sinning out of pure malice is sinning by choice, that is, willingly and knowingly. And this happens in two ways. It happens in one way by a person rejecting things that could withdraw the person from sin (e.g., the hope of pardon or the fear of divine justice), and such a circumstance constitutes a species of the sin against the Holy Spirit. And we call such a sin unpardonable. Sinning by choice can happen in a second way merely from habitual inclination, and such a circumstance does not constitute a species of sin, nor does the circumstance make a venial sin mortal, since not everyone who willingly and knowingly says an idle word sins mortally.

5. The circumstance of person, although it makes sin more serious, does not make a venial sin mortal unless it would constitute a species of sin. For example, the latter would be the case if a priest should do something contrary to a precept prescribed for priests or something contrary to his vows. And we understand Jerome's words as spoken by way of exaggeration or to illustrate an occasion of sin, since trifles from the mouth of a priest can be the occasion for others to sin by blaspheming.

Ninth Article

Are All Sins Equal?

It seems that they are, for the following reasons:

1. Jas. 2:10 says: "Whoever shall keep all the laws save one shall be guilty of violating all of them." And Jerome, commenting on Eccl. 9:18, "A person who shall offend in

one thing loses many good things," says that a person who is subject to one vice is subject to every vice.[86] But nothing can be added to what includes everything. Therefore, one cannot sin more than by sinning once, and so all sins are equal.

2. Sin is the death of the soul. But in the case of the body, one death is not greater than another, since everyone dead is equally dead. Therefore, neither is one sin greater than another.

3. Punishment corresponds to moral wrong. But there is the one punishment of hell for all sins, as Is. 24:22 says: "They will be gathered into one bundle and shut up in a prison." Therefore, all sins also have the same gravity.

4. Sinning is simply transgressing the right order of reason and the divine law. But if a judge forbids someone to transgress a fixed limit, it does not matter regarding its transgression whether the person transgresses the established limit by much or little. Therefore, regarding the transgression of sin, it does not matter what human beings do as long as they fail to observe the right order of reason and the divine law.

5. Nothing infinite is greater than infinite. But every mortal sin, since contrary to the infinite good, that is, God, is infinite and so also merits infinite punishment. Therefore, one mortal sin is not greater than another.

6. We define evil as the privation of good. But every mortal sin equally deprives persons of grace, leaving them with none. Therefore, all mortal sins are equal.

7. If we say that something is more or less such, we say this in relation to what is absolutely such. For example, we say that something is more or less white in relation to what is absolutely white. But nothing is absolutely evil, so that it lacks every good. Therefore, nothing is more or less evil than something else. And so all sins are equal.

8. Sins are contrary to virtues. But all virtues are equal, and so Rev. 21:16 says that the length and the breadth of the city are equal. Therefore, all sins are also equal.

9. If one sin is more serious than another, then a sin committed in a greater matter would be more serious than a sin committed in a lesser matter. For example, such would be the case if one should say that stealing a large amount of something is a more serious sin than to steal a little amount. But this is not true, since one who commits a lesser sin would also as a result commit a greater sin. For Lk. 16:10 says: "One who is unjust in little things is unjust in greater things." Therefore, one sin is not more serious than another.

10. Sin consists of turning away from the immutable good and turning toward a transient good. But such turning away and turning toward does not admit of more or less, since the soul, because it has no parts, totally turns to what it turns to, and totally turns from what it turns from. Therefore, one sin is not more serious than another.

11. Augustine says in his work *On the Trinity* that the magnitude of human sin is manifested by the magnitude of the remedy, namely, that Christ's death was necessary to destroy sin.[87] But this remedy is the same for all sins. Therefore, all sins are equally great.

12. As Dionysius says in his work *On the Divine Names*,[88] good results from a cause that is one and integral, and evil from any single defect. But every defect takes away the

---

86. *Commentary on Ecclesiastes* (PL 23:1090A).

87. *On the Trinity* XIII, 17 (PL 42:1031–1032).

88. *On the Divine Names* 4, n. 30 (PG 3:729C).

integrity of good. Therefore, every defect takes away the whole nature of good. There-fore, one sin is not more serious than another.

13. Virtue, since it is a form, is simple. Therefore, virtue is totally taken away if it is taken away at all. But sin is evil because it takes away virtue. Therefore, all sins are equally evil, since every one of them equally takes away virtue.

14. A thing has from the same source to be such and to be more such. Therefore, if a white color differentiates vision, a whiter color differentiates vision more. But acts have the nature of sin by reason of the turning away from God. Therefore, since all sins are the same in turning away from God, all sins are equal.

15. The greater the one offended, the more serious the sin. For example, one who strikes a king sins more gravely than one who strikes a soldier. But the one contemned in every sin is one and the same, namely, God. Therefore, all sins are equal.

16. Species belonging to the same genus equally partake of the genus. But sin is the genus of all sins. Therefore, all sins are equal, and all who sin sin equally.

17. We define evil as the privation of good, and we can know the extent of the pri-vation by what remains after the privation. But what remains of good after every sin is the same, since there remains after every sin the very nature of the soul and the freedom of choice by which human beings can choose good and evil. Therefore, one sin is not more evil than another.

18. Circumstances are related to virtue as substantial differences. But if one sub-stantial difference is taken away, the others are, since the substance of the subject is destroyed. Therefore, since every sin takes away one circumstance of virtue, every sin takes away all the circumstances of virtue, and so one sin will not be more serious than another.

On the Contrary:
1. Jn. 19:11 says: "Besides, the one who hands me over to you has the greater sin."
2. According to Augustine,[89] inordinate desire causes sin. But not every inordinate desire is equal. Therefore, not all sins are equal.

Answer:
The Stoics thought that all sins are equal. And from this opinion derives the opinion of some modern heretics,[90] who say that there is no inequality either between sins or be-tween merits, and likewise neither between rewards nor between punishments.

And the Stoics were induced to hold this position because they considered that things have the nature of sin only because they are contrary to the right order of reason. For example, it is evident that adultery is a sin, not because sexual intercourse with a woman in itself would be evil, but because the sexual intercourse is done contrary to the right order of reason, and the same is evident in other cases. And it is the same if we should say that something is contrary to divine law insofar as the latter applies to the matter under discussion, since both sins contrary to reason and sins contrary to divine law introduce privation. But privation does not seem susceptible of more and less. And so if something

89. Cf. *On Free Choice* I, 3, n. 8 (PL 32:1225).
90. The Cathars.

is evil by the privation of something, it does not seem to matter how it is disposed, insofar as it is deprived. For example, if a judge should prescribe a strict limit for a person, it does not matter whether the person should transgress the limit much or little. And they likewise said that it does not matter, insofar as a person by sinning transgresses the right order of reason, howsoever or for whatsoever reason the person does so, as if sinning were to be nothing more than crossing certain designated lines. Therefore, we need to begin the whole process of answering this argument by considering how there can be or not be more and less in things that we predicate by way of privation.

Therefore, we should consider that there are two kinds of privation. One is pure privation, such as darkness, which leaves no light, and death, which leaves nothing of life. And one is not simply privation but leaves something, and so is both a privation and a contrary, such as sickness that takes away part but not all of the balance of fluids proper to health, and the base and the dissimilar and the unequal and the false and all such like. And the latter privations seem to differ from the former in that the former are as if in a state of destroyed existence, while the latter are as if in a state of becoming destroyed. Therefore, since the whole thing is taken away in the first kind of privation, and what we predicate positively of such privations does not belong to the nature of privation, it does not matter in such privations, howsoever or for whatsoever reason a person is deprived, to say that the person is more or less deprived. For example, one who died from one wound is just as dead as one who died from two or three, nor is a house less dark if a candle is veiled by one shade than if it is veiled by two or three shades. But the whole thing is not taken away in the second kind of privation, and what is predicated positively of such privations does not belong to the nature of what is predicated privatively, and so such things admit of more or less by the difference of what we predicate positively of the privations. For example, we call sickness greater if there shall be a cause taking away health that is greater or causes more deleterious effects. And the same is true in the case of baseness and dissimilitude or such like.

Therefore, we need to consider a difference regarding sins. For sins of omission, strictly speaking, consist only of the privation of observing a disregarded precept, as I have demonstrated before.[91] And so, in sins of omission, the condition of associated acts, since they are incidental, do not make sins of omission, strictly speaking, greater or lesser. For example, if a person has a duty to go to church, we do not pay attention in a sin of omission to whether, regarding not going to church, the person lives near or far from church, except perhaps incidentally insofar as the difference in the associated act would partake of greater or lesser contempt. And yet not all sins of omission are on that account equal, since precepts are unequal either because of the different authority of the one commanding or because of the different value or need of the precepts. By contrast, sins of transgression consist of the deformity of an act, and such deformity indeed takes away part but not all of the ordination of reason. For example, if a person eats when the person ought not, it remains true that the person eats where and why the person ought. Nor, while the act persists, can the relation to reason be completely taken away, and so the Philosopher says in the *Ethics* that evil, if it is entirely such, is insupportable and destroys its very self.[92] Therefore, as not every bodily

91. A. 1.
92. *Ethics* IV, 5 (1126a12–13).

deformity is equal, but one is greater than another insofar as more things proper to come-liness or more important things are lacking, so not every deformity or disorder in human acts is equal, but one is greater than another. And so not all sins are equal.

Replies to the Objections:
1. We should not understand the words of James to mean that a person who offends regarding one commandment incurs as much guilt as if the person were to transgress every commandment. Rather, we should understand the words to mean that a person who offends regarding one, not every, commandment incurs guilt for contempt of all the commandments. For one who contemns one commandment contemns all the com-mandments inasmuch as the person contemns God, from whom all the commandments have their authority. And so Jas. 2:11 immediately adds: "For he who said 'Thou shalt not kill,' also said 'Thou shalt not commit adultery.'" And we should similarly under-stand the words of Jerome.

2. The death of the soul is the privation of grace, by which the soul is united to God. But the privation of grace is the effect and punishment of moral wrong, not essentially the moral wrong itself, as I have said before.[93] And so we call sin the death of the soul causally rather than essentially. And sin essentially consists of a deformed or disordered act.

3. There is in the punishment of the damned something common to all that corre-sponds to their contempt of God, namely, loss of the vision of God and eternal pain, and we say in that regard that they are gathered into one bundle. There is also in the punish-ment of the damned something in which they differ, insofar as some are tormented more than others, and Mt. 13:30 says in that regard that they are gathered like bundles of weeds to be burned.

4. People who cross the line that a judge has prescribed as a limit sin only because they do not contain themselves within the prescribed limit, and so their sin is directly a sin of omission. And if the judge were directly to command the person not to walk, it is evident that the further the person proceeded to walk, the more gravely the person would be punished. Or otherwise we should say that in matters that are evil only because pro-hibited, those who do not observe a precept eliminate completely what they are bound to observe. But we should say that in matters that are intrinsically evil and not only evil because prohibited, nonobservance of a precept does not completely take away the good contrary to the evil, and so the more good taken away, the more serious the sin.

5. A finite act turns a person away from the infinite good, and so sin is essentially finite, although it has a relationship to the infinite good.

6. Sin is the privation of grace causally, not essentially, as I have said.[94]

7. We predicate more or less of privations by reason of their recession from an end, not by reason of their accession to an end. And so also the Philosopher in the cited text demonstrates that there is something absolutely true because there are things more and less false. Therefore, in order for something to be more or less evil, it is necessary that there is something absolutely good, not that there is something absolutely evil.

93. Q. 1, aa. 4 and 5.
94. Reply to objection 2.

8. Not all virtues are equal in their extension, since the Apostle says that charity is greater in extension.[95] But all virtues are equal relatively, inasmuch as each virtue is equally related to its own acts. An example would be if one were to say that all the fingers of the hand are equal in relation to the hand's acts but not in the fingers' extension. But sins are not even equal relatively, since they do not depend on a single cause, as do virtues, all of which depend on practical wisdom or charity; rather, the roots of sins are diverse.

9. Sins committed in greater matters are greater, and so the theft of a more valuable object is a more serious sin, since such a theft is more contrary to the equality of justice. And we should not understand the words of the Lord to mean that one who commits a lesser sin would commit a greater, for many who would speak no blasphemy speak idle words. Rather, we should understand the words of the Lord to mean that it is easier to observe justice in lesser than in greater matters, and so one who does not observe justice in lesser matters would also not observe justice in greater matters.

10. Although the soul is essentially simple, it is nonetheless multiple as to power, both because it has many powers, and because it is related to many things by one and the same power and can be borne to them in many ways. And so not every turning away from God or turning toward a creature need be equal.

11. It was necessary that the death of Christ remedy all mortal sins because of the gravity they have by reason of their contempt of the infinite good, and yet nothing prevents one sin from being more contemptuous of God than another.

12. In every mortal sin, the integrity of good but not the whole good is taken away. Moreover, more good is taken away in one mortal sin, less in another, as I have said.[96]

13. Sins are directly contrary to virtuous acts, and many circumstances are required for virtue. And besides, there are different virtues, and one virtue is greater than another. And so all sins do not need to be equal.

14. The argument of this objection would be valid if sin were to be only a privation, but sin admits of more or less because it has in its nature a certain order, as I have said.[97]

15. We measure the degree of contempt both in relation to the one offended and in relation to the act whereby one is contemned, and such an act can be more or less extreme.

16. All animals are equally animals, but not all animals are equal. Rather, one animal is greater and more perfect than another animal. And likewise, all sins need not be equal because all sins are equally sins.

17. Both the nature of the soul and the freedom of the will remain after sin, but the aptitude for good is diminished, and more by one sin and less by another.

18. Circumstances are related neither to virtue nor to sin as substantial differences. Otherwise, every circumstance would constitute something in a genus or species of virtue or sin. Rather, circumstances are related to virtue and sin as accidents, as I have said.[98] And besides, it is not true that every essential difference is taken away when one is. For

95. Cf. 1 Cor. 13:13.
96. In the answer.
97. Ibid.
98. Aa. 6 and 7.

example, an essential difference, living, remains after an essential difference, rational, has been removed, as the *Book of Causes*[99] says, not indeed the numerically same living thing, because of the destruction of the subject, but the conceptually same living thing.

Tenth Article

Are Sins More Serious Because They Are Contrary to a Greater Good?

It seems that such sins are not more serious, for the following reasons:

1. According to Augustine,[100] we call things evil because they take away good. Therefore, things that take away more good are more evil. But the first sin of a person, even if contrary to a lesser virtue, takes away more good than the person's second sin, since the first sin deprived the person of grace and eternal life. Therefore, sins are not more serious because they are contrary to a higher virtue.

2. According to the Apostle in 1 Cor. 13:13, charity is greater than faith and hope. But hatred, which is the contrary of charity, is not a more serious sin than unbelief and despair. Therefore, sins contrary to a greater good are not more serious.

3. That a person should sin knowingly or unknowingly is accidentally related to the good of which the sin is the contrary. Therefore, if one sin is more serious than another because it is the contrary of a greater good, then one who sins knowingly would not sin more gravely than one who sins unknowingly. And this conclusion is evidently false.

4. The magnitude of punishment corresponds to the magnitude of moral wrong. But we read that some sins against one's neighbor were punished more severely than sins committed against God. For the sin of blasphemy, which is a sin against God, was punished by the stoning of only one person, as Lev. 24:16 states, while the sin of rebellion was punished by the unusual death of many persons, as Num. 26:10 states. Therefore, the sin committed against one's neighbor is more serious than the sin committed against God, although the sin committed against God is contrary to a greater good.

On the Contrary:

The Philosopher says in the *Ethics* that the worst is the contrary of the best in the same way that evil is the contrary of good.[101]

Answer:

We can weigh the gravity of sin in two ways: in one way regarding the very act; in the second way regarding the one who sins. And there are two things to consider regarding the act, namely, its species and its accidents, which we have previously called circumstances of the act.[102] And acts take their species from their object, as I have said before.[103]

---

99. *Book of Causes*, comm. 1.
100. Cf. *Enchiridion* 12 (PL 40:237).
101. *Ethics* VIII, 10 (1160b9).
102. A. 5 and a. 8 (*On the Contrary*).
103. A. 4.

Therefore, we note the gravity that sin has from its species in relation to its object or subject matter, and in considering the object or subject matter, we call sins contrary to greater virtuous goods more serious by reason of their kind. And so, since virtuous good consists of the right order of love, as Augustine says,[104] and we ought to love God above all things, we should judge that sins against God, such as idolatry, blasphemy, and the like, are by their kind the most serious. And among sins against one's neighbor, some are more serious than others inasmuch as they are contrary to the greater good of one's neighbor. But the greatest good of neighbor is the neighbor's human person, to which the sin of homicide, which takes away the actual life of a human being, is contrary. And the sin of sexual lust is contrary to the potential life of a human being, since sexual lust is a deordination regarding the act of human generation. And so of all the sins against one's neighbor, the most serious as to its kind is homicide, and adultery and fornication and such carnal sins are second, and theft and robbery and the like, which injure neighbors in their external goods, are third. And in each of these kinds of sin, there are different grades regarding which we need to take the measure of sin by its kind, insofar as charity obliges us to love the contrary good more or less.

And regarding circumstances, sins may also have a gravity that is accidental and not from the sins' species. Likewise, regarding the sinner, we note a sin's gravity insofar as the sinner sins more or less voluntarily, since the will causes sin, as I have said before.[105] But not even this gravity belongs to a sin by reason of its species.

And so if we consider the gravity of sin by its species, the greater the contrary good, the more serious the sin.

Replies to the objections:

1. Sin takes away good in two ways. One way is formal, and the right order of virtue is thereby taken away. And regarding such taking away, it does not matter whether the sin is the first or the second sin, since the second sin can take away more of the actual right order of virtue than the first sin. And the second way in which sin takes away good is the result of sin, namely, the privation of grace and glory. And regarding such taking away, the first sin takes away more than the second. But this happens by accident, since the second sin does not have the opportunity to take away grace and glory that the first sin had. And we should not presume to esteem things by what happens by chance.

2. Faith and hope are preambles to charity. And so unbelief, which is the contrary of faith, and despair, which is the contrary of hope, are most contrary to charity, since they excise charity by its roots.

3. Although sinning knowingly or unknowingly is accidental to a particular sin such as theft regarding its species, sinning knowingly or unknowingly is not accidental regarding the nature of the genus of sin, that is, regarding sin as sin, since it belongs to the nature of sin to be voluntary. And so the ignorance that diminishes voluntariness also diminishes the nature of sin.

4. The punishments that God inflicts in the future life correspond to the gravity of moral wrong, and so the Apostle says in Rom. 2:2 that "the judgment of God against

---

104. Cf. *City of God* XV, 22 (PL 41:467); *On Church Customs* I, 15, n. 25 (PL 32: 1322).
105. Aa. 2 and 3.

those who do such things is according to the true nature of things." But the punishments inflicted in the present life whether by God or human beings does not always correspond to the gravity of moral wrong. For lesser moral wrongs are sometimes punished for a time by heavier punishments in order to avoid greater dangers. For example, punishments in the present life are employed quasi-medicinally. And the sin of rebellion is the most pernicious in human affairs because it dissolves the whole governance of human society.

Eleventh Article

Does Sin Diminish Natural Good?

It seems that sin does not, for the following reasons:

1. Nothing diminished is integral. But natural goods remain intact in devils after sin, as Dionysius says in his work *On the Divine Names.*[106] Therefore, sin does not diminish natural good.

2. Accidents do not take away their subject. But the evil of moral wrong is in a natural good as the evil's subject. Therefore, the evil of moral wrong does not take away anything from the natural good and so does not diminish that good.

3. People have said that the evil of moral wrong diminishes natural good regarding the subject's suitable disposition or aptitude, not the subject's substance. But a privation takes away nothing from what is common to it and the contrary form. And as the subject's substance is common to a privation and the contrary form, so also is a suitable disposition or aptitude, since a privation requires that there be in the subject a suitable disposition for the contrary form. Therefore, a privation takes away nothing from the aptitude of the subject.

4. Being diminished is a way of being acted upon. But being acted upon consists of receiving, while acting consists rather of expending. Therefore, nothing is diminished by its act. But sin consists of an act. Therefore, sin does not diminish the natural good of the sinner.

5. People have said that sin is the act of a power that is not thereby diminished, but only the aptitude of the power is diminished. But we say that something is acted upon both if something belonging to its substance is taken away from it, and if its accidents are taken away from it. For example, we say that water is acted upon both when it loses its substantial form, and when it loses coldness upon being heated. And aptitude is the accident of a power. Therefore, if a power's aptitude is diminished, the very power will be acted upon by its act. And the second and third objections seem to render this conclusion impossible.

6. In things of nature, efficient causes are acted upon. Still, the causes are not acted upon insofar as they act, since they indeed act insofar as they are actual, while they are acted upon insofar as they are potential. For example, water cools actually hot air insofar as the air is potentially cool, and the air heats the water insofar as the air is actually hot.

---

106. *On the Divine Names* 4, n. 23 (PG 3:725C).

But it is universally true about every kind of thing that nothing is actual and potential in the same respect. Therefore, nothing is acted upon insofar as it acts. Therefore, neither are sinners diminished in their natural good by their sinful acts.

7. Diminishing is an action. But an act does not act, for that would involve an infinite regression, since whatever acts causes an act. Therefore, it seems that sin, since it is an act, does not diminish natural good.

8. Since diminution is a movement, diminishing causes movement. But nothing moves its very self, and something would move itself if it were to be moved by its own action. Therefore, sinners are not diminished in their natural good by their sinful actions.

9. Dionysius says in his work *On the Divine Names* that evil acts only by the power of good.[107] But sin does not destroy natural good by the power of good, since the power of good is salutary rather than destructive. Therefore, sin does not diminish natural good.

10. Augustine says in his *Enchiridion* that in the case of good and evil, the rule of logic denying that contraries can be present in the same thing at the same time fails.[108] But the rule would fail only if evil were to be in the good contrary to itself. Therefore, sin is in the good contrary to itself as its subject. But no accident diminishes its subject. Therefore, sin does not diminish natural good even as sin is contrary to that good.

11. If sin were to diminish natural good, the freedom of choice in which sin chiefly consists would be diminished. But Bernard says in his work *On Grace and Free Choice* that free choice suffers no detriment in the damned.[109] Therefore, sin does not diminish natural good.

12. If sin diminishes the natural aptitude for good either regarding the subject or regarding the good for which the subject is apt, we consider the aptitude to be a mean between the two. But sin does not diminish the aptitude regarding the subject, just as it does not diminish the subject itself, and the aforementioned aptitude, since it is associated with the good of virtue or grace, seems to belong to the genus of moral quality. Therefore, sin in no way diminishes natural good.

13. Augustine says in his *Literal Commentary on Genesis* that the infusion of grace is like an illumination, and so sin is like a darkening of the intellect.[110] But darkness does not take away from air the aptitude for light. Therefore, neither does sin take away any part of the aptitude for grace.

14. It seems that natural aptitude for good is the same as natural justice, and justice is rectitude of the will, as Anselm says in his work *On Truth*.[111] But rectitude cannot be diminished, since everything straight is equally straight. Therefore, neither does sin diminish the natural good that is natural aptitude.

15. Augustine says in his work *On the Immortality of the Soul* that when anything is changed, what belongs to it is changed.[112] But diminution is a species of movement. Therefore, when the subject is diminished, accidents belonging to it are. But moral wrong is in

---

107. *On the Divine Names* 4, n. 32 (PG 3:732C).
108. *Enchiridion* 14 (PL 40:238).
109. *On Grace and Free Choice* 9, n. 28 (PL 182:1016B).
110. *Literal Commentary on Genesis* VIII, 12, n. 26 (PL 34:383).
111. *On Truth* 12 (PL 158:482B).
112. *On the Immortality of the Soul* 2 (PL 32:1022).

natural good as its subject. Therefore, moral wrong, if it diminishes natural good, diminishes its very self, and this conclusion is improper.

16. According to the Philosopher in the *Ethics*,[113] there are three things in the soul: powers, habits, and emotions. But sin does not lessen emotions; rather, sin strengthens emotions, and so Rom. 7:5 even speaks of "sinful emotions." And sin completely takes away virtuous habits, but the power to perform virtuous acts remains. Therefore, there is in the soul no natural power that is diminished by sin.

On the Contrary:

1. A gloss on Lk. 10:30, "After beating him, they went away," says that sins injure the integrity of human nature.[114] But only diminution injures integrity. Therefore, sin diminishes natural good.

2. Augustine says in the *City of God* that sin is evil because it harms natural good.[115] And this would be the case only if sin were to take something away from natural good. Therefore, sin diminishes natural good.

3. Augustine says in his work *On Music* that sin makes the soul weaker.[116] Therefore, sin diminishes the natural good in the soul.

4. Rational creatures are related to grace like the eyes to light. But the eyes in darkness become less apt to see light. Therefore, the soul remaining for a long time in sin becomes less apt to receive grace. And so sin diminishes the natural good that is the aptitude to receive grace.

Answer:

Because diminishing is an action, we need to consider in how many ways we say that something acts, in order to know in what way sin diminishes natural good. And we say in a proper sense that the very cause producing an act indeed acts, while we say in an improper sense that the means whereby the cause acts acts. For example, a painter in a proper sense indeed makes a wall white, but we are also accustomed to say that the paint's whiteness makes the wall white, since the painter makes the wall white by means of the paint's whiteness. Therefore, in however many ways we say that a cause, properly so called, acts, in so many ways do we in an improper sense say that the means whereby the cause acts acts. And we say that a chief cause causes something both intrinsically and accidentally: indeed intrinsically what it causes by reason of its own form, and accidentally what it causes by removing an obstacle. For example, the sun indeed intrinsically illumines a house, and a person who opens a shuttered window that was an obstacle to light accidentally causes the house to be illumined. Again, we say that a chief cause causes one thing primarily and another thing as a consequence. For example, what causes something to come to be indeed primarily bestows a form on the thing and consequently bestows movement and everything that results from the form. And so we say that what causes something to come to be causes the movement of heavy and light things, as the

---

113. *Ethics* II, 5 (1105b20).
114. *Ordinary Gloss* (PL 92:468D–469A).
115. *City of God* XII, 6 (PL 41:353).
116. *On Music* VI, 5, n. 14 (PL 32:1170).

Physics says.[117] And we likewise need to understand regarding privative effects what I have just said regarding positive effects, since what corrupts and diminishes causes movement just as what causes things to come to be and increase does. And so we evidently can understand that as we say that removing an obstacle to light accidentally causes illumination, or even that the removal of the obstacle does, albeit in an improper sense, so also we can say that imposing an obstacle to light and even the very obstacle cause darkness.

And as the sun pours light into air, so God pours grace into the soul. And grace is indeed superior to the nature of the soul, and yet there is in the nature of the soul and of any rational creature an aptitude to receive grace, and the grace received strengthens the soul to perform requisite acts. And sin is an obstacle imposed between the soul and God, as Is. 59:2 says, "Your sins have set up a division between you and your God." And the reason for this is that God can illumine the soul by the reception of grace only if the soul is directly turned toward himself. Just so, the sun illumines the air inside a house only if the air directly faces the sun, and we call anything that blocks the air directly facing the sun an obstacle to illumination. But sin, which turns the soul to the contrary, namely, to what is contrary to God's law, prevents turning toward God. And so sin is evidently an obstacle that prevents the reception of grace.

And every obstacle to a perfection or form, along with excluding perfection or form, renders the subject less suitably disposed or apt to receive the form. And moreover, the obstacle consequently prevents the effects of the perfection or form in the subject, and especially if the obstacle is something inhering in the subject, whether habitually or actually. For example, it is evident that what moves in one direction does not move in the contrary direction and is also less suitably disposed or apt to move in the contrary direction. Similarly, something hot is less suitably disposed to be cold, since it offers greater resistance to the impact of something cold. Therefore, sin, which is an obstacle to grace, both excludes grace and renders the soul less suitably disposed or apt to receive grace, and so diminishes the suitable disposition or aptitude for grace.

And so sin diminishes natural good, since the aptitude for grace is a natural good. And since grace perfects nature both regarding the intellect and regarding the will and regarding the lower parts of the soul subject to reason, namely, the irascible and concupiscible appetites, we say that sin by excluding grace and such natural helps wounds nature. And so some say that ignorance, malice, and the like are natural wounds resulting from sin.

Replies to the Objections:

1. After sin, natural good remains integral regarding its substance, but sin diminishes the aptitude for grace, as I have said,[118] and that aptitude is a natural good.

2. Accidents, although they do not take away the substance of their subject, can nonetheless diminish aptitude for other accidents, as, for example, heat diminishes aptitude for cold. And such is the case in the matter under discussion, as I have said.[119]

---

117. Aristotle, *Physics* VIII, 4 (256a1).
118. In the answer.
119. Ibid.

3. According to the Philosopher in the *Physics*,[120] potential health and potential sickness are the same regarding the subject because the subject is one substance with the two potentialities. But potential health and potential sickness differ conceptually because we understand the nature of potentialities from actualities. Therefore, sin does not diminish the aptitude for grace regarding what is rooted in the substance of the soul—for then the contraries would belong to one common existing substance—but regarding what is ordained to the contrary as different from grace.

4. The acts of many powers of the soul, some of which powers move others (e.g., the intellect moves the will, and the will moves the irascible and concupiscible powers) work together to produce moral acts. But causes of movement make impressions on the things they move. And so moral acts involve both expending and receiving, and moral acts can for this reason cause things in the human causes, such things as habits or dispositions or even things contrary to habits or dispositions.

5. We concede the fifth objection.

6. Natural action consists only of expending. And so natural action does not cause anything in the cause, particularly in simple causes not composed of one part acting and another part being acted upon, or of one part causing movement and another part being moved. For in things so composed of one part acting and another part being acted upon, there seems to be the same nature as in moral acts.

7. We say in an improper rather than a proper sense that acts act, since they are the means whereby their causes act.

8. Nothing moves itself and is moved by itself in the same respect. But nothing prevents something moving itself and being moved by itself in different respects, as the *Physics* makes clear.[121] And this is what happens in moral acts, as I have said.[122]

9. Particular goods destroy other particular goods because of the contrariety they have to the goods they destroy, and so nothing prevents evil as acting in the power of a particular good from destroying another good, as, for example, cold destroys heat. And it is in this way that sin destroys the good of justice by turning toward a good lacking measure and order and so diminishes the suitable disposition for justice.

10. We can consider good and evil in two ways. We can consider good and evil in one way by the common aspect of good and evil. And then every evil is contrary to every good. And Augustine says in this way that the rule of logic fails insofar as there is evil in good. We can consider good and evil in a second way by the special aspect of this or that good or evil. And then not every good is contrary to every evil, but a particular good is contrary to a particular evil, as, for example, blindness is contrary to sight, and immoderation to moderation. And in this way, evil is never in the contrary good, nor does the rule of logic fail.

11. The free choice of the damned is not lessened regarding its freedom, which is neither increased nor diminished. But the free choice of the damned suffers detriment regarding freedom from moral wrong and misery.

12. We understand aptitude for grace regarding nature even as ordained for moral good.

---

120. *Physics* III, 1 (201a35–b4).
121. Ibid., VIII, 5 (257a33ff.).
122. Reply to objection 4.

13. Sin is something positively and not a pure privation like darkness, and so sin is disposed to be an obstacle to grace. But the very privation of grace is like darkness, and the obstacle to grace diminishes the aptitude for grace, as I have said.[123]

14. Aptitude for grace is not the same as natural justice but is the ordination of natural good for grace. Nor is it true that natural justice cannot be diminished, for rectitude can be diminished by something hitherto totally straight being partially bent, and natural justice is diminished in this way insofar as it is deviant in some regard. For example, natural justice in the fornicator is deviant regarding the control of sexual desires, and likewise in other matters. But in no one is natural justice completely destroyed.

15. Something belonging to something else is induced to its activity regarding the aspect wherein it depends on something else, not regarding anything else. For example, the soul existing in the body depends on the body regarding its place but not regarding its existing or magnitude, and so the soul is accidentally moved regarding place when the body is moved but not diminished when the body is diminished, nor passes away when the body passes away. But the evil of moral wrong has magnitude by reason of its departure from natural good, not from natural good, as, for example, sickness has its magnitude by reason of its departure from the body's natural disposition. And so the evil of moral wrong is not diminished when natural good is diminished, just as a weakened nature increases rather than diminishes sickness.

16. The aptitude or suitable disposition for grace is included in the powers of the soul, and that aptitude is indeed diminished, as I have said,[124] although the powers themselves are not diminished.

Twelfth Article

Can Sin Destroy the Whole Natural Good?

It seems that sin can, for the following reasons:

1. Continuous diminution can completely take away any finite thing. But the natural good that consists of aptitude for grace is a finite thing, since that natural good is created. Therefore, if sin diminishes that natural good, as I have said,[125] sin can take it away completely.

2. Turning away from grace seems to diminish or take away the natural good that consists of aptitude for grace. But turning away from grace has a fixed condition and is not an infinite process, since the contrary turning toward grace has a fixed condition, as human beings do not have unlimited charity. Therefore, the diminution of natural good has a fixed condition. And this would not be so if part of natural good were always to remain, since natural good is always constituted to be diminished by sin. Therefore, it seems that sin can completely take away natural good.

---

123. In the answer.
124. Ibid.
125. A. 11.

3. Privation takes away aptitude completely. For example, a blind man is in no way equipped to see. But moral wrong is a privation. Therefore, moral wrong completely takes away the natural good that consists of aptitude for grace.

4. Sin is spiritual darkness, as John Damascene says.[126] But darkness can completely exclude light. Therefore, moral wrong can completely exclude good.

5. The evil of moral wrong is related to the good of nature just as the good of grace is related to the evil of nature. But as is evident in the case of the blessed, grace can exclude the entire evil of nature, that is, concupiscence, which consists of the inclination to moral wrong. Therefore, the evil of moral wrong can take away the entire good of nature, which consists of aptitude for grace.

6. Aptitude for grace cannot abide where it is impossible to obtain grace. But the state of damnation, at which one arrives through moral wrong, makes it impossible to obtain grace. Therefore, moral wrong can take away the entire natural good that consists of aptitude for grace.

7. Dionysius says in his work *On the Divine Names* that evil is the deficiency of natural aptitude.[127] But this seems especially to belong to the evil of moral wrong. Therefore, it seems that sin makes completely deficient the natural good that consists of aptitude for grace.

8. Whatever puts something outside its natural position seems to take away natural good. But sin puts the sinner outside the sinner's natural position, for John Damascene says that the sinning angels fell from a position in accord with their nature to a position contrary to their nature.[128] Therefore, sin takes away natural good.

9. Privation takes away only what exists. But the sinning angels did not have grace before they sinned. Therefore, the sin of the angels did not take away the good of grace. Therefore, we conclude that their sin took away natural good.

10. Diminution is a movement. But the movement of a whole and the movement of parts of the whole are the same, for example, the movement of the whole earth and the movement of pieces of earth, as the *Physics* says.[129]

On the Contrary:

Aptitude for good remains as long as the will remains. But sin does not take away the will; rather, sin consists of willing. Therefore, it seems that sin cannot take away the entire natural good that consists of aptitude for good.

Answer:

Sin cannot completely take away the natural good that consists of the suitable disposition or aptitude for grace. But this seems to give rise to a difficulty because it seems that continuous diminution can completely take away the aptitude, since it is finite. And some indeed wanted to avoid this difficulty by understanding an analogy to a finite continuum that can be forever successively divided if the division is by the same proportion. For

---

126. Cf. *On Orthodox Faith* II, 4 (PG 94:876A).
127. *On the Divine Names* 4, n. 35 (PG 3:736A).
128. Cf. *On Orthodox Faith* II, 4 (PG 94:876A).
129. Aristotle, *Physics* III, 5 (205a11–12).

example, if a third is subtracted from a finite line, and then a third of the remainder, and so forth, the division will never end and will be able to go on indefinitely. But this is not applicable to the matter under discussion, since when the line is divided successively by the same proportion, the part subsequently subtracted is always less than the part previously subtracted. For example, one third of the whole line is greater than one third of the remainder, and so on. And we cannot say that a second sin diminishes the aforementioned aptitude less than the first does; rather, a second sin perhaps diminishes the aptitude either equally or even more if the second sin is more serious.

And so we need to say otherwise, that the aptitude can be diminished in two ways: in one way by subtraction; in the other way by adding something contrary. An aptitude is indeed diminished by subtraction, as, for example, a material substance is fit to be heated by the heat it possesses, and its aptitude to be heated is diminished when the heat it possesses is diminished. And an aptitude is diminished by adding something contrary, as, for example, heated water has a natural disposition or aptitude to grow cold, but the more heat added to the water, the less aptitude the water has to become cold. Therefore, the second kind of diminution, namely, by adding something contrary, applies more to passive or receptive powers, and the first kind more to active powers, although there are both kinds of diminution to a degree in each kind of power. Therefore, when there is diminution of an aptitude by subtraction, the aptitude can be completely taken away if the cause of the aptitude is removed. And when an aptitude is diminished by adding something contrary, we need to consider whether adding more of the contrary thing can destroy the subject of the aptitude. For if adding more of the contrary can destroy the subject, the aptitude can be completely taken away. For example, the heat in water can be increased so much that the water evaporates, and then the aptitude of the water to grow cold, which results from its species, is completely taken away. But if the addition of something contrary, howsoever much it be increased, could not destroy the subject of an aptitude, the aptitude will indeed always be diminished as more and more of the contrary is added. But the aptitude will never be completely taken away, because of the permanence of the subject in which such an aptitude is rooted. For example, heat, howsoever much it were to be increased, would not take away the aptitude of prime matter, which cannot decompose, for the form of water.

And it is evident that the aptitude of a rational nature for grace is like the aptitude of a receptive power, and that such aptitude results from rational nature as such. But I have said before that adding something contrary, namely, when the rational creature turns away from God by turning toward the contrary, diminishes this aptitude.[130] And so since a rational creature cannot be destroyed and does not cease to exist howsoever much sin is multiplied, additional sin always diminishes aptitude for the good of grace but in such a way that the aptitude is never completely taken away. And so in the matter under discussion, diminution of the aptitude for grace can go on indefinitely because there remains something contrary to the addition of sins. Just so, conversely, in the case of continuous lines, there can be an indefinite number of additions to one line by subtractions from the other, since there remains something in the other line contrary to that line's division.

130. In the answer.

Replies to the Objections:

1. The argument of this objection would be valid if natural good were to be diminished by subtraction, as I have already said.[131]

2. Turning toward a creature and turning away from God have an actually fixed state, since the turnings are not actually infinite. But they do not have a fixed state regarding what is potential, since both merits and demerits can be multiplied indefinitely.

3. A privation that takes away a power completely takes away aptitude. For example, blindness takes away the power of sight, except perhaps insofar as there remains aptitude or suitable disposition in the root of the power, that is, in the soul's essence. But a privation that takes away acts does not take away aptitude, and the privation of grace is such a privation, as is darkness, which deprives air of light. And sin is an obstacle to grace that precludes grace, not the very privation of grace, as I have said before.[132]

4. Darkness excludes light, which is its contrary, but not the suitable disposition of air for light. And likewise, sin excludes grace but not the suitable disposition for grace.

5. The propensity for evil that we call concupiscence does not result from nature as the aptitude for good does, but the propensity for evil results from the corruption of nature that consists of moral wrong. And so grace can completely take away concupiscence, but moral wrong cannot completely take away natural good.

6. The impossibility of the damned to receive grace does not result from the total subtraction of the natural aptitude for good but from the obstinacy of the will in evil and the immutability of the divine judgment that grace be denied them for all eternity.

7. We do not understand deficiency of the natural disposition for good to mean that the entire natural disposition is wanting, but that the natural disposition falls short of its perfection.

8. And we should say likewise in reply to the eighth objection that sin puts sinners outside their natural perfection, not completely outside their natural condition.

9. Privation takes away both what exists and what a thing is by nature constituted to be. For example, persons can be deprived of things they never had if nature designed the persons to have the things. And yet it is not true that angels did not have grace from the first moment of their creation, for God at the same time established their nature and bestowed grace on them, as Augustine says in the *City of God*.[133]

10. The argument of this objection would be valid if the subtraction of parts were to effect the diminution.

131. Ibid.
132. A. 11.
133. *City of God* XII, 9, n. 2 (PL 41:357).

QUESTION III

On the Causes of Sin

First Article

Does God Cause Sin?

It seems that God does, for the following reasons:

1. The Apostle says in Rom. 1:28: "God delivered them up to a depraved way of thinking, so that they do unrighteous things." And a gloss of Augustine on this text says: "God is evidently active in the hearts of human beings by inclining their wills to whatever he willed, whether to good or to evil."[1] But the inclination of the will to evil is sin. Therefore, God causes sin.

2. People have said that the will's inclination to evil is attributed to God insofar as such inclination is a punishment, and that is why Augustine in the cited text speaks of the judgment of God. But the same thing cannot in the same respect be a punishment and a moral wrong, since punishment is by its nature contrary to the will, and moral wrong is by its nature voluntary, as I have said before.[2] And the will's inclination belongs to the nature of voluntariness. Therefore, if God inclines the will to evil, it seems that he himself also causes moral wrong as such.

3. As moral wrong is contrary to the good of grace, so punishment is contrary to the good of nature. But God is not prevented from causing punishment because he causes nature. Therefore, neither is he prevented from causing moral wrong because he causes grace.

4. What causes a cause causes the effect of the caused cause. But free choice causes sin, and God causes free choice. Therefore, God causes sin.

5. God caused the objects toward which the powers he bestowed incline. But some powers bestowed by God incline to sin (e.g., the irascible power toward homicide and the concupiscible power toward adultery). Therefore, God causes sin.

---

1. Actually, Peter Lombard, *Gloss*, on Rom. 1:24 (PL 191:1332A). Cf. Augustine, *On Grace and Free Choice* 21, n. 43 (PL 44:909).

2. Q. 1, aa. 4 and 5.

6. Those who incline their own wills or the wills of others to evil cause sin. For example, such would be the case if persons giving alms should incline their wills to seek vainglory. But God inclines human wills to evil, as I have already said.[3] Therefore, God causes sin.

7. Dionysius says in his work *On the Divine Names* that there are causes of evil in God.[4] But causes in God are not in vain. Therefore, God causes evils, among which we reckon sins.

8. Augustine says in his work *On Nature and Grace* that the soul has grace as the light whereby human beings do good, and without which they cannot do good.[5] Therefore, grace causes merit. Therefore, by contrast, the withdrawal of grace causes sin. But God is the one who withdraws grace. Therefore, God causes sin.

9. Augustine says in his *Confessions*: "I ascribe to your grace whatever evils I have not committed."[6] But he would not need to impute to grace that human beings did no evil if they, lacking grace, could not sin. Therefore, sin does not cause persons to be deprived of grace; rather, the privation of grace causes sin. And so, as before, God causes sinning.

10. We should especially attribute to God everything we praise in creatures. But Sir. 31:10 says in praise of a just human being that the person "could have transgressed and did not." Therefore, much more can we say this about God. Therefore, God can sin and so cause sin.

11. The Philosopher says in the *Topics*: "God and the zealous can do evil things."[7] But to do evil things is to sin. Therefore, God can sin.

12. It is a valid argument to say: "Socrates can run if he so wills. Therefore, absolutely speaking, he can run." But it is true to say that God can sin if he so wills, since the very willing to sin is sinning. Therefore, absolutely speaking, God can sin. And so we reach the same conclusion as before.

13. One who provides the occasion for injury seems to have inflicted the injury. But God by giving the law provided the occasion for human beings to sin, as Rom. 7:7–8 says. Therefore, God causes sin.

14. Since good causes evil, it seems that the greatest good causes the greatest evil. But the greatest evil is moral wrong, which makes a good human being or a good angel evil. Therefore, the greatest good, that is, God, causes moral wrong.

15. The same person has the authority to grant dominion and to take it away. But God has the authority to grant to the soul dominion over the body. Therefore, he also has the authority to take dominion over the body away from the soul. But only sin, which subjects the spirit to the flesh, takes away the soul's dominion over the body. Therefore, God causes sin.

16. The cause of a nature causes the characteristic and natural movement of that very nature. But God causes the nature of the will, and the characteristic and natural

---

3. Objection 1.
4. *On the Divine Names* 4, n. 30 (PG 3:729C).
5. *On Nature and Grace* 26 (PL 44:261).
6. *Confessions* II, 7 (PL 32:681).
7. *Topics* IV, 5 (126a34–35).

movement of the will is turning away from God, just as the characteristic and natural movement of a stone is downward, as Augustine says in his work *On Free Choice*.[8] Therefore, God causes the will's turning away from him. And so it seems that God causes moral wrong, since the nature of moral wrong consists of turning away from him.

17. One who commands a sin causes the sin. But God has commanded sin. For example, as 1 Kgs. 22:22 says, since the spirit of lies had said, "I shall go forth and be a lying spirit in the mouth of the prophets," the Lord said, "Go forth and do so." And Hos. 1:2 says that the Lord commanded Hosea to take a wanton woman for his wife and to beget children of wantonness from her. Therefore, God causes sin.

18. Action and the power to act belong to the same subject, since action belongs to one with the power to act, as the Philosopher says.[9] But God causes the power to sin. Therefore, God causes the action of sinning.

On the Contrary:

1. Augustine says in his work *Book of the 83 Questions* that human beings are not made worse by God, their author.[10] But sin makes human beings worse. Therefore, God is not the author of sin.

2. Fulgentius say that God is not the author of what he punishes.[11] But God punishes sin. Therefore, God is not the author of sin.

3. God causes only what he loves, since Wis. 11:25 says: God loves everything that exists, "and you [God] hated nothing that you have made." And he hates sin, as Wis. 14:9 says: "The wicked and their wickedness are alike hateful to God." Therefore, God is not the author of sin.

Answer:

One causes sin in two ways: in one way because the very one sins; in the second way because one causes someone else to sin. And neither of these ways can belong to God.

For it is evident, both from the general nature of sin and from the particular nature of moral sin that we call moral wrong, that God cannot sin. For sin in the general sense, as found in things of nature and artifacts, comes about because persons' actions do not attain the ends they intend. And this happens because of a deficiency in the causal source. For example, a grammarian's poor composition, if he intends to write well, comes about because of his deficient skill. And nature's sin in forming animals, as happens in the birth of monsters, comes about because of the deficient causal power of semen. And sin as we properly speak of it in moral matters, and as it has the nature of moral wrong, comes about because the will by tending toward an improper end fails to attain its proper end. And in the case of God, the causal source cannot be deficient, since his power is infinite, nor can his will fail to attain its proper end, since his very will, which is also his nature, is the supreme goodness that is the final end and first rule of all wills. And so his will by nature adheres to, and cannot defect from, the supreme good, just as the natural appe-

---

8. *On Free Choice* III, 1, n. 2 (PL 32:1271).
9. *On Sleep and Wakefulness* 1 (454a8).
10. *Book of the 83 Questions*, qq. 3 and 4 (PL 40:11–12).
11. *To Monimus* I, 19 (PL 65:167C).

tites of things cannot fail to seek their natural good. Therefore, God cannot cause sin because he himself sins.

Likewise, he also cannot cause sin because he causes others to sin. For sin as we are now speaking of it consists of the created will's turning away from the final end. And God cannot cause anyone's will to be turned away from the final end, since he himself is the final end. For whatever created causes universally possess, they necessarily have by imitating the first cause, who gives all of them his likeness insofar as they can receive it, as Dionysius says in his work *On the Divine Names*.[12] And every created cause through its activity in some way draws other things to its very self by making the things like itself. A created cause does this either by likeness of form, as when heat makes something hot, or by directing other things to its own end, as when human beings by their commands move others to attain the ends those commanding intend. Therefore, it belongs to God to direct everything to his very self and so not to divert anything from his very self. But he himself is the supreme good. And so he cannot cause the will to turn away from the supreme good, and the nature of moral wrong, as we are now speaking about it, consists of turning away from that good.

Therefore, God cannot cause sin.

Replies to the Objections:

1. The Apostle says that God delivers some up to a depraved way of thinking or inclines their wills to evil by withdrawing his support or by not preventing evil, not indeed by his activity or movement. Just so, for example, we would say that a person who were to fail to extend a hand to someone falling would cause the latter's fall. But it is by just judgment that God does not bestow assistance on some to prevent their fall.

2. The foregoing also makes clear the reply to the second objection.

3. Punishment is contrary to a particular good. And taking away a particular good is not contrary to the nature of the supreme good, since the addition of other, sometimes better, goods takes away particular goods. For example, the addition of the form of fire takes away the form of water, and likewise the addition of a higher good, namely, that God has established an order of justice regarding things, takes away the good of a particular nature as a punishment. But the evil of moral wrong occurs by turning away from the supreme good, from which the supreme good cannot turn away. And so God can cause punishment but not moral wrong.

4. We trace to the prior cause the effect produced by the caused cause as such. But if something does not proceed from the caused cause as such, we do not need to trace the effect to the prior cause. For example, an animal's power to move its legs causes the animal's leg movement. But limping comes from the fact that a leg by reason of its deficiency lacks the capacity to receive the influence of the animal's locomotive power, not from the fact that the leg is moved by the animal's locomotive power. And so the animal's locomotive power does not cause the limping. Therefore, free choice, as it defects from God, causes sin. And so God, although he causes free choice, need not cause sin.

5. Sins do not come from the inclination of the irascible and concupiscible powers as instituted by God, but as the powers depart from the ordination that God himself

---

12. *On the Divine Names* 9, n. 6 (PG 3:913C).

instituted, for the powers were instituted in human beings to be subject to reason. And so it is not from God when they incline to sin contrary to the ordination of reason.

6. The argument of this objection is not valid, since God inclines the will by adding grace, not by activity or movement, as I have said.[13]

7. The causes of evils are particular goods that can be deficient. But such particular goods are in God as effects in their cause insofar as they are goods. And we say that the causes of evils are in God to this extent, not that he himself causes the evils.

8. God as he is in himself communicates himself to all things in proportion to their receptivity. And so if something should deficiently share in his goodness, this is because the thing has an obstacle to participating in God. Therefore, God does not cause grace not to be supplied to someone; rather, those not supplied with grace offer an obstacle to grace insofar as they turn themselves away from the light that does not turn itself away, as Dionysius says.[14]

9. We should speak in one way about human beings in the state of nature as instituted, and in another way about human beings in the state of fallen nature, since human beings in the state of nature as instituted had nothing impelling them to evil, although natural good was insufficient to attain glory. And so human beings needed the help of grace in order to merit but not in order to avoid sins, since human beings by their natural powers could remain upright. But human beings in the state of fallen nature have an impulse to evil and so need the help of grace in order not to fall. And it was regarding the latter state that Augustine attributed to divine grace the evils he did not commit. And a previous moral wrong brought about such a state.

10. Things that do not belong to the praise of higher beings can be praiseworthy in lower beings. For example, ferociousness is praiseworthy in dogs but not in human beings, as Dionysius says.[15] And likewise, not transgressing when one could belongs to the praise of human beings but is absent from the praise of God.

11. We understand the words of the Philosopher about those called gods, whether by unfounded opinion as in the case of pagan gods or by participation as in the case of human beings virtuous beyond human measure, to whom the *Ethics* attributes heroic or divine virtue.[16] Or as some say, it is possible to hold that we can say that God can do evil things because he can if he wishes.

12. The protasis of the conditional proposition, "Socrates can run if he so wills," is possible, and so it follows that the apodasis is possible. But in the case of the conditional proposition, "God can sin if he so wills," the protasis is impossible, since God cannot will evil. And so there is no similarity between the two propositions.

13. There are two ways of being an occasion of sin, namely, one when an occasion is offered for sin, the second when an occasion is taken for sin. But the commandments are occasions for sin as taken by those to whom the commandments are imparted, not indeed as given by the one who gave the commandments. And so the Apostle in Rom. 7:8 significantly adds: "Taking the occasion, sin through the law worked in me all kinds

13. In the answer.
14. *On the Divine Names* 4, n. 23 (PG 3:725C).
15. Ibid., 4, n. 25 (PG 3:728B).
16. Aristotle, *Ethics* VII, 1 (1145a19–30).

of lustful desires." For we say that persons provide an occasion for sinning when they do something less virtuous that by their example leads others to sin. And if one should perform a virtuous deed, and another should thereby be led into sinning, there will be an occasion taken but not offered for sinning. For example, such was the case when the Pharisees were scandalized at the teaching of Christ.[17] And the commandments were holy and just, as Rom. 7:12 says. And so God by the commandments does not offer an occasion to sin, but human beings take the commandments as the occasion to sin.

14. If good as such were to cause evil, it would follow that the greatest good causes the greatest evil. But good insofar as it is deficient causes evil. And so the greater the good, the lesser the cause of evil.

15. Taking away the dominion of the spirit over the flesh is contrary to the order of natural justice, and such cannot belong to God, who is justice itself.

16. We call the movement of turning away from God characteristic and natural for the will in the state of fallen nature, not in the state of nature as instituted.

17. We should not understand the statement "Go forth and do so" by way of command but by way of permission, just like the statement to Judas "What you do, do quickly,"[18] in the manner of speaking whereby we call permission by God his will. And we should understand the statement to Hosea "Take to yourself a wanton woman as your wife," etc., by way of command. But God's command causes what would otherwise be a sin not to be a sin. For as Bernard says,[19] God can dispense in regard to the commandments of the second tablet, commandments whereby human beings are directly regulated regarding their neighbor, since the good of one's neighbor is a particular good. But God cannot dispense in regard to the commandments of the first tablet, commandments whereby human beings are regulated regarding God, who cannot turn others away from his very self, since he cannot deny his very self, as 2 Tim. 2:13 says. Nonetheless, some say that we should understand that the things described about Hosea happened in a prophetic vision.

18. We understand by the words of the Philosopher that it is one thing to be able to act and another thing to act, and not what causes a power also causes the power's act.

Second Article

Do Acts of Sin Come from God?

It seems that they do not, for the following reasons:

1. We say that human beings cause sin only because they cause acts of sin, since we do not do anything aiming to do evil, as Dionysius says in his work *On the Divine Names*.[20] But God does not cause sin, as I have said before.[21]

2. Every cause of something causes what belongs to the thing by reason of its species. For example, if a person causes Socrates, then the person causes the human being

17. E.g., Mt. 15:12.
18. Jn. 13:27.
19. *On Precept and Dispensation* 3 (PL 182:864B–C).
20. *On the Divine Names* 4, n. 19 (PG 3:716C).
21. A. 1.

that Socrates is. But some acts are indeed sins by reason of their species. Therefore, if acts of sin come from God, then sin comes from God.

3. Everything from God is a thing. But acts of sin are not things, as Augustine says in his work *On the Perfection of the Justice of Human Beings*.[22] Therefore, acts of sin do not come from God.

4. Acts of sin are acts of free choice, which we call free because the will moves its very self to act. But everything whose acts are caused by another is moved by the other, and if the thing does not move itself, it is not free. Therefore, acts of sin do not come from God.

On the Contrary:

Augustine says in his work *On the Trinity* that the will of God causes every species and movement.[23] But acts of sin are indeed movements of free choice. Therefore, the acts come from God.

Answer:

Ancient thinkers held two opinions regarding this matter. For some of old, stressing the very deformity of sin, which does not come from God, said that acts of sin do not come from God. And some, stressing the very entity of the acts, said that acts of sin come from God. And we need for two reasons to hold that the entity of the acts comes from God. The first reason is general. Since God is by his essence being, for his essence is his existing, everything existing in whatever way derives from himself. For there is nothing else that can be its own existing; rather, we call everything else a being by some participation. And everything we call such a thing by participation derives from what is such by essence. For example, everything on fire derives from what is fire by essence. But acts of sin are evidently beings and classified in the category of being. And so we need to say that the acts are from God.

And second, a particular reason evidences the same thing. For every movement of secondary causes needs to be caused by the first mover, just as all the movements of earthly material substances are caused by the movements of heavenly bodies. But God is the first mover regarding all movements, both spiritual and material, just as a heavenly body is the source of all the movements of earthly material substances. And so, since acts of sin are movements of free choice, we need to say that such acts as acts come from God.

And yet we should note that the movement from the first mover is not received in all moveable things in only one way but received in each kind of moveable thing in its own way. For example, heavenly movements cause the movements of inanimate material substances, which do not move themselves, in one way, and the movements of animals, which move themselves, in another way. And further, heavenly bodies cause plants whose reproductive power is not wanting, and whose reproductive power produces perfect shoots, to sprout in one way, and plants whose reproductive power is weak and produces fruitless shoots to sprout in another way. For when something is properly disposed to receive the causal movement of the first cause, a perfect causal action in accord with

22. *On the Perfection of Human Justice* 2 (PL 44:294).
23. *On the Trinity* III, 4, n. 9 (PL 42:873).

the aim of the first mover results. But if something is not properly disposed or fit to receive the causal movement of the first mover, imperfect action results. And then we trace what belongs to the activity in it to the first mover as the cause. And we do not trace what is in it regarding deficiency to the first mover as the cause, since such deficiency in the activity results because the secondary cause defects from the ordination of the first mover, as I have said.[24] For example, everything regarding the movement in limping is from an animal's locomotive power, but everything in limping regarding deficiency is from the leg insofar as the leg lacks the aptitude to be moved by the animal's locomotive power, not from the locomotive power.

Therefore, we need to say that God, since he is the first source of the movement of everything, moves certain things in such a way that they also move their very selves, as in the case of those with the power of free choice. And if those with free choice be properly disposed and rightly ordered to receive movement by God, good acts will result, and we completely trace these acts to him as their cause. But if those with free choice should defect from the requisite order, disordered acts that are acts of sin result. And so we trace what regards the activity of those with the power of free choice to God as the cause, while only free choice, not God, causes what regards the deordination or deformity of those with the power of free choice. And that is why we say that acts of sin come from God, but that sin does not.

Replies to the Objections:

1. Although sinners do not intrinsically will the deformity of sin, the deformity of sin nonetheless in some way falls within the compass of the sinner's will, namely, as the sinner prefers to incur the deformity of sin than to desist from the act. But the deformity of sin in no way falls within the compass of the divine will; rather, the deformity results because free choice withdraws from the ordination of the divine will.

2. The deformity of sin does not result from the species of acts as the acts belong to a type of nature, and God causes the acts as they belong to a type of nature. Rather, the deformity of sin results from the species of acts as moral, as caused by free choice, as I have said in connection with other questions.[25]

3. We speak of being and thing absolutely in regard to substances but with qualifications regarding accidents. And it is in this regard that Augustine says that acts are not things.

4. When we say that something moves its very self, we posit that the same thing causes the movement and is moved. And when we say that one thing moves another, we posit that one thing causes the movement, and that the other is moved. But it is evident that when one thing moves another, we do not posit that the cause of movement, by that fact, is the first cause of movement. And so we do not preclude that the cause of movement is moved by another and has from the other the very power to cause movement. Likewise, when something moves its very self, we do not preclude that such a thing be moved by another from which it has the very power to move itself. And so it is not contrary to freedom that God cause acts of free choice.

---

24. A. 1.
25. A. 1 and q. 2, aa. 2 and 3.

Third Article

Does the Devil Cause Sin?

It seems that he does, for the following reasons:

1. Wis. 2:24 says: "Death entered the world through the devil's envy." But death is the consequence of sin. Therefore, the devil causes sin.

2. Sin consists of desire. But Augustine says in his work *On the Trinity* that the devil inspires wicked desires in his companions.[26] And Bede says in his *Commentary on the Acts of the Apostles* that the devil entices the soul to wicked desires.[27] Therefore, the devil causes sin.

3. Nature constitutes lower things to be moved by higher things. But as nature ordains that the human intellect is inferior to the angelic intellect, so does nature ordain that the human will is inferior to the angelic will, since appetitive power is proportioned to cognitive power. Therefore, a bad angel by his evil will can move human wills to evil and so cause sin.

4. Isidore says in his work *On the Supreme Good* that the devil inflames human hearts with hidden inordinate desires.[28] But the root of all evils is inordinate desire, as 1 Tim. 6:10 says. Therefore, it seems that the devil can cause sin.

5. Everything equally related to each of two things needs something to determine it in order that it proceed to act. But the power of free choice of human beings is equally related to each of two things, namely, good and evil. Therefore, in order to proceed to an act of sin, the power of free choice needs to be determined to evil by something. And the devil, whose will is determined to evil, seems especially to do this. Therefore, it seems that the devil causes sin.

6. Augustine says in his *Enchiridion* that the cause of sin is the mutable will, first indeed that of the angels and then of human beings.[29] But the first in any genus causes the others. Therefore, it seems that the devil's evil will causes the evil will of human beings.

7. Sin consists of designs, and so Is.1:16 says: "Take away the evil of your designs from my eyes." But it seems that the devil can cause us to have designs, since the cogitative power is linked to bodily organs, and the devil can change material substances. Therefore, it seems that the devil can directly cause sin.

8. Augustine says that we should not think that there is no vice when the flesh lusts against the spirit.[30] But it seems that the devil can cause such concupiscence, since the concupiscible power is the actuality of a bodily organ. Therefore, it seems that he can directly cause sin.

9. Augustine says in his *Literal Commentary on Genesis* that when images of things are so presented to human beings as not to be distinguishable from the things, disorder in the flesh results.[31] And he says that the spiritual power of a good or bad angel can accom-

---

26. *On the Trinity* IV, 12, n. 15 (PL 42:897).
27. *Commentary on Acts*, on 5:3 (PL 83:666B).
28. *On the Supreme Good* III, 5, n. 33 (PL 83:666B).
29. *Enchiridion* 23 (PL 40:244).
30. *City of God* XIX, 4, n. 3 (PL 41:629).
31. *Literal Commentary on Genesis*, XII, 12, n. 25 (PL 34:463).

plish this. But there is no disorder in the flesh without sin. Therefore, it seems that the devil can directly cause sin.

10. The Commentator in his *Commentary on the Metaphysics* cites the words of Themistius, who said that a lower nature acts as if inspired by higher causes.[32] But higher causes properly and directly cause what lower causes do. Therefore, what can inspire things in lower causes seems to cause the acts of the lower causes. But the devil can inspire in human beings things whereby they are moved to sin. Therefore, it seems that the devil can directly cause sin.

11. The Philosopher in the *Eudemian Ethics* inquires about the source of the soul's activity and shows that the source needs to be something external, since everything that begins to exist has a cause.[33] For example, human beings begin to act because they will to do so, and they begin to will because they deliberate beforehand. And if they should deliberate beforehand by reason of an antecedent deliberation, either there is an infinite regress or we need to posit an external source that first moves human beings to deliberate. (Someone may suggest that deliberation happens by chance, but then it would follow that every human act happens by chance.) And the Philosopher says that the external source in the case of good acts is indeed God, who does not cause sin, as I have demonstrated before.[34] Therefore, since human beings begin to act, to will, and to deliberate regarding sin, it seems that this process needs to have an external cause, which can only be the devil. Therefore, the devil himself causes sin.

12. To the power of whatever a cause of movement is subject, the movement caused is subject. But the cause of the will's movement is something apprehended by the senses or the intellect, both of which are subject to the power of the devil. For Augustine says in his work *Book of the 83 Questions*: "This evil," namely, the one from the devil, "creeps in through all the accesses of the senses, gives itself shapes, adapts itself to colors, adheres to sounds, is hidden in anger and false speech, underlies odors, infuses with flavors, and clouds all avenues of understanding."[35] Therefore, the devil has the power to move the will and so directly causes sin.

13. The devil buys human beings for their sins, as Is. 50:1 says: "Behold, you were sold for your sins." But buyers offer money to sellers. Therefore, the devil causes sin in human beings.

14. Jerome says that just as God perfects good, so the devil perfects evil, although human beings have certain inclinations that incite them to vices.[36] But God intrinsically causes our good acts. Therefore, it seems that the devil likewise directly causes our sins.

15. Bad angels are related to evil as good angels are related to good. But good angels lead human beings to good, since it is the divine law to lead to ultimate things through intermediaries, as Dionysius says.[37] Therefore, it seems that a bad angel can lead human beings to evil, and so that the devil causes sin.

---

32. Averroes, *On Aristotle's Metaphysics* XI, comm. 18.
33. *Eudemian Ethics* VIII, 12 (1248a17–32).
34. A. 1.
35. *Book of the 83 Questions*, q. 12 (PL 40:14).
36. *Against Jovinian* II, n. 3 (PL 23:286–87).
37. *On Ecclesiastical Hierarchy* 5, part 1, n. 4 (PG 3:504C).

On the Contrary:

1. Augustine says in his work *Book of the 83 Questions* that "the cause of the depravity of human beings is traceable to their will, whether they have been perverted at the persuasion of someone or no one."[38] But sin perverts human beings. Therefore, the human will, not the devil, causes the sin of human beings.

2. Augustine says in his work *On Free Choice* that each human being causes his or her own wickedness, and no one else causes human sin.[39]

3. The sin of human beings comes about by free choice. But the devil cannot cause movement by free choice. Therefore, the devil does not cause sin.

Answer:

We speak in many ways about causes inducing something. For example, we sometimes call what disposes or commends or commands, a cause. And we sometimes call what brings about an effect a cause. And we properly and truly call the latter a cause, since causes result in effects. But effects result directly from the activity of what brings them about, and not from the activity of what disposes or commends or commands, "since persuasion does not compel one who is unwilling," as Augustine says in his *Book of the 83 Questions*.[40] Therefore, we need to say that the devil can cause sin as one who disposes or persuades internally or externally, or even as one who commands, as is apparent in the case of those who have openly surrendered themselves to the devil. But he cannot cause sin as an efficient cause. For as the efficient causes in producing forms are the causes by whose activity the forms result, so the efficient causes in eliciting acts are the causes by whose activity human agents are induced to act. But sin is an act, not a form. Therefore, only what can directly move the will to an act of sin can intrinsically cause sin.

And we should consider that we speak in two ways about the will being induced to something: in one way by something external; in the second way by something internal. The will is indeed moved by something external, for example, an apprehended object. For we say that the apprehended object moves the will, and we say that one who commends or persuades moves the will in this way, namely, inasmuch as such a one makes something seem good. And the will is moved by something internal, for example, what produces the very act of the will. And the object proposed to the will does not necessarily move the will, although the intellect sometimes necessarily assents to a proposed truth. And the reason for this difference is that both the intellect and the will necessarily tend toward what nature has ordained as their object, for it is characteristic of nature to be determined to one thing. And so the intellect necessarily assents to the first principles known naturally, nor can it assent to their contraries, and the will likewise naturally and necessarily wills happiness, nor can anyone will unhappiness. And so regarding the intellect, things necessarily linked to naturally known first principles necessarily move the intellect. For example, such is the case of demonstrated conclusions, where it is evident that denial of the conclusions necessitates denial of the first principles from which the conclusions necessarily result. But the intellect is not compelled to assent to conclusions

38. *Book of the 83 Questions*, q. 4 (PL 40:12).
39. *On Free Choice* I, 1, n. 1 (PL 32:1223).
40. *Book of the 83 Questions*, q. 4 (PL 40:12).

if they be not necessarily linked to naturally known first principles, as is the case with contingent and probable things. Likewise, neither does the intellect necessarily assent to necessary things necessarily linked to first principles before it knows there is such a necessary connection. Therefore, regarding the will, the will will not be necessarily moved to anything that does not even seem to have a necessary connection with happiness, which is naturally willed. And it is obvious that such particular goods have no necessary connection with happiness, since human beings can be happy without any one of them. And so however much one of them is presented to human beings as good, the will does not necessarily incline to it. And the perfect good, that is, God, indeed has a necessary connection with the happiness of human beings, since human beings cannot be happy without that good, but the necessity of this connection is not fully evident to human beings in this life, since they do not in this life behold the essence of God. And so the human will in this life also does not necessarily adhere to God, but the will of those who, beholding the essence of God, evidently know that he himself is the essence of goodness and the happiness of human beings cannot not adhere to God, just as our will in this life cannot not will happiness. Therefore, it is evident that the will's object does not necessarily move the will, and so no persuasion necessarily moves the will to act.

Therefore, we conclude that the efficient and proper cause of a voluntary act is only what acts internally, and this can only be the will itself as secondary cause and God as first cause. And the reason for this is that the will's act is simply an inclination of the will to the thing willed, just as a natural appetite is simply a natural inclination to something. But a natural inclination comes from a natural form and from what gave the form. And so we say that the upward movement of fire comes from its lightness and from the cause that created such a form. Therefore, the will's movement directly comes from the will and God, who causes the will, who alone acts within the will and can incline the will to whatever he should will. But God cannot cause sin, as I have shown before.[41] Therefore, we conclude that only the will directly causes human sin. Therefore, it is clear that the devil does not, properly speaking, directly cause sin but causes sin only as a persuader.

Replies to the Objections:
1. Death entered the world through the devil's envy insofar as he persuaded the first human being to sin.

2. We say that the devil as a persuader inspires wicked desires in human beings or even draws souls to wicked desires.

3. Nature constitutes something lower, as passive, to be moved by something higher, as active, through an external change, as, for example, air is moved by fire. But external change does not impose necessity on the will, as I have shown.[42] And so the devil, although he belongs to a rank of nature superior to the human soul, cannot affect a human will necessarily. And so he does not, properly speaking, cause sin, since we properly speak of a cause as something from which something else necessarily results.

4. We say that the devil inflames the hearts of human beings by persuading them with inordinate desires.

---

41. A. 1.
42. In the answer.

5. The will, although it is equally related to each of two alternatives, is determined to one of them by something, namely, the deliberation of reason. And this determination does not need to be by an external cause.

6. The sin of the angels and the sin of human beings do not have a natural relationship to one another but only a temporal relationship. For it happens that the devil sinned before human beings did, but it could have happened conversely. And so the sin of the devil does not necessarily cause the sin of human beings.

7. There is sin in thoughts only insofar as they incline someone to evil or withdraw someone from good. And this remains subject to the will's power of free choice, no matter what thoughts arise. And so it is not necessary that something which causes thought thereby causes sin.

8. The lusting of the flesh against the spirit is an act of sensuality, which can involve sin insofar as reason can prevent or restrain its movement. And so there is no sin in the act if the movement of sensuality arises from a bodily change, and reason resists the movement. And resistance is within the will's power of choice. And so it is clear that every sin rests in the will's power of choice.

9. The fact that we do not distinguish the images and likenesses of things from the things themselves results from the fact that the higher power capable of distinguishing and judging is fettered. For example, one thing touched by two fingers seems to the sense of touch to be two things unless another power (e.g., sight) contradicts the perception. Therefore, the power of imagination, when likenesses are presented to it, is bound to them as if they were the things themselves, unless another power, namely, an external sense or reason, contradicts the perception. But if reason is fettered, and the external senses are inactive, the power of imagination is bound to the likenesses as if they were the things themselves, as happens in sleepers' dreams and the demented. Therefore, devils can cause human beings not to distinguish images from things insofar as devils, God permitting, disturb internal sense powers, and the disturbed powers fetter the operation of human reason, which needs such powers for its activity. For example, such is evidently the case with those possessed by the devil. But we impute nothing to human beings as sin when their use of reason is fettered, just as we impute nothing to irrational animals as sin. And so the devil will not cause sin even if he should cause acts that would otherwise be sins.

10. Lower natures are moved necessarily by higher causes, and so the higher causes that we speak of as inspiring lower natures cause natural effects properly and directly. But the devil's inspiration does not necessarily move the will, and so there is no comparison.

11. God is the universal source of every deliberation and willing and human act, as I have said before.[43] But every misstep and sin and deformity in deliberation, willing, and human action comes from the deficiency of human beings. Nor do we need to attribute these to another, extrinsic cause.

12. The apprehended thing does not move the will necessarily, as I have shown.[44] And so the thing apprehended by the senses or the intellect, however much it be subject to the power of the devil, cannot be sufficient to move the will to sin.

43. Ibid.
44. Ibid.

13. The devil offers sin to human beings as a persuader.

14. We do not note the cited similarity in every respect. For God is the author of our good acts both as external persuader and internal mover, while the devil causes sin only as external persuader, as I have shown.[45]

15. Good angels as persuaders, not indeed by directly moving the will, lead human beings to God. And so also does the devil induce human beings to sin.

Fourth Article

Can the Devil by Interior Persuasion Induce Human Beings to Sin?

It seems that he cannot, for the following reasons:

1. Everything acting by design knows its action's effect. But the devil cannot see internal thoughts, as the work *On Church Dogmas* says.[46] Therefore, he cannot persuade internally by causing internal thoughts.

2. Forms are impressed on the internal sense powers in a more excellent way than on material substances. But the devil can impress forms on material substances only perhaps by using certain elements, since material substances do not do the bidding of fallen angels, as Augustine says in his work *On the Trinity*.[47] Therefore, he cannot impress forms on the internal sense powers.

3. The Philosopher proves in the *Metaphysics* that forms in matter rather than those outside matter cause the forms in matter.[48] For example, the forms in particular flesh and bones cause the form of flesh and bones. But the forms of external sense powers are received in bodily organs. Therefore, the devil, who is an immaterial substance, cannot cause such forms.

4. Only the one who established the order of nature, namely, God, can act outside that order. But there is indeed a natural order of the acts of the internal sense powers of the soul, since "imagining is a movement caused by the act of an external sense," as the *De anima* says,[49] and so, in a further process, one sense power moves another. Therefore, the devil cannot cause internal movements or acts of the sense powers of the soul unless such proceed from the external senses.

5. Vital activities come from an internal source. But all the acts of the internal sense powers are kinds of vital activities. Therefore, only an internal source, not the devil, can cause the acts.

6. Only causes specifically the same cause the same effects. But the external senses cause the acts of the internal sense powers. Therefore, the devil cannot cause those acts by specifically the same action.

---

45. Ibid.
46. Gennadius, *On Church Dogmas* 81 (PL 58:999A).
47. *On the Trinity* III, 8, n. 13 (PL 42:875).
48. *Metaphysics* VII, 8 (1033b19–1034a8).
49. Aristotle, *De anima* III, 33 (429a1–2).

7. Sense powers are more excellent than nutritive powers. But the devil cannot cause acts of nutritive powers to form flesh and bones. Therefore, the devil cannot cause the acts of any of the internal sense powers of the soul.

On the Contrary:

We say that the devil both visibly and invisibly tempts human beings. But this would not be true unless he were internally to persuade human beings to things. Therefore, the devil internally incites human beings to sin.

Answer:

The devil as persuader, not as directly moving the will of human beings, can cause human sins, as I have said before.[50] And he persuades human beings to things in two ways: visibly and invisibly. He persuades visibly as when he sensibly appears to human beings in some form and sensibly speaks with them and persuades them to sin. For example, he tempted the first human being in the garden of paradise in the form of a serpent,[51] and he tempted Christ in the desert in some visible form.[52] But we should not think that he only persuades human beings in this way, since then no other sins would arise at the devil's instigation except those to which the devil in visible form persuades human beings. And so we need to say that he also invisibly induces human beings to sin.

And he does this both as persuader and as disposer. He indeed does this as persuader when he presents something to a cognitive power as good. Therefore, he can do this in three ways, since he presents either something concerning the intellect or something concerning the internal senses or something concerning the external senses. He can indeed present something concerning the intellect, since an angelic intellect can by an illumination help a human intellect to know something, as Dionysius says.[53] For an angel, although it cannot directly cause a voluntary human act, since a voluntary act is simply an inclination of the will proceeding from within, can still make an impression on the intellect, whose activity consists of receiving things from without. And it is for this reason that we say that understanding is being acted upon in a certain way. But the devil, although he could by the ordination of his nature persuade human beings of things by enlightening their intellect as good angels do, does not do this. This is so because the more an intellect is enlightened, the more it can guard itself against the deceptions that the devil intends. And so we conclude that the devil's internal persuasions and revelations are by impressions on the internal and external sense powers, not by enlightenment of the intellect.

And to see how the devil can make impressions on the internal sense powers, we should consider that nature constitutes natural material substances to be moved locally by spiritual natures but to be formed directly by material causes and not by spiritual natures, as the *Metaphysics* says.[54] And so corporeal matter is naturally subject to good or bad angels regarding locomotion, and devils can in this way collect elements that they use to produce

50. A. 3.
51. Gen. 3:1ff.
52. Mt. 4:1.
53. *On the Celestial Hierarchy* 4, n. 3 (PG 3:180).
54. *Metaphysics* VII, 8 (1033b19–1034a8).

certain wondrous effects, as Augustine says in his work *On the Trinity*.[55] But corporeal matter regarding its formation is not subject to the bidding of spiritual creatures. And so devils can form corporeal matter only by the power of material elements, as Augustine says.[56] Therefore, nothing prevents devils from doing whatever can happen by the local movement of corporeal matter, unless they are by divine intervention prevented from doing so. And the appearance or representation of the sensory forms retained in internal sense organs can be accomplished by some local movement of corporeal matter. Similarly, the Philosopher, in assigning the causes of apparitions in dreams, says in his work *On Sleep and Wakefulness* that if animals are asleep, most of their blood goes back to its sensory source.[57] And the movements or impressions left by the movements of perceptible objects, movements or impressions retained in sensory vapors, accompany the blood. And the movements or impressions move the sources of perception in such a way that they seem as if external things themselves were at that moment affecting the sources of perception.

Therefore, what happens in the case of those asleep regarding the apparitions of dreams from the local movement of vapors and fluids can happen by the like local movement achieved by devils, sometimes in those asleep, and sometimes in those awake. And in the case of those awake, devils can sometimes indeed move internal vapors and fluids even to the point that the use of reason is completely fettered, as is evidently the case with the possessed. For it is clear that great disturbance of the vapors and fluids prevent activities of reason, as is evident in the case of the insane and sleepers and drunks. And devils can sometimes move internal vapors and fluids without fettering reason. For example, even human beings who are awake and enjoy the use of reason by the voluntary movement of vapors and fluids bring interiorly retained forms from certain repositories, as it were, to the external sensory source in order to imagine particular things. Therefore, since devils do this in those who are awake and enjoy the use of reason, the more a person is fettered by an emotion, the more and the more easily the person perceives the forms brought to the sensory source and persists in thinking about them. This is so because slight likenesses move emotionally excited persons, as a slight likeness of the beloved moves the lover, as the Philosopher says in the same work.[58] And so we call devils tempters, since they learn through the actions of human beings to which emotions the human beings are more subject, so that the devils may thereby more effectively impress on the imagination of those individuals what they intend.

Likewise, devils may also by moving sensory vapors make an impression on the external senses, which by the contraction or expansion of sensory vapors perceive things more acutely or more sluggishly. And one sees or hears more acutely when the sensory vapors are abundant and pure, more sluggishly when the contrary is the case. And it is in this way that Augustine speaks of the evil introduced by devils creeping through all the external senses.[59]

Therefore, it is clear how the devil internally persuades human beings to sin by making impressions on the internal and external sense powers.

55. *On the Trinity* III, 8, n. 13 (PL 42:876).
56. Ibid.
57. Actually, *On Dreams* 3 (461b11ff.).
58. Ibid., 2 (460b5–7).
59. *Book of the 83 Questions*, q. 12 (PL 40:14).

And the devil can cause sin as a disposer insofar as he by a like movement of vapors and fluids causes some to be more disposed to anger or lust or some such thing. For it is obvious that human beings are more prone to sexual lust and anger and like emotions if the body is disposed in a certain way, and human beings are disposed to consent when these emotions arise.

Therefore, it is evident that the devil internally incites to sin by persuading and disposing but not by causing sin.

Replies to the Objections:

1. The devil can perceive internal thoughts in their effects, not in themselves.

2. The devil does not make an impression on the imagination by newly causing forms. And so he could not cause a man born blind to imagine colors. But he causes impressions on the imagination by local movements, as I have said.[60]

3. The third objection is answered in the same way.

4. The devil does not cause this outside the order of nature but by locally moving internal sources, from which nature constitutes such things to arise.

5–6. The foregoing reply makes clear the answers to the fifth and sixth objections.

7. The devil could in the same way, by heaping up vapors and fluids, cause something to digest more quickly or more slowly, but this is not very related to his design.

Fifth Article

Does the Devil Suggest Every Sin?

It seems that he does, for the following reasons:

1. Damascene says that the devil has devised every wickedness and every impurity.[61]

2. Dionysius says in his work *On the Divine Names* that the many devils cause all evils, both for themselves and for others.[62]

3. We could say about every sin what the Lord says to the Jews in Jn. 8:44: "You are from your father, the devil." But this would be so only if the devil were in some way to cause every sin. Therefore, every sin is done at the instigation of the devil.

4. Isidore says in his work *On the Supreme Good*: "The same blandishments that deceived our first parents in the garden of paradise deceive human beings now."[63] But our first parents were deceived at the instigation of the devil. Therefore, every sin even now is committed at the instigation of the devil.

On the Contrary:

The work *On Church Dogmas* says: "The devil does not stir up all our evil thoughts, but they sometimes arise from the movement of our power to choose."[64]

---

60. In the answer.
61. *On Orthodox Faith* II, 4 (PG 94:877B).
62. *On the Divine Names* 4, n. 18 (PG 3:716A).
63. *On the Supreme Good* III, 5, n. 22 (PL 83:664A).
64. Gennadius, *On Church Dogmas* 82 (PL 58:999A).

Answer:

We can speak in two ways of something causing something else: in one way directly; in the second way indirectly. Something indeed causes indirectly, as we say that a cause causing a disposition to an effect causes the effect as the occasion for the effect and indirectly. For example, such would be the case if we should say that one who dries out pieces of wood provides the occasion for burning the very wood. And we need to say in this way that the devil causes all our sins, since he himself incited the first man to sin, from whose sin a proneness to every kind of sin resulted in the whole human race. And we should understand the words of Damascene and Dionysius in this way.[65]

And we say that something that acts directly on something else directly causes it, and the devil does not cause every sin in this sense. For not every sin is committed at the instigation of the devil. Rather, some are due to the freedom of human beings to choose and to the corruption of the flesh. This is so because, as Origen says,[66] even if the devil were not to exist, human beings would have appetites for food and sex and such like, regarding which many disorders arise unless reason restrains such appetites, and especially so if we presuppose the corruption of our nature. And restraining and ordering such appetites are subject to the power of free choice. Therefore, not all sins need to come about at the instigation of the devil.

But if any sins do come about at his instigation, human beings are now deceived to commit them by the same blandishments that deceived our first parents, as Isidore says. And even if some sins are committed apart from the instigation of the devil, human sinners nonetheless become children of the devil insofar as they imitate the very one who was the first to sin. Still, there is no kind of sin that may not at times come about at the instigation of the devil.

Replies to the objections:

The foregoing makes clear the answer to the objections.

Sixth Article

Regarding Human Sinners, Can Ignorance Cause Sin?

It seems that ignorance cannot, for the following reasons:

1. Ignorance causes involuntary things, as Damascene says.[67] But involuntary things are contrary to sin, since sin is so voluntary that if there is nothing voluntary, there is no sin, as Augustine says.[68] Therefore, ignorance cannot cause sin.

2. Causes and effects are interconnected. But ignorance and sin are not interconnected, since ignorance resides in the intellect, and sin in the will, as Augustine says.[69] Therefore, ignorance cannot cause sin.

---

65. In objections 1 and 2.
66. *On First Principles* III, 2, n. 2 (PG 11:305C–D).
67. *On Orthodox Faith* II, 24 (PG 94:953B).
68. *On True Religion* 14, n. 27 (PL 34:133).
69. *On Two Souls* 10, n. 12 (PL 42:103).

3. When a cause is increased, its effect is also increased. For example, hotter fire causes more heat. But greater ignorance does not cause greater sin; rather, ignorance can be so great as to exclude sin altogether. Therefore, ignorance does not cause sin.

4. As there are two things involved in sin, namely, turning away from God and turning toward a creature, we ought to understand the cause of sin in relation to the turning toward a creature. For sin has the nature of evil regarding the turning away from God, and evil has no cause, as Dionysius says in his work *On the Divine Names*.[70] But ignorance seems to regard sin in relation to the turning away from God, not in relation to the turning toward a creature. Therefore, ignorance does not cause sin.

5. If any ignorance causes sin, this seems especially to concern malicious ignorance, which we call affected ignorance. But when a person in a willful state of ignorance falls into a sin as a result, the will to be ignorant rather than ignorance itself seems to cause the sin. Therefore, we should not say that ignorance causes sin.

6. Ignorance seems to be the reason why we are judged innocent, or why God has mercy on us, since the Apostle says in 1 Tim. 1:13: "I obtained mercy because I acted in ignorance." But mercy is contrary to sin, since the more one sins, the less one deserves mercy. Therefore, ignorance does not cause sin.

7. There are four kinds of causes, and ignorance cannot cause sin in any of these ways. For ignorance is not a final cause, since sin does not aim at it. Nor is ignorance a material cause, since the matter of sin is that about which an act of sin is concerned, as, for example, the material cause of intemperance is inordinate desire. Nor is ignorance a formal or efficient cause, since ignorance is a privation, and privation does not have the nature of a form or an efficient cause. Therefore, in no way can ignorance cause sin.

8. Ignorance is a kind of wound that results from sin, as Bede says.[71] Therefore, much more does it seem that sin causes ignorance than that ignorance causes sin.

On the Contrary:

1. Isidore says in his work *On the Supreme Good*: "Sin is committed in three ways, namely, by ignorance, by weakness, and on purpose."[72] Therefore, some sins are committed due to ignorance. Therefore, ignorance causes some sins.

2. Augustine says in his work *On Free Choice* that we rightly censure many things done out of ignorance.[73] Therefore, some sins are committed due to ignorance, and so ignorance causes some sins.

Answer:

Ignorance can cause sin, and we can trace it to the genus of efficient or active causes. But we should note that there are, as the *Physics* says,[74] two kinds of efficient causes, namely, intrinsic causes and accidental causes, which remove impediments to causal action. For example, in the locomotion of heavy and light things, intrinsic causes cause what hap-

---

70. *On the Divine Names* 4, n. 32 (PG 3:732D).
71. Scholars have found no source in the writings of Bede.
72. *On the Supreme Good* II, 17, n. 3 (PL 38:620A).
73. *On Free Choice* III, 18, n. 51 (PL 32:1295).
74. Aristotle, *Physics* VIII, 4 (255b17–256a3).

pens to the things, giving to the things the forms that result from such movement. And accidental causes cause changes that remove impediments to the movement of things. For example, we say that one who removes a pillar from beneath a block of stone causes the stone to fall. And we should note that practical sciences, since they guide us in our voluntary actions, both draw us to good things and draw us away from evil things. And so the very sciences prevent evils. Therefore, we correctly say that the ignorance that deprives us of such knowledge causes sin as a cause that takes away an impediment to evil, as is clearly evident in activity requiring skill. For example, the science of grammar guides people to speak properly and prevents them from speaking improperly, and so we can call ignorance of grammar the cause of improper speech as the remover of what prevents improper speech, or rather the very removal of such. And likewise in moral actions, practical science guides us, and so ignorance of such knowledge causes moral fault in the aforementioned way.

But we should note that there are in moral actions two kinds of knowledge that can prevent sin. One kind is universal, whereby we judge that an action is right or wrong, and such knowledge sometimes keeps persons from sin. For example, a person judging that fornication is a sin abstains from it, and if ignorance were to deprive the person of such knowledge, the ignorance would cause the fornication. And if ignorance were not to be such as altogether to excuse a person from sin, as sometimes happens, as I shall explain later,[75] such ignorance would cause sin. And the second kind of knowledge that guides us in our moral actions and can prevent sin is particular knowledge, namely, knowledge of the circumstances of the very action, since universal knowledge apart from particulars does not cause us to act, as the *De anima* says.[76]

And knowledge of circumstances may in one way draw persons away from sin absolutely, in another way prevent them from sinning by such a kind of sin but not keep them from sin absolutely. For example, suppose that a hunter, were he to know that a human being is passing by, would not shoot an arrow anywhere close, but because he does not know that a human being is passing by, and thinks he sees a deer, shoots and kills a human being. And so ignorance of a circumstance causes homicide, which is a sin, unless there be such ignorance as to excuse completely, as I shall explain later.[77] But suppose that a hunter should indeed wish to kill a person but not his father. Were he to know that a passerby is his father, he would not shoot an arrow anywhere close, but because he does not know that the passerby is his father, he shoots and kills his father. And so such ignorance evidently causes the sin of homicide, since he is guilty of homicide regarding any passerby, although he is not guilty of patricide in every murder of a passerby. Therefore, ignorance evidently may in different ways cause sin.

Replies to the Objections:

1. Ignorance may in two ways not so completely exclude something voluntary as to take away completely the nature of sin. There is indeed one way when the very ignorance is voluntary, since then we judge what results from ignorance to be voluntary. There is a second way when, although persons do not know one thing, they know something else

75. A. 8.
76. Aristotle, *De anima* III, 11 (434a16–21).
77. A. 8.

that suffices for there to be the nature of sin. For example, I have spoken about the hunter who shoots an arrow and kills someone that he knows to be a human being, but that he does not know to be his father.[78] And so the hunter, although he involuntarily commits patricide, nonetheless voluntarily commits murder.

2. Although the intellect and the will are different powers, they are still interconnected insofar as the intellect in one way moves the will, insofar as the understood good is the object of the will. And so ignorance can be connected to sin.

3. The principle that effects are increased when their causes are applies in the case of intrinsic causes, not accidental causes that are such as to remove impediments to causal action.

4. Ignorance also as to turning toward a creature causes sin insofar as ignorance removes what prevents turning to sin.

5. As we say that removing a pillar and the very act of removing the pillar cause a stone on top to fall, so also we can say that the very will of one lacking knowledge and the very privation of knowledge cause sin. But we should not say that only sinful ignorance causes sin, since ignorance of circumstances is not sinful but can cause sin, as I have said.[79]

6. Ignorance in different respects can cause contraries. For we say that ignorance insofar as it deprives persons of the knowledge that was preventing sin causes sin, and that ignorance insofar as it takes away or diminishes things being voluntary has the capacity to excuse from sin and cause God's mercy or the persons' innocence.

7. We trace ignorance to the genus of efficient causes as an accidental, not an intrinsic, cause, as I have said.[80]

8. Nothing prevents ignorance being the effect of one sin and the cause of another, just as the desires of concupiscence are effects in us of the sin of our first parent and yet causes of many actual sins.

Seventh Article

Is Ignorance a Sin?

It seems that ignorance is not, for the following reasons:

1. Contraries belong to the same genus. And so Augustine says in his work *On the Trinity* that we predicate both human being and nonhuman being as substances.[81] But ignorance is contrary to knowledge. And knowledge belongs to the genus of habit. Therefore, ignorance does also. But sin belongs to the genus of act, not the genus of habit, since "sin is a deed or word or desire contrary to the law of God."[82] Therefore, ignorance is not a sin.

---

78. In the answer.
79. Ibid.
80. Ibid.
81. *On the Trinity* V, 7 (PL 42:916).
82. Augustine, *Against Faustus* XXII, 27 (PL 42:418).

2. Grace is more contrary to sin than knowledge is, since there can be knowledge, but not grace, along with sin. But privation of grace is a punishment, not a sin. Therefore, ignorance, which is the privation of knowledge, is also a punishment, not a sin.

3. The work *Rules on Sacred Theology* says that no privation merits reward or punishment.[83] But every sin merits punishment. Therefore, no privation is a sin. But ignorance is a privation. Therefore, ignorance is not a sin.

4. We differ from irrational animals by the power of reason. Therefore, if what belongs to reason is removed from us, only what we and irrational animals have in common remains in us. But there is no sin in irrational animals. Therefore, our ignorance, which deprives us of what belongs to reason, is not a sin.

5. If any ignorance be a sin, the ignorance needs to be voluntary and so involves a prior act of the will. But when an act of the will precedes ignorance, sin consists of the very willing to be ignorant. Therefore, the willing to be ignorant rather than the ignorance is a sin.

6. Augustine says in his *Retractions*: "We can properly say that those who have unknowingly sinned have unwillingly sinned, although they themselves willingly did what they unknowingly did, since they willed the acts of sin."[84] Therefore, the act of sin consists only of the will. Therefore, ignorance itself is not a sin.

7. Augustine says in his work *On Free Choice*: "Moral wrong is imputed to you if you have neglected to know something, but not if you happen to be involuntarily in a state of ignorance."[85] Therefore, the very neglect to know something, not ignorance, is a sin.

8. Every sin is either an act elicited by the will or an act commanded by the will. But ignorance is not elicited by the will, since ignorance rests in the intellect, not the will. Likewise, ignorance is not commanded by the will. For ignorance cannot be willed, since every human being desires to know.

9. Every sin is something voluntary. But the voluntary is in the power of a knower, as the *Ethics* says.[86] Therefore, ignorance, which excludes knowledge, cannot be sin.

10. Repentance takes away every kind of sin. But ignorance abides after repentance.

11. Only original sin remains actual and passes away regarding guilt. But ignorance remains actual when guilt goes away. And ignorance is not original sin, since it would then follow that everybody would be ignorant. Therefore, it seems that ignorance is not a sin.

12. Ignorance abides continually in one who is ignorant. Therefore, if ignorance were a sin, one in a state of ignorance would sin moment by moment an endless number of times.

On the Contrary:

1. 1 Cor. 14:38 says: "If one does not acknowledge, one will not be acknowledged," namely, be rejected. But such a rejection is due to sin. Therefore, ignorance is a sin.

---

83. Alan of Lille, *Rules on Sacred Theology* 75 (PL 210:660C).
84. *Retractions* I, 15, n. 3 (PL 32:609).
85. *On Free Choice* III, 19, n. 53 (PL 32:1297).
86. Aristotle, *Ethics* III, 1 (1111a22–33).

2. Augustine says in his work *On Free Choice* that stupidity is "the wicked ignorance of the things to be desired and the things to be shunned."[87] But everything wicked is a sin. Therefore, some ignorance is a sin.

Answer:

Not knowing, ignorance, and error differ. For not knowing implies the simple negation of knowledge. And ignorance indeed sometimes means the privation of knowledge, and then ignorance is only to lack the knowledge that nature constituted a person to have, for lacking something appropriate belongs to every privation. And ignorance is sometimes contrary to knowledge, which ignorance we call the ignorance of a perverse disposition. For example, such is the case when a person has the habit of false principles and false opinions, which prevent the person from knowing truth. And error consists of assenting to false things as true. And so error adds an act over and above ignorance. For there can be ignorance without a person making judgments about unknown things, and then the person is ignorant but not erroneous. But when a person makes judgments about things of which the person is ignorant, then we speak in a strict sense about the person erring.

And since sin consists of an act, error evidently has the nature of sin. For it is presumptuous for a person to make judgments about things of which the person is ignorant, and especially in matters involving actual peril. But not knowing, of itself, has neither the nature of moral wrong nor the nature of punishment, since it is neither a moral wrong nor a punishment for a person not to know things unrelated to the person, or things that nature did not constitute the person to know. And so the blessed angels do not know certain things, as Dionysius says in his work *On Ecclesiastical Hierarchy*.[88] But ignorance of itself indicates the character of punishment, although not every ignorance has the character of moral wrong. For example, being ignorant of things that one is not bound to know involves no moral wrong, but the ignorance whereby one does not know things that one is bound to know involves sin. And everyone is obliged to know the things that guide human persons in their actions. And so every human being is obliged to know things belonging to faith, since faith guides our striving, and the commandments of the Decalogue, which enable us to avoid sin and do good. And so the commandments of the Decalogue were also promulgated before all the people, as Ex. 20:22–26 relates, while Moses and Aaron heard the more specialized precepts from the Lord. And each person is obliged to know about the latter precepts things that belong to the person's office. For example, bishops are obliged to know things that belong to their office, and priests things that belong to their office, and so forth. And ignorance of such things involves moral wrong.

Therefore, we can consider such ignorance in three ways. We can consider it in one way as such, and then it has the character of punishment but not the character or moral wrong. For I have said before that the evil of moral wrong consists of the privation of due order in human acts, and the evil of punishment consists of the privation of perfection from the subject who acts.[89] And so the privation of grace or knowledge has the nature of punishment if we consider such privation as such. We can consider such ignorance in

---

87. *On Free Choice* III, 24, n. 71 (PL 32:1306).
88. Actually, *On the Celestial Hierarchy* 7, n. 3 (PG 3:209C).
89. Q. 2, aa. 2 and 3.

a second way in relation to its cause. For just as applying the mind to acquiring knowledge causes knowledge, so not applying the mind to acquiring knowledge causes ignorance. And not applying the mind to acquiring knowledge of what one ought to know is a sin of omission. And so if we understand such privation together with its prior cause, there will be an actual sin in the way in which we call omissions sins. And we can consider such ignorance in relation to its results, and then it sometimes causes sin, as I have said before.[90]

Ignorance can also be related to original sin, as Hugo of St. Victor says.[91] And we should consider this as follows. There is in original sin something formal, namely, the lacking of original justice, which belongs to the will. And original justice, which united the will to God, produced an overflowing of perfection into other powers, namely, that knowledge of truth enlightened the intellect, and that the irascible and concupiscible appetites received direction from reason. Just so, when original justice was taken away from the will, the intellect's knowledge of truth and the irascible and concupiscible appetites' direction by reason are deficient. And so ignorance and concupiscence are the material elements in original sin, just as the turning toward a transient good is the material element in actual sin.

Replies to the Objections:

1. The privations of knowledge and grace have the nature of moral wrong insofar as we understand them along with their cause, which belongs to the genus of action. For we consider acting and nonacting to belong to the same genus, according to the rule introduced by Augustine.

2–3. The foregoing makes clear the solution to the second and third objections.

4. Ignorance, although it deprives persons of some perfection of reason, does not take away the very power of reason, by which power we differ from irrational animals. And so the argument is not valid.

5. The root of every sin consists of the will, as I have said before.[92] Nor does it thereby follow that the willed act is not a sin. And so neither also does it follow that ignorance is not a sin, although the root of the sin consists of the will of the one who is ignorant.

6. Augustine in the cited text is speaking about the sin committed due to ignorance. And this sin sometimes consists only of the will and not of the ignorance itself, for I have said before that not every ignorance is a sin that causes sin.[93]

7. Altogether involuntary ignorance is not a sin, and this is what Augustine says: "Moral wrong is not imputed to you if you are unwillingly in a state of ignorance." And by what he adds, "But if you have neglected to know something, moral wrong is imputed to you," he gives us to understand that ignorance has the character of sin from prior negligence, which is simply the failure to apply the mind to know something that one ought to know.

8. Nothing prevents us from willing something as such and by nature that we nevertheless do not will because of an additional consideration. For example, people by nature

90. A. 6.
91. *On the Sacraments* I, part 7, chap. 27 (PL 176:293D).
92. Q. 2, aa. 2 and 3.
93. A. 6.

will to preserve the integrity of their bodies, and yet they sometimes will that an infected hand be amputated should they fear a danger to the whole body from it. And likewise, human beings by nature will to know, and yet they reject knowledge because of the toil involved in learning or the fear of being kept from the sins they love. And so the will can in some way command ignorance.

9. Although people in a state of ignorance do not know the things of which they are ignorant, they still know either their very state of ignorance or the reason why they do not shun ignorance. And so ignorance can be a voluntary sin.

10. Although ignorance abides after repentance, the guilt of ignorance is taken away.

11. The sin of ignorance consists both of the privation of knowledge and the ignorance associated with its prior cause, which is the failure to acquire knowledge. And, indeed, if this neglect were actually to continue, the guilt regarding it would not pass away. But there is a condition of ignorance relating to original sin with which all of us are born, as I have said.[94]

12. As persons in other sins of omission do not continuously sin when they do not act, but only at the times when they are obliged to act, so is it also about ignorance, and we should so affirm.

Eighth Article

Does Ignorance Excuse or Diminish Sin?

It seems that ignorance does not, for the following reasons:

1. What makes sin more serious neither wholly nor partially excuses it. But ignorance makes sin more serious, for Ambrose comments on Rom. 2:4, "Do you not know that the kindness of God," etc.: "You sin most seriously if you do not know."[95] Therefore, ignorance does not excuse sin either in whole or by ever so much.

2. The *Decretum* says that those who have taken communion with heretics have sinned more seriously by the very fact that they did not know the heretics were in error.[96] Therefore, ignorance makes sin more serious and does not excuse.

3. Drunkenness results in ignorance. But the drunkard who commits homicide or any sin because he is drunk merits "double censures," as the *Ethics* says.[97] Therefore, ignorance increases rather than diminishes sin.

4. Sin added to sin becomes greater sin. But ignorance itself is a sin, as I have said.[98] Therefore, ignorance increases rather than diminishes sin.

5. What is common to every sin does not diminish sin. But ignorance is common to every sin, since every wicked person is ignorant, as the *Ethics* says.[99] And what Prov. 14:22

---

94. In the answer.
95. Actually, Peter Lombard, *Gloss*, on Rom. 2:4 (PL 191:1338D).
96. *Decretum*, c. 24, q. 1, chap. 34 (Freidberg I:979).
97. Aristotle, *Ethics* III, 5 (1113b31–32).
98. A. 7.
99. Aristotle, *Ethics* III, 1 (1110b28).

says, "Those who do evil err," is in accord with this. Therefore, ignorance does not diminish or excuse sin.

On the Contrary:
Sin consists especially of contempt of God. But ignorance diminishes or completely takes away contempt. Therefore, ignorance either wholly or partially excuses.

Answer:
Since it belongs to the nature of sin to be voluntary, ignorance has the ability to excuse sin in whole or in part insofar as ignorance takes away voluntariness. And we should consider that ignorance can take away subsequent but not antecedent voluntariness.

And since ignorance rests in the intellect, we can consider the relation of ignorance to the voluntary by the relation of the intellect to the will. For an act of the intellect necessarily precedes an act of the will, since the understood good is the object of the will. And so when ignorance takes away knowledge by the intellect, the act of the will is taken away, and so the voluntary regarding what is unknown is taken away. And so if regarding the same act, one knows something and is ignorant of something else, there can be something voluntary regarding what is known. But regarding what is unknown, there is always something involuntary. This may be because the deformity of an act is unknown. For example, a person who does not know that fornication is a sin indeed voluntarily commits fornication but does not voluntarily commit sin. Or else there is something involuntary because the circumstance of an act is unknown. For example, a person who has intercourse with a woman he thinks to be his wife indeed voluntarily has intercourse with the woman but not voluntarily with a woman not his wife. And although ignorance always causes something to be not voluntary, it does not always cause something to be involuntary. For we speak of something not being voluntary only by reason of the absence of an act of the will, but we speak of something being involuntary by reason of the fact that the will opposes what is being done. And so the involuntary results in regret, which nonetheless does not always result from something not being voluntary. For example, suppose that a man has intercourse with a woman not his wife whom he believes to be his wife. Although he does not actually will to have intercourse with a woman not his wife, since he does not know that the woman with whom he has intercourse is not his wife, he may habitually will to do so and would actually will to do so if he were to know the fact. And so when he later perceives that the woman was not his wife, he is happy rather than regretful, unless he has changed his will.

And, again, an act of the will can precede an act of the intellect, as when a person wants to understand. And by the same argument as above, willed ignorance falls within the will and becomes voluntary.

And this happens in two ways. First, indeed, it happens when a person directly wills to ignore knowledge of salvation lest the person be drawn away from the sins the person loves. And so Job 21:14 speaks of some who said to God: "Depart from us. We do not want knowledge of your ways." Second, we call ignorance indirectly voluntary because people do not exercise themselves to know, and this is the ignorance of negligence. But since we call persons negligent only when they omit to do what they ought to do, it does not seem to belong to negligence that persons do not apply their minds to know every kind of thing. And it seems that it does belong to negligence if they fail to apply their minds to know things that they ought to know, whether absolutely and at all times, and this is the reason why we reckon ignorance of the law negligence, or in a particular case. For example, we reckon a person who shoots an arrow in a place where human beings customarily pass by to be negligent if the person makes no effort to know whether anyone is passing by at the time. And we reckon such ignorance by reason of negligence to be voluntary.

Third, we speak of ignorance being accidentally voluntary, namely, because a person directly or indirectly wills something from which the very state of ignorance results. A person indeed wills such a thing directly in the evident case of the drunk who wills to drink too much wine, which deprives him of the use of reason. And a person wills such a thing indirectly when the person neglects to resist rising emotional movements that in their intensity limit the exercise of reason in particular choices. And it is in this respect that we call every wicked person ignorant.

Therefore, since we reckon in moral matters that the effects of voluntary things are voluntary, ignorance is voluntary insofar as it lacks what would cause something not to be voluntary and so what excuses from sin. Therefore, when persons directly will to be ignorant so that knowledge does not draw them away from sin, such ignorance neither in whole nor in part excuses from sin but rather increases it. For it seems that some persons out of love of sinning may prefer to suffer loss of knowledge in order to cling freely to sin. And when persons indirectly will to be ignorant because they neglect to learn something, or even when persons will ignorance accidentally by directly or indirectly willing something that results in ignorance, such ignorance does not completely cause the subsequent act to be involuntary. This is so because the subsequent act is voluntary in one respect by the very fact that it proceeds from an ignorance that is voluntary. And yet the antecedent ignorance lessens the nature of the voluntary. For an act that proceeds from such ignorance is less voluntary than if a person were knowingly without any ignorance to choose such an act. And so such ignorance does not excuse the subsequent act altogether but to a degree. Still, we should note that sometimes both the subsequent act itself and the antecedent ignorance constitute one sin in the way in which we call the will and an exterior act one sin. And so it may be the case that a sin is made more serious by the voluntariness of the antecedent ignorance no less than it is excused by the diminished voluntariness of the subsequent act.

And if ignorance is not voluntary in any of the aforementioned ways, as when the ignorance is invincible and without any disorder of the will, then the ignorance makes a subsequent evil act completely involuntary.

Replies to the Objections:

1. The statement of Ambrose is customarily explained as follows: "You sin most seriously," that is, with the greatest risk, "if you are in a state of ignorance," since you do not look for a remedy if you do not know that you are sinning.[100] Or he is speaking about the affected ignorance whereby people will to be ignorant lest they be drawn away from sin. Or he is speaking about ignorance of benefits received, since it is the highest grade of ingratitude for people not to be zealous to know the benefits they have received. Or he is

---

100. E.g., Albert the Great, *Commentary on the Sentences* II, d. 22, a. 9, *ad* 3.

speaking about the ignorance of unbelief, which in itself is the most serious sin, although even sin committed out of such ignorance is diminished, as the Apostle says in 1 Tim. 1:13: "I obtained mercy because I acted in ignorance in my unbelief."

2. The cited authority is speaking about the ignorance of unbelief.

3. Drunks who commit homicide merit double censures because they commit two sins. And yet they sin less regarding the homicide than if they were to kill when sober.

4. Even ignorance that is sinful insofar as it is voluntary diminishes the voluntariness of the subsequent act and so diminishes the subsequent sin. And it may be that such ignorance diminishes more of the subsequent sin than may be the gravity of its own sin.

5. In one who sins habitually and by choice, such ignorance is absolutely an affected ignorance and so does not diminish sin. But the ignorance of those who sin due to the state of their emotions is accidentally voluntary, as I have said,[101] and diminishes sin. For this is to sin out of weakness, by reason of which sin is diminished.

Ninth Article

Can a Person Having Knowledge Sin out of Weakness?

It seems that such a person cannot, for the following reasons:

1. We say that no one whose will has the power to keep the person from something does the thing out of weakness. But the will of everyone having knowledge has the power to keep the person from sin, for Sir. 15:16 says: "If you shall will to keep the commandments, they will keep you." Therefore, no one having knowledge sins out of weakness.

2. No one who possesses the most powerful help against sin sins out of weakness. But everyone having knowledge possesses the strongest help against sin, namely, the certainty of knowledge. Therefore, no one having knowledge sins out of weakness.

3. No power can be active except by reason of its object. For example, the power of sight cannot actually see unless it receive color from an object. But the object of the will, of whose act sin chiefly consists, is the good apprehended by the intellect, as the *De anima* says.[102] Therefore, there can be sin in an act of the will only if there be a deficiency in apprehending the good. But knowledge excludes such a deficiency. Therefore, a person having knowledge cannot sin out of weakness.

4. Only good or an apparent good is the object of the will, since evil is contrary to the will, as Dionysius says in his work *On the Divine Names*.[103] But sin is not in the will insofar as the will's object is a true good. Therefore, every sin is in the will insofar as the will's object is an apparent and not a real good. And such cannot be the case without ignorance. Therefore, a person having knowledge cannot sin out of weakness.

5. People have said that those with general knowledge can be ignorant about particular things related to action and so will sin. For example, such would be the case if a

---

101. In the answer.
102. Aristotle, *De anima* III, 10 (433b11–12).
103. *On the Divine Names* 4, n. 32 (PG 3:732D).

person should know in general that no one should commit fornication, and think that he or she should fornicate now. But as the Philosopher proves in his work *On Interpretation*,[104] contradictory opinions are contraries. And a negative universal proposition and an affirmative particular proposition are contradictory. Therefore, since no one can hold contrary opinions, as contraries cannot belong to the same thing at the same time, it seems that it is impossible for people who hold in general that no one should commit fornication, at the same time to hold in particular that they should.

6. People have said that contradictory opinions are contraries, and knowledge is not contrary to opinion, since they belong to the same genus. But knowledge differs more from false opinion than true opinion, since fear of the contrary accompanies opinion but not knowledge. Therefore, if a person cannot simultaneously hold a true opinion and a contrary false opinion, much less will the person be able simultaneously to have knowledge and a false opinion.

7. Whoever knows something universal and at the same time knows that a singular is included in the universal, draws a conclusion and knows something about the singular, as the *Posterior Analytics* says.[105] For example, one who knows that every mule is sterile and at the same time knows that this animal is a mule, knows that this mule is sterile. But we would reckon that one knowing that no one should commit fornication and not also knowing that a particular act is fornication sins in a state of ignorance, not knowingly. Therefore, if a person does not sin out of ignorance, the person has both universal and particular knowledge.

8. Words are the signs of things understood, as the Philosopher says.[106] But those who actually choose to fornicate, were they asked, would say that this act of fornication is a sin and should not be committed. Therefore, it is not true that they have general but not particular knowledge, as people have said.[107]

9. Augustine says in the *City of God* that shame extinguishes the fires of concupiscence.[108] But knowledge gives rise to shame. Therefore, knowledge extinguishes the fires of concupiscence. But weakness of spirit belongs especially to concupiscence. Therefore, knowledge takes away sins committed out of weakness. Therefore, one having knowledge cannot sin out of weakness.

10. We say that those who know that what they are doing is a sin sin knowingly. But the nature of sin consists of offending God, and the thought of offending God fetters concupiscence, as Ps. 119:120 says: "Pierce my flesh with fear of you, for I am afraid of your judgments." Therefore, knowledge prevents sins committed out of the weakness of concupiscence. And the same conclusion follows as before.

11. Bede posits weakness as one of the four wounds resulting from sin,[109] and so weakness has the nature of punishment. But punishment does not cause sin; rather, punishment is ordained to punish sins. Therefore, one having knowledge cannot commit sin out of weakness.

104. *On Interpretation* II, 14 (23b35ff.).
105. Aristotle, *Posterior Analytics* I, 1 (71a17–21).
106. *On Interpretation* I, 1 (16a3–4).
107. Objection 5.
108. *City of God* XIV, 20 (PL 41:428).
109. Scholars have found no source in the writings of Bede.

12. We take note of weakness of spirit by emotions, which reside in the sensory part of the soul, and sin consists of consent of the will, which resides in the intellectual part of the soul. But causes need to be joined to effects, since contact effects every action. Therefore, weakness cannot cause sin.

13. A proximate cause alters something passive more than a remote cause does. But knowledge, since it resides in the intellect, is closer to the will than is weakness or emotion, which we consider to come from the lower part of the soul linked to the flesh, as Mt. 26:41 says: "The spirit is willing, but the flesh is weak." Therefore, it seems impossible for a person acting against conscience to sin out of weakness.

14. The higher part of the soul, in which the intellect and will rest, also commands the lower parts of the soul in which emotions rest, namely, the irascible and concupiscible appetites, or even bodily members. But defects in bodily members affect only the execution of acts, not commands of the will. Therefore, neither do defects that the irascible and concupiscible appetites have because of the weakness of the emotions affect commands of the will. But sin consists of the will's command. Therefore, no sin is committed out of weakness.

15. We neither merit nor incur demerit because of emotions. But demerit itself is sin. Therefore, no sin is committed because of emotions, which are weaknesses of the soul.

On the Contrary:

1. Isidore says in his work *On the Supreme Good* that some sins are committed out of weakness.[110]

2. The Apostle says in Rom. 7:5: "Sinful emotions, which the Law occasioned, were operative in my members so that the emotions bore fruit unto death." But what bears fruit unto death is sin, as Rom. 6:23 says: "Death is the wage of sin." Therefore, some sins are committed due to emotions, which are weaknesses of the soul.

Answer:

Most people hold that some sins are committed out of weakness. But we would not distinguish such sins from sins of ignorance unless persons having knowledge could sin out of weakness. And so we should admit that persons having knowledge can sin out of weakness.

And to prove this, we need first to consider what we understand by the term *weakness*. And we should understand the term by analogy to bodily weakness. And the body is weak when a fluid is not subject to the governing power of the whole body. For example, such would be the case if a fluid is excessively hot or cold or some such thing. And as there is a power that governs the body, so reason is a power that governs all the internal emotions. And so when the rule of reason does not temper an emotion, and there is too much or too little emotion, we speak of a weakness of the soul. And this especially happens regarding the emotions that we call passions, such as fear, anger, sexual desire, and the like. And so ancient thinkers called such emotions of the soul sicknesses of the soul, as Augustine relates in the *City of God*.[111] Therefore, we say that human beings do

---

110. *On the Supreme Good* II, 17, n. 3 (PL 83:620A).
111. *City of God* XIV, 7, n. 2 (PL 41:411).

out of weakness what they do out of some emotion, for example, anger or fear or sexual desire or some such thing.

And as Aristotle says in the *Ethics*,[112] Socrates, noting the firmness and certainty of knowledge, held that emotion cannot overcome knowledge, namely, that human beings cannot due to emotion do anything contrary to their knowledge. And so Socrates called all virtues kinds of knowledge, and all vices or sins kinds of ignorance. And he concluded from this that no one having knowledge sins out of weakness, which is obviously contrary to things that we daily experience. And so we should consider that there are many ways in which one may have knowledge: in one way in general, in another way in particular; and in one way habitually, and in another way actually. First, it can indeed happen that, due to emotion, one does not actually consider what one knows habitually. For it is evident that whenever one power is intent on its act, another power is hindered or completely turned away from its act. For example, a person intent on hearing someone does not perceive that someone else is passing by. And this happens because all powers are rooted in one and the same soul, whose striving applies each power to its act. And so if a person should be strongly intent on the act of one power, the person's attention regarding the acts of other powers is diminished. Therefore, if there should be a strong desire, whether anger or some such thing, human beings are prevented from considering what they know.

Second, we should note that emotions, as they rest in sense appetites, regard particulars. For example, human beings desire particular pleasures and sensibly perceive particular sweet things. And knowledge regards universals. And yet universal knowledge is the source of acts only as connected to particulars, since acts regard particulars. Therefore, an emotion, if strong regarding some particular thing, resists the contrary movement regarding the same thing both by distracting a person from considering the person's knowledge, as I have just said, and by perverting one's knowledge by reason of the emotion's contrariety. And so even if a person who is constituted in a state of intense emotion should in some way consider regarding the universal, the person's consideration is nonetheless hindered regarding the particular.

Third, we should note that some bodily changes restrict the exercise of reason, so that reason either considers nothing at all or cannot freely reflect, as is evidently the case with those asleep and the insane. And emotions cause bodily changes, so that some persons at times go out of their mind due to anger or sexual desire or some such emotion. And so when such emotions are intense, they, because of the very bodily change, in some way restrict the exercise of reason, so that reason cannot freely judge about doing particular things. And so nothing prevents someone having habitual and general knowledge from sinning out of weakness.

Replies to the Objections:

1. It belongs to the power of the will of human beings to preserve them from sin, but emotions weaken them in this regard, so that they do not fully will when the exercise of reason is fettered, as I have said.[113]

---

112. *Ethics* VII, 2 (1145b21–27).
113. In the answer.

2. Although knowledge in itself is most certain, yet emotions impede it regarding particulars, as I have said,[114] and so knowledge cannot then bring assistance against sin.

3. The connection to an apprehended good moves the will, but emotions sometime impede particular desirable things being apprehended as good by judgments of reason, as I have said.[115]

4. The will always tends toward something under the aspect of good. But sometimes something not good may indeed seem good because the judgment of reason is perverted even regarding the universal, and then there is a sin out of ignorance. And sometimes something not good may seem good because reason is impeded regarding something particular because of emotion, and then there is a sin out of weakness.

5. It is impossible for a person actually to have knowledge or a true opinion about an affirmative universal proposition and a false opinion about a negative particular proposition, or vice versa. But it can well happen that a person has habitual knowledge or true opinion about one contradictory and an actual false opinion about the other, for acts are contrary to acts, not habits.

6. And the foregoing makes clear the solution to the sixth objection.

7. Since sinful and virtuous acts are done by choice, and choice is the desire for something about which one has deliberated beforehand, and deliberation is an inquiry, there needs to be a quasi-syllogistic deduction regarding every virtuous or sinful act. And yet a temperate person syllogizes in one way, an intemperate person in another way, and a continent person in one way, an incontinent person in another way. For only the judgment of reason moves the temperate person. And so the temperate person employs a syllogism with three propositions and deduces like this: no fornication should be committed; this act would be fornication; therefore, I should not do it. And the intemperate person completely follows his desires, and so even such a person employs a syllogism with three propositions and quasi-deduces like this: everything pleasurable should be enjoyed; this act would be pleasurable; therefore, I should do it. But both the continent person and the incontinent person are moved in two ways: indeed by reason to avoid sin, and by concupiscence to commit it. And the judgment of reason prevails in the case of the continent person, while the movement of concupiscence prevails in the case of the incontinent person. And so both employ a syllogism with four propositions but reach contrary conclusions. For the continent person syllogizes as follows. No sin should be committed. And although the judgment of reason proposes this, the movement of concupiscence causes the person to reflect that everything pleasurable should be pursued. But because the judgment of reason prevails in the person, the person subsumes under the first proposition and draws a conclusion as follows: no sin should be committed; this is a sin; therefore, this should not be done. And the incontinent person, in whom the movement of concupiscence prevails, subsumes under the second proposition and draws a conclusion as follows: everything pleasurable should be pursued; this is pleasurable; therefore, this should be pursued. And properly speaking, such a person is one who sins out of weakness. And so it is evident that such a person, although knowing regarding the universal, nonetheless does not know regarding the particular, since the person subsumes according to concupiscence and not according to reason.

114. Ibid.
115. Ibid.

8. As the Philosopher says in the *Ethics*,[116] just as drunks utter words that they do not inwardly understand, so a person overcome by emotion, although outwardly saying the words "This should be shunned," inwardly judges that it should be done. And so the person says one thing externally and thinks another thing internally.

9. Knowledge indeed sometimes overcomes concupiscence, whether by arousing shame or by inciting dread of offending God. But this does not prevent knowledge also being overcome by emotion in particular cases.

10. And so the solution to the tenth objection is evident.

11. Every punishment taken into consideration deflects persons from sin, but not every punishment as already inflicted does so. For example, privation of grace is a punishment, and yet persons are not deflected from sin because they are deprived of grace, but because they consider that they are deprived of grace if they should sin. And we should say the like about ignorance.

12. Consent to an act indeed belongs to the intellectual appetite, and yet there is no consent without connection to something particular, regarding which the emotions of the soul can be most powerful. And so emotions sometimes affect consent.

13. Reason is closer to the will than emotions are, but emotions are closer to particular desirable things than reason, which universalizes, is.

14. The soul governs the body like a slave, and a slave cannot resist the command of his master. But as the Philosopher says in the *Politics*,[117] reason governs the irascible and concupiscible powers by a kingly and political governance, which is the governance proper to a free people. And so the irascible and concupiscible powers can resist even the commands of reason, just as free citizens sometimes resist the commands of rulers.

15. We neither merit nor incur demerit by reason of emotions as if merit or demerit consists chiefly of them, and yet they can be a help or hindrance to meriting or incurring demerit.

Tenth Article

Do We Impute Sins Committed out of Weakness to Human Beings as Mortal Sins?

It seems that we do not, for the following reasons:

1. We impute as mortal sin nothing that human beings do not do voluntarily. But human beings do not voluntarily commit sins done out of weakness, since the Apostle says about such sins in Gal. 5:17: "The flesh lusts against the spirit, so that you do not do the things you wish to do." Therefore, we do not impute such sins to human beings as mortal sins.

2. No passive power can act except as its active power moves it to act. But properly speaking, nature constitutes reason to move the will. Therefore, if emotions should impede the judgment of reason, it seems that the will does not have the power to avoid sin.

---

116. *Ethics* VII, 3 (1147a10–b19).
117. *Politics* I, 2 (1254b5–6).

Therefore, we do not impute sin to the will as a mortal sin.

3. The soul's emotions, by reason of their proximity, impede reason and the will more than the body's undergoing change does. But the body's undergoing change completely absolves disordered deeds of moral fault, as is evidently the case regarding deeds by those asleep and by the insane. Therefore, much more do the soul's emotions excuse persons from moral fault.

4. People have said that the soul's emotions are voluntary, and that the body's undergoing change is not. But effects are not more powerful than their causes. And emotions as voluntary have only the nature of venial, not mortal, sin. Therefore, neither can emotions cause mortal sin.

5. Consequences do not make sins infinitely more serious, namely, so as to make sins mortal which are in themselves venial. But emotions themselves, were no evil choice to result, would not be mortal sins. Therefore, human beings do not incur the moral fault of mortal sin because of the fact that an evil choice results. And so sins committed out of weakness are not mortal.

On the Contrary:

The Apostle says in Rom. 7:5: "Sinful emotions were so active in our bodily members that the emotions bore fruit unto death." But only mortal sin bears fruit unto death. Therefore, sins committed due to emotions or weakness can be mortal.

Answer:

Since persons sometimes out of weakness or due to emotion commit adultery and many shameful or criminal deeds, as Peter did when he denied Christ out of fear,[118] no one should doubt that sins committed out of weakness are sometimes mortal.

And to prove this, we should note that necessity does not take away the nature of mortal sin, if we assume that the necessity belongs to something subject to the will. For example, if a sword is thrust into someone's vital organs, the person necessarily dies, but the thrusting of the sword is voluntary. And so we impute the death of the person struck by the sword to the person who struck the blow, as a mortal moral fault. We should say likewise about the matter under discussion. For granted that emotion fetters reason, an evil choice necessarily results, but the will retains the power to resist the fettering of reason. For I have said that reason is fettered because the soul's attention is powerfully focused on the activity of a sense appetite, and so reason is diverted from considering regarding the particular what it knows habitually regarding the universal.[119] And the will has the power to focus or not focus attention on something, and so the will has the power to eliminate the fettering of reason. Therefore, the deeds proceeding from such fettering are voluntary, and so the deeds are not excused from moral fault, even mortal moral fault. But if the fettering of reason by emotion were to progress to such a point that the will would not have the power to remove such fetters, as, for example, if some emotion of the soul were to make someone insane, we would not impute any deed committed to that or any other insane person as a moral fault. And yet, we might perhaps impute such

118. Mt. 27:70–72.
119. A. 9.

deeds to such persons regarding the emotion's beginning, which was voluntary, for the will could at the start have prevented the emotion going so far. For example, we impute homicide committed due to drunkenness to a human being as a moral fault, since the initial drunkenness was voluntary.

Replies to the Objections:

1. A person free of emotion does not will to do what the person fettered by emotion does, but emotion leads the person to will the deed when emotion fetters reason.

2. The will is moved by the comprehension of reason fettered by emotion. And it has the power to exclude the fetters on reason, as I have said.[120] And to that extent we impute deeds to the will as sins.

3. The will does not have the power to remove matter's subjectivity to change. But it can remove the soul's emotions, since the nature of matter is not subject to the rational will as sense appetites are. And so there is no comparison.

4. Nothing prevents something that is a mortal sin in a particular situation from not being a mortal sin absolutely. For example, not giving alms to a pauper dying of hunger is a mortal sin, but not giving alms in other circumstances would not be a mortal sin. And likewise in the matter under discussion, not willing to resist some emotion, although not a mortal sin absolutely, is a mortal sin in the situation where the emotion inclines a person to the point of consenting to mortal sin.

5. Future and unforeseen consequences do not make sins infinitely more serious, but associated and foreseen consequences can, so that there is a mortal sin that otherwise would not be mortal. For example, shooting an arrow is not a mortal sin, but shooting an arrow in conjunction with killing someone is. And likewise, not resisting an emotion that inclines one to mortal sin involves mortal sin.

Eleventh Article

Does Weakness Make Sin Less or More Serious?

It seems that weakness makes sin more serious, for the following reasons:

1. An evil emotion is related to sin just as a good emotion is related to merit. But a good emotion increases merit, since it is more praiseworthy and meritorious that a person give alms with merciful compassion than without it, as Augustine makes evident in the *City of God*.[121] Therefore, committing sin with emotion is more blameworthy and a greater sin. But sinning due to emotion is sinning out of weakness, as I have said.[122] Therefore, weakness makes sin more serious.

2. Since every sin results from inordinate desire, as Augustine says,[123] the more inordinate the desire from which a person's sin results, the more the person seems to sin.

---

120. In the answer.
121. *City of God* IX, 5 (PL 41:261).
122. A. 9.
123. *On Free Choice* I, 3, n. 8 (PL 32:1225).

But inordinate desire is an emotion of the soul and a weakness. Therefore, weakness makes sin more serious.

3. Effects are greater when their causes are greater. For example, greater heat results in greater heating. Therefore, if weakness causes sin, then greater weakness causes greater sin. And so weakness makes sin more serious.

On the Contrary:

What makes sin pardonable makes sin less, not more, serious. But we say that weakness makes sin more pardonable. Therefore, weakness makes sin less, not more, serious.

Answer:

Sinning out of weakness is sinning due to emotion, as I have said.[124] And the emotions of sense appetites are related to movements of the will in two ways: in one way as prior; in the second way as subsequent. Emotions indeed precede movements of the will, as when emotions incline the will to will something. And then emotions diminish the character of merit and the character of demerit, since merit and demerit consist of choice based on prior reasoning, and emotions cloud or even fetter the judgments of reason. And the purer the judgment of reason, the sharper the choice to gain merit or incur demerit. And so one whom the judgment of reason induces to perform a good work acts in a more praiseworthy manner than one whom only an emotion of the soul induces to do so, since the latter can sometimes err by being unduly compassionate. And likewise, one whom the deliberation of reason induces to commit sin sins more than one whom only an emotion of the soul induces to commit sin.

And we consider emotions as subsequent to movements of the will when strong movements of the will move lower appetites to emotions. And then emotions add to merit or demerit, since the emotions signify the greater intensity of the will's movements. And it is true in this sense that one who gives alms with greater compassion earns greater merit, and that one who commits sin with greater sexual lust sins more, since the emotions signify the greater intensity of the will's movements. But this is not to perform a good work or sin out of emotion; rather, it is to be affected by the choice of good or evil.

Replies to the Objections:

1–2. And so the replies to the first and second objections are clear.

3. It belongs to the nature of sin to be voluntary. And we call voluntary something whose source rests in the very one acting. And so, the greater the internal source, the more serious the sin also becomes, and the greater the external source, the less serious the sin becomes. But emotions are a source external to the will, and movements of the will the internal source. And so, the more intense the movement of the will to commit sin, the greater the sin, and the more intense the emotion inducing to commit sin, the lesser the sin.

124. A. 9.

Twelfth Article

Can a Person Sin out of Malice, That Is, Deliberate Malice?

It seems that a person cannot, for the following reasons:

1. Human beings intend what they do deliberately. But as Dionysius says in his work *On the Divine Names*,[125] no one does something with an intention to do evil. Therefore, no one does evil with deliberate malice.

2. Powers can only be moved to their objects. But the will's object is the good apprehended by the intellect. Therefore, no person can will what the person knows to be evil, and so no one can sin out of deliberate malice.

3. People have said that the will tends toward a good with an associated evil, and that the will to that extent tends toward evil. But the soul's acts of both understanding and desire can distinguish things really inseparable. For example, we can understand the spherical apart from sensibly perceptible matter, and a man may desire to be an abbot without wishing to be a monk. Therefore, although evil is associated with a good, it is nonetheless not necessary, as it seems, that one is borne to evil because one is borne to the good associated with the evil.

4. We designate things by what belongs to them intrinsically, not by what they are accidentally, since we judge things in this way. But we do not say that a person, by willing something as such, wills something else associated with it, except incidentally. For example, one who loves wine because of its sweetness, loves wine only by chance. And so when a person wills a good with an associated evil, the person wills the evil only incidentally. Therefore, we should not say that one sins out of malice, as if one wills evil.

5. Whoever sins out of weakness wills the evil associated with a good. Therefore, if we should say that one on that account sins out of malice, it also follows that one who sins out of weakness sins out of malice. And this conclusion is evidently false.

6. People have said that the will of one who sins out of malice moves itself to evil in the aforementioned way, and that the will of one who sins out of weakness does not. Rather, it is as if emotions move the will of those who sin out of weakness. But for something to move itself is for its form or nature to incline it to do something, as, for example, heavy things are of themselves moved downward. And the will by its form and nature tends toward good, not evil. Therefore, the will cannot of itself tend toward evil, and so no one will sin out of malice.

7. The will of itself tends toward the good by the general nature of good. Therefore, it is necessary regarding different kinds of good that the will tend to a good as some other determinant inclines the will. But there are different kinds of good, real good and apparent good, and the will tends toward real good by the judgment of reason. Therefore, regarding an apparent good with an associated evil, the will tends to such a good as something else inclines it, not of itself. Therefore, no one sins out of malice.

8. We sometimes understand malice as moral fault, as malice is contrary to virtue, and we sometimes understand malice as punishment, as Bede says that sin draws in four

---

125. *On the Divine Names* 4, n. 19 (PG 3:716C).

things: ignorance, weakness, malice, and concupiscence.[126] But we cannot say that one sins out of malice if we should understand malice as moral fault, since the same thing would cause its very self, namely, malice would cause malice. Nor, moreover, can we say that one sins out of malice if we should understand malice as punishment, since every punishment belongs to the aspect of weakness, and so sinning out of malice would be sinning out of weakness. And this conclusion is improper. Therefore, no one sins out of malice.

9. A person may sometimes commit a very slight sin deliberately, as, for example, when a person says an idle word or a lie in jest. But we say that sins committed out of malice are the most serious. Therefore, sinning deliberately is not sinning out of malice.

10. Dionysius says in his work *On the Divine Names* that good is the source and goal of every action.[127] But that by reason of which one sins is either the internal source inclining one to commit sin, such as a habit or an emotion or some like thing, or the intended goal. Therefore, no one sins out of malice.

11. If anyone sins out of malice, this seems especially true about one who chooses to sin. But every sin is by choice, according to Damascene.[128] Therefore, every sin would be out of malice.

12. Malice is contrary to virtue. And so inasmuch as virtue is a habit, malice is also a habit, since contraries belong to the same genus. And some virtuous habits rest in the irascible and concupiscible powers, as the Philosopher in the *Ethics* says that moderation and fortitude belong to the irrational parts of the soul.[129] But it belongs to the power of free choice, not to the aforementioned powers, to choose. Therefore, we should not say that sins committed by choice proceed from malice.

13. One who sins out of malice seems to will the very sinning and wrongdoing. But this cannot happen, since *synderesis*, which always murmurs against evil, is never extinguished. Therefore, no one sins out of malice.

On the Contrary:

1. Job 34:27 says: "They deliberately, as it were, withdrew from God and did not want to know his ways." But to withdraw from God is to sin. Therefore, some sin deliberately, and this is to sin out of malice.

2. Augustine says in his *Confessions* that when he happened to be stealing fruit, he loved his delinquency, namely, the very theft, not the fruit itself.[130] But to love evil itself is to sin out of malice. Therefore, a person can sin out of malice.

3. Envy is a kind of malice. But some sin out of envy. Therefore, some sin out of malice.

Answer:

Some thinkers held that no one voluntarily does evil, as the Philosopher says in the *Ethics*.[131] And the Philosopher says against them in the same place that it is contradictory to say that one wills to commit adultery and wills not to be unjust.[132]

126. Scholars have found no source in the writings of Bede.
127. *On the Divine Names* 4, n. 31 (PG 3:732B).
128. Actually, Nemesius, *On Human Nature* 40 (PG 40:679B).
129. *Ethics* III, 10 (1117b23–24).
130. *Confessions* II, 6, n. 12 (PL 32:680).
131. *Ethics* III, 5 (1113b14–15).
132. Ibid., III, 5 (1114a11).

And the reason for this is that we call something voluntary both if the will is borne to it primarily and intrinsically as an end, and if the will is borne to it as the means to an end. For example, a sick person wills both to regain health and in order to regain health, to swallow bitter medicine that the person otherwise would not. And similarly, a merchant voluntarily jettisons cargo to prevent a ship from sinking. Therefore, suppose that persons happen to will to enjoy some pleasure (e.g., adultery or any like desirable thing) so much that they would not shun incurring the deformity of sin that they perceive to be involved in what they will. Not only will we say that the persons will the good that they chiefly will, but also that they will the very deformity that they choose to suffer lest they be deprived of the good they desire. And so the adulterer both chiefly wills the pleasure and secondarily wills the deformity. And Augustine gives a similar example in his work *On the Lord's Sermon on the Mount*,[133] that a man because of his love of a maid servant voluntarily endures harsh servitude under her master.

And it can happen in two ways that someone wills a transient good so much as not to flee being turned away from the permanent good. It happens in one way because the person does not know that such turning away is connected with the transient good, and then we say that the person sins out of ignorance. It happens in the second way because something internal inclines the will to that good. And something is inclined to something else in two ways. It is inclined in one way as it is acted upon by something else, as when a stone is thrown up in the air. It is inclined in a second way by its own form, and then it is of itself inclined to something, as when a stone falls down to the ground. And likewise, an emotion indeed sometimes inclines the will to the transient good with which a deformity of sin is connected, and then we say that a person sins out of weakness, as I have said before.[134] And a habit sometimes inclines the will, when customary behavior has, as it were, turned the inclination to such a good into a habit or natural disposition for the transient good, and then the will of itself is inclined to the good by its own motion apart from any emotion. And this is to sin by choice, that is, deliberately, or purposely or even maliciously.

Replies to the Objections:

1. No one by acting intends evil as the object chiefly willed, and yet the very evil consequently becomes voluntary for a person when the person, in order to enjoy the desired good, does not flee incurring the evil.

2. The will is always chiefly borne to something good, and due to an intense movement to a good, the will may put up with an evil associated with such a good.

3. It sometimes happens that the will is borne to a good with which an evil is connected, and yet is not borne to the evil. For example, such would be the case if a person were to desire the pleasure in adultery but flee the deformity of adultery and so also reject the pleasure. But it also sometimes happens that a person also voluntarily incurs the deformity of moral fault.

4. What is connected with a good chiefly desired, if unforeseen and unknown, is not willed except by accident. For example, such would be the case if a person sinning

133. *On the Lord's Sermon on the Mount* II, 14, n. 47 (PL 34:1290).
134. Aa. 10 and 11.

out of ignorance wills something that the person does not know is a sin, although it is in fact a sin, since such a person wills evil only by accident. But if the person should know that it is a sin, the person consequently now wills the evil, as I have said,[135] and not only by accident.

5. When we say that a person sins "out of" something, we are given to understand that the thing is the primary source of the sin. And in the case of one who sins out of weakness, the willing of evil is not the primary source of the sin; rather, emotion causes the sin. But in the case of one who sins out of malice, the willing of evil is the primary source of the sin, since the will is of its very self and by its disposition, and not by any external source, inclined to will evil.

6. The form by which the sinner acts is both the very power of the will and the habits that internally incline the will as natural dispositions.

7. The foregoing also makes clear the solution to the seventh objection.

8. When we say that a person sins out of malice, we can understand malice in that context either as a habit contrary to a virtue or as moral fault, as we call internal acts of the will, or choices, moral faults and the causes of external acts. And so it does not follow that the same thing causes its very self.

9. Malice is contrary to the virtue that consists of the good character of the mind, and venial sins are not contrary to this virtue. And so if a person deliberately commits a venial sin, it is not done out of malice.

10. Good is primarily and chiefly the source and goal of action, but also evil can be willed secondarily and consequently, as I have said.[136]

11. There can be choice even in a sin of weakness, and yet choice is not the primary source of such sinning, since emotions cause the sinning. And so we do not say that such a person sins by choice, although the person sins when choosing.

12. As emotions resting in the irascible and concupiscible powers cause choices insofar as such emotions fetter reason for the moment, so habits belonging to those powers cause choices insofar as such habits fetter reason as immanent forms, not as presently transient emotions.

13. The universal principles of natural law, about which no one errs, belong to *synderesis*. But emotions and habits fetter reason in a person who sins regarding particular things to be chosen.

Replies to the Arguments in the Section On the Contrary:

1–2. Although the arguments presented in the section reach true conclusions, we should note regarding the second argument that when Augustine says that he loved his very delinquency, not the fruit that he was stealing, we should not so understand this statement as if the very delinquency or the deformity of moral fault could be primarily and intrinsically willed. Rather, he primarily and intrinsically willed either to exhibit typical behavior to his peers or to experience something or to do something against the rules or some such thing.

3. And we should note regarding the third argument that we cannot say that every sin that another sin causes has been committed out of malice. This is because it can be

135. In the answer.
136. Ibid.

the case that a first sin that causes another has been committed out of weakness or due to emotion, and that in order that a person sin out of malice, it is necessary that malice be the primary source of the sin, as I have said.[137]

Thirteenth Article

Does the Sinner out of Malice Sin More Seriously Than the Sinner out of Weakness?

It seems that the sinner out of malice does not, for the following reasons:

1. Rev. 3:15–16 says: "Would that you were hot or cold, but because you are lukewarm, I shall begin to vomit you out of my mouth." But one who does good deeds seems to be hot, and one who sins out of weakness (e.g., the incontinent person) seems to be lukewarm, and one who sins out of malice (e.g., the intemperate person) seems to be completely cold. Therefore, it is more dangerous to sin out of weakness than to sin out of malice.

2. Sir. 42:14 says: "The wickedness of a man is better than a woman doing a good deed." And some have understood this so that man means one who is energetic to act with courage, and woman means one who is lax and tepid about action. But the former seems to belong to the intemperate person who acts out of malice, as I have said,[138] and the latter seems to belong to the incontinent person who sins out of weakness. Therefore, it is worse to sin out of weakness than to sin out of malice.

3. The *Collations of the Fathers* says that the sinner attains the fervor for perfection more easily than the lax and tepid monk does.[139] But the sinner is especially one who acts out of malice, and the lax person is one who is weak about acting. Therefore, it is worse to sin out of weakness than to sin out of malice.

4. The person who cannot benefit from either the food or the medicine that supports others is most dangerously weak. But neither knowledge nor good intentions benefit the incontinent person who sins out of weakness, since emotions turn the person away from virtue. Therefore, the incontinent person sins most dangerously.

5. The more intense the emotion that drives a person to sin, the less seriously does the person sin. But the impulse from habits is stronger than the impulse from emotions. Therefore, one whom habits incline to commit sin, one who, we say, sins out of malice, as I have said,[140] sins less than one whom emotions incline to sin, one who, we say, sins out of weakness.

6. Inherent forms, as natural dispositions, move to evil those who sin out of malice. But insofar as nature moves something to anything, the movement is necessary, not voluntary. Therefore, those who sin out of deliberate malice do not sin voluntarily. Therefore, they sin either not at all or the least seriously.

137. Ibid.
138. Objection 1.
139. Cassian, *Collations* IV, 19 (PL 49:606C).
140. A. 12.

On the Contrary:

What leads to mercy makes sin less serious. But weakness leads to mercy, as the Ps. 103:13–14 says: "The Lord has mercy on those who fear him, since he knows our constitution." Therefore, sins committed out of weakness are less serious than sins committed out of malice.

Answer:

Sins committed out of malice, other things being equal, are more serious than sins committed out of weakness.

And three arguments make the reason for this evident. The first, indeed, is that, since we call voluntary something whose source is in the very one who acts, the more the source of an act is in the one who acts, the more something is voluntary, and so the more sin there is if the act be evil. And it is clear from what I have said before,[141] that when one sins due to emotion, the source of the sin is the emotion, which rests in a sense appetite, and so such a source is external to the will. But when one sins due to a habit, which is to sin out of malice, then the will of its very self, as now completely inclined to the act of sin by the habit as a natural inclination, tends to the act. And so the sin is more voluntary and consequently more serious.

The second argument is that in one who sins out of weakness, or emotion, the will is inclined to an act of sin as long as the emotion lasts, but immediately after the passage of the emotion, which passes quickly, the will recedes from the inclination and, repenting the sin committed, returns to its intention to do good. But in one who sins out of malice, the will is inclined to an act of sin as long as an evil habit remains, and the habit does not pass away but persists as a form already immanent and connatural. And so those who so sin continue to will to sin and do not easily repent. And so the Philosopher in the *Ethics* compares an intemperate person to a person who suffers from a chronic disease (e.g., a victim of consumption or dropsy), an incontinent person to a person who suffers intermittently from a disease (e.g., an epileptic).[142] And so it is evident that one who sins out of malice sins more seriously and more dangerously than one who sins out of weakness.

The third argument is that those who sin out of weakness have a will ordained to a good end, for they intend and seek to do good but sometimes retreat from their good intentions due to emotions. But those who sin out of malice have a will ordained to an evil end, for they have a fixed intention to sin. And it is clear that an end in matters of desire and action is like a first principle in theoretical matters, as the Philosopher says in the *Physics*.[143] And a person who errs about first principles is ignorant in the most serious and dangerous way, since there are no prior principles to lead the person away from the error. And a person who errs only about conclusions can be led away from error by first principles, regarding which the person does not err. Therefore, one who sins out of malice sins most seriously and most dangerously and cannot be recalled from sin as easily as one who sins out of weakness, in whom there remains at least a good intention.

---

141. Aa. 9 and 10.
142. *Ethics* VII, 8 (1150b32–35).
143. *Physics* II, 9 (200a34–b1).

Replies to the Objections:

1. The cited text calls cold the unbeliever, who has some excuse in that the unbeliever sins out of ignorance, as the Apostle says in 1 Tim. 1:13: "I obtained mercy because I in my unbelief acted out of ignorance." And the text calls lukewarm the Christian sinner, who sins more seriously in the same genus of sin, as the Apostle says in Heb. 10:29: "How much more severe punishments do you think one who has profaned the blood of the covenant deserves," etc. And so the authority of the cited text is not relevant to the matter under discussion.

2. According to a gloss,[144] the man in the cited text is a prudent and energetic person, who, although he sometimes sins, takes from the very sin an occasion for good (e.g., an occasion for humility and greater caution). And the cited text calls the woman an imprudent person, who takes from a good deed an occasion to endanger herself when pride in the good deed causes her to fall into sin. Or we can say in a literal sense that the wickedness of a man, that is, a wicked man to dally in conversation with a woman, is better than a woman doing a good deed. This is because a man would be more easily precipitated into sin by familiar conversation with a good woman than with an evil man. And this is made clear by what precedes in the cited text,[145] "Tarry not among women," and by what follows,[146] "A woman confusing a man to his reproach." And so the cited text is not relevant to the matter under discussion.

3. One who is lax in doing good deeds is immeasurably better than one who does evil. And by this very fact, sinners considering their evil may sometimes be so strongly moved against the evil that they achieve fervor for perfection. But those who do good, albeit laxly, have not done anything that they should much dread, and so they rest more content in their condition and are not so easily brought to better things.

4. Those who sin out of weakness, although knowledge and good intentions do not help them when they sin, can later be helped by habituating themselves to resist emotions. But it is difficult to lead away from error one who sins out of malice, just as it is in the case of one who errs regarding first principles, as I have said.[147]

5. The impulses from emotions diminish sin, since they are from an external source, as it were. But the impulses from the will increase sin, since the more intense the will's movement to commit sin, the more seriously does the person sin. And habits make movements of the will more intense, and so one who sins habitually sins more seriously.

6. Virtuous or vicious habits are forms of the rational soul, and every form is in something in the way the thing receives the form. And it belongs to the nature of a rational creature that it is free to choose, and so virtuous and vicious habits do not incline the will in a necessary way, so that a person cannot act contrary to the nature of the habits. But it is difficult to act contrary to the things to which the habits incline.

---

144. *Ordinary Gloss*, on Sir. 42:14, from Gregory the Great, *Morals* XI, 49, n. 65 (PL 75:982D).
145. Sir. 42:12.
146. Sir. 42:14.
147. In the answer.

Fourteenth Article

Is Every Sin Done out of Malice a Sin
against the Holy Spirit?

It seems that not every sin done out of malice is, for the following reasons:

1. Sins against the Holy Spirit are sins of speech, as Mt. 12:32 makes clear: "Whoever shall speak against the Holy Spirit," etc. But sins done out of malice can be sins of desire or of deed. Therefore, not every sin done out of malice is a sin against the Holy Spirit.

2. The sin against the Holy Spirit is a special genus of sin, for it has set species, namely, obstinacy, despair, and the like, as the Master makes clear in the *Sentences*.[148] But sin done out of malice is not a special genus of sin, since there may be sinning out of malice, just like sinning out of weakness or ignorance, in every genus of sin. Therefore, not every sin done out of malice is a sin against the Holy Spirit.

3. The sin against the Holy Spirit is the sin of blasphemy, as Lk. 12:10 makes clear: "There will be no pardon for one who has blasphemed against the Holy Spirit." But blasphemy is a species of sin. Therefore, since sin done out of deliberate malice is not a species of sin, as there can be such sin in every genus of sin, it seems that not every sin done out of malice is a sin against the Holy Spirit.

4. We predicate sins done out of malice of those whom malice pleases for its own sake, as goodness pleases the pious for its own sake, as the Master says in the *Sentences*.[149] But a set species of virtue is not constituted by the fact that virtue pleases someone for its own sake. Therefore, neither is a set species of sin constituted by the fact that malice pleases someone for its own sake. And so, since the sin against the Holy Spirit is a set species of sin, it seems that not every sin done out of malice is a sin against the Holy Spirit.

5. Augustine says in a letter to his companion Boniface that every sin, in whatever way human beings have estranged themselves from God unto the end of their lives, is a sin against the Holy Spirit.[150] But this may be the case regarding even sins done out of weakness and ignorance. Therefore, sinning against the Holy Spirit and sinning out of malice are not the same thing.

6. The Master says in the *Sentences* that those who think that their malice surpasses God's goodness sin against the Holy Spirit.[151] But those who think that err, and all who err are in a state of ignorance. Therefore, it seems that the sin against the Holy Spirit is more a sin of ignorance than a sin of weakness.

7. We say in two ways that a person sins due to something: in one way as due to the power, habit, or disposition eliciting the act; in a second way as due to the end that causes the will's movement. But we cannot say that one sinning against the Holy Spirit sins due to malice as a habit or disposition eliciting the act, since then every sin would be a sin against the Holy Spirit. Nor, moreover, can we say that one sinning against the Holy Spirit

---

148. *Sentences* II, d. 43, chap. 1, nn. 1–5.
149. Ibid., n. 2.
150. *Letter* 185, chap. 11, n. 49 (PL 33:814).
151. *Sentences* II, d. 43, chap. 1, n. 2.

sins due to malice as the end moving the will, since malice as such cannot be the end causing the movement. For no one acts intending to do evil, as Dionysius says in his work *On
the Divine Names*.[152] And if we should call malice a cause of the will's movement because
of the apparent good associated with it, then every sin would be due to malice, since there
is in every sin an apparent good associated with evil that is the cause of the will's movement. Therefore, a sin against the Holy Spirit is not the same as a sin done out of malice.

8.   There are two kinds of malice, namely: contracted malice (as Bede posits malice
as one of the four things that result from the sin of our first parent)[153] and committed
malice, which is actual sin. But we cannot call a sin against the Holy Spirit a sin done out
of contracted malice, since contracted malice belongs to the deficiency and weakness of
our nature, and so a sin against the Holy Spirit would be a sin done out of weakness. Nor
can we call a sin against the Holy Spirit a sin done out of committed malice, since then it
would be necessary that an actual sin precede the sin against the Holy Spirit, and this is
not true regarding every species of sin against the Holy Spirit. Therefore, a sin against
the Holy Spirit is not a sin done out of malice.

9.   The masters call sins against the Holy Spirit sins that are not easily pardoned.
But this is true about every sin that proceeds from a habit. For Augustine says in his
Confessions that inordinate desire results from a perverse will, habituation from inordinate desire, and necessity from habituation.[154] Therefore, every sin done out of habit, even
if it be done out of weakness or ignorance, not out of malice, is a sin against the Holy
Spirit, since habituation causes vicious habits. Therefore, sinning against the Holy Spirit
and sinning out of malice are not the same thing.

On the Contrary:

1.   The Master says in the *Sentences* that those whom malice pleases for its very own sake
sin against the Holy Spirit.[155] But we say that such people sin out of malice. Therefore,
sinning out of malice and sinning against the Holy Spirit are the same thing.

2.   As we appropriate power to the Father and wisdom to the Son, so we appropriate goodness to the Holy Spirit. But we can say that those who sin out of weakness, which
is the contrary of power, sin against the Father, and that those who sin out of ignorance,
which is the contrary of wisdom, sin against the Son. Therefore, we can say that those
who sin out of malice, which is the contrary of goodness, sin against the Holy Spirit.

Answer:

Particular theologians have spoken in many ways about sin against the Holy Spirit. For
example, the holy teachers who lived before Augustine, namely, Hilary,[156] Ambrose,[157]
Jerome,[158] and Chrysostom,[159] said that the sin against the Holy Spirit occurs when one

152. *On the Divine Names* 4, n. 19 (PG 3:716C).
153. Scholars have found no source in the writings of Bede.
154. *Confessions* VIII, 5, n. 10 (PL 32:753).
155. *Sentences* II, d. 43, chap. 1, n. 2.
156. *Commentary on Matthew*, 12, n. 17 (PL 9:989).
157. *Commentary on Luke*, VII, n. 119 (PL 15: 1729B).
158. *On Matthew* 12:32 (PL 26:81, 84A).
159. *On Matthew*, hom. 41, n. 3 (PG 57:449).

blasphemes the Holy Spirit, whether we consider the Holy Spirit essentially, as we can call the whole Trinity both spirit and holy, or we consider the Holy Spirit personally, as the third Person in the Trinity. And this seems to be in sufficient agreement with the text of the Gospel, from which this question originates. For example, the Pharisees, because they were saying that Christ cast out devils by Beelzebub,[160] blasphemed both Christ's divinity and the Holy Spirit through whom Christ acted, and ascribed to the prince of devils what Christ did by the power of his divinity or by the Holy Spirit. And so also the sin against the Holy Spirit is contrasted with the sin against the Son, that is, the sin against the humanity of Christ. And because Mt. 12:32 says that the sin against the Holy Spirit is not pardoned in this world or the next, it would seem to follow that those who blaspheme the Holy Spirit or the divinity of Christ could never have their sin pardoned. But the church does not deny baptism, which pardons sins, to Jews or pagans or heretics who have blasphemed Christ's divinity and the Holy Spirit, as Augustine objects in his work *On the Words of the Lord*.[161]

And so Augustine in his work *On the Lord's Sermon on the Mount* seems to limit the sin against the Holy Spirit to those who, after recognizing the truth and receiving the sacraments, blaspheme the Holy Spirit.[162] They blaspheme the Holy Spirit in words, as unbelievers do when they blaspheme the very Person of the Holy Spirit, and in desire, when they envy the truth and grace that come from the Holy Spirit, or even in hostile deeds against the Holy Spirit. Nor is this contradicted by the fact that the Pharisees to whom the Lord spoke such things were unbelievers not previously initiated into the sacraments of faith. This is so because the Lord did not mean to say that the Pharisees themselves had hitherto sinned unpardonably against the Holy Spirit, since he adds: "Either make the tree good and its fruit good," etc.[163] Rather, he meant to warn them lest they, by blaspheming as they were, at some point of time reach the level of unpardonable sin. But, again, Augustine in his work *On the Words of the Lord* objects that the Lord does not say that there is no pardon in baptism for those who have sinned against the Holy Spirit, but says that there is no pardon for them in any way in this world or the next.[164] And so this sin does not seem to fall upon the baptized rather than others, since, notwithstanding the sin, the Church does not deny forgiveness to any sinner if the sinner has repented.

And so Augustine in his work *Retractions* rejects the opinion of the teachers who preceded him, adding that those who attack known truth and envy the grace accorded brethren sin against the Holy Spirit only when they persist in this unto their dying breath.[165] And to prove this, we should consider what he says about this in his work *On the Words of the Lord*.[166] For he in that work says that we should note that we should not understand as universally true everything indistinctly presented in sacred Scripture. For example, Jn. 15:22 says: "If I had not come and spoken to them, they would have no sin."

---

160. Mt. 12:24.
161. *On the Words of the Lord*, sermon 71, chap. 3, nn. 5–6 (PL 38:447–48).
162. *On the Lord's Sermon on the Mount* I, 22, nn. 73–75 (PL 34:1266–67).
163. Mt. 12:33.
164. *On the Words of the Lord*, sermon 71, chap. 3, n. 6 (PL 38:448).
165. *Retractions* I, 19, n. 7 (PL 32:616).
166. *On the Words of the Lord*, sermon 71, chaps. 6–9 (PL 38:450–52).

But this should not be understood to mean that they would have no sin at all, but to mean that they would not have a certain sin, the one they committed by despising the preaching and miracles of Christ. Therefore, when Mt. 12:32 says distinctly, "Those who spoke against the Holy Spirit," and the Gospels of Mark and Luke say likewise,[167] "Those who blasphemed the Holy Spirit," we should understand the texts to mean those who blasphemed in a particular way.

And we should note that one may "speak" against the Holy Spirit both orally and in desire and deed, and that we call many words expressing one thought one word, as we frequently read in the prophets: "The word that the Lord spoke" to Isaiah and Jeremiah.[168]

And it is clear that the Holy Spirit is charity, and charity causes the pardon of sins on the part of the church. And so the pardon of sins is an effect appropriated to the Holy Spirit, as Jn. 20:22–23 says: "Receive the Holy Spirit; whose sins you shall remit, they are remitted." Therefore, we say that those who in desire, word, and deed resist the pardon of their sins, so that they persist in sin to their dying breath, speak unpardonably against the Holy Spirit. And so, according to Augustine,[169] impenitence persisting unto death is a sin against the Holy Spirit.

And we appropriate goodness to the Holy Spirit, just as we appropriate pardon of sins to him. And so masters following Augustine to some degree have said that one who sins out of malice, which is contrary to the goodness of the Holy Spirit, utters a word or a blasphemy against the Holy Spirit.[170]

Therefore, if we should be speaking about sins against the Holy Spirit according to the opinion of the early saints or even according to the opinion of Augustine, not every sin done out of malice is a sin against the Holy Spirit, as can be seen from what I have just said.

But if we should be speaking according to the statements of the masters, which are not to be despised, then we can say that, properly speaking about the sin against the Holy Spirit, not every sin done out of malice is a sin against the Holy Spirit. For we say, as I have said before,[171] that one sins out of malice whose will is intrinsically inclined to a particular good with an associated evil. And this indeed happens in two ways. For even in the case of natural things, something is moved in two ways: either by inclination, as heavy things move downward, or by the removal of something preventing movement, as water pours out of a glass when the glass is shattered. Therefore, the will is sometimes intrinsically borne to such a good by its own inclination from an acquired habit, and sometimes by the removal of something that keeps the person from sin, such as hope, fear of God, and other like gifts of the Holy Spirit that draw human beings away from sin. And so, properly speaking, a person sins against the Holy Spirit if the person's will tends to sin because it casts aside such bonds of the Holy Spirit. And so we posit both despair and

---

167. Mk. 3:29; Lk. 12:10.

168. E.g., Is. 38:4; Jer. 1:4.

169. *On the Words of the Lord*, sermon 71, chap. 12, n. 20 (PL 38:455).

170. William of Auxerre, *Golden Summa* II, tract. 30, chap. 4; Albert the Great, *Commentary on the Sentences* II, d. 43, a. 1; Bonaventure, *Commentary on the Sentences* II, d. 43, a. 1.

171. Aa. 12–13.

presumption and obstinacy and the like as species of the sin against the Holy Spirit, as the Master makes clear in the *Sentences*.[172]

But broadly speaking, we can say that those who sin by habitual inclination sin against the Holy Spirit, since even they thereby resist the goodness of the Holy Spirit.

Replies to the Objections:

1. According to the opinion of the older saints, the sin against the Holy Spirit is a sin of the speech whereby one blasphemes against the Holy Spirit, and it is necessary in the opinion of others to say that there are also the "words" of desires and deeds, since we also express things by desires and deeds. Accordingly, 1 Cor. 12:3 says: "No one can say 'Lord Jesus' except in the Holy Spirit," that is, by words, desires, and deeds, as a gloss on that text explains.[173]

2. According to the explanation of the older saints and also the explanation of the masters, we can call sins against the Holy Spirit a special genus of sin, provided we understand sins done out of malice properly, insofar as persons sin by casting aside the benefits of the Holy Spirit that keep them away from sin. But if we should understand sins done out of malice insofar as they derive from habitual inclinations, then there is not a special genus of sin but a circumstance of sin that can be present in every genus of sin. And we should say the same if the sin against the Holy Spirit, according to the explanation of Augustine, should be final impenitence.

3. The older saints understand blasphemy against the Holy Spirit as a special sin of speech. But in the opinion of Augustine and the masters, every resistance to the gifts of the Holy Spirit, whether in words, desires, or deeds, is included in blasphemy.

4. If virtue for its own sake were to please someone due to considering a higher cause, the character of a special virtue would accordingly result. For example, if one were to delight in chastity because of love of God, this would belong to the virtue of chastity. And similarly, if malice pleases someone because of contempt regarding hope in, or fear of, God, this belongs to the nature of special sins, namely, despair and presumption, which are species of sins against the Holy Spirit.

5. The argument of this objection is valid if we adopt the interpretation of Augustine, and then the sin against the Holy Spirit is not a special genus of sin.

6. We do not say that those in a state of despair who think that their malice exceeds God's goodness sin against the Holy Spirit regarding their opinion, for then they would commit the sin of unbelief. Rather, we say that such persons sin against the Holy Spirit because they are disposed so to think as they despair of God's goodness by considering their evil deeds.

7. As I have said before,[174] we can say that persons indeed sin out of malice in one way from a habit so inclining them, as we call malice a habit contrary to a virtue. But it is not true that everyone who sins contrary to a virtue sins out of malice. For example, not everyone who does unjust deeds already has the habit of injustice, although human beings by unjust actions develop the habit of injustice, as the *Ethics* says.[175] We can under-

---

172. *Sentences* II, d. 43, chap. 1, n. 2.
173. Peter Lombard, *Gloss*, on 1 Cor. 12:3 (PL 191:1650C).
174. Aa. 12 and 13.
175. Aristotle, *Ethics* II, 4 (1105a26ff.).

stand in a second way that persons sin out of malice because they will a good with an associated evil, and no emotion or ignorance inclines them to such a good. And so also it is clear that not every sinner sins out of malice.

8. We call contracted malice a proneness to commit evil deeds that we have from the corrupting influence of concupiscence. And when we speak of persons sinning out of malice, we do not understand malice in that sense. Rather, we then understand malice to mean committed malice, as we call the very internal choice malice. And so we should understand that, when persons sin out of malice, it is always the internal act of sin that we call malice, from which the external sinful act springs.

9. Sin committed by reason of habitual inclination indeed has such a nature that we can call it a sin against the Holy Spirit. But we can also understand sins against the Holy Spirit in other ways, as I have said.[176]

Fifteenth Article

Can Sins against the Holy Spirit Be Forgiven?

It seems that they cannot, for the following reasons:

1. Mt. 12:32 says that those "who have spoken against the Holy Spirit will not be forgiven in this world or the next." But every forgiveness is in this world or the next. Therefore, sins against the Holy Spirit are never forgiven.

2. People have argued that we say that such sins are not forgiven because they are difficult to forgive. But Mk. 3:29 says: "Those who have blasphemed against the Holy Spirit never have forgiveness and will be guilty of an eternal sin." And one whose sin is forgiven is not guilty of an eternal sin. Therefore, sins against the Holy Spirit are never forgiven.

3. We should pray for the forgiveness of every sin that can be forgiven. But we should not pray for the forgiveness of the sin against the Holy Spirit, for 1 Jn. 5:16 says: "There is sin unto death, and I do not say that one should pray for forgiveness of such sin." Therefore, the sin against the Holy Spirit can never be forgiven.

4. Augustine says in his work *On the Lord's Sermon on the Mount* that "the destruction of this sin is so great that the sinner cannot submit to the humility of begging for pardon."[177] But since sin originates in pride, as Sir. 10:15 says, no sin can be healed except through humility, inasmuch as contraries heal contraries. Therefore, the sin against the Holy Spirit cannot be forgiven.

5. Augustine says in his work *Book of the 83 Questions* that sins of weakness and ignorance but not sins of malice are venial sins.[178] But we call sins of weakness and ignorance venial because they can be forgiven. Therefore, sins done out of malice cannot be forgiven.

---

176. In the answer.
177. *On the Lord's Sermon on the Mount* I, 22, n. 74 (PL 34:1266).
178. *Book of the 83 Questions*, q. 26 (PL 40:17–18).

On the Contrary:

1. The Gospel of John says that "people shall be forgiven every sin and blasphemy."[179]

2. Persons do not sin in the hope of gaining the impossible. Therefore, if it were to be impossible for some sin to be pardoned, persons despairing of the pardon of such a sin would not sin. And this conclusion is obviously false.

3. Augustine says that we should not despair of anyone as long as the person is in the pilgrimage of this life.[180] But no sin removes a person from the condition of earthly pilgrimage. Therefore, we should not despair of any human being, and so every sin can be forgiven.

Answer:

The answer to this question is clear from what I have said before.[181] For if we understand sin against the Holy Spirit as Augustine did,[182] then it is obvious that such a sin can never be forgiven. For human beings are never forgiven sins if they persist in sin unto death without any repentance, assuming we are speaking about mortal sins. And we consider impenitence, which Augustine holds to be the sin against the Holy Spirit,[183] a mortal sin. But there are some slight and venial sins that are forgiven in the world to come, as Gregory says.[184]

And according to other understandings of the sin against the Holy Spirit, we do not call it unpardonable because it cannot be pardoned, but by reason of two other considerations. First, indeed, we can consider the pardonability of sin in relation to punishment, so that we call a sin remissible that has some excuse that makes it less deserving of punishment, just as we say that heat is remitted when it is diminished. And it is in this way that we say that sins done out of ignorance or weakness are remissible because ignorance and weakness but not malice diminish the seriousness of sin. Likewise, even those who blasphemed against the humanity of Christ by calling him a wine tippler and a glutton[185] seemed to have some excuse, since the weakness of his flesh moved them to their blasphemy. But those who blaspheme the divinity of Christ or the power of the Holy Spirit have no excuse that makes their sin less serious.

We can in another way call sin unpardonable in relation to moral wrong. And to demonstrate this, we should consider that, regarding lower things, we call something impossible by reason of the privation of an active power of the lower thing, although divine power is not excluded. For example, such would be the case if we should say that it is impossible for Lazarus to rise when his created source of life is taken away, but we do not thereby exclude that God could raise him up. And those who sin against the Holy Spirit cast aside the remedies for the remission of sin, since they contemn the Holy Spirit and his gifts whereby there is remission of sins in the church. And likewise, those who

179. Actually, Mt. 12:31.
180. *On the Words of the Lord*, sermon 71, chap. 13, n. 21 (PL 38:456).
181. A. 14.
182. *On the Words of the Lord*, sermon 71, chap. 12, n. 20 (PL 38:455).
183. Ibid.
184. *Dialogues* IV, 39 (PL 77:396A–B).
185. Cf. Mt. 11:19.

sin out of malice by habitual inclination lack knowledge of their proper end, whereby they could be led back to good, as I have said before.[186]

And so we in accord with such understandings call the sin against the Holy Spirit unpardonable because the remedies whereby human beings are assisted for the remission of sin have been removed. But the sin is not unpardonable if we should consider the power of divine grace as the active source, and the presence of a power of free choice not yet confirmed in evil as the material source of the sin's remission.

Replies to the Objections:

1. We need to understand the statement "Those who have spoken against the Holy Spirit will not be forgiven in this world or the next" in different ways according to the opinion of Augustine and the others, as I have said.[187] But Chrysostom explains himself more facilely by referring to the fact that the Jews were to suffer punishment for the blasphemies they brought against Christ, both in this life from the Romans and in the next in the damnation of hell.[188]

2. The Gospel of Mark calls the sin against the Holy Spirit an eternal sin because it, considered in itself, is eternal, though the mercy of God can bring it to an end. Just so, we say that charity, considered in itself, never falls away, although it sometimes falls away because of a sinner's sin.

3. We can understand "sin unto death" as the sin in which the sinner persists even unto death. And then we should not pray for such a person, since supplications are of no benefit for the damned who died without repentance. But if we should understand "sin unto death" as the sin committed out of malice, then no one is prohibited from praying for such a sinner. Still, not all persons are of such great merit that they could by prayer obtain grace for those who sin out of malice, since the healing of such sinners is quasi-miraculous. This is as if the text were to say: "I do not say that one," that is, anyone, "should pray for resuscitation of the dead," but that one of great merit before God should.

4. We should understand that statement to mean that such persons cannot easily become humble, not that it is altogether impossible for them to do so.

5. We speak of sins being venial in three ways: in one way by reason of their kind; in a second way by reason of their result, as, for example, we call movements of concupiscence without consent venial sins; in a third way by reason of their cause, namely, that they have a cause for indulgence that makes the sins less serious. And it is in this way that we should understand that sins of weakness and ignorance are venial, but that sins committed deliberately or maliciously are not.

---

186. Aa. 12 and 13.
187. In the answer.
188. *On Matthew*, hom. 41, n. 3 (PG 57:449).

QUESTION IV

On Original Sin

First Article

Is a Sin Contracted by Physical Descent?

It seems that no sin is so contracted, for the following reasons:

1. Sir. 15:18 says: "Life and death, good and evil are set before human beings; whichever they choose will be given to them." And we can understand from this that sin, which is the spiritual death of the soul, consists of human beings' willing sin. But nothing that human beings contract by their physical descent consists of their willing. Therefore, human beings do not contract any sin by their physical descent.

2. Accidents are transmitted only if their subject is transmitted, and the subject of sin is the rational soul. Therefore, since the rational soul is not transmitted by physical descent, as the work *On Church Dogmas* maintains,[1] it seems that neither is any sin transmitted by physical descent.

3. People have said that although the subject of sin is not transmitted, the flesh is, and the flesh causes sin. But the transmission of insufficient causes does not suffice to transmit accidents, since given the insufficiency of causes, effects do not result. And the flesh is not a sufficient cause of sin, since it rests in the power of the will to consent or not consent to sin, however much the flesh entices persons to sin. And so the will itself is the sufficient cause of sin. But the will is not transmitted. Therefore, the transmission of the flesh does not suffice to transmit any sin.

4. Sin, as we understand it here, is something that deserves punishment and reproach. But no defect contracted by physical descent deserves reproach and punishment, since, as the Philosopher says in the *Ethics*,[2] there is no reproach if one is made blind by a physical defect, but there is if one is made blind by excessive drinking. Therefore, no defect contracted by physical descent has the nature of sin.

5. Augustine in the beginning of his work *On Free Choice* distinguishes two kinds of evil: one that we commit, that is, the evil of moral wrong, and the second that we suf-

---

1. Gennadius, *On Church Dogmas* 14 (PL 58:984B).
2. *Ethics* III, 5 (1114a25–28).

fer, which belongs to the evil of punishment.[3] But every defect caused by something else has the nature of being acted upon, since undergoing something is the effect and result of an action. Therefore, everything contracted by physical descent from another has only the nature of punishment, not the nature of sin.

6. The work *On Church Dogmas* says: "Our flesh, because created by the good God, is good."[4] But good does not cause evil, as Mt. 7:18 says: "A good tree cannot bear bad fruit." Therefore, we do not contract original sin by physical descent.

7. The soul depends on the flesh more after being united to it than at the moment of the soul's very union with the flesh. But the flesh can corrupt the soul after the soul has been united to the flesh only by the soul's consent. Therefore, we cannot contract original sin by physical descent.

8. If vitiated physical descent causes sin in the soul, the more vitiated the source, the greater the resulting sin. But the source regarding those begotten as a result of fornication is more vitiated than the source regarding those begotten in the course of lawful marriage. Therefore, those begotten as a result of fornication contract greater sin in their begetting. And this conclusion is clearly false, since they do not deserve greater punishment.

9. If human beings contract original sin by physical descent, this is so only because the flesh is corrupt. Therefore, that corruption is either moral or physical. But the corruption cannot be moral, since the soul, not the flesh, is subject to moral corruption. And likewise, the corruption cannot be physical, since natural activity, namely, activity by reason of active and passive properties, would then corrupt the soul. But this conclusion is clearly false. Therefore, human beings in neither way contract original sin by physical descent.

10. The defect that resulted from the sin of our first parent is the privation of original justice, as Anselm says.[5] Therefore, since original justice is something immaterial, so also is the aforementioned defect. But corruption of the flesh is something material, and immaterial and material things belong to different genera. And so something immaterial cannot cause a material effect. Therefore, the sin of our first parent could not cause the corruption in our flesh whereby physical descent would transmit their sin to us.

11. According to Anselm,[6] original sin consists of the privation of original justice. Therefore, either original justice belonged to the soul of the first human being by nature from the moment of its creation, or original justice was something extra bestowed out of God's generosity. But if original justice was natural to the soul, the soul by sinning would never have lost it, since things bestowed by nature abide even in devils, as Dionysius says in his work *On the Divine Names*.[7] And so also all human beings would have original justice, since what is natural to one soul is natural to all souls. And so no one would be begotten with original sin, that is, without original justice. And if original justice was an extra gift bestowed out of God's generosity, then God either gives or does not give the

3. *On Free Choice* I, 1, n. 1 (PL 32:1221–22).
4. Gennadius, *On Church Dogmas* 76 (PL 58:998A).
5. *On the Virgin Conception* 27 (PL 158:461A).
6. Ibid.
7. *On the Divine Names* 4, n. 23 (PG 3:725C).

gift to the soul of human beings being begotten. If God does, the human being is begotten with original justice, and the flesh cannot corrupt the human being's soul. And if God does not, it seems that the lack of original justice should be imputed to God, who did not give it, not to the soul without it. Therefore, human beings can in neither way contract sin by physical descent.

12. The rational soul is not added to a pre-existing form, since it would not be added as a substantial form to matter but as an accidental form to an already existing subject. Therefore, there can be no pre-existing form and so no accidents when the rational soul comes. Therefore, the semen's very corruption, if there was any from the begetter, also ceases. Therefore, the flesh cannot corrupt the soul when the soul comes.

13. Movements result from the nature of the dominant element in composite material substances, and so all the properties of such composites result from the dominant element. But the soul dominates the body in human beings, who are composed of both, and the soul is by reason of its origin untainted. Therefore, even if the flesh by reason of its origin contracts some taint, it nonetheless seems that human beings at the time of their begetting deserve to be called untainted, not tainted, with sin.

14. Sin is something deserving a punishment. But sin contracted by physical descent does not deserve any punishment. For privation of the vision of God, which theologians generally attribute as punishment for such sin,[8] does not seem to be a punishment. It does not seem to be punishment because persons, if they were to die without any sin and without sanctifying grace, could not attain the vision of God. And eternal life consists of that vision, as Jn. 17:3 says, "This is eternal life, that they know you, the one true God," and as the Apostle says in Rom. 6:23, "The gift of God is eternal life." Therefore, no sin is contracted by physical descent.

15. As primary causes are more excellent than secondary causes, so secondary causes are more excellent than their effects. But if our first parent transmits sin, the soul of the first human being, by sinning, caused corruption in his flesh, and his flesh causes corruption in the souls of the human beings begotten of him. And so the soul of the first human being is like a primary cause, and his flesh like a secondary cause, and the souls of human beings subsequently begotten like final effects. Therefore, the first human being's soul will be more excellent than his flesh, and his flesh more excellent than the begotten human beings' souls. But this conclusion is improper. Therefore, physical descent cannot transmit sin.

16. Things can only cause insofar as they are actual. But there is no actual sin in semen. Therefore, discharged semen cannot corrupt souls with any sin.

17. The same thing cannot cause the corruption of sin and cause merit. But acts of begetting can at times be meritorious, as when a man in the state of grace has intercourse with his wife to beget offspring or fulfill his marital duty. Therefore, such acts could not cause the corruption of sin in the offspring.

18. A particular cause does not bring about a universal effect. But Adam's sin was something particular. Therefore, his sin could not corrupt the whole human race with a sin.

19. In Ez. 18:4 and 20, the Lord says: "All souls are mine; sons will not be burdened with the iniquity of their fathers." But sons will be so burdened if those begotten of the

---

8. Cf. Peter Lombard, *Sentences* II, d. 33, chap. 2, n. 5.

first human being were to be condemned for his sin. Therefore, sin is not transmitted to Adam's descendants because of his sin.

On the Contrary:

1. Rom. 5:12 says: "Sin entered the world through one human being." But this does not happen by imitation, since it was thus that sin entered the world through the devil, as Wis. 2:24–25 says: "Death entered the world through the devil's envy, and his followers imitate him." Therefore, sin is transmitted from the first human being to his descendants through a vitiated physical origin.

2. Augustine in *City of God* says that the first human being, corrupted of his own volition, begot corrupted offspring.[9] But only sin causes corruption. Therefore, the offspring of Adam contract sin by their physical descent from him.

Answer:

The Pelagians denied that any sin can be transmitted by physical descent.[10] But this in large part eliminates the need for the redemption achieved by Christ, which seems to have been especially necessary to eradicate the corruption of sin that was transmitted from our first parent to all of his posterity. Just so, the Apostle says in Rom. 5:18 that "as the sin of one human being resulted in the condemnation of all human beings, so also the justice of one human being resulted in life-giving acquittal for all human beings." The Pelagian position also eliminates the need to baptize infants, which the universal practice of the church, derived from the Apostles, affirms, as Dionysius says in his work *On Ecclesiastical Hierarchy*.[11] And so we should say absolutely that physical descent from our first parent transmits sin to his posterity.

And to prove this, we should note that we can consider particular human beings in two ways: in one way as individual persons; in the second way as members of a community. And acts can belong to human beings in both ways. For example, acts that human beings do by their own choice and by their very selves belong to them as individual persons. And acts that are not done by their own choice or by their very selves but by the whole community or by the majority of the community or by the ruler of the community belong to human beings as members of the community. Just so, we say that the political community does what the ruler of the community does, as the Philosopher says.[12] For we reckon such a community as if one human being, so that different human beings with different functions are united as if different members of the same natural body, as the Apostle points out in 1 Cor. 12:12 regarding members of the church. Therefore, we should consider the whole population of human beings receiving their nature from our first parent as one community, or rather as the one body of one human being. And regarding this population, we can indeed consider each human being, even Adam himself, either as an individual person or as a member of the population that originates by physical descent from one human being.

9. *City of God* XIII, 14 (PL 41:386).
10. Cf., e.g., Augustine, *On Heresies* 88 (PL 42:48).
11. *On Ecclesiastical Hierarchy* 7, part 3, n. 11 (PG 3:568A–B).
12. *Ethics* IX, 8 (1168b31–32).

And we should consider that God had bestowed a supernatural gift, namely, original justice, on the first human being at his creation. And by that original justice, that human being's reason was subject to God, and his lower powers subject to his reason, and his body to his soul. And God had given this gift to the first human being both as an individual person and as a source of the whole human race, namely, that he transmit the gift to his posterity by physical descent. And the first human being, when he by his free choice sinned, lost the gift in the same habitual condition in which he received it, namely, for himself and all his descendants. Therefore, the privation of this gift extends to all of his descendants, and so the privation is transmitted to them in the way in which human nature is transmitted. And human nature is indeed not transmitted totally but only partially, namely, regarding the flesh into which God infuses the soul. Therefore, as the souls infused by God belong to the human nature originating from Adam because of the flesh to which the souls are united, so also the aforementioned privation of original justice belongs to the souls because of the flesh that Adam propagated. The privation is due to the flesh propagated by Adam both regarding the material substance of the flesh and regarding the seminal source of the flesh, that is, both as matter and as proceeding from its active source, for it is thus that children receive human nature from their fathers.

Therefore, if we should consider this privation so transmitted by physical descent to a particular human being insofar as the human being is an individual person, then such privation cannot have the nature of moral fault, for which voluntariness is a prerequisite. But if we should consider a particular begotten human being as a member of the whole human nature propagated by our first parent, as if all human beings were one human being, then the privation of original justice has the nature of moral fault because of its voluntary source, that is, the actual sin of our first parent. This is as if we should say that the movement of a hand to commit homicide, insofar as we consider the hand as such, does not have the character of a moral fault, since something else moves the hand in a determined way. But if we should consider the hand as part of the human being who acts willingly, then the hand's movement shares the character of the moral fault, since then the movement is voluntary. Therefore, as we call the homicide the moral fault of the whole human being and not of the hand, so we call the privation of original justice a sin of the whole human nature and not a personal sin. Nor does the privation belong to the person except insofar as human nature corrupts the person. And different parts of a human being, namely, the will, reason, hands, eyes, and the like, are used to commit one sin, and yet there is only one sin because of its one source, namely, the will, from which the character of sin is transmitted to all the acts of the other parts. Just so, we consider original sin as if one sin by reason of its source in the whole human nature. And it is for this reason that the Apostle says in Rom. 5:12: "In which all sinned." And according to Augustine,[13] we can understand "in which" in two ways: as in which person, that is, in the first human being, or as in which thing, that is, in the sin of the first human being, so that that sin is, so to speak, the common sin of human beings.

---

13. *On the Punishment and Forgiveness of Sins and on the Baptism of Infants* I, 10, n. 11 (PL 44:115).

Replies to the objections:

1. We call the sin contracted by physical descent voluntary by reason of its source, namely, the will of our first parent, as I have said.[14]

2. This sin extends to the whole human nature. And so the subject of the sin is the soul as part of human nature. And so as human nature is transmitted although the soul is not, so also original sin is transmitted although the soul is not.

3. The flesh is not the sufficient cause of actual sin but is the sufficient cause of original sin, just as transmission of the flesh is the sufficient cause of human nature, albeit as to the matter.

4. Something contracted by physical descent does not deserve punishment or reproach if we regard the person contracting it, since such a thing does not have a voluntary character. But if we regard the nature contracting it, then it has a voluntary character, as I have said.[15] And it is in this way that it deserves reproach and punishment.

5. The privation of original justice contracted by physical descent indeed has the nature of being from another if we regard the person contracting the privation, but not if we regard the nature contracting it. For then it is from an internal source, as it were.

6. Our flesh in its natural condition is good. But because of the sin of our first parent, our flesh causes original sin insofar as our flesh is deprived of original justice.

7. Strictly speaking, original sin is a sin of human nature and only of the person by reason of the corrupted nature, as I have said.[16] But the reproductive act properly serves nature, since the act is ordained for the preservation of the species, and it belongs to the constitution of a human person that the flesh is already united to the soul. And so the flesh as considered in the process of generation rather than as already united to the soul causes original sin.

8. Regarding those begotten by fornication, there is indeed a doubly vitiated origin, namely, the moral fault of nature, which Adam transmits, and the moral fault of the person, that is, of the father who begets, from which defect no corruption abides in the offspring. For every father in begetting offspring transmits original sin because he begets as Adam, not because he begets as Peter or Martin, that is, he transmits original sin because he begets by what he has from Adam, not by what is particular to himself.

9. The corruption in the flesh is indeed actually physical, although moral in its orientation and power. For the sin of our first parent deprived his flesh of the power to be capable of ejecting semen that would propagate original justice in others. And so the privation of this power in the semen is a defect involving moral corruption and an orientation of the flesh's corruption, just as we say that the orientation of color is in the air, and that the orientation of the soul is in the semen. And so as the semen has the power to produce human nature in the offspring begotten, the semen also has the power to produce like corruption in them.

10. Nothing prevents an immaterial cause from producing a material effect. For Boethius too says in his work *On the Trinity* that the forms in matter came from forms

14. In the answer.
15. Ibid.
16. Ibid.

without matter.[17] And regarding ourselves, the will moves lower appetites, and the movements of those appetites cause material changes.

11. Original justice was additionally bestowed on the first human being out of God's generosity. But that God does not bestow original justice on the souls of the first human being's posterity is not due to God but to human nature, in which there is something contrary that prevents the condition of original justice.

12. The corruption of original sin is virtually, not actually, in the semen in the same way that human nature is virtually in the semen. And the active power in the semen resides in its foaming effluence, as Aristotle says in his work *On the Generation of Animals*,[18] not in the matter that loses one form and gains another.

13. As Dionysius says in his work *On the Divine Names*,[19] good results from the whole and integral cause, while evil results from even a single defect. And so the defect regarding the body suffices to take away the integrity of human nature.

14. Persons may lack the vision of God in two ways. They lack the vision of God in one way if they do not possess in themselves the means whereby they could attain the vision. And it is in this way that persons endowed only with natural powers who were to be without sin would lack the vision, for then lacking the vision is not a punishment but a deficiency resulting in every created nature. This is so because no creature by its own natural powers can attain the vision of God. In the second way, persons can lack the vision if they possess in themselves something whereby they deserve to lack the vision, and then lacking the vision is a punishment of both original and actual sin.

15. There are two kinds of efficient causes. One is the chief cause, which acts by its own form, and this cause as such is more excellent than its effect. The second is the instrumental cause, which acts insofar as something else moves it, not by its own form, and this cause need not be more excellent than the effect. For example, a saw used to build a house is not more excellent than the house. And it is in the latter way that bodily semen causes the human nature in offspring and also the original moral fault in the offspring's soul.

16. An efficient cause is active in several ways. It is active in one way by its own form, which either contains the form of the effect by specific likeness, as fire causes fire, or only by its power, as the sun causes fire. An efficient cause is active in another way by being moved by something else, and then the instrument acts as an actual being. And so also semen is active insofar as it has its movement and orientation from the soul begetting, as the Philosopher says in his work *On the Generation of Animals*.[20] And so semen has the power to cause both human nature and original sin.

17. An upright man in having intercourse with his wife merits by what belongs to himself. And he transmits original sin by what he has from Adam, not by what belongs to himself, as I have said before.[21]

---

17. *On the Trinity* 2 (PL 64: 1250D).
18. *On the Generation of Animals* II, 3 (736b29ff.).
19. *On the Divine Names* 4, n. 30 (PG 3:729C).
20. *On the Generation of Animals* II, 3 (736b29ff.).
21. Reply to objection 8.

18. Adam, insofar as he was the source of the whole of human nature, had the nature of a universal cause, and so his act of disobedience corrupted the whole human nature that he propagates.

19. The sin of the first human being is in a way a sin common to the whole human nature, as I have said.[22] And so persons punished for the sin of our first parent are punished for their own sin, not the sin of another.

Second Article

What Is Original Sin?

I

It seems that original sin is concupiscence, for the following reasons:

1. Augustine says in his work *On the Punishment and Forgiveness of Sins and on the Baptism of Infants*: "Adam, besides providing an example to imitate, has by the hidden corruption of his carnal concupiscence corrupted in himself all of those who are to come from his stock."[23] And so the Apostle correctly says in Rom. 5:12 that Adam is the one "in whom all have sinned." But original sin is that in which all have sinned, as I have said.[24] Therefore, original sin is concupiscence.

2. Anselm says in his work *On the Virgin Conception*: "He [Adam] was so constituted that he did not have to experience disordered desires."[25] But as Anselm says in the same work,[26] there is sin both when human beings do not have what they ought to have, and when they have what they ought not to have. Therefore, contracted concupiscence is original sin.

3. Augustine says in his work *Retractions* that the guilt of concupiscence is absolved in baptism. But properly speaking, the guilt of original sin is absolved in baptism.[27] Therefore, concupiscence is original sin.

On the Contrary:

1. Damascene says in his work *On Orthodox Faith* that sin exists because persons turn themselves from what is according to nature to what is contrary to nature.[28] And so we hold that sin is contrary to nature. But desire is natural, for nature has taught every animal to desire. Therefore, concupiscence is not original sin.

2. People have said that concupiscence is natural in our corrupted nature but not in our nature as originally constituted. But desires are the proper acts of concupiscible

22. In the answer.
23. *On the Punishment and Forgiveness of Sins and on the Baptism of Infants* I, 9, n. 10 (PL 45: 115).
24. A. 1.
25. Actually, *On the Harmony of Foreknowledge and Predestination*, q. 3, chap. 7 (PL 158:530C).
26. Actually, *Why God Became Man* I, 24 (PL 158:397A).
27. *Retractions* I, 15, n. 2 (PL 32:609).
28. *On Orthodox Faith* II, 30 (PG 94:976A).

powers. And concupiscible powers are natural even in our nature as originally constituted. Therefore, concupiscence is also natural.

3. No sin is related to good and evil. But we can desire both good (e.g., wisdom)
and evil (e.g., stealing). Therefore, concupiscence as such is not original sin.

4. Concupiscence designates either a habit or an act. But as designating an act,
concupiscence is actual sin, not original sin. And as designating a habit, concupiscence
cannot be original sin, since habits that human beings acquire by their own evil acts are
not sins; otherwise, they would continually sin and continually incur demerit. And so
much less do we designate as sin the habitual concupiscence caused in particular human
beings by the disobedient act of our first parent. Therefore, in neither way is concupiscence
original sin.

5. Every habit is either given by nature or acquired or infused. But original sin is
not a habit given by nature, since nothing belonging by nature to something is evil for it,
as Dionysius says in his work *On the Divine Names*.[29] Likewise, neither is original sin an
acquired habit, since acts cause acquired habits, as the Philosopher makes clear in the
Ethics,[30] and original sin is contracted by physical descent, not acquired by acts. Likewise, original sin is not an infused habit, since only God acting internally on the soul
causes such habits, and he cannot cause sin. Therefore, in no way is original sin habitual concupiscence.

6. In the common opinion of theologians,[31] good habits precede good acts, since God
infuses the habits, and we then perform the acts. But bad acts precede bad habits. Therefore, if original sin should be habitual concupiscence, then the evil acts that are actual
sins would precede original sin. And this conclusion is improper.

7. Original sin is the incendiary source of every sin. But malice and ignorance as
well as concupiscence cause sins, as I have maintained before.[32] Therefore, original sin is
not concupiscence.

8. Concupiscence, if it is original sin, is such by its essence, and then baptism would
not have absolved original sin, since concupiscence abides after baptism. And to conclude
that baptism does not absolve original sin is improper. Or else we call concupiscence
original sin because of something associated with concupiscence, and then that other thing
is more properly original sin. Therefore, original sin is not concupiscence.

9. The sources of subjects cause the subjects' accidents. But the subject of original
sin is the soul, and the flesh rather than the soul causes concupiscence. Therefore,
concupiscence is not original sin.

10. Concupiscence seems to be original sin especially insofar as concupiscence implies the necessity of desiring. But we can understand such necessity in two ways. We
can understand the necessity in one way to be the necessity to consent to movements of
concupiscence, and we indeed cannot call this necessity original sin, since the necessity
does not remain after baptism, although the effects of original sin, with moral guilt remitted, remain actual. And the other way is the necessity of experiencing the movements

---

29. *On the Divine Names* 4, n. 25 (PG 3:728B).
30. *Ethics* I, 13 (1103a18ff.).
31. Cf. Peter Lombard, *Sentences* II, d. 27, chap. 1, n. 1.
32. Q. 3, aa. 7 and 12.

of concupiscence, but neither can this be original sin. For either this of itself would be original sin, or it would be original sin because of something else. If of itself, it would follow that original sin would remain after baptism, since such necessity remains after baptism. And if because of something else, namely, because of the lack of original justice, neither does this seem possible. It seems impossible because the necessity of experiencing such movements is related to original sin as actually experiencing the movements is related to actual sin. And actually experiencing movements of concupiscence is not an actual sin because grace does not accompany the experience. Otherwise, every concupiscible movement in those without grace would be a sin. And this conclusion is clearly false, since those without grace sometimes by their natural reason resist the movements of concupiscence. Therefore, neither is the necessity of experiencing such movements original sin because of the associated lack of original justice. And so in no way is concupiscence original sin.

11. Concupiscence, if it is original sin, is such either essentially or causally. But concupiscence is not original sin essentially, since concupiscence causes original sin according to Augustine,[33] and causes are extrinsic to the essences of the things they cause. And likewise, concupiscence is not original sin causally, since causes precede effects, and concupiscence does not precede the lack of original justice, of which the nature of original sin especially consists. Rather, concupiscence results from the lack of original justice. Therefore, in neither way is concupiscence original sin.

12. As the concupiscible powers rebel against reason in the condition of our corrupt nature, so also do the irascible powers. Therefore, we ought no more call concupiscence original sin than we ought to call anger original sin.

II

Original sin has likewise been shown to be ignorance, for the following reasons:

1. Anselm says in his work *On the Harmony of Foreknowledge and Predestination* that we attribute to human nature as original sin the inability to have and understand justice.[34] But the inability to understand belongs to ignorance. Therefore, original sin is ignorance.

2. The same work says that we attribute the diminished excellence of human nature to it as sin.[35] But the excellence of human nature consists especially of the splendor of knowledge. Therefore, it seems that the original sin that we impute to human nature consists of the diminution of knowledge, namely, ignorance.

3. Hugo of St. Victor says that the evil contracted at our begetting consists of mental ignorance and carnal concupiscence.[36] But such evil is original sin. Therefore, original sin is just as much ignorance as concupiscence.

33. See, e.g., *Against Julian* V, 3, n. 8 (PL 44:787).
34. *On the Harmony of Foreknowledge and Predestination*, q. 3, chap. 7 (PL 158:529D).
35. Ibid. (PL 158:530A).
36. *On the Sacraments* I, part 7, chap. 1, n. 2ff.

On the Contrary:

1. Ignorance differs from concupiscence and has a different subject. But the same thing does not belong to different genera and does not belong to different subjects. Therefore, original sin, since it is concupiscence, cannot be ignorance.

2. As the intellect suffers deficiency because of original sin, so also do lower powers like the reproductive, and even the body itself. Therefore, if we hold that ignorance, which is a deficiency of the intellect, is original sin, we should by like argument also hold that all the deficiencies of the lower powers and even of the body itself are original sin. And this conclusion seems inappropriate.

III

Original sin has likewise been shown to be the lack of original justice, for the following reasons:

1. Anselm in his work *On the Virgin Conception* argues as follows: Every sin is injustice and so excludes some justice.[37] But original sin excludes only original justice. Therefore, original sin is the lack of original justice.

On the contrary:

1. We speak of moral fault by reason of the privation of sanctifying grace. But original justice does not include sanctifying grace, since the first human being was constituted in original justice without sanctifying grace, as the Master makes clear in the *Sentences*.[38] Therefore, the lack of original justice does not constitute the nature of a sin.

2. Baptism does not restore original justice, since lower powers continue to rebel against reason. Therefore, if original sin were to be the lack of original justice, then baptism would not absolve original sin. And this conclusion is heretical.

3. We ought to posit subjects in the definition of accidents. But if we say that original sin consists of the lack of original justice, we make no mention of the subject of original sin. Therefore, the definition is inadequate.

4. As original sin takes away original justice, so actual sin takes away grace. But lack of grace is the effect of sin, not itself the actual sin itself. Therefore, neither is lack of original justice original sin itself.

IV

Original sin has likewise been shown to consist of punishment and moral fault, for the following reasons:

1. On the words of Ps. 84:2, "Lord, you have blessed your earth," a gloss says that what we contract from Adam consists of punishment and moral fault.[39] But what we

---

37. *On the Virgin Conception* 24 (PL 158:458C).
38. Peter Lombard, *Sentences* II, d. 24, chap. 1, n. 2ff.
39. Peter Lombard, *Gloss* (PL 191: 795D).

contract from Adam is original sin. Therefore, original sin consists of punishment and moral fault.

2. Ambrose says that defects or punishments corrupt nature, and that moral fault offends God.[40] But original sin does both. Therefore, original sin is both moral fault and punishment.

On the Contrary:

1. Hugo of St. Victor says that original sin is a mortal weakness from which the necessity of concupiscence results.[41] But weakness designates a punishment. Therefore, original sin is only a punishment.

2. Anselm, speaking about original sin, compares it to the slavery that persons suffer for the sin of fathers who committed the crime of treason.[42] But such slavery is only a punishment. Therefore, original sin is only a punishment.

3. Augustine says in his work *City of God* that original sin is a debility of human nature.[43] But debility designates a punishment. Therefore, original sin is only a punishment.

Answer:

We can understand the answer to this question from what I have said before.[44] For I have said before that original sin belongs to particular persons considered as parts of the population descended from Adam as if they were particular bodily members of the same human being. I have also said that original sin is one sin of one human sinner regarding the whole sin and the first cause of the sinning, although the sin is executed in different members.[45] Therefore, original sin regarding particular human beings consists only of what accrues to them from the sin of our first parent by reason of their physical descent from him. Just so, sin regarding hands or eyes consists only of what accrues to them from the action of the first cause of sinning, that is, the will, although physical descent causes the action in the case of original sin, and the command of the will causes the action of hands and eyes in the case of actual sin. And what accrues to hands from the sin of an individual human being is indeed an effect and imprint of the first disordered action, which belonged to the will, and so needs to bear a likeness to the disorder of the will. And the disordered action of the will consists of turning toward a transient good without proper ordination to the requisite end. And this disorder is indeed a turning away from the immutable good. And the turning away from God is the quasi-formal element, and the turning toward a transient good the quasi-material element, since we understand the formal aspect of a moral act in relation to the act's end. And so also what belongs to hands regarding a sin of one human being consists only of their use to produce an effect lacking any ordination of justice. And moreover, if the will's action reaches to something incapable of sin (e.g., a lance or a sword), we say that the thing has sin only virtually and

40. *Second Apology of David* 3, n. 19 (PL 14:893B).
41. *On the Sacraments* I, part 7, chap. 31 (PL 176:302A).
42. *On the Virgin Conception* 28 (PL 158:462A).
43. *City of God* XIV, 19 (PL 41:427).
44. A. 1.
45. Ibid.

in terms of the effect, namely, as the act of sin causes the motion of the lance or sword that accomplishes the effect. We do not say that the very lance or the very sword sins, since they, unlike hands or eyes, are not parts of the human being who sins.

Therefore, the sin of our first parent had a formal element, namely, turning away from the immutable good, and a material element, namely, turning toward a transient good. And our first parent lost the gift of original justice because he turned away from the immutable good. And his lower powers, which should have been elevated to reason, have been dragged down to lower things because he inordinately turned toward a transient good. Therefore, even regarding those who come from his stock, both the higher part of the soul lacks the requisite ordination to God, which it had through original justice, and the lower powers are not subject to the power of reason. Rather, the lower powers by their own impulse are turned toward lower things, and even the body itself tends toward dissolution by the inclinations of the contraries of which it is composed. And the higher part of the soul and even some lower powers subject to the will and constituted by nature to obey it incur this consequence of the first sin as moral fault, since such parts can incur moral fault. But lower powers not subject to the will, namely, powers of the vegetative soul, and also the body itself incur this consequence as punishment. They do not incur the consequence as moral fault except perhaps virtually, namely, as such punishment resulting from sin causes sin, as the reproductive power by discharging semen works to transmit original sin along with human nature.

And among the higher powers that incur the defect transmitted by physical descent as moral fault, there is one that moves all the others, namely, the will, and the will moves all the other powers to their own acts. And what regards an efficient cause and a cause of movement is always like form, and what regards the subject undergoing motion and being acted upon is like matter. And so the lack of original justice regards the will, and the proneness to desire inordinately, which we may call concupiscence, regards the lower powers moved by the will. Therefore, original sin in particular human beings consists only of concupiscence and the lack of original justice but in such a way that the lack of original justice is the quasi-formal element in original sin, and concupiscence the quasi-material element. Just so, the turning away from the immutable good is the quasi-formal element in actual sin, and the turning toward a transient good may be the quasi-material element. As a result, we may understand that the soul in the case of original sin is turned away from God and toward a creature just as acts in the case of actual sin are turned away from God and toward a creature, so to speak.

Replies to the Objections (I):
Therefore, we need to admit the arguments proving that original sin is concupiscence.

Replies to the Arguments in the Section On the Contrary (I):
1. Things can be natural to human beings in two ways. Something can be natural to human beings in one way insofar as they are animals, and then it is natural to them that their concupiscible powers are, generally speaking, borne to what is sensibly pleasurable. Something can be natural to human beings in a second way insofar as they are such, that is, rational animals, and then it is natural for them that their concupiscible powers are borne to what is sensibly pleasurable according to the ordination of reason. Therefore, the concupiscence whereby concupiscible powers are prone to be borne to sense plea-

sures beyond the ordination of reason is contrary to the nature of human beings as such. And so concupiscence belongs to original sin.

2. As concupiscible powers are natural to human beings as their nature was instituted, so also it is natural to them that the powers are subject to reason, according to the statement of the Philosopher in the *De anima* that sense appetites follow the rational appetite just as one sphere moves another.[46]

3. The object of desire is indeed good insofar as desire follows the ordination of reason, and the object of desire is evil insofar as the desire is contrary to the ordination of reason. This is so because, as Dionysius says in his work *On the Divine Names*,[47] it is evil for human beings to be beyond the bounds of reason. And so being angry beyond the bounds of reason is evil for human beings although good for dogs.

4. Concupiscence as belonging to original sin is habitual rather than actual. But we should understand that habits make us apt to do things. And causes can in two ways be apt to do things. Causes can be disposed in one way to do something by forms that incline them to do it, as, for example, the forms that heavy material substances have from what produced them incline the substances to move downward. Causes can be disposed in another way to do something by the removal of an impediment, as, for example, wine pours out of a cask when the hoops preventing the outpouring are broken, and excited horses rush headlong when their restraining bridles are snapped. Therefore, we can speak about habitual concupiscence in two ways. We can speak about habitual concupiscence in one way as a disposition or habit inclines one to desire inordinately, as, for example, if frequent actual concupiscence were to cause habitual concupiscence. And then we do not call the concupiscence original sin. We can understand habitual concupiscence in a second way as the very proneness or disposition to desire inordinately, which happens because the concupiscible powers are not completely subject to reason when the restraint of original justice has been removed. And then original sin in a material sense is habitual concupiscence.

And yet it does not follow that if habitual concupiscence positively understood does not have the nature of actual sin as caused by personal acts, habitual concupiscence understood as the removal of an impediment does not on that account have the nature of original sin as caused by the act of our first parent. This is so because we do not call original sin sin for the same reason we call actual sin sin. For actual sin consists of a person's voluntary act, and so what does not belong to such an act does not have the nature of actual sin. But original sin belongs to a person by reason of the nature that the person gets from another by physical descent, and so every defect in the nature of offspring derived from the sin of our first parent has the character of original sin, provided the defect is in a subject capable of moral fault. For as Augustine says in his *Retractions*,[48] we call concupiscence sin because it was caused by sin.

5. As vicious habits belonging to particular persons have been acquired by the persons' acts, so also habitual concupiscence, which belongs to the sin of nature, has been acquired by the voluntary act of our first parent. But habitual concupiscence is not, properly speaking, natural, nor is it infused.

---

46. *De anima* III, 11 (434a12–15).
47. *On the Divine Names* 4, n. 32 (PG 3:733A).
48. *Retractions* I, 15, n. 2 (PL 32:608).

6. The argument of this objection is valid about a personal habit in the positive sense. But such a habit is not original sin.

7. We include both malice and ignorance in original sin. For as concupiscence contracted by physical descent consists only of stripping lower powers of the restraint of original justice, so contracted malice consists only of stripping the will itself of original justice. And so the will incurs every kind of proneness to choose evil things. And so as I have said before,[49] malice belongs to original sin as a formal element, and concupiscence as a material element. And I shall speak later about ignorance.[50]

8. We call something such because of something else both as it is such because of an accidental characteristic, and as it is such because of its formal source. For example, we call the body alive because of the soul, and yet it does not follow that the body is not a part of the living thing. And likewise, we call concupiscence original sin because of the lack of original justice, which is related to concupiscence as a formal element to a material element, as I have said.[51] And so it does not follow that concupiscence is not part of original sin.

9. The sources of a subject cause the subject's natural accidents but not accidents that do not belong to the subject's nature. And original sin is of the latter kind of accident. And yet even original sin is caused by the will of our first parent.

10. Concupiscence as part of original sin does not designate a necessity to consent to the disordered movements of concupiscence. Rather, concupiscence as part of original sin designates a necessity to experience those disordered movements, which indeed remain after baptism but are no longer accompanied by the lack of original justice, from which lack the guilty condition of punishment results. And so we say that the effects of original sin remain, but its guilt is taken away. And yet the necessity of experiencing movements of concupiscence need not lack the character of original sin because lack of grace does not cause the experience of such movements to have the character of actual sin. For actual sin, as a disordered act, consists of an act. And so the defect that constitutes actual sin is the very disorder of the act and not the absence of grace, which is a defect in the subject who sins. But original sin is a sin of human nature. And so the disorder of human nature by the removal of original justice causes the character of original sin.

11. We can consider concupiscence in two ways. We can consider it in one way as it belongs to a person other than the one contracting original sin, and it is in this way that we hold that a father's concupiscence causes original sin in his offspring. And this concupiscence does not belong to the essence of the original sin in the offspring but rather precedes it. We can consider concupiscence in a second way as it belongs to the same person contracting original sin. And then concupiscence causes original sin as matter, which belongs to the essence of things, and precedes original sin in a material way, just as the body precedes the soul in the order of material causality. For I have said before that the flesh, to which concupiscence belongs, corrupts the soul,[52] to which the lack of original justice belongs.

---

49. In the answer.
50. Replies to the objections (II).
51. In the answer.
52. A. 1.

12. Corruption of the irascible powers, just like corruption of the concupiscible powers, is included in original sin in a material way. But we designate original sin by the corruption from the concupiscible powers rather than the irascible powers for two reasons. The first reason is indeed because all the irascible emotions arise from love, which rests in the concupiscible powers, and terminate in joy or sadness, which also rest in the concupiscible powers. And so we can generally call both concupiscible and irascible movements concupiscence. The second reason is because original sin is transmitted by the reproductive act, in which there is the highest degree of pleasure, and regarding which the disorder of a concupiscible power is obvious. And so we call the concupiscible powers both corrupt and tainted, since the acts of such powers transmit original sin.

Replies to the Objections (II):
Even the intellect is one of the powers moved by the will. And so a deficiency of the intellect is also included materially in original sin, and this deficiency indeed consists of the lack of the natural knowledge that human beings would have possessed in their original state. And it is in this way that ignorance is included materially in original sin.

Replies to the Arguments in the Section On the Contrary (II):
1. Since original sin is a sin of human nature, as human nature is composed of many parts, so many things, namely, the defects of different parts of human nature, compose original sin.

2. Things not constituted by nature to be subject to reason are not capable of moral fault. And so transmitted defects in them have only the nature of punishment, not the nature of moral fault. But the intellect is capable of moral fault, since one can merit or incur demerit by acts of the intellect insofar as they are voluntary. And so there is no comparison.

Replies to the Objections (III):
Lack of original justice is a quasi-formal element in original sin, as I have said.[53]

Replies to the Arguments in the Section On the Contrary (III):
1. Original justice includes sanctifying grace, nor do I think that it is true that human beings were created with purely natural powers. But if original justice does not include sanctifying grace, it still does not on that account exclude the lack of original justice having the nature of moral fault. This is so because one incurs moral fault by the very fact that one sins contrary to a dictate of natural reason. For the rectitude of grace accompanies the rectitude of human nature.

2. Baptism restores original justice as to the union of the higher part of the soul to God, by the privation of which the guilty condition of moral fault is present. But baptism does not restore original justice as to the subjection of lower powers of the soul to reason. For concupiscence, which remains after baptism, results from such defect.

3. We posit the will in the definition of justice, for justice is the rectitude of the will, as Anselm says.[54] And so, because we posit justice in the definition of original justice,

---

53. In the answer.
54. *On Truth* 12 (PL 158:482B).

original justice does not lack a subject. Just so, if we should posit pug-nosed in the definition of something, we would not need to posit nose in the definition, since nose is included in the definition of pug-nosed.

4. The privation of grace belongs to the subject who acts, not to acts themselves, and so does not belong to actual sin. But the lack of original justice belongs to human nature and so can belong to original sin, which is a sin of human nature.

Replies to the Objections and Arguments (IV):
As I have said before,[55] if we relate original sin to particular human beings as particular persons without regard to their nature, then original sin is a punishment. But if we relate original sin to the source in which all sinned, then original sin has the nature of moral fault. And this makes readily clear the reply to the arguments in the section *On the contrary*.

Third Article

Is Flesh or the Soul the Subject in Which
Original Sin Inheres?

It seems that original sin inheres in the flesh and not in the soul, for the following reasons:

1. God created the soul. But the soul does not have the impurity of sin from God, or from itself, since then the impurity would be actual sin. Therefore, in no way does original sin inhere in the soul.

2. Persons in whom there is original sin have sinned in Adam, as the Apostle says of Adam in Rom. 5:12: "In whom all have sinned." But the souls of particular human beings have not sinned in Adam, since those souls were not in him. Therefore, original sin does not inhere in the soul.

3. Augustine says in his work *Against Five Heresies* that the rays of the sun filter through refuse and are not soiled.[56] But the soul is an immaterial light and so more powerful than material light. Therefore, the soul is not soiled by the impurities of the flesh.

4. Punishment corresponds to moral fault. But the punishment for original sin is death, which belongs to the composite, not only to the soul. Therefore, original sin inheres in the composite, not the soul.

5. Characteristics belong more truly to causes than to effects. Therefore, if the flesh causes the soul's corruption, it seems that original sin inheres in the flesh rather than the soul.

On the contrary:
Ambrose says that the same thing is the subject of virtue and vice.[57] But flesh is not the subject of virtue. Therefore, neither is flesh the subject of vice.

---

55. A. 1.
56. Augustine (Pseudo), *Against Five Heresies* 5, n. 7 (PL 42:1107).
57. *On Noah and the Ark* 12, n. 41 (PL 14:379A).

Answer:

We need to consider two distinctions in order to understand this question. First, indeed, we need to consider that we speak in two ways about something being in something: in one way as in its proper subject; in the second way as in its cause. And the proper subject of an accident is proportioned to the accident itself. For example, if we wish to consider the proper subject of happiness and virtue, the proper subject of both, since they are properties of human beings, will be what is proper to human beings, namely, the rational part of the soul, as the Philosopher argues in the *Ethics*.[58] And there are two kinds of causes, namely, the instrumental and the chief. An effect is indeed in its chief cause by a likeness of form, either of the same species if the cause is univocal (e.g., when human beings beget human beings, or fire generates fire) or regarding a more excellent form if the cause is nonunivocal (e.g., as the sun generates human beings). And an effect is in an instrumental cause by the power that the instrument receives from the chief cause insofar as the latter moves the former. For example, a house's form is in one way in the house's stones and wood as the form's proper subject, and in another way in the mind of the builder as the chief cause, and in another way in the saw and ax as instrumental causes.

And to be a subject of sin is evidently proper to human beings, and so the proper subject of every sin needs to be what is proper to human beings, namely, the rational soul by reason of which human beings are human beings. And so original sin inheres in the rational soul as the sin's subject. But as the bodily semen is the instrumental cause of the transmission of human nature to offspring, so is it the instrumental cause of the transmission of original sin. And so original sin inheres virtually in the flesh, that is, the bodily semen, as instrumental cause.

Second, we should consider that there are two ways of ordering, namely, the ordering of nature and the ordering of temporal succession. In the ordering of nature, the perfect is prior to the imperfect, and actuality is prior to potentiality, but in the ordering of generation and temporal succession, conversely, the imperfect is prior to the perfect, and potentiality is prior to actuality. Therefore, in the ordering of nature, original sin inheres in the soul as in a proper subject prior to inhering in the flesh as in an instrumental cause. But in the ordering of generation and temporal succession, original sin inheres first in the flesh.

Replies to the Objections:

1. The rational soul has the impurity of original sin from its union with the flesh, not from itself or from God. For it is thus that the soul becomes part of the human nature transmitted by Adam.

2. Original sin, since it is a sin of human nature, belongs to the soul only insofar as the soul is part of human nature. And our human nature partially originated in Adam, namely, regarding the flesh and the aptitude for a soul. And we accordingly say that human beings have sinned in Adam by original sin.

3. Augustine introduces this example to show that the Word of God was not stained by the incarnation, since the Word of God is not united to the flesh as a form and so is like light unmixed with matter, as the sun's rays are unmixed with refuse. But the soul

58. *Ethics* I, 7 (1097b22–1098a20).

is united to the body as a form and so is comparable to light immersed in matter. And the soul is soiled by the immersion, just as the sun's rays passing through cloudy air are evidently darkened.

4. Death as a punishment of original sin is caused by the fact that the soul lost the power to preserve its body free of dissolution. And so even this punishment belongs chiefly to the soul.

5. Something is more excellent in a chief cause than in an effect, but something is not more excellent in an instrumental cause than in an effect. And both human nature and original sin are in the bodily semen as their instrumental cause. And so as human nature is not more truly in the semen than in an already integrated body, so neither is original sin more truly in the flesh than in the soul.

Fourth Article

Does Original Sin Inhere in the Powers of the Soul Prior to Being in the Soul's Essence?

It seems that original sin does, for the following reasons:

1. Original sin consists of the lack of original justice according to Anselm,[59] as I have said before.[60] But original justice inheres in the will, as he himself says.[61] Therefore, original sin inheres first in the will, which is a power.

2. Original sin is concupiscence according to Augustine,[62] as I have said before.[63] But concupiscence belongs to the powers of the soul. Therefore, original sin inheres first in the powers.

3. We say that original sin insofar as it inclines persons to acts of sin is the incendiary source of sin. But the inclination to acts belongs to powers. Therefore, original sin inheres in the powers of the soul.

4. Original sin is a disorder contrary to the ordination of original justice. But order and disorder presuppose the distinction of parts, and the soul's essence has no parts. And so there can be no disorder in the soul's essence. But the powers of the soul are distinct. Therefore, original sin inheres in the soul's powers prior to being in the soul's essence.

5. The original sin in particular begotten human beings derives from the sin of Adam, which corrupts the powers of the soul prior to corrupting the soul's essence. But effects are like their causes. Therefore, original sin also corrupts the soul's powers prior to corrupting the soul's essence.

6. The soul is essentially the form of the body, and the soul gives being and life to the body. Therefore, the defect belonging to the soul's essence is deficiency of life, that is, death or the necessity of dying. But such defect has the nature of punishment, not the nature of moral fault. Therefore, original sin does not inhere in the soul's essence.

59. *On the Virgin Conception* 27 (PL 158:436A).
60. A. 1, objection 10.
61. Anselm, *On the Virgin Conception* 3 (PL 158:436A).
62. *Retractions* I, 15, n. 2 (PL 32:608).
63. A. 2, the fourth reply to the arguments in the section *On the contrary* (*I*).

7. The soul is capable of sin only insofar as it is rational. But we call the soul rational by reason of certain rational powers. Therefore, sin inheres in powers of the soul prior to inhering in the soul's essence.

On the Contrary:

1. The soul contracts original sin by its union with the flesh. But the soul is essentially united to the flesh as the form of the flesh. Therefore, original sin inheres first in the soul's essence.

2. Original sin is first a sin of human nature, not a personal sin, as I have said before.[64] But the soul as form of the body constitutes an essential part of human nature. And the soul by its powers is the source of acts, which belong to persons, since acts belong to individuals, as the Philosopher says.[65] Therefore, original sin inheres in the soul's essence prior to being in the soul's powers.

3. There is one original sin in each human being, and there are many powers in each human being, which are nonetheless united in the one essence of each soul. But one accident belongs to several subjects only insofar as they are united. Therefore, original sin inheres in the soul's essence prior to being in the soul's powers.

4. We contract original sin by physical descent. But the soul's essence is the terminus of our origin, since the end of generation is the form generated. Therefore, original sin directly regards the soul's essence.

5. According to Anselm,[66] original sin consists of the lack of original justice. But original justice was a gift bestowed on human nature, not to the person of Adam; otherwise, it would not have been transmitted to his offspring. And so original justice belonged to the essence of the soul, which is the nature and form of the body. Therefore, by like reasoning, original sin also inheres in the soul's essence prior to being in the soul's powers.

6. Whatever inheres in the soul's powers prior to being in the soul's essence inheres in the soul as related to objects. And what is in the soul by a relation to the subject is in the soul's essence prior to being in the soul's powers. But original sin does not inhere in the soul by a relation to objects; rather, original sin inheres in the soul by a relation to the subject, that is, the flesh, from which the soul contracts corruption. Therefore, original sin inheres in the soul's essence prior to being in the soul's powers.

Answer:

Original sin in some respect inheres both in the soul's essence and in the soul's powers, since the defect from the moral fault of our first parent extends to the whole soul. And we need to consider whether original sin inheres in the soul's essence prior to being in the soul's powers. And at first glance, it may indeed seem to some that original sin inheres first in the soul's essence because there is one original sin, and the soul's powers are unified in the soul's essence as their common source. But this argument is not convincing, since the powers of the soul are also unified in another way, namely, by the unity of their orderly arrangement as well as by the unity produced by the primary power moving and directing them.

---

64. A. 1.
65. *Metaphysics* I, 1 (981a16–17).
66. *On the Virgin Conception* 27 (PL 158:461A).

And we need to undertake our inquiry into this question from another perspective. And indeed, since the flesh transmits original sin to the soul, there can be no doubt that original sin in some way, at least in the process of generation and temporal succession, inheres in the soul's essence prior to being in the soul's powers. This is so because the soul is by its essence and not by its powers directly united to the body as the body's form, as I have shown elsewhere.[67] But one cannot maintain that original sin in the order of generation and temporal succession inheres in the soul's essence prior to being in the soul's powers but in the order of nature inheres first in the soul's powers, as I have previously said about the soul and the flesh as the subject of original sin.[68] For the soul's essence is not related to its powers as the body is to the soul, since the body is related to the soul as matter is to form. And matter precedes form in the process of generation and temporal succession, and form precedes matter in the process of perfection and nature. But the soul's essence is related to its powers as substantial form to resulting natural properties, and substances are prior to accidents both in the order of temporal succession and in the order of nature and conceptually, as the *Metaphysics* proves.[69]

And so original sin in every way inheres in the soul's essence prior to being in the soul's powers, and original sin is transmitted from the soul's essence to its powers, just as nature progresses from the soul's essence to its powers. And original sin concerns human nature, as I have said.[70]

Replies to the Objections:

1. Original justice, since it was a gift conferred on human nature, was not in the will so as not to be first in the soul's essence.

2. Concupiscence is original sin materially and by derivation from something higher, as it were, as I have said before.[71]

3. The soul's essence is related to its powers as substantial form to resulting properties, as, for example, the form of fire is related to its heat. But heat acts only by reason of fire's substantial form; otherwise, it would not act to induce the substantial form of fire. And so substantial form is the first source of activity. And so also the soul's essence is the source of activity prior to its powers.

4. The disorder of the soul's powers is from the defect of human nature, which first and chiefly regards the soul's essence.

5. Regarding Adam, the person corrupted his nature, and so the corruption in him was first in the powers of his soul rather than in its essence. But regarding human beings begotten from Adam, nature corrupts the person, and so corruption in them belongs to their souls' essence prior to belonging to their souls' powers.

6. The soul's essence is both the form of the body giving the body life and the source of powers. And so original sin is first in the soul's essence.

67. *De anima*, a. 9.
68. A. 3.
69. *Metaphysics* VII, 1 (1028a31–b2).
70. A. 1.
71. A. 2.

7. The rational powers themselves are derived from the soul's essence insofar as the soul causes human nature. And so the soul's essence transmits the capacity to be the subject of sin to its powers.

Fifth Article

Does Original Sin Inhere in the Will Prior to Being in Other Powers?

It seems that original sin does not, for the following reasons:

1. Original sin is a corruption. But of the powers of the soul, we say that the reproductive is the most corrupted. Therefore, original sin inheres in the reproductive power prior to being in the will.

2. We discern the lack of original justice, of which Anselm says that original sin consists,[72] in the rebellion of lower powers against reason. But such rebellion belongs to lower powers. Therefore, original sin inheres first in lower powers.

3. In the case of actual sin, turning away from the immutable good results from turning toward a transient good. But in the case of original sin, concupiscence is like the turning toward a transient good in actual sin, as I have said before.[73] Therefore, since concupiscence rests in lower powers, original sin is first in lower powers.

4. Original sin consists of the lack of original justice, as I have said.[74] But justice is a moral virtue, and all moral virtues rest in the nonrational parts of the soul, as a commentator on the *Ethics* says.[75] Therefore, original sin as well inheres first in the nonrational parts of the soul.

5. Original sin is a warping of the soul's governance. But the soul's governance belongs to reason. Therefore, original sin as well inheres in the power of reason prior to being in the power of the will.

6. The punishment of original sin consists of being deprived of the vision of God, which belongs to the intellect. But punishment corresponds to moral fault. Therefore, original sin inheres in the intellect prior to being in the will.

On the Contrary:
Anselm says in his work *On the Virgin Conception* that justice consists of rectitude of the will.[76] But original sin consists of the privation of original justice. Therefore, original sin inheres first in the will.

Answer:
We find that the subjects of virtues or vices are parts of the soul insofar as the subjects partake of something from a higher power. For example, the irascible and concupiscible

---

72. *On the Virgin Conception* 27 (PL 158:461A).
73. A. 2.
74. Objection 2.
75. Anonymous.
76. *On the Virgin Conception* 27 (PL 158:461A).

powers are subjects of certain virtues insofar as the powers partake of reason. And so we need to say that something rational is primarily and intrinsically the subject of virtue. Therefore, in order to discover the first subject of original sin among the powers of the soul, we need to consider which is the power from which all the others are capable of being subjects of sin. For it is to that power that original sin must necessarily be first transmitted from the soul's essence. And it is clear that sin, as we are now speaking of sin, deserves punishment. And our acts, because they are voluntary, deserve punishment and reproach. And so the will transmits the capacity of being a subject of sin to other powers. And so it is evident that original sin inheres in the will prior to being in other powers.

Replies to the Objections:

1. As I have said before,[77] we say that the corruption of sin is in something either actually, as in its proper subject, or virtually, as in its cause. But the cause of original sin is the reproductive act. And the reproductive act indeed belongs to the reproductive power regarding the power of execution, to concupiscible power regarding the power of desiring and commanding, and to the sense of touch regarding the power of experiencing and communicating pleasure. And so we say that the corruption of original sin inheres first in those powers virtually, as in its cause, and not actually, as in its proper subject.

2. The rebellion of the lower powers against the higher powers is due to the loss of power previously present in the higher powers, as I have said before.[78] And so original sin inheres in the higher powers rather than the lower powers.

3. In the reproductive process, turning away from the immutable good results from turning toward a transient good, but the character of actual sin is accomplished in the turning away. And likewise, the character of original sin is accomplished in the privation of original justice. And so original sin inheres first in the will.

4. The statement of the commentator is only true about those moral virtues that regard emotions, which belong to the nonrational parts of the soul. But justice regards activities, not emotions, as the *Ethics* says.[79] And so justice does not inhere in the irascible and concupiscible powers but in the will. And so there are four chief virtues in four powers capable of being subjects of virtue: practical wisdom in the power of reason; justice in the power of the will; temperance in concupiscible powers; fortitude in irascible powers.

5. The warped governance of reason has the nature of moral fault only insofar as it is voluntary. And so also reason has from the will the capacity to be the subject of sin.

6. The lack of the vision of God is a punishment insofar as the lack is contrary to the will of the person lacking the vision. For such contrariness belongs to the nature of punishment, as I have said before.[80] And so the lack as punishment relates to the will.

---

77. A. 3.
78. A. 2.
79. *Ethics* V, 1 (1129a3–5).
80. Q. 1, a. 4.

Sixth Article

Is Original Sin Transmitted by Adam to All Descendants from His Seed?

It seems that original sin is not, for the following reasons:

1. Death is punishment for original sin. But at the end of the world, when the Lord comes to render judgment, some of the living will not die, as Jerome says to Marcella.[81] Therefore, they will not be begotten with original sin.

2. People have said that not everybody held the position of Jerome on this matter, and so the argument is not absolutely conclusive. But a necessary inference from a probable proposition is not falsified nor contrary to faith any more than a possible but false proposition yields an impossible conclusion. And it is probable that some human beings begotten of Adam do not die. Therefore, the conclusion from the latter proposition, that some human beings are begotten without original sin, is also not falsified. Rather, the conclusion is probable.

3. As Augustine says in his *Enchiridion*,[82] we ask for eternal things in the first three petitions of the Lord's Prayer and earthly things in the other four petitions. But among the latter, we ask forgiveness of out debts, one of which is the necessity to beget children with original sin. Therefore, since it is inappropriate to say that the prayer of the whole church is not heard, it seems that some could in this earthly life beget children without original sin.

4. No one can receive from another what the other does not have. But the baptized do not have original sin, since baptism takes away original sin. Therefore, no one begotten by a father who has been baptized contracts original sin.

5. The Apostle says in Rom. 11:16, "If the trunk is holy, so are the branches," and the Lord says in Mt. 7:17, "A good tree bears good fruit." Therefore, a father, if he is both holy and good, does not beget children tainted by original sin.

6. If the contrary species belongs to the contrary genus, the species in question also belongs to the genus in question. But human beings who are sinners beget sinners. Therefore, by the same token, human beings who are just beget just human beings. Therefore, just human beings do not beget human beings corrupted by original sin.

7. The Apostle says in Rom. 5:15 that "the gift of Christ is not like the sin of Adam," and that the gift of Christ is much more powerful. But the sin transmitted by Adam to someone is transmitted by that one to his children. Therefore, the gift of Christ transmitted by baptism to someone is also transmitted by that one to his children. And so the children of the baptized are begotten without original sin.

8. Augustine says in his work *On the Punishment and Forgiveness of Sins and on the Baptism of Infants*: "The transgression of the first sinner did not do more harm to human beings than the incarnation and redemption of the Saviour brought them profit."[83] But

---

81. *Letter 59*, n. 3 (PL 22:587).
82. *Enchiridion* 115 (PL 40:285).
83. *On the Punishment and Forgiveness of Sins and on the Baptism of Infants* II, 30 (PL 44:180).

the redemption of the Savior did not bring profit to all human beings. Therefore, neither did the transgression of Adam harm all human beings. And so not all begotten of Adam's seed contract original sin from him.

9. The more general is not destroyed when the less general is. For example, it does not follow that if there is no human being, there is no animal; rather, the converse is true. But human nature is more general than any person possessing human nature. Therefore, the personal corruption of Adam himself could not corrupt the whole human nature by original sin.

10. Baptism either does or does not take away the corruption of human nature. If baptism does, then no act of human nature transmits original sin to offspring. And if baptism does not, the corruption is equally related to the soul of the begetter and to the soul of the offspring begotten. Therefore, if the corruption does not corrupt the soul of the begetter with original sin, neither will original sin corrupt the soul of the offspring begotten.

11. Anselm says in his work *On the Virgin Conception* that sin is no more in semen than in spittle.[84] But nothing can convey to another what it does not possess. Therefore, the generation produced by Adam's seed does not cause original sin in his offspring.

12. Augustine says in his work *On the Perfection of Human Justice*: "What comes about by natural necessity lacks moral fault."[85] But semen by natural necessity causes everything it causes in offspring. Therefore, everything semen causes lacks moral fault. Therefore, those begotten of Adam's seed do not contract original sin.

13. Semen is a material substance. But the action of material substances is successive, not instantaneous, and moral fault corrupts the soul instantaneously. Therefore, semen does not cause such corruption.

14. The Philosopher says in his work *On the Generation of Animals* that semen is an overflow of nutriment,[86] and so the semen that begets particular human beings was not in Adam. But particular human beings contract original sin insofar as they sinned in Adam, as the Apostle says in Rom. 5:12. Therefore, impregnation of semen does not transmit original sin from Adam to all human beings.

15. A proximate cause has a greater impact than a remote cause does. And the proof of this is that a proximate cause produces something specifically like itself, and a remote cause does not. For example, the human being begotten is specifically like the human being who begets, not like the sun. But the corruption of human nature as it was in Adam is also in the same way in the immediate parent. Therefore, we ought to say that those presently begotten contract original sin from their immediate parents, not from Adam.

16. Augustine says in his work *On Marriage and Concupiscence* that lust, not propagation, transmits original sin to offspring,[87] and so it seems that if there were generation without lust, sin would not be transmitted to offspring. But generation when with or without lust causes different dispositions of the semen only by a greater or lesser inten-

---

84. *On the Virgin Conception* 7 (PL 158:441C).
85. *On the Perfection of Human Justice* 4 (PL 44:295).
86. *On the Generation of Animals* I, 18 (726a26).
87. *On Marriage and Concupiscence* I, 24 (PL 44:429).

sity of heat. For as semen is a material substance composed of elements, we trace its different disposition in activity to active properties of the elements. But causes distinguished only by greater or lesser intensity of heat do not produce specifically different effects. Therefore, as propagation without lust would not transmit original sin, so neither does propagation accompanied by lust.

17. Charity lessens sexual lust. But charity can be increased endlessly. Therefore, since sexual lust is not infinite, it seems that charity can completely eliminate it. And so some human beings need not be begotten with original sin.

18. Sexual lust belongs either to disordered sensuality or to a wicked will. But neither one of these alternatives is true about the just begetting offspring. Therefore, those begotten of the just do not contract original sin.

19. As good pours itself out, as Dionysius says,[88] so evil draws itself in. But the good that Adam did (e.g., his repentance) is not poured out to all human beings. Therefore, much less is the evil he did.

20. Sin is transmitted from Adam to others insofar as they sinned in him. But Adam sinned by eating the forbidden apple, and we cannot say that all human beings ate the forbidden apple when Adam did. Therefore, neither can we say that they sinned when he did. And so original sin is not transmitted from Adam to all human beings.

On the Contrary:

1. The Apostle says in Rom. 5:12: "Sin entered the world through one human being, and death through sin, and so death passed to all human beings from Adam, in whom all sinned."

2. Augustine says in his work *On Faith, to Peter* that as human beings cannot copulate without lust, so they cannot be conceived without original sin.[89]

Answer:

It is false to say that any are descended from Adam's seed without original sin. For then there would be some human beings who would not need the redemption accomplished by Christ. And so we should absolutely concede that all propagated from Adam's seed contract original sin immediately at the very moment of their conception.

And we can demonstrate this from things that I have said before.[90] For I have said before that original sin is related to the whole of human nature propagated from Adam as actual sin is related an individual human person, as if all human beings as descendants of the one Adam should be one human being whose different bodily members are different persons. And it is clear that actual sin inheres first in its source, namely, the will, which is the first subject of sin, as I have said before.[91] And actual sin is transmitted from the will to other powers of the soul and even bodily members insofar as the will moves these powers and members, since it is in this way that acts are voluntary, and acts need to be voluntary in order to have the nature of sin. Therefore, we ought also consider origi-

---

88. *On the Divine Names* 4, n. 4 (PG 3:700A).
89. Augustine (Pseudo) = Fulgentius, *On Faith, to Peter* 2, n. 16 (PL 40:758).
90. A. 1.
91. A. 5.

nal sin first in Adam as its source, from which it is transmitted to all produced by that source. And as the command of the will moves the parts of one and the same human being, so fathers by their reproductive power produce children. And so the Philosopher says in the *Physics* that fathers by impregnating semen cause offspring,[92] and he says in his work *On the Generation of Animals* that semen has its causal power from the soul of the begetter that disposes matter to receive the form of the begotten.[93] Therefore, such movement, which originated from our first parent, is transmitted to all who come from his seed. And so all who come from his seed contract original sin from him.

Replies to the Objections:

1. Jerome does not propose this as his own opinion but as the opinion of some people, as is evident in the letter that he writes to Minerius about the resurrection of the flesh,[94] in which letter he posits several opinions on the subject. And of these opinions, he reports that some people thought that those alive at the coming of the Lord will not die because of what the Apostle speaking in their person says in 1 Thes. 4:17: "We who are alive will along with them be snatched up into the clouds to meet Christ in the air." And others explain this text to mean that those alive at the coming of the Lord, rising immediately, would be dead only for a little while, not that they do not die. And this is the more common opinion.

2. Granted that those alive at the coming of the Lord would never die, it does not necessarily follow that they did not contract original sin. For the special punishment of original sin is the necessity of dying, as the Apostle says in Rom. 8:10, "The body is indeed dead because of sin," that is, consigned to the necessity of death, as Augustine explains.[95] And it may happen that some have the necessity of dying but will never die due to the power of God preventing death, just as it may happen that something by nature heavy is not borne downward due to some impediment.

3. The debt of begetting offspring with original sin is remitted in this life as to Christ's power cleansing of sin some begotten with sin, not as to one begetting offspring without sin. For debts mean sins, as Augustine explains in his work *On the Lord's Sermon on the Mount*.[96]

4. Original sin is the contrary of original justice. And by reason of original justice, the higher power of the soul both was joined to God and commanded lower powers and could even preserve the body from corruption. Therefore, baptism takes away original sin regarding the gift of grace, which unites the superior part of the soul to God, but baptism does not give the soul the power to be able to preserve the body from corruption, or the higher part of the soul the power to be able to preserve the lower powers from every kind of rebellion. And so there remains after baptism both the necessity of dying and concupiscence, which is the material element in original sin. And so as to the higher part of the soul, it shares in the new condition of Christ. But as to the lower powers of the soul and

---

92. *Physics* II, 3 (194b30–31).
93. *On the Generation of Animals* II, 3 (736b29ff.).
94. *Letter 119*, n. 7 (PL 22:971).
95. *On the Punishment and Forgiveness of Sins and on the Baptism of Infants* I, 6 (PL 44:112).
96. *On the Lord's Sermon on the Mount* II, 8, n. 28 (PL 34:1281).

the body itself, there still remains the old condition that comes from Adam. And it is clear that the baptized beget offspring by their lower powers and the body, not by the higher part of the soul. And so the baptized transmit to their offspring the old condition of Adam, not the new condition of Christ. And so, although the baptized do not themselves have original sin regarding moral fault, they still transmit original sin to their offspring.

5. And the foregoing makes clear the reply to the fifth objection.

6. This way of arguing is valid regarding what belongs to contraries as contraries but not regarding what is common to both contraries. For example, it follows that if black concentrates vision, white disperses vision, but it does not follow that if black is visible, white is invisible, since visibility belongs to black as a color, and color is the genus of both black and white. And the old condition of Adam regarding lower powers and the body itself is common to the just and to sinners, and sinners in that respect beget sinners. And so it does not follow that the just beget offspring without original sin.

7. The gift of Christ is more powerful than the sin of Adam, since Christ's gift restores human beings to a higher state than Adam had before he sinned, namely, the state of glory, which involves no risk of sinning. But this needs to be accomplished by conforming oneself to Christ, so that the effect is like its cause. For Christ assumed the old condition of punishment in order by his death to redeem us from death, and so he by his resurrection restored our life. Just so, human beings through Christ are first conformed to Christ through grace, with the old condition of punishment remaining, and are at last brought to glory at the resurrection. And by reason of the penal condition that remains in the baptized regarding their lower powers, they transmit original sin. Nor is it inappropriate that punishment cause moral fault, since lower powers can be subjects of moral fault only insofar as higher powers can move them. And so when moral fault has been removed from the higher part of the soul, the nature of moral fault does not actually remain in the lower powers, but the nature of moral fault remains in those powers virtually insofar as the powers are the source of human generation.

8. As the sin of Adam harms all those begotten of his seed, so the redemption of Christ profits all those spiritually begotten of him.

9. Human nature absolutely considered belongs to more things than a person does, but human nature considered as belonging to the person is included in the bounds of the person. And the person can corrupt human nature in this way. And since all those propagated from the seed of our first parent receive human nature from him, such corruption of human nature is transmitted to all of them. Just so, if water were to be tainted at its source, the taint would affect the whole stream coming from the source.

10. The soul of a baptized parent has something that resists the corruption of original sin, namely, the sacrament of Christ, and the soul of the begotten offspring indeed does not have this impediment to corruption. Or we should say that the corruption of human nature passes to the soul only by the reproductive act, which is a natural act, and so the corruption passes to the soul of the begotten, who is the end product of generation, and not to the soul of the begetter.

11. Original sin is virtually, not actually, in the semen, inasmuch as the semen is the source of human generation, as I have said before.[97]

---

97. A. 1.

12. The defect of original sin does not have the nature of moral fault because generation from semen necessarily transmits the sin. Rather, the defect has the nature of moral fault because human nature has been corrupted by a taint that is imputed as voluntary on account of its source, as I have said before.[98]

13. Semen causes corruption of the soul in the same way it causes completion of human nature. Therefore, as the causal action of the semen is successive, but the completion of human nature instantaneous at the advent of the ultimate form, so also the corruption of original sin is caused instantaneously, although the causal action of the semen is not instantaneous.

14. Some believed that original sin could be transmitted from our first parent to his posterity only if all human beings were materially in Adam, and so they held that semen is matter transmitted from Adam himself, not an overflow of nutriment.[99] But this cannot be the case, since then semen would be something distinct from the substance of the begetter. And what is distinct from the substance of something is separate from its nature and in the process of dissolution, and so cannot be the source of generating the same nature. And the Philosopher concludes from this that semen is an overflow of nutriment, not something distinct. But this does not preclude original sin being contracted from our first parent. For the condition of the begotten depends on the efficient cause that disposes its matter and gives it its form rather than on the matter, which, leaving its prior disposition and losing its prior form, receives a new disposition and form from the cause. And so, regarding the contraction of original sin, it does not matter whencesoever the matter of the human body came. Rather, it matters by what cause the matter of the human body was changed into the human species.

15. We can distinguish proximate and remote causes in two ways: in one way intrinsically; in the second way accidentally. We can indeed distinguish them accidentally when we consider remoteness and distance only spatially or temporally or some such thing accidental to the cause as cause. And then it is true that the proximate cause causes a deeper imprint on the effect than the remote cause does. For example, a fire at hand heats something more than a distant fire does, and an evil at hand causes more anxiety than a remote evil does. And we distinguish proximate and remote causes intrinsically by the natural ordering of the causes in causing, and then the remote cause has more influence on the effect than the proximate cause does. For the *Book of Causes* says that every primary cause has more influence on its effect than a secondary cause does, since the secondary cause acts only by the power of the primary cause.[100] And that the effect sometimes receives the species of the proximate rather than the remote cause is due to the deficiency of matter that is incapable of receiving so excellent a form, not to lack of efficacy on the part of the remote cause. And so matter will receive the form of the chief cause rather than the form of the proximate cause if the matter is capable of doing so, just as a house receives the form of the builder's craft rather than the form of his tools. Therefore, since all human beings have the old condition of original sin insofar as they are caused by our first parent, as I have said before,[101] so no one

98. Ibid.
99. Cf., e.g., Bonaventure, *Commentary on the Sentences*, d. 30, a. 3, q. 1.
100. *Book of Causes*, prop. 1 and comm.
101. A. 1.

transmits original sin except insofar as he begets in virtue of the first cause. And that is why we say that offspring contract original sin from Adam rather than from their immediate parents.

16. Lust designates actual inordinate desire. And I have said before that the material element in original sin is habitual concupiscence,[102] which comes from the fact that reason does not have the power completely to restrain lower powers. Therefore, the actual lust in sexual intercourse is evidence of the habitual concupiscence that is the material element in original sin. And the reason why human beings transmit original sin to offspring is because there remains in them even after baptism something of original sin, namely, concupiscence or the incendiary source of sin, as I have said.[103] Therefore, it is clear that actual lust is not the reason why original sin is transmitted. Rather, it is evidence of the sin. And so, if actual lust were miraculously to be completely eliminated from sexual intercourse, the offspring would nonetheless contract original sin, since the cause of original sin remains. And so when Augustine said that lust transmits original sin, he posited the sign of original sin for the thing signified. And the objection was arguing on the basis of such actual lust, with which more intense heat is associated. But the heat is not the whole cause; rather, the more important cause derives from the power of such a soul, which power is chiefly active in the semen, as the Philosopher says.[104]

17. Charity lessens actual lust insofar as the concupiscible powers obey reason. But concupiscible powers in the present condition of corrupted human nature do not obey reason in such a way that they do not partially retain their own spontaneous movement, even movement contrary to the ordination of reason. And so sexual lust is not altogether taken away, however much the charity of one's life is increased.

18. Even the just experience actual lust in the sexual act when the concupiscible appetite tends unrestrainedly for the pleasures of the flesh, and the will, even if it does or wills nothing contrary to reason, nonetheless, due to the emotional intensity, does not pay attention to the ordination of actual reason.

19. We are the source of sin, and God is the source of meritorious good. And so there was in Adam some good that could have been communicated to all human beings, namely, original justice, which he notwithstanding had from God. But he had from himself the evil that he transmitted to others. And so we could rather say that God would have been the transmitter of good, and the human being is the transmitter of evil. And the good of Adam's very repentance is not transmitted to others, since its source was the grace personally bestowed on him.

20. Eating signifies a personal act, but sinning can belong both to a person and to human nature. And so we say that those who receive their human nature from Adam sinned in Adam, not that they ate in Adam.

102. Reply to objection 4.
103. Reply to objection 7.
104. Cited in the answer (conclusion).

Seventh Article

Do Those Begotten Only from Adam's
Matter Contract Original Sin?

It seems that they do, for the following reasons:

1. The corruption of the flesh to which the soul is united taints the soul with original sin. But the corruption of sin actually tainted the flesh of the human being who sinned, and the corruption of sin only virtually tainted his semen, since the semen, lacking a rational soul, is incapable of receiving the taint of sin. Therefore, a human being miraculously formed out of the flesh of one having original sin (e.g., out of the rib or hand or foot) would contract the stain of original sin to a greater degree than a human being begotten from the semen of such a man.

2. A gloss on Gen. 4:1 says that the whole posterity of Adam was corrupted in his loins, since his posterity was not previously separated from him when he lived in paradise but was later separated from him when he was exiled.[105] But if a human being were to be formed out of the body of another human being (e.g., out of the hand or the foot), the flesh of the former would be separated from the flesh of the latter when the latter's flesh was in a penal condition. Therefore, the human being so formed would contract original sin.

3. Original sin is a sin of the whole human nature, as I have said before.[106] But a human being formed out of the flesh of another human being would belong to human nature. Therefore, the human being so formed would contract original sin.

4. In the begetting of human beings and all animals, the female provides the matter of the body. But the corruption of sin taints the soul because the soul is united to the matter of the body. Therefore, even if Adam were not to have sinned, and Eve did, the offspring begotten of both would contract original sin simply because of the matter, not because of the corruption of Adam's semen.

5. Death and every corruption results from a property of matter. But mothers provide the matter of offspring. Therefore, if Eve by sinning were to have become subject to death and suffering, and Adam did not sin, the children begotten would have been subject to death and suffering. But there is no punishment without moral fault. Therefore, the children would have contracted original sin.

6. Damascene says in his work *On Orthodox Faith* that the Holy Spirit came over Mary and purified her.[107] But we cannot say that her purification was superfluous, since no created nature, much less the Holy Spirit, does anything superfluous. Therefore, the body of Christ, if it were to have been taken from the Virgin without her being previously purified, would still have contracted original sin. And so it seems that the very fact that one receives flesh from Adam's matter suffices to contract original sin.

---

105. *Ordinary Gloss*, on Gen. 4:1.
106. Aa. 1, 2, and 6 (reply to objection 9).
107. *On Orthodox Faith* III, 2 (PG 94:986B).

On the Contrary:

Augustine says in his *Literal Commentary on Genesis* that Christ did not sin in Adam, nor was he destined for punishment in the loins of Abraham, since Christ was in the loins only regarding their bodily substance, not regarding their reproductive nature.[108]

Answer:

We can understand the answer to this question from what I have explained before.[109] For I have said before that original sin is transmitted from our first parent to his descendants insofar as our first parent caused them by physical descent. And it is clear that it is the nature of matter to undergo motion, not to cause motion. And so howsoever a person comes from Adam's matter or from his descendants, the person would contract original sin only if the person were to be propagated from Adam's seed. Just so, neither would a person contract original sin if the person were to be freshly formed out of the earth. For regarding the condition of a person, it matters by what cause the person is formed, not out of what matter the person is formed, since human beings receive their form and dispositions from their efficient causes, as I have said,[110] and matter, losing its prior form and disposition, acquires a new one by generation.

Replies to the Objections:

1. If a human being were to be formed out of the finger or flesh of another human being, this could only be the case if the flesh of the other ceased to be such and abandoned its prior disposition, since the coming to be of one thing is the ceasing to be of something else. And so the previous corruption in the flesh would not remain to corrupt the soul.

2. We should not understand the gloss as if the condition of exile causes a human being to contract original sin, since if Adam were to have remained in the earthly paradise after sinning, he would still have transmitted original sin to his posterity. Rather, the cause of the transmission of original sin is the corruption of human nature in our first parent, and the condition of exile accompanies the corruption. And so the gloss posits the condition as something accompanying the cause, not as the cause of the transmission of original sin.

3. Original sin does not belong to human nature absolutely, but Adam transmits human nature through his semen, as I have said.[111]

4. Children begotten of an Adam who did not sin and of an Eve who did would not contract original sin, since original sin is contracted through the power that causes the movement toward human nature, and this power is in the semen of the male, as the Philosopher says.[112] And so, although Eve sinned first, the Apostle nonetheless expressly says in Rom. 5:12 that sin entered the world through one man.

5. Some thought that those begotten of an Adam who did not sin and of an Eve who did would be subject to death and suffering because those things result from the

---

108. *Literal Commentary on Genesis* X, 19 and 20 (PL 34:423–24).
109. A. 6.
110. A. 6, reply to objection 14.
111. A. 6.
112. *On the Generation of Animals* II, 3 (736b29ff.).

matter, which mothers provide, and then mortality and suffering would be natural and not punitive defects.[113] But we should more accurately say that those so begotten would not be subject to suffering or death. For if Adam had not sinned, he would have transmitted original justice to his descendants, to which justice belongs both that the soul is subject to God, and that the body is subject to the soul. And this excludes the capacity to suffer and die.

6. Christ was unable to contract original sin because he was conceived of the Virgin without semen from a man. And the Virgin was previously purified because complete purity befitted the flesh that the Word of God received, not because her purification was necessary in order that Christ should be conceived without original sin.

Eighth Article

Are the Sins of Immediate Parents Transmitted by Physical Descent to Their Posterity?

It seems that those sins are, for the following reasons:

1. David, begotten of a lawful marriage, says in Ps. 51:5: "Behold, I was conceived in iniquities, and my mother conceived me in sins." And it seems from this that one and the same human being has many original sins. But this could not be if the sins of immediate parents were not to be transmitted by physical descent to their posterity, and if only the sin of the first man were to be. Therefore, the sins of immediate parents are transmitted by physical descent to their posterity.

2. As human nature belonged to Adam, so does human nature belong to individual human beings. But Adam by his actual sin corrupted human nature and also transmitted the corrupted nature to his posterity, since he communicated the nature as he possessed it. Therefore, every other man by his actual sin also corrupts human nature in himself and transmits such corruption to his posterity. And so the actual sins of immediate parents pass by physical descent to their posterity just as the sin of our first parent does.

3. People have said that Adam had an integral human nature, and so he could corrupt it by his actual sin, but other human beings have a corrupt human nature, and so their actual sins cannot corrupt that nature. But Rev. 22:11 says: "Let the holy be made holier, and let the filthy become filthier." And to be in the filth of sin is to be corrupt. Therefore, the corrupt nature in someone can still be further corrupted.

4. People have said that the corruption of human nature that the sin of our first parent brought about corrupted an integral human nature and so could cause the transmission of original sin, but that other corruptions of human nature, which our immediate parents' actual sins bring about, do not corrupt an integral human nature. And so other corruptions do not cause the transmission of original sin. But the mean in relation to one of the extremes has the nature of the other extreme; for example, gray is related to

---

113. Cf. Thomas himself, *Commentary on the Sentences*, d. 31, q. 1, a. 2, in the reply to objection 4, and Bonaventure, *Commentary on the Sentences*, d. 31, doubt 3.

white as blacker, and to black as whiter. And the less corrupt is the mean between the integral and the more corrupt. Therefore, the corruption by which human nature is transformed from integral to corrupt, and the corruption by which human nature is transformed from less corrupt to more corrupt, produce the same effect.

5. People have said that human nature belonged to the first man as its first source, and so it could be corrupted in him but not in others. But if the first man were not to have sinned, and a male of his posterity were to have sinned, the latter would have a corrupted human nature and would transmit such a nature to his posterity. And yet human nature would not belong to him as the first source. Therefore, in order to transmit an original sin, the first source of human nature need not corrupt that nature.

6. Ex. 20:5 says: "I am a jealous God, visiting the iniquity of fathers on sons unto the third and fourth generations." And this can only be referring to the actual sins of immediate parents. Therefore, the actual sins of immediate parents are transmitted by physical descent to their posterity.

7. People have said that we should understand the foregoing text about the transmission of sins regarding punishment and not moral fault. But there can be no effect without its cause. And punishment is an effect of moral fault. Therefore, if punishment be transmitted, it is necessary that moral fault also be transmitted.

8. People have said punishment does not always suppose moral fault in the same person but sometimes supposes moral fault in another. But punishment is from God, and it is just. And justice is a certain equality between the wrong and the punishment. Therefore, punishment needs to reduce the inequality of moral fault to equality. But this could only be so if the punishment were to bring about equality in the same person in whom moral fault previously brought about inequality, that is, that one who by sinning of his or her own will acted contrary to the will of God suffer something contrary to his or her will by the will of God. Therefore, punishment needs to be transmitted to the same person to whom moral fault is transmitted.

9. According to Mt. 27:25, the Jews said: "His blood be upon us and our children." And explaining this, Augustine in a sermon on the Lord's passion says: "Behold what goods they transmit to their heirs by such a testimonial to their sacrilege; they imbue themselves with the stain of his blood, and they ruin their posterity."[114] Therefore, the actual sin of men other than Adam are transmitted to posterity even regarding moral stain.

10. All of us sinned in Adam when he sinned, as the Apostle says in Rom. 5:12, and this is so because we were in him by reason of the power of his semen to beget us, as Augustine says.[115] But as we were in Adam by his seminal power, so also are we in our immediate parents by their seminal power. Therefore, we also sinned in them when they sinned, and so their sins are transmitted to us by physical descent.

11. Death, which is the privation of life, is a punishment of original sin. But the life of human beings is ever being shortened more and more, since human beings at the beginning lived longer than they do now. Therefore, since the punishment is increasing, it

114. *Sermon 28* (Mai I:62, n. 3).
115. *Literal Commentary on Genesis* X, 20, n. 35 (PL 34:424).

seems that it is increasing from moral fault. So actual sins of immediate parents add something to the original sin that we contract from our first parent.

12. Before the institution of circumcision, male children were saved only by the faith of their parents, as Gregory says.[116] Therefore, the children were damned by their parents' lack of faith. But lack of faith is an actual sin. Therefore, the actual sin of immediate parents is transmitted to their posterity.

13. It is a greater effect to produce something that exists in the imagination and in reality than to produce something that exists only in the imagination. But an imaginary bodily ugliness, which exists only in the imagination of a begetter, is transmitted to offspring, and so Jerome in his work *Book of Hebraic Questions on Genesis* relates that a certain woman gave birth to a black child after looking at the picture of an Ethiopian on the wall.[117] Therefore, much more is the ugliness of sin, which is in a father's soul both in reality and in his imagination, transmitted to his offspring.

14. Persons can better share with others what they possess of themselves than what they possess from others. But immediate parents transmit to their descendants the corruption of original sin transmitted to them by Adam. Therefore, much more do they transmit the corruption of their actual sins.

15. Canon and civil law hold children liable for the sins of their parents. For example, the children of pagan priests, although born of free women, are bound to slavery,[118] and canon law holds the heirs of a thief liable for the theft of their father even if they do not share in the proceeds of the theft,[119] and even if no suit was brought against the father. And the children of traitors bear the shame of their parents.[120] Therefore, the sins of parents are transmitted to their children.

16. Children have more in common with their immediate parents than with their first parent and are more directly related to their immediate parents. Therefore, if the sin of the first parent is transmitted to all of his posterity, much more are the sins of immediate parents transmitted to their children.

17. Things of the body are transmitted when the body is transmitted. But some actual sins belong to the body. For example, the Apostle says in 1 Cor. 6:18: "Every other sin that a human being shall commit is outside his body, but a fornicator sins in his body." Therefore, such actual sins are transmitted by physical descent from immediate parents to their offspring.

On the Contrary:

1. Sin is contrary to merit. But the merits of parents are not transmitted to their offspring; otherwise, all of us would not be begotten children of wrath. Therefore, neither are the actual sins of immediate parents transmitted to their offspring.

2. Ez. 18:20 says: "Children shall not incur the iniquity of their fathers." But they would if their fathers' iniquity were to be transmitted to them. Therefore, the sins of immediate parents are not transmitted to their children.

---

116. *Morals* IV, 3 (PL 75:635B).
117. *Book of Hebraic Questions on Genesis* 30 (PL 23:985).
118. *Decretum*, c. 15, q. 8, chap. 3 (Friedberg I: 759).
119. Cf., e.g., Raymond of Penafort, *Summa of Penances* (Ochoa-Diaz:498).
120. *Decretum*, c. 6, q. 1, chap. 22 (Friedberg I: 560).

Answer:

Augustine considers this question in his *Enchiridion* and leaves it unresolved.[121] But if we should consider the question carefully, we would conclude that the actual sins of immediate parents cannot be transmitted by physical descent to their offspring.

And to prove this, we need to note that a univocal begetter transmits the nature of his species to the begotten, and so all the accidents that result from the species. For example, as a human being begets a human being, so a being capable of laughter begets a being capable of laughter. And if the power of the begetter happens to be intense, he transmits his likeness to the begotten even regarding individual accidents. But this is so regarding accidents that in some way belong to the body and not regarding accidents that belong to the soul, especially the rational soul, which is not a power in a bodily organ. For example, a light-skinned father usually begets a light-skinned son, and a tall father usually begets a tall son, but a grammarian does not beget a grammarian, nor a natural scientist a natural scientist.

And because sin takes away the gift of grace, we should consider regarding sin the same thing that we consider regarding the gift of grace taken away by sin. And at the beginning of the human condition, God bestowed on the first human being a gratuitous gift both regarding his person and regarding the whole human nature transmitted by him, and this gift was original justice. And the power of this gift did not rest only in the higher part of the soul, that is, the rational part. It was also diffused to the lower parts of the soul, which the power of the aforementioned gift kept completely subject to reason, and even diffused to the body, in which nothing contrary to the gift's presence in the soul could happen as long as the gift remained. And so this gift would have been transmitted to Adam's posterity for two good reasons: first, indeed, because it was befalling human nature by God's gift, albeit not by the ordination of nature; second, because it reaches even to the body, which is transmitted by generation. But the first sin of our first parent took away this gift. And so it was also reasonable that that sin for the same reasons be transmitted to Adam's posterity by physical descent.

But other actual sins, whether of the first parent himself or also of other ancestors, are contrary to the gift of grace that God bestows on someone only regarding the person. And moreover, the power of this gift of grace rests only in the rational soul and is not transmitted to the body so that such grace takes away dissolubility of the body. And so the very grace is not transmitted, nor are the actual sins of any ancestors, even the actual sins of Adam himself aside from his first sin, transmitted to offspring by way of physical descent. But the actual sins of immediate parents can be transmitted to their children by way of example, because of the continuous interaction of children with their parents.

Replies to the Objections:

1. Original sin in a human being is only one sin. But the text, "My mother conceived me in sins," uses the plural for four reasons. First, it is customary for Scripture to use the plural for the singular, as Mt. 2:20 does when it says, "Those who were seeking the life of the child are dead," meaning only Herod. Second, original sin is in a way the cause of

---

121. *Enchiridion* 47 (PL 40:255).

subsequent sins and so includes many sins virtually. Third, there were in the actual sin of our first parent, who causes original sin, many deformities of sin; for example, there were pride, disobedience, gluttony, and theft. Fourth, the corruption of original sin belongs to different parts of human beings. And yet we can accordingly speak of original sin being many in one human being only relatively.

2. Adam by his actual sin corrupted human nature by taking away the gratuitous gift that could be transmitted to his posterity. And the actual sins of our immediate parents do not do this, as what I have said makes clear,[122] although the sins add to the corruption by taking away grace or the disposition for grace itself, which is a personal gift.

3–4–5. And the foregoing makes clear the replies to the third, fourth, and fifth objections.

6. The cited text says this because sin is transmitted from parents to offspring regarding punishment. But we should consider that there are two kinds of punishment. One kind of punishment is spiritual, and such punishment belongs to the soul. And children are never punished for their fathers by such punishment. And this is so because the souls of children do not come from the souls of fathers; rather, God directly creates the children's souls. And Ez. 18:4 and 20 gives this explanation: "As the soul of a father belongs to me, so also does the soul of his son," and "the son will not incur the iniquity of his father." The second kind of punishment is bodily or of things belonging to the body, and regarding such punishment, children are sometimes punished for their parents, especially when the children are likened to the parents in moral fault. For regarding the body that is transmitted by the parent, the child is part of the father.

7. The temporal punishment with which a child is sometimes punished has as its cause the previous moral fault in the child's parent.

8. Insofar as the child is part of the father, so also is the father punished in the punishment of the child.

9. The descendants of the Jews are liable for the blood of Christ insofar as the descendants imitate the wickedness of their ancestors by approving it.

10. We were in our first parent and our immediate parents by sharing their nature, not by sharing their persons. And so we share in the sin that takes away the gift bestowed on the nature but not in sins that take away gifts of the persons.

11. The fact that human beings now live shorter lives than at the beginning of the world is not due to the original sin becoming more punitive or the continual weakening of human nature, as some have said;[123] otherwise, the human lifespan would in the course of time become ever shorter and shorter. And this conclusion is evidently false, since human beings now live as long as in the time of David, who said in Ps. 90:10: "The span of our years is three score and ten." Therefore, the extended duration of life at the beginning of the world was due to God's power in order to secure the multiplication of the human race.

12. From the beginning of the world, only Jesus Christ, the mediator between God and human beings, could apply a remedy for original sin. Therefore, the ancients' faith and its profession did not profit their children for salvation as if their faith was a merito-

---

122. In the answer.
123. Cf. Alexander of Hales, *Summa of Theology* II–II, n. 252.

rious act of believers, and so it was not necessary that their faith be an act of perfect faith. Rather, their faith profited their children regarding the object of their faith, namely, the very mediator. For it is also in this way that the subsequently instituted sacraments profit us insofar as they are professions of faith. And so it does not follow that the parents' lack of faith would harm their children, except by accident, for example, by taking away the remedy for sin.

13. Imagination is a power in a bodily organ. And so as to an image in the imagination, there is a change in the bodily effluence, on which the causal power at work in the semen is based. And so a change comes about in the offspring through the imagination of the parent in sexual intercourse itself, if the intercourse is intense. But the corruption of sin, especially actual sin, abides entirely in the soul and does not belong to the body. And so there is no comparison.

14. The argument of this objection is valid, other things being equal.

15. The argument of this objection is valid regarding the transmission of sin as to bodily punishment.

16. Human beings would contract sin from their immediate parent rather than from their first parent if the sin of the immediate parent were to take away a gift bestowed on human nature, as the sin of our first parent did.

17. We do not say that the fornicator sins in his body because the stain of this sin is in his body; rather, the stain is in the soul just as grace, its contrary, would be. But we say that the fornicator sins in his body because the sin abounds in bodily pleasure and relaxation of the body unlike any other sin. For example, there is no relaxation of the body in the sin of gluttony, and there is no bodily pleasure in spiritual sins.

On the Punishment of Original Sin

First Article

Is Privation of the Vision of God a Fitting Punishment for Original Sin?

It seems that the privation of the vision of God is not, for the following reasons:

1. As the *Physics* says,[1] means that do not attain their end are pointless. But nature ordains human beings for happiness as their ultimate end, and this happiness consists of the vision of God. Therefore, the existence of human beings is pointless if they should not attain the vision of God. But God did not cease to cause the generation of human beings because of original sin, as Damascene says.[2] Therefore, since nothing regarding the works of God is pointless, it seems that human beings do not incur the guilty condition of privation of the vision of God because of the sin that they contract by their physical descent.

2. Ez. 18:4 says: "All souls belong to me; as the soul of a son is mine, so also is the soul of the father." And we can understand from this that God directly creates all souls, and that one is not transmitted by another. Therefore, a person should not be punished for the original sin transmitted by our first parent with a punishment that belongs only to the soul. But the privation of the vision of God is a punishment that belongs only to the soul, just as the very vision of God belongs only to the soul. Therefore, the privation of the vision of God is not a proper punishment for original sin.

3. Augustine says in his *Enchiridion* that the punishment of those punished only for original sin is the mildest.[3] But Chrysostom says in a homily on the Gospel of Matthew that the privation of the vision of God is the greatest punishment and worse than hell.[4] Therefore, the privation of the vision of God is not a fitting punishment for original sin.

---

1. Aristotle, *Physics* II, 6 (197b25–26).
2. *On Orthodox Faith* IV, 24 (PG 94:1208A).
3. *Enchiridion* 93 (PL 40:275).
4. *On Matthew*, hom. 23, n. 7 (PG 57:317).

4. People have said that the privation of the vision of God by itself is a lesser punishment than the privation along with the punishment of the senses incurred for actual sins. But punishment as an evil consists of the privation of a good. And the relation of privations to one another is like the relation of the things deprived to one another. For example, deafness is related to blindness as hearing is to sight. But the privation of the vision of God deprives human beings of God, and punishment of the senses deprives human beings of created goods, namely, sense pleasures or the like. And created goods added to the uncreated good do not make human beings happier. For Augustine, addressing God, says in his *Confessions*: "Those who know you and them," namely, creatures, "are happy because of you alone and not happier because of them."[5] Therefore, those whom the privation of the vision of God deprives of the uncreated good alone are not less unhappy than those who suffer punishment of the senses along with the privation.

5. People have said that although human beings may not be less happy regarding the essential reward, they are nonetheless less happy regarding the accidental reward. But the accidental reward is accidentally related to happiness. And increasing an accident does not increase the thing to which the accident belongs. For example, if something is whiter, it is not on that account more a human being. Therefore, happiness, which consists essentially of enjoying the highest good, is not increased by adding any created good.

6. Since the uncreated good infinitely surpasses created goods, a created good is related to the uncreated good like a point to a line. But adding a point does not make a line greater. Therefore, neither does adding a created good make greater the happiness that consists of enjoying the uncreated good.

7. People have said that although God is infinite good, the vision of God is not, since a finite intellect beholds God in a finite way, and so a person deprived of the vision of God is not deprived of infinite good. But those whose perfection is taken away are deprived of their perfection. And the object seen is the perfection of those who see. Therefore, those whose vision is taken away are deprived of the very object seen. And so those deprived of the vision of God are deprived of infinite good, since the object seen in the vision of God is infinite good.

8. God himself is human beings' reward, since he said to Abraham in Gen. 15:1: "I am your exceedingly great reward." Therefore, those deprived of their ultimate reward, which consists of the vision of God, are deprived of God himself, who is infinite good.

9. Original sin deserves less punishment than venial sin does; otherwise, the punishment of original sin would not be the mildest, as Augustine says.[6] But venial sin deserves punishment of the senses and not privation of the vision of God. Therefore, since privation of the vision of God without punishment of the senses is undoubtedly greater than punishment of the senses without privation of the vision of God, it seems that original sin does not deserve privation of the vision of God as its punishment.

10. People have said that even venial sin deserves privation of the vision of God for a time, just as it deserves punishment of the senses for a time. But adding eternity worsens the punishment of the privation of the vision of God more than adding tem-

---

5. *Confessions* V, 4 (PL 32:708).
6. *Enchiridion* 93 (PL 40:275).

poral punishment of the senses does, since no rightly disposed person would not will to undergo every temporal punishment rather than to lack the everlasting vision of God. Therefore, if original sin is punished with the everlasting privation of the vision of God, original sin is punished more than venial sin and so is not the mildest punishment.

11. According to the law, one who has suffered for another's wrongdoing deserves mercy. But those who are punished only for original sin have suffered for the wrongdoing of another, namely, our first parent. Therefore, they deserve mercy. Therefore, they do not deserve the worst punishment, that is, privation of the vision of God.

12. Augustine says in his work *On Two Souls*: "To hold anyone a criminal because he did not do what he could not do partakes of the greatest injustice and insanity."[7] But no such thing is consistent with God. Therefore, since the child who is begotten could not avoid original sin, it seems that the child accordingly would not incur the guilty condition of any punishment.

13. Original sin is the privation of original justice, as Anselm says.[8] But the vision of God is not due to those having original justice, since they could have original justice without grace. Therefore, neither does privation of the vision of God correspond to original sin as punishment.

14. As we read in Gen. 3:12, Adam excused himself, saying: "The woman you gave me gave it to me, and I ate." And this would have been an excuse sufficient not to merit punishment if he were to have been unable to resist the woman's prompting. But God gave our souls flesh whose corruption they cannot resist. Therefore, it does not seem that our souls accordingly deserve any punishment.

15. The privation of the vision of God, which human beings can attain only through grace, would be proper for them as constituted in their natural powers even if they had never sinned. But sin properly deserves punishment. Therefore, we cannot call the privation of the vision of God a punishment of original sin.

On the Contrary:

1. Gregory says in his work *Morals*: "The mind in its pilgrimage cannot see the light as it is, since the captivity of its condemnation hides the light from the mind."[9]

2. Innocent III says in the *Decretals* that original sin deserves the privation of the vision of God as punishment.[10]

Answer:

Privation of the vision of God is a fitting punishment of original sin. And to prove this, we should consider that although two things seem to belong to something's perfection, one of being capable of a great good or of actually possessing it, and the second of needing no or little external help, the first condition outweighs the second. For it is far better

---

7. *On Two Souls* 12, n. 17 (PL 42:107).
8. *On the Virgin Conception* 27 (PL 158:461A).
9. *Morals* IV, 25, n. 46 (PL 75:660A).
10. *Decretals* III, title 42, chap. 3 (Friedberg II: 646).

to be capable of a great good although needing much help to attain it than to be capable of only a little good that can be attained with little or no external help. For example, we say that the body of a human being is better disposed if it could attain perfect health albeit with much help from medicine than if it could attain only imperfect health without the help of medicine. Therefore, rational creatures surpass every other kind of creature in being capable of the highest good in beholding and enjoying God, although the sources from their own nature do not suffice to attain it, and they need the help of God's grace to attain it.

And we should note regarding this point that every rational creature without exception needs a particular divine help, namely, the help of sanctifying grace, in order to be able to attain perfect happiness, as the Apostle says in Rom. 6:23: "The grace of God is eternal life." But in addition to this necessary help, human beings needed another supernatural help because of their composite nature. For human beings are composed of soul and body, and of an intellectual and a sensory nature. And if the body and the senses be left to their nature, as it were, they burden and hinder the intellect from being able freely to attain the highest reaches of contemplation. And this help was original justice, by which the mind of human beings would be so subject to God that their lower powers and their very bodies would be completely subject to them, nor would their reason impede them from being able to tend toward God. And as the body is for the sake of the soul, and the senses for the sake of the intellect, so this help whereby the body is under the control of the soul, and sense powers under the control of the intellect, is almost a disposition for the help whereby the human mind is ordained to see and enjoy God. And original sin takes away this help of original justice, as I have said before.[11]

And when persons by sinning cast away the means whereby they were disposed to obtain a good, they deserve that the good that they were disposed to obtain be taken away. And the very taking away of the good is a fitting punishment for the sin. And so the fitting punishment of original sin is the taking away of grace and thereby of the vision of God for which grace ordains human beings.

Replies to the Objections:

1. Human beings would have been created uselessly and in vain if they were to be unable to attain happiness, as would be the case with anything that cannot obtain its ultimate end. And so, lest human beings begotten with original sin be created uselessly and in vain, God from the beginning of the human race intended a remedy for them by which they would be freed from such frustration, namely, Jesus Christ, the very mediator between God and human beings. And the impediment of original sin could be removed through faith in him. And so Ps. 89:47 says: "Remember what my substance is, for have you constituted all the children of human beings in vain?" And an explanatory gloss says that David is asking for the incarnation of the Son, who was to take his flesh from David's substance and to free human beings from empty purpose.[12]

2. The souls of children who die without baptism are not punished with the privation of the vision of God because of the sin of Adam as his personal sin. Rather, those

---

11. Q. 4, a. 8.
12. Peter Lombard, *Gloss*, on Ps. 89:47 (PL 191:830D).

children are so punished for the taint of original sin, which they incur by union with the body transmitted from their first parent by physical descent. For it would be unjust that the guilty condition of punishment be transmitted unless there were to be the taint of moral fault. And so also the Apostle in Rom. 5:12 explains the transmission of punishment by the transmission of moral fault, saying: "Sin entered the world through one man, and death through sin."

3. We can consider the gravity of punishments in two ways. We consider it in one way regarding the very good that the evil of punishment takes away, and then lacking the vision and enjoyment of God is the worst punishment. We consider the gravity of punishments in a second way in relation to the one punished, and then the punishment is worse as the thing taken away is proper and connatural to the one from whom it is taken away. For example, we would say that human beings would be punished more if they were deprived of their inheritance than if they were prevented from coming into possession of a kingdom to which they had no right. And we say in this way that the privation of the vision of God by itself is the mildest of all punishments, insofar as the vision is an altogether supernatural gift.

4. Created goods added to the uncreated good do not make good or happiness greater. This is so because if two things sharing in something are combined, what they share in can be increased in them, but if a sharing thing is added to what is by its essence such, nothing greater results. For example, two conjoined hot things can cause greater heat, but if there were to be something that was by its essence subsistent heat, no added hot thing would increase the heat. Therefore, since God is the very essence of goodness, as Dionysius says in his work *On the Divine Names*,[13] and everything else is good by participation, no added good makes God a greater good, since the goodness of every other thing is included in his very self. And so since happiness is simply attainment of the perfect good, no other good added to the vision and enjoyment of God will cause greater happiness; otherwise, God would have become happier by creating creatures. But the reasoning about happiness and the reasoning about unhappiness differ, since as happiness consists of union with God, so unhappiness consists of withdrawal from God, and a person indeed departs from his likeness and partaking of him by the privation of any good. And so every privation of good causes greater unhappiness, although not every addition of good causes greater happiness. This is so because human beings are not more united to God by an added good than if they be directly united to him, although they are more separated from him when a good is taken away.

5. The addition of an accidental reward does not cause greater happiness, since we recognize an accidental reward as a created good, and the happiness of human beings as the uncreated good. But as a created good is a likeness and sharing of the uncreated good, so the attainment of a created good is a happiness analogous to true happiness, although true happiness is not thereby increased.

6. As a point does not increase the size of a line, so a created good does not increase happiness.

---

13. *On the Divine Names* 1, n. 5 (PG 3:593C).

7–8. We concede the seventh and eighth objections, since those deprived of the vision and enjoyment of God are deprived of God himself.

9. Venial sin is in one respect greater and in another respect lesser in relation to original sin. For venial sin in relation to this or that person has more of the nature of sin than original sin does, since venial sin is something willed by the will of such a person, and original sin is not. But original sin in relation to human nature is more serious, since original sin deprives human nature of a greater good, namely, the good of sanctifying grace, than the good of which venial sin deprives the person. And so those with original sin ought to lack the vision of God, since they attain that vision only through sanctifying grace, which venial sin does not preclude.

10. The perpetuity of punishment results from the perpetuity of moral fault, and the perpetuity of moral fault results from the privation of grace, since moral fault cannot be remitted except through grace. And since original sin excludes grace, and venial sin does not, original sin deserves perpetual punishment, and venial sin does not.

11. The child who dies without baptism has indeed suffered for the sin of another regarding the sin's cause, namely, because the child contracted the sin from another, but the child has suffered for its own sin insofar as the child contracted moral fault from its first parent. And so the child deserves mercy that lessens but does not completely remit punishment.

12. The child who dies without baptism does not have a guilty condition because the child did not do anything, for this would be a sin of omission. Rather, the child has a guilty condition because the child contracted the taint of original sin.

13. The argument of this objection is valid in the opinion of those who hold that sanctifying grace is not included in the nature of original justice.[14] But I believe that opinion to be false. I so believe because inasmuch as original justice would originally consist of the subordination of the human mind to God, which can be steadfast only through grace, there could be no original justice without grace. And so one having original justice deserved the vision of God. But still, assuming the aforementioned opinion, the conclusion does not follow, since original justice, although it would not include grace, was nonetheless a disposition prerequisite for grace. And so what is contrary to original justice is also contrary to grace, just as what is contrary to natural justice, such as theft, murder, and the like, is contrary to grace.

14. If Adam were not to have been able to resist Eve's influence, he would have been excused from actual sin, which one commits with one's own will. And so also the soul of a child is excused from the guilty condition of actual sin but not that of original sin, the corruption of which the soul contracted by union with the flesh.

15. Human beings constituted only with natural powers would indeed lack the vision of God if they were to die in that condition. Nevertheless, they would not deserve not to have the vision. For it is one thing not to deserve to have something, which nonpossession has the nature only of a deficiency and not the nature of punishment, and it is another thing to deserve not to have something, which nonpossession has the nature of punishment.

14. Cf., e.g., Peter Lombard, *Sentences* II, d. 24, chaps. 1 and 2.

Second Article

Does Original Sin Deserve Punishment of the Senses?

It seems that original sin does, for the following reasons:

1. Augustine says in his *Hypognosticon* that infants who die without baptism experience hell.[15] But hell designates punishment of the senses. Therefore, original sin deserves punishment of the senses.

2. Augustine says in his work *On Faith, to Peter*:[16] "Firmly believe and doubt not that infants who have departed this life without the sacrament of baptism are to be punished by eternal torment." But torment designates punishment of the senses. Therefore, original sin deserves punishment of the senses.

3. On Job 9:17, "He has multiplied my wounds without cause," Gregory in his work *Morals* says that "the sacraments do not free them [infants who die without baptism] from the moral fault of their origin, and although they themselves have done nothing wrong in this world, they arrive at torments in the next world."[17] But torments designate punishment of the senses. Therefore, original sin deserves punishment of the senses.

4. The original sin of such a child seems to belong to the same species as the actual sin of our first parent, since the former sin derives from the latter sin as an effect from a proper cause. But the actual sin of our first parent deserves punishment of the senses. Therefore, the original sin of such a child also deserves punishment of the senses.

5. An efficient cause in contact with something capable of suffering brings about punishment of the senses. But the souls of children as well as their bodies after the resurrection are capable of punishment, since they do not have the gift of incapacity to suffer. Therefore, they will suffer punishment of the senses surrounded by fire.

6. After the judgment, the punishment of sinners will be consummated. But the punishment of children who die without baptism, who are punished only for original sin, could not be consummated after the judgment unless a punishment of the senses were to be added to the privation of the vision of God, which they already suffer. Therefore, original sin deserves punishment of the senses.

7. Moral fault deserves punishment. But the flesh causes original sin. Therefore, since the flesh deserves only punishment of the senses, it seems that original sin especially deserves punishment of the senses.

8. If persons should die with original sin as well as venial sin, they will perpetually suffer punishment of the senses. But venial sin does not deserve perpetual punishment. Therefore, original sin deserves perpetual punishment of the senses.

On the Contrary:

1. Bernard says that only one's own will burns in hell.[18] But original sin is not a sin of one's own will; rather, it results from the will of another. Therefore, original sin does not deserve punishment of the senses.

---

15. Augustine (Pseudo), *Hypognosticon* V, 1ff. (PL 45:1647).
16. Augustine (Pseudo) = Fulgentius, *On Faith, to Peter* 27, n. 70 (PL 40:774).
17. *Morals* IX, 21, n. 32 (PL 75:877A).
18. *Sermons on the Liturgical Seasons, sermon 3 on Eastertide*, n. 3 (PL 183:290A).

2. Innocent III says in the *Decretals* that actual sin deserves punishment of the senses.[19] But original sin is not actual sin. Therefore, original sin does not deserve punishment of the senses.

Answer:

According to the common opinion, original sin deserves only the punishment of loss, namely, privation of the vision of God, not punishment of the senses. And this seems convincing for three reasons. First, it indeed seems convincing because every person is an individual substance of a certain nature, and so persons of themselves are directly ordained for things that belong to that nature, and indirectly, by means of the nature, ordained for things superior to the nature. Therefore, it can be due to a fault of human nature or a personal fault that persons suffer harm regarding things superior to human nature, but it seems that it can be due only to a person's own fault that persons suffer harm regarding things that belong to human nature. And as is evident from what I have explained before,[20] original sin is a fault of human nature, and actual sin is a fault of the person. And grace and the vision of God are superior to human nature, and so persons deserve privation of grace and privation of that vision both for their actual sins and for original sin. But punishment of the senses is contrary to the integrity of human nature and its right disposition, and so persons deserve punishment of the senses only for their actual sins.

Second, original sin does not deserve punishment of the senses because punishments are proportioned to moral fault. And so actual mortal sin, in which there is a turning away from the immutable good and a turning toward a transitory good, deserves both the punishment of loss, namely, the privation of the vision of God corresponding to the turning away from God, and punishment of the senses corresponding to the turning toward a creature. But there is no turning toward a creature in original sin and only a turning away from God, or something corresponding to such turning away, namely, the soul's forsaking original justice. And so original sin deserves only the punishment of loss, namely, the privation of the vision of God, not punishment of the senses.

Third, original sin does not deserve punishment of the senses because habitual dispositions never deserve such punishment. For example, persons are not punished because they are disposed to steal but because they actually steal. Nonetheless, habitual privations unaccompanied by any act deserve to lose things; for example, one who is illiterate is by that very fact unworthy of elevation to the episcopal dignity. And original sin indeed involves concupiscence by way of an habitual disposition that renders infants apt to desire inordinately, as Augustine says,[21] and causes adults actually to desire inordinately. And so an infant who died with original sin does not deserve punishment of the senses but deserves only the punishment of loss, namely, that the privation of original justice render the child unsuitable to attain the vision of God.

Replies to the Objections:

1. We should understand the words *torment*, *anguish*, *hell*, and *torture*, or any other like expressions of the saints to mean punishment in a broad sense, as we posit the specific

---

19. *Decretals* III, title 42, chap. 3 (Friedberg II: 646).
20. A. 1, reply to objection 9.
21. Cf. *On the Punishment and Forgiveness of Sins and on the Baptism of Infants* II, 4 (PL 44:152).

for the general. And so the saints used such a way of speaking to make abominable the error of the Pelagians, who asserted that infants have no sin and deserve no punishment.

2–3. The foregoing makes evident the replies to the second and third and all like objections.

4. All sinned in the one sin of our first parent, as the Apostle says in Rom. 5:12. But not everyone is related to that one sin in the same way. For the sin belongs to Adam by his own will and is his actual sin, and so he deserved actual punishment for such sin. But the sin belongs to others by reason of their physical descent and not by reason of their own will, and so others do not deserve punishment of the senses for such sin.

5. In the condition of the future life, fire and other like causes do not act on the souls or bodies of human beings by a necessity of nature but rather by the ordination of divine justice, since that condition is one of receiving reward according to one's deserts. And so since divine justice does not require that children who die only with original sin deserve punishment of the senses, they suffer nothing from such causes.

6. The punishment of children who die with original sin will be consummated after the judgment insofar as the very children punished with this punishment will be consummated by the restoration of their bodies.

7. Original sin, although it is transmitted to the soul by the flesh, has the nature of moral fault only insofar as it extends to the soul. And so the disposition of the flesh does not deserve punishment, and if the flesh is sometimes punished, this is because of the moral fault in the soul.

8. Many deem impossible the position that some die with original sin and only venial sin. Lack of maturity, since it sometimes excuses from mortal sin due to lack of the use of reason, far more excuses from venial sin. And after persons attain the use of reason, they are obliged to attend to their salvation. And if they have done this, they will now be free from original sin with the advent of grace, and if they have not done this, such omission on their part will be a mortal sin. But if it were to be possible for persons to die with original and only venial sin, I say that they would be punished with eternal punishment of the senses. For eternal punishment accompanies privation of grace, which results in eternal moral fault, as I have said.[22] And so venial sin in one who dies with mortal sin, since it is never remitted, is punished with eternal punishment due to the person's privation of grace. And the argument would be the same if one were to die with original and only venial sin.

Third Article

Do Those Who Die with Only Original Sin Suffer the Torment of Internal Anguish?

It seems that they do, for the following reasons:

1. Everything naturally desired, if not possessed when it should be, causes torment and anguish, as is evidently the case if one lacks food when nature requires it. But human beings by nature desire happiness, and they should possess it after this life. Therefore,

---

22. A. 1, reply to objection 10.

since those who die with original sin do not attain happiness, in that they lack the vision of God, it seems that they suffer torment.

2. As baptized children are disposed to receive the merit of Christ, so unbaptized children are disposed to receive the demerit of Adam. But baptized children are joyful because of the merit of Christ. Therefore, unbaptized children are sorrowful because of the demerit of Adam.

3. It belongs to the nature of punishment to be contrary to the will of the one punished. But everything contrary to one's will makes one sorrowful, as the Philosopher says in the *Metaphysics*.[23] Therefore, if persons suffer any punishment, they are necessarily made sorrowful.

4. To be perpetually separated from one's beloved is especially a source of torment. But unbaptized children by nature love God. Therefore, since they know that they are eternally separated from him, it seems that they cannot be in this condition without torment.

On the Contrary:

The pleasure in moral fault deserves the pain or torment of punishment, as Rev. 18:7 says: "Give her as much torment and grief as she indulged herself in pride and pleasures." But there was no pleasure in original sin. Therefore, neither will there be any pain or torment in its punishment.

Answer:

Some have held that children who die with original sin experience an internal anguish and torment from their privation of the vision of God, although the anguish does not have the nature of the worm of conscience, since they are not conscious of having been able to avoid original sin.[24] But there seems to be no reason why we should deny that they suffer external punishment of the senses if we affirm that they suffer internal anguish, which is far more a punishment and more contrary to the mildest punishment that Augustine ascribes to them.[25] And so it seems to others, and with better reason, that the children experience no internal torment.

And particular theologians explain this in different ways. For example, some say that the souls of children who die with original sin are so darkened with ignorance that they do not know that they have been created for happiness, nor do they think at all about it, and so they suffer no anguish about it.[26] But this does not seem to be properly stated. First, indeed, it is not properly stated because inasmuch as the children have no actual sin, which is personal sin in the proper sense, they do not deserve to suffer any loss in natural goods, for the reason previously ascribed.[27] And it is natural for separated souls to be more rather than less endowed with knowledge than souls in the present life, and so it is unlikely that separated souls suffer such great ignorance. Second, the aforemen-

23. *Metaphysics* V, 5 (1015a28).
24. Cf. Albert the Great, *Commentary on the Sentences IV*, d. 1, a. 20.
25. *Enchiridion* 93 (PL 40:275).
26. Alexander of Hales, *Commentary on the Sentences* II, d. 33, n. 9.
27. A. 2.

tioned opinion is inappropriately expressed because those condemned to hell, having less darkness of ignorance, would accordingly be in a better condition regarding their most excellent part, namely, their intellect. And as Augustine says,[28] there is no one who would not prefer to suffer anguish being of sound mind than to be joyful being of unsound mind.

And so some ascribe the children's lack of torment to the disposition of their will.[29] For the disposition of the will in the soul, whether to good or evil, is not changed after death. And so, since children before they reach the use of reason do not have a disordered act of the will, neither will they have a disordered act of the will after death. But there is disorder of the will if one should grieve about not having what one could never obtain. For example, it would be inordinate if a peasant were to grieve about not inheriting a kingdom. Therefore, since the children after death know that they could never have obtained that heavenly glory, they will not grieve over its privation.

But combining the two positions, we can hold a middle position. And so we say that the children's souls indeed do not lack the natural knowledge that the separated soul by its nature deserves. And the separated souls lack the supernatural knowledge that faith implants in us in this life, since they did not actually have faith in this life, nor did they receive the sacrament of faith. And it belongs to natural cognition that the soul know that it is created for happiness, and that happiness consists of attainment of the perfect good. But that the perfect good for which human beings have been created is the glory that the saints possess is beyond natural knowledge. And so the Apostle says in 1 Cor. 2:9 that "the eye has not seen, nor the ear heard, nor has it entered into the heart of human beings, what things God has prepared for those who love him," and then (v. 10) adds: "And God has revealed them to us through his Spirit." And this revelation indeed belongs to faith. And so the children's souls do not know that they are deprived of such a good, and they accordingly do not grieve. But those souls possess without anguish what they have by natural knowledge.

Replies to the Objections:

1. The souls of children who die in original sin indeed know happiness in general regarding its common aspect but not in particular. And so they do not grieve about losing it.

2. As the Apostle says in Rom. 5:15, Christ's gift is greater than Adam's sin. And so it is not necessary that unbaptized children should be sorrowful because of Adam's sin if baptized children are joyful because of Christ's merit.

3. Punishment does not always correspond to one's actual will. For example, punishment does not correspond to one's actual will when persons are defamed in their absence or despoiled of their possessions without their knowing about it. But it is necessary that punishment should always be either contrary to one's actual will or contrary to one's habitual will or at least contrary to one's natural inclination, as I have said before when I dealt with the evil of punishment.[30]

4. Children who die in original sin are indeed eternally separated from God regarding their loss of the glory of which they are ignorant but not regarding their partaking in the natural goods that they know.

---

28. *City of God* XI, 27, n. 2 (PL 41:341).

29. Thomas himself, *Commentary on the Sentences* II, d. 33, q. 2, a. 2.

30. Q. 1, aa. 4 and 5.

Fourth Article

Are Death and Other Ills of This Life Punishment of Original Sin?

It seems that they are not, for the following reasons:

1. Seneca says: "Death is the nature, not a punishment, of human beings."[31] Therefore, by the same reasoning neither are other ills connected with death punishment.

2. What many things have in common belongs to them by reason of something common to them. But death and other ills connected with death are common to human beings and other animals. Therefore, human beings and animals have death and other ills by reason of something common. But death and other ills do not belong to other animals by reason of moral fault, which the animals cannot incur. Therefore, death and other ills do not belong to human beings by reason of moral fault and so are not punishment of original sin.

3. Punishment should be proportional to sin, as Dt. 25:2 says: "The number of scourges will be proportioned to the crime." But original sin equally befalls all begotten of Adam, and the aforementioned ills do not equally befall all of them, since some at the first moment of their existence are begotten sickly, some maimed, some well disposed. Therefore, such ills are not punishment of original sin.

4. Such ills are punishments of the senses. But sin deserves punishment of the senses because of an improper turning toward a transitory good, and there is indeed no such turning in original sin. Therefore, such ills do not correspond to such turning as punishment of original sin.

5. Human beings are punished more severely after this life than during it. But original sin does not deserve punishment of the senses after this life, as I have said.[32] Therefore, neither does original sin in this life, and so the same conclusion follows as before.

6. Punishment corresponds to moral fault. But moral fault belongs to human beings as such. Therefore, since death and the like do not belong to human beings as such, inasmuch as other living things suffer them, it seems that such ills do not belong to punishment.

7. Original sin is the privation of original justice, and original sin belonged to Adam as regards his soul. But death and like ills belong to the body. Therefore, they do not correspond to original sin as punishment.

8. If Adam were not to have sinned, his offspring could have. And if they were to have, they would die. But their death would not be due to original sin, since they would not have had it. Therefore, death is not punishment for original sin.

On the Contrary:

1. Rom. 6:23 says: "The wages of sin are death." And Rom. 8:10 says: "The body is dead because of sin." And Gen. 2:17 says: "On whatever day you shall eat it, you shall die the death."

---

31. *On Remedies for Chance Events* II, n. 1.
32. A. 2.

2. Augustine says in his works *On the Trinity*[33] and *City of God*[34] and *Against the Letter of the Foundation*[35] that such ills derive from the condemnation of sin. Isidore also says in his work *On the Supreme Good* that water would not drown human beings, nor fire burn them, nor other like things come about, if a human being were not to have sinned.[36] Therefore, all such ills are punishment of original sin.

Answer:

In accord with the Catholic faith, we undoubtedly need to hold that death and all such ills of our present life are punishment for original sin.

But we should note that there are two kinds of punishment: one, indeed, as a penalty for sin; the second as something concomitant. For example, we perceive that a judge sentences men to be blinded for their crimes, and that many ills, such as the need to beg and the like, result from their blindness. But the blindness itself is the punishment allotted for sin, since the judge intends to deprive the sinner of his sight because of his sin, and the judge does not consider the ills that result from blindness. And so if the judge sentences several persons to be blinded for the same kind of sin, more ills may result in one person than in another. And yet this does not redound to the injustice of the judge, since he did not inflict such concomitant ills as punishment for sin; rather, they resulted incidentally as regards the judge's intention. And we can say the same about the matter under discussion. For God had bestowed on human beings in their original condition the help of original justice, which preserved them from all such ills. And the whole human nature was indeed deprived of that help because of the sin of our first parent, as is evident from what I have said before.[37] And different ills result from the privation of this help, and different persons have these deficiencies in different ways, although they equally share the moral fault of original sin.

But there seems to be a difference between God punishing and a human judge imposing punishment. The human judge cannot foresee ensuing events, and so he cannot consider them when he imposes punishment for wrongdoing. Therefore, the inequality of such ills does not plausibly derogate from his justice. But God foreknows all future events, and so it would seem to belong to his justice if such ills unequally befall those equally linked to moral fault.

Therefore, in order to remove this difficulty, Origen proposed that souls earned different merits before their union with the body, and in proportion to such merits, greater or lesser ills result in the bodies with which the souls are united.[38] And so some are troubled by evil spirits soon after birth or are born blind or suffer some such ills, as he himself says.[39] But this is contrary to the teaching of the Apostle. For the Apostle, speak-

---

33. *On the Trinity* XIII, 16, n. 20 (PL 42:173).

34. *City of God* XV, 6 (PL 41:442).

35. *Against the Letter of the Foundation* 1 (PL 42:173).

36. Actually, Isidore (Pseudo), *On the Order of Creatures* 10, n. 8 (PL 83:940A).

37. A. 1.

38. Related by Jerome, *Letter* 124, chap. 1, n. 3 (PL 22:1061). Cf. Origen, *On First Principles* II, 8, n. 4 (PG 11:224A).

39. Related by Jerome, *Letter* 124, chap. 3, n. 8 (PL 22:1066). Cf. Origen, *On First Principles* III, 3, n. 5 (PG 11:318).

ing of Jacob and Esau, says in Rom. 9:11: "Before they were yet born or had done anything good or evil," etc. And the argument is the same regarding all human beings. And
so we should not say that souls earned merits or demerits before their union with the
body. And it is also contrary to reason. For the soul, inasmuch as it is by nature part of
human nature, is incomplete when it is without the body, as is any part separated from
the whole. And it would have been inappropriate for God to begin his work of creation
with incomplete things. And so it is just as unreasonable to suppose that God created
souls before he created bodies as it is to suppose that he formed hands apart from human
beings.

And so we need to say otherwise, that God indeed sometimes foresees and ordains
such difference as occurs in human beings regarding those ills because of the sins of parents, not indeed because of merits that come from another life. For inasmuch as an offspring is part of its father regarding the body that it takes from its father but not regarding its soul, which God directly creates, it is not improper that an offspring for the sin of
its father suffer corporal punishment but not spiritual punishment, which belongs to the
soul. Just so are human beings punished in other affairs of theirs. And such ills are sometimes ordained as a remedy against future sin or to develop the virtue either of the one
who suffers the ill or of another, not as the punishment of any sin. For example, the Lord
says in Jn. 9:3 of the man born blind: "Neither this man nor his parents sinned, but the
works of God were to be manifested in him." And this was helpful for human salvation.
But the very fact that human beings are in such a condition that such ills or deficiencies
help them either to avoid sin or develop virtue is due to the weakness of human nature,
which weakness results from the sin of our first parent. Just so, the fact that the body of
a human being is so disposed as to need surgery in order to cure it belongs to its weakness. And so all these ills correspond to original sin as a concomitant punishment.

Replies to the Objections:

1. The help bestowed on human beings by God, namely, original justice, was gratuitous,
and so reason could not account for it. And so Seneca and other pagan philosophers did
not consider such ills under the aspect of punishment.

2. Such help was not conferred on other animals, nor did they previously lose anything through moral fault, from which such ills would result, as in the case of human
beings. And so the reasoning is not the same. Just so, in the case of those who stumble
along because of the blindness with which they have been born, their stumbling walk
has the character of a natural defect, not of a punishment relating to human justice. But
in the case of those who have been blinded because of their crimes, their stumbling walk
has the character of punishment.

3. Such ills are not a punishment imposed for sin but a concomitant punishment, as
I have said.[40]

4. Only actual turning toward a transitory good deserves the imposition of punishment of the senses, but there is another argument regarding a concomitant punishment.

5. The condition of persons after death is one of receiving reward or punishment
according to one's merits, not one of advancing in virtue or failing through sin. And so

---

40. In the answer.

all ills imposed after death are imposed for moral fault and ordained neither for the advancement of virtue nor for the avoidance of sin. And so unbaptized children after death do not deserve punishment of the senses.

6. Anything that in human beings has the nature of moral fault (e.g., killing a human being) can indeed be found in other animals but without having the nature of moral fault. And moral fault consists of the fact that something is willed, and irrational animals do not have this power. And similarly, ills common to human beings and other animals have in human beings the nature of punishment, which consists of the fact that something is contrary to the will, but not so in other animals. For the nature of punishment and moral fault belongs to human beings as such.

7. Original justice, although it belonged to the soul, preserved the proper relationship of the body under control of the soul. And so bodily ills properly result from original sin, which took away original justice.

8. According to certain theologians,[41] if Adam when tempted had not sinned, he would have been immediately confirmed in justice, and all his posterity would have been begotten confirmed in justice. And if one accepts that view, the objection is irrelevant. But I believe the opinion to be false, since the condition of the body in its first state corresponded to the condition of the soul, and so as long as the body was animal, the soul, not yet made completely spiritual, was also capable of change. And generation belongs to animal life. And so it follows that the offspring of Adam would not be begotten confirmed in justice. Therefore, if one of Adam's posterity sinned, while Adam did not, such a person would indeed die for his own actual sin as Adam did, but his posterity would die because of original sin.

Fifth Article

Are Death and Like Ills Natural to Human Beings?

It seems that death and like ills are, for the following reasons:

1. The body of human beings is composed of contrary things. But everything composed of contrary things can by nature dissolve. Therefore, human beings are by nature mortal and so subject to other ills.

2. People have said that the fact that the body of human beings is dissolved because of the contrariety present in it results from the withdrawal of original justice and so is a punishment rather than something natural. But if the withdrawal of original justice, which prevents those ills, brings about death and dissolution in human beings, it follows that sin causes such ills by removing an impediment to them. And the movement resulting from the removal of an impediment is natural even if what removes the impediment is a free cause. For example, when someone removes a column, a stone on top of it falls, and the stone's movement is natural. Therefore, notwithstanding the withdrawal of original justice, death and dissolution are natural to human beings.

3. Human beings in their first condition were immortal insofar as they could not die, and they in their final condition will be immortal insofar as they will be unable to die, and

41. Cf. Alexander of Hales, *Summa of Theology* I–II, n. 501.

they in their intermediate condition are in every respect mortal insofar as they are necessarily subject to death. But the immortality of the final condition will not be natural; rather, that immortality will be consummated by the grace that consists of glory. Therefore, neither was the immortality of the first condition natural. Therefore, dying was natural.

4. Human beings in their natural condition, if left to themselves, die. And in their first condition, a gift bestowed by God would have preserved them from death. But if God causes something in a thing above the thing's nature, the contrary disposition is nonetheless natural to the thing. For example, if God were to cause water to boil, the water would still be cold by nature. Therefore, human beings in their first condition were by nature mortal notwithstanding God's gift.

5. As it was supernaturally given to human beings to have been able not to die, so it is supernaturally given to them to be able to see God. But the fact that human beings lack the vision of God is not contrary to their nature. Therefore, neither is it contrary to their nature that they lack immortality. Therefore, death is not contrary to their nature.

6. The human body, even before sin, was composed of four elements, and so there were active and passive qualities in it. But these qualities naturally bring about dissolution of the body. For active qualities naturally assimilate passive qualities. And when this is done, the passive qualities cease to be, and so the very composite ceases to be. Therefore, the human body, even before sin, was by nature capable of dissolution.

7. The action of natural heat, which is a natural cause, preserves human life. But every natural cause in causing undergoes some diminution, since it acts after it has been acted upon, according to the Philosopher.[42] And it is necessary that every finite thing be completely consumed if parts of it are continuously cast off. Therefore, since the natural heat in the human body was finite, it is necessary that it would by its nature be finally consumed. And so human beings, even before sin, would have naturally died.

8. The human body was finite. But it underwent depletion; otherwise, it would not have needed food. Therefore, since continuous depletion at some time consumes every finite thing, it seems that it was by nature necessary that the human body be dissolved, even before sin.

9. Augustine says that the ability not to die belonged to human beings by benefit of the tree of life.[43] But this seems to be impossible, since the tree of life could not bestow indissolubility if it was dissoluble, and it could not be useful for human beings as nourishment if it was indissoluble. Therefore, human beings did not have the ability not to die and would naturally and necessarily have died.

10. Something of itself contingent is never made necessary by something else. And so something of itself dissoluble is never made indissoluble by something else, for the dissoluble and the indissoluble differ generically, as the *Metaphysics* says,[44] and generically different things are not transformed into one another. But the human body as such was dissoluble, since it was composed of contrary things. Therefore, nothing else could in any way make it indissoluble. Therefore, human beings would naturally die even if no human being had sinned.

---

42. *Physics* III, 1 (201a23).
43. *Literal Commentary on Genesis* VI, 25 (PL 34:354).
44. Aristotle, *Metaphysics* X, 10 (1058b28–29).

11. If human beings before sin could not die, the ability not to die was due either to grace or to nature. If due to grace, then human beings could merit it, and this is contrary to the Master.[45] And if due to nature, then human beings could be wounded but not completely destroyed, since sin stripped them of their gifts and wounded them in their natural powers, as a gloss says.[46] Therefore, in neither way did human beings before sin have the ability not to die.

12. According to philosophers,[47] there is necessarily inequality in everything composed of contrary things. For example, if contrary things were to belong equally to the constitution of composite matter, one would not be more a form than the other; rather, everything would be equally actual. And several things do not constitute one thing unless one of them is related to the other as potentiality to actuality. And inequality is necessarily a source of dissolubility, since what is stronger destroys what is weaker. Therefore, the human body was by natural necessity dissoluble even if no human being had sinned.

13. Human beings before and after sin have substantially the same nature; otherwise, they would not belong to the same species. But the necessity of dying belongs to human beings after sin by reason of the nature of their substance, namely, because matter has potentiality for other forms. Therefore, human beings before sin would also have died by natural necessity.

14. People have said that, before sin, God preserved human beings from dying. But God never causes something whose logical consequence is that contradictory propositions are simultaneously true. And from the assertion that something potential is subject to causal activity and does not dissolve, it logically follows that contradictory propositions are simultaneously true, namely, that something is and is not potential. For it belongs to the nature of something potential that a cause bring it into actuality. Therefore, the human body before sin would not have been indissoluble if God prevented the dissolution.

15. Augustine says in his *Commentary on the Book of Genesis* that God so administers things that he allows them to cause their own movements.[48] But the proper and natural movement of a material substance composed of contrary things is to tend toward dissolution. Therefore, God did not prevent this.

16. Created powers cannot cause things superior to the natural order, since every created power acts by causal principles implanted by nature, as Augustine says in his work *On the Trinity*.[49] But original justice was a created gift. Therefore, its power could not preserve human beings from dissolution.

17. Something in all or most is not contrary to nature. But death belongs to all human beings after sin. Therefore, death is not contrary to nature.

On the Contrary:

1. Every means is proportioned to an end. But human beings were created for everlasting happiness. Therefore, they by their nature have everlasting life. Therefore, death and dissolution are contrary to their nature.

---

45. Peter Lombard, *Sentences* II, d. 24, chap. 1, n. 2.
46. Scholars have found no source for this gloss.
47. Cf., e.g., Aristotle, *On Generation and Corruption* I, 10 (328a28ff.).
48. Actually, *City of God* VII, 30 (PL 41:220).
49. *On the Trinity* III, 8, n. 13 (PL 42:876).

2. Matter is by nature proportioned to form. But the rational soul, which is the form of the body, cannot be dissolved. Therefore, the human body is also indissoluble, and so death and dissolution are contrary to the nature of the human body.

Answer:

According to the Philosopher in the *Physics*,[50] we speak of natural in two ways: either of what has a nature, as we call material substances natural, or of what results from a nature, something in accord with a nature, as we say that it is natural for fire to be borne upward. And so we are now speaking about the natural that is in accord with a nature. And so since we speak of a nature in two ways, namely, as form and as matter, we call things natural in two ways, either regarding their form or regarding their matter. We indeed call things natural regarding their form. For example, it is natural for fire to cause heat, for causal action results from something's form. And we call things natural regarding their matter. For example, it is natural for water to be capable of being heated by fire. And since form is more the nature than matter is, it is more natural to be natural regarding form than to be natural regarding matter.

And we can in two ways understand what results from matter: in one way as befitting form, and this is what the cause chooses in matter; in the second way not as befitting form but rather as perchance contrary to both the form and the end although due to a necessity of matter, and the cause does not choose or strive for such a condition. For example, a blacksmith making a saw for cutting wood seeks out iron, since iron because of its hardness is matter fit for the saw's form and end. But iron has a condition by which it is unsuitable for both the form and end of the saw, for instance, that it can break or rust or some such thing, and these things impede attainment of the end. And so the blacksmith does not choose these things but rather would reject them if he were able to do so. And so also the Philosopher says in his work *On the Generation of Animals* that we should look only for the material and not the final cause of something in the accidental characteristics of an individual of that kind of thing.[51] We should do so because accidental things result from the disposition of the matter, not the aim of the cause. Therefore, some things are natural to human beings regarding their form, for example, understanding, willing, and the like, and other things are natural to them regarding their matter, that is, their body.

And we can consider the condition of the human body in two ways: in one way as befitting the form; in the second way as what results in it only by a necessity of the matter. Regarding the disposition for the form, it is indeed necessary that the human body be composed of elements and harmoniously composed. For inasmuch as the human soul is potentially intellectual, it is united to the body so that it may through the senses acquire intelligible forms, by means of which it actually understands. For the union of the soul with the body is for the sake of the soul, not for the sake of the body, since matter exists for the sake of form, not form for the sake of matter. And the primary sense is that

---

50. *Physics* II, 1 (192b32–193a1).
51. *On the Generation of Animals* V, 1 (778a30–b10).

of touch, which is in a way the foundation of the other senses, and the organ of touch needs to be a mean between contraries, as the *De anima* says.[52] And so the body befitting such a soul was a body composed of contrary things, and it follows from a necessity of the matter that the body is dissoluble.

But the body in this condition opposes rather than befits the form. And every dissolution of every physical thing is indeed not by reason of its suitability for form. For inasmuch as form is the source of existing, dissolution, which is the process leading to nonexisting, is contrary to it. And so the Philosopher says in *On Heaven and Earth* that the disintegration of the elderly and all deficiencies are contrary to the particular nature of a particular thing as determined by its form, although in accord with the whole of nature, by whose power matter is brought into the actuality of every form for which matter has potentiality.[53] And he says that when one thing comes to be, another thing necessarily passes away. And the dissolution resulting from a necessity of matter is in a special way unbefitting the form that is the rational soul. For other forms can pass away at least incidentally, but the rational soul can pass away neither intrinsically nor incidentally. And so if there could be in nature a body composed of elements, and the body were to be indissoluble, such a body would undoubtedly be naturally suitable for the soul. Just so, if one could find iron incapable of breaking or rusting, it would be most suitable matter for a saw, and a blacksmith would seek it. But because one cannot find such iron, the blacksmith takes such as he can find, namely, hard but breakable iron. And likewise, since there can be no body composed of elements that is by the nature of matter indissoluble, an organic but dissoluble body is by nature suitable for the soul that cannot pass away.

But since God, who creates human beings, could by his omnipotence prevent this necessity of matter from coming about, his power conferred on human beings before sin that they be preserved from death, until they by sinning proved themselves unworthy of such a benefit. Just so, a blacksmith, if he could, would endow the iron he molds with the incapacity to break.

Therefore, death and dissolution are natural to human beings by reason of a necessity of matter, but immortality would befit them by reason of the form's nature. And yet natural sources do not suffice to provide immortality. Rather, a natural disposition for it indeed befits human beings by reason of their soul, and supernatural power fulfills it. Just so, the Philosopher says in the *Ethics* that we by nature have a disposition for moral virtues, but habits perfect them in us.[54] And death and dissolution are contrary to our nature insofar as immortality is natural for us.

Replies to the Objections:

1. The argument of this objection is valid regarding the necessity of matter.

2. And we need to say likewise in reply to the second objection.

3. The argument of this objection is valid about immortality with respect to its consummation and not with respect to the disposition for it.

---

52. Aristotle, *De anima* II, 2 (413b4–5).
53. *On Heaven and Earth* II, 6 (288b15–16).
54. *Ethics* II, 1 (1103a24–26).

4. Boiling is contrary to water by reason of water's form, but immortality is not contrary to being human, as I have said,[55] and so the two situations are dissimilar. And yet we need to say that what God directly effects in things is indeed beyond nature but not contrary to it, since every created thing is by nature subject to its creator. Indeed, every created thing is much more subject to God than lower material substances are to heavenly bodies, although what the influence of heavenly bodies brings about in lower material substances, such as the ebb and flow of the sea, are not contrary to nature, as the Commentator says in his *Commentary on On Heaven and Earth*.[56]

5. The vision of God is superior to human nature not only regarding the matter of human nature but also regarding its form, since the vision surpasses the nature of the human intellect.

6. There are contrary qualities in composite material substances in the same way that there are contrary elements in the world. And contrary elements do not destroy one another, since the power of a heavenly body, which governs their activities, preserves them. Just so, substantial forms, which bear an imprint from a heavenly body, govern and preserve contrary qualities in composite material substances so that the contrary qualities do not destroy one another, since earthly material substances act to preserve their species only through the power of a heavenly body. And so as long as a form has its force from the imprint of a heavenly body, a composite material substance is preserved in existence. And so a heavenly body by drawing closer and more distant causes the coming to be and the passing away in earthly material substances, and the cycle of heavenly bodies measures the duration of all earthly material substances. And so if there were to be a form whose force would ever abide from the imprint of its cause, dissolution would never result from the activity of active and passive qualities.

7. The power of a physical cause, although it is diminished by being acted upon, can be restored. And so we observe restoration of active power happening in parts of the universe because warm elements, whose power is diminished by the absence of the sun in winter, are restored by the nearness of the sun in summer. And this happens in every composite material substance as long as the power of the form preserving the composition of elements perdures.

8. Adam's consumption of food restored the loss of water that the action of natural heat caused in his body, and so he could be preserved from being completely wasted away.

9. What food produces is almost extraneous regarding the initial basis of the power of the human species. And so as adding water gradually dilutes the strength of wine and finally destroys it, so adding nutrient fluids gradually weakens the power of the species and finally destroys it. And so animals necessarily become weaker and finally die, as the work *On Generation and Corruption* says.[57] And the tree of life provided assistance against this deficiency, by restoring the power of the species to its pristine force by the tree's power. But the tree did not do this in such a way that it, once taken as nourishment, would bestow the power to last forever, for it was perishable, and so it could not be the intrinsic

---

55. In the answer.
56. Averroes, *Commentary on Aristotle's On Heaven and Earth*, comm. 20.
57. *On Generation and Corruption* I, 15 (322a31–33).

cause of perpetuity. But it strengthened the natural power to endure longer by a fixed period of time, at the conclusion of which it could be ingested again in order to live longer, and so on until human beings would be brought to the condition of glory, in which they would no longer need nourishment. Therefore, the tree of life was an aid to immortality, but the chief cause of immortality was the power conferred by God on the soul.

10. Something of its nature contingent is never made necessary regarding its nature by something else, namely, that it have a necessary nature. Still, something of itself contingent is made necessary by something else, although not by nature necessary, as happens in the case of everything coerced, which we call necessary by reason of something else, as the *Metaphysics* says.[58]

11. The ability not to die was due to grace but not sanctifying grace according to some theologians,[59] and so human beings in that condition could not merit. But according to others,[60] the gift of immortality resulted from sanctifying grace, and human beings in that condition could merit.

12. The power of the form preserves the inequality of the elements in a composite material substance as long as the form's cause preserves it.

13. Matter has potentiality for other forms, and yet an external cause cannot bring the potentiality into actuality unless the cause is stronger than the force of the form that the form has from the influence of its cause. And God alone, whose power infinitely surpasses every power of other causes, causes the form that is the human soul. And so no external or internal cause could cause human beings to pass away as long as God willed to preserve them in existence by his power. Just so do we also clearly perceive that the power of a heavenly body preserves material forms in existence against the action of destructive causes.

14. It belongs to the nature of potentiality that a cause bring it into actuality, but an actuality in the potentiality prevents the potentiality being brought to another actuality. And so an external cause will not bring a potentiality into actuality unless the cause be stronger than the power of the form existing in the matter, whether the power that the form has of itself, or the power that the form has from what preserves it. For example, a small fire cannot destroy a large quantity of water. And so it is not surprising if the human soul in the condition of innocence could by the influence of God resist every contrary cause.

15. God by his governance does not prevent the proper movements of things, movements that belong to the things' perfection. But God out of the abundance of his goodness sometimes takes away movements that belong to the things' deficiency.

16. The form itself is the effect of the cause. And so what the cause causes as efficient cause, and what the form causes as formal cause are one and the same thing. For example, a painter, and also the color of paint, color a wall. In this way, therefore, God alone is the efficient cause of the immortality of human beings, and the soul is the formal cause of immortality by a gift conferred by God on the soul, whether in the state of innocence or in the state of glory.

58. Aristotle, *Metaphysics* V, 5 (1015a28).
59. Alexander of Hales, *Summa of Theology* I–II, n. 492.
60. Bonaventure, *Commentary on the Sentences* II, d. 29, a. 2, q. 1.

17. The argument of this objection is valid regarding things absolutely contrary to nature, for such in no respect belong to all or to many. But death is in one respect in accord with nature and in another respect contrary to nature, as I have said.[61]

Replies to the Arguments in the Section On the Contrary:
What I have explained easily makes clear the answer to those arguments. For the eternal happiness for which human beings are ordained is superior to human nature, and so immortality need not belong by nature to human beings. And likewise, even the body, although dissoluble, is proportioned to the human soul, as I have explained.[62]

61. In the answer.
62. Ibid.

On Human Choice

On Human Choice

Do Human Beings Have Free Choice in Their Acts, or Do They Choose Necessarily?

It seems that human beings choose necessarily and not freely, for the following reasons:

1. Jer. 10:23 says: "The path of human beings is not theirs, nor do they walk and direct their steps." But acts regarding which human beings enjoy liberty are their own, as acts in their control. Therefore, it seems that human beings do not enjoy free choice regarding their paths and acts.

2. People have said that the aforementioned text refers to the execution of choices, and human beings sometimes do not have the power to execute their choices. But the Apostle says in Rom. 9:16: "It," that is, willing, "does not belong to the one willing, nor does it," that is, running, "belong to the one running," but willing belongs to God showing mercy. And as running belongs to the external execution of acts, so willing belongs to internal choice. Therefore, human beings do not have power even over their internal choices, and God moves human beings to their choices.

3. People have said that internal impulses, namely, those from God himself, inevitably cause human beings to choose what they choose, and this is not contrary to human freedom. But although every animal moves itself by its appetites, animals other than human beings do not have free choice. Other animals do not have free choice because an external cause, namely, the power of a heavenly body or the action of another material substance, moves their appetites. Therefore, if God inevitably moves the wills of human beings, then human beings do not enjoy free choice in their acts.

4. Something is coerced if its cause is from without, and what is being coerced contributes nothing. Therefore, if an external cause should cause the will's choice, it seems that coercion and necessity determine the will to act. Therefore, the will does not have free choice in its acts.

5. The human will cannot fail to be in accord with God's will, since either human beings do what God wills, or God fulfills his will regarding them, as Augustine says in his *Enchiridion*.[1] Therefore, all human choices result from an inevitable choice.

6. The acts of every power can relate only to their proper object. For example, the acts of sight can relate only to visible things. But the will's object is the good. Therefore, the will can only will the good. Therefore, the will necessarily wills the good and does not have free choice of good or evil.

7. Every power to which an object is related as a cause of movement to something moveable is a passive power, and its function is to be acted upon. For example, a sensibly perceptible object moves the external senses, and so the senses are passive powers, and sense perception is a condition of being acted upon. But the object of the will is related to the will as a cause of movement to something moveable. For the Philosopher in the *De anima*[2] and the *Metaphysics*[3] says that the desirable causes movement without itself being moved, and the appetite causes movement and is moved. Therefore, the will is a passive power, and willing consists of being acted upon. But an efficient cause if sufficient necessarily moves every passive power. Therefore, it seems that the desirable necessarily moves the will. Therefore, human beings are not free to will or not to will.

8. People have said that the will has a necessity regarding the ultimate human end, since human beings necessarily will to be happy, and that the will does not have any necessity regarding means to that end. But both the end and the means are the will's object, since both have the nature of good. Therefore, if the will is necessarily moved to the end, it seems that it is also necessarily moved to the means.

9. Where the cause of movement is the same, and the moveable thing is the same, there is the same kind of movement. But when one wills the end and the means, the thing moved, namely, the will, is the same, and the cause of movement is the same, since one wills the means only insofar as one wills the end. Therefore, there is the same kind of movement, namely, that just as one necessarily wills the ultimate end, so one necessarily wills the means.

10. The will, just like the intellect, is a power distinct from matter. But the intellect's object necessarily moves the intellect, since the force of reason necessarily compels human beings to assent to truths. Therefore, by the same reasoning, the will's object also necessarily moves the will.

11. The disposition of a first cause of movement is imparted to all subsequent causes of movement, since all secondary causes of movement cause movement insofar as the first cause of movement has moved them. But in the ordering of voluntary movements, the first cause of movement is the desirable object the intellect understands. Therefore, since intellectual understanding of a desirable object admits necessity, it seems that necessity results in all subsequent movements if reason demonstrates something to be good. And so the will is necessarily, not freely, moved to will.

12. Real things cause movement more than mental things do. But according to the Philosopher in the *Metaphysics*,[4] good belongs to things, and truth to the mind. And so

1. *Enchiridion* 100 (PL 40:279).
2. *De anima* III, 10 (433b11–12).
3. *Metaphysics* XII, 7 (1072a26).
4. Ibid., VI, 4 (1027b25–27).

good is a real thing, and truth is a mental thing. Therefore, good rather has the character of a cause of movement more than truth does. But truth necessarily moves the intellect, as I have said.[5] Therefore, the good necessarily moves the will.

13. Love, which belongs to the will, is a more intense movement than knowledge, which belongs to the intellect, since knowledge assimilates things, but love transforms them, as we learn from Dionysius in his work *On the Divine Names*.[6] Therefore, the will is more moveable than the intellect. Therefore, if the intellect is necessarily moved, it seems that much more is the will.

14. People have said that the intellect's activity concerns a movement to the soul, and the will's acts concern movements away from the soul. And so the intellect has more the nature of something passive, and the will more the nature of something active. And so the will's object does not necessitate the will. But assent belongs to the intellect as consent belongs to the will. And assenting signifies a movement toward the thing to which the intellect assents, just as consenting signifies a movement toward the thing to which the will consents. Therefore, the will's movement is no more away from the soul than the intellect's movement is.

15. If the will is not necessarily moved regarding the objects willed, we need to say that it is disposed toward contrary things, since something that need not exist can not exist. But everything that has potentiality for contrary things is brought into the actuality of one of contraries only by an actual being that makes what had potentiality have actuality. And we call what makes something actual the thing's cause. Therefore, if the will definitively wills something, there is necessarily a cause that makes the will itself so will. And given a cause, we necessarily posit its effect, as Avicenna proves,[7] since if the effect can not exist when the cause is posited, the effect will still need something else to bring potentiality to actuality, and so the first thing was not a sufficient cause. Therefore, the will is necessarily moved to will things.

16. No power disposed toward contrary things is active, since every active power can do that regarding which it is active. And if something is possible, nothing implied by it is impossible. And if a power were active regarding contrary things, it would follow that two contrary things would simultaneously exist, which is impossible. But the will is an active power. Therefore, it is not disposed to contrary things and is necessarily determined to one of them.

17. The will sometimes begins to choose when it did not previously choose. Therefore, the disposition in which it previously was either was or was not altered. If not, then the will no more chooses now than it did previously. And so the will not choosing would choose, and this is impossible. And if the will's disposition is changed, something needs to change it, since everything moved is moved by something else. But a cause of movement imposes necessity on the moveable thing; otherwise, the cause would be insufficient to move the thing. Therefore, the will is necessarily moved.

18. People have said that such arguments reach valid conclusions about natural powers, which belong to matter, and not about an immaterial power like the will. But

---

5. Objection 10.
6. *On the Divine Names* 4, n. 13 (PG 3:712A).
7. *Metaphysics* I, 7.

the senses are the source of all human knowledge. Therefore, human beings can know things only insofar as either the things themselves or their effects fall within the power of the senses. But the very power disposed toward contrary things does not fall within the power of the senses. And regarding the power's effects that fall within the power of the senses, no two contrary acts exist simultaneously; rather, we always perceive that only one actually results in a definite way. Therefore, we cannot judge that human beings have an active power disposed toward contrary things.

19. Since we speak of powers in relation to their acts, one power is related to another power as one kind of act is related to another kind of act. But two contrary acts cannot exist simultaneously in the same power. Therefore, neither can one power be disposed toward two contrary things.

20. According to Augustine in his work *On the Trinity*,[8] nothing is the cause of its own existence. Therefore, by like reasoning, nothing is the cause of its own movement. Therefore, the will does not move itself. But something needs to move the will, since the will, hitherto inactive, begins to act, and what begins to act is in some respect moved. And so also we say about God, because of his immutability, that he does not begin to will after not willing. Therefore, something else needs to move the will. But something moved by another undergoes necessity from the other. Therefore, the will wills necessarily, not freely.

21. We trace everything of many kinds to something of one kind. But human movements are various and of many kinds. Therefore, we trace the cause of human movements to a uniform movement, that is, the motion of the heavens. But what the motion of the heavens causes results necessarily, since natural causes necessarily produce their effects unless there is an impediment. And nothing can prevent the motion of a heavenly body from attaining its effect, since we would need to trace the cause of even an impediment's property to a heavenly source. Therefore, it seems that human movements result from necessity, not free choice.

22. Those who do what they do not will do not have free choice. But human beings do what they do not will, as Rom. 7:15 says: "I do the evil I hate." Therefore, human beings do not have free choice in their acts.

23. Augustine says in his *Enchiridion* that "human beings who use their free choice wrongly have lost themselves and it."[9] But choosing freely is simply enjoying free choice. Therefore, human beings do not have free choice.

24. Augustine says in his *Confessions* that "there is necessity where there is no resistance to habits."[10] Therefore, it seems that the will, at least in those habituated to do things, is necessarily moved.

On the Contrary:

1. Sir. 15:14 says: "God from the beginning constituted and left human beings in the hands of their own deliberation." But this would only be the case if they were to have

---

8. *On the Trinity* I, 1, n. 1 (PL 42:820).
9. *Enchiridion* 30 (PL 40:246).
10. *Confessions* VIII, 5, n. 10 (PL 32:753).

free choice, which is the desire for things about which there has been deliberation, as the *Ethics* says.[11] Therefore, human beings have free choice in their acts.

2. Rational powers are disposed toward contrary things, as the Philosopher says.[12] But the will is a rational power, since the will belongs to reason, as the *De anima* says.[13] Therefore, the will is disposed toward contrary things and is not moved necessarily to one of them.

3. As the Philosopher says in the *Ethics*,[14] human beings are masters of their acts, and they have the power to act or not to act. But this would not be the case if they were not to have free choice. Therefore, human beings have free choice in their acts.

Answer:

Some have held that the human will is necessarily moved to choose things. But they did not hold that the will is coerced, since only something from an external source, not everything necessary, is coerced. And so also some necessary movements are natural but not coerced. For what is coerced is as contrary to what is natural as to what is voluntary, since the source of both the natural and the voluntary is internal, and the source of what is coerced is external.

But this opinion is heretical. For it takes away the reason for merit and demerit in human acts, as it does not seem meritorious or demeritorious for persons to do necessarily what they could not avoid doing.

It is also to be counted among the oddest philosophical opinions, since it is not only contrary to faith but also subverts all the principles of moral philosophy. For if nothing is within our power, and we are necessarily moved to will things, deliberation, exhortation, precept, punishment, and praise and blame, of which moral philosophy consists, are destroyed. And we call like opinions that destroy the foundations of parts of philosophy odd, as, for example, the position that nothing is moving, which destroys the foundations of natural science. And some individuals were indeed led to hold such positions partly because of impudence, partly because of sophistical arguments that they could not refute, as the *Metaphysics* says.[15]

Therefore, to show the answer to this question, we need first to consider that human beings, like other things, have a source of their proper acts. And properly speaking, the intellect and the will are the active or causal source in human beings, as the *De anima* says.[16] And this source partially accords with, and partially differs from, the active source in things of nature. There is indeed agreement. For things of nature have forms, which are the source of action, and inclinations resulting from the forms, which we call natural appetites, and actions result from these inclinations. Just so, human beings have an intellectual form and inclinations of the will resulting from understood forms, and external acts result from these inclinations. But there is this difference, that the form of a thing of nature is a form individuated by matter, and so also the inclinations resulting from the form are determined to one thing, but the understood form is universal and includes many

11. Aristotle, *Ethics* III, 6 (1112a14–15).
12. *Metaphysics* IX, 2 (1046b4–5).
13. Aristotle, *De anima* III, 9 (432b5).
14. *Ethics* III, 1 (1110a17–18), and VI, 12 (1144a10–11).
15. Aristotle, *Metaphysics* IV, 5 (1009a19–22).
16. Aristotle, *De anima* III, 10 (433a13–18).

individual things. And so since actualities regard singular things, and none of them exhausts the potentiality of the universal, inclinations of the will remain indeterminately disposed to many things. For example, if an architect should conceive the form of house in general, under which different shapes of house are included, his will can be inclined to build a square house or a round house or a house of another shape.

And the active source in irrational animals is midway between both those sources. For forms perceived by the senses, like the forms of things of nature, are individual, and so forms perceived by the senses, like the forms of things of nature, result in inclinations to act in only one way. And yet the senses do not always receive the same form, as in the case of the things of nature (since fire is always hot), but forms perceived by the senses are at one time one form and at another time another. For example, forms perceived by the senses are at one time pleasurable and another time disagreeable. And so animals sometimes flee and at other times seek what they perceive. And in this respect, the active source in irrational animals is like the human active source.

Second, we need to consider that powers are moved in two ways: in one way regarding the subject; in a second way regarding the object. A power is indeed moved regarding the subject, as, for example, the alteration of the disposition of a bodily organ causes the power of sight to see more or less clearly. And a power is moved regarding the object, as, for example, the power of sight sometimes perceives white, sometimes black. And the first kind of alteration indeed belongs to the very performance of the act, namely, that it be or not be performed, or performed better or worse. And the second kind of alteration belongs to specifying the act, since objects specify acts.

And we need to consider that the specification of acts in things of nature indeed comes from the things' forms, and that the very performance of the acts comes from the cause that causes the very movement. And the cause of movement acts for the sake of an end. And so we conclude that the first source of movement as to the performance of an act comes from the end. And if we should consider the objects of the will and the intellect, we find that the object of the intellect belongs first and chiefly to the genus of formal cause, since its object is being and truth. But the object of the will belongs first and chiefly to the genus of final cause, since its object is the good, in which all ends are included, just as all understood forms are included in the true. And so good itself, insofar as it is a comprehensible form, is included in the true as something true, and the true itself, insofar as it is the end of intellectual activity, is included in the good as something good.

Therefore, if we should consider the movement of the soul's powers regarding the object specifying the act, the first source of movement comes from the intellect, since the understood good in this way moves even the will itself. And if we should consider the movement of the soul's powers regarding performance of the act, then the source of the movement comes from the will. For the power to which the chief end belongs always moves to action the power to which the means to the end belongs. For example, the art of war causes a bridle maker to make bridles. And thus does the will move both itself and all the other powers. For example, I understand because I will to do so, and I also use all my other powers and habits because I will to do so. And so also the Commentator in his *Commentary on the De anima* defines habit as what a person uses at will.[17]

---

17. Averroes, *On Aristotle's On the Soul* III, comm. 18.

Therefore, in order to show that the will is not moved necessarily, we need to consider the movement of the will both regarding performance of the will's act and regarding specification of the act, which is by the object.

Therefore, regarding performance of the act, it is indeed first of all evident that the will moves its very self. For just as it moves other powers, so also does it move itself. Nor does it follow from this that the will is potential and actual in the same respect. For human beings by using their intellect in the process of discovery move themselves to knowledge, as they move from things actually known to unknown things that were only potentially known. Just so, they by actually willing something move themselves actually to will something else. For example, human beings, by willing health, move themselves to will to take medicine, since they, because they will health, begin to deliberate about things that conduce to health and finally will to take medicine when deliberation has so determined. Therefore, deliberation, which indeed results from the will of one willing to deliberate, precedes the will to take medicine. Therefore, since the will moves itself by deliberation, and deliberation is an inquiry that does not yield only one conclusion but leads to contrary conclusions, the will does not move itself necessarily. And since the will has not always willed to deliberate, something else needs to move the will to will to deliberate. And if the will indeed moves itself to deliberate, it is also necessary that deliberation precede the movement of the will, and that an act of the will precede the deliberation. And since there cannot be an infinite regression, we need to hold that regarding the first movement of the will, something external, at whose instigation the will would begin to will, moves the will of anyone not always actually willing.

Therefore, some have held that that instigation comes from a heavenly body.[18] But this cannot be so. For as the will belongs to the power of reason, as the Philosopher says in the *De anima*,[19] and the power of reason, that is, the intellect, is not a material power, the power of a heavenly body cannot directly move the will itself. And to hold that an imprint of a heavenly body moves the human will itself, as such an imprint moves the appetites of irrational animals, follows the opinion of those who hold that the intellect does not differ from the senses. For the Philosopher in the *De anima* attributes to them the words of those who say that the human will is such "that the source of human beings and the gods," that is, the heavens or the sun, "daily induces the will to act."[20]

Therefore, we conclude, as Aristotle concludes in the chapter on good fortune in the *Eudemian Ethics*,[21] that what first moves the intellect and the will is something superior to them, namely, God. And since he moves every kind of thing according to the nature of the moveable thing, for example, light things upward, and heavy things downward, he also moves the will according to its condition, as indeterminately disposed to many things, not in a necessary way. Therefore, if we should consider the movement of the will regarding the performance of an act, the will is evidently not moved in a necessary way.

And if we should consider the movement of the will regarding the object determining the act of the will to will this or that, we need to note that the object moving the will

---

18. Some ancient philosophers, according to Aristotle, *De anima* III, 3 (427a26).
19. Ibid., III, 9 (432b5).
20. Ibid., III, 3 (427a26).
21. *Eudemian Ethics* VIII, 2 (1248a17–32).

is a good apprehended as suitable. And so a good, if it is presented to us as good but not as suitable, will not move the will. And since deliberations and choices regard particular things, which are the objects of the will's acts, we need to apprehend good and suitable things as good and suitable in particular and not only in general. Therefore, if we apprehend something as a suitable good in every conceivable particular, it will necessarily move the will. And so human beings necessarily seek happiness, which Boethius says is "a condition made complete by combining all good things."[22] And I say "necessarily" regarding specification of the act, since human beings cannot will the contrary, and not regarding performance of the act, since a person may at a particular time not will to think about happiness, as even the very acts of the intellect and the will are particular acts.

But if the good is such as not to be found good in every conceivable particular, it will not necessarily move the will even regarding specification of the act. This is so because a person will be able to will its contrary, even when thinking about it, since the contrary is perhaps good or suitable regarding some other particular consideration. For example, something good for health is not good for enjoyment, and so forth.

And that this or that particular condition moves the will toward what is presented to it can happen in three ways. It happens in one way, indeed, as one particular predominates, and then reason moves the will. For example, such is the case when human beings prefer what is useful for health to what is useful for pleasure. And it happens in a second way when a person thinks about a particular circumstance and not about another, and this often happens through a favorable opportunity offered either from within or from without, so that such consideration absorbs the person. And it happens in a third way from the disposition of a human being, since "ends seem to a person as the person is disposed," as the Philosopher says.[23] And so the will of one who is angry and the will of one who is calm are moved in different ways regarding an object, since the same object is not suitable to both persons, just as a healthy person and a sick person regard food in different ways.

Therefore, if the disposition whereby something seems good and suitable to a person is natural and not subject to the will, the will by natural necessity will choose it. For example, all human beings by nature desire to exist, live, and understand. But if the disposition is such as to be subject to the will and not a natural disposition, as, for example, when a habit or emotion so disposes a person that something seems to the person to be either good or evil in a particular respect, the will will not necessarily be moved. This is so because persons will be able to alter such a disposition, so that the thing does not seem the same to them, as, for example, if persons calm their anger so as not to judge in anger about something. And yet emotions are more easily altered than habits.

Therefore, regarding its object, the will is necessarily moved toward some but not all things. And regarding performing its act, the will is not moved necessarily.

Replies to the Objections:

1. We can understand the cited authority in two ways. We can understand it in one way such that the prophet is speaking about the execution of choice, since human beings do not have power to put into effect what they deliberate about in their minds. We can

---

22. *On Consolation* III, prose 2 (PL 63:724A).
23. *Ethics* III, 5 (1114a32–b1).

understand the authority in a second way as regards the fact that a superior power, that is, God, moves even the internal will. And regarding this, the Apostle says in Rom. 9:16 that something, namely, willing, does not belong to the one willing, nor does something, namely, running, belong to the one running, as the first source of the acts. Rather, the acts belong to God who inspires them as their first source.

2. And so the reply to the second objection is evident.

3. The impulse of a higher cause moves irrational animals to definite things by way of particular forms, and the perception of these forms activates animals' sense appetites. And God indeed inevitably moves the will because of the efficacy of his causal power, which cannot fail. But because the nature of the will so moved is indifferently disposed to different things, no necessity results, and freedom abides. Just so, God's providence works infallibly in every kind of thing, although effects result contingently from contingent causes, insofar as God moves every kind of thing proportionally, each in its own way.

4. The will when moved by God contributes something, since the will itself acts even though God moves it. And so the will's movement, although from an external source as the first source, is nevertheless not coerced.

5. The human will is not in accord with God's will in one way, namely, insofar as the human will wills something that God does not will, as when the human will wills to sin. But God also does not will that the human will not will this, since the human will would not if God were so to will. For the Lord accomplished everything that he willed. And although the human will is in this respect not in accord with God's will regarding the human will's movement, the human will nonetheless can never be in discord with God's will regarding the outcome or result, since the human will always achieves the result that God fulfills his will regarding human beings. And as to the way the human will wills, the human will is not necessarily the same as God's will, since God eternally and infinitely wills everything, but human beings do not. And so Is. 55:9 says: "As the heavens are exalted above the earth, so are my ways exalted above your ways."

6. Because good is the object of the will, we can conclude that the will wills things only under the aspect of good. But because many and different kinds of things are included in the aspect of good, we cannot conclude from the necessity to will things under the aspect of good that the will is necessarily moved to this or that.

7. Something active necessarily causes only when it overcomes the power of something passive. And since the will is potential regarding good in general, only something good in every respect overcomes the power of the will so as necessarily to move the will, and the only such good is the perfect good that is happiness. And the will cannot not will this good; that is, the will cannot will the contrary. Nevertheless, the will is able not actually to will happiness, since the will can avoid thinking about happiness insofar as the will moves the intellect to its activity. And in this respect, neither does the will necessarily will happiness itself. Just so, persons would not necessarily become warm if they could at will repel heat.

8. The end is the reason for willing means, and so the will is dissimilarly related to each.

9. If there is only one possible way to achieve the end, then the reason for willing the end and the reason for willing the means are the same. But such is not the case in the matter under discussion, since there are many ways to achieve happiness. And so human

beings, although they necessarily will happiness, do not necessarily will any of the things leading to happiness.

10. The intellect and the will are similar in one respect and dissimilar in another. They are indeed dissimilar regarding performance of their acts, for the will moves the intellect to activity, and the will is moved by itself, not by another power. But both the intellect and the will are similar regarding their objects. For as an object good in every respect necessarily moves the will, and an object that can be understood as evil in some respect does not, so also necessary truths (truths that cannot be conceived to be false) necessarily move the intellect, and contingent truths (which can be conceived to be false) do not.

11. The disposition of the first cause of movement abides in the things it moves insofar as it itself moves them. For it is thus that they receive the first cause's likeness. But they do not need to receive the first cause's likeness completely. And so the first cause of movement cannot be moved, and the other causes can.

12. Because the true is a concept that exists in the mind, it has a more formal element than the good does, and more power to move as regards the object. But the good has more power to move as regards the end, as I have said.[24]

13. We say that love transforms the lover into the beloved as love moves the lover toward the very thing beloved, and knowledge assimilates as the likeness of the known thing is produced in the knower. And the former belongs to the alteration that the efficient cause seeking the end causes, but the latter belongs to the alteration that the form causes.

14. Assenting designates the movement of the intellect toward rightly understanding something one has in one's mind rather than a movement of the intellect toward the thing, and the intellect assents to conceptions when it judges them to be true.

15. Not every cause necessarily brings about an effect even if the cause is sufficient, since the cause can be prevented from sometimes achieving its effect. For example, natural causes produce their effects for the most part but not necessarily, since they are prevented from so doing in relatively few cases. Therefore, the cause that makes the will will something need not necessarily achieve this, since the will itself can present an obstacle, whether by removing the consideration that induces the will to will it or by considering the contrary, namely, that what is presented as good is not good in some respect.

16. The Philosopher in the *Metaphysics* by this means shows that an active power disposed toward contrary things does not necessarily produce its effect, not that a power disposed toward contrary things is not an active power.[25] For if we suppose that an active power disposed toward contrary things necessarily produces its effect, it would obviously follow that contradictory things would exist simultaneously. But if we should grant that an active power is disposed toward contrary things, it does not follow that the contraries exist simultaneously, since one is not compatible with the other even though each contrary toward which the power is disposed is possible.

17. The will, when it freshly begins to choose, is transformed from its prior disposition regarding its previous potentiality to choose and its subsequent actual choice. And

---

24. In the answer.
25. *Metaphysics* IX, 2 (1046b4–5).

a cause indeed effects this change as the will moves itself to act and also as an external cause, namely, God, moves the will. And yet the will is not moved necessarily, as I have said.[26]

18. The source of human knowledge comes from the senses, but not everything that human beings know needs to be subject to the senses or known directly through perceptible effects. For the intellect also knows itself through its activity, which is not subject to the senses. And it likewise also knows internal acts of the will as acts of the intellect in one respect move the will, and the will in another respect causes acts of the intellect, as I have said,[27] as effects are known through causes, and causes through effects. But granted that we can know the power of the will as a power disposed toward contrary things only through perceptible effects, the argument of the objection is still invalid. For we know universals, which are everywhere and always, through singulars, which are here and now, and we know prime matter, which has potentiality for different forms, through the succession of forms, which nonetheless do not exist simultaneously in matter. Just so, we know the power of the will as a power disposed toward contrary things because contrary acts follow one another successively from the same source, not indeed because contrary acts exist simultaneously.

19. The proposition, "As one kind of act is related to another kind of act, so one power is related to another power," is true in one respect and false in another. For if we understand the acts of powers to be as commensurate with the powers as the powers' universal objects, the proposition is true, since then hearing is related to sight as sound is to color. But if we understand what is included in the universal object as a particular act, then the proposition is false. For example, there is one power of sight although white and black are different colors. Therefore, although human beings have the power of the will as a power disposed toward contrary things, the contraries toward which the will is disposed do not exist simultaneously.

20. The same thing as such does move itself; rather, the same thing as different can move itself. For it is thus that the intellect as it actually understands first principles moves itself from potentiality to actuality regarding conclusions, and that the will as it wills the end moves itself to act regarding the means.

21. We trace movements of the will, since they are of different kinds, to a uniform source. But this source is God, not a heavenly body, as I have said,[28] if we should mean the source that directly moves the will. And if we should be speaking about movements of the will as external perceptible objects on favorable occasions move the will, then we trace the movements to a heavenly body. And yet the will is not necessarily moved, since the will does not have to desire pleasurable things when they are presented to it. Nor is it true that things heavenly bodies directly cause result necessarily from the heavenly bodies. For as the Philosopher says in the *Metaphysics*,[29] if every effect were to result from a natural cause, and every natural cause necessarily to produce its effect, then everything would be necessary. But both of these suppositions are false. For some causes, even if they

---

26. In the answer and the reply to objection 15.
27. In the answer.
28. Ibid.
29. *Metaphysics* VI, 1 (1027a29ff.).

be sufficient, do not produce their effects, since the causes can be prevented from doing so, as is evident in the case of every kind of natural cause. Neither, moreover, is it true that everything that happens has a natural cause. For natural efficient causes do not cause things that happen by accident, since things that happen by accident are neither beings nor intrinsically one. Therefore, we do not trace encountering an obstacle to a heavenly body as the cause, since encountering the obstacle is due to chance. For heavenly bodies act in the way of natural causes.

22. Persons who do what they do not will do not have free action, but they can have free will.

23. Human beings who sin have lost free choice regarding freedom from moral fault and unhappiness but not regarding freedom from coercion.

24. Habits do not cause necessity absolutely, although they especially do so in sudden situations. For however much persons are habituated, they can still by deliberation act contrary to habit.

QUESTION VII

On Venial Sin

First Article

Do We Properly Contradistinguish Venial Sin from Mortal Sin?

It seems that we do not, for the following reasons:

1. As Augustine says in his work *Against Faustus*, "Sin is a word or deed or desire contrary to the eternal law."[1] But every sin contrary to the eternal law is mortal. Therefore, every sin is mortal. Therefore, we do not properly distinguish sin into mortal and venial sin.

2. Sin by its nature deserves punishment. But pardon, which takes away punishment, is contrary to punishment. Therefore, the venial is contrary to the nature of sin. But no specific difference dividing a genus is contrary to the genus. Therefore, the mortal and the venial cannot properly distinguish sin.

3. Whoever turns inordinately, turns toward a transitory good and away from the immutable good, since in every movement, one who approaches one terminus recedes from the other. Therefore, whoever sins turns away from the immutable good. But this is to sin mortally. Therefore, whoever sins sins mortally. Therefore, there are not two kinds of sin: one mortal, the other venial.

4. Every sin consists of an inordinate love of a creature. But whoever loves loves either as one using a means or as one enjoying an end. And whoever loves a creature as one using it as a means does not sin, since the person relates the creature to the end of happiness, which is to make use of it as a means, as Augustine says in his work *On Christian Doctrine*.[2] And if a person loves a creature as one enjoying it, the person sins mortally, since the person makes a creature the ultimate end. Therefore, one who loves a creature either does not sin or sins mortally, and so the same conclusion follows as before.

---

1. *Against Faustus* XXII, 27 (PL 42:418).
2. *On Christian Doctrine* I, 3 (PL 34:20).

5. If two things are contrary, one does not pass into the other. For example, whiteness never becomes blackness, nor the converse. But venial becomes mortal, for a gloss on Ps. 32:1, "Blessed are they whose iniquities are forgiven," says: "Nothing is so venial that it could not become mortal when one approves it."[3] Therefore, we should not contradistinguish the venial from the mortal.

6. If one does not approve something evil, it is not a sin, since it is not voluntary. But if one approves it, it is a mortal sin, as the cited gloss makes clear.[4] Therefore, either it is not a sin, or it is a mortal sin.

7. We do not contradistinguish what inclines to something from the thing, since one contrary does not incline to the other. But venial sin disposes toward mortal sin. Therefore, we should not contradistinguish venial sin from mortal sin.

8. Anselm says in his work *Why God Became Man* that a rational creature's will ought to be subject to God's will; whoever takes away this subordination takes away the honor due to God and dishonors him.[5] But to dishonor God is to sin mortally, and whoever sins dishonors God thereby, since the person does not subject his or her will to God's will. Therefore, whoever sins sins mortally.

9. Human beings are obliged by precept to ordain everything they do to God as their end. For 1 Cor. 10:31 says: "Whether you are eating or drinking or are doing anything else, do everything for the glory of God." But we cannot ordain venial sin to God. Therefore, whoever sins venially acts contrary to the precept. Therefore, such a person sins mortally.

10. Augustine says in his work *Book of the 83 Questions*: "Using as the means what ought to be enjoyed as the end or enjoying as the end what ought to be used as the means is the whole and sole evil for human beings."[6] But both of these things are mortal sins. For those who use as the means what ought to be enjoyed as the end do not make God their ultimate end, whom alone they should enjoy as their end. And those who enjoy as the end what ought to be used as the means make creatures their ultimate end. And both of these constitute mortal sin. Therefore, every evil of moral fault is mortal sin.

11. Since punishment corresponds to moral fault, it seems that there is the same nature of moral fault wherever there is the same punishment. But venial sin deserves the same punishment as mortal sin, since Augustine says in a sermon on purgatory that it is a venial sin to flatter persons of higher station,[7] and yet clerics are defrocked for such adulation, as the *Decretum* maintains.[8] Therefore, the nature of venial and mortal moral fault is the same. Therefore, we do not properly contradistinguish venial sin from mortal sin.

12. People have said that venial and mortal sin differ in their subject, since venial sin belongs to sense powers, and mortal sin to the power of reason. But consent to an act belongs to higher reason, as Augustine says in his work *On the Trinity*.[9] And venial sin

---

3. Under the name of Augustine in *Decretum*, d. 25, chap. 3, n. 4 (Friedberg I:92).
4. Ibid.
5. *Why God Became Man* I, 11 (PL 158:376B–C).
6. *Book of the 83 Questions*, q. 30 (PL 40:19).
7. *Sermon 104*, n. 3 (PL 39:1947).
8. *Decretum*, d. 46, chap. 3 (Friedberg I:168).
9. *On the Trinity* XII, 12, n. 17 (PL 42:1008).

involves some consent to an act, for example, consenting to an idle word. Therefore, the attributed difference is improper.

13. The first movements of spiritual sins are venial sins. But spiritual sins belong to the power of reason rather than to sense appetites. Therefore, venial sin does not belong only to sense appetites.

14. What we share with irrational animals does not seem to be the subject of sin, since irrational animals have no sin. But we share sense appetites with irrational animals. Therefore, there cannot be either mortal or venial sin in sense appetites.

15. Necessity excludes the character of sin, since there is neither praise nor blame regarding things done out of necessity. But sense appetites are subject to necessity, since they are linked to bodily organs. Therefore, sin cannot belong to sense appetites.

16. Anselm says that only the will is punished.[10] But sin deserves punishment. Therefore, sin belongs only to the will. Therefore, sin does not belong to sense appetites.

17. If mortal sin belongs to higher reason, this will be so either directly or indirectly. But mortal sin cannot belong to higher reason directly and as such, since higher reason cannot err, inasmuch as it has the power according to Augustine to contemplate the eternal natures of things, regarding which there is no error.[11] "And they err who do evil," as Prov. 14:22 says. Likewise, neither can mortal sin belong to higher reason indirectly, since higher reason does not control lower powers. For higher reason does not have this power, inasmuch as it lost the power to control lower powers as a result of original sin, as Augustine says.[12] Therefore, mortal sin cannot belong to higher reason.

18. People have likewise said that venial and mortal sins differ in that one who sins mortally loves a creature more than God, and one who sins venially loves a creature less than God. But let us suppose that one thinks that plain fornication is not a mortal sin, and that the person fornicates while holding that view but would forgo fornicating were he or she to know that the action is contrary to the will of God. It is evident that the person sins mortally, since ignorance of the law does not excuse the person, and yet he or she loves God more than fornication. For that is loved more for which something else is forgone. Therefore, not everyone who sins mortally loves a creature more than God.

19. More and less do not distinguish species. But mortal and venial distinguish species. Therefore, mortal and venial do not differ in the fact that one loves a creature more or less than God.

20. We can find equality wherever we find more and less, since if we take away what is surplus, equality results. But a person may love a creature more than God and also less than God. Therefore, a person may love a creature equally as much as God. Therefore, there will be a sin in between mortal and venial, and so the division into mortal and venial sin will be inadequate.

21. People have likewise said that mortal and venial sins differ in their effects, in that mortal sin deprives one of grace, and that venial sin does not. But there can be no grace without virtue. And venial sin takes away virtue, which consists of rightly ordered love, as Augustine says in his work *On Church Customs*.[13] And venial sin takes away the

---

10. *On the Virgin Conception* 4 (PL 158:438B).

11. E.g., *On the Trinity* XII, 7, n. 12 (PL 42:1005).

12. *On the Punishment and Forgiveness of Sins and on the Baptism of Infants* II, 22 (PL 44:172).

13. *On Church Customs* I, 15, n. 25 (PL 32:1322).

right order of love; otherwise, it would not be sin. Therefore, even venial sin takes away grace.

22. It belongs to grace to direct human beings to God as their end. But venial sin takes away their ordination to God as their end, since sin cannot be ordained to God as its end. Therefore, venial sin takes away grace.

23. Whoever offends God does not have God's grace. But one offends God by venial sin, since God punishes such a person. Therefore, venial sin takes away grace.

24. People have likewise said that venial sin differs from mortal sin regarding liability to punishment, since mortal sin makes a person liable to eternal punishment, and venial sin makes a person liable to temporal punishment. But Augustine says in his *On the Gospel of John* that lack of faith is a sin whose retention causes all sins to be retained.[14] And so it is evident that the venial sins of unbelievers are not forgiven. But liability to punishment is not taken away as long as moral fault remains. Therefore, the venial sins of unbelievers are punished with eternal punishment. Therefore, venial sin does not differ from mortal sin, and so venial sin cannot be contradistinguished from mortal sin.

On the Contrary:

1. 1 Jn. 1:8 says: "We deceive ourselves if we say that we have no sin." But we cannot understand this about mortal sin, since, as Augustine says,[15] there is no mortal sin in the saints. Therefore, there is some venial sin that we can contradistinguish from mortal sin.

2. Augustine says in a homily on the Gospel of John that serious sins deserve damnation, and venial sins do not.[16] Therefore, we properly contradistinguish venial sin from mortal sin.

Answer:

We derive the word "venial" from "pardon" [Latin: *venia*]. And we call something venial from pardon in three ways. First, indeed, we call something venial from pardon because something obtained pardon, as Ambrose says that confession makes mortal sin venial,[17] and some call such venial by reason of the outcome.[18] And it is obvious that we do not contradistinguish venial in this sense from mortal sin. Second, we call sin venial because it has in itself a reason for pardon, not that it be unpunished, but that it be less punished. And it is thus that we call sin venial that is done out of weakness or ignorance, since weakness either totally or partially excuses from sin. And some call such sin venial by reason of its cause.[19] But we also do not contradistinguish venial in this sense from mortal sin, since someone sinning out of ignorance or weakness may sin mortally, as I have maintained in previous questions.[20] We call a sin venial in a third way because, inasmuch as it does not of itself exclude pardon, that is, a limit to punishment, and it is

14. *On the Gospel of John*, tr. 89, n. 1 (PL 35:1856).
15. Actually, Peter Lombard, *Gloss*, on 1 Tit. 1:5 (PL 192:386A).
16. Actually, *On the Gospel of John*, tr. 41, n. 9 (PL 35:1697).
17. *On Paradise* 14, n. 71 (PL 14:310B).
18. Cf. Albert the Great, *Commentary on the Sentences* II, d. 22, a. 4.
19. Ibid.
20. Q. 3, aa. 8 and 10.

in this way that we contradistinguish venial from mortal sin, which of itself deserves eternal punishment and so excludes pardon, that is, a limit to punishment. And some call such sin venial in general.[21]

And in order for us to seek the specific difference that distinguishes venial sin from mortal sin, we need to consider that they indeed differ regarding punitive liability. For mortal sin deserves eternal punishment, and venial sin temporal punishment. But this difference results from rather than constitutes the nature of mortal and venial sin. For a sin is not such a kind of sin because it deserves such a punishment. Rather, conversely, a sin deserves such a punishment because it is such a kind of sin. Likewise, they differ regarding their effects. For mortal sin deprives one of grace, and venial sin does not. But neither is this the difference we are looking for, since the difference results from the nature of the sin. For a sin has such an effect because the sin is such a kind of sin, and not the converse.

And the difference regarding the subject of sin would constitute a different nature of sin if venial sin were always to belong to sense appetites, and mortal sin always to the power of reason. For it is thus that we essentially distinguish intellectual virtue from moral virtue, according to the Philosopher in the *Ethics*,[22] since moral virtue belongs to reason insofar as reason participates in the activities of sense appetites, that is to say, moral virtue belongs to sense appetites, and intellectual virtue belongs to the very power of reason. But this is not true, since venial sin can also belong to the power of reason, as one of the objections indicates,[23] and so this difference does not explain the different nature of each kind of sin.

And the fourth difference, which regards the way of loving, indeed constitutes a different nature of sin but only regarding the act of the will, which relates to the efficient cause of sin. And venial sin consists both of internal acts of the will and of external acts. For there are certain external acts that are venial sins by reason of their kind, as, for example, to utter an idle word or a lie in jest or the like. And there are certain sins that are mortal by reason of their kind, such as homicide, adultery, and the like. And the difference that regards acts of the will does not differentiate kinds of external acts. For one can do something generically good with an evil will. For example, such would be the case if one should give alms for the sake of vainglory. Likewise, something generically venial can be mortal because of the will of the doer. For example, such would be the case if one should utter an idle word in contempt of God. But external acts differ generically by reason of their objects. And so theologians commonly say that acts in regard to proper subject matter are generically good, and that acts in regard to improper subject matter are generically evil.[24] Therefore, we need to call evil generically venial and generically mortal because it concerns certain improper subject matter.

Therefore, in order to pursue this inquiry, we need to consider that sin consists of a disorder of the soul, just as physical disease consists of a disorder of the body. And so sin is a disease of the soul, as it were, and pardon is for sin what healing is for disease. There-

---

21. See n. 18 above.
22. *Ethics* I, 13 (1103a1–5).
23. Objection 13.
24. E.g., Alexander of Hales, *Commentary on the Sentences* II, d. 36, n. 8.

fore, as there are some curable diseases and some incurable diseases, which we call mortal, so there are some quasi-curable sins, which we call venial, and some sins of themselves incurable, which we call mortal, although God can cure them.

And we call incurable and mortal a disease that destroys a life principle. For if such a principle is taken away, there remains nothing whereby the principle might be restored, and so such a disease cannot be cured and brings about death. And there is a kind of disease that does not destroy anything belonging to life principles but destroys something that results from life principles, something that life principles can restore. For example, there is tertian fever, which consists of an overabundance of heat, and the power of nature can overcome the fever. And according to the Philosopher in the *Ethics*,[25] the source in human activity is the end. And so the source of spiritual life, which consists of right action, is the end of human actions. And the end of human actions is love of God and neighbor: "For the end of the commandments is love," as 1 Tim. 1:5 says. For the virtue of charity unites the soul to God, who is the life of the soul as the soul is the life of the body. And so if charity be excluded, there is mortal sin. For there remains no life principle that would restore the deficiency, and only the Holy Spirit can do so, since "the Holy Spirit given to us pours love of God in our hearts," as Rom. 5:5 says. And if the deficiency of rectitude be such as not to exclude charity, there will be venial sin. For charity, remaining as a life principle, as it were, can restore all deficiencies: "For love covers all sins," as Prov. 10:12 says.

And it can happen in two ways that a sin does or does not exclude charity: in one way regarding the sinner; in the second way from the very type of sin.

It can indeed happen regarding the sinner in two ways. It happens in one way because the act of sin belongs to a kind of power that is not constituted to ordain its acts to the end, and so not to be turned away from the end. And so the movements of sense appetites can be only venial sins, not mortal sins, since ordaining things to the human end belongs only to the power of reason. It happens in the second way because the power that can ordain things toward or away from the end can ordain to the contrary of the end acts that are not also of themselves such. For example, if one should utter an idle word in contempt of God, which would be contrary to charity, this will be a mortal sin because of the evil will of the doer, not because of the type of deed.

It happens in the second way that a sin be or not be contrary to charity from the very type of deed, which regards the object or matter that is or is not contrary to charity. Analogously, some food (e.g., poisonous food) is of itself opposed to life, and some food (e.g., coarse and not easily digestible food or even easily digestible food consumed in excessive amounts) is not opposed to life although such food offers an impediment to one's proper vital disposition. Just so regarding human acts, there are things of themselves contrary to love of God and neighbor, namely, things that destroy the obedience and reverence that human beings owe to God, for example, blasphemy, devil worship, and the like. And there are also things that destroy the common life of human society, for example, theft, homicide, and the like. For human beings could not live in harmony with one another where such things were to be perpetrated promiscuously and indiscriminately. And such things are mortal sins by reason of their kind with whatever intention

25. *Ethics* VI, 5 (1140b16–17).

or will they are done. And there are some things that, although containing a disorder, nonetheless do not directly exclude either of the aforementioned things (love of God, love of neighbor). For example, such would be the case if a person should tell a lie to please or even help someone, not in a position of trust or to harm the person's neighbor, or if a person should be excessive in eating or drinking or the like. And so these things are venial sins by reason of their kind.

Replies to the Objections:

1. There are two kinds of division. One is the kind that divides a univocal genus into its species, species that equally share the genus, as, for example, the division of animal into ox and horse. The other is a division of a common analogue regarding the things of which we predicate the analogue by what is prior and what is subsequent, as, for example, we divide being into substance and accident and into potentiality and actuality. And in such things, the common aspect is in one contained completely but in the others contained in a respect and by what is subsequent. And such is the division of sin into venial and mortal. And so the cited definition of sin indeed belongs completely to mortal sin but incompletely and in a respect to venial sin. And so we properly say that venial sin is beyond the law but not contrary to it, namely, that venial sin somewhat recedes from the ordination of the law but does not destroy the very ordination of the law. For venial sin does not destroy love, which is the fullness of the law, as Rom. 13:10 says.

2. Venial is a difference that takes away from the nature of sin, and such a difference belongs to all the things that in some respect incompletely share something common.

3. An end has the nature of a terminus, and a means does not. But venial sin is not turned toward a transitory good as an end. And so venial sin is not turned to that very good as a terminus other than God, so that the sinner is necessarily on that account turned away from God.

4. One who sins venially uses a creature as a means rather than enjoys it as an end, since the person relates it habitually but not actually to God. Nor does the person in so doing act against precept, since the person is not always bound actually to relate creatures to God.

5. Venial sin as venial never becomes mortal sin, just as whiteness does not become blackness. But an act generically venial can become a mortal sin from the will of one who constitutes a creature as the person's end, since even something by its nature cold, like water, can become hot.

6. Venial sin becomes mortal sin when one approves it as an end, not when one approves it in any way.

7. We sometimes contradistinguish one thing from another because they are essentially contrary, as, for example, white from black, hot from cold, and the one does not incline to the other. But things are sometimes distinguishable in relation to one another because they are contrary by reason of being complete and incomplete. And one of these contraries is ordained for the other, as, for example, accident for substance, and potentiality for actuality. And we in this way also contradistinguish venial sin from mortal sin, and venial sin inclines to mortal sin.

8. The will of a rational creature is obliged to be subject to God, but this is achieved by affirmative and negative precepts, of which the negative precepts oblige always and on all occasions, and the affirmative precepts oblige always but not on every occasion.

Therefore, when one sins venially, one indeed does not render due honor to God by actually observing an affirmative precept. But this is not to sin mortally, as one sins mortally who dishonors God by transgressing a negative precept or not fulfilling an affirmative precept on an occasion when it obliges.

9. Since the cited precept of the Apostle is affirmative, it does not always oblige one actually to observe it. And one always observes it habitually when one habitually has God as one's ultimate end. And venial sin does not exclude this habitual disposition.

10. Augustine in the cited text is speaking about the complete evil of moral wrong, and such evil is mortal sin.

11. Flattering only to please is a venial sin by reason of its genus, since it is a form of vanity. But flattering to deceive is a mortal sin, as Is. 3:12 says: "O my people, those who are calling you happy are deceiving you." And the canon speaks of such flattery. And so the canon says that clerics who spend their time in flatteries and deceits should be defrocked.

12. The difference regarding the subject does not constitute sin as mortal or venial, but the difference accompanies the two kinds of sins. And so nothing prevents a venial sin belonging to higher reason.

13. And the reply to objection 13 is the same.

14. The sense appetites of irrational animals do not in any way share in reason, as they do in us, as the *Ethics* says.[26] And so the sense appetites of irrational animals cannot be the subjects of sin.

15. The bodily organs themselves obey reason to some degree, and there can accordingly be sin in their acts, and likewise in the acts of sense appetites.

16. Sin belongs only to the will as the first cause of movement but also to other powers as commanded and moved by the will.

17. Mortal sin can belong to higher reason both directly and indirectly. For higher reason, although it does not err insofar as it contemplates the eternal natures of things, can still err insofar as it can be turned away from the natures. Likewise, we need to say that original sin does not result in lower powers in no way obeying reason, but results in lower powers not completely obeying reason, as they did when human beings were in the condition of innocence.

18. The cited difference is proper insofar as we understand the difference between mortal and venial sin regarding the will. But some sins are mortal by reason of their kind, and these are always mortal sins, with whatever will they are done, and the argument of the objection is valid regarding these sins. And in such things, the very deed is by reason of its kind contrary to the love of God, as, for example, one acts against charity by the very deed if one harms someone.

19. More and less resulting from different considerations differentiate species of sin, and so it is in the case of the matter under discussion. For example, loving something as an end and loving something as a means do not consider love in the same way.

20. One without charity may well love a creature more than God, a creature as much as God, and a creature less than God. But such a person cannot love a creature as much

26. Ibid., I, 13 (1102b30–31).

as God without loving some creature more than God, since human beings necessarily constitute the ultimate end of their will in one thing.

21. The cited difference results from and does not constitute mortal and venial sin. And one who sins venially lacks rightly ordered love in an act regarding means, not absolutely regarding the end itself. And so venial sin does not take away virtue or grace.

22. It is one thing not to be rightly ordered to God, which belongs to venial sin, and another thing to exclude the right ordination to God, which belongs to mortal sin.

23. God does not hatefully punish the person who sins venially; rather, he punishes such a person as a father who purifies and corrects the son whom he loves.

24. The venial sins of those who die in a state of unbelief or any mortal sin are eternally punished because of the conjoined mortal sin, which takes away grace, not because of the venial sins, which do not.

Second Article

Does Venial Sin Diminish Charity?

It seems that venial sin does, for the following reasons:

1. Augustine says in his *Confessions*: "Those love you less who love anything besides you that they do not love for your sake."[27] But those who sin venially love something besides God that they do not love for God's sake; otherwise, they would not sin in so loving. Therefore, those who sin venially love God less.

2. Contraries are constituted to concern the same kind of thing, and increase and decrease are contraries. And charity is increased, as Phil. 1:9 says: "I pray that your charity more and more abound." Therefore, it is also diminished. But mortal sin does not diminish charity; rather, mortal sin takes away charity. Therefore, venial sin diminishes charity.

3. People have said that venial sin diminishes charity regarding its acquisition, namely, that venial sin causes persons to receive less charity but cannot diminish the charity already received. But according to the Philosopher in the *Ethics*,[28] the same things produce, destroy, and diminish virtue. Therefore, venial sin, if it causes less charity to be infused, also causes the charity possessed to be diminished.

4. Whatever diminishes the constitutive difference of a species diminishes the species' essence. But difficulty to change is the constitutive difference of habits, and venial sin diminishes a habit, since venial sin makes human beings more prone to fall into mortal sin, and they lose charity by mortal sin. Therefore, venial sin diminishes the habit of charity.

5. Every love is either a love of desire or a love of charity, as Augustine says in his work *On the Trinity*.[29] But one who sins venially indeed does not love a creature with the love of charity, since "charity does not act perversely," as 1 Cor. 13:4 says. Therefore, one

---

27. *Confessions* X, 29 (PL 32:796).
28. *Ethics* II, 1 (1103b6–8).
29. *On the Trinity* IX, 8 (PL 42:967–68).

who sins venially loves a creature with a love of desire. But an increase of desire seems to decrease charity, since the very nourishment of charity diminishes desire, as Augustine says in his work *Book of the 83 Questions*.[30] Therefore, it seems that venial sin diminishes charity.

6. Augustine says in his *Literal Commentary on Genesis* that charity or grace is related to the soul as light is to air.[31] But the light in air is diminished if there is an obstacle to light, for example, if steam makes air denser. Therefore, it is also the case that venial sin, which is an obstacle to charity and a clouding of the mind, diminishes charity or grace.

7. Everything that is being continuously destroyed can be diminished. But charity is being continuously destroyed. Therefore, venial sin can diminish charity. We prove the minor of that syllogism in two ways. The first argument is indeed as follows: everything being destroyed is a subject of destruction; but charity is being destroyed; therefore, charity is a subject of destruction. Therefore, part of it is destroyed, and part of it still remains and so is being continuously destroyed. The second argument is as follows: Charity is not destroyed when it exists; nor is it being destroyed when it does not exist at all, since it has already been destroyed; therefore, it is being destroyed when part of it exists, and part of it does not. Therefore, charity is being continuously destroyed. Therefore, it can be diminished. But mortal sin does not diminish it. Therefore, venial sin does.

8. As there is disorder in mortal sin absolutely, so there is disorder in venial sin in some respect. But disorder without qualification, which belongs to mortal sin, takes away the order of charity absolutely. Therefore, disorder in some respect takes away the order of charity in that respect. Therefore, venial sin diminishes charity.

9. Many acts of venial sin produce a habit. But acts of venial sin prevent acts of charity. Therefore, habits of venial sin prevent the habit of charity. Therefore, venial sin diminishes charity.

10. Every offense diminishes love. But venial sin is an offense, since it has the nature of moral wrong. Therefore, venial sin diminishes the love of charity.

11. Bernard says in a sermon on the purification of Mary that not to progress in the way of God is to regress.[32] But those who sin venially do not progress in the way of God. Therefore, they regress. And this would not be the case unless venial sin were to diminish charity.

12. All integrated virtue is stronger than diversified virtue. And so also is integrated love stronger than love dispersed to many things. And the Philosopher accordingly says in the *Ethics* that one cannot love many things intensely.[33] But those who sin venially disperse their love to things other than God. Therefore, the virtue of charity is thereby diminished.

13. Prov. 24:16 says, "The upright person falls seven times a day and rises again," and a gloss interprets this as the falls occasioned by venial sin.[34] But human beings do not fall out of charity through venial sin. Therefore, they fall out of the full degree of charity. Therefore, venial sin diminishes charity.

30. *Book of the 83 Questions*, q. 26, n. 1 (PL 40:25).
31. *Literal Commentary on Genesis* VIII, 12, n. 26 (PL 34:383).
32. *On the Purification of Mary*, sermon 2, n. 3 (PL 183:369C).
33. *Ethics* VIII, 6 (1158a10–15).
34. *Ordinary Gloss*, on Prov. 24:16.

14. Human beings through charity earn the glory of eternal life. But venial sin retards human beings from attaining eternal life. Therefore, venial sin diminishes charity.

15. Things that impede the body's life or its health diminish its very life. But venial sin is an obstacle to the spiritual life, which thrives by charity, as I have said before.[35] Therefore, venial sin diminishes charity.

16. Activity results from form. Therefore, what hinders activity diminishes form. But venial sin hinders acts of charity. Therefore, venial sin diminishes charity itself.

17. Fervor is a property of charity, and so Rom. 12:11 speaks of the "fervent in spirit." But according to the common opinion,[36] venial sin diminishes the fervor of charity. Therefore, venial sin diminishes charity.

On the Contrary:
1. Additions and subtractions to something infinitely distant from another thing neither increase nor decrease the other thing, as is clear in the case of adding points to or subtracting points from a line. But venial sin is infinitely distant from charity, since charity loves God as the infinite good, and venial sin loves a creature as a finite good.

2. The reward of eternal life is proportionate to the amount of charity and is diminished when charity is diminished. But venial sin does not diminish the reward of eternal life; otherwise, the punishment of venial sin would be an eternal punishment, namely, the eternal diminution of glory. Therefore, venial sin does not diminish charity.

3. Continuous diminution will completely destroy any finite thing. But charity is a finite habit of the soul. Therefore, venial sin, if it should diminish charity, will destroy charity itself when there are many such sins. And this conclusion is improper.

Answer:
Since we consider increase and decrease in quantitative terms, we need to consider what the quantity of charity is in order to answer this question. And since charity is a form and a habit or virtue, we need to consider its quantity in two ways: in one way, indeed, insofar as it is a form; in the second way insofar as it is the kind of form that is a habit or virtue.

And some quantity of forms is accidental, and some quantity of forms intrinsic. Some quantity of forms is indeed accidental, as, for example, we say that a form has a magnitude by reason of the subject, as we say that whiteness has a magnitude by reason of the surface in which it inheres. But such quantity is irrelevant to the matter under discussion, since the soul, which is the subject of charity, is not quantified. And we consider the intrinsic quantity of a form in two ways. We consider it in one way regarding the efficient cause, since the stronger the causal power, the more perfect the form it induces, more perfectly bringing the subject from potentiality to actuality. For example, a great deal of heat heats more than a little heat does. We consider the intrinsic quantity of a form in the second way regarding the subject, which indeed receives form more perfectly from the activity of the cause the more disposed the subject is to do so. For example, dry wood can be more easily heated than green wood, and air more easily heated than water, by the same fire.

---

35. A. 1.
36. E.g., William of Auxerre, *Golden Summa* III, tr. 5, chap. 5.

We consider the quantity of a form in a third way insofar as the form is a virtue or habit, regarding the object of the virtue. For we call virtues that are capable of doing great things great virtues, and every habit derives its species and its magnitude from its object. Therefore, if we should consider the magnitude of charity regarding its object, then the magnitude can in no way be increased or decreased, since things whose nature consists of something indivisible cannot be increased or decreased. And this is the reason why no specific number increases or decreases, since the unit completes the species. For example, an added unit always causes a new specific number. And the object of charity has an indivisible nature and consists of the terminus, for the object of charity is God as the highest good and ultimate end.

But charity can be greater or lesser regarding the efficient cause and the subject. Charity can indeed be greater or lesser regarding the cause, not because of God's greater or lesser power, but because of his wisdom and virtue, according to which he distributes different measures of grace and charity to human beings. Just so, Eph. 4:7 says: "Grace has been given to each one of us according to the measure of Christ's gift." And charity can be greater or lesser regarding the subject insofar as one by good deeds disposes oneself more or less to receive grace or charity. But we should note that the good deeds of human beings are related in one way to the magnitude of charity regarding the very coming to be of charity and in another way regarding the charity already actually existing. For the deeds of human beings before charity are related to charity itself and its magnitude only by way of a material disposition, not by way of merit, since charity is the source of meriting. On the other hand, charity, when already possessed, itself merits to be increased because of its deeds, so that increased charity also merits to be perfected, as Augustine says.[37]

And venial sin cannot cause the charity possessed to be diminished either regarding the efficient cause, namely, God, or regarding the recipient, namely, the human being. Venial sin indeed cannot cause diminution of charity regarding the cause, since venial sin cannot merit diminution of charity as acts done out of charity merit its increase, inasmuch as persons merit that to which their will is inclined. And one who sins venially is not so inclined to a creature as to be in any way turned away from God. For such a person is turned to a creature as a means, not as the person's end, and the affection for the end by those who are inordinately disposed to certain means is not thereby diminished. For example, if persons are inordinately disposed regarding the taking of medicine, their desire for health is not thereby diminished. And so it is clear that venial sin does not merit the diminution of charity already possessed.

Likewise regarding the subject, neither can venial sin diminish charity itself. And this is evident for two reasons. First, it is indeed evident because venial sin does not belong to the soul in the same way that charity belongs to the soul. For charity belongs to the soul regarding the soul's higher part, inasmuch as the soul is ordained for something as its highest good and ultimate end, while venial sin has some disorder but not one that extends to the soul's ordination to its ultimate end. And so venial sin, even if it were to be contrary to charity, would not diminish charity, as, for example, blackness in a foot does not diminish whiteness in the head. Second, it is evident because the form in a subject is

---

37. *Letter* 186, chap. 3, n. 10 (PL 33:819).

diminished by any admixture of its contrary, as the Philosopher says that something is "whiter that is less mixed with black."[38] But venial sin has no contrariety to charity, since they do not by their nature concern the same object. For venial sin is not a disorder regarding the ultimate end, which is the object of charity.

And so venial sin in no way diminishes the charity possessed. But venial sin can cause less charity to be initially infused, namely, insofar as it impedes the acts of free choice whereby human beings are disposed to receive grace. And venial sin can in this way prevent the charity possessed from increasing, namely, by preventing the meritorious acts whereby persons merit an increase of charity.

Replies to the Objections:

1. Those who sin venially love something as well as God, something that they habitually, although not actually, love for the sake of God.

2. Things meritorious on the part of human beings and efficacious on the part of God's goodness, to which the movement toward good always belongs, can cause an increase of charity. But charity cannot be diminished by things either demeritorious on the part of human beings, as I have said,[39] or inefficacious on God's part, since God does not make human beings worse, as Augustine says in his *Book of the 83 Questions.*[40]

3. The argument of this objection would be valid if venial sin were directly to cause less charity to come to be. But venial sin by accident, as it were, and indirectly causes less charity to come to be, namely, as it impedes the acts of free choice whereby persons are disposed to receive charity. And regarding adults, acts of free choice are required for the infusion of grace or charity but not for the preservation of the habit already possessed. And so the charity possessed is not diminished when such acts are prevented.

4. Difficulty to change is not the difference constitutive of habits. For dispositions and habits are not different species of things; otherwise, one and the same quality that was previously a disposition could not subsequently become a habit. But facility and difficulty to change are related as perfect and imperfect regarding the same thing. And granted that difficulty to change were to be a constitutive difference, the argument would still fail. This is so because a habit may be easily changeable for two reasons. It may be easily changeable in one way intrinsically, namely, because the habit is not so perfect in the subject. And so whatever would diminish the resistance of a habit to change would diminish the habit itself. A habit may be easily changeable in a second way by accident, namely, because a disposition to the contrary is introduced, as if, for example, we should say that the form of water becomes less difficult to change when the water is heated, and yet the substantial form is obviously not diminished. And it is also in this way that venial sin diminishes the resistance of charity to change. And it is in this way that we should understand the opinion of those who say that venial sin diminishes charity at its roots in the subject,[41] by accident and indeed not intrinsically, as I have said.[42]

---

38. *Topics* III, 5 (119a27–28).
39. In the answer.
40. *Book of the 83 Questions*, qq. 3 and 4 (PL 40:11 and 12).
41. E.g., William of Auxerre, *Golden Summa* III, tr. 5, chap. 5.
42. In the answer.

5. Augustine says that the decrease, not the increase, of desire nourishes or preserves charity, namely, in that decrease of desire decreases venial sins, which dispose one to loss of charity.

6. Dense steam is received in the same part of the air in which light is received, and so diminishes the light. But venial sin does not extend to the highest part of the soul regarding the soul's disposition toward the highest good and so cannot diminish the charity already possessed, although venial sin can limit its magnitude regarding its acquisition. Just so, the darkness of air outside the house would not diminish the brightness inside the house produced by a source of light inside the house, although the darkness would diminish the intense brightness of rays of the sun coming into the house from outside. And the perfection of the higher part of the soul regarding the acquisition of charity depends on the right disposition of the lower parts of the soul, but the perfection of the higher part of the soul regarding the preservation of charity does not. For example, human beings by their natural constitution arrive at internal intelligible things by means of lower and sensibly perceptible external things. And so also deficiency of sight or hearing can prevent human beings acquiring knowledge but not diminish the knowledge they have already acquired.

7. It is not universally true that everything successively ceasing to be is diminished, since a substantial form is being successively lost if we should consider the preceding changes. Accordingly, the Philosopher says in the *Physics* that what is ceasing to be was ceasing to be and will cease to be, and yet its substantial form is not diminished.[43] And so charity is sometimes being successively lost if we should consider the preceding disposition for the loss. But charity is not being successively lost if we should consider the very loss as such. And it is altogether false to say that charity, because it is being destroyed, is the subject of the dissolution. Just so, we do not say that whiteness or any form ceases to be because it itself is the subject of the dissolution. Rather, the subject of whiteness is the subject of dissolution because it ceases to be white. Likewise, we should say that being dissolved and the first moment of having been dissolved are the same thing if we should consider the very dissolution of the form as such as it belongs to the terminus of the dissolution. Just so, being illumined and the first moment of having been illumined are the same thing. And something ceases to exist at the very moment when it has been dissolved, as the *Physics* says.[44] And so charity ceases to exist at the moment it is being destroyed.

8. Disorder without qualification destroys the right order of charity without qualification, since such disorder extends to the higher part of the soul. And disorder in a qualified sense destroys the right order of charity in a qualified sense by certain acts, as the right order of charity is transmitted from the higher part of the soul to the lower parts. But disorder in a qualified sense does not at all diminish charity itself, just as blackness in a foot does not at all diminish whiteness in the head.

9. Many venial sins can cause a habit, but the habit so acquired neither destroys nor diminishes charity, since the habit does not belong to, nor concern, the same thing as charity does.

10. Venial sin, since it does not imply turning away from God, does not have the nature of an offense in the strict sense.

---

43. *Physics* VI, 6 (237b17–19).
44. Ibid., VI, 5 (235b28–29).

11. One advances in the way of God both when charity is actually increased, and when one is disposed to receive an increase of charity. Just so, a child does not actually grow during the whole span of its growing to maturity; rather, the child sometimes actually grows and sometimes is disposed to grow. And likewise, one regresses in the way of God not only by a decrease of charity but also by being retarded from progressing, or even by being disposed to fall into mortal sin. And venial sin causes both of the latter.

12. Love is diminished when it is diffused to many things in the same respect. But the diffusion of love in one respect does not diminish love in other respects. For example, if a man should have many friends, he would not on that account love his son or wife less, but if he were to love many wives, the love for each of them would be diminished, and if he were to have many sons, the love that would be for an only son is diminished. And venial sin does not disperse the love of human beings for creatures in respect to the end, since they love God as their end. And so their habitual love for God is not diminished, although their actual love perhaps is.

13. Venial sin causes one to fall away from acts of charity, not indeed from charity itself or the perfect degree of charity.

14. Venial sin does not at all diminish glory but only retards the acquisition of glory. And likewise, venial sin does not at all diminish charity but only retards its acts and its increase.

15. Some things impede perfect health and healthy functioning but do not diminish health. For example, some foods are hard to digest because they prevent easy digestion.

16. Action can be diminished in two ways. It is diminished in one way regarding the capacity to act, as, for example, if a person could not do so much, and then what diminishes the action diminishes the source of the action, that is, the form. It is diminished in a second way regarding the performance of acts, and then what diminishes the action need not diminish the form. For example, a column that keeps a stone from falling down does not diminish the weight of the stone, nor does one who ties up another diminish the power of the other to walk. And venial sin diminishes the action of charity in the second, not the first, way.

17. We can understand fervor in two ways. We understand it in one way insofar as it implies the intensity of the inclination of the lover for the beloved, and such fervor is essential for charity and not diminished by venial sin. We speak of fervor in a second way insofar as the movement of love even redounds to lower powers, so that both the heart and the flesh in some way praise God. And venial sin diminishes such fervor without diminishing charity.

Third Article

Can Venial Sin Become Mortal?

It seems that venial sin can, for the following reasons:

1. Augustine says in his *On the Gospel of John*, explaining Jn. 3:6, "Whoever does not believe in the Son will not see life": "Many small sins, if they are not attended to, kill."[45]

---

45. *On the Gospel of John*, tr. 12, n. 14 (PL 35:1492).

But we call a sin mortal because it kills spiritually. Therefore, many small sins, that is, venial sins, produce mortal sin.

2. On the words of Ps. 40:13, "They are more than the hairs on my head," a gloss says: "You have avoided rocks; beware lest you be crushed by grains of sand."[46] But grains of sand mean small, namely, venial, sins. Therefore, many venial sins crush or kill human beings, and so the same conclusion follows as before.

3. People have said that we say that many venial sins kill or crush insofar as they dispose one to mortal sin. But Augustine says in his *Rule* that "pride creeps into good deeds in order to destroy them,"[47] and so it seems that even good deeds dispose toward mortal sin. And yet we do not say that good deeds kill or crush human beings. Therefore, neither can we say that venial sins kill or crush human beings for the cited reason. Therefore, it seems that venial sin of itself becomes mortal.

4. Venial sin is an inclination toward mortal sin. But inclinations become habits, as the Philosopher says in the *Categories*.[48] Therefore, venial sin becomes mortal.

5. The movements of sense appetites are venial sins. But they become mortal sins when reason consents, as Augustine makes clear in his work *On the Trinity*.[49] Therefore, venial sins can become mortal.

6. A movement of unbelief may arise surreptitiously in higher reason itself, and such a movement is a venial sin. But the advent of consent does not destroy the essence of the prior movement that was a venial sin, and yet the consent makes the sin mortal. Therefore, venial sins can become mortal.

7. Venial and mortal sins sometimes differ by reason of the different stations of persons. For example, the *Decretum* says that not to reconcile enemies is a venial sin for the laity,[50] but it seems to be a mortal sin for bishops, since they are to be deposed for that offense, as the *Decretum* holds.[51] But persons of lower station can be transferred to a higher station. Therefore, venial sins can become mortal.

8. According to Chrysostom,[52] laughter and jesting are venial sins. But laughter can become a mortal sin, for Prov. 14:13 says: "Laughter will be mixed with sorrow, and lamentation takes possession of the extremities of joy." (A gloss says "perpetual lamentation.")[53] And yet only mortal sin deserves this. Therefore, venial sins can become mortal.

9. [Of things distinguished only by accident, one can become the other. But venial and mortal sin are distinguished only by accident. For things distinguished intrinsically are not transformed into one another, and venial and mortal sin are transformed into one another, since nothing is so venial that it does not become mortal when approved. And likewise, confession renders every mortal sin venial. Therefore, venial sins can become mortal.][54]

46. Peter Lombard, *Gloss*, on Ps. 40:13 (PL 191:405A).
47. *Rule for the Servants of God*, n. 2 (PL 32:1379).
48. *Categories* 8 (9a10–13).
49. *On the Trinity* XII, 12, n. 17 (PL 42:1007).
50. *Decretum*, d. 25, chap. 3, n. 7 (Friedberg I:93).
51. Ibid., d. 90, chap. 11 (Friedberg I:315).
52. *On Matthew*, hom. 6, n. 6 (PG 57:70–71).
53. *Interlinear Gloss*, on Prov. 14:13.
54. The text of this objection is missing from the earliest manuscripts, but the Leonine editors have reconstructed it from later printed versions.

10. By access to God, the least good becomes the greatest good. For example, movements of free choice informed by grace become meritorious. Therefore, by withdrawal from God, the least evil can become the greatest evil. But the least evil in the genus of sin is venial sin, and the greatest such evil is mortal sin. Therefore, venial sins can become mortal.

11. Boethius says in his work *On Consolation* that sins are related to the soul as sicknesses are to the body.[55] But the least sickness can become the greatest if it grows worse. Therefore, the least sin, namely, venial sin, can become the greatest sin, namely, mortal sin.

12. The gifts of graces formally constitute the orders of angels. But the orders of angels differ specifically. Therefore, the gifts of graces also differ specifically. But those who initially merited to be assumed to a lower order of angels later merit to be assumed to a higher order through an increase of merit. Therefore, a lesser grace becomes a greater grace, although they differ specifically. Therefore, by like reasoning, venial sins can become mortal.

13. The condition of innocence does not infinitely surpass the condition of corrupted human nature. But every venially sinful movement in the condition of innocence would have been mortally sinful. Therefore, venial sins can also now become mortal in the condition of corrupted human nature.

14. Good and evil differ more than the two kinds of evil, namely, venial and mortal sin, do, since good and evil differ generically, and the two kinds of evil belong to the same genus. For good and evil are the genera of other things, as the *Categories* says.[56] But the numerically same action can be good and evil, for example, if a slave grudgingly gives alms at the command of his master, who commands it out of charity. Therefore, much more can the numerically same action be venial and mortal sin.

15. Sin is a weight upon the soul, as Ps. 38:5 says: "My iniquities have fallen on my head, and they as a heavy burden have weighed me down." But the least weight can by addition become so great that it exceeds the strength of the bearer. Therefore, venial sins can by addition become mortal and exclude virtue.

16. As Augustine says in his work *On the Trinity*,[57] the process in every sin is like the process in the sin of our first parents, and so sense appetites represent the serpent, reason the woman, and higher reason the man. But it was impossible for the man to eat from the forbidden tree without sinning mortally. Therefore, sin in higher reason can only be mortal. Therefore, a sin venial in lower reason, when brought to higher reason, will become mortal.

17. If a habit deserves condemnation, the acts proceeding from it also will. But there remains in unbaptized infidels with unpardoned original sin the habit of the original condemnation, to which the corruption of concupiscence belongs. Therefore, even the first movements arising from such corruption deserve condemnation and are mortal sins, and yet the movements as such are evidently venial sins. Therefore, venial sins can become mortal.

---

55. *On Consolation* IV, prose 6 (PL 63:818A).
56. Aristotle, *Categories* 11 (14a23–25).
57. *On the Trinity* XII, 12, n. 17 (PL 42:1007).

On the Contrary:

1. Things that infinitely differ do not change into one another. But mortal and venial sins differ infinitely, since one deserves temporal punishment, and the other deserves eternal punishment. Therefore, venial sins cannot become mortal.

2. Things that generically or specifically differ do not change into one another. But venial and mortal sins differ generically or even specifically. Therefore, venial sins can never become mortal.

3. One kind of privation does not become another. For example, blindness never becomes deafness. But mortal sin encompasses privation of the end, and venial sin privation of ordination to the end. Therefore, venial sins can never become mortal.

Answer:

We can understand this question in three ways. For we can understand the question in one way as to whether a sin numerically one and the same that was previously venial can afterward become mortal. Second, we can understand the question as to whether a sin by its kind venial can in some respect become mortal. Third, we can understand the question as to whether many venial sins constitute one mortal sin.

Therefore, if we understand the question in the first way, we need to say that venial sin cannot become mortal. For inasmuch as the sin of which we are now speaking presumes a morally evil act, the sin needs to be one act morally for it to be numerically one and the same sin. And it is a moral act because it is voluntary, and so we need to consider the unity of the moral act regarding the will. For an act may sometimes be numerically one insofar as it belongs to a physical genus, and not one insofar as it belongs to a moral genus, because of different acts of the will. For example, such would be the case if one on the way to church should initially intend vainglory and later on intend to give service to God. Therefore, in an act that is one regarding its physical species there may be a venial sin at the beginning and a mortal sin later if the will should grow into so immoderate desires as to perform a venially sinful act (e.g., uttering an idle word, or the like) also in contempt of God. And so there are two sins, not one, since there is not one act regarding the moral genus of acts.

And if we should understand the question in the second way, then we need to say that what is a venial sin by reason of its kind can become a mortal sin, not indeed by reason of its kind but by reason of its end. And to prove this, we need to consider that we can note two objects, namely, the object of the external act and the object of the internal act, since an external act belongs to the moral genus insofar as it is voluntary. And the two objects sometimes coincide, as, for example, if one willing to go somewhere goes there. And sometimes the two objects are different, and one may be good, and the other evil, as, for example, if one gives alms wanting to please people, the object of the external act is good, and the object of the internal act evil. And because the external act is constituted in the moral genus insofar as it is voluntary, we need to consider the moral species of the act formally according to the object of the internal act. For we consider the species of acts by their objects. And so the Philosopher says in the *Ethics* that one who commits adultery in order to steal is an avaricious person rather than an adulterer.[58] Therefore,

---

58. *Ethics* V, 2 (1130a24–28).

an external act that is a venial sin by reason of the species it has from its external object changes into the species of mortal sin by reason of the object of the internal act. For example, such would be the case if one utters an idle word intending to incite someone to lustful desire. Something as such may also be a venial sin because of its incomplete state, not because of its object. For example, movements of concupiscence to commit adultery, which movements belong to a sense appetite, indeed belong to the genus of mortal sin regarding their object. But such movements do not completely attain moral wickedness, since they lack the deliberation of reason, and so they cannot be mortal sins, which are complete wickedness in the moral genus. And such sins may become mortal if they should reach completion, as, for example, happens with the advent of the deliberate consent of reason.

And if we should understand the question in the third way, then we need to say that many sins indeed do not directly and as efficient causes constitute one mortal sin, namely, so that many venial sins have the punitive liability of one mortal sin. And this is evident for two reasons. First, indeed, it is evident because whenever many accumulated things constitute one thing, there needs to be the same measure of magnitude regarding both the many things and the one thing. For example, many small lines constitute one long line. And where there are different measures of magnitude, many things do not constitute one thing. For example, many numbers do not constitute one line, nor the converse. And venial sin does not have the same measure of magnitude as mortal sin. For the magnitude of mortal sin results from turning away from the ultimate end, and the magnitude of venial sin regards a disorder concerning a means. Second, many venial sins do not constitute one mortal sin because venial sin does not diminish charity, as I have said before,[59] and mortal sin destroys charity. Dispositively, however, many venial sins lead to the commission of mortal sin, since the repetition of acts produces habits, and the eagerness and pleasure in sin increase and can increase so much that one is inclined more easily to sin mortally. But this disposition is not necessarily prerequisite for mortal sin, since human beings can sin mortally even without previous venial sins, and human beings through charity can resist mortal sin when there is the aforementioned previous disposition from venial sins.

Replies to the Objections:
1. Many small sins kill in a dispositive way, as I have said.[60]
    2. We should reply likewise to the second objection.
    3. Good deeds do not dispose one to sin mortally as venial sins do, but good deeds can by accident be an occasion of mortal sin.
    4. Inclinations are related to habits as the imperfect to the perfect. But this occurs in two ways. It occurs in one way such that the perfect and the imperfect belong to the same species, and then an inclination becomes a habit. It occurs in the second way such that the perfect and the imperfect belong to different species, and then an inclination never becomes that to which it inclines. For example, heat does not become the form of fire. And likewise, neither does venial sin become mortal sin.

---

59. A. 2.
60. In the answer.

5. The movements that were venial sins in sense appetites will never become mortal sins. But the very advent of consent will intrinsically constitute mortal sin.

6. Disbelief does not always creep into higher reason but can sometimes creep into the imagination, as, for example, if one imagines the three persons in God like three human beings and is suddenly moved to unbelief. And unbelief sometimes creeps into lower reason, as, for example, if one considers certain things in creatures repugnant to belief in the Trinity. And unbelief sometimes creeps into higher reason, as, for example, if one suddenly begins to think disrespectfully about the Trinity of persons in God, such surreptitious intrusion belongs to higher reason, and the added consent is a different movement. And so it does not follow that the same sin is venial and mortal.

7. A person is something abiding and so can be promoted to a higher station. But an act is something that immediately passes away, and so there is no comparison.

8. Extreme lamentation takes possession of the extremities of the joy whereby one enjoys a creature as an end, not of every kind of joy.

9. Mortal sin by reason of its kind is always such and never becomes venial sin if we understand the sin to be venial by reason of its kind. And we understand equivocally the word "venial" in the saying that repentance renders mortal sin venial, as the previously posited distinction of venial makes clear.[61]

10. We can understand the least good in the genus of human acts as an act that is generically good but not meritorious because not informed by grace. And such a numerically identical act never becomes a meritorious act that we can call the greatest good in the genus of human acts, just as a venial sin never becomes a mortal sin.

11. Sickness, like health, is a disposition or habit, not an act, and so something numerically the same can be changed from less imperfect to more perfect. But sin is a transient act, and so there is no comparison in that respect. But we note a comparison only regarding the fact that as sickness is a physical disorder, so sin is the disorder in a human act.

12. Since we hold angelic orders to be parts of a hierarchy that constitutes a sacred dominion, it is evident that the orders consist essentially of gifts of grace. And we distinguish angelic orders by the different gifts gratuitously bestowed, although we presuppose different natural goods as the matter endowed and as disposing angelic orders for the gifts. But we should note that we can consider the gifts of grace in two ways. We can consider the gifts of grace in one way regarding what unites the angels to God, and the angelic orders do not differ in this respect. Rather, they are the same, and so Dionysius says that the entire hierarchy of angels is related to God as much as likeness and unity allow.[62] We can consider the gifts of grace in a second way insofar as they are ordained for the angels' work, and the different angelic orders have different kinds of grace as the angelic orders are ordained for different duties. But we do not say in this connection that human beings are assumed into angelic orders because of their duties but because of their measure of glory and enjoyment of God. And so it does not follow that human beings have specifically different graces according to their different condition of perfection.

13. Human beings in the condition of innocence could not sin venially because they could not do anything that is venial sin by reason of its kind, not indeed because they could

---

61. A. 1.
62. *On the Celestial Hierarchy* 3 (PG 3:165A).

not do things venially sinful by reason of their kind that would be mortally sinful for them to do. For there could not be disorder in the lower parts of their soul regarding means unless there would be a previous disorder in the higher part of their soul regarding the end.

14. The action of the servant and the action of the master proceed from different wills, and so there is not one action morally.

15. There is one measure of magnitude regarding all material weights but not regarding mortal and venial sin. And so the argument is invalid.

16. By tasting of the tree of the knowledge of good and evil, Adam acted contrary to God's command and so sinned mortally. And likewise, higher reason, whenever it sins by acting against God's command, sins mortally. But higher reason does not always sin by acting against God's command. And so the argument is invalid.

17. The cited proposition, namely, that if a habit deserves condemnation, so do its acts, is false. For mortal sin consists of an act, not a habit. And so not every movement resulting from the inclination of a habit need be a mortal sin if many acts of mortal sin should produce the habit. For example, no one has so confirmed a habit of sexual lust or another vice that the person may not sometimes by the use of reason resist the vice's movements, and it would be stupid to say that such movements would be imputed as mortal sins to those who resist the movements. And so although habitual concupiscence deserves condemnation in the case of an unbeliever not yet baptized, every movement of concupiscence does not need to deserve condemnation in the way of mortal sin. And yet we call concupiscence habitual in a privative way, namely, by the withdrawal of original justice, as I have said before,[63] not in a positive way. And so the movements resulting from natural powers themselves do not always need to be sin, still less mortal sin. Therefore, we should not say that the first movements of sense appetites in unbelievers are mortal sins, since they would much more be mortal sins for the faithful. For the faithful sin more regarding the same kind of act than unbelievers do, other things being equal, as the Apostle in Heb. 10:29 makes clear: "How much more severe punishments do you think those who made the blood of the covenant unclean deserve?" And 2 Pet. 2:21 says: "It was better for them not to know the way of truth than for them after they have known the truth to go back on what the holy commandments had transmitted to them."

Replies to the Arguments in the Section On the Contrary:
What I have said before makes clear the reply to the arguments in the section *On the Contrary*.[64]

Fourth Article

Do Circumstances Make Venial Sins Mortal?

It seems that circumstances do, for the following reasons:

1. Augustine says in his sermon on purgatory that if anger should be retained for a long time, and inebriation is constantly repeated, they become numbered with mortal

---

63. Q. 5, a. 2.
64. In the answer.

sins.[65] But such sins are venial by reason of their kind; otherwise, they would always be mortal sins. Therefore, venial sins become mortal sins by reason of the circumstance of constant repetition or long duration.

2. Prolonged pleasure in sinful thoughts is a mortal sin, as the Master says in the *Sentences*.[66] But if the pleasure is not prolonged, the sin is venial. Therefore, the circumstance of prolongation makes venial sins mortal.

3. In human acts, good differs from evil more than venial sin differs from mortal sin, since good and evil, inasmuch they are the genera of other things, as the *Categories* says,[67] differ generically. But circumstances make good acts evil. Therefore, much more do circumstances make venial sins mortal.

4. We posit among other circumstances of a human act the reason for which it is done, and this circumstance belongs to the end of the act. But venial sins become mortal sins on account of their ends, as I have said.[68] Therefore, circumstances make venial sins mortal.

On the Contrary:

A circumstance is something accidental to a moral act, as the very name indicates. But being a mortal sin belongs to the species of sin. Therefore, since no accident constitutes the species of that of which it is an accident, it seems that circumstances cannot make venial sins mortal.

Answer:

We call moral acts generically good or evil by reason of their object. And two kinds of goodness or wickedness can be added to the generic goodness or wickedness of moral acts: one, indeed, from the intended end; the second from circumstances. And because an end is the first object of the will, the internal act acquires its species from its end, and if the internal act has the nature of mortal sin from its end, the external act will move into the species of the internal act and be constituted a mortal sin, as I have said before.[69] But circumstances do not always specify moral acts but only do so when they add a new deformity belonging to a different species of sin. For example, such would be the case if a man in addition to having intercourse with a woman who is not his wife has intercourse with a woman who is the wife of another, and then the act has the incidental deformity of injustice. And so this circumstance give a new species to the act, and properly speaking, it is not now a circumstance but becomes the specific difference of the moral act.

Therefore, if an added circumstance should add a deformity such that the act be against God's command, then the circumstance will make what is venial sin by reason of its kind to be mortal sin. Therefore, what is venial sin by reason of its kind can become mortal sin only by reason of a circumstance that transfers the sin into another species, not by reason of a circumstance that remains in the nature of a circumstance. But some-

---

65. *Sermon* 104, n. 2 (PL 39:1946).
66. Peter Lombard, *Sentences* II, d. 24, chap. 12, n. 2.
67. Aristotle, *Categories* 11 (14a23–25).
68. A. 3.
69. Ibid.

thing may sometimes be a venial sin because of the incomplete character of the act, since the act does not attain the deliberate consent of reason, which consent completes the nature of a moral act, and not because of the thing's kind, namely, regarding its object. And then such a circumstance completing the moral act, for example, the advent of deliberate consent, makes venial sin mortal.

Replies to the Objections:

1. Anger implies a movement to harm one's neighbor. And to cause harm to one's neighbor is by reason of its kind a mortal sin, since it is contrary to charity regarding love of neighbor. And when the movement remains in a lower appetite, and reason does not consent to cause serious harm to one's neighbor, there is only a venial sin due to the incomplete character of the act. And anger cannot be long continued without the deliberation of reason being added. And we do not understand anger to be retained for a long time whenever it persists for a long time. Rather, we understand anger to be retained because one has the power to resist it by the use of reason, in which case the movement of anger is not retained even if it should persist. We should say the same about inebriation, since it as such actually turns reason away from God, namely, so that reason cannot turn toward God while the condition of inebriation lasts. And since human beings are not obliged always actually to turn their reason toward God, inebriation is accordingly not always a mortal sin. And if human beings are repeatedly inebriated, it seems that they are not solicitous that their reason be turned toward God, and inebriation under that hypothesis is a mortal sin. For then it seems that one because of the love of wine contemns the turning of reason toward God.

2. We should say the same about prolonged pleasure in sinful thoughts as we said about anger that persists for a long time.

3. A circumstance, when it changes a good act into an evil one, constitutes a new species of sin and so transfers the act into another moral genus. And also in such a case, a circumstance can make a venial sin mortal.

4. An end as the object of an act specifies the moral act and can for that reason make a venial sin mortal.

Fifth Article

Can Venial Sin Belong to Higher Reason?

It seems that venial sin cannot, for the following reasons:

1. In his work *On the Trinity*, Augustine says that higher reason cleaves to the eternal natures of things,[70] and so it seems that sin can belong to higher reason only by turning away from the eternal natures. But every such sin is a mortal sin. Therefore, only mortal sin can belong to higher reason.

2. Sin can belong to a power only by reason of a disorder of the power's act in relation to its object. For example, there can be error in acts of sight only in relation to color.

---

70. *On the Trinity* XII, 7, n. 12 (PL 42:1005).

But the object of higher reason is the ultimate end consisting of the eternal good. Therefore, sin can belong to higher reason only by reason of disorder regarding the ultimate end. But every such sin is a mortal sin, since venial sin concerns means, and mortal sin concerns the end, as I have said.[71] Therefore, only mortal sin can belong to higher reason.

3. Higher reason is the power of reason that partakes of the light of grace. But the light of grace is more powerful than material light. And material light unless destroyed or diminished is not deficient in its activity, and so much less is spiritual light. Therefore, no deficient act can belong to higher reason unless grace is either destroyed or diminished. But venial sin neither destroys nor diminishes grace, as I have said before.[72] Therefore, the deficiency of venial sin cannot belong to higher reason.

4. The object of higher reason is the good to be enjoyed, that is, the eternal good. But as Augustine says in his *Book of the 83 Questions*,[73] every human evil consists of enjoying means as the end or using the end as means. Therefore, sin can belong to higher reason only by using the end, which is God, as a means. But this is to love something more than God, and to do so constitutes mortal sin. For using something is to relate it to something else as the end. Therefore, only mortal sin can belong to higher reason.

5. Higher and lower reason are not different powers but differ in that higher reason reaches conclusions from the eternal natures of things, and lower reason from their temporal aspects, as Augustine maintains in his work *On the Trinity*.[74] But there can be error when one reaches conclusions from the eternal natures only because one errs regarding the natures, and that is always a mortal sin. Therefore, only mortal, not venial, sin can belong to higher reason.

6. According to the Philosopher in the *De anima*,[75] reason is always correct. But sin is contrary to rectitude. Therefore, venial sin cannot belong to higher reason.

7. The Philosopher says in the *Ethics* that we praise the reason of the temperate and the intemperate person, and so he praises reason in both the good and the wicked.[76] But sin does not belong to what is praised. Therefore, no sin, either mortal or venial, belongs to reason.

8. Reason implies deliberation. Therefore, if a sin belongs to reason, it needs to belong to reason by deliberation, since everything in something else belongs to it in the way of the subject. But deliberate sin is intentional or committed out of pure malice, which is especially mortal because it is a sin against the Holy Spirit. Therefore, only mortal sin can belong to higher reason.

9. Consulting the eternal nature of things belongs to higher reason. But consultation is a kind of deliberation. Therefore, higher reason never sins except by deliberate consent, and so the same conclusion follows as before.

10. Venial sin becomes mortal sin because of one's contempt, as I have said before.[77] But that a person deliberately sin seems to be done with contempt. Therefore,

71. A. 1.
72. Ibid.
73. *Book of the 83 Questions*, q. 30 (PL 40:19).
74. *On the Trinity* XII, 7, n. 12 (PL 42:1005).
75. *De anima* III, 10 (433a26).
76. *Ethics* I, 13 (1102b14–15).
77. A. 3.

it seems that a sin of higher reason, since done deliberately, is always mortal and never venial.

11. We observe that venial sin creeps into the lower powers of the soul. But sin, insofar as it creeps into higher reason, apparently cannot be venial. Therefore, venial sin can in no way belong to higher reason. We prove the minor as follows. The advent of deliberate consent makes a venial sin that occurs surreptitiously a mortal sin, since reason in deliberating considers another, greater good, and to act against such a good is a more serious sin. For example, when concupiscence arises surreptitiously, a person considers only the pleasurable aspect in the object desired. But reason in deliberating considers something higher, namely, the law of God contrary to concupiscence, and a human being sins mortally by contemning that law through concupiscence. And we cannot understand anything higher than the object of higher reason that is the eternal good. Therefore, if a sin arising surreptitiously were to be venial regarding its object, deliberate consent could not make the sin mortal as belonging to higher reason, although the sin is evidently mortal by reason of the deliberate consent. Therefore, the sin is mortal by reason of deliberate consent even if it arises surreptitiously. Therefore, in no way can a venial sin belong to higher reason.

12. Higher reason is the source of spiritual life as the heart in animals is the source of their material life. And so also does Prov. 4:23 compare higher reason to the heart: "Guard your heart with every protection, since life comes from it." But only mortal sickness can belong to the material heart. Therefore, no venial sin and only mortal sin can belong to higher reason.

On the Contrary:

1. Augustine says in his work *On the Trinity*[78] that every consent to an act belongs to higher reason. But some actual consent constitutes a venial sin, as, for example, when one consents to utter an idle word, since consent to a venial sin is venial in the same way that the consent in mortal sin is mortal. Therefore, venial sin can belong to higher reason.

2. As the will takes delight in the good, so reason takes delight in the truth. But the will can sin venially if it loves a created good inferior to the uncreated good. Therefore, higher reason can sin venially if it should take delight in a created truth inferior to the uncreated truth.

Answer:

Since reason directs our desire, sin may belong to reason in two ways. Sin belongs to reason in one way regarding reason's own activity, as when one errs in some regard by embracing the false and rejecting the truth. Sin belongs to reason in a second way because our desire after the deliberation of reason is borne inordinately toward something. And if the deliberation of reason rests on certain temporal considerations (e.g., that something is useful or not, becoming or unbecoming in the common estimation), we shall indeed say that the sin belongs to lower reason. And if the deliberation rests on the eternal natures of things (e.g., that something is in accord or discord with the commandments of God), we shall say that the sin belongs to higher reason. For we call the reason that

78. *On the Trinity* XII, 12, n. 17 (PL 42:1008).

fastens on the eternal natures higher reason, as Augustine says in his work *On the Trinity*.[79] And reason fastens on them in two ways, namely, in contemplating them and in deliberating about them. Reason indeed fastens on the eternal natures by contemplating them as its proper object and by deliberating about them as the means that it uses to direct a desire or action.

And both venial and mortal sin can belong to higher reason in both ways. For reason, insofar as it fastens on the eternal natures, which constitute its proper object, can in contemplating them have deliberate acts, or indeliberate acts, which we call surreptitious movements. And although it belongs to reason to deliberate, every deliberation still needs to include an absolute consideration, since deliberation is simply a discursive process and a process of successive consideration, and every movement has irreducible elements (e.g., moments in time and points in lines). Therefore, if sin arising surreptitiously should belong to higher reason regarding its proper object, there will be a venial sin. For example, such would be the case if one should without reflection think that God cannot be triune and one. For this is not a mortal sin before reason adverts to the fact that the thought is contrary to the command of God, since going contrary to his command belongs to the nature of mortal sin. Therefore, when reason through deliberation has perceived that disbelief is contrary to his command, the sin will become mortal if one were to disbelieve.

And no sin can arise surreptitiously in one who consults and fastens on the eternal natures as the means to direct a desire or action, since consultation itself causes deliberation. Nevertheless, venial and mortal sin can belong to higher reason in this way, since we in deliberating seek both how something can be done, and how something can be done better. Therefore, there can be sin regarding deliberation in two ways. There is sin regarding deliberation in one way insofar as we as a result of such deliberation approve something altogether contrary to our end, such that one cannot attain the end if the act is posited, and then there is mortal sin. For example, the person who in deliberating considers that fornication is contrary to God's law and nonetheless chooses to fornicate sins mortally. But if the person approves something that does not preclude the person's end, and yet the person could attain the end better without it, since the thing in some respect impedes one from the end or disposes one to the contrary of the end, then there is venial sin. For example, such would be the case if one utters an idle word also considering in deliberation that such an act is a venial sin that disposes the person to mortal sin and in some respect falls short of the rectitude of justice leading to God.

Replies to the Objections:

1. Higher reason does not need to turn away from the eternal natures of things whenever it sins, since it sometimes sins by approving something not contrary to them, as I have said.[80]

2. There can in two ways be disorder regarding the end: either because one withdraws from the end, and this is mortal sin, or because one approves something that retards one from the end, and this is venial sin.

---

79. Ibid., XII, 7, n. 12 (PL 42:1005).
80. In the answer.

3. Material light acts out of natural necessity, and so as long as the whole of it abides, it always acts, and its activity is never diminished. But putting charity and grace into practice is subject to the will's choice. And so human beings in possession of charity do not always make use of its perfection and sometimes act less perfectly.

4. Augustine in the cited text speaks of mortal sin, which is wickedness and evil in an absolute sense. But we can in a proper sense call venial sin wickedness only relatively, as I have said.[81]

5. Reason sins mortally when it draws the right conclusion from the eternal natures of things but approves something contrary to them. But sometimes reason sins because it disposes one to something contrary to the natures and impedes one from the end, not because what one approves may be contrary to them.

6. We say that reason is always correct either in that it is disposed toward first principles about which it does not err, or in that error results from defective reasoning rather than the properties of reason. And error results from a property of imagination insofar as imagination perceives the images of things not at hand.

7. Both the temperate and the intemperate person at least possess right reason about the universal, since even the intemperate person by right reason judges that it is evil to approve unworthy pleasure, although passion leads the person to rebel against this general consideration. But it does not thereby follow that every sinner's reason in relation to the universal is praiseworthy, since the intemperate person even when free of passion, as one making evil use of reason, judges it good to enjoy unworthy pleasure.

8. Although reason may deliberate, it is still necessary that it have an absolute consideration included in the very deliberation, as I have said.[82] But one does not necessarily sin out of pure malice whenever one deliberately sins. Rather, one necessarily sins out of pure malice only when one approves something contrary to virtue, as the *Ethics* says.[83] And venial sin is not contrary to virtue. Therefore, when one deliberately consents to venial sin, one does not on that account sin out of malice.

9. The above makes clear the answer to objection 9.

10. Deliberate consent does not cause contempt of God unless one should approve as contrary to God that to which one consents.

11. Both higher and lower forms of knowledge can consider the object of higher reason, which is the most exalted object. For the knowledge that God has of the eternal good that is himself is superior to the knowledge that human beings have of him by human reason. And so the knowledge human beings have about God insofar as they believe his revelation of himself corrects the knowledge human beings have of him by their reason. Therefore, when one spontaneously thinks that God is not triune and one, one does so according to human reason, and it is a venial sin. But when a person deliberates, the person, considering that disbelief in the Trinity of the one God is contrary to what God has revealed, adds to the knowledge by human reason the knowledge from God. And so the sin becomes a mortal sin, brought into contrariety by a higher means of knowledge, as it were.

---

81. A. 1, reply to objection 1.
82. In the answer.
83. Aristotle, *Ethics* VII, 4 (1148a2–4).

12. Sickness that alters the heart's components or what flows from it is always mortal, but sickness that brings about a disorder in its movement is not always mortal. And likewise, sin that takes away charity from higher reason is mortal, but sin that causes disorder in an act of reason is not.

Sixth Article

Can Venial Sin Belong to Sense Appetites?

It seems that venial sin does not, for the following reasons:

1. Ambrose says that only what is capable of virtue is capable of vice.[84] But sense appetites are not capable of virtue, since the serpent represents the sense appetites, as Augustine says in his work *On the Trinity*.[85] Therefore, sense appetites cannot cause vice.

2. According to Augustine,[86] every sin belongs to the will, "since only the will sins." But sense appetites are different from the will. Therefore, sense appetites are not venial sin.

3. Irrational animals have no sin. But sense appetites are common to us and irrational animals. Therefore, sin cannot belong to sense appetites.

4. People have said that the sense appetites in irrational animals do not obey reason, but that those in us do. And so the sense appetites in us can be the subject of sin in us but not in irrational animals. But sense appetites according to this opinion will be the subject of venial sin only insofar as they are subject to reason. And that on account of which things are such is such more and first. Therefore, we should ascribe reason rather than sense appetites as the subject of venial sin, since the Philosopher says in the *Topics* that they err who do not ascribe a first subject to accidents.[87]

5. Disposition and habits belong to the same subject. But venial sin is a disposition to mortal sin. Therefore, since mortal sin cannot belong to sense appetites, neither will venial sin be able to belong to sense appetites.

6. Augustine says in his *On Genesis against the Manicheans* that one is rewarded rather than endangered if one does not consent to the movements of sense appetites.[88] But no one sinning venially is on that account rewarded. Therefore, the movements of sense appetites are not venial sins.

7. Augustine says in his sermon on the works of mercy: "Every sin is contempt of God, since his commandments are contemned."[89] Therefore, sin can belong to the part of the soul that can perceive the commands of God. But only reason, not sense appetites, can perceive the commands of God. Therefore, venial sin cannot belong to sense appetites.

---

84. *On Noah and the Ark* 12, n. 41 (PL 14:379A).
85. *On the Trinity* XII, 12, n. 17 (PL 42:1007).
86. *On Two Souls* 10, n. 14 (PL 42:104).
87. *Topics* VI, 9 (147b29–34).
88. *On Genesis against the Manicheans* II, 14, n. 21 (PL 34:207).
89. This work is missing but mentioned by Possidius (PL 46:17).

8. No one sins in what one cannot avoid by the power of the will. But human beings cannot by the power of their will avoid movements of concupiscence arising, as Rom. 7:15 says: "For I do not do the good that I will," namely, not to desire inordinately, as a gloss explains.[90] Therefore, the movements of sense appetites are not sin.

On the Contrary:
The Master says in the *Sentences* that movements of concupiscence, if they belong only to sense appetites, will be venial sins,[91] and this is taken from Augustine's work *On the Trinity.*[92]

Answer:
Strictly speaking, sins regard acts, as is clear from what I have said before.[93] And since we are now speaking of sin in moral matters, sin may belong to a power's act that can be a moral act. And an act is moral because reason and the will ordain and command it. And so sin can belong to the act of every part of a human being that obeys reason. And both bodily members regarding external acts and sense appetites regarding some internal movements obey reason and the will. And so also sin can belong to external acts and the movements of the sense appetites that we call sensuality.

And we should consider that because we attribute acts to their chief and primary cause rather than to their instrumental cause, we attribute sin to reason, not to sense appetites or bodily members, when internal sense appetites or external bodily members act at the command of reason. And it never happens that an external bodily member acts unless it is moved to act either by reason or at least by imagination or memory in conjunction with a sense appetite. And so we never say that sin belongs to external bodily members (e.g., a hand or a foot). But sense appetites are sometimes moved to act without any command of reason and the will, and then we say that the sin belongs to the sense appetites. And yet this sin can be only venial, not mortal. For mortal sin consists of turning away from the ultimate end ordained by reason, and sense appetites cannot reach so far. And so only venial sin, not mortal sin, can belong to sense appetites. And when reason commands movements of sense appetites, as is evidently the case regarding one who wills to lust for something mortally sinful, such movements are mortal sins, but we attribute them to reason commanding them, not to the sense appetites.

Replies to the Objections:
1. Ambrose is speaking about the vice of mortal sin, which is contrary to virtue. But venial sin is not contrary to virtue, although certain virtues belong to the nonrational parts of the soul, according to the Philosopher in the *Ethics,*[94] insofar as the parts can partake of reason, not indeed insofar as they belong to the senses.

---

90. *Interlinear Gloss,* on Rom. 7:15.
91. Peter Lombard, *Sentences* II, d. 24, chap. 9, n. 3.
92. *On the Trinity* XII, 12, n. 17 (PL 42:1007).
93. Q. 2, aa. 1 and 2.
94. *Ethics* III, 10 (117b23–24).

2. Augustine means that every sin belongs to the will as the first cause of sensual movements or the first power causing the movements. For movements of sense appetites are venial sins because the will can prevent them.

3. Sense appetites are the subject of sin insofar as they are subject to reason, and they are not in this respect common to us and irrational animals.

4. When an act of the will or reason is involved in a sin, we can directly attribute it to reason or the will as the first cause of the movement to sin and the sin's first subject. But when no act of the will or reason is involved in a sin but only the act of a sense appetite, which we call sin because reason and the will can forbid it, we attribute the sin to the sense appetite.

5. When a disposition and a habit differ as the perfect and the imperfect regarding the same species of thing, they belong to the same subject; otherwise, it is not necessarily the case. For example, the goodness of the imagination consists of its disposition for knowledge, and the movement of sense appetites can also be a disposition for mortal sin, which belongs to reason.

6. When an illicit movement belongs to a sense appetite, reason can be related to it in three ways. Reason can be related to the illicit movement of a sense appetite in one way as resisting the movement, and then there is the merit of reward and no sin. And reason is sometimes related to the illicit movement as commanding it. For example, when one deliberately arouses the movement, there will be mortal sin if the illicit object belongs to the genus of mortal sin. And reason is sometimes related to the illicit movement as neither prohibiting it nor commanding or consenting to it, and then there is venial sin.

7. Augustine in the cited text is speaking about mortal sin, which is sin without qualification, since venial sin is sin in a qualified sense, as I have said.[95]

8. Since sense perceptions affect sense appetites, and yet sense appetites are powers belonging to bodily organs, the movements of sense appetites can arise in two ways: in one way from the disposition of the body; in the second way from sense perception. And the disposition of the body is not subject to the command of reason, but every sense perception is subject to the command of reason. For reason can forbid the exercise of any power of sense perception, especially in the absence of something perceptible by touch, which sometimes cannot be removed. Therefore, since sin belongs to sense appetites insofar as they can obey reason, the first movements of sense appetites, which arise from the disposition of the body, are not sin, and some call these movements the very first movements.[96] And the second movements, which sense perceptions arouse, are sin. For reason cannot in any way avoid the first movements, and reason can avoid some but not all second movements, since reason, turning its attention from one thing, encounters another, from which an illicit movement can arise.

---

95. A. 6, reply to objection 4.
96. E.g., William of Auxerre, *Golden Summa* II, tr. 28, q. 2, chap. 2 (incidental question).

Seventh Article

Could Adam in the Condition of Innocence Have Sinned Venially?

It seems that he could, for the following reasons:

1. On 1 Tim. 2:14, "Adam was not deceived," a gloss says: "Having no experience of God's severity, he could have been deceived to believe that he was committing venial sin."[97] And so it seems that Adam in the condition of innocence believed that he could sin venially even before he sinned mortally. But he himself knew the condition of his state better than we do. Therefore, we should not say that he could not have sinned venially.

2. People have said that the cited text does not understand venial to mean generically venial as we call an idle word a venial sin, but venial as we call a sin easily pardoned a venial sin. But Gregory says in his work *Morals* on Job 10:9, "Remember, I urge you, that you made me like clay": "Human beings commit venial sins, but such sins are unpardonable in angels."[98] Therefore, Adam would not have been deceived if he were to have thought that his sin was pardonable. Therefore, we should not explain the gloss in such a way that we understand venial to mean pardonable.

3. Venial sin is a disposition for mortal sin. But dispositions precede habits. Therefore, venial sin preceded mortal sin in Adam.

4. Since we can sin venially, it was only because of the integrity of Adam's condition if he could not. But venial sin is less contrary to the integrity of the original condition than mortal sin is, and yet he committed mortal sin. Therefore, much more could he commit venial sin.

5. Sins are contrary to acts of virtue. But acts of virtue did not in the condition of innocence belong to a different genus than they do now. Therefore, neither do acts of sin. Therefore, if some sins are now venial, they would also have been such in the condition of innocence.

6. We reach the less distant before we reach the more distant. But mortal sin is more distanced from the rectitude of the original condition than venial sin is. Therefore, Adam arrived at venial sin before he arrived at mortal sin.

7. Adam could sin or act rightly. But he could do something more or something less good. Therefore, he could do something more or something less evil, by sinning mortally or venially.

8. There is a condition of rational creatures in which they can sin mortally or venially, as happens in us. There is also another condition of rational creatures in which they cannot sin either venially or mortally, as is the case in the condition of glory. There is also a condition of rational creatures in which they can only sin mortally, not venially. Therefore, there is a condition in which they can sin venially but not mortally as long as the condition lasts. But the latter condition can only be the condition of innocence. Therefore, it was possible in the condition of innocence to sin venially as long as the condition lasted.

---

97. Peter Lombard, *Gloss*, on 1 Tim. 2:14 (PL 192:341C).

98. Actually, *Ordinary Gloss*, on Job 10:9; from Gregory the Great, *Morals* IX, 50, n. 76 (PL 75:900C)

9. The soul had rightly ordered governance in the condition of innocence, and so Eccl. 7:29 says that God made human beings rightly ordered. But rightly ordered governance can be weakened before it is destroyed. Therefore, venial sin could weaken the soul's governance before mortal sin completely destroyed it.

10. Grace does not take away human nature. But the free choice of human beings has the power to act rightly and the power to sin mortally and venially. Therefore, the gratuitous gift of original justice did not preclude the possibility of sinning venially.

11. Nothing prevents the activity of a secondary cause being deficient although there is no deficiency in the activity of the primary cause. For example, a plant's power to germinate may be deficient with no deficiency in the causal action of the sun. But reason and sense appetites in the soul are related as superior and inferior powers. Therefore, venial sin could belong to acts of sense appetites without mortal sin belonging to acts of reason even in the condition of innocence.

12. Augustine says in his *Literal Commentary on Genesis* that "Adam was tempted by an inordinate desire to acquire knowledge because he saw that the woman did not die after she ate the fruit. And yet he, if he was already endowed with a spiritual way of thinking, could in no way believe that God would out of envy have forbidden them to eat of the fruit of that tree."[99] But Adam did not have a spiritual way of thinking after he sinned. Therefore, he was tempted before his sin by the inordinate desire to acquire knowledge. But an inordinate desire to acquire knowledge is a venial sin. Therefore, Adam committed a venial sin before he committed mortal sin.

13. A sudden movement to unbelief is a venial sin. But Eve had a sudden movement to unbelief before she sinned, and this is evident by what she said while in a state of doubt, as it were: "Lest we perhaps die."[100] Therefore, she sinned venially before she sinned mortally.

14. According to Augustine in his work *Enchiridion*,[101] sins belong to the soul as sicknesses belong to the body. But Adam incurred a sickness that weakened his powers before he incurred death. Therefore, by like reasoning, he incurred weakness through venial sin before he incurred spiritual death through mortal sin.

15. Augustine says in his *Literal Commentary on Genesis*: "We should not think that the tempter would have caused Adam to fall unless some pride that ought to be checked were to have previously belonged to his soul."[102] But that pride could not be checked after he consented to it. Therefore, it had arisen in him even before he should have checked it by rejecting it. But such movements that ought to be checked are venial sins. Therefore, Adam committed venial sin before he consented.

16. The tempter caused Adam to fall through mortal sin. But pride warranting suppression preceded the fall, as the very words of Augustine imply.[103] Therefore, Adam committed venial sin before he committed mortal sin.

99. *Literal Commentary on Genesis* XI, 42, n. 60 (PL 34:454).
100. Gen. 3:3.
101. *Enchiridion* 11 (PL 40:236).
102. *Literal Commentary on Genesis* XI, 5 (PL:432).
103. Ibid.

On the Contrary:

1. The first sin of Adam caused death according to the Apostle in Rom. 5:12: "Sin entered the world through one man, and death through the sin." But we call sin mortal because it causes death. Therefore, the first sin of Adam was necessarily a mortal sin.

2. Anselm says in his work *On the Virgin Conception* that as irrational animals are ordained to act without reason, so human nature is ordained to act with reason.[104] But those who sin venially act without reason; otherwise, their actions would not be evil, since Dionysius says in his work *On the Divine Names* that it is evil for human beings to act without reason.[105] Therefore, human beings could not sin venially in the condition of innocence, in which the order of human nature was integral.

3. Every movement comes from a source that prevails. But justice prevailed in human beings during their innocence. Therefore, every movement in that condition was in accord with justice. Therefore, human beings could not sin venially while that condition lasted.

Answer:

Theologians commonly hold that Adam in his original condition did not sin venially before he sinned mortally.[106] And one could think that this is so because sins venial in us would have been mortal for human beings in the condition of innocence due to the excellence of their condition.

But we cannot say this. For one and the same sin may be more serious because of the status of a person. And the circumstance of a person's station does not infinitely increase the seriousness of sin so as to make a venial sin mortal unless the circumstance transfer the sin to another species, since only such a circumstance makes a venial sin mortal, as I have maintained before.[107] And this transformation happens when something becomes contrary to a precept for a person because of a condition of the person's station, something that in a person of lower station does not have the nature of being contrary to the precept. For example, for a priest to marry is contrary to the precept to observe one's vow of continence, but not for a layman who has taken no such vow, and so what is either a venial sin or no sin for a layman is a mortal sin for a priest. And if the act of a person of higher station be not contrary to a precept specifically constituted for such a person, there is no mortal sin, since every mortal sin is contrary to a precept of God's law, as I have said before.[108] (But such an act may by accident be a mortal sin by reason of resulting scandal, since it is also contrary to a precept of God's law to provide a brother with the occasion of his destruction.) And we cannot say that venially sinful acts would have been for the first man in his condition of innocence contrary to a precept in a different way than the acts are for us. And so we cannot say that acts that are venial sins for us would have been mortal sins for him, if he were to have committed them, because of the excellence of his station.

---

104. *On the Virgin Conception* 10 (PL 158:444A).
105. *On the Divine Names* 4, n. 32 (PG 3:733A).
106. E.g., Albert the Great, *Commentary on the Sentences* II, d. 21, a. 10.
107. A. 4.
108. A. 1, reply to objection 1.

Rather, we should say that the condition of Adam's status was such that he could in no way commit venial sin as long as the status lasted. And this is because human beings were instituted in the condition of innocence in such a way, as Augustine says in the *City of God*,[109] that as long as the higher part of human beings clung firmly to God, all lower things, both lower parts of the soul and the body itself and other external things, were subject to the higher part. And only mortal sin, which consists of turning away from God, could remove the higher part of human beings, namely, the intellect, from the rectitude whereby it was subject to God. Therefore, no disorder could belong to lower parts of the soul before Adam sinned mortally. And so the venial sin that belongs to sense appetites without the deliberation of reason was evidently impossible in the condition of innocence, since every movement of lower parts would follow the ordination in the higher part.

And because venial sin may also belong to higher reason in the way I previously explained,[110] it could seem to some that there could be at least such venial sin in Adam in the condition of innocence. But we also find the same explanation regarding this if we should carefully consider the matter. For inasmuch as we distinguish powers by their objects, there is also a ranking of the powers by the ranking of their objects. And there may also be a ranking of higher and lower reason regarding the objects of reason in both theoretical and practical matters. For as self-evident first principles are the highest in theoretical matters, so ends are the highest in practical matters. And so as long as the higher reason of human beings were to have been well disposed regarding the human end, in no way could it have been deficient regarding the means, because of the indefectible ordination of lower things for higher things by the condition of the state of innocence. Just so in theoretical matters, no defect regarding conclusions will be possible as long as human beings properly esteem first principles unless there be a defect in connecting the principles to the conclusions. And it is clear from what I have said before that mortal sin results from turning away from the end, and venial sin is a disorder regarding means.[111] And so Adam in the condition of innocence could not sin venially before he sinned mortally.

Replies to the Objections:

1. The gloss does not understand venial to mean generically evil, as we are now speaking about venial, but to mean easily pardonable.

2. The sin of Adam was indeed venial as Gregory uses the term, since it could be pardoned, although not so easily as he himself thought, namely, that it be pardoned without loss of Adam's condition.

3. Something disposes to something else in two ways. Something disposes in one way by a necessary and natural ordination, as heat disposes to the form of fire, and such a disposition always precedes that to which it disposes. Something disposes in the second way contingently and as if by accident, as anger disposes to, but does not necessarily precede, a rise in the body's temperature, and venial sin in this way disposes one to mortal sin without venial sin always preceding mortal sin.

109. *City of God* XIV, 15 (PL 41:422–24).
110. A. 5.
111. A. 1.

4. Both venial and mortal sin are so contrary to the integrity of the original condition that integrity is incompatible with either. But mortal sin is so much more contrary that it could destroy the integrity of the original condition, and venial sin could not.

5. The argument of this objection is valid on the supposition that Adam could have done things that are venial sins for us, and yet those things would be mortal sins for him. And what I have explained before makes clear that such a supposition is false.[112]

6. The argument of this objection is valid when one cannot arrive at a more distant terminus except by way of a fixed less distant terminus. But when one can arrive at a more distant terminus by way of different less distant termini, no one of the less distant termini need pre-exist. For example, if one could go to a destination by several routes, it is not necessary that, before reaching a more distant point, one arrive at a less distant point on one of those routes. And likewise, human beings do not necessarily sin venially before they sin mortally.

7. Adam originally could commit a more serious or a less serious mortal sin. But it does not follow that he could sin venially, since not every lesser sin is a venial sin.

8. Such arguments are not always valid. For there can be one thing without a second thing (e.g., a substance without accidents, or a form without matter), and yet there cannot be the second thing without the first. And likewise, we can say that although there is a condition in which there could be only mortal sin, it is not thereby necessary that there be a condition in which there is necessarily only venial sin. But we may say that there is a condition in which there could be venial sin but not mortal sin, as in the case of those sanctified in the womb, namely, Jeremiah and John the Baptist and the Apostles. And Scripture says of those so sanctified: "I have strengthened their pillars,"[113] and we believe them to have been so confirmed in grace that they could sin only venially, not mortally.

9. The fact that a governance is weakened before it is completely overturned can result either from the deficiency of a ruler who is lacking in wisdom or justice, or from the deficiency of subjects who are not completely obedient. But Adam's intellect in the condition of innocence was perfect in wisdom and justice, and his lower powers were completely subject to him. And so venial sin could not weaken his soul's governance before mortal sin destroyed its governance.

10. Grace takes away the deficiency of human nature, not its perfection. And the capacity to sin belongs to the deficiency, and so also grace can take away such a capacity, so that it is impossible to sin, as is evident especially in the blessed.

11. The action of a lower cause may be deficient without the action of a higher cause being deficient because the lower cause is not completely subject to the higher. But this was not the case in the condition of innocence, and so the argument does not follow.

12. That inordinate desire to acquire knowledge was subsequent to the pride that Adam conceived at the words of Eve, and Augustine so states when he says that the inordinate desire to acquire knowledge tempted Adam because of an intellectual pride. And that pride was the first sin and was a mortal sin consisting of pride against God. And yet the inordinate desire to know something forbidden by God can be a mortal sin.

---

112. In the answer.
113. Ps. 75:3. The psalm actually indicates that the pillars belong to the earth.

And the statement that Adam was endowed with a spiritual way of thinking needs to be related to the time before the arousal of his pride, although we could say that Adam even after his sin had a spiritual way of thinking by reason of the spirituality of keen intelligence, not indeed of the spirituality of grace.

13. We cannot call a movement of unbelief or doubt also expressed in words a sudden movement. And yet the pride arising in Eve's mind at the words of the serpent, whereby the serpent tempted her about what the precept of her superior would restrain, preceded even that expressed doubt of hers. For the pride whereby she shrank from the constraints of God's precepts arose immediately in Eve's mind, and her doubt resulted from this.

14. We call the very necessity of dying that Adam immediately incurred a death of humankind, as Rom. 8:10 says: "The body is indeed dead because of sin." Just so, we call mortal sin the death of the soul. But actual death corresponds analogously to future damnation.

15. When Augustine says that the arousal of pride should be checked, he is saying that pride should not be permitted to arise. For at the words set forth by the tempter, Adam should have so disposed himself as not to allow pride to enter.

16. We can understand Adam's fall so described as the externally sinful act or even the loss of the condition of innocence, which is subsequent to the pride, as effects are subsequent to causes.

Eighth Article

Are the First Movements of the Sense Appetites
of Unbelievers Venial Sins?

It seems that such movements are not, for the following reasons:

1. Anselm says in his work *On Grace and Free Choice*: "Those experiencing fleshly desires who do not belong to Christ are following the path of damnation even if they do not act according to fleshly desires."[114] But experiencing fleshly desires and not acting according to them is the first movement of concupiscence. Therefore, since only mortal sin deserves condemnation, it seems that the first movements of concupiscence in unbelievers, who do not belong to Christ Jesus, are mortal sins, not venial sins.

2. The Apostle says in Rom. 7:15: "For I do not do the good that I will," namely, willing not to experience concupiscence. And on that account he concludes that he cannot be condemned, provided he does not act according to the flesh, since he belonged to Christ Jesus. For he says in Rom. 8:1: "Therefore, there is no condemnation," namely, for experiencing concupiscence, "for those who belong to Christ Jesus and do not act according to the flesh." But when a cause is removed, its effect is removed. Therefore, concupiscence is condemnable in those who do not belong to Christ Jesus.

---

114. *On Grace and Free Choice* (= *On the Harmony of Foreknowledge and Predestination*), q. 3, chap. 7 (PL 158:530C).

3. As Anselm says in the same work, human beings were created in such a way that they would not be required to experience concupiscence.[115] And the grace of baptism that unbelievers do not possess seems to remit the liability of human beings to experience concupiscence. Therefore, whenever unbelievers experience concupiscence, even if they do not consent, they act contrary to the way they ought to act. Therefore, they sin mortally.

On the Contrary:
Other things being equal, Christians sin more seriously in a sinful act than unbelievers do, as is evident by what the Apostle says in Heb. 10:29: "How much worse punishment do you think those deserve who have trodden Christ under foot," etc. But Christians experiencing concupiscence do not sin mortally if they do not consent. Therefore, much less do unbelievers.

Answer:
Some have held regarding unbelievers that even their first movements of concupiscence are mortal sins.[116] But this cannot be. For we can consider the movements of sense appetites in two ways. We can consider such movements in one way as such, and then there evidently cannot be mortal sin, since mortal sin consists of turning away from the ultimate end and out of contempt for the command of God. But sense appetites are not capable of moral response to a divine command, and they cannot arrive at the ultimate end. And so their movements considered as such can in no way be mortal sins. We can consider the movements in a second way regarding their source, which is original sin. And they cannot in this way have more of the nature of sin than original sin would have, since an effect as such cannot be more powerful than its cause. And original sin indeed belongs to unbelievers as to both moral fault and punishment, and regarding believers, punishment indeed remains, but moral fault is taken away, as I have said before when I discussed original sin.[117]

And so movements of sense appetites in believers are indeed venial sins insofar as they are personal acts, but insofar as they arise as a consequence of original sin, they belong only to a punishment, not to culpable condemnation. And regarding unbelievers, there is likewise venial sin insofar as the movements are personal acts, but insofar as they derive from original sin, they incur some culpable condemnation by reason of the condemnation that belongs to original sin, not indeed by reason of actual mortal sin.

Replies to the Objections:
1. Those experiencing fleshly desires who do not belong to Christ obtain the condemnation due to original sin, not the condemnation due to mortal sin.

2. The Apostle, when he says: "Therefore, there is no condemnation," etc., intends us to conclude that the rebellion of concupiscence in those who belong to Christ Jesus does not incur the condemnation of original sin. And we can infer from this that the

115. Ibid.
116. No known source.
117. Q. 4, a. 6, reply to objection 4.

incendiary material of sin along with original sin belong to those who have not obtained the grace of Christ Jesus.

3. The nonliability to experience fleshly desires is due to having original justice. And so it follows that those not having original justice or anything in its place, such as the grace of baptism, have original sin, but not that they incur mortal sin in every movement of their sense appetites.

Ninth Article

Can a Good or Bad Angel Sin Venially?

It seems that a good or bad angel can, for the following reasons:

1. As Gregory says in a homily on the Ascension, human beings share with angels the capacity to understand.[118] But venial sin can belong to human beings even regarding the intellectual part of their soul, namely, higher and lower reason, as I have said before.[119] Therefore, by like reasoning, venial sin can belong to angels.

2. Mortal sin consists of the fact that one loves a creature more than God, and in venial sin, one loves something lesser than God. But angels could love a creature more than God, since they sinned mortally. Therefore, they could also sin venially by loving a creature lesser than God, since one who can love more can also love less.

3. Mortal sin is infinitely different from venial sin, and this is evidenced by their different punishments, since venial sin deserves temporal punishment, and mortal sin eternal punishment. But angels are not infinitely different from human beings. Therefore, the bad angels we call devils sometimes do things that are venial sins for human beings, as, for example, when bad angels utter a few idle words or induce others to utter them. Therefore, it seems that such sins by angels are venial sins, not mortal sins.

4. Sin that is venial by reason of its kind becomes mortal only from some contempt. But devils sometimes induce human beings to things venial by reason of their kind, and as devils themselves sometimes say, they do not do this out of contempt of God, nor to induce human beings to mortal sin. Therefore, they sin venially.

On the Contrary:
Venial sin especially happens surreptitiously. But there are no surreptitious movements in good or bad angels, since they have a godlike intellect, as Dionysius says.[120] Therefore, neither good nor bad angels can commit venial sin.

Answer:
No angel, good or bad, can commit venial sin. And the reason for this is that angels do not have a discursive intellect as we do. And it belongs to the nature of a discursive intellect sometimes to consider first principles and conclusions separately, and so the discursive in-

---

118. *On the Gospels* II, hom 29, n. 2 (PL 76:1214B).
119. Aa. 5 and 6.
120. *On the Divine Names* 7, n. 2 (PG 3:869C).

tellect may go from one to the other, considering now the one, now the other. But this cannot belong to a godlike, nondiscursive intellect; rather, such an intellect always considers conclusions in considering the principles themselves without any discursive reasoning. And I have said that the end is related to the means in matters of desire and action as self-evident principles are related to conclusions in theoretical matters.[121] And so we may sometimes think or be affected only about the means or sometimes only about the end. And this cannot be so in the case of angels. Rather, movements of the angelic intellect are always borne simultaneously to the end and the means. And so angels can never have any disorder regarding the means without a simultaneous disorder regarding the end itself. But we may have a disorder through venial sin regarding the means to our end with our intellect habitually fixed on the end. And so human beings but not angels may commit venial sin without mortal sin. And angels have every disorder as a result of turning away from their ultimate end, and this turning away constitutes mortal sin. For angels sin because they adhere to a created good by turning themselves away from the uncreated good.

Replies to the Objections:

1. We indeed share with the angels regarding the capacity to understand but only in general. There is still a specifically big difference, since the angelic intellect is godlike, and out intellect is discursive, as I have said.[122]

2. Angels do not have a composite nature as human beings do. And the sentient and material nature of human beings induces them to love something they ought not love or ought not love so much. But angels can sin only because they love an agreeable good without relating it to God, which is to be turned away from God and to sin mortally. And so they can desire something inordinately only by turning away from God.

3. The devil sins mortally in all of his voluntary acts, since his acts of free choice proceed from his intention to do evil.

4. The very fact that the devil induces human beings to exaggerated speech shows that he has the wicked intention of leading them into mortal sin. We impute to human beings as sin even the very familiarity with him, since we should not even look for truth from him, as Chrysostom says.[123] And so also the Lord forbade the devil to profess truths about the Lord's divinity, as Mk. 1:24 and Lk. 4:34–35 hold. Nor should we believe the words of the devil, since he is a liar and the father of lies, as Jn. 8:44 says.

Tenth Article

Is Venial Sin by One without Charity Punished by
Eternal Punishment?

It seems that such venial sin is not, for the following reasons:

1. When a cause is taken away, its effect is also. But the reason why mortal sin is punished by eternal punishment is because it destroys the eternal good. For Augustine

121. A. 7, in the answer.
122. In the answer.
123. From St. Thomas, *Golden Chain*, on Mk. 1:25.

says in his work the *City of God* that "the man who destroyed in himself the good that could be eternal became worthy of eternal evil."[124] And venial sin does not do this. Therefore, venial sin accompanied by mortal sin is not punished by eternal punishment.

2. As Dt. 25:2 says, "The number of lashes shall also be in proportion to the crime." But venial sin does not become greater because it is accompanied by mortal sin. Therefore, it is not punished by a greater punishment. But it is not punished with eternal punishment when it is unaccompanied by mortal sin in one who has charity. Therefore, neither will it be punished by eternal punishment when it is accompanied by mortal sin.

3. People have said that the addition of mortal sin makes venial sin more serious in one who dies without charity, because of the person's final impenitence. But according to Augustine in a sermon on the words of God, final impenitence is a sin against the Holy Spirit.[125] Therefore, venial sin, if final impenitence should make it more serious, will become a sin against the Holy Spirit. And so the sin will now be mortal rather than venial.

4. Even persons who possess charity may not repent before their death of venial sins they have committed, and yet they are not punished for such sins with eternal punishment. Therefore, final impenitence does not make venial sin accompanied by mortal sin so much more serious that the impenitence makes the venial sin deserving of eternal punishment.

5. The higher a person's station, the more serious the person's sin seems to be. But a person who has charity seems to have a higher station than a person who has mortal sin. Therefore, venial sin is more serious in one who has charity.

6. Persons dying in a state of mortal sin may sometimes repent of venial sins they have committed, changing the will they had during their life about sinning venially. But the soul remains with the same condition of the will that the soul has when it leaves the body. Therefore, those who die in this state will be free of such venial sin after death. Therefore, they will not be eternally punished for such venial sin.

7. God always punishes less than one deserves. And so also Ps. 77:9 says that God does not in anger withhold his mercies. But God does not mitigate the severity of the punishment of venial sin in the future life, since the punishment of purgatory is greater than any present punishment, as Augustine says,[126] and the punishment of hell is much greater. Therefore, he mitigates the duration of the punishment of venial sin. Therefore, venial sin accompanied by mortal sin is not eternally punished.

8. Original sin, like mortal sin, is the condition of one without grace. But venial sin accompanied by original sin is not punished eternally. For venial sin is not punished in the limbo of unbaptized children, since there is no punishment of the senses there, and it is not punished in the hell of the damned, since only mortal sin is punished there. And one is not punished eternally in purgatory. Therefore, neither will venial sin accompanied by mortal sin be eternally punished.

9. People have said that venial sin can accompany original sin only if mortal sin is simultaneously present. They have said this because human beings cannot sin venially before they have the use of reason, and after they have the use of reason, they are in a

---

124. *City of God* XXI, 12 (PL 41:727).
125. *On the Words of the Lord*, sermon 71, chap. 12, n. 20 (PL 38:455).
126. *Expositions on the Psalms*, Ps.37:2, n. 3 (PL 36:397).

condition of mortal sin unless they be turned toward God, and if they be turned toward God, they will already have the grace that destroys original sin. But an affirmative precept requires that one actually turn oneself to God, and affirmative precepts, although always obligatory, do not oblige under all circumstances. Therefore, a person does not instantly sin mortally if the person be not actually turned toward God at the moment the person acquires the use of reason. And a person can then sin venially. Therefore, there can be venial sin without mortal sin in the state of original sin.

10. The punishment of mortal sin is proportionate in severity to the punishment of venial sin, since the severity of both punishments is finite, and everything finite is proportional to every other finite thing. Therefore, if venial sin accompanied by mortal sin, just like mortal sin, deserves eternal punishment, the punishments of the two kinds of sin will differ only regarding the severity of the punishments. Therefore, the punishment of a mortal sin surpasses the punishment of venial sin proportionally. Therefore, venial sins could be so great in number that they will deserve the punishment equivalent to one mortal sin. But this conclusion is false, since many venial sins do not constitute one mortal sin, as I have said before.[127] Therefore, the premise of the conclusion, namely, that venial sin accompanied by mortal sin is punished by eternal punishment, is also false.

On the Contrary:
That the punishment of venial sins comes to an end is due to the merit of the sinner's fundamental condition, as the Apostle makes clear in 1 Cor. 3:11–12. And this fundamental condition is indeed habitual faith, as Augustine says in his works *City of God*[128] and *On Faith and Works*.[129] But one who dies in a condition of mortal sin does not have this fundamental condition. Therefore, the punishment of venial sins in such a one will not end.

Answer:
Moral wrong deserves punishment because punishment rectifies the moral wrong, since human beings by their own willing to sin neglect to follow the proper order of God's justice. And that order is repaired only by justice being administered to human beings when they are punished according to God's will contrary to their own.

And perpetual punishment corresponds to mortal sin according to the ordination of God's justice both by reason of the sin's very species and by reason of the sin's inherence in the sinner. The punishment corresponds to mortal sin by reason of the sin's species because mortal sin is directly contrary to love of God and neighbor, which remits the punishment due sin. And those who sin against something deserve for that very reason to be deprived of its benefit. For example, in human affairs, those who commit crimes against the commonwealth are for that very reason perpetually deprived of fellowship in the commonwealth, whether by perpetual exile or even by death. And regarding the punishment of death, as Augustine says in his work *City of God*,[130] the span of time re-

---

127. A. 3.
128. *City of God* XXI, 26, n. 1 (PL 41:743).
129. *On Faith and Works* 16, n. 27 (PL 40:215).
130. *City of God* XXI, 11 (PL 41:726).

quired to execute the criminal is irrelevant. Rather, the relevant consideration is that death forever deprives the criminal of the benefit of the commonwealth, although the crime committed was perchance momentary or perpetrated in a short span of time. And so also those who sin mortally, insofar as they sin against charity, deserve to be deprived of pardon, which is the product of charity. And if the Lord does pardon such sinners, he does so out of his mercy, not because of the merits of human beings.

And regarding the inherence of mortal sin in the human subject, the sin has perpetual punishment because the sin deprives the human being of the grace whereby the sin can be pardoned. But the punishment is not remitted as long as the sin remains, since there can be nothing disordered in the works of God. And so just as a man who were to jump into a well from which he could not by his own power extricate himself would cause himself to be there forever insofar it lies within his power, so also those who sin mortally bring themselves to eternal punishment insofar as it lies within their power.

But venial sin, since it is not contrary to charity, does not deserve eternal punishment by reason of its species of sin, nor, properly speaking, by reason of the sin's inherence in the human subject, since venial sin does not deprive the human subject of grace. Nonetheless, venial sin by accident becomes unpardonable when it is accompanied by mortal sin, insofar as it belongs to a subject deprived of grace. And then it is by accident punished by eternal punishment.

Replies to the Objections:

1. The argument of this objection is valid regarding the cause of eternal punishment by reason of the species of the act. But venial sin deserves eternal punishment in another way, not this way, as I have said.[131]

2. The severity of punishment corresponds to the magnitude of sin, but the eternity of punishment corresponds to the indelibility of sin. And such indelibility indeed sometimes befits venial sin by accident, as I have said.[132]

3. That final impenitence constitutes a sin against the Holy Spirit and is contrary to charity, which is the special gift of the Holy Spirit. And so not to repent of venial sin, since it is not contrary to charity, does not constitute a sin against the Holy Spirit. But venial sin, insofar as it is accompanied by mortal sin and final impenitence, by accident has indelibility, as I have said.[133]

4. One who repents of mortal sin but not venial sin does not have an impenitence contrary to the remission of sin. And so there is no reason for eternal punishment.

5. Venial sin accompanied by mortal sin is punished longer because of the indelibility that comes from what accompanies venial sin, not because of the gravity of venial sin itself, as I have said.[134] And yet it is not always true that venial sins accompanied by mortal sin are lesser than those accompanied by charity; rather, the former are very often greater because they result from a more disordered desire that charity does not restrain. And in those with complete charity, venial sins for the most part arise surreptitiously

---

131. In the answer (conclusion).
132. Ibid.
133. Ibid.
134. Ibid.

and are quickly pardoned in virtue of charity, as 2 Chr. 30:18–19 says: "The good Lord will grant mercy to all who with their whole heart seek the Lord God of their fathers, and he will not impute to them the fact that they are not sanctified."

6. Sin, after it actually ceases, can abide in liability to punishment, which only the alteration that charity causes, not any change of the will, takes away.

7. The punishment of venial sin, even in hell, is mitigated regarding its severity, although it is punished more severely than human beings would punish it. It is punished more severely because it has greater gravity in relation to God, as punished by God, than in relation to human beings, as punished by human beings.

8. A person cannot die with original and venial sin but without mortal sin. A person cannot because a child before having the use of reason is excused from mortal sin, so that it does not incur the punitive liability of mortal sin even if it should commit an act that is by reason of its kind a mortal sin, since the child does not yet have the use of reason. And so much more is the child excused from the guilt of venial sin, since what excuses the greater sin much more excuses the lesser sin. But the child, after it has the use of reason, sins mortally if it does not do what lies in its power to acquire its salvation, and if it should do so, it will obtain the grace whereby it will be free from original sin.

9. Although affirmative precepts, commonly speaking, do not oblige under all circumstances, the natural law still obliges human beings to be first of all solicitous about their salvation, as Mt. 6:33 says: "Seek first the kingdom of God." For their ultimate end is by nature the first thing to fall within their will, just as first principles are the first thing to fall within their comprehension. For all desires presuppose the desire of the ultimate end, just as all theoretical considerations presuppose the theoretical consideration of first principles.

10. [Although a finite proportion belongs to things of the same nature, something of a less perfect nature, however much it be perfected, cannot become equal to something of a more perfect nature. For example, blackness, however much intensified, is always less perfect than whiteness. And the punishment properly deserved for mortal sin is the privation of the vision of God, and this kind of punishment does not correspond to venial sin. And so the punishment deserved for venial sin cannot be made equal to the punishment deserved for mortal sin.

Or we should say that the punishments of the senses inflicted in hell for mortal and venial sin are not infinitely different. We should say this because both punishments are finite and correspond to the creature's turning toward a transient good, which even in mortal sin is finite, although perhaps the remorse of conscience called the worm of conscience is incomparably greater in one than in the other sin. But the infinite difference between mortal and venial sin is due to the turning away from God, and this turning away belongs only to mortal sin, which eternally deprives the sinner of the vision of God. And venial sin does not cause this except by accident, as I have said.[135] Nor does it follow that more venial sins cause punishment equal in intensity to the punishment of mortal sin. Rather, more venial sins cause more extensive punishment, since they will be punished in more ways. And so the argument is invalid.][136]

135. In the answer (conclusion).

136. The text of this reply is missing from the earliest manuscripts, but the Leonine editors have reconstructed it from later printed versions.

Eleventh Article

Are Any Venial Sins Remitted in Purgatory
after This Life Ends?

It seems that none are, for the following reasons:

1. Eccl. 11:3 says: "If a tree be cut down, it will lie wherever it falls, whether point-ing to the south or to the north." But death causes human beings to be cut down. There-fore, human beings after death will ever remain in the condition in which they die. There-fore, no sin of human beings is remitted after their death.

2. Only a change in the will of the sinner that caused the very sin can transform the sin, since an effect is not removed as long as its cause remains. But the will after death cannot be changed, as angels cannot change after their fall. For death is for human beings what the fall was for the angels, as Damascene says.[137] Therefore, venial sin cannot be remitted after this life ends.

3. People have said that mortal sin, because absolutely voluntary, requires for its remission an actual change in the will. But this is not true about original sin, which is not a voluntary sin by the person's will. Nor is it true about venial sin, which is not abso-lutely voluntary, since human beings cannot avoid sinning venially, although they can avoid particular venial sins. But Augustine says in his sermon on repentance that human beings cannot begin the new life unless they repent of their old ways of life.[138] And the pardon of sin belongs to the beginning of the new life, and every sin, even original and venial sin, belongs to the old ways of life. Therefore, since he calls repentance a change of one's actual will, it seems that neither original sin nor venial sin can be remitted with-out an actual change of the will.

4. By the same habit, one is pleased with one contrary and displeased with the other. For example, by the habit of generosity, one is pleased to be generous and displeased to be stingy. But we are pleased with the goodness of grace by the habit of charity. There-fore, we are displeased with the evil of moral fault by the habit of charity. Therefore, if habitual displeasure were to suffice for the pardon of venial sin, venial sin would never be simultaneously present with charity.

5. Pardon of venial sin belongs to perfecting the spiritual life. But perfecting the spiritual life, since it belongs to the condition of pilgrimage, cannot happen after death, which ends the condition of pilgrimage. Therefore, venial sin cannot be pardoned after this life ends.

6. It seems to belong to the same consideration that one merits a substantial or an accidental reward, and that one's sins are pardoned, since by the same consideration whereby something advances toward one contrary, the thing retreats from the other. But human beings after death cannot merit either a substantial or an accidental reward. Therefore, by like reasoning, they cannot obtain the pardon of sin, whether mortal sin or venial sin.

7. Human beings fall into sin more easily than they are forgiven their sins, since human beings are spiritual beings who enter into sin of their own accord and do not by

---

137. *On Orthodox Faith* II, 4 (PG 94:877C).
138. *Sermon* 351, chap. 2 (PL 39:1537).

their own effort abandon sin. But human beings after death cannot sin venially. Therefore, neither can they then be forgiven venial sin.

8. No sin meriting eternal punishment is forgiven after this life ends. But venial sin seems to merit eternal punishment. For if human beings can merit eternal life for avoiding venial sin, they can, conversely, merit eternal punishment for committing venial sin. Therefore, venial sin cannot be pardoned after this life ends.

9. There is both grace and punishment in purgatory. But venial sin is not pardoned in purgatory by reason of the sin's punishment, both because punishment as the product of moral fault does not affect the moral fault, and because every punishment would by like reasoning take away moral fault. And the latter proposition is evidently false about the punishment of hell. Likewise, venial sin is not pardoned in purgatory by reason of grace, since grace is compatible with, and not contrary to, venial sin. Therefore, venial sin is not pardoned in purgatory.

10. People have said that venial sin is remitted in purgatory because human beings in this life merited its remission. But the merits of Christ are more efficacious than the merits of any human being. And the sacraments, which derive their efficacy from the merits of Christ, can absolve no one from a future sin. Therefore, much less can human beings merit the remission of a future sin.

11. As mortal sin is contrary to charity, so venial sin is contrary to the intensity of charity. But the intensity of charity that destroys venial sin cannot take place in the future life, since there will be no new movement of the will then. Therefore, venial sin cannot be remitted then, just as mortal sin cannot be remitted without the fresh advent of charity.

12. Whatever is compatible with the antecedent is compatible with the consequent. For example, if white is compatible with human, white is compatible with animal; otherwise, it would follow that contrary things would be simultaneously asserted. But glory, with which venial sin is incompatible, necessarily results from the final state of grace. Therefore, venial sin is incompatible with the final state of grace. Therefore, venial sin cannot be remitted after this life ends.

13. Purgatory is a condition in between the condition of our present life and the condition of future glory. But there is both moral fault and punishment in the present life, and there is neither moral fault nor punishment in the condition of glory. And between these conditions, there is either moral fault without punishment or punishment without moral fault. But there cannot be moral fault without punishment, since this is contrary to the ordination of God's justice. Therefore, there will be punishment without moral fault in purgatory. Therefore, no sin can be remitted in purgatory after this life ends.

14. No sacrament of the church has been instituted in vain. But extreme unction, because instituted for the remission of venial sins, would seem to have been instituted in vain if venial sin were able to be remitted in purgatory after this life ends. Therefore, venial sins cannot be remitted after this life ends.

15. A disposition resulting from a form does not remain in matter when the form withdraws. For example, heat does not remain in ignited matter when the fire has been extinguished. Therefore, neither does the disposition of matter remain in a form separated from matter. But venial sin is a disposition of human beings regarding their matter. For venial sins arise from the body's corruption that burdens the soul, since there

could be no venial sins in the condition of integral human nature, as I have said before.[139] Therefore, venial sin does not remain in the soul separated from the body and so cannot be remitted after this life ends.

16. When a great good is deferred, and a great evil threatens, there arises an intense desire to acquire the good and to avoid the evil. But a great evil, namely, the bitter pain of purgatory, threatens the separated soul liable to the punishment of purgatory, and the separated soul is kept from the good most hoped for, namely, eternal life. Therefore, an intense desire immediately arises in the separated soul. But intensity of charity is incompatible with venial sin. Therefore, the separated soul in purgatory cannot have venial sin. Therefore, venial sin cannot be remitted in purgatory.

17. The fire of purgatory as the instrument of God's justice punishes the soul. But we do not suppose that the fire is the instrument of God's mercy, to which it belongs to remit sins. Therefore, venial sin is not remitted in purgatory after this life ends.

On the Contrary:

1. Gregory says in his *Dialogues*: "We are given to understand that some slight sins are remitted after this life ends."[140]

2. On Mt. 3:11, "He himself will baptize you in the Holy Spirit and with fire," a gloss says: "He cleanses in the present life with the Spirit; he purifies afterwards with the fire of purgatory if any stain of sin has arisen."[141] And we should believe this purification to concern less serious sins.

3. Augustine says that "the transitory fire of purgatory purges slight sins, not capital sins."[142]

4. Ambrose says in his work *On a Good Death*: "As our physical eyes cannot see the physical sun if they have any injury, so injured spiritual eyes cannot see the spiritual sun."[143] But venial sin is an injury of the soul. Therefore, the soul cannot arrive at the vision of God as long as it has the stain of venial sin. Therefore, such stain needs to be cleansed in purgatory.

Answer:

To establish the answer to this question, we need first to understand what remission of sin is, and it is simply that sin not be imputed to the sinner. And so Ps. 32:1–2, when it says, "Blessed are those whose sins are forgiven," adds as if in explanation: "Blessed is the man to whom God has not imputed sin." And sin is imputed to someone inasmuch as it prevents a human being from attaining the ultimate end consisting of eternal happiness, which sin prevents human beings from attaining both by reason of moral fault and by reason of liability to punishment. Sin indeed prevents human beings from attaining their ultimate end by reason of moral fault because eternal happiness, as the perfect good of human beings, is incompatible with any diminution of goodness. And by the very

139. A. 7.
140. *Dialogues* IV, 39 (PL 77:396A–B).
141. *Ordinary Gloss*, on Mt. 3:11.
142. *Sermon* 104, n. 1 (PL 39:1946).
143. *On the Good of Death* 11, n. 49 (PL 14:563A).

fact that human beings committed an act of sin, they incurred some diminution of goodness, namely, insofar as they became blameworthy and unworthy of so great a good. And because they deserve punishment, they are also prevented from attaining perfect happiness, which excludes all sorrow and punishment. "For sorrow and pain in Sion shall flee away," as Is. 35:10 says.

And both mortal and venial sin prevent perfect happiness, mortal sin in one way, venial sin in another way. For human beings by mortal sin suffer diminution of goodness by being deprived of the chief thing that leads to their end, namely, charity. And human beings by venial sin suffer diminution of goodness and an impediment by reason of something unbecoming in the sinful act, as if by an impediment in the very act whereby they were advancing toward their end, but with the source directing their actions to their end intact. Just so, something heavy can be prevented from moving downward either because it has lost its heaviness, or because there arises an impediment that prevents its movement from attaining its natural end. There is also a difference regarding the liability to punishment, since one by mortal sin merits destructive punishment as an enemy, and one by venial sin merits corrective punishment.

Therefore, venial sin is pardoned in one way, and mortal sin in another. For regarding moral fault, in order for mortal sin not to be imputed, a new infusion of charity and grace needs to take away the impediment that resulted from the destruction of their source. And this is not required in the case of venial sin, since charity abides, although a strong impulse contrary to the impediment attached by the obstacle of venial sin needs to be removed. Just so, the impediment that results from the destruction of the heaviness of something can be removed only by reproducing the same heaviness, and a violent movement removing an attached obstacle takes away the impediment that would result from the very obstacle. And so regarding moral fault, intensity of charity even remits venial sin, but the infusion of new grace remits mortal sin. And regarding punishment, mortal sin is not remitted, since it incurs endless and eternal punishment, but venial sin is remitted by the discharge of finite temporal punishment. And this indeed makes sufficiently clear how both the moral fault and punishment of venial sin are remitted in this life.

And in the future life, mortal sin can never be remitted regarding moral fault, since no new infusion of grace and charity transforms the soul essentially after this life ends. And because the moral fault has not been remitted, neither is the punishment, as I have said.[144]

And some have said about venial sin that, in those who possess charity, it is always remitted in this life regarding moral fault, and remitted after this life only regarding punishment, namely, by discharge of the punishment.[145] And this indeed seems probable enough in the case of those who depart this life with the use of reason, since it is unlikely that one possessing charity and conscious of imminent death would not be moved by an impulse of charity both toward God and contrary to every sin committed, even venial sins. And this suffices for the remission of venial sins regarding moral fault, and

144. A. 10.
145. Alexander of Hales, *Summa of Theology* II–II, n. 286.

perhaps also regarding punishment if there be intense love. But it sometimes happens that some during their very acts of venial sin or while intending to sin venially are drowsy or overcome by emotions that take away the use of reason, and death overtakes them before they can use reason. And for such persons, venial sins are evidently not remitted in this life. And yet such persons are not on that account kept forever from eternal life, and they in no way attain eternal life unless they are completely free of every moral fault they have committed.

And so we need to say that venial sins are remitted after this life even regarding moral fault in the same way that they are remitted in this life, namely, by an act of love of God contrary to venial sins committed in this life. Nonetheless, because there is no condition of meriting after this life ends, the movement of love in persons in purgatory indeed takes away the impediment of venial sin but does not merit the discharge or diminution of punishment, as the movement of love in this life would.

Replies to the Objections:

1. Venial sin does not alter the condition or status of human beings but is an impediment whereby human beings are put off from attaining their ultimate end.

2. In the future life, there is no essential change of the will, namely, change of the will regarding the ultimate end or charity or grace, but an accidental change can result from the removal of an impediment, since the removal of an impediment causes incidentally, as the *Physics* says.[146]

3. It belongs to the same consideration that the will is borne to desire one contrary and to detest the other. But persons possessing the exercise of free choice can begin the new life that results from the infusion of grace only if they desire and love the goodness of grace. And so they need to detest every contrary evil. They need to do so in such a way that they specifically detest the mortal sins that they have personally committed, and which are directly contrary to grace. As a result, the infusion of grace takes away the effect of mortal sin, namely, the privation of grace, when the displeasure with mortal sin has removed the cause taking away grace. And original sin is not contracted by such a person's own will, and venial sin is indeed committed by the person's own will but does not cause the privation of grace. And so such a person needs to have only displeasure with venial sin in general, insofar as it has a nature contrary to grace, and not in particular.

4. Habitual displeasure with venial sin does not suffice for remission of such sin. Rather, actual displeasure is required, although general displeasure suffices.

5. The remission of venial sin does not intrinsically cause spiritual progress, namely, regarding an increase of spiritual goodness. Rather, the remission of venial sin does so only incidentally, namely, regarding the removal of an impediment to the increase.

6. The merit of substantial or accidental glory belongs intrinsically to the spiritual progress that is due to the increase of spiritual goodness. And so the reasoning is dissimilar to that regarding the remission of sin.

7. The soul after death passes into another condition, one like that of the angels. And so for the same reason, separated souls, like angels, cannot sin venially. But the soul's

---

146. Aristotle, *Physics* VIII, 4 (255b24).

venial sins can be remitted even after death because the soul nonetheless retains the exercise of charity, which causes the remission of venial sin.

8. We can understand avoidance of venial sin in two ways. We can understand it in one way as a pure negation, and then it does not merit eternal life, since those asleep also do not sin venially and yet do not merit. We can understand it in a second way as an affirmation, insofar as we say that one who wills not to commit venial sin avoids it. And because such a will can be due to charity, avoiding venial sin can for that reason merit eternal life. But committing venial sin is not contrary to charity. And so venial sin does not merit eternal punishment.

9. Purgatory effects the remission of venial sin regarding punishment, and human beings by suffering the punishment of purgatory discharge the debt they owe, and so their punitive liability ceases. But regarding moral fault, punishment does not remit venial sin insofar as one actually undergoes punishment, since punishment is not meritorious. Nor does punishment remit venial sin insofar as one reflects on the punishment, since it would not be a movement of charity for one to detest venial sin because of the punishment; rather, it would be a movement of servile or natural fear. Therefore, the power of grace remits venial sin in purgatory regarding moral fault both as grace is habitual, for then it is compatible with venial sin, and as grace issues in an act of charity detesting venial sin.

10. No one can merit the remission of a future moral fault, but one can merit the condition of purgatory, where moral fault can be remitted.

11. There will be after death no new movement of the will that did not previously have in this life a foundation in either nature or grace. But there will be after this life many new actual movements of the will, since the soul will additionally have movements of the will regarding what the soul then knows and learns.

12. When the antecedent and the consequent of a conditional proposition relate to the same time, everything compatible with the antecedent is compatible with the consequent. But when the antecedent and the consequent relate to different times, that is not necessarily so. For example, it follows that an animal will die if it is alive, but it is not true that everything compatible with life is compatible with death. And likewise, it is not true that everything compatible with the final state of grace is compatible with glory.

13. Something intermediate in one respect is not necessarily intermediate in every respect. Therefore, the condition of purgatory is indeed intermediate regarding things between the condition of our present life and the condition of glory, but not intermediate regarding there being moral fault without punishment or punishment without moral fault.

14. All the sacraments of the new law were instituted to confer grace. But the infusion of new grace is not needed to remit venial sins, as I have said.[147] And so neither extreme unction nor any sacrament of the New Law was chiefly instituted against venial sins, although the sacraments do remit venial sin. Rather, extreme unction was instituted to remove the remains of sins.

15. Although the corruption of the body is a cause of venial sins, venial sins belong to the soul, not to the body, as their subject. And so they are dispositions of our form, not of our matter.

147. In the answer.

16. The argument of this objection validly concludes that venial sin is instantly remitted in purgatory, not that venial sin is not remitted there. And this seems quite likely.

17. As I have already said, punishment does not cause the remission of sin, but the use of grace, which God's mercy produces, does.[148]

Twelfth Article

Does Sprinkling Holy Water, Anointing the Body,
and the Like Remit Venial Sins in This Life?

It seems that such things do not, for the following reasons:

1. Conferring grace belongs to the sacraments of the New Law. But we do not call such things as sprinkling holy water, etc., sacraments. Therefore, such things do not confer grace. Therefore, such things do not remit any sin.

2. Mortal sin is not simultaneously compatible with grace, but venial sin is. And so the infusion of grace suffices for the remission of mortal but not venial sin. Therefore, it seems that more is required for the remission of venial sin than for the remission of mortal sin. But sprinkling holy water and the like cannot remit mortal sin. Therefore, much less can they remit venial sin.

3. Acts of charity remit venial sin. But acts of charity come from within and cannot be caused by sprinkling holy water and the like. Therefore, sprinkling holy water and the like cannot remit venial sin.

4. Sprinkling holy water and the like are equally related to all venial sins. Therefore, if such things remit one venial sin, they by like reasoning remit all venial sins. And so if venial sins are remitted regarding moral fault, those without mortal sin can very frequently say: "We have no sin." But this is contrary to 1 Jn. 1:8. And if sprinkling holy water and the like should remit venial sin regarding punishment, most will immediately after death escape without experiencing the punishment of purgatory. And this conclusion seems inappropriate. Therefore, sprinkling holy water and the like do not remit venial sins.

On the Contrary:

Nothing about the church's customs are done in vain. But the formula for blessing water mentions the remission of sin. Therefore, sprinkling holy water remits some sin. But sprinkling holy water does not remit mortal sin. Therefore, it remits venial sin.

Answer:

Intensity of charity remits venial sins, as I have said.[149] And so things constituted by their nature to arouse the intensity of charity can cause the remission of venial sins. And acts of charity belong to the will, which is indeed inclined to things in three ways. They are indeed sometimes inclined by reason alone demonstrating something, and sometimes by

148. Ibid.
149. A. 11.

reason accompanied by an internal impulse from a higher cause, namely, God, and sometimes additionally by the inclination of a settled habit. Therefore, some things cause the remission of venial sins insofar as they incline the will to intense acts of charity in the three mentioned ways. And the sacraments of the New Law remit venial sins in all of these ways, since reason also considers them to be salutary remedies, and God's power in the sacraments effects salvation in hidden ways, and the sacraments confer the gift of habitual grace. And some things cause the remission of venial sin in two of the mentioned ways, since they, although not causing grace, cause reason to consider something that arouses intensity of charity, and we also piously believe that God's power by arousing intensity of love is at work interiorly. And holy water, papal blessings, and like sacramentals cause the remission of sin in this way. And some things (e.g., the Lord's prayer, striking one's breast, and the like) cause the remission of venial sin only by arousing the intensity of charity by way of contemplation.

Replies to the Objections:

1. The conferring of new grace is not necessary for the remission of venial sin. And so something not a sacrament can remit venial sin.

2. A person possessing the exercise of free choice receives an infusion of new grace with an intensity of charity. And so more things are required for the remission of mortal sin than for the remission of venial sin.

3. Sprinkling holy water and the like cause intensity of charity by inclining the will itself, as I have said.[150]

4. Although sprinkling holy water and the like are equally related to all venial sins, the intensity such things arouse is still not always equally so related but sometimes concerns particular venial sins and acts more efficaciously against them. And the intensity, if it concerns venial sin generally, may not have an effect on all venial sins. This is so because the affections of human beings are sometimes habitually inclined to commit certain venial sins, namely, so inclined that if the person were to recall the sins, the person would not disapprove them, or the person would perhaps commit the sins if an opportunity were to present itself. And it rarely happens that human beings during the course of their mortal life are free from such defects. And so we cannot say with confidence that we have no sin. And if human beings by such remedies should acquire even for an hour freedom from all venial sins regarding moral fault, it still does not follow that they are freed regarding all punishment, unless there perhaps be so much intensity of love as to suffice for the remission of all punishment.

150. In the answer.

QUESTION VIII

On the Capital Sins

First Article

How Many Capital Sins Are There, and Which Sins Are?

It seems that there are seven capital sins, for Gregory says in his work *Morals*: "There are seven chief sins, namely, vainglory, envy, anger, spiritual apathy, avarice, gluttony, and lust."[1] But there are not, for the following reasons:

1. We seem to call sins capital from which other sins arise. But all sins arise from one or two sins. For 1 Tim. 6:10 says: "Covetousness is the root of all evils." And Sir. 10:15 says: "Pride is the origin of all sin." Therefore, there are not seven capital sins.

2. People have said that the Apostle in 1 Tim. 6:10 is speaking about covetousness to signify a general disorder of desire, not a special kind of sin. But covetousness as a special kind of sin is the inordinate desire of riches that we call avarice. And the Apostle is speaking in the cited text about such covetousness, which is evident from what he says in 1 Tim. 6:9: "Those who wish to become rich fall into temptation and the snare of the devil." Therefore, the covetousness that is the root of all evils is a special kind of sin.

3. Vices are the contraries of virtues. But there are only four cardinal virtues, as Ambrose says in commenting on Lk. 6:20–22, "Blessed are the poor," etc.[2] Therefore, there are only four capital vices.

4. Other sins seem to arise from the sins whose ends they serve. For example, if a person should lie in order to acquire money, the lie arises from avarice. But every sin can be ordained for the end of any other sin. Therefore, one sin is not more capital than another.

5. We cannot hold that things of which one by nature arises from another are equally of chief rank. But envy by nature arises from pride. Therefore, we ought not to hold that envy is a capital sin equal to pride.

---

1. *Morals* XXXI, 45, n. 87 (PL 76:621A).
2. *Commentary on Luke* V, n. 62 (PL 15:1653C).

6. Sins that have ends of chief rank seem to be chief or capital. But there are more than seven capital sins if we should understand by ends the proximate ends of sins. And if we should understand by ends the remote ends of sins, we shall not distinguish gluttony from sexual lust, both of which aim at pleasures of the flesh as their remote end. Therefore, we do not appropriately assign seven as the number of capital sins.

7. Heresy is a sin. But none of the aforementioned sins causes heresy in a person who incurs it out of pure ignorance. Therefore, there is a sin that does not arise from the aforementioned sins, and so we insufficiently assign those sins as the chief sins.

8. A sin may arise from a good intention, as, for example, is evidently the case if one steals in order to give alms. But such a sin does not derive from one of the aforementioned sins. Therefore, not every sin arises from those sins.

9. Gluttony seems designed for the pleasures of taste, and sexual lust for the pleasures of touch. But there are also pleasurable objects of the other senses. Therefore, we ought to understand chief sins by the other senses.

10. All sins seem to belong to the will, since it is by the will that we sin or live righteously, as Augustine says.[3] But movements of the will come from the soul to things. And things have either good or evil, as the *Metaphysics* says.[4] Therefore, there ought to be only two capital sins, one with respect to good and the other with respect to evil.

11. The will, to which sin belongs, is the intellectual appetite, which seems to belong to things in general, since activity of the will results from intellectual cognition, which regards universals. But the universals regarding the genus of appetite are good and evil, which universals are the genera of other things and do not belong to a genus, as the *Categories* says.[5] Therefore, we ought to distinguish capital sins only in general, so that there are two capital sins corresponding to the difference between good and evil, not into any particular goods and evils.

12. Evil happens in more ways that good does, since good results from a unified and integral cause, and evil from individual defects, as Dionysius says in his work *The Divine Names*.[6] But we seem to understand four capital sins by their relations to good. For example, gluttony and sexual lust concern pleasurable goods, avarice useful goods, pride worthy goods, since "it [pride] sneaks into good works in order to destroy them," as Augustine says.[7] Therefore, there ought to be more than three other capital sins.

13. There are different sources of different genera of things, as the *Metaphysics* says.[8] But ends in practical matters and desirable things are like first principles in theoretical matters, as the *Ethics* says.[9] Therefore, we cannot trace different genera of sins to the end of one sin, and so many kinds of sin cannot arise from one kind of sin.

14. If one sin arises from another as if the former sin is ordained for the end of the latter sin, then both sins would have the same end. Therefore, both sins would have the

3. *Retractions* I, 9, n. 4 (PL 32:596).
4. *Metaphysics* VI, 4 (1027b25–27).
5. *Categories* 11 (14a23–25).
6. *On the Divine Names* 4, n. 30 (PG 3:729C).
7. *Rule for the Servants of God*, n. 2 (PL 32:1379).
8. Aristotle, *Metaphysics* XII, 4 (1070a31–33).
9. Aristotle, *Ethics* VII, 8 (1151a16–17).

same end either in the same respect or in different respects. If in different respects, we shall need to say that there are several ends, not one end, since we note the multiplicity and diversity of the objects corresponding to powers, habits, and acts of the soul by the natures of the objects rather than materially by the very things. And so one sin will not be subordinated to the end of another; rather, each will intrinsically in equal measure have its own end. And if the end of each sin is the same in the same respect, then both sins are specifically the same. Just so, things of nature possessing one and the same form belong to the same species, since ends specify moral acts as forms specify things of nature. And so one sin will not originate from another, but sins will rather be of one kind. Therefore, we ought not hold that the aforementioned sins are capital sins.

15. The Philosopher says in the *Ethics* that one who commits adultery in order to steal is a thief rather than an adulterer.[10] And so it seems that a sin subordinated to the end of another sin passes into the species of the latter sin. Therefore, one sin will accordingly not arise from another.

16. On Ps. 19:13, "I shall be washed clean of the greatest sin," a gloss says that "the greatest sin is pride, and those without pride are free of every sin."[11] And so it seems that pride is sin in general. But we do not contradistinguish the general from the particular. Therefore, we should not hold that pride is a capital sin on a par with the others, as some theologians hold.[12]

17. On Rom. 7:7, "I would not have known what it was to covet had the law not said, 'Thou shalt not covet,'" a gloss says: "The law that in forbidding covetousness forbids every evil is good."[13] And so also it seems that covetousness is sin in general. Therefore, we ought not hold that covetousness or avarice is specifically one of the seven capital sins.

18. We call sins that have ends of the first rank capital sins, as I have said.[14] But riches, which are the goal of avarice, do not have the nature of an end of first rank, since people seek riches only as useful and a means to other things. And so the Philosopher demonstrates in the *Ethics* that happiness cannot consist of riches.[15] Therefore, we should not hold that avarice is a capital sin.

19. The soul's emotions incline us to sins, and so also Rom. 7:5 calls them "sinful emotions." But the primary emotion is love, whence all the affections of the soul arise, as Augustine says in the *City of God*.[16] Therefore, we should in particular hold that disordered love is a capital sin, especially since Augustine says in the same work that self-love unto the contempt of God causes the city of Babylon.[17]

20. We designate four chief emotions of the soul, namely, joy and sadness, hope and fear, as Augustine makes clear in the *City of God*.[18] But there are among the seven capi-

10. Ibid., V, 2 (1130a24–28).
11. Peter Lombard, *Gloss*, on Ps. 19:13 (PL 191:214A).
12. Cf. Albert the Great, *Commentary on the Sentences*, d. 42, a. 8, *ad* 3.
13. Peter Lombard, *Gloss*, on Rom 7:7 (PL 191:1416C).
14. Objection 6.
15. *Ethics* 1, 7 (1097a24–b6).
16. *City of God* XIV, 7, n. 2 (PL 41:410).
17. Ibid., XIV, 28 (PL 41:436).
18. Ibid., XIV, 7, n. 2 (PL 41:411).

tal sins some that belong to joy or delight, like gluttony and sexual lust, and some that belong to sadness, like spiritual apathy and envy. Therefore, we ought also to designate some capital sins that belong to hope and fear. We ought to do so especially because some sins arise from hope, since we say that only hope causes interest-taking. And likewise, some sins arise from fear, since on Ps. 80:16, "Things set on fire and undermined," etc., Augustine says that every sin arises from a love that wickedly inflames or from a fear that wickedly undermines.[19]

21. We do not designate anger a chief emotion. Therefore, it seems that we also ought not to designate anger a capital sin.

22. The chief vices are the contraries of the chief virtues. But charity is a chief virtue that we call both the mother and the root of virtues, and hate is its contrary. Therefore, we ought to designate hate a capital vice.

23. 1 Jn. 2:16 says: "Everything in the world is either lust of the flesh or lust of the eyes or pride of life." But we call persons worldly or belonging to the world because of their sin. Therefore, we ought to designate only these three things capital sins.

24. Augustine says in his homily on the fire of purgatory that there are several capital sins, namely, sacrilege, murder, adultery, fornication, false testimony, rape, theft, pride, envy, avarice, anger if it is retained for a long time, and inebriation if it is habitual.[20] And the *Decretum* holds the same. Therefore, the previously cited seven capital sins seem to be inappropriately assigned.[21]

Answer:

We call sins capital from the word "head" [Latin: *caput*], and we understand head in three ways.

For we first of all call one member of an animal's body the head, and 1 Cor. 11:4 so understands head: "Every man praying or prophesizing with covered head disgraces his head." And second, since the head is a source of animal life, the word "head" has been given an extended meaning to signify every kind of source. For example, Lam. 4:1 says: "The stones of the sanctuary are scattered at the head of all the streets leading from it." And Ez. 16:25 says: "You have erected a sign of your prostitution at the head of every street." Third, head signifies the chief or ruler of a people. For the head of a political body in some way also rules the other bodily members. And 1 Sam. 15:17 understands head in this way: "When you were an infant in your eyes, you were constituted head of the tribes of Israel." And Am. 6:1 so understands head: "Heads of the people processing in state into the house of Israel."

And we can call sins capital in these three meanings of head. For we sometimes call sins capital from head in the sense of the bodily member, and we in this way call crimes capital that are punished by capital punishment. But we are not now speaking about capital sins in this sense. Rather, we are now speaking about capital sins as we speak of head meaning source. And so Gregory calls capital sins fonts of sin.[22]

19. *Expositions on the Psalms*, on Ps. 80:16, n. 13 (PL 36:1027).
20. *Sermon* 104, n. 2 (PL 39: 1946).
21. *Decretum* 25, chap. 3, n. 6 (Friedberg I:93).
22. *Morals* XXXI, 45, n. 88 (PL 76:621A–C).

And we should note that one sin can arise from another sin in four ways. The first way indeed regards the withdrawal of grace, which keeps human beings from sin, as 1 Jn. 3:9 says: "Every person born of God does not commit sin, since God's seed abides in the person." And so the first sin that takes away grace causes the sins resulting from the privation of grace. And so any sin can be caused by any other sin. And this way of causing is through the removal of an impediment to sin. And removing an impediment causes by accident, as the *Physics* says.[23] And no practical or theoretical knowledge contemplates accidental causes, as the *Metaphysics* says.[24] And so we do not assign capital sins by this way of causing or being the source. In the second way, one sin causes another by way of inclination, namely, insofar as a previous sin causes a disposition or habit that inclines one to sin, and every sin in this way of causing causes another specifically the same. And so we also do not call sins capital in this way of originating. In the third way, one sin causes another regarding the matter, namely, insofar as one sin serves as the matter for the other sin. For example, gluttony serves as the matter for sexual lust, and avarice for dissension. But we also do not call sins capital in this way of originating, since what serves as the matter for sin causes sin potentially and as the occasion of sin, not actually. In the fourth way, one sin causes another regarding the end, namely, insofar as human beings commit one sin to attain the end of another sin. For example, avarice causes fraud because avaricious persons commit fraud in order to acquire money. And one sin in this way actually and formally causes another. And so we call sins capital in this way of originating, to which the third meaning of head also consequently belongs. For a ruler evidently directs his subjects to attain his objective, as, for example, a commander deploys his army to attain his objective, as the *Metaphysics* says.[25] And so capital sins are commanders, and the sins arising from capital sins the army, as it were, as Gregory says.[26]

And it can happen in two ways that one sin is subordinated to the end of another sin. It happens in one way regarding the very sinner, whose will is more prone to the end of one sin than to the end of another. But this is incidental to the sins, and so we do not in that way call any sins capital. It happens in the second way regarding the very relationship of two ends, one of which befits the other, so that one is for the most part designed for the other. For example, deception, which is the end of fraud, is ordained to amass riches, which is the end of avarice. And we should understand capital sins in this way. Therefore, those sins are capital that have ends chiefly desirable as such, so that other sins are subordinated to such ends.

And we should note that it belongs to the same consideration that one pursues a good and shuns the contrary evil. For example, a glutton seeks pleasure in food and shuns the distress that results from the absence of food, and it is likewise regarding other sins. And so we can appropriately distinguish capital sins by different goods and evils, namely, so that one capital sin is distinguished from others whenever there is a particular aspect of desirability or avoidance. Therefore, we should consider that good by its nature attracts the will to itself, and that the will avoids a good because of a particular aspect that one

---

23. Aristotle, *Physics* VIII, 4 (255b24).
24. Aristotle, *Metaphysics* VI, 2 (1026b4–5).
25. Ibid., XII, 10 (1075a13–15).
26. *Morals* XXXI, 45, n. 88 (PL 76:621A–C).

apprehends regarding such a good. And so we need by such aspects to consider capital sins that differ from those ordained to pursue a good.

And there are three kinds of human good, namely, goods of the soul, goods of the body, and goods consisting of external things. Therefore, pride or vainglory aims to attain a good of the soul, which is a good conceived in the mind, namely, the excellence of honor and glory. And gluttony aims to attain a good of the body relating to preservation of the individual, which consists of food. And sexual lust pertains to a good of the body relating to preservation of the species as regards sexual intercourse. And avarice pertains to a good consisting of external things. And a good is avoided insofar as it is an impediment to another good inordinately desired. And the will indeed has two movements regarding a good that is an impediment, namely, the movement of aversion and the movement of resistance against it. Therefore, regarding the movement of aversion, we understand two capital sins as we consider in itself or something else a good that prevents a desired good. There is indeed one capital sin as we consider the impediment in itself, as a spiritual good prevents tranquility or bodily pleasure, and then there is spiritual apathy, which is simply apathy about a spiritual good as that good prevents a bodily good. And there is a second capital sin as we consider the impediment as belonging to another, as the good of another prevents one's own excellence, and then there is envy, which is chagrin at the good of another. And anger imports resistance against a good preventing a desired good.

Replies to the Objections:

1. Regarding virtues, we consider two kinds of ends, namely, the ultimate and general end, that is, happiness, and the particular end of each virtue. So also regarding vices, we can understand their particular ends, by which we understand capital sins, as I have said,[27] and an ultimate and general end that is a particular good, since all the mentioned capital sins aim at a particular good. But a particular good can be the end of sins only insofar as one inordinately desires that good, and one inordinately desires that good insofar as one desires it contrary to the ordination of God's law. And so also we say that two things are involved in every sin, namely, turning toward a transitory good and turning away from the immutable good. Therefore, regarding the turning toward a creature, we designate as the source of every sin a general covetousness, which consists of an inordinate desire for one's own good. And regarding the turning away from God, we designate as the source of sins a general pride, insofar as human beings do not make themselves subject to God. And so Sir. 10:14 says that "the source of pride in human beings is their turning away from God." Therefore, we indeed do not call covetousness and pride, understood in a general way, capital sins, since they are not particular vices. Rather, we call covetousness and pride in general certain roots and sources of vices, just as if we were to say that the desire for happiness is the root of all virtues. But we can say that even covetousness and pride as particular sins, by reason of their ends, have a general causal influence on all sins. For example, the end of avarice is related to the ends of all other sins as a source, since human beings can with riches acquire everything that other vices desire. For money by its power includes all such objects of desire, as Sir. 10:19 says: "Everything obeys

---

27. In the answer.

money." And the particular end of pride, namely, the excellence of honor or glory, is the end of all such ends, as it were, since human beings can obtain honor or glory by great riches and by indulging certain desires. And although one of these ends in the course of executing the ends is the first, and another the last, so to speak, we still ought not on that account to designate only these two sins capital, since the will's intention is not chiefly ordained only to those two ends.

2. The foregoing makes clear the answer to objection 2.

3. Virtue is constituted by the fact that the ordination of reason is imposed on an appetitive power, and vice derives from the fact that an appetitive movement withdraws from the ordination of reason. But the same thing brings about the imposition of the ordination of reason on an appetite and the withdrawal of an appetite from the ordination of reason. And so although vices are the contraries of virtues, the chief vice does not have to be contrary to the chief virtue, since there is a different reason for the origin of virtue and vice.

4. The disposition of the sinner can bring it about that any sin is subordinated to the end of any other sin. But by reason of the relationship that the objects and ends of sins have for one another, certain sins arise in a settled way from other sins, and the former also result more frequently from the latter. And in considering moral matters, as in considering things of nature, we attend to what happens for the most part.

5. It is clear from what I have said that envy for the most part arises from pride.[28] For example, human beings are especially chagrined at the good of another because that good prevents their own pre-eminence. But we designate envy as a capital sin distinct from pride because the movement of envy has a particular nature.

6. We understand capital sins by reason of the proximate ends of certain sins from which other sins for the most part naturally arise, not the proximate ends of all particular kinds of sins. And so also we distinguish gluttony from sexual lust, since the pleasure that is the object of gluttony and the pleasure that is the object of sexual lust have different natures.

7. Four things seem to belong to deficient knowledge, namely, lack of knowledge, ignorance, error, and heresy. Of these, lack of knowledge is the most common, since it signifies the simple absence of knowledge, and so also Dionysius supposes some lack of knowledge in angels, as his work *On Ecclesiastical Hierarchy* makes clear.[29] And ignorance is a kind of lack of knowledge, namely, of things that human beings are by nature constituted to know and ought to know. And error adds to ignorance the turning of the mind to the contrary of truth, since it belongs to error to approve the false as true. And heresy adds to error something both regarding the matter, since heresy consists of error about things that belong to faith, and regarding the one in error, since heresy implies obstinacy, which alone produces a heretic. And this obstinacy indeed arises from pride, since it belongs to great pride that persons prefer their own opinion to divinely revealed truth. Therefore, heresy arising out of pure ignorance, if it is a sin, arises out of one of the aforementioned capital sins. For if persons do not take care to learn things they are

28. Ibid.
29. *On Ecclesiastical Hierarchy* 6, part 3, n. 6 (PG 3:537B).

obliged to know, we impute the ignorance to them as sin. And this seems to result from spiritual apathy, to which belongs avoidance of a spiritual good insofar as it prevents a bodily good.

8. We call the aforementioned sins capital because other sins for the most part arise from them, although sins sometimes arise from good. And yet we can say that even when one steals in order to give alms, even this sin in one respect arises from one of the capital sins, since to do evil for the sake of good derives from some ignorance or error, and we trace ignorance or error to spiritual apathy, as I have said.[30]

9. Sexual lust and gluttony concern the pleasure of touch. For we call someone a glutton because the person as if delighted by the touch takes pleasure in the consumption of food, not because the person takes pleasure in its taste, as the Philosopher says in the *Ethics*.[31] And the pleasures of other senses are not chief ends, since other senses are related either to knowledge of truth, as in the case of human beings, or to the pleasures of touch, as in the case of other animals. For example, a dog scenting a rabbit takes pleasure in the food he expects to consume, not in the smell of the rabbit. And so we do not designate capital sins by the pleasures of other senses.

10. Things have good or evil in different respects. And so there does not need to be only one capital sin in relation to good.

11. Many more particular universals can be subsumed under a general universal, just as particular genera are subsumed under a universal genus, and the more particular universals also fall within our understanding. So also can the intellectual appetite be borne in different ways to different specific goods.

12. We do not distinguish sins by the difference of good and evil, since the same sin concerns a good and its contrary evil, as I have said.[32]

13. Things that belong to different most general genera, as it were, have really different, although analogously the same, sources, as the *Metaphysics* says.[33] But things included in a universal genus, although they belong to different particular genera, can have the same sources regarding the commonality of that genus. And we can in this way trace the particular sins of different genera to the same source, which is the end that is the common ground of their origin.

14. When one sin is subordinate to the end of another sin, the end of both sins is the same and in the same respect, although not by the same relation, since the end of one sin is the proximate end, and the end of the other sin is the remote end. And so it does not follow that both sins belong to the same species, since moral acts take their species from their proximate, not their remote, end.

15. We designate persons thieves or adulterers from their habits, as the Philosopher speaks in the *Ethics* about the just and the unjust, not from their acts or emotions.[34] And the strivings of human beings come from their habits, and so when one steals in order to commit adultery, one indeed actually commits the sin of theft. And yet the striving derives from the habit of adultery, and so we call the person an adulterer, not a thief.

30. Reply to objection 7.
31. *Ethics* III, 10 (1118a33–b1).
32. In the answer.
33. Aristotle, *Metaphysics* XII, 4 (1070a31–33).
34. *Ethics* V, 6 (1134a17–23).

16. We can understand pride in two ways, as I have said.[35] We understand it in one way as it signifies a rebellion against the law of God, and then it is the universal root of all sins, as Gregory says.[36] And so he lists vainglory, not pride, among the capital sins. We can understand pride in the second way as an inordinate desire for a pre-eminence, and then we posit it as a capital sin on a par with the others. And because human glory seems to belong especially to such pre-eminence, Gregory substitutes vainglory for this particular kind of pride.

17. And we need to say the like in reply to objection 17, since the objection also understands covetousness as a general root of sin.

18. Riches, because they have the nature of a useful good, indeed lack the nature of a chief end, but this deficiency is compensated because of the general utility of riches, which in one respect by their power include all worldly objects of desire.

19. Love consists of willing good for another, as the Philosopher says in the *Rhetoric*.[37] Therefore, in that human beings desire certain goods for themselves, it seems that they love their very selves. And so love of self is not separately designated either the root of sin or even a capital sin, since all roots and sources of sin include disordered love of self.

20. Fear and hope are irascible emotions, and all irascible emotions derive from concupiscible emotions. And so we understand the first sources of sins to belong to joy and sadness rather than fear and hope. For although some sins spring from fear and hope, yet even fear and hope themselves spring from other emotions, namely, love or covetousness of some good.

21. Anger signifies a particular movement, namely, resistance against something. And so although even that movement arises from other movements, we designate it separately as a capital sin, since it has a different particular nature from the others.

22. We do not call a vice chief by reason of its contrariety to a chief virtue. And so hate does not need to be a chief vice even though charity is a chief virtue.

23. The three things that John designates indicate certain first sources and roots of sins, namely, pride and covetousness. For both lust of the flesh and lust of the eyes are included in general covetousness.

24. Augustine calls sins punishable by capital punishment capital sins.[38] For capital sins are thus the same as mortal sins.

Second Article

Is Pride a Special Kind of Sin?

It seems that pride is not, for the following reasons:

1. Every particular kind of sin destroys a particular kind of virtue and power of the soul. But pride destroys all virtues and powers of the soul. For Gregory says in his work

---

35. In the answer.
36. *Morals* XXXI, 45, n. 87 (PL 76:621A).
37. *Rhetoric* II, 4 (1380b35–36).
38. *Sermon* 104, n. 2 (PL 39:1946).

Morals: "Pride, in no way satisfied with destroying one virtue, spreads through all parts of the soul, and like a pervading and deadly disease corrupts the whole body."[39] And Isidore says in his work *On the Supreme Good* that pride is the ruin of all the virtues.[40] Therefore, pride is not a special kind of sin.

2. To prefer one's own will to the will of a superior is to be proud. But those who sin mortally prefer their own will to the will of a superior, namely, God. Therefore, they are proud. Therefore, every sin is pride, and so pride is not a special kind of sin.

3. People have said that pride as love of one's own excellence is a special kind of sin, but pride as signifying contempt of God is sin in general. But every special kind of sin has its own matter. For example, gluttony has food as its matter, lust sexual pleasures, avarice riches. And pride as love of one's own excellence does not have its own matter, since, as Gregory says in his work *Morals*: "One person takes pride in gold, another in eloquence, another in base and earthly things, another in exalted and heavenly virtues."[41] Therefore, pride as love of one's own excellence is not a special kind of sin.

4. It likewise seems that pride as signifying contempt of God is not sin in general, since those who sin out of weakness or ignorance do not sin out of contempt. But many who sin mortally sin out of weakness or ignorance. Therefore, not every mortal sin is committed out of contempt of God, and so pride as signifying contempt of God is not sin in general.

5. Good in general, not a particular good, is the contrary of evil in general. But the particular good consisting of reverence for God, which belongs particularly to the gift of religious fear, is the contrary of contempt for God. Therefore, contempt of God is not sin in general and so not pride as signifying contempt of God. And so the aforementioned distinction does not avail.

6. What completes every sin in the aspect of wickedness is sin in general. But pride is such, as Gregory says in his *Commentary on Ezekiel*.[42] Therefore, pride is sin in general.

7. We distinguish sins by their objects, just as we distinguish virtues. But pride has the same object as other sins. For example, pride has the same object as envy, which in seeking a person's own excellence grieves at the good of another, and the same object as vainglory, which seeks a person's excellence in courting human favor, and the same object as anger, which seeks vengeance, which belongs to an excellence of victory. Therefore, pride is not a special kind of sin distinct from other sins.

8. That without which there can be no sin is common to all sins. But pride is such, for Augustine says in his work *On Nature and Grace* that you will not find any sin without the name of pride.[43] And Prosper says in his work *On the Contemplative Life* that there neither can nor could nor will be able to be any sin without pride.[44] Therefore, pride is sin in general.

---

39. *Morals* XXXIV, 23, n. 48 (PL 76:744D).
40. *On the Supreme Good* II, 17, n. 3 (PL 83:639C).
41. *Morals* XXXIV, 23, n. 49 (PL 76:745C).
42. Actually, *Morals* XXXIV, 23, n. 48 (PL76:744D).
43. *On Nature and Grace* 29 (PL 44:263).
44. Pseudo Prosper (Julian Pomerius), *On the Contemplative Life* III, 2, n. 2 (PL 59:476B).

9. What is convertible with every sin is sin in general. But pride is such. For Augustine says in his work *On Nature and Grace* that "as to be proud is to sin, so to sin is to be proud."[45] Therefore, pride is sin in general.

10. On Sir. 10:14, "The origin of sin by human beings is apostasy from God," a gloss says: "There is no greater apostasy than to withdraw from God, which we rightly call pride."[46] But those who sin mortally withdraw from God. Therefore, they are proud, and so pride is sin in general.

11. On the same text, another gloss says: "Let us beware covetousness and pride, which are one thing, not two things."[47] Therefore, pride is not a special kind of sin distinct from other sins.

12. On Job 33:17, "To turn human beings from evil," etc., a gloss says: "To be proud against the creator is to transgress his commands by sinning."[48] But those who sin transgress God's commands. For Augustine says in his work *Against Faustus* that "sin consists of a word or deed or desire contrary to the eternal law."[49] Therefore, those who sin are proud, and every sin is pride.

13. Anselm says that the soul necessarily seeks its own good.[50] And what necessarily happens is not sin. Therefore, pride is not a sin and so not a special kind of sin.

14. If pride were to be a special kind of sin, it would be one of the seven chief sins. But Isidore in his work *On the Supreme Good* does not list pride among the seven chief sins and lists vainglory in its place.[51] Therefore, pride is not a special kind of sin.

15. Augustine says in his work *On Free Choice* that pride is the love of one's own good.[52] But this is common to every sin. Therefore, pride is sin in general.

16. What is the formal element in every sin is not a special kind of sin. But pride is such. For Augustine says in his work *On Free Choice* that to sin is to spurn the immutable good and to embrace transitory goods.[53] And the former, namely, spurning the immutable good, belongs to the turning away from God that is the formal element in every sin, just as the turning toward God, which is accomplished by charity, is the formal element in virtues. And spurning God belongs to pride. Therefore, it seems that pride is sin in general.

17. Nothing ordained by God is a sin. But God ordains pride. For on Is. 60:15, "I shall put you in a condition of everlasting pride," a gloss of Jerome says that there is good and evil pride.[54] And in Prov. 8:18, the wisdom of God says: "Riches and glory, proud riches and justice, are with me." Therefore, pride is not a special kind of sin.

45. *On Nature and Grace* 29 (PL 44:263).
46. *Ordinary Gloss*, on Sir. 10:14.
47. Ibid.
48. Ibid., on Job 33:17.
49. *Against Faustus* XXII, 27 (PL 42:418).
50. *On the Fall of the Devil* 13 (PL 158:345D).
51. *On the Supreme Good* IV, 40, n. 2 (PL 83:1178D).
52. *On Free Choice* III, 24, n. 72 (PL 32:1307).
53. Ibid., I, 6, n. 35 (PL 32:1240).
54. *Ordinary Gloss*, on Is. 60:10.

On the Contrary:

1. Augustine says in his work *On Nature and Grace*: "Let a person seek, and the person will find that according to the law of God, pride is a sin very different from other sins."[55]

2. Augustine says in the same place that many things are done wickedly but not with pride.[56] Therefore, pride is not sin in general.

3. No other sin is prior to sin in general. But another sin is prior to pride, for Sir. 10:14 says: "The origin of pride in human beings is apostasy from God." Therefore, pride is not sin in general.

4. Every sin on a par with other sins is a special kind of sin. But pride is such, as 1 Jn. 2:16 makes clear: "Everything belonging to the world is lust of the flesh or lust of the eyes or pride of life." Therefore, pride is a special kind of sin.

5. Every sin involving a particular act is a particular kind of sin. But pride is such. For as Augustine says in his work *On Nature and Grace*,[57] we need be wary only of pride in good deeds. And Gregory says that the first pride withdraws from God, the last returns.[58] Therefore, pride is a special kind of sin.

6. What we predicate as a superlative belongs to only one thing. But pride is the greatest sin, as a gloss says on Ps. 19:13, "I shall be washed clean of the greatest sin."[59] Therefore, pride is a special kind of sin.

Answer:

To answer this question, we need to perceive what a sin of pride is, so that we can afterward perceive if it be a special kind of sin.

Therefore, we should consider that every sin is based on a natural appetite. And human beings by every natural appetite seek likeness to God, inasmuch as every good naturally desired is a likeness of God's goodness. Therefore, Augustine, speaking to God, says in his *Confessions*: "The soul commits fornication," namely, in sinning, "when it is turned away from you and seeks apart from you what it cannot find pure and clean except when it returns to you."[60] But it belongs to reason to direct appetites, and especially insofar as the law of God informs reason. Therefore, an appetite will be morally right and virtuous if the appetite is borne to a naturally desired good by the rule of reason, and there will be sin whether the appetite exceeds the rule of reason or falls short of it. For example, the desire to know is natural to human beings, and so it will be virtuous and praiseworthy if human beings strive for knowledge as right reason dictates. And there will be the sin of excessive striving for knowledge if one exceeds the rule of reason, and there will be the sin of negligence if one strives too little for knowledge.

And one of the things that human beings naturally desire is excellence. For it is natural for both human beings and everything to seek in desired goods the perfection that consists of a certain excellence. Therefore, the will will indeed be morally right and

---

55. *On Nature and Grace* 29 (PL 44:257).
56. Ibid. (PL 44:263).
57. Ibid., 32 (PL 44:265).
58. Actually, Peter Lombard, *Gloss*, on Ps. 19:13 (PL 191:213D).
59. Ibid., on Ps. 19:13 (PL 191:214A).
60. *Confessions* II, 6, n. 14 (PL 32:681).

belong to loftiness of spirit if it seeks excellence in accord with the rule of reason informed by God. Just so, the Apostle says in 2 Cor. 10:13: "And we do not glory in something beyond our measure," as if in the measure of another, "but by the measure by which God has measured us." And one will incur the sin of pusillanimity if one should fall short of the rule of reason. And there will be the sin of pride if one should exceed the rule, as the very name "pride" [Latin: *superbia*] demonstrates, since to be proud is simply to exceed the proper measure in the desire for excellence. And so Augustine says in the *City of God* that pride is "the appetite for perverse eminence."[61] And because not all things have the same measure, something that would be imputed to one person as pride may not be so imputed to another. For example, we do not impute pride to a bishop if he happens to perform functions belonging to his excellent state, but we would impute pride to an ordinary priest if he were to attempt to perform functions reserved to a bishop. Therefore, pride is evidently a special kind of sin if excellence has the proper nature of a particular desirable object, although materially present in many things. For we specifically distinguish acts and habits by the formal aspects of their objects. And so also Augustine, specifically assigning to individual sins their proper objects, in the desire for which our acts faintly represent likeness to God, speaks thus of pride when he addresses God: "Pride mimics eminence, since you are a God exalted above all things."[62]

But pride may be sin in general in two ways: indeed in one way by diffusion; in a second way by its effects.

Regarding the first way, we should consider what Augustine says in the *City of God*.[63] He says that as the love of God produces the city of God, so disordered love of self produces the city of Babylon. And he says that as God himself is the ultimate end in his love, and all things loved with a proper love are ordained for him, so we find that the excellence in loving him is the ultimate end for which all other things are ordained. For those who seek to abound in riches or knowledge or honors or anything else strive for an excellence through all such things. And we should consider regarding all skills and practical habits that the skill or habit to which their end belongs governs the movements of the skills or habits regarding the means to achieve the end. For example, the skill of piloting, to which navigation, that is, the end of piloting, belongs, governs the skill of shipbuilding, and we can see the same thing regarding all skills. And so also charity, that is, love of God, governs all the other virtues. And so charity, although it is a special virtue if we should consider its proper object, is nonetheless common to all the virtues by reason of the diffusion of its governance. And so we call charity the form and mother of all the virtues. And likewise, pride, although it is a special kind of sin by reason of its proper object, is nonetheless a sin common to all sins by reason of the diffusion of its governance. And so also we call pride the root and queen of all sins, as Gregory makes clear in his work *Morals*.[64]

And regarding the second way, we should note that we can consider every sin regarding both the person's intent and the sin's effect. For there may sometimes be a sin as

---

61. *City of God* XIV, 28 (PL 41:420).
62. *Confessions* II, 6, n. 13 (PL 32:680).
63. *City of God* XIV, 28 (PL 41:436).
64. *Morals* XXXI, 45, n. 87 (PL 76:620–21).

to its effect but not as to the person's intent. For example, if one should kill one's father thinking the father to be an enemy, the person indeed commits the sin of patricide as to the sin's effect but not as to the person's intent. And it has also been said of certain Milesians that "they are indeed not simpletons, but they act like simpletons."[65] Therefore, if we should understand the sin of pride by its effect, it is common to every sin, since it is an effect of pride that one refuses to be subject to the rule of a superior, which every sinner does insofar as the sinner does not subject himself or herself to the law of God. But if we should consider the sin of pride regarding the sinner's intent, the sin of pride does not always belong to every sin, since sinners do not always commit particular sins out of actual contempt of God or his law. Rather, they sometimes commit sins out of ignorance and sometimes out of weakness or because of an emotional state. And so Augustine says in his work *On Nature and Grace* that the sin of pride is distinct from other sins.[66]

Replies to the Objections:

1. Pride extinguishes all the virtues and weakens all the powers of the soul by the diffusion of its governance, as I have said.[67]

2. To prefer one's own will to the will of a superior is indeed an act of pride but does not always arise from an intent to be proud, as I have said.[68]

3. Pride has its own matter if we understand by pride the formal character of its object, as I have said,[69] although this character can be in every kind of thing. Similarly, loftiness of spirit is a special kind of virtue and yet strives for greatness in every virtuous act, as the Philosopher says in the *Ethics*.[70]

4. Pride, insofar as it signifies intentional contempt of God, cannot be sin in general. Rather, such pride is an even a more particular kind of sin than pride as signifying the desire for perverse eminence, since there can be a desire for perverse eminence both if one should contemn God and if one should contemn a human being. But if we should understand pride as contempt of God by reason of its effect, then there is pride in every sin, even those committed out of weakness or ignorance, as I have said.[71]

5. As pride, although a special kind of sin, belongs to every sin by reason of its diffusion and effect, so also fear of God, although a special gift, can belong to every virtuous act in the same ways.

6. Pride complements all the cited sins by reason of their wickedness, not that pride is essentially every kind of wickedness but that pride is wickedness in the two aforementioned ways.[72]

7. Envy, vainglory, and anger do not have the same object as pride, and the objects of envy, vainglory, and anger are subordinated to the object of pride as their end. For

---

65. Cf. Aristotle, *Ethics* VII, 8 (1151a9–10).
66. *On Nature and Grace* 29 (PL 44:263).
67. In the answer.
68. Ibid.
69. Ibid.
70. *Ethics* IV, 3 (1123b30).
71. In the answer.
72. Ibid.

envy is chagrined at a neighbor's good, and vainglory seeks praise, and anger seeks vengeance, so that one gain a pre-eminence through such means. And we can conclude from
this that pride governs envy, vainglory, and anger, not that pride is the same thing, as
what I have said makes clear.[73]

8. We understand the cited authorities to mean pride as regards its effect, without
which there can be no sin, and not as regards the intention to be proud.

9. We need to say the same in reply to objection 9, since pride as regards its effect is
then convertible with sin. But one can say in reply to objections 8 and 9 that Augustine
in his work *On Nature and Grace* introduces those words as the words of another person,
against whom he is arguing, and not as his own opinion. And so also he afterward rejects them, saying that one does not always sin out of pride.[74]

10. Withdrawal from God is pride as regards pride's effect.

11. We need to reply to objection 11 in the same way, since to transgress God's commands by sinning is to be proud as regards pride's effect but not as regards the sinner's
intent.

12. If we should understand pride as it belongs to every sin by pride's effect, then
pride is simply turning away from the immutable good, and covetousness turning toward a transitory good. And one sin is constituted by these two turnings as the formal
and material elements, since every sin is a turning away from the immutable good and a
turning toward a transitory good.

13. There may be sin in desiring the soul's own good if there is a withdrawal from
the rule of reason, as I have said.[75]

14. Gregory in his work *Morals* likewise does not list pride as one of the chief sins,
but he does list it as the queen and root of all sins insofar as it diffuses its governance to
all sins.[76] And the latter does not preclude pride being a special kind of sin.

15. Disordered love of one's own good belongs generally to all sins and so also belongs to pride insofar as what belongs to a genus belongs to its species. But we can say
that pride is in a strict sense love of one's own good if we understand what we call "one's
own" with a precision, namely, in such a way that one loves one's own good not as if a
good belonging to a superior. And this way of loving one's own good belongs in a strict
sense to pride; in other words, in such a way that one does not acknowledge that one's
own good comes from another.

16. The argument of this objection is valid about pride as regards its effect, since
we in such a way spurn the immutable good in every sin, but not as regards the sinner's
intent.

17. We can call something pride in one way because it exceeds the rule of reason, and
then pride is always a sin. And people commonly so understand pride. We can call
something pride in a second way because it exceeds something else, and then pride can
be good, as Jerome says. For example, such would be the case if one wishes to perform
works of the evangelical counsels, which surpass the general works of the command-

---

73. Ibid.
74. *On Nature and Grace* 29 (PL 44:263).
75. In the answer.
76. *Morals* XXXI, 45, n. 87 (PL76:620–21).

ments. Or one can say that, by the words "I shall put you in a condition of everlasting pride," we understand pride in a material sense, that is, "I shall give you great excellence, of which worldly persons are proud." And we can similarly understand the words "proud riches," that is, the riches about which persons are usually proud.

Third Article

Does Pride Belong to Irascible Power?

It seems that pride does not, for the following reasons:

1. Since irascible power belongs to sense appetites, movements of such power are necessarily emotions because the soul's emotions are the movements of sense appetites. But pride does not seem to consist of any emotion belonging to irascible power, no emotion of fear or daring or hope or despair or anger. Therefore, pride does belong to irascible power.

2. Since irascible power belongs to the sensory part of the soul, the object of irascible power can only be a sensibly perceptible good. But pride seeks pre-eminence in both perceptible goods and immaterial and purely intelligible goods, as Gregory says in his work *Morals*.[77] Therefore, irascible power cannot be the subject to which pride belongs.

3. Devils have no sensory part of the soul, since they have no body. Therefore, if pride were to belong to irascible power, then devils could not have pride. And this conclusion is obviously false.

4. Pride in the strict sense is contempt of God. But irascible power cannot attain such an object, that is, God, since irascible power is power of the sensory soul. Therefore, irascible power is not the subject to which pride belongs.

5. Avicenna defines irascible power as the power that moves to repel or destroy the harmful, seeking to vanquish it.[78] But this does not belong to pride, since pride strives to excel in what is good, not to repel the harmful. Therefore, pride does not belong to irascible power.

6. Pride causes envy. But envy belongs to concupiscible power, since envy consists of "hatred of another's happiness."[79] Therefore, pride does not belong to irascible power.

7. Pride seems to belong to the power of reason, not to irascible power. For Gregory, designating four kinds of pride, says in his work *Morals*: "There are four kinds of pride that manifest the inflated egos of the arrogant: either when they judge that they have their goodness from themselves, or when if they believe that goodness has been given to them from above, they think that they have received it because of their merits, or surely when they boast of having what they do not have, or when, in despising others, they desire to appear to have in a singular way what they have."[80] But all of these things, namely,

77. *Morals* XXXIV, 23, n. 49 (PL 76:745C).
78. Thomas himself, *De anima* I, 5.
79. *Expositions on the Psalms*, on Ps. 105:25, n. 17 (PL 37:1399).
80. *Morals* XXIII, 6, n. 13 (PL 76:258C).

judging, thinking, believing, and comparing themselves to others, belong to reason. Therefore, pride belongs to reason.

8. Prov. 11:2 says: "Where there is humility, there is wisdom." But wisdom belongs to reason. Therefore, humility also does. Therefore, pride, which is the contrary of humility, also does, since contraries are by nature constituted to belong to the same kind of thing.

9. Bernard in his work *On the Degrees of Humility* says that the perfection of humility consists of knowledge of truth.[81] But knowledge of truth belongs to reason. Therefore, humility belongs to reason. Therefore, pride also does.

10. The Philosopher says in the *Ethics* that the proud person pretends to be brave.[82] But pretension belongs to reason, since to pretend is to represent, which belongs only to reason, as the Philosopher says in the *Poetics*.[83] Therefore, pride belongs to reason.

11. A gloss on Hab. 2:5, "How wine deceives the tippler," says that pride first makes a person believe loftier things about self.[84] But believing is an act of reason. Therefore, the first act of pride belongs to reason. Therefore, pride itself belongs to reason.

12. Ambrose says on Ps. 119:1, "Blessed are the blameless," that only the law of God can repel the powerful movements of pride.[85] But the law of God belongs to reason. Therefore, the pride that it repels also does.

13. Gregory says in his work *Morals* that pride is the queen of all sins.[86] But ruling belongs to reason. Therefore, pride belongs to reason.

14. A gloss on Jer. 49:16, "Your pride and your arrogance," etc., says: "Pride, not error, produces the heretic."[87] But heresy belongs to reason. Therefore, pride also does.

15. Augustine says in his work *On the Trinity* that sin belongs to lower reason insofar as higher reason does not restrain it, or even insofar as higher reason consents to it.[88] And so it seems that the first sin belongs to higher reason. But pride is the first sin. Therefore, pride belongs to higher reason.

16. Augustine says,[89] and the *Decretum*[90] maintains, that pride is a movement to obtain what justice forbids. But justice belongs to reason, since reason obliges human beings to render to others their due. Therefore, pride belongs to reason.

17. Augustine says,[91] and the *Decretum*[92] maintains: "God would never bring destruction on vessels of his wrath unless he were to find voluntary sins in them." But we call things subject to the command of reason voluntary. Therefore, since vessels of

81. *On the Degrees of Humility* 2, nn. 3 and 5 (PL 182:943A).
82. *Ethics* III, 7 (1115b29–30).
83. Actually, Averroes, *Explanation of the Poetics* (Minio-Paluello [Averroes]:44–45).
84. *Ordinary Gloss* and *Interlinear Gloss*, on Hab. 2:5.
85. *Exposition on Ps. 119*, sermon 7, n. 10 (PL 15:1283D).
86. *Morals* XXXI, 45, n. 87 (PL 76:620D).
87. *Interlinear Gloss*, on Jer. 49:16.
88. *On the Trinity* XII, 12, n. 17 (PL 42:1007).
89. *On Two Souls* 11 (PL 42:105).
90. *Decretum*, c. 15, q. 1, part 1, n. 5 (Friedberg I:745).
91. Actually, Fulgentius, *To Monimus* I, 26 (PL 65:174A).
92. *Decretum*, c. 23, q. 4, chap. 23 (Friedberg I:907).

his wrath especially incur destruction because of pride, it seems that pride belongs to reason.

18. Seneca says in a letter that the highest good of human beings consists of the rational.[93] But the rational is the power that pride corrupts, as I have said.[94] Therefore, pride likewise belongs to reason, not irascible power.

19. It seems that pride belongs to the will, not to irascible power, since a gloss on Mt. 3:15, "Thus it becomes us to fulfill all justice," adds: "That is, perfect humility."[95] But justice belongs to the will. Therefore, humility also does.

20. The desire for honor seems especially to belong to pride. But desiring honors belongs to the will. Therefore, pride belongs to the will.

21. To be proud is to be exalted, and so it seems that pride especially belongs to a higher power that transcends other powers. But transcending other powers belongs to the will, which moves all the other powers. Therefore, pride seems to belong to the will and not to irascible power.

22. It seems that pride belongs to concupiscible power, for Prosper says in his work *Sentences Derived from Augustine* that "pride is love of one's own excellence."[96] But love belongs to concupiscible power. Therefore, pride also does.

23. Seeking joys and avoiding sorrows belong to pride, according to Augustine.[97] But these things belong to concupiscible power. Therefore, pride belongs to concupiscible power.

24. It belongs to pride to take pleasure in one's own goodness. But this belongs to concupiscible power. Therefore, pride seems to belong to concupiscible, not irascible, power.

On the Contrary:

1. Gregory in his work *Morals* designates the gift of fear of God the contrary of pride.[98]

2. Augustine says in the *City of God* that pride is "the desire for perverse eminence."[99] But the difficult is the object of irascible power. Therefore, pride belongs to irascible power.

3. Pusillanimity seems to be the vice contrary to pride. But pusillanimity, like loftiness of spirit, belongs to irascible power. Therefore, pride also belongs to irascible power.

Answer:

To answer this question, we need first to consider to which power of the soul sin or virtue can belong, so that we can consider to which power of the soul, as subject, pride belongs.

---

93. *Moral Letters* IX, letter 5:9.
94. A. 2.
95. *Ordinary Gloss*, on Mt. 3:15.
96. Prosper of Aquitaine, *Sentences Derived from Augustine*, 294 (PL 51:471B).
97. Actually, Bernard, *On the Degrees of Humility* 12, n. 40 (PL 182:963C).
98. *Morals* II, 49, n. 77 (PL 75:593A).
99. *City of God* XIV, 13, n.1 (PL 41:420).

Therefore, we should consider that every virtuous or sinful act is voluntary. And we have two sources of voluntary acts, namely, reason or intellect, and will, since these are two causes of movement, as the *De anima* says,[100] and especially causes of movement regarding the proper acts of human beings. And reason, since it is cognitive, differs from the will in that the activity of reason and every cognitive power is actualized by the known object belonging to the knowing subject. For the intellect actually understanding is the object actually understood, and the senses actually perceiving are the objects actually perceived. But the activity of appetitive powers consists of the desiring subject being moved to the object desired. And it evidently belongs in the strict sense to pride that one inclines to one's own excellence inordinately, by magnifying oneself, as it were, as Ps. 10:18 says: "To judge in favor of the orphan and lowly, so that human beings do not presume to magnify themselves further over the earth." And so pride evidently belongs to an appetitive power.

And since a cognitive power in one respect moves an appetitive power, inasmuch as a known good moves an appetite, we need to distinguish appetitive powers by the different ways of knowing. We need to do so because things acted upon are proportioned to the things acting upon them and to the causes of the movements, and we distinguish powers by their objects. And there is a power to know universals, namely, the intellect or reason, and a power to know singulars, namely, the external senses and imagination. And so there are two kinds of appetitive powers: one belonging to the rational part of the soul, the one we call the will, and the other belonging to the sensory power of the soul, the one we call sensuality or sense appetite.

Therefore, the rational appetite, that is, the will, has good in general as its own formal object and is not divided into several powers. And sense appetites attain particular aspects of perceptible or imaginable goods, not the universal nature of good. And so we need to distinguish sense appetites by the particular aspects of such goods. For things have the nature of being desirable because they are pleasurable to the senses, and they are in this respect the object of concupiscible power. And other things have the nature of being desirable because animals imagine them to have an excellence enabling the animals to repel everything harmful and use their powers to enjoy their good. And such desirable goods indeed completely lack sensory pleasure and are sometimes even accompanied by physical pain, as when animals fight in order to survive. And we understand the object of irascible power by this aspect of imagined goods. And every particular is obviously included in the universal, although the converse is not true. And so the will can be borne to whatever the irascible and concupiscible powers can be borne, and to many other things. But the will is borne to its object without emotion, since the will does not have any bodily organ, although the irascible and concupiscible powers are borne to their objects accompanied by emotions. And so all the movements of the irascible and concupiscible powers accompanied by emotions, such as the emotions of love, joy, hope, and the like, can belong to the will but without emotion.

And it is clear from what I have said before that the object of pride is excellence.[101] Therefore, if only the excellence of perceptible or imaginable things belongs to pride, we would need to hold that pride belongs only to irascible power. But pride also regards

100. Aristotle, *De anima* III, 10 (433a13–18).
101. A. 2.

intelligible excellence, which belongs to spiritual goods, as Gregory says in his work *Morals*,[102] and pride in addition belongs even to purely spiritual substances, in which there are no sense appetites. Therefore, we need to say that pride belongs both to irascible power, insofar as pride regards a perceptible or imaginable excellence, and also to the will, insofar as pride regards an intelligible excellence, and insofar as devils have pride.

Replies to the Objections:

1. Pride is the inordinate desire for pre-eminence. And so hope is related to a difficult future good as desire is related to good absolutely considered. And so it is clear that pride chiefly regards hope, which is an irascible emotion, since presumption, which is inordinate hope, also seems especially to belong to pride.

2. The pride that regards intelligible excellence belongs to the will, not to irascible power, as I have said.[103] And yet intelligible excellence sometimes results in an imagined effect, with respect to which pride can belong to irascible power. For example, such would be the case if persons are praised for the excellence of their knowledge or receive some sensibly perceptible honor.

3. The pride of devils, although it does not belong to an irascible power, nonetheless belongs to the will, as I have said.[104]

4. Things are objects in two ways. There is one object considered as the terminus at which an action is directed, and God cannot be such an object of irascible power. There is an object in a second way considered as the terminus from which an action originates, and then what is contemned is the object of the very act of contempt. And nothing prevents God being the object of irascible power in the latter way, namely, insofar as irascible power, unrestrained by reverence for God, is borne to its own object.

5. We designate irascible power, although the subject of many emotions, from anger as the ultimate emotion. And so Avicenna designates irascible power only by the emotion of anger and not other emotions.

6. Envy belongs to concupiscible, not irascible, power, since there is chagrin at the good of another, and sadness, like pleasure, belongs to concupiscible power, and hate and love belong to the same kind of power. But if envy were to belong to irascible power, pride would not on that account be prevented from belonging to irascible power, since pride causes envy. For nothing prevents one act or emotion of a power causing another act or emotion of the same power, as, for example, love causes desire, although both belong to concupiscible power.

7. An act can belong to a sin in three ways: in one way directly; in the second way antecedently; in the third way as a consequence. For example, the desire for vengeance indeed belongs directly and essentially to anger, and resentment over an injury inflicted belongs to anger antecedently, and pleasure over the punishment of the one who inflicted the injury belongs to anger as a consequence. Therefore, the intemperate desire for excellence indeed belongs to pride directly and quasi-essentially. And the judgment that

---

102. *Morals* XXXIV, 23, n. 49 (PL 76:745C).
103. In the answer.
104. Ibid.

one is so great that such excellence is due to oneself belongs to pride antecedently. And that one proceeds from such a judgment and desire to ostentatious words and deeds belongs to pride as a result of pride. And of these three, the first belongs to irascible power, and the other two to reason, since the cognition of reason precedes the movement of desire, and the command of reason regarding external execution results from the very desire.

8. We find humility and wisdom in the same individuals insofar as humility disposes them to wisdom, since those who are humble subject themselves to the wise in order to learn and do not rely on their own perceptions. But wisdom and humility need not belong to the same part of the soul, since what belongs to the soul's lower part can dispose one toward what belongs to the higher part. For example, good imagination disposes one to acquire knowledge.

9. Knowledge of truth is related antecedently to humility, since persons do not exalt themselves beyond their measure as long as they are mindful of the truth.

10. Pretense is related to pride as a consequence. For the consequence of desiring one's pre-eminence is that one shows oneself externally to be such that one excels in some way in comparison to others.

11. We say that thinking lofty thoughts about oneself is the first act of pride because it precedes the desire for pre-eminence.

12. Reason insofar as it governs lower powers and moves them draws them away from inordinate movements. And so the law of God insofar as it belongs to reason excludes pride effectively, as a painter excludes blackness, not indeed formally, as blackness excludes whiteness, for then the law of God and pride would have the same subject. And so pride does not need to belong to reason, to which the law of God belongs.

13. Gregory says that pride is the queen of other sins insofar as it diffuses its commands to all the other sins because of the ordination of its end for the ends of other sins, not because it belongs to reason.

14. The cited authority proves that heresy is an effect of pride. And nothing prevents what belongs to one power of the soul having an effect on another power of the soul.

15. Augustine says the first sin belongs to reason antecedently and to desire essentially, namely, insofar as appetitive powers incline toward something illicit, or a judgment of reason restrains them from it.

16. Sin belongs to a lower power of the soul because the lower power withdraws from the rectitude of reason. And so if justice belongs to reason in one respect, reason need not on that account be the subject to which every sin essentially belongs.

17. The cited authorities say that sin is voluntary or spontaneous both when the will elicits the sinful act, and when the will, which commands the acts of lower powers, commands it. And so nothing prevents a voluntary sin belonging to a lower power of the soul.

18. Socrates held that all virtues are certain kinds of knowledge, as the *Ethics* says.[105] And so he and the Stoics,[106] who agreed with him on this, held that all virtues belong essentially to reason. But because moral virtue directly perfects appetitive powers rather than reason itself, we should more accurately say, as Aristotle does, that moral virtues

---

105. Aristotle, *Ethics* VI, 13 (1144b29–30).
106. E.g., Seneca. See n. 93 above.

belong to appetitive powers, which are rational by participation insofar as the commands of reason move them.[107]

19. Every virtue is justice in one respect, insofar as justice ordains us to obey the law, as the *Ethics* says.[108] And so although justice belongs to the will, we nonetheless need not say that all virtues, which receive the name of justice in the cited way, belong to reason or the will, since reason and the will can also move other powers of the soul.

20. To receive perceptible or imaginary honors insofar as they have the nature of the difficult or excellent belongs both to the will and to irascible power.

21. To be proud is to be exalted by exceeding one's own measure, which can belong both to higher and lower powers.

22. All the emotions of irascible power originate from love, which is an emotion of concupiscible power, and terminate in pleasure or sadness, which also belong to concupiscible power. And so nothing prevents things belonging to concupiscible power, if they be attributed antecedently or consequently to pride, which belongs to irascible power.

23 and 24. The foregoing makes clear the answers to objections 23 and 24.

Fourth Article

Does Gregory Appropriately Assign Four Species of Pride?

Gregory assigns four species of pride, saying: "There are indeed four species that manifest the inflated egos of the arrogant: either when they judge that they have their goodness from themselves, or when if they believe that their goodness has been given to them from above, they think that they have received it because of their merits, or surely when they boast that they have what they do not have, or when, despising others, they desire to appear to have in a singular way what they have."[109] And it seems that Gregory inappropriately does so, for the following reasons:

1. Judging that one has one's goodness from oneself, not from another, belongs to unbelief, since correct belief holds that God causes all good. Therefore, we ought to hold that judging one has goodness from oneself is a species of error or unbelief rather than a species of pride.

2. Of all the goods we have in this life, the good of grace, even about which some may be proud, is the most powerful. But to believe that grace is given to human beings because of their merits belongs to the heresy of the Pelagians. Therefore, we ought not designate as a species of pride that persons believe that God has because of their merits given to them what they have.

3. To boast that one has what one does not have belongs to lying, which is a different sin than pride. Therefore, we ought not designate such boasting a species of pride.

---

107. *Ethics* VI, 13 (1144b28–30).
108. Aristotle, *Ethics* V, 1 (1129b29–31).
109. *Morals* XXIII, 6, n. 13 (PL 76:258C).

4. Wishing to be noticed belongs to vainglory, which is the daughter of pride, not pride, as Gregory says in his work *Morals*.[110] Therefore, we ought not designate as a species of pride that one wishes to be noticed in a singular way.

5. Jerome says that nothing is so proud as to seem ungrateful.[111] But Gregory does not list ingratitude among the four species of pride. Therefore, it seems that Gregory insufficiently enumerates the species of pride.

6. Augustine says in the *City of God* that to excuse oneself from a sin one has committed belongs to pride.[112] But Gregory does not list such among the species of pride. Therefore, Gregory insufficiently deals with the species of pride.

7. It seems especially to belong to pride that one presumptuously strive to acquire something above oneself. But Gregory does not mention this among the four species of pride. Therefore, it seems that he insufficiently deals with the species of pride.

On the Contrary:
The cited authority of Gregory suffices.

Answer:
A unified and integral cause causes good, and individual defects cause evil, as Dioynisius says in his work *On the Divine Names*.[113] For example, beauty results because all parts of the body are becomingly disposed, and ugliness will result if even one of them is unbecomingly disposed. Therefore, it belongs to virtue that the rule of reason and the measure of the will convey the will of human beings to an excellence, and the evil of pride consists of a person who desires an excellent good exceeding the person's due measure. And so there are as many species of pride as there may be ways of exceeding one's due measure in the desire for one's own excellence.

And this happens in three ways. It happens in one way regarding the excellent good itself that one desires, namely, as when one's desire is borne to something that exceeds one's measure. And this corresponds to the third species of pride, namely, when one boasts that one has what one does not. It happens in a second way regarding the way of obtaining the good, namely, that one attributes to oneself or one's merits an excellence that one can obtain only by the favor of another. And then we understand the first two species of pride, since something can be from us in two ways, either absolutely, as when we do something, or by some preparation for it, as when we merit something. In the third way, one can exceed one's due measure regarding the way one possesses an excellence, namely, as one affects to have something above others that it belongs to the person to have in the same way as others do.

Replies to the Objections:
1. The judgment of reason is corrupted in two ways: in one way regarding a universal proposition; in the second way regarding a particular proposition because of an emotion.

---

110. Ibid., XXXI, 45, n. 87 (PL 76:621A).

111. *Letter* 148, n. 4 (PL 22:1206).

112. *City of God* XIV, 14 (PL 41:422).

113. *On the Divine Names* 4, n. 30 (PG 3:729C).

Therefore, corruption of judgment regarding things that belong to faith or good morals belongs to the sin of heresy if the corruption should indeed regard a universal proposition, but not if the corruption should regard a particular proposition because of emotion, as Prov. 14:22 says: "All who do evil err." For example, one who were to hold as a universal proposition that fornication is not a sin would lack faith, but we do not think that a fornicator who chooses fornication as good because of a lustful emotion lacks faith. And likewise it would pertain to heresy if one were to judge universally that God does not cause every good, or that the good of grace is due to one's merits. But it would not belong to heresy if the judgment of reason is corrupted regarding a particular proposition because of an inordinate love of excellence that originates in inordinate desires, so that one imagines that one can have some good from oneself or from one's own merits. And such belongs to pride.

2. The foregoing makes clear the reply to objection 2.

3. We do not designate boasting a species of pride regarding the external act itself, which is related to pride as a consequence, as I have said.[114] But we designate boasting a species of pride regarding the internal desire from which such an external act derives, namely, when human beings imagine themselves to have what they do not, and their will strives for such excellence, which is appropriate for them only if they were to have what they do not.

4. Even wishing to be noticed in a singular way belongs to pride as a consequence. But the fourth species of pride essentially consists of human beings imagining themselves to excel all others in a singular way, and their will is moved to such excellence.

5. The first two species of pride belong to ingratitude, since persons who do not acknowledge that a benefit has been gratuitously bestowed on them, or who judge that they have obtained a benefit due to their merits, are ungrateful.

6. We understand that to lack evil belongs to the nature of good, as the Philosopher says.[115] And so as it belongs to the third species of pride that one should boast that one has what one does not, so also it belongs to that species that one excuses oneself from a sin that one has committed.

7. The sin of pride sometimes seems more evident by reason of its antecedents and consequences than by reason of that of which it essentially consists. And so Gregory assigns species of pride by certain antecedent and consequent acts, although all species of pride consist essentially of a presumption of the soul.

---

114. A. 3.
115. *Ethics* V, 1 (1129b8–9).

QUESTION IX

On Vainglory

First Article

Is Vainglory a Sin?

It seems that vainglory is not, for the following reasons:

1. Vainglory consists of persons wishing their good deeds to be apparent to others. But this is praiseworthy rather than a sin. For Mt. 5:16 says: "Let your light shine before human beings, so that they see your good works." Therefore, vainglory is not a sin.

2. The desire for vainglory consists of persons seeking that human beings praise their good deeds. But the Apostle in Rom. 12:17 commands this of us: "Provide good deeds both in the sight of God and in the sight of all human beings." Therefore, vainglory is not a sin.

3. Every sin consists of the disorder of a natural appetite. But vainglory does not seek anything that is not naturally desirable, since it is by nature desirable that human beings know truth, and that they themselves be known. Therefore, vainglory is not a sin.

4. Eph. 5:1 says: "Model yourselves on God as his dearly beloved children." But human beings in seeking glory imitate God, who seeks his own glory. Therefore, it seems that seeking glory is not a sin.

5. Seeking what recompenses human beings as their reward is not a sin. But glory is promised human beings as their reward, for Job 22:29 says: "The lowly will be in glory." And Prov. 3:35 says: "The wise will possess glory." Therefore, the desire for glory is not a sin.

6. What arouses virtuous deeds does not seem to be a sin. But the desire for glory is such, for Cicero says in his *Tusculan Disputations*: "Glory inflames everyone to zealous endeavors."[1] Therefore, the desire for glory is not a sin.

7. What the good and the wicked equally desire does not seem to be a sin. But Sallust says in the *Catilinarian War*: "The good and the wicked equally desire glory, honor, and power for themselves."[2] Therefore, the desire for glory is not a sin.

---

1. *Tusculan Disputations* I, 2, n.4.
2. *Catilinarian War* 11, n. 2.

8. Augustine says that vainglory is the judgment of others thinking well of one.[3] But seeking this is not a sin, since "those who neglect their reputation are unfeeling," as he himself says.[4] Therefore, vainglory is not a sin.

9. The object of covetousness is not a sin, although the covetousness itself is, as is evident in the case of money and greed for money. But vainglory is the object of covetousness, as is evident from what Gal. 5:26 says: "Let us not become covetous of vainglory." Therefore, vainglory is not a sin.

10. Sin is contrary to virtue regarding the same matter. But vainglory is not contrary to true glory, since they can belong to the same thing, so it seems. Therefore, vainglory is not a sin.

On the Contrary:

What keeps human beings from faith, which gives access to God, is a sin. But the desire for human vainglory is such, for Jn. 5:44 says: "How can you believe who receive glory from one another and seek not the glory that is from God alone?" Therefore, vainglory is a sin.

Answer:

To answer this question, we first need to perceive what glory is, and second, what vainglory is, and then, third, we shall be able to determine how vainglory is a sin.

Therefore, we should note that, as Augustine says in his his work *On the Gospel of John*,[5] glory signifies a clarity, and so the Gospel understands being glorified and being clarified to be the same. And clarity implies some evidence that makes something apparent and manifest in its splendor, and so glory implies a manifestation of someone's goodness. And if someone's wickedness be manifested, we then call it ignominy rather than glory. And Ambrose on that account says that glory is "clear recognition accompanied by praise."[6]

And we consider glory in three conditions. For in its greatest condition, glory consists of someone's goodness being manifested to the people, since we call clear what all or most people can clearly see. And so also Cicero says that "glory is a persistent good reputation accompanied by praise."[7] And Livy introduces Fabius, who says: "It is not the time for me to glory when I am with only one person."[8] And yet we speak of glory in a second way regarding its condition as the goodness of one person is manifested even to a few or only one person. We also speak of glory in a third way insofar as one's goodness consists of reflecting on it, namely, insofar as one considers one's own goodness under the aspect of its clarity, as something to be manifested to, and admired by, many people. And we accordingly say that one glories when one desires or even takes pleasure in the manifestation of one's own goodness, whether to the people or to a few or to one person or only to one's very self.

3. *City of God* V, 12, n. 4 (PL 41:156).
4. *Sermon* 355, 1, n. 1 (PL 39:1569).
5. *On the Gospel of John*, tr. C, n. 1 (PL 35:1891).
6. Actually, Augustine, *Against Maximinus* II, 13, n. 2 (PL 42:770).
7. *On Invention* II, 55, n. 166.
8. *From the Founding of the City* XXII, 39, n. 9.

And in order to know what vainglory or vainly taking glory is, we should note that we are accustomed to understand vain in three ways. For we sometimes understand vain to mean what lacks subsistence, as we call false things vain. And so Ps. 4:2 says: "Why do you love vanity and seek after lying?" And we sometimes understand vain to mean what lacks solidity or stability, as Eccl. 1:2 says: "Vanity of vanities, and all is vanity," which we say because of the transitory nature of things. And we sometimes call things vain when they do not attain their due end, as we say that a person who did not recover health took medicine in vain. And so Is. 49:4 says: "I have labored in vain, and I have wasted my strength without cause and in vain."

Accordingly, therefore, we can speak of vainglory in three ways. First, we indeed speak of vainglory when one glories in something false, for example, in a good one does not have. And so 1 Cor. 4:7 says: "What do you have that you have not received? And if you have received it, why do you glory as if you have not received it?" Second, we speak of vainglory when one glories in a good that easily passes away, as Is. 40:6 says: "All flesh is grass, and all its glory like the flowers of the field." We speak of vainglory in a third way when the glory of a human being is not subordinated to the human being's proper end. For example, it is natural for human beings to desire knowledge of truth, since this perfects their intellect. But to desire that others know one's goodness is not a desire for one's own perfection. And so such a desire involves a vanity unless it is useful for an end.

And we can laudably ordain such a desire for three things. First, we can indeed ordain such a desire for the glory of God, since manifesting one's goodness glorifies God, to whom as first cause that goodness chiefly belongs. And so Mt. 5:16 says: "Let your light shine before human beings, so that they see your good deeds and glorify your Father who is in heaven." Second, such a desire is useful for the salvation of one's neighbors, who, per-ceiving one's goodness, are drawn to imitate it, as Rom. 15:2 says: "Let all please their neighbors for good in order to build up the community." One can in a third way ordain such a desire for the benefit of oneself, who when considering that others praise one's good deeds, gives thanks for them and persists in them more resolutely. And so also the Apostle often calls to the mind of the Christian faithful their good deeds, that they may more resolutely persist in them.[9]

Therefore, there will be vainglory if one should desire to manifest one's good deeds or even to take pleasure in such manifestation for any reason other than the three just cited. But vainglory in any of the cited ways evidently denotes a disordered desire that constitutes the nature of sin. And so vainglory howsoever understood is sin. And yet vainglory understood in the third way is the most general, for one can in this way vainly glory both in what one has and in what one does not, and in both spiritual and material goods.

Replies to the Objections:

1. The Lord in the cited text commands us to make our good deeds known to others for the glory of God. And so he adds: "That they see your good deeds and glorify your Father who is in heaven."[10] And this is not vainglory.

9. E.g., Rom. 12:17.
10. Mt. 5:16.

2. The Apostle commands that we do good deeds in the sight of human beings for their benefit, and so he adds: "Having peace with everyone, if possible, insofar as it lies within your power."[11] And this aim excludes vainglory.

3. Every perfect thing by nature communicates itself to other things as much as it can, and this belongs to everything because everything imitates the first perfect thing, namely, God, who communicates his goodness to everything. And one's goodness is communicated to others regarding both others' existence and others' knowledge. And so it seems to belong to a natural appetite that one wish one's goodness to become known. Therefore, if one relates this desire to a proper end, it will belong to virtue, and if one does not, it will belong to vanity.

4. To know God's goodness is the ultimate end of a rational creature, since happiness consists of this. And so the glory of God is not to be related to anything else. Rather, it is proper to God himself that rational creatures seek his glory for its very self. But the knowledge of no creature's goodness makes a rational creature happy. And so we should seek no glory of a creature for its own sake but for the sake of something else.

5. True, not vain, glory is promised as a reward, and true glory consists of knowledge of God. And such glory is never sin.

6. Many human beings are stirred to spiritual deeds for the sake of some temporal goods, but the disordered covetousness of temporal goods is not on that account sinless. So also although many perform virtuous deeds for the sake of glory, the disordered desire for glory is not on that account sinless, since we should perform virtuous deeds for their own sake, or rather for God's sake, not for the sake of glory.

7. As Sallust in the cited text adds, "The good strive for glory by the true path,"[12] that is, by virtue. And this is to strive for it in a proper way and not to desire glory vainly.

8. The judgment of those thinking well of one so belongs to vainglory when one desires it without spiritual benefit to others or oneself.

9. Glory insofar as it pertains to those who know our goodness is an object of covetousness. And then it is not a sin, since one can desire it rightly or wrongly. Glory is in another way insofar as it belongs to the covetous appetite itself, and then it has vanity and the nature of sin.

10. True glory and vainglory can belong to the same person but not in the same respect.

Second Article

Is Vainglory a Mortal Sin?

It seems that vainglory is, for the following reasons:

1. Only mortal sin precludes eternal reward. But vainglory precludes eternal reward, for Mt. 6:1 says: "Beware lest you perform your justice in the sight of human beings in order that they notice you; otherwise, you will not have reward with your Father in heaven." Therefore, vainglory is a mortal sin.

11. Rom. 12:18.
12. *Catilinarian War* 11, n. 2.

2. Chrysostom commenting on the same text says of vainglory that "it enters secretly and imperceptibly steals all our interior goods."[13] But only mortal sin takes away interior and spiritual goods. Therefore, vainglory is a mortal sin.

3. Job 31:26–28 says: "If I saw the sun when it were to shine, and the moon when it processes brightly, and my heart rejoiced secretly, and I kissed my hands, this is the greatest evil." And Gregory in his work *Morals* interprets this to mean vainglory.[14] Therefore, vainglory is the greatest sin and mortal sin.

4. Jerome says nothing is so dangerous as the inordinate desire for glory and the sin of boasting and a spirit swollen with consciousness of its own virtues.[15] But what is especially dangerous seems to be mortal. Therefore, vainglory is a mortal sin.

5. [Every capital sin is a mortal sin. But vainglory is a capital sin. Therefore, vainglory is a mortal sin.][16]

6. Whoever steals what is proper to God sins mortally much more than one who steals property belonging to a neighbor. But those who desire vainglory usurp for themselves what is proper to God, for Is. 42:8 says: "I shall not give my glory to another." And 1 Tim. 1:17 says: "To God alone be honor and glory." Therefore, it seems that vainglory is a mortal sin.

7. It seems to be the sin of idolatry that one attribute the glory of God to a creature, as Rom. 1:23 says: "They have transformed the glory of the indestructible God into the likeness of the image of a destructible human being." But those who desire glory seem to desire for themselves what belongs to God, since glory in the strict sense belongs to God, as I have said.[17] Therefore, vainglory is the sin of idolatry. And so it follows that vainglory is a mortal sin.

8. Augustine says in the *City of God* that to contemn glory belongs to great virtue.[18] But great evil is the contrary of great good. Therefore, to desire glory is a great sin.

9. Vainglory seeks to please fellow human beings, since "glory is something that one would not rush to possess if no one were around to know it," according to the Philosopher.[19] But to seek to please fellow human beings is a mortal sin, since it excludes us from the service of Christ, as Gal. 1:10 says: "If I were still to please human beings, I would not be a servant of Christ." Therefore, vainglory is a mortal sin.

10. As form bestows species in the case of things of nature, so the object specifies in moral matters. But things that share in one natural form do not differ specifically. Therefore, in moral matters, things that share in one object do not differ specifically. Therefore, since vainglory has only one object, it seems that it cannot be that some vainglory is a mortal sin, and some vainglory is a venial sin. But some vainglory is evidently a mortal sin. Therefore, all vainglory is a mortal sin.

---

13. *On Matthew*, hom. 19, n. 1 (PG 57:273).

14. *Morals* XXII, 6 (PL 76:218D).

15. *Letter* 78, station 41 (PL 22:722).

16. The text of this objection is missing from the earliest manuscripts, but the Leonine editors have reconstructed it from later printed versions.

17. Objection 6.

18. *City of God* V, 19 (PL 41:165).

19. *Topics* III, 3 (118b21–22).

On the Contrary:

1. A gloss on Mt. 10:14, "Shake the dust from your feet," says: "Dust is the shallowness of earthly knowledge, from which not even the loftiest teachers are immune when they minister to the cares of those subject to them."[20] But what even the loftiest teachers cannot avoid is venial sin. Therefore, the shallowness of earthly knowledge, which belongs especially to vainglory, is a venial sin.

2. Chrysostom says in his *Unfinished Work on Matthew* that while other sins are found in the servants of the devil, vainglory is found in the servants of Christ.[21] But no mortal sin is found in those who serve Christ. Therefore, vainglory is not a mortal sin.

3. A sin of word or deed is more serious than a sin of desire. But not every vanity in deeds or words is a mortal sin. Therefore, we should in no way say that all vainglory that consists of desire is a mortal sin.

Answer:

The answer to the previous question can show the answer to this question. For I have said that we call glory vain when one glories either in something false or something temporal, or when one does not relate one's glory to a proper end.[22]

Therefore, regarding the first two, it is evident that not every vainglory is a mortal sin. For example, no one would say that persons sin mortally who glory in their singing, judging that they sing well when they sing poorly, or who glory in possessing a horse that is a good racer. But there seems to be a more serious cause for doubting about the third way of vainglory. For inasmuch as it is vain for something not to be related to a proper end, it seems that the glory of a human being either is not vain if it is related to God, or it is a mortal sin if it is not related to God and one posits in it the end of one's striving. For then one would enjoy a creature as an end, and one cannot do this without mortal sin.

And so we should consider that it can happen in two ways that an act is not related to God as its end. It happens in one way regarding the act, namely, because the very act is not ordained to that end, and no such disordered act can be related to the ultimate end, whether the sin be mortal or venial. For a disordered act is not a proper means to achieve a good end, just as a false proposition is not a proper means to arrive at true knowledge. It happens in the second way regarding the one who acts, namely, the one whose mind is not actually or habitually ordained to our proper end. For then the act proceeding from such a frame of mind is ordained to something else as the ultimate end, and then the human act not related to God as the ultimate end is a mortal sin. And I am speaking about a mind that is not actually or habitually ordained to our proper end, since it sometimes happens that human beings do not actually ordain their acts for God although the acts of themselves include no disorder by reason of which the acts cannot be related to God. And yet these acts are not only not sins but also meritorious, since the mind of such human beings is habitually related to God as their end.

20. *Ordinary Gloss*, on Mt. 10:14.
21. John Chrysostom (Pseudo), *Unfinished Work on Matthew*, hom. 13 (PG 56:704).
22. A. 1.

Therefore, we need to say that if we should call glory vain because it is not related to God as its end inasmuch as the mind of a human being glorying in something is not actually or habitually turned toward God, then vainglory is always a mortal sin. For then a human being glories in a created good not related actually or habitually to God. And if we should call glory vain because it is not related to God as its end regarding the act itself, namely, an act that cannot be related to the end because it is disordered, then vainglory is not always a mortal sin, since disordered glory of any kind makes glory incapable of being ordained to God. For example, there is a disordered act if one glories in something about which one ought not glory or glories more than one ought or does not observe some other due circumstance, but mortal sin results only when the disordered act is contrary to the law of God, not because any due circumstance is not observed.

Therefore, we should say that vainglory is not always a mortal sin.

Replies to the Objections:

1. The Lord is speaking about situations when a person relates works of justice to human glory as the person's ultimate end, since vainglory is then a mortal sin and completely excludes the person from eternal reward. And we can say that vainglory, even when a venial sin, excludes a person from eternal reward, not indeed absolutely but by the nature of a particular act, namely, insofar as vainglory causes the act that proceeds from it to be incapable of receiving eternal reward, just as venial sin does. But vainglory that is venial sin does not absolutely exclude a person from the reward of eternal life.

2. Vainglory takes away the interior goods of human beings in two ways. It takes them away in one way regarding the acts of interior virtues, for which one does not merit the reward of eternal life if one does them for the sake of vainglory, even if the vainglory be a venial sin. Vainglory takes interior goods away in a second way regarding interior habits themselves, namely, as it deprives human beings of interior virtues, but vainglory does not do this unless it is a mortal sin.

3. The argument of this objection is valid regarding vainglory insofar as one glories in one's goods in oneself, neither actually nor habitually relating them to God, that is, as vainglory is mortal sin.

4. What easily leads a person to perish is dangerous, and vainglory easily leads human beings to perish inasmuch as it causes them to trust in themselves. And so we say that vainglory is the most dangerous sin both because of its seriousness and because it disposes one to sin more seriously.

5. We should not judge that all sins called capital are mortal sins by reason of their kind. Otherwise, it would follow that every sin of gluttony and anger would be a mortal sin, and this is clearly false. And so neither need every vainglory be a mortal sin, although vainglory is a capital sin. But because we call capital a sin from which other sins arise, whether the other sins be venial or mortal, we can say that every sin capital in relation to other mortal sins is a mortal sin, if we should understand capital sins to be such insofar as one sin arises from another as if ordained for its end. For it is evident that a person so greatly influenced by one sin that the person wills to sin mortally in order to attain the end of that sin also sins mortally in the first sin. For example, if one is so greatly drawn to the pleasure of taste that one wills to sin mortally because of it, the very gluttony will also be a mortal sin for the person. And so also vainglory is a mortal sin when one commits a mortal sin for the sake of vainglory.

6. As in a kingdom, we owe honor and glory to the king in one way, to commanders and soldiers in another way, so also in the universe, we owe certain honor and glory only to God, and if one were to will to usurp such honor and glory for oneself, one would attribute to oneself what belongs to God. Just so, were a soldier in a kingdom to desire the glory that he owes to the king, he would thereby desire the kingly dignity for himself. But not everybody who vainly desires glory desires the honor or glory due only to God. Rather, some who vainly desire glory desire the glory due to a human being because of some excellence. Still, they sometimes sin against God in not relating such glory to its proper end. And then although they do not substantially usurp God's glory for themselves, they still usurp God's glory for themselves in the way they possess glory. For it belongs to God alone that his glory not be related to another end.

7. Those who would usurp for themselves the glory and honor of the Godhead, as we read many tyrants to have done, would truly be idolaters. But not all who vainly glory usurp God's glory in this way. And so not all who are vainglorious are idolaters.

8. Avoiding lesser sins belongs to more abundant virtue, as what the Lord says in Mt. 5:21–22 makes clear, that the justice that avoids both homicide and anger abounds more than the justice of the Old Law forbidding homicide does. And so we cannot conclude from the fact that contemning vainglory belongs to great virtue that vainglory is a serious sin.

9. We can rightly or wrongly desire to please human beings. For example, if one should wish to please human beings in order to be able to inspire them for good, this is virtuous and praiseworthy. And so also the Apostle says in 1 Cor. 10:33 and Rom. 15:2: "Let all of you please your neighbor for good to build up the community, just as I please all persons in all things." But wishing to please human beings only for the sake of worldly glory is the sin of vainglory, indeed sometimes mortal sin, namely, if one, loving human favor more than observance of God's commandments, constitutes one's end in human favor and accordingly excludes oneself from the service of God. And wishing to please human beings only for the sake of worldly glory is sometimes a venial sin, when one takes inordinate pleasure in the favor of human beings, but subject rather than contrary to God.

10. In moral matters, the object constitutes the species by reason of the formal aspect of the object, not by its material element. And the object of vainglory, insofar as vainglory is a venial or mortal sin, has different formal aspects, that is, different ends and means. For there is mortal sin when one constitutes one's end in human glory, and there is venial sin when one does not.

Third Article

Do We Appropriately Assign Disobedience, Boasting, Hypocrisy, Contention, Obstinacy, Discord, and Audacity for Novelties as the Daughters of Vainglory?

It seems that we do not, for the following reasons:

1. All these things seem to belong to pride, whose daughter is also vainglory itself. Therefore, we ought not to designate such sins the daughters of vainglory, but we ought to designate them daughters of pride accompanied by vainglory.

2. We ought not to derive sin in general from another sin. But disobedience is sin in general, for Ambrose says that sin is "transgression of the law and disobedience of the heavenly commandments."[23] Therefore, we ought not to designate disobedience a daughter of vainglory.

3. Boasting is the third species of pride, as is clear from what I have said before.[24] Therefore, if boasting is the daughter of vainglory, pride is the daughter of vainglory. And this conclusion is clearly false, since pride is the mother of all sins, as Gregory says in his work *Morals*.[25]

4. Contentions and discords seem especially to originate from anger. But anger is a capital sin contradistinguished from vainglory. Therefore, we ought not to designate discord and contention daughters of vainglory.

On the Contrary:

The authority of Gregory in his work *Morals* says that these are daughters of vainglory.[26]

Answer:

We call a sin capital and the mother of sins by the same consideration, namely, insofar as other sins arise from it, ordained to its end. For such a consideration belongs to the nature of head insofar as the head has the power to rule over things subject to the head, and we understand the nature of every governance from its end. And such a consideration also belongs to the nature of mother, since a mother conceives offspring within her very self. And so we say that a sin from which other sins arise is the mother of the others, which result from the sinner conceiving their end.

Therefore, since the special end of vainglory is to manifest one's own excellence, we call the sins whereby human beings strive to manifest their own excellence daughters of vainglory. And human beings can manifest their own excellence in two ways: in one way directly, and in a second way indirectly. Human beings can indeed manifest their own excellence directly either by words, and then there is boasting, or by real deeds that are a source of astonishment, and then there is audacity for novelties. (For novelties are usually a greater source of astonishment to human beings.) Or human beings can manifest their own excellence directly by imaginary deeds, and then there is hypocrisy. And human beings manifest their excellence indirectly by striving to show that they are not inferior to others. And human beings do this as regards four things. First, they do this as regards the intellect, and then there is obstinacy, by which they, unwilling to accept a sounder opinion, rely on their own opinion. Second, they do this as regards their will, and then there is discord when human beings do not accommodate their will to the will of their superiors. Third, they do this as regards their words, and then there is contention when they do not wish to be outdone by others in argument. Fourth, they do this as regards deeds when they do not wish to subject their deeds to the commands of superiors.

23. *On Paradise* 8 (PL 14:292D).
24. Q. 8, a. 4, objection 1.
25. *Morals* XXXI, 45, n. 87 (PL 76:620D).
26. Ibid., XXXI, 45, n. 88 (PL 76:621A).

Replies to the Objections:

1. We designate pride generally as the mother of all sins and the seven capital sins under it, among which vainglory is especially akin to it, as I have said before.[27] Vainglory is so related to pride because vainglory strives to manifest the excellence that pride desires, and because pride seeks an excellence by that very manifestation. And so all the daughters of vainglory have an affinity with pride.

2. We designate disobedience a daughter of vainglory insofar as disobedience is a particular sin, for then it is simply contempt of a precept. But disobedience as sin in general denotes an absolute withdrawal from the commands of God, which is sometimes done out of weakness or ignorance, not contempt, as Augustine says in his work *On Nature and Grace*.[28]

3. We designate boasting a species of pride regarding the internal desires whereby persons desire an excellence exceeding their measure, as I have said.[29] But regarding the external acts whereby persons manifest their excellence in words, boasting belongs to vainglory.

4. Anger only in conjunction with vainglory causes contention and discord, when persons do not wish to seem inferior by subjecting their wills to the will of others or by having their arguments seem less valid that those of others.

---

27. Objection 3.
28. *On Nature and Grace* 29 (PL 44:263).
29. Q. 8, a. 4.

QUESTION X

On Envy

First Article

Is Envy a Sin?

It seems that envy is not, for the following reasons:

1. We do not praise or blame emotions, as the Philosopher says in the *Ethics*.[1] But envy is an emotion, for Damascene says in his work *On Orthodox Faith* that "envy is chagrin at the good things belonging to others."[2] Therefore, we blame no one on that account. But one is rendered blameworthy because of sin. Therefore, envy is not a sin.

2. The involuntary is not a sin, as Augustine says.[3] But envy, inasmuch as it is the emotion of sadness, is involuntary, for "sadness concerns things that befall us against our will," as Augustine says in the *City of God*.[4] Therefore, envy is not a sin.

3. Since good is the contrary of evil, good does not move one to sin, which is evil, just as one contrary never moves anything to the other contrary. But the cause of envy is good, for Remigius says that envy is sorrow over the good of another.[5]

4. Augustine says in *The City of God* that there is in every sin a disordered turning toward a transitory good.[6] But envy is a turning away from, rather than a turning to, a transitory good, since envy is chagrin at the good of another. Therefore, envy is not a sin.

5. Augustine says in his work *On Free Choice* that every sin results from inordinate desire.[7] But envy, inasmuch as it consists of sadness, does not result from inordinate desire, which is the desire for pleasure. Therefore, envy is not a sin.

6. What cannot exist cannot be a sin. But it is apparently impossible for a person to envy, since inasmuch as good is what everything desires, no one can sorrow over the good, which is to envy. Therefore, envy cannot be a sin.

---

1. *Ethics* II, 5 (1105b31–32).
2. *On Orthodox Faith* II, 14 (PG 94:932B).
3. *On True Religion* 14, n. 27 (PL 34:133).
4. *City of God* XIV, 6 (PL 41:409).
5. Scholars have found no source of this citation.
6. *City of God* XIV, 13, n. 1 (PL 41:420).
7. *On Free Choice* I, 3, n. 8 (PL 32:1225).

7. Every sin consists of an act. But envy, inasmuch as it consists of sadness, lessens activity, which pleasure induces. Therefore, envy lessens sin. Therefore, envy is not a sin.

8. We call moral acts good or evil by the formal aspect of their object. But the object of envy is a good, as I have said,[8] since envy consists of sorrow over the good of another, as I have said.[9] Therefore, acts of envy are good. Therefore, they are not sins.

9. We contradistinguish the evil of punishment from the evil of moral fault, as Augustine makes clear in his work *On Free Choice*.[10] But envy is a penal evil, as Isidore in his work *On the Supreme Good* says that "spite, that is, envy, punishes its author."[11] Therefore, envy is not a sin.

10. Augustine says in the *City of God* that every sin consists of wicked love.[12] But envy is not wicked love, since love makes one rejoice at the good fortune of friends and be sad at their misfortunes. Therefore, envy is not a sin.

11. It seems more serious to envy someone about spiritual goods than material goods. But envy of spiritual goods is not a sin, for Jerome says to Leta regarding the education of her daughter: "Let her have companions with whom she may learn, whom she may envy, whose praises may influence her."[13] Therefore, envy is not a sin.

On the Contrary:

Extremes in moral matters are sinful. But envy is an extreme, as the *Ethics* makes clear.[14] Therefore, envy is a sin.

Answer:

Envy is a sin by reason of its kind.

Since moral acts take their species or are assigned to a genus by reason of their object, we can know that a moral act is evil by reason of its kind if the very act is not properly related to its matter or object.

And we should consider that a good or evil object belongs to the appetitive power just as objects of the intellect are true or false. And we trace all acts of the appetitive power to two common things, namely, to pursuit or avoidance, just as the acts of the intellectual power is related to affirmation or negation. And this consists of pursuit regarding the will and affirmation regarding the intellect, and avoidance regarding the will and negation regarding the intellect, as the Philosopher says in the *Ethics*.[15] And good has the nature of attracting, since good is what everything desires, as the *Ethics* says.[16] And conversely, evil has the nature of repelling, since evil is contrary to the will and other appetites, as Dionysius says in *On the Divine Names*.[17]

---

8. Objection 3.
9. Ibid.
10. *On Free Choice* I, 1, n. 1 (PL 32:1221–22).
11. *On the Supreme Good* III, 25, n. 1 (PL 83:700A).
12. *City of God* XIV, 7, n. 2 (PL 41:410).
13. *Letter* 107, n. 4 (PL 22:871).
14. Aristotle, *Ethics* II, 7 (1108b4–5).
15. Ibid., VI, 2 (1139a21–22).
16. Ibid., I, 1 (1094a2–3).
17. *On the Divine Names* 4, n. 32 (PG 3:732C–D).

Therefore, every act of the appetitive power pertaining to pursuit whose object is evil is an act not proper for its matter or object. And so all such acts (e.g., loving evil and rejoicing in evil) are evil by reason of their kind, just as it is a mistake of the intellect to affirm what is false. And likewise, every act pertaining to avoidance whose object is good is an act not proper for its matter or object. And so every such act (e.g., hating good and despising good and being saddened at good) is a sin by reason of its kind, just as it is a mistake of the intellect to deny what is true. But it does not suffice for an act to be good that the act involve pursuit of good or avoidance of evil unless it involve pursuit of a suitable good and avoidance of the evil contrary to such a good. This is so because more things are required for good, which the entire and integral cause accomplishes, than for evil, which results from individual defects, as Denis says in his work *On the Divine Names*.[18] But envy implies sadness over good. And so the sadness is a sin by reason of its kind.

Replies to the Objections:

1. Since emotion is the movement of a sense appetite, as Damascene says in his work *On Orthodox Faith*,[19] emotion considered as such cannot be a virtue or a vice, or something praiseworthy or something blameworthy, since these things belong to reason. But insofar as sense appetites are in one respect rational inasmuch as they can obey reason, so also even emotions themselves can be praiseworthy or blameworthy insofar as they can be ordained or restrained. And so the Philosopher says in the same place that a person who is angry in a certain way, that is, according to the ordination of reason or contrary to it, is praised or blamed, but a person who is angry without qualification is not.[20]

2. The cited authority does not say that sadness is an involuntary movement, but that the object of sadness is involuntary in a qualified sense. But nothing prevents a voluntary human action regarding something involuntary being good or evil, namely, insofar as one can bear something involuntary rightly or wrongly.

3. Good as such always induces one to good, but an evil affective disposition may move a person to the evil of envy, just as a bad disposition of the body may make healthy food harmful for it.

4. We understand lack of a good as an evil, as the Philosopher says in the *Ethics*.[21] And so to oppose good through sadness comes to the same thing as to turn toward the evil associated with an inordinately loved transitory good.

5. As good by nature is prior to the evil that is its privation, so also the soul's desires whose object is good are by nature prior to the soul's desires whose object is evil. And so desires for evil originate from desires for good. And so a love, desire, or pleasure causes hate and sadness, and an inordinate desire causes envy in such a way.

6. Good as such cannot make a person sad, but one can be sad about good as understood under the aspect of evil, whether real or apparent. And envy in this way consists of chagrin at the good of another, namely, insofar as the good of another is an impediment to one's own excellence.

---

18. Ibid., n. 30 (PG 3:729C).
19. *On Orthodox Faith* II, 22 (PG 94:940D).
20. *Ethics* II, 5 (1105b33–1106a1).
21. Ibid., V, 1 (1129b8–9).

7. As pleasure perfects the activity belonging to it, so pleasure prevents extraneous activity, as the Philosopher says in the *Ethics*.[22] For example, one who takes pleasure in learning studies more and is less concerned about other things. Therefore, chagrin about the good of neighbor prevents actions that strive for the neighbor's good and moves a person to contrary activities that hinder the neighbor's good.

8. As there can be sin in love of good only insofar as something loved, although understood under the aspect of good, is nonetheless evil, not really good, so also sadness regarding a good understood as an evil that is an apparent, not really, an evil is nonetheless evil. This is so because such sadness does not befit an object that is really good. For moral acts are good by reason of their object insofar as they befit the object.

9. Certain penalties are affixed to certain sins, and then the same thing is a punishment and a moral fault in different respects. The thing is indeed a moral fault insofar as it proceeds from the disordered will of a human being, and then God is not the cause. And it is a punishment insofar as it has a conjoined penal affliction, and God does cause this, as Ps. 50:21 says: "I shall reprove you, and I shall set myself against your face." And Augustine says in his *Confessions*: "You have commanded, O Lord, and so it is that every disordered affection is its own punishment."[23] And envy can in this way be both punishment and sin.

10. Every sin is a love that is wicked by reason of its cause, not by reason of its essence, since every emotion of the soul, even sadness, proceeds out of love, as Augustine says in the cited work.[24]

11. Aristotle in the *Rhetoric*, distinguishing between zeal and envy, says that zeal out of goodness belongs to the virtuous, but "envy is wicked and belongs to the wicked."[25] For the zealous out of emulation prepare themselves to obtain good things, but the envious out of envy want their neighbor not to have good things. For example, there is envy when persons are saddened at the fact that their neighbor has good things that they themselves do not, but there is zeal when persons are saddened at the fact that they themselves do not have the good things that their neighbor does. And Jerome in the cited authority understood envy as zeal, since it is praiseworthy for persons to strive to learn what others are learning, as the Apostle says in 1 Cor. 12:31: "You are to be zealous for better gifts."

Second Article

Is Envy a Mortal Sin?

It seems that envy is not, for the following reasons:

1. Gregory says in his work *Morals*: "It very often happens that the ruin of enemies gladdens us, and their glory saddens us, without our loss of charity."[26] But this is to envy. Therefore, envy does not take away charity, and so we do not call envy a mortal sin.

---

22. Ibid., X, 5 (1175a29–b24).
23. *Confessions* I, 12 (PL 32:670).
24. *City of God* XIV, 7, n. 2 (PL 41:410).
25. *Rhetoric* II, 11 (1388a33–34).
26. *Morals* XXII, 11, n. 23 (PL 76:226D).

2. Damascene says in his work *On Orthodox Faith* that emotion is the movement of a sense appetite.[27] But we call this movement of sense appetites sensuality, as Augustine says in his work *On the Trinity*.[28] Therefore, envy, inasmuch as it is an emotion of the soul, belongs to sensuality, in which there is only venial sin, as Augustine says in the same place. Therefore, envy is not a mortal sin.

3. Things good by reason of their kind can be done in an evil way, but things evil by reason of their kind cannot be done in a good way, as Augustine says in his work *Against Lying*.[29] Just so, things venial by reason of their kind can become mortal, but things mortal by reason of their kind cannot in any respect be venial. The latter is, for example, evident in the case of homicide and adultery. But not all envy is a mortal sin. Therefore, envy is not a mortal sin by reason of its kind.

4. A sin of deed is more serious than a sin of desire, assuming both sins belong to the same kind of sin. But actively to prevent a neighbor's good is not always a mortal sin. Therefore, it is not always a mortal sin to grieve at a neighbor's good, which is to envy.

5. Mortal sin cannot belong to perfect human beings. But a movement of envy arising surreptitiously can belong to them. Therefore, envy is not a mortal sin.

6. Children not yet able to talk cannot commit mortal sin, since they do not yet have the use of reason, only in which there is mortal sin. But children can have envy, for Augustine says in his *Confessions*: "I have seen and known a jealous child; he was not yet able to talk, but he became pale, casting bitter looks at his foster-brother."[30] Therefore, envy is not a mortal sin.

7. Every mortal sin is contrary to the ordination of charity. But envy, which is chagrined at the good of another, inasmuch as it redounds to one's own harm is not contrary to the ordination of charity. And all people by that ordination ought to love themselves more than others, and neighbors more than strangers, as Ambrose says.[31] Therefore, envy is not a mortal sin.

8. Every mortal sin is the contrary of some virtue. But envy is not the contrary of any virtue but rather the contrary of an emotion that the Philosopher in the *Ethics* calls just anger.[32] Therefore, envy is not a mortal sin.

On the contrary:

1. Gregory, explaining Prov. 14:30, "Envy is rottenness of the bones," says: "The sin of envy causes even strong acts of virtue to vanish before the eyes of God."[33] But only mortal sin does this. Therefore, envy is a mortal sin.

2. The *Journey Reading of Clement* relates that Peter said that three sins merit equal punishment: when one kills with one's hands, when the tongue detracts, and when the heart envies or hates.[34] But homicide is a mortal sin. Therefore, envy also is.

---

27. *On Orthodox Faith* II, 22 (PG 94:940D).
28. *On the Trinity* XII, 12, n. 17 (PL 42:1007).
29. *Against Lying* 7, n. 18 (PL 40:528–29).
30. *Confessions* I, 7, n. 11 (PL 32:665–66).
31. Acually, Origen, *On the Song of Songs*, hom. 2, n. 8 (PG 13:54A).
32. *Ethics* II, 7 (1108a30–b1).
33. *Morals* V, 46, n. 85 (PL 75:728D).
34. Actually, Clement (Pseudo), *Letter I to James* (PG 1:480C).

3. Isidore says in his work *On the Supreme Good*: "There is no virtue of which envy is not the contrary, since only misery lacks envy."[35] But only mortal sin is the contrary of every virtue. Therefore, envy is a mortal sin.

4. As Augustine, on Ps. 105:25, "He [God] turned their hearts to hate his people," says: "Envy is hatred of another's happiness."[36] But hatred is long-standing anger, as he himself says.[37] Therefore, all envy is something long-standing and so cannot be a venial sin arising suddenly, as it were.

5. Only mortal sin kills spiritually. But envy kills spiritually, as Job 5:2 says: "Envy slays the childish." And a gloss on 2 Cor. 2:15, "We are the sweet fragrance of Christ," says: "This fragrance brings life to those who love and death to those who envy."[38] Therefore, envy is a mortal sin.

Answer:

As I have said,[39] we note the genus or species of a moral act by its matter or object. And so also we call a moral act good or evil by its genus. But the soul lives by charity, which joins us to God, who gives life to the soul. And so 1 Jn. 3:14 says: "One who does not love abides in death," since death is the privation of life.

Therefore, when we understand something as contrary to charity by the relation of an act to its matter, the act is necessarily a mortal sin by reason of its kind. For example, killing a human being imports something contrary to charity, by which we love our neighbor and wish our neighbor to live and to exist and to have other good things. For such belong to the nature of friendship, as the Philosopher says in the *Ethics*.[40] And so homicide is a mortal sin by reason of its kind. And if there should not seem to be anything contrary to charity by the relation of an act to its object (e.g., uttering an idle word or the like), there is not mortal sin by reason of its kind. And yet such things can become mortal sins by something else being added, as I have maintained before.[41] And envying implies something contrary to charity by the very relation of the act to its object, since it belongs to the nature of friendship that we wish as good things for our friends as we do for ourselves, as the *Ethics* says,[42] inasmuch as a friend is in one respect another self. And so for a person to be chagrined at the happiness of another is evidently contrary to charity, since one loves one's neighbor through charity. And so Augustine says in his work *On True Religion*: "One who envies a good singer does not love the good singer."[43] And so envy is a mortal sin by reason of its kind.

But we should consider that there can belong to the genus of mortal sin an act that is not a mortal sin because it is not completely such a sin, namely, because the act does not attain the complete nature of that genus of sin. And this indeed happens in two ways.

---

35. *On the Supreme Good* III, 25, n. 4 (PL 83:700B).
36. *Expositions on the Psalms*, on Ps. 105:25, n. 17 (PL 37:1399).
37. Cf., e.g., *Sermon 49*, chap. 7 (PL 38:324).
38. Peter Lombard, *Gloss*, on 2 Cor. 2:15 (PL 192:20D).
39. A. 1.
40. *Ethics* IX, 4 (1166a4–5).
41. Q. 7, a. 3.
42. *Ethics* IX, 4 (1166a30–32).
43. *On True Religion* 47, n. 90 (PL 34:162).

It happens in one way regarding the efficient cause, namely, that the act does not proceed from deliberative reason, which is the proper and chief efficient cause of human acts. And so sudden movements, even in the genus of homicide or adultery, are not mortal sins, since they do not completely attain the nature of moral acts, whose source is reason. It can happen in a second way regarding the object, namely, that an act's object because of its slight gravity does not attain the complete nature of the object, since reason understands something small as if it were nothing. For example, this is evident in the case of theft; if one should take an ear of corn or the like from the field of another, we should not think that such a person sins mortally, since both the one who takes the thing and the one from whom it is taken regard it as nothing.

Therefore, it can accordingly happen that although envy is a mortal sin by reason of its kind, a movement of envy is not a mortal sin because of the incompleteness of the movement itself. A movement of envy may be incomplete either because the movement is sudden and does not proceed from deliberative reason, or because a human being is chagrined at a good of another so little as to seem to be nothing. For example, the latter would be the case if one playing a game, such as running a race or some such sport, should envy the winner.

Replies to the Objections:
1. We posit in the definition of something only what is intrinsic, not what is accidental. Therefore, when we say that envy is sadness at the happiness or glory of another, we need to understand this insofar as one is saddened at the very happiness of another as such, at which one is saddened because one wants to excel in a singular way. And so we say in a strict sense that one who is surpassed by someone in glory or happiness and grieves over it is envious. But one can be saddened at the happiness of another for other reasons, which sometimes belong to other sins, not to envy. For example, one who hates someone is not saddened at that person's happiness insofar as it is an excellence, but insofar as it is simply a good of the person one hates. For inasmuch as one wishes evil on an enemy, one is consequently saddened at any good the enemy has. And so the difference between the envious and the hateful is that the envious are saddened at the good of another only if the other should thereby excel, or the envious should lose the uniqueness of their glory, while the hateful are saddened at every good of their enemy. There can also be still another reason why persons are saddened at the happiness of another, namely, because they fear that some harm may come to them or those they love because of the other's good. And this sadness belongs to fear rather than envy, as the Philosopher says in the *Rhetoric*.[44] And fear can be good or evil. And so it can occur either with sin, when the fear is evil, or without sin, when the fear is good. And so Gregory, explaining the cited words, adds that "we believe this when we think that some justly rise at the fall of someone, and when we fear that many are unjustly crushed at rise of another."[45] And so he also adds that such sadness is without the moral fault of envy.

44. *Rhetoric* II, 9 (1386b22–25).
45. *Morals* XXII, 11, n. 23 (PL 76:226D).

2. There cannot be mortal sin when there is only the movement of a sense appetite, but there is the movement both of a sense appetite and of reason when the movement of sadness results from the deliberation of reason. And so there can be mortal sin. But we can also say that such names of emotions sometimes signify only the very acts of the will, and sadness in this way will belong to the rational part of the soul, not to a sense appetite.

3. What is mortal sin by reason of its kind cannot become venial if the act be completely such an act, but this can happen because of the incomplete nature of the act, as I have said.[46]

4. One can without mortal sin prevent the good of someone because of the incomplete nature of the act, since the good impeded does not have the complete nature of good, either because the good is slight, or because the good is undeserved.

5. A surreptitious movement of envy is incomplete, and even such a movement of envy belongs to children lacking the use of reason.

6. And so the reply to objection 6 is evident.

7. When persons are saddened at the happiness of another because of the harm that thereby threatens them or their families, such sadness belongs to fear, not envy. And so it can sometimes be without sin, as I have said.[47]

8. Envy regards two objects, since it consists of sadness at the prosperity of a good person. And envy can accordingly be contrary to two virtues. For regarding the prosperity at which one grieves, pity, which grieves at the adversity of good persons, is the contrary of envy. And regarding the good person at whose prosperity one is saddened, the zealous anger that we understand as retribution, namely, when one is saddened at the fact that evil persons prosper in their wickedness, is the contrary of envy. And although pity and zealous anger seem to be emotions that regard the nature of sadness, they take the nature of virtue insofar as rational choice supervenes.

Replies to the Arguments in the Section On the Contrary:

1. Gregory is speaking in the cited text about envy insofar as it is a mortal sin. And St. Peter is also speaking about such envy of desire,[48] which indeed merits the same punishment as homicide as to the kind of punishment, since both merit eternal punishment.

2. And so the reply to argument 2 is clear.

3. Mortal sin is contrary to the virtue of the one who sins, and envy is contrary to every virtue of another, not every virtue of the one who sins, as Isidore says. And so he could not prove from this that envy is a mortal sin.

4. Envy consists of hatred of another human being's happiness, not of the human being, as we include under hatred all the emotions of the soul inclining toward evil that originate from hatred. And we should not understand the statement of Augustine that hatred is long-standing anger as if all hatred be such, as a condition of the movement of hatred, but because long-standing anger causes hatred.

5. The cited authorities are speaking about envy as a mortal sin.

---

46. In the answer.
47. Reply to objection 1.
48. In argument 1 of the section *On the contrary*.

Third Article

Is Envy a Capital Sin?

It seems that envy is not, for the following reasons:

1. It belongs to a capital sin to have daughters but not to be the daughter of anything else. But envy is the daughter of pride, as Augustine says in his work *On Holy Virginity*.[49] Therefore, envy is not a capital sin.

2. Envy is a sadness, as I have already said.[50] But sadness signifies the terminus of an appetitive movement, since human beings are saddened when they incur an evil they hitherto hated. Therefore, envy is not a capital sin, since it belongs to the nature of a capital sin that all other sins originate from it.

3. We attribute daughters to any capital sin. But envy does not seem to have any daughters, for Gregory in his work *Morals* attributes five daughters, which are: hatred, gossiping, detraction, exultation over those suffering adversity, and distress about those prospering.[51] And none of these seem to be daughters of envy, since it is rather hatred and gossiping and detraction and exultation over those suffering adversity that produce hatred, and distress about those prospering seems to be the same as envy. Therefore, envy is not a capital sin.

On the Contrary:

Gregory in his work *Morals* lists envy among the capital sins.[52]

Answer:

Capital sins are those from which other sins naturally arise by reason of being the final causes of other sins, as I have said before.[53] But ends have the nature of good, and the appetite strives in the same way for good and the enjoyment of good, that is, pleasure. And so as the desire for good moves the appetite to do something, so also does the desire for pleasure.

And we should consider that as good is the end of the appetitive movement that consists of pursuit, so evil is the end of the appetitive movement that consists of avoidance. For as one who wills to acquire a good pursues it, so one who wills to be without an evil avoids the evil, and as pleasure is the enjoyment of good, so sadness is a malaise by which an evil depresses the spirit. And so human beings, because they reject sadness, are induced to do many things that repel sadness or to repel things inclining them to sadness. Therefore, since envy is sadness at the glory of another as conceived to be an evil, it follows that human beings out of envy strive to do disordered deeds against their neighbor, and envy is accordingly a capital sin.

And regarding this striving of envy, one thing is like a starting point, and another thing like an end point. The starting point is indeed that a person excludes the glory of another that causes the person to be sad. And one indeed does this by disparaging the

49. *On Holy Virginity* 31 (PL 40:413).
50. A. 2, *ad* 1.
51. *Morals* XXXI, 45, n. 88 (PL 76:621B).
52. Ibid., n. 87 (PL 76:621A).
53. Q. 8, a. 1.

virtues of the other or by saying bad things about the other, both in a disguised way by gossiping and openly by detraction. And we can in two ways consider the end point of this striving. We can indeed consider it in one way regarding the one who is envied, and then the movement of envy sometimes ends in hate, namely, that a human being both is saddened regarding the abundant excellence of the other and further wishes the other's misfortune absolutely. And we can in the second way consider the end point of the striving regarding the one who envies. Persons, if they could indeed attain their intended end of diminishing the glory of another, rejoice, and then we designate the daughter of envy exultation over those suffering adversity. And persons, if they could not attain their purpose, namely, to prevent the glory of neighbor, are saddened, and then we designate the daughter of envy distress at those prospering.

Replies to the Objections:

1. As Gregory says in his work *Morals*, pride is the common mother of all sins.[54] And so the fact that envy is the daughter of pride does preclude envy being a capital sin.

2. Sadness, although the end point in execution, is nonetheless first in intention, namely, insofar as many other movements result from avoidance of sadness.

3. Nothing prevents the same sins arising from different sins in different respects. Therefore, anger produces hate as one provoked to anger inflicts an injury, and envy produces hate as one conceives the good of the person envied as an impediment to one's own excellence. Likewise, gossiping and detraction and exultation over those suffering adversity arise out of hate as persons belittle every good and exaggerate every evil of their enemy. These things result from envy only in respect to taking away another's excellence. And distress at those prospering is in one respect envy itself and in another respect envy's daughter. For insofar as one is saddened at another prospering as much as one is adverse to the other's singular excellence, then the distress is envy itself. And insofar as one is saddened at another's prosperity because it results despite one's own striving to prevent it, then the distress is the daughter of envy.

---

54. *Morals* XXXI, 45, n. 87 (PL 76:620D).

QUESTION XI

On Spiritual Apathy

First Article

Is Spiritual Apathy a Sin?

It seems that spiritual apathy is not, for the following reasons:

1. Virtue and sin, since they are contraries, belong to the same genus. But virtue belongs to the genus of love, for Augustine in his works *On Church Customs*[1] and *City of God*[2] says that virtue is the right ordination of love. Therefore, since spiritual apathy does not belong to the genus of love and is rather a sadness, as Damascene says,[3] it seems that spiritual apathy is not a sin.

2. A gloss on Ps. 107:1, "Give thanks to God," designates four temptations, namely, error, the difficulty of overcoming inordinate desires, apathy, and worldly turmoil.[4] But error and difficulty and worldly turmoil are not sins. Therefore, neither is apathy, which is spiritual apathy, a sin.

3. Every sin is due to human beings, as Hos. 13:9 says: "Your destruction is due to you, O Israel." But spiritual apathy, since it is a sadness, is not attributable to human beings. For a gloss on 2 Cor. 9:7, "Not glumly or by compulsion," etc., says: "If you act with sadness, the deed is done regarding you, but you do not do it."[5] Therefore, spiritual apathy is not a sin.

4. An act cannot simultaneously be meritorious and a sin. But an act done with spiritual apathy is meritorious. For example, such would be the case if one fasts out of devotion or obedience and yet the very fasting makes the person sad, and then there is in the fasting spiritual apathy, which is apathy about a virtuous spiritual good. Therefore, spiritual apathy is not always a sin.

---

1. *On Church Customs* I, 15, n. 25 (PL 32:1322).
2. *City of God* XV, 22 (PL 41:467).
3. *On Orthodox Faith* II, 14 (PG 94:932B).
4. Peter Lombard, *Gloss*, on Ps. 107:1 (PL 191:973A).
5. Ibid., on 2 Cor. 9:7 (PL 192:63B).

5. Damascene says in his work *On Orthodox Faith* that spiritual apathy is oppressive sadness.[6] But oppression seems to be punishment rather than sin. Therefore, spiritual apathy is punishment rather than sin.

6. Spiritual apathy seems to be sadness or boredom concerning an interior good, about which a gloss on Ps. 107:18 says: "Their souls abhorred every kind of food."[7] Therefore, if spiritual apathy is a sin, either it is a sin because it does not receive a spiritual good, or it is a sin because, spurning the spiritual good, it receives a bodily good. But it cannot be sin because it does not receive a spiritual good, since not to receive is a privation, not an act, and every praise or blame results from an act, as the Philosopher says in the *Ethics*,[8] and blame is due to sin. Therefore, if spiritual apathy be a sin, we conclude that it is a sin because, contemning a spiritual good, it pursues a bodily good. But pursuit of good belongs to concupiscible power, as avoidance of evil belongs to irascible power. Therefore, it seems that spiritual apathy, although it seems rather to belong to irascible power, belongs to concupiscible power.

7. Gregory says in his work *Morals* that spiritual apathy is an interior sadness of mind whereby one prays or chants psalms less devoutly.[9] But human beings do not have the power to pray devoutly. Therefore, they do not have the power to avoid spiritual apathy. Therefore, spiritual apathy is not a sin, since no one sins regarding what one cannot avoid.

8. Damascene in his work *On Orthodox Faith* designates spiritual apathy a species of sadness,[10] which is one of the four emotions. But emotions are not sins, since we are neither praised nor blamed on their account. Therefore, spiritual apathy is not a sin.

9. What the wise choose is not a sin. But the wise choose spiritual apathy or sadness, for Eccl. 7:4 says that "the heart of the wise is where there is sadness." Therefore, spiritual apathy or sadness is not a sin.

10. What God rewards is not a sin. But God rewards sadness, for Mal. 3:14 says in the person of the wicked: "What reward have we because we kept his ordinances and walked sorrowful before him?" Therefore, spiritual apathy or sadness is not a sin.

On the Contrary:

Gregory in his work *Morals* lists spiritual apathy with other sins,[11] and so does Isidore in his work *On the Supreme Good*.[12]

Answer:

As Damascene makes clear, spiritual apathy is a certain sadness,[13] and so also Gregory in his work *Morals* sometimes substitutes sadness for spiritual apathy.[14] And the object of

6. *On Orthodox Faith* II, 14 (PG 94:932B).

7. Peter Lombard, *Gloss*, on Ps. 107:18 (PL 191:977A).

8. *Ethics* I, 12 (1101b14–15).

9. Actually, a conflation of *Morals* XXXI, 45, n. 88 (PL 76:621B), and Peraldus, *Summa on Vices and Virtues*, tr. 5, part 2, chap. 13.

10. *On Orthodox Faith* II, 14 (PG 94:932B).

11. *Morals* XXXI, 45, n. 87 (PL 76:621A).

12. *On the Supreme Good* IV, 40, n. 2 (PL 83:1178D).

13. *On Orthodox Faith* II, 14 (PG 94:932B).

14. *Morals* XXXI, 45, n. 87 (PL 76:621A).

sadness is a present evil, as Damascene says.[15] And there are two kinds of good, one that is truly good, and one that appears to be good because it is good in some respect, but is not truly good because it is not good in every respect. Just so, there are two kinds of evil, one that is truly and absolutely evil, and one that is apparently and in some respect evil but, in reality, absolutely good.

Therefore, love and desire and pleasure regarding a true good are praiseworthy, and love and desire and pleasure regarding an apparent but false good are blameworthy. So also, hate, aversion, and sadness concerning a true evil are praiseworthy, and hate, aversion, and sadness regarding what is in some respect and apparently an evil but absolutely good are blameworthy and sins. And spiritual apathy consists of boredom or sadness regarding a spiritual and interior good, as Augustine says on Ps. 107:18, "Their souls abhorred every kind of food."[16] And so since interior and spiritual good is truly good and can only be apparently evil, namely, insofar as it is contrary to carnal desires, spiritual apathy as such is evidently sinful.

But we should note that we can consider spiritual apathy in two ways, since it is a sadness: in one way as the act of a sense appetite; in the second way as the act of the intellectual appetite, that is, the will. For all names of such dispositions as indeed acts of sense appetites designate emotions, but as acts of the intellectual appetite designate only movements of the will. And sin intrinsically and in the strict sense belongs to the will, as Augustine says.[17] And so spiritual apathy, if it should designate an act of the will avoiding an internal and spiritual good, can have the complete nature of sin. But if we should understand spiritual apathy as the act of a sense appetite, it has the nature of sin only from the will, namely, insofar as the will can forbid such a movement. And so if the movement is not forbidden, it has some nature of sin but not the complete nature.

Replies to the Objections:

1. Love is the source of all dispositions, as Augustine makes clear in his work *City of God*.[18] And so when he says that virtue is the right ordination of love, the predication is by virtue's cause, not by its essence. For not every virtue is essentially love, but every disposition to virtue originates from a rightly ordered love, and likewise, every disposition to sin originates from a disordered love.

2. The mode of argument of this objection is not valid. For it is not necessary that everything predicated of a subdivision of something common should also be predicated of other subdivisions. For things listed one after another as subdivisions of something common share in that common thing but not necessarily in anything else. And so the four temptations share in the common nature of temptation, but nothing prevents one of them being a sin, and the others not being sins. For example, temptation from the flesh is not without sin, but temptation from an enemy can be altogether without sin.

3. Acts done out of sadness or fear are mixtures of the voluntary and the involuntary, as the *Ethics* says,[19] and insofar as they are partially involuntary, they are not attributable to us. But the very movement of sadness is attributable to ourselves.

15. *On Orthodox Faith* II, 12 (PG 94:929B).
16. *Expositions on the Psalms*, on Ps. 107, n. 6 (PL 37:1422).
17. *On True Religion* 14, n. 27 (PL 34:133).
18. *City of God* XIV, 7, n. 2 (PL 41:410).
19. *Ethics* III, 1 (1110a11–12).

4. Nothing prevents a deed considered in itself being a source of sadness and yet being a source of pleasure as related to the service of God. And so also we say that even the martyrs in their tears produced fruit, as Augustine explains.[20] Nor is emotional sadness spiritual apathy, since such sadness concerns an external evil, not an interior good. For example, the martyrs rejoiced over their interior good, and the more the external evil saddened them, the more their joy gained them merit. And likewise if one willingly fulfilling obedience or a precept should be sad about some distressful or difficult assignment, such sadness is not spiritual apathy, since it relates to an external evil, not an interior good.

5. We say that sadness is oppressive insofar as it suppresses the desire to act, and the oppression of sadness regarding good deeds accordingly has the nature of sin rather than punishment, since it springs from ourselves.

6. We do not distinguish irascible and concupiscible powers by pursuit and avoidance, since it belongs to the same power to seek good and avoid the contrary evil. Rather, we distinguish them by the fact that pursuit of a good difficult to obtain or avoidance of an evil difficult to avoid belongs to irascible power, and pursuit or avoidance of good absolutely belongs to concupiscible power. And accordingly, as hope and fear belong to irascible power, so joy and sadness belong to concupiscible power. And so spiritual apathy insofar as it belongs to a sense appetite belongs to concupiscible power. And yet spiritual apathy is not necessarily without sin because it avoids a spiritual good. This is so both because the very avoidance is an appetitive movement and not only a privation, and because even if it were to be only a privation, which is not to receive a spiritual good, this also could have the nature of moral fault, in which case we say that there is a sin of omission.

7. The devotion of human beings originates from God. But insofar as human beings can dispose themselves to having or preventing devotion, lack of devotion is for that reason a sin. Nevertheless, the cited authority does not say that spiritual apathy is lack of devotion, but that lack of devotion results from spiritual apathy.

8. Damascene is not speaking about spiritual apathy as a sin, namely, as it consists of sadness about an interior spiritual good, but generally as sadness about any evil. And so he is speaking about spiritual apathy as a species of emotion, not as a sin.

9–10. In reply to objections 9 and 10, we should say that the arguments are valid about the sadness over something absolutely evil, and such sadness is praiseworthy.

Second Article

Is Spiritual Apathy a Special Kind of Sin?

It seems that spiritual apathy is not, for the following reasons:

1. Spiritual apathy, since it is sadness, is contrary to pleasure. But pleasure is not a special kind of virtue, since virtuous persons take pleasure in their virtuous acts, as the *Ethics* makes clear.[21] Therefore, sadness over a spiritual good is not a special kind of sin.

20. *Sermon* 31, chap. 1, nn. 1–2 (PL 38:192–93).
21. *Ethics* I, 13 (1099a7–21).

2. What results from every sin is not a special kind of sin. But sadness over a spiritual good results from every sin, since what is contrary to a person's good is a source of sadness for the person, and a virtuous spiritual good is contrary to every sin. Therefore, spiritual apathy is not a special kind of sin.

3. People have said that spiritual apathy is sadness over a spiritual good in a particular respect, namely, inasmuch as spiritual apathy prevents bodily rest. But to desire bodily rest belongs to carnal sins. And to desire something and to be sad at its prevention belong to the same consideration. Therefore, if spiritual apathy be a special kind of sin only because it prevents bodily rest, then spiritual apathy would be a sin of the flesh, although Gregory lists spiritual apathy with spiritual sins, as his work *Morals* makes clear.[22] Therefore, spiritual apathy is not a special kind of sin.

On the Contrary:
Gregory in his work *Morals* lists spiritual apathy with other kinds of sin.[23] Therefore, it is a special kind of sin.

Answer:
If spiritual apathy were to be absolutely sadness at whatever spiritual good in whatever respect, then it would necessarily be a consequence of every sin, not a special kind of sin. Therefore, in order that spiritual apathy be designated a special sin, we need to say that there is sadness about a spiritual good in a particular respect. And we cannot say that there is a particular respect insofar as the sadness prevents a bodily good, since spiritual apathy accordingly would not be a sin distinct from the sin that concerns the bodily good. This is so because it is regarding the same consideration that we take pleasure in something and flight from its impediment. Just so, in the case of things of nature, it is by the same natural power that heavy things go down from higher places and strive for lower places. And so we see that as one takes pleasure in food because of gluttony, so also one by reason of the same sin is saddened over abstinence from food. What prevents a bodily good is the reason why a spiritual good causes sadness, but it is not the reason why sadness about the good is a special kind of sin.

Therefore, we should consider that nothing prevents something considered in itself being a particular kind of good, something that is nonetheless the general end of many things. And so charity is a particular virtue, since it is first and chiefly love of the divine good and secondarily love of our neighbors' good, and such good is the end of all or many other goods. Therefore, a deed of a special virtue (e.g., chastity) can be loveable and pleasurable in two ways: in one way as the act of such a virtue, and this belongs to chastity; in the second way as the act is ordained for the divine good, and then it belongs to charity.

Therefore, we should say that to be saddened over the special good that is the interior and divine good causes spiritual apathy to be a special kind of sin, as loving this good causes charity to be a special virtue. And this divine good is a source of sadness for human beings because of the contrariety of the spirit to the flesh, since "the flesh lusts against the spirit," as the Apostle says in Gal. 5:17. And so when desire of the flesh is

22. *Morals* XXXI, 45, n. 88 (PL 76:621C).
23. Ibid., n. 87 (PL 76:621A).

dominant in human beings, they have distaste for spiritual good as contrary to their good. Just so, human beings with infected taste buds have distaste for healthy food and grieve over it whenever they need to consume such food. Therefore, such sadness and abhorrence or boredom regarding a spiritual and divine good is spiritual apathy, which is a special sin. And so, in order to repel this apathy, the wise man in Sir. 6:26 warns: "Bow your shoulders and bear it [spiritual wisdom], and do not grow weak in its bonds."

Replies to the Objections:

1. Pleasure over a spiritual and divine good belongs to the special virtue that is charity, as Gal. 5:22 says: "The fruit of the spirit is charity, joy, peace."

2. Every sinner is saddened at spiritual good by reason of the special nature of the virtue that is contrary to the sinner's sin. But a sinner is saddened at spiritual apathy itself by reason of the nature of a divine spiritual good, which is the special object of charity.

3. The reply to objection 3 is evident from what I have said.[24] For the contrariety to bodily rest causes a spiritual good to be a source of sadness but does not cause a special nature of sin.

Third Article

Is Spiritual Apathy a Mortal Sin?

It seems that spiritual apathy is not, for the following reasons:

1. Perfect human beings have no mortal sin. But spiritual apathy is a sadness we find in perfect human beings, and the Apostle in 2 Cor. 6:10 says in their person: "As if sad but always rejoicing." Therefore, spiritual apathy is not a mortal sin.

2. Every mortal sin is contrary to a precept of God. But spiritual apathy does not seem to be contrary to any precept, since no precept about pleasure is included in the precepts of the Decalogue. Therefore, spiritual apathy is not a mortal sin.

3. Since sadness concerns a present evil, as Damascene says in his work *On Orthodox Faith*,[25] spiritual apathy, which is a sadness, needs to concern a present evil, which is indeed truly good but apparently evil. Spiritual apathy cannot concern the truly good, which is the uncreated good. This is so both because the presence of such good involves no boredom or sadness, as Wis. 8:16 says about divine wisdom that "no conversation or company with her is boring," and because there can be no mortal sin if the uncreated good be present. Therefore, we conclude that spiritual apathy is sadness over a present created good. But turning away from a created good does not cause mortal sin. Rather, only turning away from the immutable good does. Therefore, spiritual apathy is not a mortal sin.

4. A sin of deed is not less than a sin of desire if they belong to the same genus. But to refrain in deed from a created spiritual good leading to God is not a mortal sin. For example, one who does not fast or pray does not sin mortally. Therefore, even withhold-

---

24. In the answer.
25. *On Orthodox Faith* II, 12 (PG 94:929B).

ing of desire from a created good through sadness is not always a mortal sin. And so spiritual apathy is not a mortal sin by reason of its kind, since then it would always be a mortal sin like homicide and adultery.

5. People have said that withdrawal in deed from an obligatory created good causes mortal sin. But deeds that are not obligatory are sometimes more spiritual, and yet to withdraw from them is a mortal sin only if a vow makes them obligatory. Indeed, there is also no sin if one does not observe virginity or poverty. Therefore, neither is every sadness over a spiritual good a mortal sin.

6. To refrain in deed from a spiritual good is a mortal sin only insofar as human beings are obliged to do that good deed. But even if human beings are obliged to do a spiritual good deed, they are still not obliged to do it with pleasure, since the pleasure realized in a deed is the sign of an inherent habit. And so those without a virtuous habit cannot be obliged to do it with pleasure. Therefore, even spiritual apathy concerning an obligatory spiritual good is not a mortal sin.

7. Every mortal sin is contrary to the spiritual life. But the spiritual life does not require that we do things with pleasure; it suffices that we do them; otherwise, all who were to do something that they ought to do, if they were to find no pleasure in it, would sin mortally. Therefore, spiritual apathy, which is contrary to spiritual joy, is not a mortal sin.

8. Not every inordinate desire is a mortal sin, since proneness to inordinate desire threatens us from the corruption of our nature. But proneness to seek rest and to avoid toil, which seems to belong to spiritual apathy, threatens us from the same corruption. Therefore, not all spiritual apathy is a mortal sin.

On the Contrary:

1. Damascene says that spiritual apathy is a sadness.[26] But it is not sadness in accord with God, since then it would not be a sin. Therefore, it is worldly sadness. But worldly sadness produces death, as the Apostle says in 2 Cor. 7:10. Therefore, spiritual apathy is a mortal sin.

2. Augustine says in his *Literal Commentary on Genesis* that Jacob, saying to his sons: "You will bring my old age with sadness down to hell,"[27] seems to have feared that he would be so disturbed by excessive sorrow that he would go to the hell of sinners and not to the repose of the blessed.[28] And everything that withdraws persons from the repose of the blessed and brings them to the hell of sinners is a mortal sin. Therefore, the sadness that is spiritual apathy is a mortal sin.

3. On Ps. 43:5, "Why are you sad, O my soul?" a gloss says that "it teaches that we should avoid worldly sadness, which extinguishes patience and charity and hope and confounds the whole good life."[29] Therefore, spiritual apathy is a mortal sin, since we call what extinguishes charity and the other virtues mortal sin.

---

26. Ibid., 14 (PG 94:932B).
27. Cf. Gen. 44:29.
28. *Literal Commentary on Genesis* XII, 33, n. 64 (PL 34:482).
29. Peter Lombard, *Gloss*, on Ps. 43:5 (PL 191:426C–D).

Answer:

We can easily show from what I have said before[30] that spiritual apathy as a special sin is a mortal sin by reason of its kind. For spiritual apathy signifies a sadness arising out of the repugnance of human desires for divine spiritual good, since such repugnance is obviously contrary to charity, which belongs to a divine good and rejoices in possession of that good. Therefore, since what is contrary to charity, which gives life to the soul, is a mortal sin, it evidently follows that spiritual apathy is a mortal sin by reason of its kind, since "Those who do not love abide in death," as 1 Jn. 3:14 says.

And we should consider that envy, which is sadness at a neighbor's good, is a mortal sin by reason of its kind insofar as it is contrary to charity regarding love of neighbor. Just so. spiritual apathy, which is sadness over a divine spiritual good, is a mortal sin by reason of its kind insofar as it is contrary to charity regarding love of God. But it is true regarding all sins mortal by reason of their kind that movements incompletely belonging to the genus of such sins, namely, movements without the deliberation of reason, are not mortal sins. And so such movements of spiritual apathy are venial sins, as I have said before about movements of envy.[31] Nonetheless, when carnal desire so prevails over reason that human beings are deliberately saddened over a divine spiritual good, such movements of the will are evidently mortal sins.

Replies to the Objections:

1. Perfect human beings can have incomplete movements of spiritual apathy at least regarding sense appetite, since no human beings are so perfect that they retain no opposition of the flesh to the spirit. But the Apostle in the cited text seems to be speaking about sadness over temporal evils, not about sadness over a spiritual good.

2. Spiritual apathy is contrary to the precept to keep holy the Sabbath, which as a moral precept commands repose of the mind in God.

3. God as present in our minds does not allow sadness or mortal sin to accompany his presence. And so spiritual apathy is sadness about a good that is divine by way of participation, not sadness about the presence of God himself.

4. Spiritual apathy is not withdrawal of the mind from every spiritual good but withdrawal from a spiritual good to which the mind is necessarily obliged to adhere, and that spiritual good is a divine good, as I have already said.[32]

5. [And the foregoing makes clear the reply to objection 5.][33]

6. The argument of this objection is valid about the spiritual good of the particular acts of particular virtues, since no precept commands that human beings take pleasure in everything. But a precept does command that human beings take joy in God, just as a precept commands that they love God, since pleasure results from love.

7. The pleasure resulting from charity, to which spiritual apathy is contrary, necessarily belongs to the spiritual life, just as charity itself does, and so spiritual apathy is a mortal sin.

---

30. A. 2.

31. Q. 10, a. 2.

32. In the answer.

33. The text of the reply to objection 5 is missing from the earliest manuscripts, but the Leonine editors have reconstructed it from later printed versions.

8. As inordinate desire belongs only to a sense appetite, which results from the corruption of human nature, is not a mortal sin because it is an incomplete movement, so also neither is such spiritual apathy a mortal sin.

Fourth Article

Is Spiritual Apathy a Capital Sin?

It seems that spiritual apathy is not, for the following reasons:

1. As pleasure results from love, so sadness results from hate. But hate is not a capital sin. Therefore, much less is spiritual apathy, which is a sadness.

2. Capital sins are those that dispose us to the acts of other sins. But spiritual apathy seems to render us immobile rather than dispose us to the acts of other sins. For it is oppressive sadness, as Damascene says.[34] Therefore, spiritual apathy is not a capital sin.

3. A capital sin has daughters. But spiritual apathy does not seem to have the daughters Gregory in his work *Morals* assigns to it.[35] For malice is common to all sins. And rancor belongs to hate, which anger generates. And pusillanimity and despair belong to irascible power, but spiritual apathy belongs to concupiscible, not irascible, power. And torpor regarding precepts seems to be the same as spiritual apathy. And letting the mind wander seems to be contrary to the nature of sadness, which restricts the mind. Therefore, we ought not designate spiritual apathy a capital sin.

On the Contrary:
The authority of Gregory in his work *Morals* lists spiritual apathy or sadness among the capital sins.[36]

Answer:
Those sins are capital from which other sins arise by reason of the capital sins being the final causes of other sins, as I have said before.[37] And as human beings proceed to do or avoid many things in order to seek pleasure, so also they proceed to do or avoid many things in order to avoid sadness. For both ways of proceeding seem to have the same nature, that is, to seek good and avoid evil. And spiritual apathy is sadness over an interior divine good, as envy is sadness over a neighbor's good, as I have said.[38] Therefore, as many sins arise out of envy because human beings do many things inordinately to repel the sadness that results from a neighbor's good, so also is spiritual apathy a capital sin.

And no human being can long remain pleasureless and sad, as the Philosopher says in the *Ethics*.[39] Therefore, two things result from sadness, one of which is that human

34. *On Orthodox Faith* II, 14 (PG 94:932B).
35. *Morals* XXXI, 45, n. 88 (PL 76:621B).
36. Ibid., n. 87 (PL 76:621A).
37. Q. 8, a. 1.
38. A. 3.
39. *Ethics* VIII, 5 (1157b15–16).

beings withdraw from things that make them sad, and the other of which is that they turn to other things in which they find pleasure. And the Philosopher accordingly says in the *Ethics* that those who cannot enjoy spiritual pleasures turn their endeavors for the most part to bodily pleasures.[40] And so due to the sadness conceived regarding spiritual goods, their minds then wander over the illicit things in which the carnal spirit takes pleasure. And in avoiding such sadness, we note the progression wherein human beings indeed first avoid spiritual goods and then attack them. And both withdrawal from a divine good hoped for, which is despair, and withdrawal from spiritual good deeds to be done belong to avoidance of spiritual goods. And the latter withdrawal as regards the general things necessary for salvation is indeed torpor concerning the commandments. And withdrawal from spiritual good deeds as regards difficult things falling within the counsels is pusillanimity. And further, persons may, indeed, if they be unwillingly made to engage in spiritual good deeds that cause them sadness, first conceive indignation at prelates or any persons who make them engage in such deeds, and this is rancor. And they may then conceive indignation and hatred against even the spiritual good deeds, and this is malice in the strict sense.

Replies to the Objections:

1. Among the virtues, we designate love, from which pleasure results, the chief virtue, that is, charity, since the divine good and the good of neighbor are loveable as such. And the divine good and the good of neighbor are not hateable as such but only insofar as they incidentally cause sadness. And so we understand capital sins by reason of sadness rather than by reason of hatred.

2. Spiritual apathy indeed immobilizes the persons subject to it from the things that cause their sadness but renders them prone to contrary things.

3. Gregory does not understand malice insofar as it is common to every sin, but insofar as it signifies hostility to spiritual goods. And nothing prevents anger and spiritual apathy generating rancor, since different causes can cause the same thing in different respects. And that pusillanimity and despair belong to irascible power does not prevent spiritual apathy causing them, since concupiscible emotions cause all irascible emotions. And torpor regarding the very deeds to be done is not sadness itself but an effect of sadness. And so spiritual apathy results in sadness, as if the heart is weighed down because apathy restricts it, and so the heart shrugging off such heaviness escapes to other things.

40. Ibid., X, 6 (1176b19–21).

QUESTION XII

On Anger

First Article

Is All Anger Evil, or Is Some Anger Good?

It seems that all anger is evil, for the following reasons:

1. Jerome, explaining Mt. 5:22, "Everyone angry with his brother," etc., says: "Some codices add 'without cause,' but the statement is unqualified in authentic codices, and anger is completely reproved. For if we are commanded to pray for our persecutors, every occasion for anger is removed. Therefore, we should delete 'without cause,' since human anger does not accomplish God's justice."[1] Therefore, all anger is evil and forbidden.

2. As Dionysius says in his work *On the Divine Names*, anger is natural to dogs but unnatural to human beings.[2] But what is contrary to the nature of human beings is evil and sin, as Damascene makes clear in his work *On Orthodox Faith*.[3] Therefore, all anger is sin.

3. Evil for the human soul consists of being contrary to reason, as Dionysius says in the same chapter.[4] But anger is always contrary to reason, for the Philosopher says in the *Ethics*: "Anger seems in some respect to listen to reason but to mishear it,"[5] that is, not to hear it perfectly, as he afterwards explains.[6] Therefore, anger is always evil.

4. The Lord in Mt. 7:3–4 reproves those who have a beam in their own eye and wish to cast out a mote from a brother's eye. Therefore, much more are those to be reproved who put a beam in their own eye in order to cast out a mote from another's eye. But such are those who become angry in order to correct another, for Cassian says in his work *The Institutes*: "Intense emotion of anger for whatever reason blinds the eye of the heart."[7]

---

1. *On Matthew* I, on 5:22 (PL 26:36).
2. *On the Divine Names* 4, n. 25 (PG 3:728B).
3. *On Orthodox Faith* II, 30 (PG 94:976A).
4. *On the Divine Names* 4, n. 32 (PG 3:733A).
5. *Ethics* VII, 6 (1149a25–26).
6. Ibid.
7. *The Institutes (for Monasteries)* VIII, 6 (PL 49:333A).

Therefore, those are to be reproved who become angry in correcting their brother, and much more are those who become angry for any other reason.

5. The perfection of human beings consists of imitation of God. And so Mt. 5:48 says: "Be perfect as your Father is perfect." But "God judges with tranquility," as Wis. 12:18 says. "Anger, however, takes away peace of mind," as Gregory says in his work *Morals*.[8] Therefore, all anger detracts from human perfection, as it separates us from the likeness of God.

6. Everything good or morally indifferent is useful for virtuous acts, since the use of good things is a virtuous act, as Augustine says in his work *On Free Choice*.[9] But no anger is useful for virtue, for Cassian says in the cited work: "When the Apostle says in Eph. 4:31: 'Let us put all anger away from us,' he makes absolutely no exception for what is necessary or useful for us."[10] And Cicero says in his *Tusculan Disputations*: "Courage does not need to call on anger; it is perfect enough when armed with its own weapons."[11] Therefore, no anger is good.

7. Gregory says in his work *Morals*: "When anger strikes down peace of mind, anger brings the mind torn and rent into complete confusion, so that the mind is not in harmony with its very self and loses the force of its inner likeness."[12] And so it is evident that anger especially harms the soul. But we call something evil because it causes harm, as Augustine says in his *Enchiridion*.[13] Therefore, all anger is evil.

8. A gloss on Lev. 19:17, "Hate not your brother in your heart," says that anger is inordinate desire for revenge.[14] But to seek revenge is contrary to God's law, for Lev. 19:18 adds: "Do not seek revenge." Therefore, anger is always a sin.

9. There is like judgment about like things. Therefore, we ought also to judge similarly about things with the same name. But we designate anger among the capital sins, and every one of the other things called capital sins is always evil and never good, as is evident to anyone going through the capital sins one by one. Therefore, anger is always evil and never good.

10. Causes can be most powerful even if they be least in size, as the Philosopher says.[15] But capital sins cause sins. Therefore, they are the greatest in evil. Therefore, they have no admixture of good. And so no anger is good.

11. What prevents the best activity of human beings is evil. But even anger out of zeal for rectitude prevents the best activity of human beings, namely, contemplation. For Gregory says in his work *Morals*: "When even striving for righteousness troubles a person, the contemplation that only a tranquil heart can perceive is destroyed."[16] Therefore, all anger is evil.

8. *Morals* V, 45, n. 78 (PL 75:724C).
9. *On Free Choice* II, 19, n. 50 (PL 32:1268).
10. *The Institutes (for Monasteries)* VIII, 5 (PL 49:330B–332A).
11. *Tusculan Disputations* IV, 23.
12. *Morals* V, 45, n. 78 (PL 75:723D).
13. *Enchiridion* 12 (PL 40:237).
14. *Ordinary Gloss*, on Lev. 19:18.
15. *On Heaven and Earth* I, 5 (271b12).
16. *Morals* V, 45, n. 82 (PL 75:726D).

12. As Cicero says in his *Tusculan Disputations*, emotions are diseases of the soul.[17] But all bodily diseases are evils of the body. Therefore, all emotions of the soul are evils of the soul. Therefore, all anger is evil.

13. The Philosopher says in the *Topics* that one who undergoes emotion but refrains from it is one who undergoes emotion but is not controlled by it, and a gentle and temperate person is one who does not undergo emotion.[18] And the Philosopher thereby holds that being virtuous consists of undergoing no emotion, and so every emotion is contrary to virtue. But everything contrary to virtue is evil. Therefore, all anger, since it is an emotion, is evil.

14. All those who usurp for themselves what belongs to God sin. But all those who become angry usurp to themselves vengeance, which belongs only to God, as Dt. 32:35 says: "Vengeance is mine, and I shall repay." For anger is the desire for vengeance, as the Philosopher says.[19] Therefore, all those who become angry sin.

15. Valerius Maximus relates of Archytas of Tarentum that when his slave had offended him, he said: "I would punish you severely were I not angry with you."[20] Therefore, it seems that anger prevents due correction.

16. If any anger be good, only anger that rises up against sin is. But no anger is such, since anger, as the emotion of a sense appetite, arises only against evils perceived by the senses. Therefore, no anger is good.

On the Contrary:

1. Chrysostom says: "Those who become angry without cause will be guilty, and those who become angry with cause will not. For if there be no anger, teaching is bootless, the judicial process undermined, and crimes unchecked."[21] Therefore, some anger is good and necessary.

2. Divine precepts lead only to good. But a divine precept instructs us to be angry, as Eph. 4:26 says: "If you are angry, do not sin." And a gloss explains: "Be angry at sinners, for this is a natural movement of the soul customarily associated with correction of the wayward. Therefore, it tells us to be angry at sinners, indicating that such anger is good."[22] Therefore, not all anger is evil.

3. Gregory says in his work *Morals*: "Those who wish us to be angry only with ourselves and not also with our wayward neighbors do not understand correctly. For if we are commanded to love our neighbors as ourselves, it follows that we should be as angry at their sins as with our own."[23]

4. Damascene says in his work *On Orthodox Faith* that Christ was angry,[24] and yet Christ had no sin, as 1 Pet. 2:22 says. Therefore, not all anger is sin.

---

17. *Tusculan Disputations* III, 10.
18. *Topics* IV, 5 (125b22–27).
19. *Rhetoric* II, 2 (1378b1–2).
20. *Extraordinary Deeds and Sayings* IV, 1, extract 1.
21. John Chrysostom (Pseudo), *Unfinished Work on Matthew*, hom. 11 (PG 56:690).
22. Peter Lombard, *Gloss*, on Eph. 4:26 (PL 192:206A).
23. *Morals* V, 45, n. 82 (PL 75:726C).
24. *On Orthodox Faith* III, 20 (PG 94:1081B–C).

5. Every sin is blameworthy. But some who become angry are not blameworthy, as the Philosopher says in the *Ethics*.[25] Therefore, not all anger is a sin.

Answer:

There was a controversy about this question among ancient philosophers, for the Stoics said that all anger is evil, and the Aristotelians said that some anger is good.[26]

Therefore, in order to perceive what is closer to the truth in this matter, we should note that we can consider two things regarding anger or any other emotion: one the formal element, as it were; the other the material element, as it were. The formal element in anger indeed concerns the appetitive soul, namely, that anger desires vengeance, and the material element belongs to a bodily disturbance, namely, that anger increases the circulation of blood around the heart.

Therefore, if we should consider anger by its formal element, then it can belong both to a sense appetite and to the intellectual appetite, that is, the will, insofar as one can will to take vengeance. And so anger can evidently be either good or evil. For it is evidently virtuous for one to seek vengeance according to the proper ordination of justice, as, for example, when one seeks vengeance for the correction of sin without violating what the law prescribes. And this is to be angry at sin. And anger is a sin when one inordinately desires vengeance, or because one seeks vengeance contrary to what the law prescribes, or because one seeks vengeance with the aim of doing away with the sinner rather than the sin—and this is to be angry at one's brother. And there would have been no disagreement between the Stoics and the Aristotelians on this point, for even the Stoics conceded that willing vengeance is sometimes virtuous. But the whole controversy concerned the second element, the material element in anger, namely, the disturbance of the heart, since such disturbance prevents the judgment of reason, of which virtuous good chiefly consists. And so for whatever reason one is angry, this seems to be to the detriment of virtue, and all anger to that extent seems to be evil.

But if one should consider the matter rightly, one will find that the Stoics in their evaluation erred in three ways. First, they indeed erred regarding their failure to distinguish between the unconditionally best and the best in a particular case. For something better unconditionally may not be better in a particular case. For example, it is better, absolutely speaking, to philosophize that to have money, but for one in need of necessities, it is better to have money, as the *Topics* says.[27] And it is good for dogs by reason of their natural condition to be ferocious, although this is not good for human beings. Therefore, since human nature is a composite of soul and body, and of an intellectual nature and a sensory nature, it belongs to the human good that the whole composite as such be subject to virtue, namely, both regarding the intellectual part and the sensory part and the body. And so the virtue of human beings requires that a desire for due vengeance belong to both the rational part of the soul and the sensory part and the body itself, and that the body itself be moved to observe virtue.

25. *Ethics* II, 5 (1105b33–1106a1).
26. Cf. Augustine, *City of God* IX, 4 (PL 41:258).
27. *Topics* III, 2 (118a10–11).

Second, the Stoics did not consider that anger and other such emotions can be related to judgments of reason in two ways. Anger can be related to judgments of reason in one way antecedently, and then anger and all such emotions necessarily always prevent judgments of reason, since the soul can best judge truth in a certain tranquility of mind. And so also the Philosopher says that the soul becomes knowledgeable and prudent when at rest.[28] Anger can be related to judgments of reason in a second way as a consequence, namely, because after reason has judged and ordained a mode of vengeance, then emotion arises to achieve it. And then anger and other such emotions do not prevent the previous judgments of reason but rather help to execute the judgments more readily, and the emotions in this way are useful for virtue. And so Gregory says in his work *Morals*: "One should take the greatest care lest the anger that we adopt as an instrument of virtue dominate the mind and give orders as if our mistress. Rather, let anger never withdraw from following reason like a handmaid ready to render service. For anger stands up more firmly against sin when it serves reason as a subject."[29]

Third, the Stoics erred in not correctly understanding anger and other emotions.[30] For although not all appetitive movements are emotions, they failed to distinguish emotions from other appetitive movements in that the other appetitive movements belong to the will, and emotions to sense appetites, since they did not distinguish the two kinds of appetite. But they did distinguish the appetites by calling emotions appetitive movements that transgress the moderation of well-ordered reason. And so they called emotions diseases of the soul, as diseases of the body transgress the moderation of health. And so all anger and emotion was necessarily evil. On the other hand, we rightly call anger any movement of the sense appetite, and reason can ordain such movements, and anger insofar as it results from a judgment of reason serves reason in readily executing the judgment. And the condition of human nature requires that reason control sense appetites. Therefore, we need to say in agreement with the Aristotelians that some anger is good and virtuous.

Replies to the Objections:

1. Jerome is speaking about the anger whereby one is angry at one's brother, as the words of the Lord that he explains make clear. And all such anger is evil, but the anger at sin is good, as I have said.[31]

2. Anger prevailing over reason is not natural to human beings. Rather, it is natural for them that they obey reason.

3. The Philosopher is speaking in the cited text about intemperate anger, which is not subject to reason.

4. Anger, when it obeys judgments of reason, indeed disturbs reason to a degree, but it helps to promote readiness to execute the judgments. And so such anger does not take away the ordination of reason that judgments of reason have already previously

28. *Physics* VII, 3 (247b19–20).
29. *Morals* V, 45, n. 83 (PL 75:727A–B).
30. Cf. Cicero, *Tusculan Disputations* III, 10.
31. In the answer.

established. And so Gregory says in his work *Morals* that sinful anger blinds the eye of the mind, but zealous anger only disturbs rather than blinds the eye of the mind.[32]

5. God is incorporeal. Therefore, as he does not act with bodily members, so he does not act with sense appetites. But it belongs to the virtue of human beings that they use the movements of sense appetites, just as they use bodily instruments.

6. The anger preceding judgments of reason is useless for, and harmful to, virtue. But the anger subsequent to judgments of reason is useful for executing the judgments of reason, as I have said.[33]

7. We should understand the words of Gregory about sinful anger. And so he himself also shows in what follows that there is another kind of anger that is praiseworthy and virtuous.

8. God's law prohibits punishment inflicted only out of malicious vengeance but not punishment inflicted out of zeal for justice.

9. We should make judgments based on the nature of things, not their names. And so things with the same name need not be judged the same way; otherwise, the fallacy of equivocation would be ignored. Therefore, we should note that sins contrary to gentleness lack a name, as the Philosopher says in the *Ethics*.[34] And so we substitute the word "emotion" for the expression "capital sin." And because emotions can be good or evil, anger can be good or evil. But we designate other capital sins by the names proper to the sins, and so the other capital sins are always evil.

10. Evil causes only through the power of good, as Dionysius says in his work *On the Divine Names*.[35] And so capital sins have the power to be sources of sins by reason of good, insofar as the capital sins' ends are desirable and cause movements to certain acts, not by reason of evil. And so capital sins do not need to be especially and simply evil. And yet we can say that anger as a capital sin is never good.

11. Not everything that prevents something better is evil; otherwise, matrimony would be evil, since it prevents virginity. And moreover, what prevents something good at a particular time can also be better for the moment. And so although contemplation is the best of human activities, absolutely speaking, an action that anger supports can be better in a particular case.

12. The argument of this objection is valid about anger insofar as anger designates a disordered movement, as the Stoics understood it.

13. The Philosopher in the *Topics* introduces as examples things he thinks to be false, but others think to be probable. And such is his statement that virtue consists of undergoing no emotion, since this was the position taken by the Stoics. And he in the *Ethics* argues against the opinion of those who said that virtues are emotionless states.[36] And yet we can say that virtue consists of undergoing no disordered emotion.

14. Those who are angry at the sin of their brother seek the vengeance of God, not their own vengeance. For sin is only an offense against God, and so those who are justly angry do not usurp for themselves what belongs to God.

---

32. *Morals* V, 45, n. 82 (PL 75:726C).
33. In the answer.
34. *Ethics* IV, 5 (1125b26–27).
35. *On the Divine Names* 4, n. 32 (PG 3:732C).
36. *Ethics* II, 5 (1105b31–32).

15. Archytas had not determined the means of avenging the wrong, and so he was unwilling to determine it while angry lest he punish too much.

16. We can consider two things regarding anger, namely, the reason for anger that reason communicates, and this can be sinful, and second, the harm to which a sense appetite inclines, and this is always something perceptible.

Second Article

Can Anger Be a Sin?

It seems that anger cannot, for the following reasons:

1. Anger is an emotion. But we neither merit nor incur demerit for our emotions, nor are we praiseworthy or blameworthy because of them, as the Philosopher makes clear in the *Ethics*.[37] Therefore, anger is not a sin.

2. As a lame man is a human being, so our fallen nature is a nature. But getting angry belongs to our fallen nature. Therefore, anger is something befitting our nature. But nothing such is a sin. Therefore, anger is not a sin.

3. We should not judge that what of itself can be ordained for good or evil is a sin. But anger can be ordained for good or evil. Therefore, anger as such is not a sin.

4. The proper acts of the natural powers of the soul are not sins, since sin is contrary to nature, as Damascene says in his work *On Orthodox Faith*.[38] But anger is an act of irascible power, which is a natural power of the soul. Therefore, anger is not a sin.

5. Every sin is voluntary, as Augustine says.[39] But anger is not voluntary, since an angry person acts with sadness, as the Philosopher says in the *Ethics*,[40] and sadness concerns things that happen to us against our will, as Augustine says in the *City of God*.[41] Therefore, anger is not a sin.

6. Things beyond our power are not sins, since no one sins regarding what one cannot avoid, as Augustine says.[42] But anger is beyond our power, since a gloss on Ps. 4:4, "If you are angry, do not sin," says that movements of anger are beyond our power.[43] Therefore, anger is not a sin.

7. The Philosopher says that anger consists of increased circulation of blood around the heart.[44] But this does not imply any sin. Therefore, anger is not a sin.

8. Jerome says in his *Letter to Antoninus the Monk* that becoming angry belongs to human beings, but that not inflicting injury belongs to Christians.[45] But what belongs to human beings as such is not a sin. Therefore, anger is not a sin.

---

37. Ibid.
38. *On Orthodox Faith* II, 30 (PG 94:976A).
39. *On True Religion* 14, n. 27 (PL 34:133).
40. *Ethics* VII, 6 (1149b20–21).
41. *City of God* XIV, 6 (PL 41:409), and 15, n. 2 (PL 41:424).
42. *On Free Choice* III, 18, n. 50 (PL 32:1295).
43. Peter Lombard, *Gloss*, on Ps. 4:4 (PL 191:86C).
44. *De anima* I, 2 (403a31).
45. *Letter* 12 (*to Antoninus*) (PL 22:346).

9. Every sin involves a turning toward a transitory good. But anger is a turning toward an evil, that is, harm to be inflicted on a neighbor, not toward a transitory good. Therefore, anger is not a sin.

On the Contrary:

The Apostle says in Eph. 4:31: "Every indignation and anger is removed from us." But he would not say this unless anger were to be a sin. Therefore, anger is a sin.

Answer:

Anger signifies a certain appetitive movement. But it signifies pursuit, not avoidance. And because the proper object of pursuit is a good, not an evil, all appetitive movements whose objects are evil (e.g., loving or desiring an evil, and rejoicing at an evil) are evil if they belong to pursuit of the objects, as I have said.[46] And anger indeed signifies a desire for some evil, that is, the harm one seeks to inflict on a neighbor, but anger desires that evil under the aspect of good, namely, righteous vengeance, not under the aspect of evil. For an angry person seeks to injure another in order to avenge an injury inflicted on the person. And we judge appetitive movements by the formal rather than the material element of their object. And so we should say that anger is the pursuit of good rather than the pursuit of evil, since what anger seeks is good in a formal sense but evil in a material sense. And although every pursuit of evil is evil, not every pursuit of good is good. Rather, we need to consider whether the good is really and absolutely good or apparently and relatively good. For the pursuit of something really and absolutely good (e.g., the love of and desire for and joy over wisdom) is good. And the pursuit of something apparently and relatively good but really and absolutely evil is evil, as is evident in the case of gluttony and sexual lust, regarding which we condemn the desire for something apparently and falsely good. Therefore, we should say regarding the question at issue that anger will be good and virtuous and called zealous if it be a desire for vengeance insofar as it is really righteous. But anger is a sin if it should belong to a vengeance apparently and falsely righteous. And Gregory in his work *Morals* calls such anger sinful.[47]

And a vengeance so desired is apparently righteous because of a previous injury that reason dictates should be avenged, but the vengeance is not really and absolutely righteous, since it does not observe the proper ordination of justice. This may be so because a person seeks a greater retribution than the person ought, or because a person seeks vengeance on the person's own authority when such is not permitted to the person, or because a person does not seek vengeance for a proper end. And so the Philosopher says in the *Ethics* that an angry person indeed begins to hear reason, namely, as the person judges that an injury should be avenged, but does not fully listen to reason because the person does not take heed to follow the right ordination of vengeance as reason dictates.[48] And so the Philosopher compares anger to servants who hasten to carry out commands before they hear them in their entirety, and so make mistakes.

46. Q. 10, a. 1.
47. *Morals* V, 45, n. 82 (PL 75:726C).
48. *Ethics* VII, 6 (1149a25–28).

Replies to the Objections:

1. We say that emotions are neither praiseworthy nor blameworthy because they, as such, do not signify anything in accord with, or contrary to, reason. But if we add to emotions something that renders them in accord with reason, such emotions will be praiseworthy. And if we add to emotions something that renders them contrary to reason, such emotions will be blameworthy. And so we designate anger a sin insofar as anger does not fully listen to reason, as I have said.[49] And yet we say that anger is a sin both as an emotion, that is, the movement of a sense appetite, and as designating an act of the intellectual appetite, that is, the will, as I have said.[50]

2. Something can belong to a lame man as a human being, and this belongs to him intrinsically as a human being and accidentally as a lame man. For something accidentally related to the man as a human being can belong to him insofar as he is lame. And likewise, anger can belong to our fallen nature insofar as it is fallen, for this results in movements of anger departing from the ordination of reason.

3. As I have said before,[51] we substitute the name of the emotion, which is intrinsically indifferent, for the name of the vice, since the vice contrary to gentleness lacks a name. And it is in this way that we call anger a sin. And so such anger is related only to evil.

4. And we should say the same in reply to objection 4. For anger designates the act of a natural power insofar as anger is an emotion indifferently related to good or evil.

5. An angry person acts with a sadness that results from an injury inflicted on the person. And so we cannot conclude from this that anger is involuntary. Rather, we can conclude that something involuntary causes anger, since people would never become angry unless something were to be inflicted on them against their will.

6. The gloss is speaking about a disordered anger as belonging to a sense appetite before full deliberation by reason. And such movements of sense appetite are indeed within our power in particular cases, since we can prevent such movements by turning our thoughts to other things, although we cannot prevent disordered movements from arising.

7. The Philosopher gives that definition of anger by its material element, since the increased circulation of blood around the heart belongs to a bodily alteration. But such a bodily disturbance results from the will's movement that constitutes the formal element in anger. And the nature of sin consists of that movement.

8. We sometimes understand the name "human being" to mean human weakness, as 1 Cor. 3:3 does: "Since there are still jealousy and strife among you, are you not carnal and walking in a human way?" And this is the way in which we speak of disordered anger belonging to human beings, since such anger belongs to human weakness.

9. The object of anger is an evil under the aspect of something good, and so it signifies a turning toward a good.

49. In the answer.
50. A. 1.
51. A. 1.

Third Article

Is Anger a Mortal Sin?

It seems that anger is, for the following reasons:

1. A gloss on Eph. 4:26, "Do not let the sun set on your anger," says that Christ never dwells where there is anger.[52] But only mortal sin is incompatible with Christ dwelling in our soul. Therefore, anger is a mortal sin.

2. The Lord says in Mt. 5:21–22: "You have heard that it was said to our forefathers, 'Thou shalt not kill, and whoever kills will be liable to judgment.' But I say to you that everyone who is angry with his brother will be liable to judgment." And it is clear from this that anger deserves the same punishment in the New Law that murder deserved in the Old. But murder was always a mortal sin in the Old Law. Therefore, anger is a mortal sin in the New Law.

3. Everything that deserves eternal damnation is a mortal sin. But anger deserves eternal damnation, for a gloss on Mt. 5:22 says these three things, namely, judgment, the court, hell, express in particularity different stages in the process of eternal damnation corresponding to different kinds of sin.[53] Therefore, anger is a mortal sin.

4. Gregory says in his work *Morals*: "Through anger, justice is abandoned, peace disrupted, the splendor of the Holy Spirit expelled."[54] But only mortal sin does these things. Therefore, anger is a mortal sin.

5. Every willful desire for what Christ has reserved to himself is a mortal sin. But "anger is the lust for vengeance," as Augustine says in the *City of God*.[55] And Christ reserves vengeance to himself, as Dt. 32:35 says: "Vengeance belongs to me, and I shall repay." And that text says in other words: "Mine is punishment." Therefore, anger is a mortal sin.

6. What increases evil deeds seems to be an evil deed, that is, a mortal sin. But anger increases evil deeds, as a gloss on Prov. 29:22, "An angry man provokes quarrels," says.[56] Therefore, anger is a mortal sin.

7. Only a remarkable sin weakens the intellect, since the remarkable qualities of perceptible objects similarly weaken the senses. But anger weakens the intellect, for Gregory says in his work *Morals* that anger blinds the eye of reason.[57] Therefore, anger is a remarkable sin, and such sin is mortal.

8. What is contrary to reason seems to be a mortal sin. But inordinate anger is contrary to the judgment of reason, as is clear from what I have said before.[58] Therefore, anger is a mortal sin.

9. What is contrary to the nature of human beings is a mortal sin. But anger is such, for human beings are by nature gentle animals, and anger is contrary to gentleness. Therefore, anger is a mortal sin.

---

52. Peter Lombard, *Gloss*, on Eph. 4:26 (PL 192:206C).
53. *Ordinary Gloss*, on Mt. 5:22.
54. *Morals* V, 45, n. 78 (PL 75:724A–C).
55. *City of God* XIV, 15, n. 2 (PL 41:424).
56. *Ordinary Gloss*, on Prov. 29:22.
57. *Morals* V, 45, n. 82 (PL 75:726C).
58. A. 1.

10. Whatever is contrary to acts of charity is a mortal sin. But anger is contrary to acts of charity that will good for a neighbor, and anger wills harm to a neighbor. Therefore, anger is a mortal sin.

11. We call sins mortal because they kill spiritually. But Job 5:2 says that "anger kills a stupid man." Therefore, anger is a mortal sin.

On the Contrary:

1. A gloss on Ps. 4:4, "If you are angry, do not sin," says: "Anger that is not carried into effect is venial."[59] But consent by itself never renders venial things that are mortal sins by reason of their kind even before they are carried into effect. Therefore, anger is not a mortal sin by reason of its kind.

2. A sin of deed is no less a sin than a sin of desire. But an angry deed is not always a mortal sin. For example, such is the case when one through anger inflicts a slight harm on a neighbor, whether by striking the neighbor lightly or by rebuking the neighbor or by doing some such thing. Therefore, neither is anger a mortal sin by reason of its kind.

3. Augustine says in the *City of God* that Christian teaching does not consider whether one is angry but rather why a pious soul is angry.[60] But no mortal sin can accompany piety. Therefore, anger is not a mortal sin.

4. Some anger is virtuous, as I have maintained before,[61] and some anger is a mortal sin. Therefore, some anger in between is a venial sin.

5. No mortal sin can coexist with the Holy Spirit. But anger can coexist with the Holy Spirit, for we read in 2 Kgs. 2:15 that the spirit of Elijah rested on Elisha, and yet Elisha immediately afterward cursed the young boys, and "two bears came out of the forest and mauled forty two of them."[62] And the cursing seems to belong to extreme anger. Therefore, anger is not a mortal sin.

6. The New Law permits no mortal sin. But the New Law permits anger, as a gloss on Eph. 4:26, "If you are angry, do not sin," makes clear.[63] Therefore, anger is not a mortal sin.

7. Concupiscence is baser than anger, as the Philosopher says in the *Ethics*.[64] But concupiscence is not always a mortal sin. Therefore, neither is anger.

8. No appetitive movement prior to full deliberation by reason is a mortal sin. But anger is always prior to the full deliberation of reason, since anger never fully listens to reason, as the Philosopher says in the *Ethics*.[65] Therefore, anger is not a mortal sin.

Answer:

We should consider whether moral acts are good or evil by reason of their kind, and whether the acts, if evil, are mortal or venial sins, in relation to their objects, since the

---

59. Peter Lombard, *Gloss*, on Ps. 4:4 (PL 191:86C).

60. *City of God* IX, 5 (PL 41:260).

61. A. 1.

62. 2 Kgs. 2:24.

63. Peter Lombard, *Gloss*, on Eph. 4:26 (PL 192:206A).

64. *Ethics* VII, 6 (1149b23–25).

65. Ibid. (1149a25–26).

acts derive their species from their objects. And I have said that the object of anger as sin is unrighteous anger, which is simply the harm that one inflicts on a neighbor contrary to the obligations of justice.[66] And such anger by its nature signifies mortal sin. For inasmuch as the duty of justice falls under a precept, everything contrary to the obligations of justice is contrary to the precept and so is a mortal sin. And so sinful anger is a mortal sin by reason of its kind, since such anger is simply the will to harm one's neighbor unjustly because of a previous offense by the neighbor.

But a sin may be mortal by reason of its kind and nonetheless venial because of the incompleteness of the act, as I have said regarding other sins.[67] I have said before that acts of human beings can be incomplete in two ways.[68] The acts are incomplete in one way regarding the one who acts, and then the incomplete acts of human beings belong only to sense appetites prior to judgments of reason, which is the proper source of activity by human beings. And such movements of sense appetites to commit mortal sins, even to commit adultery or homicide, are venial sins. We call acts incomplete in the second way regarding their object, which we consider as if nothing because it is slight. For reason understands something slight as if it were nothing, as the Philosopher says in the *Politics*.[69] And so although taking someone else's property is a mortal sin by reason of its kind, taking something trivial, which is as if of no value or no importance, is not a mortal sin. For example, such would be the case if one were to take a small bunch of grapes from someone's vineyard. And there may be venial sins in the genus of sins of anger in both ways: in the first way as a sudden movement of anger to which reason does not consent is a venial sin; in the second way because the harm inflicted is slight. For example, the harm may be slight if one angry at a child wants to pull the child's hair or ear a little, or do some other slight thing, to punish the child. But when one desires to avenge oneself without observing justice, by inflicting serious harm with the consent of deliberative reason, such anger is always a mortal sin.

And since some anger is a mortal sin, and some anger a venial sin, we need to reply to both sets of arguments.

Replies to the Objections:
1. The gloss is speaking about sinful anger, when the movement of anger is complete both regarding the one who acts and regarding the object. For then there is always mortal sin, as I have said.[70]

2–4. And we should say the like in reply to objections 2, 3, and 4.

5. God reserves part of retribution to himself alone. For he has committed infliction of retribution regarding public sins to others legally constituted in positions of power, as Rom. 13:4 says of those holding legitimate power that they are "avengers of God's wrath on evildoers." But he has reserved to himself alone judgment and retribution regarding hidden sins, as 1 Cor. 4:5 says: "Do not judge before the appointed time." God has also reserved to himself alone that he be avenged for his own sake, since human beings

66. A. 2.
67. Q. 10, a. 2, and q. 11, a. 3.
68. Q. 10, a. 2.
69. Actually, *Rhetoric* II, 2 (1378b12–13).
70. In the answer.

should be avenged because of the moral fault committed against them that is an offense against God, not for their own sakes. Therefore, when one seeks vengeance for one's own sake or contrary to the prescriptions of legally constituted authority, one usurps to oneself what belongs to God, and so one sins mortally unless the act be incomplete, as I have said.[71]

6. Both adding evil deeds to evil deeds and providing the occasion for sin can cause an increase of sins. And anger that is a venial sin can cause an increase of sins by providing an occasion for sin.

7. Something can weaken the intellect or reason in two ways. Something weakens the intellect or reason in one way intrinsically and directly by reason of a contrariety, and only mortal sin does so in this way. Something weakens the intellect or reason in a second way indirectly and by accident insofar as a bodily alteration prevents the use of reason. And even anger that is a venial sin can in this way prevent the use of reason, but we do not in the strict sense say that anger blinds reason except when anger leads reason to consent to sin.

8. Reason directs everything for an end. Therefore, what excludes our proper end is directly contrary to reason, and only mortal sin does this. But if the disorder regards means without excluding our proper end, the disorder is, strictly speaking, outside reason but not contrary to it, and a venial sin.

9. Anger is contrary to the nature of human beings, who are rational animals, insofar as anger is contrary to reason, and such anger belongs only to the anger that is mortal sin.

10. Charity wills the good of one's neighbor under the aspect of good, and so hatred is strictly contrary to charity. But anger desires evil for one's neighbor under the aspect of retributive justice, not as evil, as I have said.[72] And so anger regarding an object apparently but not really just is contrary to justice, and anger as an emotion is contrary to gentleness, which is the mean regarding anger.

11. We should understand the cited authority to be speaking about completely sinful movements of anger.

Replies to the Arguments in the Section On the Contrary:

1. The gloss is speaking about anger that consists only of sense appetite, and the gloss says that such anger is carried into effect both in external deeds and by internal consent, which God imputes as a deed.

2. The argument of this objection is valid regarding anger that is incomplete regarding its object.

3. A pious soul is angry with zealous anger, which is virtuous, as I have said.[73]

4. There is nothing in between just and unjust vengeance, and so also neither is there anything in between virtuous and mortally sinful anger, except perhaps incomplete anger, which is a venial sin.

5. Elisha cursed the young boys out of zeal for divine justice, not out of sinful anger as if because of vengeful spite.

71. A. 2.
72. Ibid.
73. A. 1.

6. The Apostle allows movements of incomplete anger that consist solely of sense appetite.

7. If complete inordinate desire should belong to something a mortal sin by reason of its kind, it is also a mortal sin. But if the inordinate desire is incomplete, it is a venial sin, just as I have said about anger.[74]

8. Anger does not fully listen to dissuading reason, but anger sometimes fully listens to consenting reason.

Fourth Article

Is Anger a Less Serious Sin Than Hate and Envy and the Like?

It seems that anger is not, for the following reasons:

1. We call things evil because they harm, as Augustine says in his work *Enchiridion*.[75] Therefore, the more harm something causes, the more serious the sin. But anger causes greater harm to human beings than envy does, for Hugo of St. Victor says in his work *On the Five Sevens* that "pride takes God away from human beings, envy takes away their neighbor, anger takes away themselves."[76]

2. Effects are like their causes. But anger is the effect of envy, as Hugo says in the same work.[77] Therefore, anger is not a less serious sin than envy.

3. It likewise seems that anger is not a lesser sin than hate, since we note the seriousness of sins by their effects. But hate and anger have the same effects, namely, inflicting harm on one's neighbor. Therefore, hate is not a more serious sin than anger.

4. It likewise seems that anger is a more serious sin than concupiscence of the flesh, since one thing is greater than another if the greatest of the one is greater than the greatest of the other, as the Philosopher says in the *Topics*.[78] But the greatest sin in the genus of anger, namely, homicide, is more serious than any sin in the genus of concupiscence of the flesh. Therefore, anger is absolutely a more serious sin than concupiscence of the flesh.

5. The more serious a sin, the greater repentance it induces. But repentance is more associated with anger than with concupiscence of the flesh, since an angry person sins with sadness, but a concupiscent person does not, as the Philosopher says in the *Ethics*.[79] Therefore, anger is a more serious sin than concupiscence.

6. Ez. 16:44 says: "Like mother, like daughters." But blasphemy, which Gregory calls the daughter of anger,[80] is the most serious sin. Therefore, anger is a more serious sin than all the aforementioned sins.

---

74. In the answer.
75. *Enchiridion* 12 (PL 40:237).
76. *On the Five Sevens* 2 (PL 175:406B–C).
77. Ibid. (PL 175:407A).
78. *Topics* III, 2 (117b33–39).
79. *Ethics* VII, 6 (1149b20–21).
80. *Morals* XXXI, 45, n. 88 (PL 76:621B).

On the Contrary:

Augustine in his *Rule* compares anger to a mote, hate to a beam.[81]

Answer:

We should look for the differences in these sins where we find some agreement. The sin of anger agrees with the three sins regarding their object. For the object of anger is an evil to be inflicted under the aspect of a good, as I have said.[82] Therefore, regarding the evil, anger agrees with hate, which desires evil for another, and with envy, which grieves at the good of another. And regarding the desired good, anger agrees with concupiscence, which is also a disordered desire of a good.

But absolutely speaking, anger is less serious than the three aforementioned sins. For hate seeks the evil of neighbor under the aspect of evil, and envy is contrary to the good of neighbor under the aspect of good, but anger seeks a neighbor's evil and prevents a neighbor's good only under the aspect of good, that is, just retribution. And so what causes hate and envy to strive intrinsically for an evil and accidentally for a good causes anger to strive intrinsically for a good and accidentally for an evil. And an intrinsic cause is always more powerful than an accidental cause. And so envy and hate surpass the sin of anger in malice. Likewise, the sin of concupiscence results from striving for a sensibly pleasurable good, while anger strives inordinately for an apparently righteous good in accord with reason. And so since the good proper to reason is better than the good proper to the senses, movements of anger come closer to virtue than movements of concupiscence do. And so absolutely speaking, anger is a lesser sin. And so the Philosopher says in the *Ethics* that the lack of restraint in concupiscence is baser than the lack of restraint in anger.[83] And we indeed note this comparison by the very kinds of sins, since nothing prevents anger being more serious than the others by reason of additional circumstances.

Replies to the Objections:

1. Envy takes one's neighbor away from oneself by a contrariety to oneself, but anger does not take oneself away from oneself in this way. Rather, anger takes oneself away from oneself indirectly insofar as the bodily disturbance of anger prevents the exercise of reason whereby human beings are self-composed.

2. According to the Philosopher,[84] sadness causes anger, and so envy, since it is a sadness, may cause anger. But anger need not be equal to envy, since effects are not always equal to their causes, although effects are like their causes.

3. Anger and hatred come to inflict harm on our neighbor in different ways. And we can consider the difference in several respects, as the Philosopher says in the *Rhetoric*.[85] First, indeed, anger, because it strives for harm only under the aspect of just retribution, seeks to harm only those who have injured us or our relatives, in order to inflict some retribution.

---

81. *Rule for the Servants of God*, n. 10 (PL 32:1384).

82. A. 2.

83. *Ethics* VII, 6 (1149b23–25).

84. Ibid. (1149b20–21).

85. *Rhetoric* II, 4 (1381b37ff.).

But there can be hatred against strangers who have never injured us at all, because their disposition is contrary to ours. Second, anger and hatred differ because anger is always directed at particular persons, since injurious acts cause anger, and acts belong to particular persons. But hatred can be directed at a group with a common characteristic, as, for example, human beings hate the whole class of robbers. Third, anger and hatred differ because angry people seek their neighbor's harm only up to the measure that seems to them just retribution, and anger is indeed quieted when just retribution is obtained. But hatred is not satisfied with any evil, since it seeks the neighbor's evil as such. Fourth, anger and hatred differ because an angry person seeks that the other on whom the person inflicts harm perceive the fact that the evil happens to the other because of the injury the other has committed. But a hateful person does not care howsoever undeservedly the evil befalls the other. And these things also make clear that hate is a more serious sin than anger.

4. The argument of this objection would be valid if homicide were a species of anger, but homicide is an effect of anger, not one of its species. And a greater evil may sometimes result from a lesser evil.

5. Concupiscence can be repented of even more than anger, since anger belongs more to reason. And the sadness associated with anger does not belong to repentance, since the sadness regards the cause provoking to anger, namely, the injury inflicted, not the act of anger.

6. Since evil causes only by the power of good, sinners in sinning progress from what has a greater semblance of good, and so lesser sins very often lead human beings to commit greater sins. And so anger is not necessarily as serious as blasphemy.

Fifth Article

Is Anger a Capital Sin?

It seems that anger is not, for the following reasons:

1. There is no head of a head. But anger has a head, for sadness causes anger, as the Philosopher also says.[86] Therefore, anger is not a capital sin.

2. Every capital sin is a special kind of sin. But anger, since it is contrary to many virtues, not only to one, seems to be sin in general. For example, anger is contrary to charity and justice and gentleness. Therefore, anger is not a capital sin.

3. Other sins are contrary to other capital sins. For example, pusillanimity is contrary to pride, vain joy to spiritual apathy. But no other sin is contrary to anger. Therefore, anger is not a capital sin.

On the Contrary:
A gloss on Prov. 29:22, "An angry man provokes quarrels," says: "Anger is the gateway to all sins. And if it be shut, virtues will bestow internal peace; if it be open, the spirit will be armed to commit every kind of villainy."[87]

---

86. *Ethics* VII, 6 (1149b20–21).
87. *Ordinary Gloss*, on Prov. 29:22.

Answer:

A capital sin is one from which other sins arise by reason of the capital sin being their final cause, as I have said before.[88] And many things may for the most part be done inordinately to attain the end of anger, that is, to take vengeance, and those inordinate deeds are indeed sins. And so anger is a capital sin. And Gregory in his work *Morals* designates six daughters of anger, namely, quarrels, inflated ego, insults, exclamations, indignation, blasphemies.[89] And he does so because we can consider anger in three ways: in one way as in desire; in a second way as in speech; in a third way as also resulting in deeds.

And as in desire, a sin indeed arises from anger regarding the cause of anger, that is, the injury inflicted. For the harm inflicted provokes one to anger only insofar as one considers the harm under the aspect of injustice, since retribution is then warranted for it. And the more inferior and subject one person is to another, the more unjust the harm inflicted on the superior person. And so angry persons contemplating the harm inflicted on them magnify the injustice in their minds and go on from this to avenge the lack of respect by the person who inflicted the harm. And this is indignation in the strict sense. And anger in desire causes another sin regarding what an angry person desires. For angry people mull over different ways and means whereby they can avenge themselves, and such thoughts inflate their egos, as Job 15:2 says: "The wise will never fill their bellies with fire." And then an inflated ego results from anger. Anger also issues in speech, both against God, who permits the injury to be inflicted, and then anger causes blasphemy, and against the neighbor who inflicted the injury, and then there are two grades of anger, on which Mt. 5:22 touches. And one of these grades of anger in speech occurs when a person bursts into inordinate speech without expressing injurious words toward an individual, as in the case of one who says to a brother, "Fool," which is the exclamation of an angry person. The second grade of anger in speech occurs when a person bursts into even injurious words toward an individual, as in the case of one who says to a brother, "You fool," and insults belong to such anger in speech. And anger, as it culminates in action, causes quarrels, in which all the deeds resulting from anger, such as wounds, homicides, and the like, are included.

Replies to the Objections:

1. The sadness from which anger arises is not only the sadness that is a capital sin [spiritual apathy], and so anger is not included under a capital sin.

2. Anger is a special kind of sin, but it is contrary to different virtues in different respects. For example, it is contrary to gentleness regarding its very disorder of emotion, and contrary to charity regarding the harm that an angry person strives to inflict, and contrary to true justice regarding the aspect of apparent justice that an angry person contemplates. But it is more contrary to gentleness, which moderates anger.

3. There is also a sin contrary to anger, namely, inordinate abatement of anger. And Chrysostom on Mt. 5:22, "Everyone angry at a brother," etc., says: "Unreasonable patience begets sins, nourishes negligence, and invites both the wicked and the virtuous to evil."[90] But because this sin lacks a name, no other sin seems to be contrary to anger.

---

88. Q. 10, a. 3.
89. *Morals* XXXI, 45, n. 88 (PL 76:621B).
90. John Chrysostom (Pseudo), *Unfinished Work on Matthew*, hom. 11 (PG 56:690).

On Avarice

First Article

Is Avarice a Special Kind of Sin?

It seems that avarice is not, for the following reasons:

1. Every special kind of sin has a special kind of matter, since the objects of moral acts always determine the species of the acts. But avarice has a general, not a special, kind of matter, for Augustine says in his work *On Free Choice*: "We should understand avarice, which is called *philarguria* in Greek, both regarding silver or coins and regarding all immoderately desired things whenever one at all wants more than is sufficient."[1] Therefore, avarice is not a special kind of sin.

2. What includes in itself different kinds of sins is not a special kind of sin. But avarice includes in itself different kinds of sins, since even pride, which is the disordered desire for pre-eminence, is included in avarice. For Gregory in a homily on Mt. 4:1, "Jesus was led," etc., says: "There is avarice not only for money but also for high position when one desires a status above one's measure."[2] Therefore, avarice is not a special kind of sin.

3. Cicero says that "avarice is the immoderate love of possessing."[3] But we are said to possess everything that belongs to us, both our substantial parts and our qualities and our size and our external accidents, as the Philosopher says in the *Categories*.[4] Therefore, avarice is not a special kind of sin.

4. Every special kind of sin has another sin contrary to it, as the *Ethics* says.[5] But avarice has no other sin contrary to it, as the Philosopher makes clear in the *Ethics*.[6] Therefore, avarice is not a special kind of sin.

---

1. *On Free Choice* III, 17, n. 48 (PL 32:1294).
2. *On the Gospels* I, hom. 16, n. 2 (PL 76:1136A).
3. *Tusculan Disputations* IV, 11, n. 26.
4. *Categories* 1415 (15b17–33).
5. Aristotle, *Ethics* II, 8 (1108b11ff.).
6. Ibid., V, 5 (1133b32–33).

5. What is related to all kinds of sins does not seem to be a special kind of sin. But avarice is related to all kinds of sins, for 1 Tim. 6:10 says: "Covetousness is the root of all evils." And we understand covetousness to mean avarice, as Augustine says in his *Literal Commentary on Genesis*.[7] Therefore, avarice is not a special kind of sin.

6. If avarice should be a special kind of sin, this is especially so inasmuch as avarice is an inordinate desire for money. But avarice is in this way sin in general, since every sin consists of a turning toward a transitory good, as Augustine says, and almost every temporal good can be acquired with money, as Eccl. 10:19 says: "Everything obeys money."[8] Therefore, avarice is in no way a special kind of sin.

7. No special kind of sin is contrary to different virtues, since only one thing is contrary to another, as the *Metaphysics* says.[9] But avarice is contrary to different virtues. For it is contrary to charity, as Augustine says in his *Literal Commentary on Genesis*.[10] And it is contrary to generosity, as people generally say. And it is contrary to justice as a special virtue, as Chrysostom, explaining Mt. 5:6, "Blessed are those who hunger and thirst for justice," says, since he says that justice is either virtue in general or a special virtue contrary to avarice.[11] Therefore, avarice is not a special kind of sin.

8. It belongs to avarice to hoard things that should not be hoarded. But we should especially not hoard spiritual things, since shared spiritual things are increased, not diminished. Therefore, avarice regards spiritual goods. And it is evident that avarice regards material goods. Therefore, avarice regards all goods. Therefore, avarice is a general sin, not a special kind of sin.

On the Contrary:

1. We do not contradistinguish general things from special things. But we contradistinguish avarice from special kinds of sins. For Gregory in his work *Morals* contradistinguishes avarice from other capital sins.[12] And a gloss on Gen. 3:1 says the devil tempted the first human being regarding gluttony, pride, and avarice, and so the gloss contradistinguishes avarice from other kinds of sins.[13] Therefore, avarice is a special kind of sin.

2. A special kind of sin is contrary to a special virtue. But avarice is contrary to justice as a special virtue, as the cited authority of Chrysostom makes clear.[14] Therefore, avarice is a special kind of sin.

3. A root has the nature of a source. But we distinguish sources by the things of which they are the sources, since nothing is the source or cause of itself. Therefore, since avarice is the root of all evils, as the Apostle says, it seems that avarice is a sin distinct from other sins.[15] And so it is a special kind of sin, not sin in general.

---

7. *Literal Commentary on Genesis* XI, 15, n. 19 (PL 34:436).
8. *On Free Choice* I, 6, n. 35 (PL 32:1240), and III, 1, n. 1 (PL 32:1269).
9. *Metaphysics* X, 4 (1055a19–20).
10. *Literal Commentary on Genesis* XI, 15, n. 19 (PL 34:437).
11. St. Thomas, *Golden Chain*, on Mt. 5:6; cf. Chrysostom, *On Matthew*, hom. 15, n. 3 (PG 57:227).
12. *Morals* XXXI, 45, n. 87 (PL 76:621A).
13. *Ordinary Gloss*, on Gen. 3:1.
14. See objection 7.
15. 1 Tim. 6:10.

Answer:

Avarice as to the primary application of the name signifies the inordinate desire for money, for we call a person avaricious as if to say avid for money, as Isidore says in his work *Etymologies*.[16] And it is consonant with this that avarice is called *philarguria* in Greek, love of silver, as it were. And so inasmuch as money is a special matter, it seems that avarice as to the primary application of the name is a special kind of sin. But we by an analogy amplify the name *avarice* to signify inordinate desire for any good, and avarice in this sense is sin in general, since every sin involves a turning toward a transitory good through inordinate desire. And so Augustine says in his *Literal Commentary on Genesis* that there is avarice in general when one desires anything more than one ought, and there is special avarice commonly called love of money.[17]

And we make this distinction for the following reason. Since avarice is the inordinate love of possessing, we can understand possessing in a general way and in a second, special way, as we say we possess the things with which we can do whatever we want. Just so, we understand avarice in a general way to mean the inordinate love of possessing anything, and in a special way to mean love of possessing all of the things that we understand under the name *money*, since money measures their value, as the Philosopher says in the *Ethics*.[18]

But because sins are contrary to virtues, we need to consider that both justice and generosity are concerned about possessions or money, although in different ways. For the mean of the equality constituted in the very things possessed belongs to justice, namely, that every person possess what is due the person. And generosity constitutes the mean in the very dispositions of the soul, namely, that no one love or desire money too much, and that everyone dispense them with pleasure or without sadness when and where one should. Therefore, some speak of avarice as the contrary of generosity, and then avarice signifies a defect regarding dispensing money and surplus goods, a defect regarding the acquisition and retention of such things due to an excessive love of money.[19] And the Philosopher in the *Ethics* speaks of avarice as the contrary of justice, and he accordingly calls avaricious a person who takes or keeps another's goods contrary to the obligations of justice.[20] For he contrasts lack of generosity, not avarice, with generosity, as the *Ethics* makes clear.[21] And the cited authority of Chrysostom is consonant with this.[22] And so is what Ez. 22:27 says: "Her rulers in her midst are like wolves seizing their prey to shed blood and to pursue plunder avariciously."

Replies to the Objections:

1. Augustine is speaking in the cited text about avarice in the general sense.

   2. We should say the like in reply to objection 2.

---

16. *Etymologies* X, 9 (PL 82:369A).
17. *Literal Commentary on Genesis* XI, 15, n. 19 (PL 34:436 and 437).
18. *Ethics* IV, 1 (1119b26–27).
19. E.g., Alexander of Hales, *Summa of Theology* II–II, n. 581.
20. *Ethics* V, 1 (1129a31b10).
21. Ibid., IV, 1 (1122a13–14).
22. See n. 11, supra.

3. We say that we possess especially the possessions of which we are completely the masters. And so we should understand in the strict sense the statement of Cicero that avarice is the immoderate love of possessing, as when we speak of having possessions.

4. The argument of this objection is valid regarding avarice as contrary to justice. For justice is indeed the mean between too much and too little and not the mean between two vices, as other virtues are, as the *Ethics* says.[23] But for a person to abound in taking or keeping things beyond the obligations of justice is a vice and belongs to avarice. And for a person to have less than the person's due is to suffer injustice, not to commit it, and a punishment rather than a moral fault. And so avarice is not contrary to any other sin.

5. Avarice belongs to all sins as their root and source, not as their genus. And so one can conclude from this that avarice is a general cause of sins, not that avarice is sin in general.

6. We acquire with money things that are desirable in the same respect as money, namely, as they are useful for the necessities of life, so that all the things we call possessions both are included under the name "money" and constitute the matter of avarice in the special sense. And there are some things that we can acquire with money but have a different aspect of desirability. And such things belong to other special kinds of sins, for example, exalted honors to inordinate desire for fame, and excessive praise to vainglory, and pleasure in food to gluttony, and pleasure in sex to lust.

7. Avarice as conceived in different ways is contrary to justice and generosity, but avarice is contrary to charity just as every mortal sin constitutes its end in a created good.

8. Spiritual goods are to be shared, not hoarded, but there is not the same way of possessing or sharing those goods as one possesses or shares possessions. And so they do not belong to avarice in the strict sense.

Second Article

Is Avarice a Mortal Sin?

It seems that avarice is, for the following reasons:

1. Only mortal sin excludes one from the kingdom of God. But avarice excludes one from the kingdom of God, for Eph. 5:5 says: "No fornicator or unclean person or avaricious person, that is, a worshiper of idols, inherits the kingdom of Christ and God." Therefore, avarice is a mortal sin.

2. Every sin contrary to charity is mortal, since charity brings life to the soul, as 1 Jn. 2:15 says: "The perfect love of the Father is not in one who loves the world." But avarice is contrary to charity, for Augustine says in his work *Book of the 83 Questions* that covetousness poisons charity.[24] Therefore, avarice, which is the same as covetousness, is a mortal sin.

3. 1 Jn. 2:15 says: "The love of the Father is not in one who loves the world." But avarice results from inordinate love of the world. Therefore, avarice excludes the love of God from human beings and so is a mortal sin.

---

23. Aristotle, *Ethics* V, 5 (1133b32–33).
24. *Book of the 83 Questions*, q. 36, n. 1 (PL 40:25).

4. What is contrary to justice seems to be mortal sin, since justice has the nature of an obligation that falls under a precept. But avarice is contrary to justice, since avarice withholds things that can bring about the benefit of neighbors. For Basil says: "It is the bread of the hungry that you hoard, the cloak of the naked that you keep to yourself, the money of the needy that you retain. And so you could help as many as you have wronged."[25] Therefore, avarice is a mortal sin.

5. A gift of the Holy Spirit is more perfect than virtue. But avarice is contrary to a gift of the Spirit, namely, piety, as a gloss on Lk. 6:35 holds.[26] Therefore, avarice is a mortal sin.

6. Mortal sin is a turning away from the immutable good and a turning toward a transitory good. But such especially belongs to avarice, which is the inordinate desire of a transitory good. Therefore, avarice is a mortal sin.

7. What presses the mind down to earthly things so that it cannot rise to heavenly things seems to be mortal sin. But avarice is such, for Gregory says in his work *Morals* that "avarice renders the mind it has infected so heavy that the mind cannot be lifted to seek lofty things."[27] Therefore, avarice is a mortal sin.

8. Incurability is the condition of a most serious sin, since we call the sin against the Holy Spirit, which is the most serious, unforgivable. But avarice is incurable, as the Philosopher says in the *Ethics*.[28] Therefore, avarice is a mortal and most serous sin.

On the Contrary:

1. A gloss on 1 Cor. 3:12, "If one has built on this foundation," etc., says that "one who thinks about worldly things, how one pleases the world, builds on wood, hay, and straw," and this belongs to the sin of avarice.[29] But this signifies venial, not mortal, sin, for 1 Cor. 3:15 adds: "Such a one will be saved as if by fire." Therefore, avarice is not a mortal sin.

2. Avarice is contrary to prodigality. But prodigality is not by reason of its kind a mortal sin. Therefore, neither is avarice, since contraries belong to the same genus.

3. Superfluous accumulation of temporal things belongs to avarice in the strict sense. But such is not always a mortal sin, since it is not contrary to a precept. Therefore, avarice is not a mortal sin.

4. It seems that it is praiseworthy not to take things belonging to another. But avaricious persons sometimes do not want to take things belonging to another, as the Philosopher says in the *Ethics*.[30] Therefore, avarice is sometimes not evil and so not a mortal sin.

Answer:

We speak of avarice in two ways, as I have said.[31] For we sometimes understand avarice as the contrary of justice, and then avarice is always a mortal sin, except perhaps because

---

25. *Homily on Luke* 12:18, n. 7 (PG 31:277A).
26. *Ordinary Gloss*, on Lk. 6:35.
27. *Morals* XIV, 53, n. 63 (PL 75:1072A).
28. *Ethics* IV, 1 (1121b12–13).
29. Peter Lombard, *Gloss*, on 1 Cor. 3:12 (PL 191:1557A).
30. *Ethics* IV, 2 (1121b23).
31. A. 1.

the act is incomplete, as I have said before about other sins.[32] For then unjustly taking or keeping the things of another belongs to avarice, and this is always a mortal sin, although the first movements in this type of act are not mortal sins. And we sometimes understand avarice as the contrary of generosity, which contrary the Philosopher in the *Ethics* calls stinginess, and then it belongs to avarice to be excessive in the love and desire of money and all the things that money can buy.[33] And so if we are speaking of such love and desire in a general way, avarice is not always a mortal sin. But if we are speaking of such love and desire in the strict sense, then avarice is always a mortal sin. For good is the object of love and desire, and good is in the strict sense and chiefly an end, and what is ordained to an end has the intrinsic nature of good only because of its ordination to the end. Therefore, the end is in the strict sense and chiefly the object of love and desire, and the means are the object of love and desire secondarily.

Therefore, if we call avarice the love and desire of temporal goods in such a way that we make them our end, avarice will always be mortal sin. For turning toward a created good as our end causes turning away from the immutable good, which ought to be our ultimate end, since there cannot be several ultimate ends. But if we in a general way of speaking call avarice an inordinate love or desire for things of this world, then avarice is not always a mortal sin. This is so because some still love worldly things and are wrapped up in earthly affairs but in such a way that their hearts do not withdraw from Christ, and they put nothing ahead of Christ, as a gloss on 1 Cor. 3:12, "If one builds," etc., maintains.[34]

Replies to the Objections:

1. The Apostle does not say absolutely that an avaricious person does not participate in the kingdom of Christ and God but adds the qualification: "That is, a worshiper of idols." For avarice as idolatry excludes one from the kingdom of Christ and God because, inasmuch as one makes temporal goods one's end, one gives a creature the honor owed to God, and one ought to give such honor to God alone.

2. The covetousness extinguishing charity is one that makes temporal goods a person's end. But the covetousness that does not make temporal goods a person's end, although exceeding due measure, impedes the virtue of charity from its acts but does not extinguish it.

3. The foregoing makes clear the reply to objection 3.

4. The argument of this objection is valid about avarice as contrary to justice. But the avarice that is the same as lack of generosity is not always contrary to justice. For persons may be ungenerous because they do not give what it would be praiseworthy to give, although they are not under an obligation of justice to give it, or because they give with regret or niggardly even what they do give. Basil is speaking about the case where people are obliged to disburse their goods to the poor, as when the goods are superfluous for a person's needs, as Lk. 11:41 says: "Give your surplus goods as alms." And avarice in such a case is contrary to piety, as the gloss cited in objection 5 says.

32. Q. 10, a. 2, and q. 12, a. 3.
33. *Ethics* IV, 5 (1122a13–14).
34. Peter Lombard, *Gloss*, on 1 Cor. 3:12 (PL 191:1557B).

5. And the foregoing makes clear the reply to objection 5.

6. The argument of this objection is valid about avarice as constituting temporal goods one's end.

7. And we should say the like in reply to objection 7.

8. There is incurable avarice in one way, and the sin against the Holy Spirit in another. For we call the sin against the Holy Spirit incurable because the will adheres completely to sin. For a sinner out of ignorance chooses sin only incidentally, as the sinner chooses something sinful without knowing that it is a sin. And a sinner out of weakness indeed chooses what is intrinsically a sin but due to an impulse that quickly passes away, namely, an emotional impulse. And a sinner out of pure malice chooses sin as desirable as such, and so such incurability belongs to the seriousness of the sin. But we call avarice incurable because of the condition of the subject, since human life continually verges on deficiency of temporal goods, and every such deficiency incites to avarice. For we seek temporal goods in order to relieve the deficiencies of the present life.

Replies to the Arguments in the Section On the Contrary:

1. The argument of this objection is valid about avarice as not constituting temporal goods one's end, goods that one loves or desires inordinately.

2. Avarice or lack of generosity is more contrary to the virtue of generosity than prodigality is, as the Philosopher shows in the *Ethics*.[35] And so prodigality is not a mortal sin as easily as lack of generosity or avarice is.

3. The accumulation of temporal goods contrary to justice is always a mortal sin. And so Hab. 2:6 says: "Woe to those who pile up things not their own." Likewise, the accumulation of temporal goods, even if not contrary to justice, is a mortal sin if one makes them one's end.

4. Considered as such, not taking things belonging to another does not have the nature of sin, but not taking things given by another in order not to be obliged to give to others is blameworthy.

Third Article

Is Avarice a Capital Sin?

It seems that avarice is not, for the following reasons:

1. Avarice is in one way contrary to generosity, as I have said.[36] But generosity is not a chief virtue. Therefore, neither is avarice a capital sin.

2. We call a sin from which other sins arise because the sin is the final cause of the other sins a capital sin, as I have said before.[37] But such does not seem to be the case with avarice, since money, which is the matter of avarice, does not have the nature of end but

---

35. *Ethics* IV, 1 (1122a13–16).
36. A. 1.
37. Q. 12, a. 5.

is always desired as the useful means for an end, as the Philosopher says in the *Ethics*.[38]
Therefore, avarice is not a capital sin.

3. A capital sin is a sin from which other sins arise. But avarice arises from other sins. For Gregory says in his work *Morals* that avarice sometimes arises out of feeling superior, sometimes out of fear, as some, fearing that they will lack things necessary for their expenses, let their minds contemplate avarice. And he says there are others who, desiring to seem more powerful, are inflamed to strive for things that belong to others.[39] Therefore, avarice is not a capital sin.

On the Contrary:
Gregory in his work *Morals* lists avarice among the capital sins.[40]

Answer:
We should count avarice among the capital sins. The reason why is that we call a sin with a chief end for which many other sins are by nature ordained a capital sin, as I have said before, and thus many other sins arise from such a sin as their final cause.[41] But the end of all human life is happiness, which all human beings seek. And so insofar as something regarding human affairs apparently or actually shares any condition of happiness, that thing has a chief place in the genus of ends.

And there are three conditions of happiness, as the Philosopher says in the *Ethics*, namely, that it be a complete good and intrinsically sufficient and accompanied by plea-sure.[42] And a good seems to be complete insofar as it has an excellence, and so excel-lence seems to be something chiefly desirable, and we accordingly designate pride or vainglory a capital sin. And regarding perceptible things, the greatest pleasure regards touch in foods and sex, and so we designate gluttony and sexual lust capital sins. And riches especially promise sufficiency of temporal goods, as Boethius says in his work *On Consolation*, and so we also designate avarice, which is the inordinate desire of riches, a capital sin.[43]

And Gregory in his work *Morals* designates seven daughters of avarice, namely, treachery, fraud, falsehood, perjury, restlessness, violence, and hardheartedness against mercy.[44] And we can understand the distinction of these things as follows. For two things belong to avarice, one of which is to be excessive in retaining things, and this part of ava-rice results in hardheartedness against mercy, or lack of humanity, namely, that avari-cious persons harden their hearts so as not to dispense their possessions to help someone out of mercy. And the second thing belonging to avarice is to be excessive in taking things, and we can accordingly indeed first consider avarice as it belongs to an avaricious person's heart. And then avarice leads to restlessness, since avarice brings unnecessary anxieties

---

38. *Ethics* I, 5 (1096a6–7).
39. *Morals* XV, 25, n. 30 (PL 75:1096B).
40. Ibid., XXXI, 45, n. 87 (PL 76:621A).
41. Q. 12, a. 5.
42. *Ethics* I, 7 (1097a30ff.), and 8 (1099a24–25).
43. *On Consolation* III, prose 3 (PL 63:732B).
44. *Morals* XXXI, 45, n. 88 (PL 76:621B).

and cares to human beings, "for money does not satisfy an avaricious person," as Eccl. 5:9 says. And second, we can consider avarice in excessive taking as executed in deed, and then an avaricious person indeed sometimes uses force in taking things belonging to another, and so there are acts of violence. And sometimes an avaricious person uses deceit, which if done by words will be falsehood in the ordinary speech whereby one deceives another for gain, and which if done by words confirmed under oath will be perjury. And if one perpetrates deceit in deeds, then there will be fraud regarding things and treachery regarding persons, as is evident in the case of Judas, who betrayed Christ out of avarice.[45]

Replies to the Objections:

1. Reason brings about virtue, and the inclination of sense appetites brings about vice. And so a chief vice is not necessarily contrary to a chief virtue, since we note the chiefness in virtue and vice by different considerations.

2. Money, although it has the nature of utility, is analogous to happiness because it has an aspect of universality, for "everything obeys money," as Eccl. 10:19 says. And so avarice is accordingly a capital sin, as I have said.[46]

3. Nothing prevents a capital sin, from which many sins for the most part arise, also sometimes arising from other sins, as I have also said before.[47]

Fourth Article

Is Lending at Interest a Mortal Sin?

It seems that lending at interest is not, for the following reasons:

1. The divine law permits no mortal sin. But the divine law permits lending at interest, for Dt. 23:19–20 says: "You shall not lend money to your brother at interest, nor the fruits of the earth, nor any other thing. But you may to the foreigner." Therefore, lending at interest is not a mortal sin.

2. Some have said that this was not approved for the people but rather tolerated because of the people's hardness of heart, just as bills of divorce were. But what is tolerated as an evil is not assured as a just reward. For what is assured as a reward is introduced as good and something to be desired. And lending at interest is assured in the law of God as a just reward, for Dt. 28:12 says: "You shall lend to many peoples, and you yourself shall not borrow from anyone." Therefore, lending at interest is not a mortal sin.

3. To forgo a counsel is not a mortal sin, since as 1 Cor. 7:28 says, a woman does not sin if she marries, although she forgoes the counsel of virginity. But Lk. 6:27 and 35 designates lending without interest among the counsels when it says: "Love your enemies,

---

45. Cf. Mt. 26:14–16; Mk. 14:10–11; Lk. 22:3–6.
46. In the answer.
47. Q. 8, a. 1.

and do good to those who hate you, and lend expecting no return," whereby interest-taking is enjoined, as many explain.[48] Therefore, lending at interest is not a mortal sin.

4. As human beings own their homes or horses, so also they own their money. But human beings can lease their homes or horses for a price. Therefore, human beings by like argument can take interest for the money they loan.

5. A contract obliging a person to do what the natural law obliges the person to do does not seem to be illicit. But the natural law obliges human beings to recompense those who have bestowed benefits on them, and the lender of money bestows a benefit, for the lender comes to the aid of those in need. Therefore, if the lender should oblige the borrower by a fixed contract to recompense the lender for such a benefit, this does not seem to be an illicit contract.

6. Positive law derives from natural law, as Cicero says in his *Rhetoric*.[49] But civil law allows interest-taking.[50] Therefore, it is not contrary to the natural law to lend at interest. Therefore, lending money at interest is not a sin.

7. Lending at interest, if it be a sin, needs to be contrary to a virtue. And lending at interest, since it consists of a transaction, namely, the loan, seems to be especially contrary to justice if it be a sin, for justice consists of such transactions, as the *Ethics* says.[51] But lending at interest is not contrary to justice. This is so because we cannot say that the borrower paying interest suffers injustice, neither from himself or herself, since no people do injustice to themselves, as the Philosopher shows in the *Ethics*, nor from another, since one suffers injustice from another only through the other's deceit or coercion.[52] And neither deceit nor coercion is involved in the matter under discussion, since the borrower pays interest knowingly and willingly. Therefore, neither does the lender at interest commit injustice. Therefore, the lender at interest does not sin.

8. People have said that there is partial coercion in a loan at interest, since the borrower pays interest as if coerced. And there is partial coercion when a necessity threatens, as is evident in the case of one who jettisons cargo into the sea to save a ship. But people sometimes borrow at interest without any great need. Therefore, it is not a mortal sin to lend at interest at least in such a case.

9. Anyone can alienate what one owns. But a borrower paying interest owns the money he pays the lender. Therefore, the borrower can alienate the money, and so the lender receiving it can licitly keep it.

10. In contracting a loan, two persons, namely, the debtor and the creditor, come to an agreement. But the creditor can licitly forgo what the debtor owes. Therefore, the debtor can also give more without committing sin.

11. It is far more serious to kill a human being than to take interest for money lent. But to kill a human being is sometimes licit. Therefore, it is sometimes far more licit to lend money at interest.

---

48. E.g., Alexander of Hales, *Gloss on the Sentences* III, d. 37, nn. 19 and 25.
49. *On Invention* II, 22, n. 65, and 53, n. 160.
50. Cf. Justinian, *Institutes* II, title 4, n. 2.
51. Aristotle, *Ethics* V, 2 (1130b30–32).
52. Ibid., V, 11 (1138a4–28).

12. What human beings obligate themselves to do can be licitly exacted of them. But those who pay interest obligate themselves to do this when they take a loan. Therefore, the lender at interest can licitly exact it.

13. One commits simony no matter what recompense is received, whether praise or money or service. Therefore, if receiving recompense in money for money lent were to be a mortal sin, it would also seem by like argument that even any service one were to receive for money lent would be a mortal sin. And this seems very harsh.

14. There are two kinds of compensation. There is indeed one kind of compensation because something is not present, namely, that one did not acquire what one could have acquired, and one is not obligated to compensate for this. There is another kind of compensation because something is wanting, namely, that something a person had has been taken away from the person, and an obligation for such compensation is generated. But persons may sometimes because of money lent suffer loss regarding what they had. Therefore, it seems that one can without sin receive some compensation for this.

15. It seems more praiseworthy to lend someone money for a useful purpose than only for show. But when one lends someone money for show, to show that one is rich, one can on that account receive recompense without sin. Therefore, far more can one receive recompense if one lends money to alleviate the need of another.

16. Sacred Scripture proposes the deeds of Christ for us to imitate, as Jn. 13:15 says: "I gave you an example so that you may do as I have done." But the Lord in Lk. 19:23 says of himself: "I on my return might have exacted it," namely, the money lent, "with interest." Therefore, to exact interest is not a sin.

17. Those who consent to others sinning mortally also themselves sin mortally. For Rom. 1:32 says that "both those who do such things and those who consent to those doing the things deserve death." But those who borrow money at interest consent to those who lend at interest. Therefore, if lending money at interest is a mortal sin, borrowing money by a loan subject to interest will also be mortal sin. And this seems to be false because of the contrary practice of many good people.

18. Those who assist sinners sinning mortally seem to sin, as, for example, if one were to lend weapons to an enraged person or one bent on killing. Therefore, if lenders lending money at interest sin mortally, it seems that those who deposit money with them also sin mortally.

19. People have said that those who without necessity borrow money by loans subject to interest, or who deposit their money with moneylenders, sin mortally, and that those who do so out of necessity are excused from sin. But people commonly need to borrow money at interest to avoid a temporal loss. And we should not consent to, or furnish the matter for, another's sin, since we ought to love a neighbor's soul more than all temporal goods. Therefore, the aforementioned borrowers are not excused from mortal sin because of such necessity.

20. Theft seems to be a greater sin than lending money at interest, since the former is altogether involuntary regarding the victim, while the latter is in a respect voluntary regarding the borrower paying interest. But theft can sometimes be licit, as is evident in the case of the children of Israel who took vessels from the Egyptians and did not return them, as Ex. 12:35–36 says. Therefore, much more can lending money at interest be without sin.

On the Contrary:

1. Gregory of Nyssa says: "If anyone should call the malign contrivances of interest-taking theft or homicide, that person will not be in error, for what does it matter whether one possesses things snatched through a breached wall or things illicit by compelling payment of interest?"[53] But homicide and theft are mortal sins. Therefore, lending money at interest is also a mortal sin.

2. "If what is affirmed in a proposition is true, the contrary in a contrary proposition is true," as the Philosopher says.[54] But not lending money at interest leads human beings to life, for Ez. 18:17 says that those who do not lend at interest live, and Ps. 14:5 and Ps. 24:5 say, "One who has not lent at interest . . . will receive a blessing from the Lord." Therefore, lending at interest leads to death and takes away God's blessing, Therefore, lending at interest is a mortal sin.

3. Everything contrary to a precept of the divine law is a mortal sin. But lending money at interest is contrary to a precept of the divine law, for Ex. 22:25 says: "If you lend your money at interest to poor people of mine who dwell with you, you shall not squeeze them as if a tax collector nor oppress them with interest charges." Therefore, lending money at interest is a mortal sin.

Answer:

Lending money at interest is a mortal sin. And it is not a sin because it is prohibited, but rather prohibited because it is as such a sin. For lending money at interest is contrary to natural justice. And this is evident if one should correctly consider the nature of interest. For we call interest [Latin: *usura*] such from the word *use*, namely, because one receives a recompense for the use of money, as if one should sell the very use of lent money.

And we should consider that there are different uses of different things. For there are some things whose use consists of consuming the things themselves. For example, the proper use of wine consists of drinking it, and the substance of the wine is thereby consumed, and the proper use of wheat or bread likewise consists of eating it, and this consumes the wheat or bread itself. So also the proper use of money consists of spending it in exchange for other things, since money was devised to facilitate exchange, as the Philosopher says in the *Politics*.[55]

And there are some things whose use does not consist of consuming the things themselves. For example, the use of a house is as a dwelling, and it does not belong to the nature of inhabitation that the house be razed. And if the house by people dwelling in it should happen to be improved or suffer deterioration, this is incidental. And we should say the same about horses and clothes and the like. Therefore, since use does not consume such things, strictly speaking, the thing itself or its use can be separately leased or sold, or both together can be alienated. For example, one can sell a house while retaining one's use of the house for a time, and one can likewise sell the use of a house while retaining one's title and ownership of the house. But regarding the things whose use con-

---

53. St. Thomas, *Golden Chain*, on Lk. 6:35; cf. Gregory of Nyssa, *On Ecclesiastes*, hom. 4 (PG 44:672B–C).

54. *Topics* IV, 4 (124b4–5).

55. *Politics* I, 3 (1257a35–36).

sists of consuming them, the use of the thing is only the thing itself, and so whoever is granted the use of such things is also granted the ownership of the things themselves, and vice versa. Therefore, when a person lends money with the stipulation that the entire sum be returned, and the person in addition wants to have a fixed recompense for the use of the money, the person evidently sells separately the use of the money and the very substance of the money. And the use of money is only its substance, as I have said,[56] and so the lender of money at interest sells nothing or sells the same thing twice, namely, the very money whose use consists of its consumption. And this is evidently contrary to the nature of natural justice. And so lending money at interest as such is mortal sin. And the same argument applies to everything else whose substance is consumed in its use, as is evidently so in the case of wine, wheat, and the like.

Replies to the Objections:

1. The divine law allowed the Jews to take money as interest from foreigners as something tolerated but not licit, namely, that the Jews would not be punished for it by temporal punishment. And the reason for this was that the Jews were prone to avarice. And so the lesser evil, namely, taking interest from Gentiles, was permitted to the Jews in order to avoid a greater evil, namely, taking interest from Jews, who worship God. But the prophets later warned them that they should completely abstain from taking interest, as the authorities introduced in the section *On the Contrary* make clear.

2. Lending is sometimes broadly understood to mean lending with or without taking interest, as Sir. 29:7 evidences: "And many out of wickedness have not lent," that is, have not lent without taking interest. And lending without taking interest pertains to those who have surplus goods, and so we should understand the statement "You shall lend" to mean "You shall lend without taking interest," so that we are thereby given to understand that the Jews will so abound in temporal goods that they could lend to others without taking interest and would not need to borrow from anyone.

3. Superficially, the meaning of the Gospel text can be that lending is a counsel, but if a loan be made, it is a precept that it be made without expecting interest as profit. And regarding the first point, lending is listed with the counsels. Or we can say that some things are really prescriptions or prohibitions that are above the precepts as understood by the Pharisees. For example, in Mt. 5:21–22, the Lord, commenting on the precept "Thou shall not kill," which the Pharisees understood to mean external homicide, adds: "Those who hate their brother will be liable to judgment." And it is in this way that regarding the opinion of the Pharisees that lending money at interest is not absolutely forbidden, the Lord lists among the counsels that one lend without expecting interest as profit. Or we can say that the Lord is not speaking there about expecting interest as profit but about the hope we put in human beings, for we ought not do our good deeds expecting reward from human beings but only expecting reward from God.

4. Some say that homes and horses, unlike money, suffer deterioration through use, and so lenders can receive something as compensation for this.[57] But this is no argument, since one accordingly could not justly receive greater compensation for a rented house

---

56. In the answer.
57. E.g., Alexander of Hales, *Summa of Theology* III, n. 380.

than the house would thereby lose value. Therefore, we should say that it is licit to sell the use of a house but not the use of money, for the reason I mentioned before.[58]

5. As the Philosopher says in the *Ethics*, one makes recompense in one way for a benefit received in the case of a useful friendship and in another way in the case of a virtuous friendship.[59] This is so because the utility that the beneficiary of the benefit received should be the measure of recompense in the case of useful friendship, and the disposition of the donor of the benefit given should be the measure of recompense in the case of virtuous friendship. And to oblige one by a fixed contract to recompense a benefit does not belong to virtuous friendship. This is so because a beneficent friend in such a friendship affects the disposition of the friend receiving the benefit, namely, that the beneficiary freely and generously recompense the donor when the opportunity will arise. But to oblige one by a fixed contract to recompense a benefit is proper to useful friendship, and so the beneficiary ought not be obliged to render more than the benefit received. And the beneficiary did not receive anything more than the very sum of money, since its use, which consumes the money, is only the very money, and so the beneficiary ought not be obliged to do more than return the money.

6. Positive law strives chiefly for the common good of the people. And it sometimes happens that the greatest harm comes to the community if an evil is prevented, and so positive law sometimes permits something as an exception lest the community suffer greater disadvantage, not because it is just that the thing permitted be done. For example, even God permits that some evils be done in the world so as not to prevent the good deeds that he knows how to elicit from the bad deeds. And it is in this way that positive law permits interest-taking because of the many advantages that some gain from money lent, albeit lent subject to interest.

7. Those who pay interest on loans do not suffer injustice from themselves but from lenders. And lenders, although not compelling borrowers absolutely, nonetheless compel borrowers in a partially voluntary way, namely, in that the lender imposes a heavy burden on one in need of a loan, namely, that the borrower pay back more than the lender lends. And this is as if one were to sell something to another in need for much more than the value of the thing, for such a sale would be unjust, just as loans at interest are unjust.

8. Things are necessary in two ways, as the *Metaphysics* says.[60] Something is indeed necessary in one way if something else cannot exist without it, as, for example, food is necessary for human life. And something is necessary if something else can exist without it but not so well or suitably, and we accordingly call all useful things necessary. And the borrower is under necessity in either the first or the second way.

9. A borrower paying interest to a lender does not pay interest completely voluntarily but under some compulsion, as I have said.[61]

10. As creditors can of their own accord licitly accept less payment of a debt, so also debtors can of their own accord pay more than the debt, and the creditor licitly receive more payment. But if this is included in a contract for a loan, the contract and receiving more payment are illicit.

58. In the answer.
59. *Ethics* IX, 1 (1164a33b10).
60. Aristotle, *Metaphysics* V, 5 (1015a20–26).
61. Reply to objection 7.

11. We should consider killing in general as we consider lending in general, and each can be done righteously or unrighteously. But killing an innocent person brings in a species of evil, and this cannot be done righteously, just as lending at interest cannot.

12. When an obligation is licit, one can licitly exact from another that to which the other obligated self. But the very obligation to pay interest is by nature unjust, and so the lender at interest cannot exact that to which the borrower illicitly obligated self.

13. A lender of money by reason of making a loan can in two ways expect a recompense from a borrower, whether in money or praise or service. A lender of money can expect a recompense from a borrower in one way as if the recompense is a debt by reason of a tacit or express obligation. And then the lender illicitly expects any such recompense. A lender of money can expect a recompense from a borrower in a second way as if the recompense is gratuitous and offered without obligation, not as if a debt. And then the lender can licitly expect a recompense from the borrower, as one who does a service for another trusts that the other will in the spirit of friendship return the favor. But the considerations regarding the simonist and regarding the lender of money differ. The simonist gives what belongs to Christ, not what belongs to self, and so the simonist ought expect only the honor of Christ and the benefit of the Church, not any recompense for self, but the lender of money gives to another only what belongs to the lender, and so the lender can expect a friendly recompense in the aforementioned way.

14. A lender by reason of money lent can in two ways incur the loss of something already possessed. The lender incurs loss in one way because the borrower does not return the money lent at the specified date, and then the borrower is obliged to pay compensation. The lender incurs loss in a second way when the borrower returns the money lent within the specified time, and then the borrower is not obliged to pay compensation, since the lender ought to have taken precautions against loss to self, and the borrower ought not incur loss regarding the lender's stupidity. And it is similar regarding buying, for the buyer of something justly pays for it as much as it is worth and not as much as the seller is hurt by its privation.

15. As the Philosopher says in the *Politics*, things can have two uses: one specific and primary; the other general and secondary.[62] For example, the specific and primary use of shoes is to wear them, and the their secondary use is to exchange them for something else. And conversely, the specific and primary use of money is as a means of exchange, since money was instituted for this purpose, and the secondary use of money can be for anything else, for example, as security or for display. And exchange is a use consuming, as it were, the substance of the thing exchanged insofar as the exchange alienates the thing from the one who exchanges it. And so if persons should lend their money to others for use as a means of exchange, which is the specific use of money, and seek a return for this use over and above the principal, this will be contrary to justice. But if persons lend their money to others for another use in which the money is not consumed, there will be the same consideration as regarding the things that are not consumed in their very use, things that are licitly rented and hired out. And so if one gives money sealed in a purse to someone to post it as security and then receives recompense, this is not interest-taking, since it involves a renting or hiring out, not a contract for a loan. And the

---

62. *Politics* I, 3 (1257a5–14).

reasoning is the same if a person gives money to another to use for display, just as, conversely, if one gives shoes to another to use as a means of exchange and on that account were to seek a recompense over and above the value of the shoes, there would be interest-taking.

16. The cited text calls an increase of the spiritual goods that God demands of us for our benefit interest in a metaphorical sense, and no proof can be drawn from metaphorical expressions.

17. It is one thing to consent with someone in wickedness; it is another thing to use the wickedness of someone for good. For one who approves that another practice wickedness, and who perhaps induces the other to do so, consents with the other in wickedness, and this is always a mortal sin. But one who turns the evil that another does to some good uses the wickedness of the other for good, and even God in this way uses the sins of human beings and brings some good out of the sins. And so also it is licit for human beings to use the sin of another for good. And when Publicola inquired whether it would be licit to use the oath of persons who swear by false gods, in which the persons evidently sin, Augustine gave the following reply.[63] One who uses the trustworthiness of those who have openly sworn by false gods, and does so for good, not for evil, does not associate himself or herself with their sin of swearing by devils but with their virtuous promise to tell the truth. But one who were to approve that another swear by false gods, and who were to induce the other to do so, would sin. We should likewise say regarding the matter under discussion that a person does not sin if the person borrows at interest and uses the wickedness of the lender for some good. But if one were to urge a lender who was not ready to lend at interest to do so, one would undoubtedly in every such case sin as consenting with the other sinning.

18. If a person were to deposit money with someone who lends at interest with the aim of seeking profit thereby from the interest, such a person would undoubtedly sin as one consenting to the sin. And it seems that we should say the same about persons who knowingly give their money to another whom the persons believe will use it to acquire profit from interest that the other could not otherwise acquire. But if people give their money to a lender who at other times lends at interest, in order that the lender's need occasioned by the loan be alleviated, not that the lender make profit, the people use the lender's wickedness rather than consent to the lender's sin. Or they provide the lender only with the matter for sinning. And so this can be done without sin.

19. Human beings ought not to consent to the sin of others to avoid any material inconvenience. And yet human beings to avoid a material inconvenience can licitly use the wickedness of others or provide, not remove, the matter of sin. For example, if a robber were to intend to slay someone, and the victim were to reveal the location of his treasure to the robber, who would plunder it, in order to avoid death, the victim would not sin. And we have the example of the ten men who said to Ismael: "Do not kill us, since we have treasure in the fields," as Jer. 41:8 relates.

20. It was not theft for the children of Israel to have carried off the borrowed vessels, since the authority of the one who is master of all transferred the vessels to their ownership.

63. *Letter* 47, n. 2 (PL 33:184).

QUESTION XIV

On Gluttony

First Article

Is Gluttony Always a Sin?

It seems that gluttony is not, for the following reasons:

1. No one sins regarding what one cannot avoid, as Augustine says in his work *On Free Choice*.[1] But no one can avoid gluttony, for Gregory says in his work *Morals* that "in eating, pleasure is mixed with need; we do not know what need requires, or what pleasure suffices."[2] Therefore, gluttony is not a sin.

2. Augustine says in his *Confessions*: "Who is there, O Lord, who does not partake of food a little beyond the measure of need?"[3] But doing such belongs to gluttony. Therefore, we cannot avoid gluttony. Therefore, gluttony is not a sin.

3. Augustine says in his work *On Free Choice* that there is no moral fault where nature and need dominate.[4] But nature and need move us to gluttony. Therefore, it seems that gluttony is not a sin.

4. Hunger is a desire for food, as the Philosopher says in the *De anima*.[5] Therefore, intemperate hunger is an intemperate desire to consume food, and the nature of gluttony consists of this. But it is not within our power not to be intemperately hungry. Therefore, it is not within our power to avoid gluttony. Therefore, gluttony is not a sin.

5. Augustine says in his *Confessions*: "You have taught me to approach the consumption of food as I would medicine."[6] But we do not hold there to be any sin in the consumption of medicine. Therefore, it seems that gluttony, which consists of the consumption of food, is not a sin.

---

1. *On Free Choice* III, 18, n. 50 (PL 32:1295).
2. *Morals* XXX, 18, n. 62 (PL 76:558B).
3. *Confessions* X, 31, n. 47 (PL 32:799).
4. *On Free Choice* III, 1, n. 1 (PL 32:1270).
5. *De anima* II, 3 (414b12).
6. *Confessions* X, 31, n. 44 (PL 32:797).

6. Every sin is contrary to a virtue as an extreme to a mean, as the Philosopher makes clear in the *Ethics*.[7] But gluttony is not contrary to moderation or sobriety as an extreme to a mean, since inadequate consumption of food would necessarily destroy the virtue. And this seems to be false, since inadequate consumption of food belongs to abstinence, as is evident in the case of penitential fasts and the like. Therefore, gluttony is not a sin.

On the Contrary:

What as an enemy keeps us from spiritual combat seems to be a sin. But gluttony is such, for Gregory says in his work *Morals* that "we do not rise to the conflict of spiritual struggle unless we first conquer the enemy posited within us, namely, our gluttonous appetite."[8]

Answer:

The evil of the soul consists of being contrary to reason, as Dionysius says in his work *On the Divine Names*.[9] And so there may be sin regarding anything that can depart from the rule of reason, since only a disordered or evil act is a sin.

And there can be a departure from the rule of reason regarding both external actions and the internal emotions of the soul that the rule of reason should direct. And the more difficult emotions are to subject to the rule of reason, the more sin may belong to the emotions. And of all emotions, the most difficult for reason to regulate is pleasure, and especially the natural pleasures that are "integral parts of our life," such as the pleasures in food and drink, without which we cannot live a human life.[10] And so there is often a departure from the rule of reason regarding such pleasures. Therefore, there is the sin of gluttony when the desire for such pleasures goes beyond the rule of reason. And so there is the saying that "gluttony is the intemperate desire to eat."[11]

And the sin of gluttony does not consist of the external acts regarding the very consumption of food except as a consequence, namely, insofar as the consumption results from an inordinate desire for food, as is also the case regarding all the other sins related to emotions. And so Augustine says in his *Confessions*: "I do not fear the uncleanness of food eaten with bread but the uncleanness of inordinate desire."[12] And so it is evident that gluttony chiefly regards emotions and is contrary to moderation regarding the desires and pleasures in food and drink.

Replies to the Objections:

1. The rule of reason in this matter is that human beings consume the food appropriate to sustain their substance and good condition and to enjoy the company of those with whom they live, as the *Ethics* says.[13] Therefore, when human beings desire and consume food according to this rule of reason, they consume food according to their need. And

---

7. *Ethics* II, 6 (1107a2–6).
8. *Morals* XXX, 18, n. 58 (PL 76:555D).
9. *On the Divine Names* 4, n. 32 (PG 3:733A).
10. Aristotle, *Ethics* II, 3 (1105a3).
11. Hugo of St. Victor, *On the Sacraments* II, part 13, chap. 1 (PL 176:526A).
12. *Confessions* X, 31, n. 46 (PL 32:799).
13. Aristotle, *Ethics* III, 11 (1119a16–20).

when they exceed this limit, they go beyond the rule of reason and depart from the virtuous mean in order to satisfy their appetite for pleasure. But as the Philosopher says in the *Ethics*, there is indeed sometimes a great departure from the virtuous mean, which can be easily perceived, and there is sometimes a slight departure, which is imperceptible, and so has little of the nature of sin.[14] And we should understand the words of Gregory in this way.

2. Not everyone who consumes food beyond the measure of need sins by the sin of gluttony. For it may be the case that what one thinks necessary for oneself is superfluous, and then the desire for food is not intemperate, since the desire does not depart from the rule of reason. And gluttony primarily and intrinsically signifies the intemperate desire to consume food, not the intemperate consumption of food, as I have said.[15] And we understand the measure of the consumption of food by the norm of our bodily nature. And so medical skill can ascertain that norm better than practical reason can. But practical reason can determine whether the desire for food is moderate or immoderate, even if this cannot be easily discerned when there is no great departure from reason, as I have said.[16] Nonetheless, human beings can do so, especially with the help of God. And so Augustine after the cited words adds: "Whoever the persons are," namely, the persons who do not consume food beyond the measure of need, "they are great; let them magnify your name."[17]

3. Nature and need induce us to consume food, but the natural need for food, in accord with which reason moderates desire, is exceeded in acts of gluttony.

4. There are two kinds of appetites for food. One is indeed a natural appetite, by which the appetitive, ingestive, digestive, and excretive powers serve the nutritive power of the vegetative soul, and hunger, which results from a natural need, not any sense perception, is such an appetite. And so excessive hunger is not a moral fault but rather lessens or completely excuses fault. The second kind of appetite is a sense appetite that results from sense perception, and emotions of the soul belong to such appetites. And the immoderate desire of such an appetite to consume food has the nature of gluttony. And so the argument of the objection was based on an equivocation.

5. Food and medicine are similar in that we take both to counter the deficiencies of our bodily nature. But we can consider two differences regarding them. We note first, indeed, that we take medicine according to the rules of medical skill, and so if there be something out of order in taking medicine, we impute the mistake to the doctor administering it rather than the patient taking it. But human beings for the most part impart food by their own choice, and so we impute it to them as sin if they take too much food out of the immoderate desire for the pleasure of food. Second, taking food and taking medicine differ in that the taking of medicines, unlike the taking of food, is not pleasurable, and so in taking medicine, unlike taking food, there is no sin out of an inordinate desire for pleasure. But if a sick person, contrary to the advice of the person's doctor, were to take more of a pleasurable medicine than prescribed because of a desire for pleasure, the person would likewise sin by the sin of gluttony.

14. Ibid., II, 9 (1109b18–20).
15. In the answer.
16. Reply to objection 1.
17. *Confessions* X, 31, n. 47 (PL 32:799).

6. We understand the excessive and the deficient and the mean regarding moral virtues in relation to right reason, which determines the virtuous mean, and not as to absolute quantity, as the very definition of virtue in the *Ethics* makes clear.[18] And so virtue may sometimes belong to an extreme as to absolute quantity but belong to the mean in relation to right reason. Just so, the Philosopher says in the *Ethics* that the greatsouled person "is indeed extreme in greatness," namely, in that such a person strives for the greatest things, but the person "is at the mean by what is proper."[19] Therefore, virginity and poverty and penitential fasting belong to an extreme as to absolute quantity but to the mean in relation to right reason, and it is a sin if one should likewise fail to observe the mean by excessive abstinence. And so also Gregory says in his work *Morals*: "The flesh when restrained more than right is often weakened even for the performance of good deeds, so that while hastening to stifle the forces of sin within, it does not have enough strength to pray or preach. And so while pursuing the enemy, we slay the citizen we love."[20]

Second Article

Is Gluttony a Mortal Sin?

It seems that gluttony is, for the following reasons:

1. A gloss on Heb. 12:16, "Lest there be a fornicator or profane person like Esau," etc., says that Esau was profane because he was a voracious eater, that is, a glutton.[21] But we call someone profane because of mortal sin. Therefore, gluttony is a mortal sin.

2. Only mortal sin destroys virtues. But gluttony destroys virtues, for Gregory says in his work *Morals*: "When the sin of gluttony prevails, human beings lose everything they have done bravely, and all their virtues are destroyed when they do not restrain their belly."[22] Therefore, gluttony is a mortal sin.

3. Everything that destroys a virtuous mean destroys virtue, which consists of the mean, and so is a mortal sin. But gluttony destroys a virtuous mean, as I have said.[23] Therefore, gluttony is a mortal sin.

4. It is a more serious sin for a human being to commit suicide than to kill another, and it likewise seems to be a more serious sin to inflict harm on one's own body than on the body of another. But gluttony inflicts harm on one's own body, for Sir. 37:33–34 says: "There will be sickness in eating much food," and "Many have perished because of drunkenness." Therefore, gluttony is a mortal sin just like anger, which strives for the harm of neighbor.

---

18. Aristotle, *Ethics* II, 6 (1106b36–1107a2).
19. Ibid., IV, 3 (1123b13–14).
20. *Morals* XXX, 18, n. 63 (PL 76:558C).
21. Peter Lombard, *Gloss*, on Heb. 12:16 (PL 192:505C).
22. *Morals* XXX, 18, n. 59 (PL 76:556A–B).
23. A. 1.

5. As the priority of affirmative precepts is evident in the good deeds prescribed, so the priority of prohibitions is evident in the sins forbidden. But the first prohibition enjoined on human beings concerned the sin of gluttony, as Gen. 2:17, where God commanded Adam not to eat of the tree of the knowledge of good and evil, makes clear. Therefore, the sin of gluttony is the first and greatest sin and so seems to be a mortal sin.

6. Mortal sin consists of turning away from God. But gluttony turns human beings away from God, since it makes human beings idolaters, as Ex. 32:6 says: "The people sat down to eat and drink, and they rose to play," that is, to worship an idol. Gluttony also causes human beings to fornicate, for Hos. 4:10 says: "They shall eat and not be satisfied, they have fornicated and not stopped fornicating." Therefore, gluttony is a mortal sin.

7. Jerome says in his work *Against Jovinian*: "Greed for food, which is the mother of avarice, binds the soul with fetters."[24] But only mortal sin binds the soul. Therefore, gluttony is a mortal sin.

8. Jerome says in the same work that it is contrary to nature to sink into pleasures.[25] But what is contrary to nature is a mortal sin, since such is necessarily contrary to reason. Therefore, gluttony, which consists of a stream of pleasures, is a mortal sin.

9. Everything whose effect is always a mortal sin is a mortal sin. But the effects of gluttony are always mortal sins, since a gloss on Ps. 136:10, "Who struck down Egypt in their firstborn," says: "Sexual lust, pride, avarice are sins that the belly first begets."[26] Therefore, gluttony is a mortal sin.

10. Sir. 39:31–32 says: "The sources of things necessary for human life are water, fire and iron, salt and milk and wheat bread and honey and clusters of grapes, and oil and clothing. All these things will be turned into blessings for the holy but into curses for the wicked and sinners." A gloss on this says: "For sinners, that is, for those who abuse these things, the things will be turned into evils, that is, into eternal damnation."[27] But gluttony for the most part causes abuse of these goods. Therefore, gluttony deserves eternal damnation and so is a mortal sin.

11. What makes human beings bestial is a mortal and most serious sin. But lack of moderation, part of which consists of gluttony, makes human beings bestial, as the Philosopher says in the *Ethics*.[28] Therefore, gluttony is a mortal sin.

12. Idolatry is a mortal sin. But gluttony is a form of idolatry, for Rom. 16:18 says that some worship their belly rather than Christ the Lord, and Phil. 3:18–19 says: "Many have a way of life whose end is destruction, whose god is their belly." Therefore, gluttony is a mortal sin.

On the Contrary:

1. Holy persons have no mortal sin. But holy persons are sometimes gluttonous, for Augustine says in his *Confessions*: "Drunkenness sometimes crept upon your servant. You

---

24. *Against Jovinian* II, n. 8 (PL 23:297C).
25. Ibid., II, n. 9 (PL 23:299A).
26. Peter Lombard, *Gloss*, on Ps. 136:10 (PL 191:1197D).
27. *Interlinear Gloss*, on Sir. 39:31–32.
28. *Ethics* III, 10 (1118b34).

will be merciful, so that it be far from me."[29] But drunkenness belongs to gluttony. Therefore, gluttony is not a mortal sin.

2. Every mortal sin is contrary to a precept of the law. But gluttony is not contrary to any precept of the law, as is evident to anyone who goes through the precepts of the decalogue one by one. Therefore, gluttony is not a mortal sin.

3. Gregory, explaining Job 11:11, "He knows the vanity of human beings," says in his work *Morals*: "We are led, Job says, from vanity to iniquity when we first sink into slight sins, so that from habit making light of all things, we are not at all afraid later to commit more serious sins."[30] And Gregory adds among other examples an example about gluttony: "When we rest in gluttony, we immediately hand ourselves over to the folly of levity."[31] And so he lists gluttony with slight sins. But we do not call mortal sins slight. Therefore, gluttony is not a mortal sin.

4. Augustine says in his sermon on purgatory: "As often as a person takes more in food or drink than necessary, the person should know that this belongs to little sins."[32] But taking more in food or drink than necessary belongs to gluttony. Therefore, gluttony is not a mortal sin.

Answer:

When we ask whether a sin is generally a mortal sin, we should understand the question to mean whether the sin is mortal by reason of its kind. This is so because, as we have said many times previously, one can find a movement that is venial sin in any kind of mortal sin (e.g., homicide or adultery).[33] And one can likewise find an act that is mortal sin in any kind of venial sin. For example, the latter would be the case regarding the genus of idle word when an idle word is related to the end of a mortal sin. And we take the species of a moral act from its object. And so if the object of a sin is contrary to charity, of which the spiritual life consists, the sin is necessarily a mortal sin by reason of its genus or species. For example, blasphemy by reason of its object would be contrary to charity regarding love of God, and homicide by reason of its object would be contrary to charity regarding love of neighbor. And so both are mortal sins.

And the sin of gluttony consists of inordinate desire for the pleasure of food. And the very pleasure in food considered as such is contrary to charity neither regarding love of God nor regarding love of neighbor. But insofar as a disorder is or is not added, the desire can in that way be or not be contrary to charity. For the desire for such pleasure can be disordered in two ways. It can be disordered in one way such that it excludes the ordination of the ultimate end. And this indeed happens when human beings desire such pleasure as their ultimate end, since a single human being cannot have many ultimate ends. And such disorder is contrary to charity regarding love of God, whom we ought to love as our ultimate end. There can be disordered desire in a second way regarding means that leave the ordination of the ultimate end intact. For example, such is the case if one

29. *Confessions* X, 31, n. 45 (PL 32:798).
30. *Morals* X, 11, n. 21 (PL 75:933A).
31. Ibid.
32. *Sermon 104*, n. 3 (PL 39:1946).
33. Q. 10, a. 2; q. 11, a. 3; q. 13, a. 2.

desires too much food but not in such a way that the person would want to transgress the divine precepts to obtain it. And such disorder is not contrary to charity. And a disorder in the desire for food but not a disorder taking away the ordination of the ultimate end belongs to the nature of gluttony. And so gluttony is not a mortal sin by reason of its species, but it can sometimes be a mortal or venial sin in the two aforementioned ways of disorder.

Replies to the Objections:

1. The gloss called Esau profane on account of his gluttony because he had so great a disordered desire for food that he sold his birthright for food.[34] And so he seemed in some respect to desire the pleasure of food as his end.

2. A sin takes away virtues in two ways. A sin takes away virtues in one way directly by its contrariety to virtue, and gluttony as a mortal sin in this way takes away virtues just as other mortal sins do. A sin takes away virtues in a second way dispositively, and even venial sins take away virtues in this way, since "one who contemns little things falls little by little," as Sir. 19:1 says.

3. Every sin, both venial and mortal, takes away an actual virtuous mean, since there would be sin only if one were to depart from the mean fixed by reason. But only a sin contrary to charity, on which all virtues depend, takes away habitual virtue, and gluttony that is a venial sin accordingly takes away an actual, not the habitual, virtuous mean.

4. Harm of neighbor is intrinsically the object of anger, for anger desires just retribution, which consists of harm of neighbor. But harm of one's own body is not the proper object of gluttony. Rather, harm of one's own body sometimes results from the object apart from one's aim, and such harm is not part of the nature of gluttony. But if one knowingly out of an immoderate desire for food inflicts serious harm on one's own body by eating too much or consuming harmful foods, one would not be excused from mortal sin.

5. The prohibition enjoined on Adam was not a prohibition of the sin of gluttony, since Adam could have eaten the apple without any sin were there to have been no added prohibition. But the precept was disciplinary, namely, that Adam would learn the difference between the good of obedience and the evil of disobedience, as Augustine says in his *Literal Commentary on Genesis*.[35] And so the first sin of Adam was disobedience or pride, not gluttony.

6. Gluttony induces one to idolatry and lust dispositively but not in such a way that the latter two sins belong to the nature of gluttony. And so it does not follow that the sin of gluttony is a mortal sin, since even a venial sin can dispose one to mortal sin.

7. Mortal sin absolutely binds the soul insofar as mortal sin prevents the soul from being capable of itself to return to the ordination of charity. But venial sin binds the soul in one respect insofar as venial sin prevents actual virtue. And so gluttony as a venial sin binds the soul in one way, and as mortal sin binds the soul in another way.

---

34. Cf. Gen. 25:33.
35. *Literal Commentary on Genesis* VIII, 14, n. 31 (PL 34:384).

8. Reason belongs to human beings by nature. And so whatever is contrary to reason is contrary to the nature of human beings. Therefore, to sink in pleasure insofar as this goes beyond the rule of reason is contrary to the nature of human beings. This is so whether one goes beyond the rule of reason by taking away the ordination of the end, which is to be absolutely contrary to reason, or by taking away the ordination of means to the end, which is to be contrary to reason in one respect, or rather, outside reason.

9. We say that these three things are effects of gluttony insofar as gluttony disposes one to these sins. But it does not follow from this that gluttony is always a mortal sin.

10. To use as a means is to relate things to the ultimate end that makes us happy. And so, properly speaking, those who constitute created things as their end by not relating the things to their ultimate end abuse the things, and this deserves damnation in the case of gluttony as in the case of other sins whereby human beings abuse created things in this way.

11. The Philosopher does not say that intemperance in an absolute sense makes human beings bestial, but that enjoying such pleasures and especially loving them is bestial. And enjoying and loving such pleasures is bestial because such pleasures belong to things that we share with beasts. For there are other pleasures that are proper to human beings, and those who constitute their end in such pleasures love them above other pleasures.

12. Those who constitute their end in the pleasure of foods pertaining to the belly, which end ought to be constituted in God alone, worship their belly as their god.

Replies to the Arguments in the Section On the Contrary:
The replies to those arguments are readily evident, since the arguments are valid regarding gluttony as a venial sin.

And we need to reply to the second argument that it seems to demonstrate that gluttony, since it is not contrary to any precept, is never a mortal sin. For we should say that precepts of the Decalogue command and forbid things that natural reason clearly judges should or should not be done, since they fall within everyone's understanding. And so not all mortal sins are directly contrary to the precepts of the Decalogue, but some are reductively. For example, we can trace the prohibition of plain fornication to the precept "Thou shalt not commit adultery." And the prohibition of gluttony as a mortal sin is likewise by implication contrary to the precept about keeping holy the Sabbath, by which precept we understand spiritual tranquility, and the intemperance of gluttony prevents such tranquility.

Third Article

Does Gregory Appropriately List the Species of Gluttony?

Gregory in his work *Morals* lists the species of gluttony, saying: "The sin of gluttony tempts us in five ways. For it sometimes anticipates times of needing food. It sometimes seeks more sumptuous foods. It sometimes desires that foods to be consumed be prepared more meticulously. It sometimes exceeds the measure of replenishment in the very quantity of consumption. One sometimes sins in the very fervor of ravenous desire."[36] And these are summarized in the verse: "Hastily, sumptuously, excessively, ravenously, fastidiously."[37] And it seems that he inappropriately distinguished these five species of gluttony, for the following reasons:

1. The aforementioned modes of gluttony differ regarding different circumstances, since *hastily* regards time, *sumptuously* regards the quality of the food, and so forth regarding the other modes. But circumstances, since they are accidents of acts, do not differentiate species. Therefore, we should not distinguish different species of gluttony by the aforementioned five modes.

2. One may in any sin transgress the rule with respect to different circumstances. For example, an ungenerous person takes things when and where that person should not, and likewise regarding other circumstances, but we do not distinguish different species of lack of generosity in this way. Therefore, neither should we distinguish different species of gluttony by the aforementioned five modes.

3. As we designate time as one kind of circumstance, so also we designate place and the person of the sinner as circumstances. Therefore, if we understand time as a species of gluttony, we should also understand place and the seven other kinds of circumstance as other species, so that there be seven or eight species of gluttony.[38]

4. As the Philosopher says in the *Ethics*, moderation, which is the contrary of gluttony, does not regard pleasures of taste as such but as pleasures of touch.[39] But *sumptuously* and *fastidiously* seem to belong to the good flavor of food, which is the proper object of taste. Therefore, Gregory inappropriately lists these two modes as species of gluttony.

5. Augustine says in his *Confessions* that "the people in the desert deserved to be reproved because they murmured against God in their desire for food, not because they desired fleshmeat."[40] But Gregory says in his work *Morals* that the people "disdained the manna and sought fleshmeat that they esteemed more sumptuous."[41] Therefore, desiring sumptuous food does not seem to belong to the sin of gluttony, and so it seems that Gregory inappropriately assigns the aforementioned species of gluttony.

On the Contrary:
The authority of Gregory, who distinguishes such species, stands to the contrary.[42]

Answer:
In distinguishing species of moral acts, we need especially to consider the causes of movement that are the proper objects of voluntary acts, since the object moving the will is as if the will's form. And so we distinguish voluntary acts by the different causes of move-

36. *Morals* XXX, 18, n. 60 (PL 76:556–57).
37. Alexander of Hales, *Summa of Theology* II–II, n. 591.
38. Cf. q. 2, a. 6.
39. *Ethics* III, 10 (1118a26–32).
40. *Confessions* X, 31, n. 46 (PL 32:799).
41. *Morals* XXX, 18, n. 60 (PL 76:557A).
42. Ibid., XXX, 18, n. 60 (PL 76:556–57).

ment, as we distinguish the acts of things of nature by the different forms of efficient causes. And the same cause of movement may sometimes be the reason why human beings transgress the virtuous mean regarding different circumstances, and then we do not understand different species of sin by different inordinate circumstances. For example, one and the same cause of movement, namely, to accumulate money, moves human beings to take things belonging to another both at a time when they ought not and in a place where they ought not and from persons from whom they ought not. And so we do not distinguish species of avarice in this way. But if there were to be different causes of movement to sin, then there would be different species of avarice, as, for example, if one were to aim to transgress some circumstances by giving too little and to transgress other circumstances by taking too much. Therefore, we should say that we distinguish the aforementioned species of gluttony by the different causes of movement. For the sin of gluttony consists of an inordinate desire for food, as I have said, and the disorder can be related either to the pleasure or the very desire.[43]

And the cause of the pleasure can be natural or the product of human skill. The cause is indeed natural, for example, when one excessively takes pleasure in eating expensive and choice foods, as Am. 6:4 says: "You who eat lambs of the flock and calves from the midst of the herd." And the cause of the pleasure is the product of human skill, for example, when one excessively desires foods that are overdelicately prepared. Therefore, regarding the first kind of cause, we speak of eating sumptuously, and regarding the second kind of cause, we speak of eating fastidiously.

And regarding the desire, we can in three ways distinguish the disorder regarding the causes of movement. For the desire is indeed the movement of an appetitive power aiming at pleasure. And we can consider the inordinate vehemence of the movement even regarding its bodily elements in three stages. First, we can indeed consider the vehemence of the movement before the movement arrives at its intended term, and then the vehement movement hastens to arrive at the term. And likewise, desire when inordinately vehement cannot brook delay in taking food and hastens to eat. And we understand the expression *hastily* in this sense. Second, we consider the vehemence of the movement regarding the very arrival at the movement's term, since anything moved violently in a material way is inordinately united with the object for which it strives. And likewise, human beings are inordinately disposed regarding the consumption of food when they have a vehement desire for food. And the expression *ravenously* pertains to this aspect of disorder. Third, we consider inordinate the vehemence of a bodily movement after the movement has arrived at the object for which it strives, since it does not rest there but continues further. And likewise, human beings are inordinately disposed regarding the consumption of food when they desire food inordinately and their desire does not rest in the moderate amount of food that nature requires but they take more. And the expression *excessively* pertains to this aspect of disorder.

Replies to the Objections:

1. We differentiate the aforementioned species because of different causes of movement, not different circumstances, as I have said.[44]

43. A. 1.
44. In the answer.

2–3. The foregoing makes clear the replies to objections 2 and 3, since transgressions of different circumstances do not always have different causes of movement.

4. A glutton does not take pleasure in sumptuous and meticulously prepared foods in order to judge flavors, as wine testers do, which is proper to taste as such. For the disorder of such pleasure belongs to curiosity rather than gluttony, but a glutton takes pleasure in the very consumption of sumptuous and meticulously prepared food, and this consumption is indeed the result of touching.

5. Eating sumptuous food is not a sin, as Augustine says. But inordinate desire for sumptuous food can be a sin according to Gregory's scheme.

Fourth Article

Is Gluttony a Capital Sin?

It seems that gluttony is not, for the following reasons:

1. As pleasure may belong to the senses of taste and touch, so also pleasures may belong to the other senses. But we do not designate capital sins regarding the pleasures of other senses. Therefore, neither should we designate gluttony, which regards the pleasure of taste, a capital sin.

2. As Gregory says in his work *Morals*, pride is designated the queen of sins, not a capital sin, because all kinds of sins arise from it.[45] But drunkenness is the root of all kinds of sins, for the *Decretum* says: "Before all else, clerics should avoid drunkenness, which inflames and nourishes all kinds of sins."[46] And drunkenness is a species of gluttony. Therefore, we ought not list gluttony among the capital sins.

3. One capital sin is not listed among the daughters of another. But sexual impurity, which Gregory in his work *Morals* designates a daughter of gluttony, belongs to lust, as Eph. 5:3 says: "Every fornication is sexual impurity," etc.[47] Therefore, since sexual lust is a capital sin, it seems that gluttony is not a capital sin but superior to capital sins.

4. Desiring joyful things belongs in the strict sense to the proud, as Bernard says.[48] But pride is not the daughter of any capital sin. Therefore, since Gregory designates improper joy a daughter of gluttony, it seems that gluttony is not a capital sin.[49]

On the Contrary:
Gregory in his work *Morals* lists gluttony among the capital sins.[50]

Answer:
As I have said regarding previous questions, we call sins capital because they give rise to other sins as the final cause of the other sins.[51] That is to say, a capital sin gives rise to

---

45. *Morals* XXXI, 45, n. 87 (PL 76:620D).
46. *Decretum* 35, chap. 9 (Friedberg I:133).
47. *Morals* XXXI, 45, n. 88 (PL 76:621B).
48. *On the Degrees of Humility* 12, n. 40 (PL 182:963C).
49. *Morals* XXXI, 45, n. 88 (PL 76:621B).
50. Ibid., n. 87 (PL 76:621A).
51. Q. 13, a. 3, and q. 12, a. 5.

other sins insofar as that sin's object is very desirable and desirable from the beginning, and especially insofar as the object simulates happiness, which everybody by nature desires. And one of the conditions of happiness is pleasure, without which there can be no happiness. And so the sin of gluttony, which regards one of the greatest pleasures, consisting of food and drink, is a capital sin.

Some sins arise from gluttony and are called its daughters as sins that can result from immoderate pleasure in food and drink. And we can indeed consider this regarding the body, whose sexual impurity readily results from excessive consumption of food, and then we designate sexual impurity a species of gluttony. Or else we can consider sins that can result from gluttony regarding the soul, to which governance of the body belongs, and immoderate pleasure in food and drink prevents that governance in many ways. And immoderate pleasure in food and drink indeed first prevents the soul's governance of the body by reason, whose sharpness is blunted by excessive consumption of food or excessive concern regarding its consumption, since reason itself is impeded when the lower powers of the body are disturbed by the inordinate consumption of food. And then we designate dullness of the senses in relation to the use of intelligence a daughter of gluttony. Second, a disorder results in one's disposition, which is inordinately affected when the governance of reason is lulled to sleep, and then there is improper joy. Third, disordered speech results, and then there is garrulousness, since human beings fall into verbosity when reason does not weigh their words. Fourth, disordered deeds result, and then there is rudeness, that is, a jeering in external gestures that comes from lack of reason, to which composure of external bodily members belongs. Therefore, gluttony is a capital sin, and it has five daughters, as Gregory says in his work *Morals*, namely, improper joy, rudeness, garrulousness, sexual impurity, and dullness of the senses in relation to the use of intelligence.[52]

Replies to the Objections:

1. The pleasures of other senses result from being united with the pleasurable object only by a cognitive likeness, but the pleasures of touch result from being united with the pleasurable object physically. And so we designate capital sins regarding the pleasures of touch as more important and greater pleasures, and not regarding the pleasures of other senses except taste insofar as it is a form of touch.

2. All kinds of sins result from drunkenness by the removal of an impediment to the sins, namely, insofar as drunkenness removes the judgments of reason whereby human beings are kept from sin, not by way of final causality. And so it does not follow that gluttony or drunkenness is the source of all sins, as pride is, but the source of some sins in particular that directly result out of gluttony as its special effects.

3. Emission of semen can result from a cause related to the animal nature of human beings, for example, from the desire for a perceived sense pleasure, and such belongs chiefly to sexual lust. Or emission of semen can result from an internal bodily cause,

52. *Morals* XXXI, 45, n. 88 (PL 76:621B).

namely, from surplus fluid abounding within the body, surplus fluid that causes a man to have an emission of semen, and we accordingly designate sexual impurity a daughter of gluttony.

4. It belongs to pride to desire joyful things, but it belongs to gluttony that improper joy result from gluttony, since reason is impeded, as I have said.[53]

53. In the answer.

QUESTION XV

On Sexual Lust

First Article

Is Every Act of Sexual Lust a Sin?

It seems that not every act of sexual lust is, for the following reasons:

1. Fornication is an act of sexual lust. But we list fornication with things permitted, not with things that are sinful as such. For Acts 15:28–29 says: "It seemed good to the Holy Spirit and us not to impose on you any burden beyond what is necessary, that you abstain from foods sacrificed to idols, from the blood of animals, from the meat of strangled animals, and from fornication." And no consumption of food as such is sinful, since 1 Tim. 4:4 says: "We should reject nothing that we receive with thanksgiving to God." Therefore, neither is fornication a sin, and so not every act of sexual lust is sinful.

2. Having intercourse with a woman is a natural act, and so the act considered as such is not a sin, just as looking at a woman is not, since each of these acts is the act of a natural power. But looking at a woman who is not one's wife is not a sin. Therefore, neither is having intercourse with a woman not one's wife a sin.

3. If fornication is a sin, this is so either because of the power that elicits the act or because of the matter or because of the purpose. But fornication is not sinful because of the power, since the power that elicits the act is natural. And fornication is not sinful because of the matter, since the matter consists of women created by God for this purpose, as Gen. 2:18 says: "Let us make for the man a helper like himself." It also may be the case that fornication is not sinful because of its purpose, as, for example, if one fornicates with the intention of begetting a child in order to foster worship of God. Therefore, it seems that not every act of fornication is sinful.

4. As the Philosopher says in his work *On the Generation of Animals*, semen is surplus food.[1] But it is licit to discharge other surplus foods in any way, and one does this without sin. Therefore, it seems that the like happens in the emission of semen. Therefore, not every act of sexual lust is sinful.

---

1. *On the Generation of Animals* I, 18 (726a26).

5. We are not permitted to do for any good end what is sinful by reason of its kind, as Rom. 3:8 says: "It is not as some accuse us of saying, that we may do evil things in order to bring about good things." But a just man, a virtuous man, commits adultery with the wife of a tyrant in order to kill the tyrant and liberate his country, as a commentator says in his *Commentary on the Ethics*.[2] Therefore, even adultery as such is not a sin. Therefore, much less are other acts of sexual intercourse outside of marriage, as such, sins.

6. No act of a just person as such is sinful. But fornication seems to be a just act, for Gen. 38:26 says that Judas said of Tamar, with whom he had fornicated, "She is more just than I," or "She acted justly because I was guilty," as in the Hebrew text cited by Jerome.[3] Therefore, fornication is not a sin.

7. Augustine says in *City of God* that every sin is contrary to nature.[4] But fornication is not contrary to nature, since a gloss on Rom. 1:26, "Their women substituted unnatural for natural intercourse," says "Natural intercourse consists of a man and a woman copulating together."[5] Therefore, fornication is not a sin.

8. One commits no sin following the command of God. But some have fornicated at the command of God, for Hos. 1:2 says: "The Lord said to Hosea, 'Go, take to yourself a harlot wife and beget of her a harlot's children.'" Therefore, fornication as such is not sinful.

9. Contrary to every vice consisting of excess is a vice consisting of deficiency. But sexual lust designates excess regarding desires for sexual pleasures, and its contrary deficiency, virginity or perpetual continence, is not a sin but something praiseworthy. Therefore, neither is sexual lust sinful.

On the Contrary:

1. Heb. 13:4 says: "Honor marriage in every respect and keep the marriage bed undefiled, for God will condemn fornicators and adulterers." But things for which human beings are subject to God's condemnation are sins. Therefore, fornication and adultery and all such acts of sexual lust are sins.

2. Tob. 4:13 says: "Be careful, my son, to keep from all fornication and never allow yourself to have intercourse with a woman not your wife." But we call acts of intercourse other than those with one's lawful wife acts of sexual lust. Therefore, every act of sexual lust is sinful.

Answer:

Sexual lust is a sin contrary to temperance insofar as temperance moderates desires for things pleasurable to touch regarding sex, just as gluttony is contrary to temperance insofar as temperance moderates desires regarding things pleasurable to touch in food and drink. And so sexual lust indeed chiefly signifies a disorder by reason of excess regarding desires for sexual pleasures. And such disorder can belong either to internal emotions alone or also in addition to external acts that are of their very selves disordered and

---

2. Anonymous author, *Commentary on the Ethics* V, 11 (1137b22) (Heylbut:249).
3. *Book of Hebraic Questions on Genesis* 38 (PL 23:996B).
4. *City of God* XI, 17 (PL 41:331).
5. Peter Lombard, *Gloss*, on Rom. 1:26 (PL 191:1333C).

not only because of the disordered desires from which they spring. For it belongs to disordered desire that, because of a desire for something pleasurable, one does something intrinsically disordered. For example, such is evidently the case regarding desires for money. For one can inordinately desire to acquire or keep money that belongs to oneself, and then such acquisition or retention of money is sinful only because it springs from excessive desire, and not as such. But the disordered desire for money sometimes leads human beings also to want to acquire or keep things that belong to another, and then such acquisition or retention is disordered as such and not only because the product of disordered desire. And both of these sins belong to the vice of lack of generosity, as the Philosopher makes clear in the *Ethics*.[6]

We should say the like about sexual lust. For sexual lust indeed sometimes signifies only the disorder of internal desire, as is evidently the case regarding one who out of disordered desire has intercourse with his wife, since the very act is disordered only because it springs from disordered desire and is not disordered as such. And sometimes the disorder of desire is also accompanied by a disorder in the very external act as such, as happens in every use of the genital organs outside the conjugal act.

And every such act is evidently disordered of its very self, since we call every act that is not properly related to its requisite end a disordered act. For example, eating is disordered if it be not properly related to bodily health, for which as end eating is ordained. And the end of using genital organs is to beget and educate offspring, and so every use of the aforementioned organs that is not related to begetting and properly educating offspring is as such disordered. And every act of the aforementioned organs outside the sexual union of a man and a woman is obviously unsuitable for begetting offspring.

And every sexual union of a man and a woman outside the law of marriage is disproportional to the proper rearing of offspring. For the law of marriage was instituted to prohibit promiscuous copulation, which would prevent ascertaining the father of offspring. This is so because if any man could indiscriminately have intercourse with any woman, and no woman were to be limited to intercourse with him, ascertaining the father of offspring would be impossible, and so the care of fathers in rearing their children would be removed. And this is contrary to what befits human nature, since human beings are by nature solicitous to identify their offspring and to rear their children. This concern also belongs more to fathers than to mothers, since the rearing of children for which mothers are responsible concerns the children's infancy, and it is subsequently the responsibility of fathers to educate and instruct and enrich the children throughout their lives. And so we see even in other animals that in any species in which the newborn need to be commonly reared by the male and the female, copulation is not promiscuous but of males with particular females, as is evident in the case of all kinds of birds who build their nests together. And so it is evident that every sexual union of a man and a woman outside the law of marriage, which prohibits extramarital copulation, is of itself disordered. And we are not now considering whether this limitation is to one wife or several, whether several successively or simultaneously, for these matters belong to questions about marriage. But howsoever these questions are resolved, every sexual union of a man and a woman outside the law of marriage is necessarily disordered.

6. *Ethics* IV, 1 (1121b14–1122a14).

Therefore, every act of sexual lust is a sin either because of the disorder of the act or even because of the disorder of the desire alone, which disorder primarily and intrinsically belongs to sexual lust. For Augustine says in the *City of God*: "Sexual lust is not the sin of beautiful and pleasant bodies but of souls wickedly loving bodily pleasures to the neglect of moderation, which makes us fit for things that are spiritually more beautiful and pleasant."[7]

Replies to the Objections:

1. The Apostles, wishing to unify the Gentile and Jewish converts of the primitive Church, excluded obstacles to this union by cutting out from each group what would be burdensome to the other. And so they forbade to the Gentiles certain things offensive to the Jews only because the things were causing scandal, but without considering whether such things would be sins. And the Gentiles thought that every kind of food as such was licit to eat, which is true, but the Jews abhorred this because of their ancient customary law. And so the Apostles for the time being forbade to the Gentiles foods most abominable to the Jews. Conversely, the Gentiles falsely judged that fornication, absolutely speaking, was not a sin, and the Jews, instructed by the Law, rightly abominated fornication as a sin. And so the Apostles also forbade this as a sin as well as a cause of dissension.

2. Nothing prevents something proper for me to look at being nonetheless not proper for me to use in another way. For example, gold displayed in the street is proper for me to look at but not to possess. Likewise, a woman can be proper for someone to look at or even to possess as a maidservant but not for me to use for sexual intercourse except by prescription of the law of marriage.

3. Acts of sexual lust are sinful because of the power involved, namely, insofar as concupiscible power is not kept subordinate to reason, and because of the matter, since acts fit for begetting and rearing offspring require both women as the matter and women appointed by marriage, as I have said.[8] The end of acts of sexual lust is also by its nature disordered, even if the human agent intends a good end. And the good end intended by a human agent does not suffice to excuse such acts, as is evident in the case of one who steals in order to give alms.

4. As the Philosopher says in the same place, semen is indeed surplus regarding the nutritive power's activity but necessary for begetting offspring, and so every voluntary emission of semen is licit only if suitable for the end for which nature strives.[9] But other surplus things, such as sweat, urine, and the like, are unnecessary for begetting offspring, and so it does not matter how they are discharged.

5. We should not agree with the commentator on this point, since one ought not commit adultery for any benefit, just as one ought not tell a lie for any benefit, as Augustine says in his work *Against Lying*.[10]

6. The text says that Tamar acted justly because she did not want her offspring to be from a stock other than the one from which a husband was proper for her, not because of the fornication she committed.

---

7. *City of God* XII, 8 (PL 41:356).
8. In the answer.
9. *On the Generation of Animals* I, 18 (724b22ff.).
10. *Against Lying* 14 (PL 40:505).

7. We can speak in two ways about acts of sexual lust being contrary to nature. We can say this in one way absolutely, namely, because they are contrary to the nature of every kind of animal. And then we say that every act of sexual lust outside the sexual union of male and female is contrary to nature insofar as the act is not related to begetting, which the sexual union of the two sexes effects in every species of animal. And the gloss speaks in this sense. We say in a second way that something is contrary to nature because it is contrary to the proper nature of human beings, to whom it belongs to ordain the reproductive act for the proper rearing of offspring, and then every act of fornication is contrary to nature.

8. What would otherwise have been theft was not theft for the children of Israel when they despoiled the Egyptians, as Ex. 12:35–36 relates, because of the command of God, to whose power all things belong. Just so, the copulation that would otherwise have been fornicacious was not such because of the authority of God himself, who is superior to the law of marriage. And so the cited text speaks of the harlot wife and the harlot children, meaning that there would otherwise have been fornication, not that there was fornication on that occasion.

9. Virginity or perpetual continence is not contrary to sexual lust as an extreme but as a mean, since we measure the mean in virtues by right reason, not quantity, as the Philosopher says of the magnanimous person in the *Ethics*.[11] But there would be an extreme by deficiency if one were, contrary to right reason, to abstain from sexual intercourse, as is evidently the case when a husband disdains to fulfill his marital duty to his wife, or when one abstains because of fear of devils, as sorcerers do, and vestal virgins did.

Second Article

Is Every Act of Sexual Lust a Mortal Sin?

It seems that not every act of sexual lust is, for the following reasons:

1. A gloss of Ambrose on 1 Tim. 4:8, "Godliness is beneficial for all sorts of things," says: "The whole of Christian training consists of mercy and godliness. And if a person following this path suffers lapses of the flesh, the person will undoubtedly be punished but will not perish."[12] But whoever sins mortally both is punished and perishes. Therefore, not everyone who suffers lapses of the flesh through acts of sexual lust sins mortally.

2. Every mortal sin is contrary to a precept of the divine law. But of the sins of sexual lust, only adultery is contrary to a precept of the divine law, namely, the precept "Thou shalt not commit adultery."[13] Therefore, of the acts of sexual lust, only adultery is a mortal sin.

---

11. *Ethics* IV, 3 (1123b12–14).

12. Peter Lombard, *Gloss*, on 1 Tim. 4:8 (PL 192:348D); from Ambrose (Pseudo), *Commentary on 1 Tim.*, 4:8 (PL 17:474).

13. Ex. 20:14; Dt. 5:18.

3. People have said that we are to understand a prohibition of every illicit copulation to be included in the prohibition against marital infidelity, that is, against adultery. But we do not understand the prohibition of a lesser sin to be included in the prohibition of a greater sin. And adultery is a greater sin than plain fornication. Therefore, we are not to understand the prohibition of plain fornication to be included in the prohibition of adultery.

4. Every mortal sin is contrary to charity, which gives life to the soul, as 1 Jn. 3:14 says: "We have been brought from death to life because we love our brothers." But plain fornication is neither contrary to love of God, since it is not a sin against God, nor contrary to love of neighbor, since it inflicts no injury on one's neighbor. It inflicts no injury on neighbor because a woman free to do as she wishes suffers no injury when she consents to an act of plain fornication, as no one suffers injustice if the person wills it, as the Philosopher says in the *Ethics*.[14] Therefore, fornication is not a mortal sin by reason of its kind.

5. Isidore says in his work *On the Supreme Good* that if the pleasure of fornicating pleases a person more than the love of chastity, sin still reigns in the person.[15] And it seems from this that fornication and the virtue of chastity can coexist in a person. But no mortal sin in a person can coexist with virtue. Therefore, fornication is not a mortal sin.

6. Sins are less serious in two ways: in one way due to an individual's weakness; in the second way due to the magnitude of a temptation. But human beings experience greater weakness regarding sins of sexual lust than sins of gluttony, since the reproductive power, to which sins of sexual lust belong, is both weakened like the nutritive power, to which the sins of gluttony belong, and tainted. Likewise, the temptations of the enemy regarding sexual lust are greater than the enemy's temptations regarding gluttony, since the devil especially assails human beings in regard to sexual lust. Just so, the statement in Job 40:11, "His strength is in his loins, and his power is in the navel of his belly," which Gregory relates to sins of sexual lust, makes this clear.[16] Therefore, it seems that sins of sexual lust are less serious than sins of gluttony. But not every act of gluttony is a mortal sin, as I have said before.[17] Therefore, not every sin of sexual lust is a mortal sin.

7. The corruption of human nature consists of the flesh's rebellion against the spirit. But this rebellion resulted from the sin of gluttony, since Bernard, explaining what Gen. 3:6 recounts, "The woman saw that the tree was good for food," says that rebellion of the flesh against the spirit resulted from the disordered desire for the forbidden tree.[18] Therefore, the nutritive power, to which such desire belongs, is more corrupt than the reproductive power. And so inasmuch as not every act of gluttony is a mortal sin, it seems that much less is every act of sexual lust.

8. Punishment corresponds to moral fault. But the sin of our first parent resulted in greater punishment for the nutritive power than any other power of the soul, since hunger and thirst and the like, which sometimes bring human beings even to the point

14. *Ethics* V, 11 (1138a12).
15. *On the Supreme Good* II, 39, n. 17 (PL 83:642B).
16. *Morals* XXXII, 14, n. 20 (PL 648A).
17. Q. 14, a. 2.
18. *Sermon on the Song of Songs* 72, chaps. 7 and 8 (PL 183:1132).

of death, belong to the nutritive power. Therefore, greater moral fault regards the nutritive power than the reproductive power, and so we reach the same conclusion as before.

9. Mortal sin can belong only to the power of reason, as Augustine makes clear in his work *On the Trinity*.[19] But acts of sexual lust sometimes take place without deliberation by reason, as is evident in the case of Lot, who unwittingly had intercourse with his daughters, as Gen. 19:33–37 relates. Therefore, it seems that acts of sexual lust are not always mortal sins.

10. When reason is preoccupied, we do not impute deeds as mortal sins. But in acts of sexual lust, reason is totally preoccupied. For a gloss on 1 Cor. 6:18, "A fornicator sins against his own body," says: "Here the soul is in a proper sense the slave of the body inasmuch as a human being at the very moment and experience of so great shame cannot plan or strive for anything else, since the very submersion and absorption in sexual lust holds the mind captive."[20] Therefore, it seems that acts of sexual lust are not mortal sins.

11. A gloss on Dt. 23:17, "There shall be no whore in your midst," says: "It forbids intercourse with those whose wickedness is venial."[21] Therefore, intercourse with whores is a venial sin.

12. The sexual union of a man and a woman is ordained for the begetting and rearing of offspring. But fornication can sometimes fittingly result in begetting and rearing offspring. Therefore, not every fornication is a mortal sin.

13. A man who intends to be perpetually continent prevents the good of begetting and rearing offspring more than the man who has fornicacious intercourse with a woman. Therefore, if fornication were to be a mortal sin because it impedes the rearing of offspring, much more would observing continence be a mortal sin, since observing continence completely prevents the begetting of offspring.

14. Obviously, the begetting of offspring cannot result from intercourse with a sterile and somewhat old woman. But there can sometimes be such intercourse in the state of marriage without mortal sin. Therefore, even other acts of sexual lust from which no begetting or requisite rearing of children results can be without mortal sin.

15. Mt. 5:28 says that if desire has excited the soul, there is no serious sin even if there is sin.[22] But such excitement is an act of sexual lust. Therefore, not every act of sexual lust is a serious or mortal sin.

16. The pleasure in only thinking about fornication is not a mortal sin. But consenting to sin venially is not a mortal sin. Therefore, neither is the consent of reason to such pleasure a mortal sin, although it is an act of sexual lust. Therefore, not every act of sexual lust is a mortal sin.

17. What is a mortal sin for one person is not a mortal sin for another. But consent to pleasure is not a mortal sin for a man who is having intercourse with his wife, since the act itself is not a mortal sin for him. Therefore, neither is consent to pleasure in sexual lust a mortal sin for others. Therefore, not every act of sexual lust is a mortal sin.

---

19. *On the Trinity* XII, 12, n. 17 (PL 42:1008).
20. Peter Lombard, *Gloss*, on 1 Cor. 6:18 (PL 191:1584A).
21. *Ordinary Gloss*, on Dt. 23:17.
22. Actually a gloss: *Interlinear Gloss*, on Mt. 5:28.

18. Acts of sexual lust also include touches, embraces, and kisses. But such things do not seem to be mortal sins. For although the Apostle in Eph. 5:3–4 had said: "Let not fornication or sexual impurity or greed or obscenity," which things consist of embraces and kisses, as a gloss says, "or foolish talk or scurrility even be mentioned among us," [23] he then adds (v. 5): "Every fornication or sexually impure or greedy person has no inheritance in the kingdom of Christ or God." He thereby omits obscenity and foolish talk and scurrility. Therefore, it seems that the latter such things are not mortal sins excluding one from the kingdom of God.

On the Contrary:

1. The Apostle says in Gal. 5:19: "The deeds of the flesh, which include fornication, sexual impurity, shamelessness, sexual lust, are manifest," and he then adds (v. 21): "Those who do such things will not possess the kingdom of God." But only mortal sin excludes one from the kingdom of God. Therefore, every act of sexual lust is a mortal sin.

2. Mt. 5:28 says: "Anyone who looks at a woman with lust has already committed adultery with her in desire." And so such a person sins mortally. But of all the acts of sexual lust, the first and least is the act of gazing lustfully at a woman. Therefore, much more are all other acts of sexual lust mortal sins.

Answer:

As I have said before acts of sexual lust can be disordered in two ways: in one way only because of the disorder in the desire; in a second way also because of the disorder of the very act.[24]

Therefore, when there is a sin of sexual lust only because of the disorder of the desire, for example, when one has intercourse with one's wife lustfully, we need to make a distinction. We need to make the distinction because the disorder is sometimes such as to exclude the ordination of one's ultimate end. For example, such is the case when a man desires sexual pleasure to such a degree that he would not abstain from it because of God's precept and would will to have intercourse with his wife, or even another woman, contrary to the law of marriage. And then there is mortal sin, since the desire for sex is not kept within the bounds of marriage. And the disorder of the desire sometimes does not eliminate the ordination of the ultimate end, namely, when a man, although excessively desiring sexual pleasure, would abstain from it before he would act contrary to God's precept, and he would not have intercourse with any woman unless she were his wife. And then the desire stays within the bounds of marriage and is a venial sin. (We have previously made just such a distinction in the case of gluttony.)[25]

But if acts of sexual lust are sins because of the very disorder of the acts, namely, because the acts are not properly related to the begetting and rearing of offspring, then I say that they are always mortal sins. For we perceive that mortal sin includes both homicide, which takes away the life of a human being, and theft, which takes away external goods

23. Peter Lombard, *Gloss*, on Eph. 5:4 (PL 192:209C).
24. Q. 15, a. 1.
25. Q. 14, a. 2.

ordained to sustain human life. And so Sir. 34:25 says: "The bread of the needy is the life of the poor; the person who defrauds the poor takes blood." And human semen, in which there is a potential human being, is more closely ordained for human life than any external things. And so also the Philosopher says in the *Politics* that there is something divine in human semen, namely, inasmuch as there is a potential human being. And so the disorder regarding the emission of semen concerns human life in proximate potentiality.[26]

And so it is clear that every such act of sexual lust is a mortal sin by reason of its kind. And since an interior desire derives its goodness or wickedness from the object desired, it follows that even the desire for such a disordered act is a mortal sin if the act be fully desired, namely, with the deliberation of reason. Otherwise, there is venial sin.

Replies to the Objections:

1. Ambrose is speaking in the cited text about lapses of the flesh as venial sins, as is evident in conjugal acts, as I have said.[27] Or we can say, and better, that he is even speaking about the lapses of mortal sin. But we should not understand in an absolute sense that if a person were to persevere in such lapses of the flesh even to the time of death, the person would escape condemnation because of works of piety. Rather, we should understand that repeated works of piety dispose human beings to repent more easily, and after they have repented, to expiate their past sins more easily. And it is also for this reason that the Lord in Mt. 25:41–46 imputes lack of mercy to the damned, namely, that they did not endeavor to expiate their past sins by works of mercy, as Augustine says in *City of God*.[28]

2. We understand by the commandment "Thou shalt not commit adultery" that every illicit use of the genital organs, which is a mortal sin by reason of its kind, is forbidden.

3. God directly transmitted the commandments of the Decalogue to his people. And so he transmitted them in that format exactly as they are evident to the natural reason of every human being, even ordinary human beings. And everyone by natural reason can immediately perceive that adultery is a sin, and so the prohibition of adultery is included among the commandments of the Decalogue. But subsequent prescriptions of the law, which God transmitted to the people through Moses, prohibited fornication and other corrupt practices.[29] God did so because the disorder of those acts, inasmuch as it does not clearly include injury to neighbor, is not evident to everybody but only to the wise, who ought to transmit knowledge about it to others.

4. All the corruptions of sexual lust besides legitimate conjugal acts are sins against neighbor inasmuch as the corruptions are contrary to the good of begetting and rearing children, as I have said.[30]

5. Love of chastity can please both one who has the virtue and one who does not, inasmuch as human beings by natural reason esteem the good in the virtue and love it and are pleased with it even if they lack it.

---

26. Actually, *On the Generation of Animals* II, 3 (737a7–17).

27. In the answer.

28. *City of God* XXI, 27, n. 3 (PL 41:747).

29. Ex. 20:15–17.

30. A. 1.

6. The argument of this objection is valid regarding the gravity of sin we note by reason of its circumstances, which gravity is outweighed by the gravity of sin we note by reason of the act's species. And so it is clear that however much one is induced to commit homicide, homicide is a more serious sin than uttering an idle word even without inducement. Likewise, although human beings are more severely tempted to commit acts of sexual lust than acts of gluttony and are weaker regarding acts of sexual lust, it does not follow that sins of sexual lust are less serious than sins of gluttony. For acts of sexual lust as such are mortal sins, since they have improper matter contrary to charity, and acts of gluttony do not. But it would perhaps follow that a sin of sexual lust is less serious than a sin of gluttony in a case in which the act of sexual lust is a venial sin. For a person who consumes food needlessly, just like a man who has intercourse with his wife needlessly, sins venially, unless there be something else to make the sin mortal in both cases. And a person who eats stolen or legally forbidden food sins mortally but less than a fornicator, inasmuch as food and every external thing is more remotely related to human life than human semen is, as I have said.[31]

7. In the sin of our first parent, gluttony was the material element, but the formal and chief element was the sin of pride in which Adam was unwilling to be subject to the rule of God's command. And the rebellion of the flesh against the spirit resulted from this, as Augustine says in *City of God*, and not from the sin of gluttony.[32]

8. The rebellion of the flesh, which we experience especially in the genital organs, is a greater punishment than hunger and thirst, since the latter punishment is purely material, and the former spiritual.

9. Since it belongs to reason to consent to an act, as Augustine says in his work *On the Trinity*, there cannot be an act of fornication without the deliberation of reason, except perhaps in the case of one lacking the use of reason.[33] And then if an illicit cause should be responsible for preventing the use of reason, the person is not altogether excused from sin. For example, such was evidently the case with Lot, who committed incest because he was drunk, unless perhaps his drunkenness happened without him sinning, as happened to Noah because he did not know the strength of wine.[34] And if the cause of such deficiency of reason is blameless, as is evidently so in the case of maniacs and the insane, then ensuing acts of sexual lust or whatever sin are not imputed as sin.

10. Reason cannot deliberate in the very act of sexual lust, but it could deliberate beforehand, when it consented to the act. And so we impute acts of sexual lust to persons as sins.

11. The copy of the gloss has been corrupted. For it should read: "whose wickedness is venal," not "whose wickedness is venial."

12. The reproductive act is ordained for the good of the species, which is the common good. And law can ordain the common good, but private good is subject to the ordination of each person. And so individuals regarding acts of the nutritive power, which

---

31. In the answer.
32. *City of God* XIV, 15, n. 1 (PL 41:423).
33. *On the Trinity* XII, 12, n. 17 (PL 42:1008).
34. Cf. Gen. 9:21.

is ordained for the preservation of individuals, can determine for themselves the food suitable for themselves. But it belongs to the lawmaker, to whom it belongs to make ordinances regarding the procreation of children, and not to individuals, to determine under what conditions the reproductive acts should take place, as the Philosopher in the *Politics* also says.[35] And law considers what is wont to happen generally, not what can happen in a particular case. And so although the aim of nature regarding the begetting and rearing of offspring can be provided for in particular cases of acts of fornication, the acts as such are still disordered and mortal sins.

13. Both human and divine law made it sinful that one abstain completely from reproductive acts at the time in which abstinence needed to be prohibited in order to multiply the human race. But in the present period of grace, we need more to pursue spiritual growth, for which those living celibate are more fit. And so we esteem it more virtuous in this period of time to abstain from reproductive acts.

14. General laws are laid down regarding general conditions, not accidental particulars. And so we say that an act in the genus of sexual lust is contrary to nature if begetting offspring cannot result from the act by reason of the act's species, not if begetting offspring cannot result from the act because of an accidental particular such as old age or infirmity.

15. The argument of this objection is valid regarding acts of sexual lust in which there is sin only because of a disordered desire, but which do not exclude the ordination of one's ultimate end.

16. Consent to what is a venial sin by reason of its kind is not a mortal sin. But pleasure in thinking about fornication is a mortal sin by reason of its kind just as much as fornication itself. And that pleasure in thinking about fornication happens to be a venial sin is accidental to it because of the incomplete nature of the act, the deliberation of reason being lacking. And at the advent of deliberation, deliberate consent restores the act to the nature of its kind so as to constitute a mortal sin.

17. As the Philosopher says in the *Ethics*, the goodness or wickedness of pleasures results from the activities that are pleasurable.[36] And so as copulation is not a mortal sin for the married but is for the unmarried, there is also a like difference between the pleasure in copulation and consent to the pleasure. For consent to a pleasure cannot be a more serious sin than consent to the act, as Augustine makes clear in his work *On the Trinity*.[37]

18. Touches, embraces, and kisses, insofar as they are ordained for acts of fornication, result from consent to fornication, and insofar as they are ordained only for the pleasure in them, result from consent to the pleasure, which consent constitutes a mortal sin. And so they are mortal sins in both cases. But because such things are not specifically mortal sins, like fornication and adultery, but only mortal sins because they are ordained for something else, that is, the aforementioned consents, the Apostle does not repeat mention of obscenity and scurrility and foolish talk but only of things that are as such mortal sins.

---

35. *Politics* VII, 13 (1334b29ff.).
36. *Ethics* X, 5 (1175b24–36).
37. *On the Trinity* XII, 12, n. 17 (PL 42:1007).

Third Article

Are Fornication, Adultery, Incest, Seduction of a Virgin, Rape, and Sins Contrary to Nature the Species of Sexual Lust?

It seems that we unsuitably distinguish these acts as species of sexual lust, for the following reasons:

1. Different matter does not distinguish species. But we distinguish the aforementioned acts only by reason of their matter, namely, as one defiles either a married woman or a virgin or a woman neither married nor a virgin. Therefore, the aforementioned acts do not constitute different species of sexual lust.

2. Sexual lust consists intrinsically of the sexual pleasures in the copulation of a man and a woman. But it is accidental to a woman whether she is married or single or a virgin. Therefore, the aforementioned acts differ only accidentally and so are not different species, since accidental differences do not distinguish species.

3. Sexual lust is intrinsically contrary to moderation. But some of the aforementioned acts, especially adultery and rape, are contrary to justice. Therefore, it seems that the aforementioned acts inappropriately designate the species of sexual lust.

On the Contrary:
The Master in the *Sentences* designates these species.[38]

Answer:
As I have said before, sins of sexual lust can be disordered in two ways: in one way regarding the desire, and such disorder does not always cause mortal sin; in a second way regarding the acts themselves, which are of themselves disordered, and then there is always mortal sin.[39] And so we understand the aforementioned species of lust in the latter regard whereby the sins are more serious. And so acts of sexual lust are disordered because the acts cannot result in the begetting of offspring, and then there are sins contrary to nature, or because the acts cannot result in the proper rearing of offspring, namely, in that the woman is not bound to the man so as to be his by the law of marriage. And this indeed happens in three ways. It happens in one way because the woman is not absolutely specified as his, and then there is fornication, which is the sexual union of an unmarried man and an unmarried woman. And we derive the name *fornication* from *fornice*, that is, a decorative arch, because women prostitutes gathered at such public places. Second, it happens because the law of marriage does not permit the woman to be bound to the man. And this can happen by reason of kinship, whereby the man owes the woman a respect contrary to performing such an act, and then there is incest, which is sexual union with a woman who is a relative by blood or marriage. Or else the law of marriage does not permit the woman to be bound to the man because of an inviolability or purity of the woman, and then there is seduction of a virgin, which is illicit intercourse with a

---

38. Peter Lombard, *Sentences* IV, d. 41, chaps. 5–9.
39. Q. 15, aa. 1 and 2.

virgin. Third, it happens because the woman belongs to another either by the law of marriage, and then there is adultery, or in another way, and then there is rape, as, for example, when a girl is abducted from the home of her father, to whose care she is entrusted.

Replies to the objections:

1. The aforementioned six categories of acts differ both materially and by different kinds of deformity, and so the six categories constitute different species of sin.

2. Although the aforementioned acts are accidental to women as such, they are nonetheless intrinsic considerations regarding women in relation to marriage.

3. Because the deformity of the injustice in acts of sexual lust is related to the end of intemperance, the entirety of the acts belongs to the genus of lack of moderation.

Fourth Article

Is Sexual Lust a Capital Sin?

It seems that sexual lust is not, for the following reasons:

1. Gregory in his work *Morals* designates sexual impurity a daughter of gluttony.[40] But we do not designate one capital sin the daughter of another. Therefore, since sexual impurity belongs to sexual lust, as Eph. 5:3 makes clear, it seems that sexual lust is not a capital sin.

2. Isidore says in his work *On the Supreme Good*: "Those in the grip of pride fall into lust of the flesh."[41] Therefore, sexual lust is a daughter of pride. Therefore, sexual lust is not a capital sin.

3. Despair is a daughter of spiritual apathy, as Gregory makes clear in his work *Morals*.[42] But despair causes sexual lust, as Eph. 4:19 says: "Those who despair of themselves have given themselves over to unchastity." Therefore, sexual lust is not a capital sin.

On the Contrary:

Gregory in his work *Morals* lists sexual lust among the capital sins.[43]

Answer:

As I have said before,[44] since pleasure is one of the conditions for happiness, sins that have pleasure for their object are capital sins inasmuch as they have an especially desirable end to which other sins are by nature related.

---

40. *Morals* XXXI, 45, n. 88 (PL 76:621B).
41. *On the Supreme Good* II, 38, n. 1 (PL 83:639B).
42. *Morals* XXXI, 45, n. 88 (PL 76:621B).
43. Ibid., n. 87 (PL 76:621A).
44. Q. 14, a. 4.

And pleasure in sex, which is the end of sexual lust, is the greatest of physical pleasures. And so we ought to designate sexual lust a capital sin, and it has eight daughters, namely, "blindness of mind, lack of consideration, inconstancy, temerity, self-love, hatred of God, love of this world, and despair of the next," as Gregory makes clear in his work *Morals*.[45] For when the attention of the soul is strongly concentrated on the activity of a lower power, the soul's higher powers are evidently weakened and disordered in their activity. And so when the whole attention of the soul is drawn to lower powers (i.e., the concupiscible power and the sense of touch) in acts of sexual lust because of the strong pleasure therein, the higher powers, namely, reason and the will, necessarily suffer deficiency.

And there are four acts of reason insofar as reason directs human acts. And the first of the acts is an understanding whereby a person correctly esteems the ultimate end, which is the starting point, as it were, in practical matters, as the Philosopher says in the *Physics*.[46] And insofar as sexual lust prevents this understanding, we designate blindness of mind a daughter of sexual lust, as Dan. 13:56 says: "Beauty has deceived you, and lustful desire has perverted your heart." The second act of reason consists of deliberation about what is to be done, which deliberation sexual lust takes away. For example, Terence says regarding Eunuchus: "And there is no deliberation or moderation in this matter; you cannot control it by deliberation."[47] And Terence is speaking about lustful love. And in this respect, we designate sexual lust lack of consideration. The third act of reason consists of judging what is to be done, and sexual lust also prevents this. For Dan. 3:9 says that "they averted their minds so as not to be mindful of right judgments." And in this regard, we designate sexual lust temerity, namely, when one is inclined to consent rashly without awaiting the judgment of reason. The fourth act of reason consists of a command about doing something, which sexual lust also prevents inasmuch as human beings do not persist in their decisions, as Terence also says regarding Eunuchus, "These words," namely, the ones whereby you tell your mistress that you will leave her, "are undone by a small false tear."[48] And in this regard, we designate sexual lust lack of constancy.

And we should note two things regarding the disorder of desire in sexual lust. The first is that there is a desire for pleasure toward which the will is borne as one's end. And in this regard, we designate sexual lust self-love, namely, that one inordinately desires pleasure for self. And by contrast, one has hatred for God, namely, inasmuch as God forbids the desired pleasure. And the second thing to be noted is the desire of the means whereby one attains the end of pleasure. And in this regard, we designate sexual lust love of this world, that is, of all the things whereby those who belong to this world attain the end they strive for. And we by contrast designate sexual lust despair of the next world, since the more one desires pleasures of the flesh, the more one despises spiritual pleasures.

---

45. *Morals* XXXI, 45, n. 88 (PL 76:621B).
46. *Physics* II, 9 (200a34b1).
47. Terence, *Eunuchus*, Act 1, v. 12.
48. Ibid., Act 1, v. 23.

Replies to the Objections:

1. We designate sexual impurity a daughter of gluttony insofar as a physical cause, that is, an excess of fluids, and not a perceived cause, namely, desire, which especially belongs to sexual lust, causes an emission of semen.

2. It is not contrary to the nature of a capital sin that it arise out of pride, from which all sins originate.

3. Despair incidentally causes sexual lust insofar as it takes away the hope of future happiness, for the sake of which one desists from sexual lust. But we note the origin of capital sins by their intrinsic causes, not their accidental causes.

QUESTION XVI

On Devils

First Article

Do Devils Have Bodies Joined to Them by Nature?

It seems that devils do, for the following reasons:

1. Augustine says in his *Literal Commentary on Genesis*: "Regarding the spirit of a rational creature, the very fact that it lives and gives life to bodies is good, whether ethereal bodies, as in the case of the spirit of the devil himself and other devils, or earthly bodies, as in the case of the souls of human beings."[1] But a body given life is by nature joined to the spirit giving life, since life is something natural. Therefore, devils have ethereal bodies joined to them by nature.

2. Many memories of the same thing from past sense perceptions produce experience, as the opening of the *Metaphysics* says.[2] And so there is sense perception wherever there is experience. And there is no sense perception without a body joined by nature to one with experience, since sense perception is the activity of a bodily organ. But devils have experience, for Augustine says in his *Literal Commentary on Genesis* that they know some truths in part because they thrive with more subtle mental powers, in part because of their shrewder experience, in part because they learn from holy angels.[3] Therefore, devils have bodies joined to them by nature.

3. Dionysius says in his work *On the Divine Names* that the evil in devils is "an irrational rage, a demented desire, and a shameless imagination."[4] But these three things belong to the sensory part of the soul, which possesses the power of imagination and the irascible and concupiscible powers, and the sensory part of the soul does not exist apart from a body. Therefore, devils have bodies joined to them by nature.

4. The higher something belonging to a lower rank, the greater the link it has with a higher rank. And so the *Book of Causes* says that of faculties of mental perception, there

---

1. *Literal Commentary on Genesis* XI, 13 (PL 34:436)
2. Aristotle, *Metaphysics* I, 1 (980a29–981a7).
3. *Literal Commentary on Genesis* II, 17, n. 37 (PL 34:278).
4. *On the Divine Names* 4, n. 23 (PG 3:725B).

is a kind that is only a faculty of mental perception, namely, the lower, and a kind that is divine. And of souls, there is a kind that is only a soul, as in the case of irrational animals, and a kind that is an intellectual soul, as in the case of human beings. And of material substances, there is a kind that is only a material substance and a kind that is a living material substance.[5] And so Dionysius says in *On the Divine Names* that "divine wisdom joins the highest qualities of lower things to the lowest qualities of higher things."[6] But air is a more excellent material substance than earth. Therefore, since there are some living earthly material substances, much more will there be some living ethereal material substances. And we call such living ethereal material substances devils.

5. That whereby something belongs to another can receive more of that thing. For example, if diaphanous material substances are the means whereby opaque material substances are illumined, diaphanous substances can receive more illumination. But living spirits, that is, ethereal material substances, give life to the earthly bodies of human beings and other animals. Therefore, ethereal material substances are more endowable with life than earthly material substances. And so we reach the same conclusion as before.

6. A mean partakes of the nature of extremes. But the highest material substances, namely, heavenly bodies, partake of life, since philosophers call them living.[7] Likewise, in lower material substances, namely, the earth, water, and the lower atmosphere, there are some living material substances. Therefore, there are some living material substances in the middle atmosphere. But only devils are such, since birds cannot climb so high. Therefore, devils are animals with bodies joined to them by nature.

7. What a creature has in relation to God the creature has by its nature, since the relations of creatures to God are grounded in creatures. But Gregory says in his work *Morals* that the spirits of angels in comparison with the spirits of our bodies are indeed spirits, but "in comparison with the highest and boundless spirit are bodies."[8] And Damascene says in his work *On Orthodox Faith* that we call angels "incorporeal and spiritual in relation to us, as everything is both gross and material in comparison to God, since God alone is by his essence spiritual and incorporeal."[9] Therefore, devils have bodies joined to them by nature, since they have the same nature as angels.

8. What we posit in the definition of something belongs by nature to the thing, since a definition signifies the thing's nature. But we posit body in the definition of devils. For example, Calcidius says in his *Commentary on the Timaeus*: "Devils are rational animals, immortal, capable of experience in their soul, ethereal in their bodies."[10] And Apuleius says in his work *On the God of Socrates* that devils are animal by their kind, capable of experience in their soul, rational of mind, ethereal of body, everlasting in time."[11] And Augustine brings this description of devils into the *City of God*.[12] Therefore, devils have bodies joined to them by nature.

5. *Book of Causes*, prop. 19.
6. *On the Divine Names* 7, n. 3 (PG 3:872B).
7. Cf., e.g., Aristotle, *On Heaven and Earth* II, 2 (285a30)
8. *Morals* II, 3 (PL 75:557A).
9. *On Orthodox Faith* II, 3 (PG 94:868A).
10. *Commentary on the Timaeus* 15 (Waszink:175).
11. *On the God of Socrates*; related by Augustine, *City of God* VIII, 16 (PL 41:241)
12. Ibid.

9. Things that are by reason of their bodies subject to the punitive action of material fire have bodies joined to them by nature. But devils are such, for Augustine says in the *City of God* that "fire will be applied to punish devils as well as human beings, since devils also have evil bodies."[13] Therefore, devils have bodies joined to them by nature.

10. What things have from the beginning of their creation and ever after belong to the things by nature. But devils have bodies from the beginning of their creation and ever after, for Augustine says in the *City of God*: "Plotinus thought that it belongs to the mercy of God the Father that human beings be mortal regarding the body in order that they not be eternally bound to the misery of this life. The devils' wickedness was deemed unworthy of such mercy and has received, not a mortal body as in the case of human beings, but an everlasting body in the wretched condition of a soul capable of suffering."[14] Therefore, devils have bodies joined to them by nature.

11. Augustine says in the *City of God*: "That we were to understand that we should not estimate the worth of souls by the qualities of bodies, the wickedest devil possesses an ethereal body, while human beings, both in the present age (although they have far less and far less harsh wickedness than the devils) and before the advent of sin, have received a body of clay."[15] But human beings have bodies of clay joined to them by nature. Therefore, devils likewise have ethereal bodies joined to them by nature.

12. The more perfect a substance, the more it possesses what it needs for its activity. But the human soul, which has a lower nature than devils, has joined to it by nature the bodily organs that it needs for its activities. Therefore, since devils need bodies for some activities (otherwise, they would not assume bodies), it seems that they have bodies joined to them.

13. More goods are better than fewer goods. But body and spirit are more goods than spirit alone. Therefore, since human beings, who have a lower nature than devils, are composed of body and spirit, much more are devils, who have a higher nature than human beings, so composed.

14. Only the intellect and the will are powers distinct from bodily organs. But devils effect some things in lower material substances, as Job 1:2 and 2:7 make clear. And the will alone does not effect these things, since it belongs to God alone that corporeal matter obey him at his bidding, as Augustine says in his work *On the Trinity*,[16] and so also neither does the intellect alone, which has effects on external things only through the will. And so devils have other active powers besides the intellect and the will. Therefore, they have bodies joined to them by nature.

15. Nothing can act on something distant unless some medium conveys its power to the distant object. But a material medium cannot convey the power of a pure spirit, since a material substance is incapable of spiritual power. Therefore, since devils act on distant things, it seems that devils are not pure spirits but things composed of body and spirit.

16. There is no power of imagination without a bodily organ. But angels and devils have a power of imagination, for Augustine says in his *Literal Commentary on Genesis*

---

13. Ibid., XXI, 10, n.1 (PL 41:724).
14. Ibid., IX, 10 (PL 41:365).
15. Ibid., XI, 23, n. 2 (PL 41:337).
16. *On the Trinity* III, 8, n. 13 (PL 42:875).

that they by their knowledge of future events preform in their spirit the images of material things.[17] Therefore, angels and devils have bodies joined to them by nature.

17. Augustine says in the same work that "when a spirit takes and seizes a soul, that soul is carried off to perceive the images of material substances."[18] But the soul could not perceive the images of material substances in completely spiritual substances. Therefore, the spirit of an angel or a devil seizing a soul has bodily organs in which such forms are preserved.

18. Matter causes numerical multiplicity. But both angels and devils are numerically multiple, for we designate them as distinct persons. Therefore, they have matter that causes their numerical multiplicity. But such is matter bounded by dimensions, and its substance is indivisible if the dimensions are severed from the substance, as the *Physics* says.[19] And then the division of matter could not cause numerical multiplicity. Therefore, angels and devils have material dimensions and so matter joined to them by nature.

19. Wherever there is the property of a material substance, there is also a material substance. But locomotion and change belong in the strict sense to material substances, and such belong to devils, for Job 1:12 says that Satan departed from the presence of the Lord. Therefore, devils have matter joined to them by nature.

On the Contrary:
1. We do not call anything composed of soul and body a spirit. And so Is. 31:3 says: "The Egyptians are human beings and not gods, and their horses have flesh and not spirit." But we call devils spirits, as Mt. 12:43 makes clear: "When an unclean spirit has gone out of a human being," etc. Therefore, devils do not have bodies joined to them by nature.

2. Devils and angels have the same nature, for Dionysius says in his work *On the Divine Names* that "devils were not always, nor are they by nature, evil; rather, they are evil by reason of lacking angelic virtues."[20] But angels are immaterial, as he himself says in the same chapter.[21] Therefore, neither do devils have bodies joined to them by nature.

3. Mk. 5:9 says that when the Lord asked the devils, "What is your name?" they replied: "Legion, for we are many." But a legion comprises 6,666 soldiers, as Jerome says in his work *On Matthew*.[22] But it would be impossible for so many devils to belong to one human body if they were to be material. Therefore, devils do not have bodies joined to them by nature.

4. Damascene says in his work *On Orthodox Faith* that angels "are not circumscribed or contained, nor are they confined by walls or doors or bolts or seals."[23] But if they were to have bodies joined to them by nature, they would be able to be confined by doors and bolts, since many material substances cannot simultaneously occupy the same space. Or the death of the devils would result if cleaving them were to free them from confinement. Therefore, devils do not have bodies joined to them by nature.

17. *Literal Commentary on Genesis* XII, 22, n. 48 (PL 34:473).
18. Ibid., XII, 23 (PL 34:474).
19. Aristotle, *Physics* I, 2 (185a32–b5).
20. *On the Divine Names* 4, n. 23 (PG 3:725B).
21. Ibid., 4, n. 1 (PG 3:693C).
22. *On Matthew* IV, on 26:53 (PL 26:200).
23. *On Orthodox Faith* II, 3 (PG 94:869A).

Answer:

Whether devils have bodies joined to them by nature does not matter much for the doctrines of Christian faith. For Augustine says in the *City of God*: "As it seemed to some learned persons, devils also have bodies made of the dense and humid air whose impact we feel when the sirocco is blowing. But if anyone were to assert that devils have no bodies, we ought not belabor the point or contest the issue with laborious inquiry or contentious debate."[24] Still, in order to learn the truth of the matter, we should consider what we find some have perceived about the material and the immaterial, and about devils.

For those who first began to investigate these matters thought that only material substances existed, as was the case with the first philosophers, who studied things of nature.[25] And the error of the Manicheans, who held that even God was a material light,[26] derived from that opinion, which arose because the first philosophers were unable to use their understanding to transcend their imagination. But the activity of understanding itself, which could not be the activity of a bodily organ, evidently demonstrates that something immaterial exists, as the *De anima* proves.[27]

Therefore, with the opinion of the first philosophers excluded, some held that there is indeed something immaterial but always such as to be united to a body. And so they even held that God is the soul of the world, as Augustine relates about Varro in the *City of God*.[28] But Anaxagoras indeed rejected this opinion by reason of the universality of the power to move everything, holding that the intellect that moves everything ought not be mixed with anything.[29] And Aristotle rejected the opinion by reason of the eternity of movement, which perpetual motion is only possible by reason of the infinite power of the first cause of movement, and a finite magnitude cannot possess infinite power. And so Aristotle concludes in the *Physics* that the first cause of movement lacks material magnitude.[30] And Plato rejected the opinion by way of abstraction, holding that the good and the one, which we can understand without reference to material substance, subsist in the first cause without materiality.[31]

And so assuming that the first cause, that is, God, is neither a material substance nor joined to material substance, some held that such a condition belongs only to God, and that other spiritual substances are joined to material substances. And so Origen says in his work *On First Principles* that "it belongs only to God that we understand him to exist apart from material substances and any union with a material supplement."[32] But an obvious argument excludes this position. For what is joined to something by reason of something else and not by reason of the thing's own nature can always exist without what is added. For example, fire exists without a mixture of other elements that do not belong to its nature, and accidents do not exist apart from substances, since inhering in a

---

24. *City of God* XXI, 10, n. 1 (PL 41:724).
25. Related by Aristotle, *Metaphysics* I, 3 (983b6–8)
26. Related by Augustine, *On Heresies* 46 (PL 42:35).
27. *De anima* III, 4 (429a24–27).
28. *City of God* VII, 6 (PL 41:199).
29. Aristotle, *Physics* VIII, 5 (256b25–27).
30. Ibid., VIII, 10 (267b17–19).
31. Cf. Proclus, *Theological First Principles (Elementatio theologica)*, props. 12 and 13.
32. *On First Principles* I, 6, n.4.

substance belongs to the nature of accidents. And it is evident that intellects are joined to bodies regarding other powers and not as such. And so it is evident that other intellects exist without bodies. But God is superior to such intellects.

Therefore, with these things understood about the material and the immaterial, we need to consider regarding devils that the followers of Aristotle held that devils do not exist. And the followers of Aristotle claimed that the things ascribed to devils come about from the power of heavenly bodies and other things of nature. And so Augustine says in the *City of God* that it seemed to Porphyry that "human beings, by plants and stones and animals, and by definite sounds and words, and by forms and figments, some of which human beings even observe in the heavenly motions of the stars, construct earthly powers fit to bring about various effects."[33] But this position is obviously false, since there are some activities of devils that can in no way result from natural causes, as, for example, that a person possessed by a devil speaks an unknown language. And there are many other deeds of devils both in cases of possession and in the arts of black magic that only an intellect can produce.

And so still other philosophers were forced to admit that devils exist. And as Augustine relates in the *City of God*,[34] one of these, Plotinus, "said that devils are human souls, and the souls change from human beings to deities if they should deserve reward, and to malevolent ghosts or shades if they should deserve punishment, and benevolent spirits if it is uncertain whether they deserve reward or punishment." But as Chrysostom says in a homily on the Gospel of Matthew, "Devils came forth out of the tombs in order to spread a pernicious doctrine, namely, that the souls of the dead become devils. And so many soothsayers even killed their children in order to have the children's souls as co-workers. But there is no reason why an immaterial power should be able to be transformed into a different substance, namely, a human soul into the substance of a devil. Nor is there any reason why a soul separated from the body should wander here on earth, for the souls of the just are in the hands of God, and the souls of sinners are immediately taken away from here."[35]

And so with the latter opinion eliminated, as Augustine relates in the *City of God*, others held that "there is a triple division of animals having a rational soul: gods, human beings, and devils. And they said that gods have heavenly bodies, devils ethereal bodies, human beings earthly bodies."[36] And so Plato held that these three ranks of substances united to bodies were lower than intellectual substances entirely separated from matter.[37]

But regarding devils, the latter position seems to be impossible. First, indeed, it seems impossible because, as the air is like in its entirety and its parts, the whole would be alive if we assume that some parts of it are. And this conclusion is plainly false, since we perceive no vital activity in the whole air by reason of its movement or anything else. Sec-

---

33. *City of God* X, 11 (PL 41:290).
34. Related, ibid., IX 11 (PL 41:265).
35. The text as quoted is from St. Thomas, *Golden Chain (Catena aurea)*, on Mt. 8:28; cf. Chrysostom, *On Matthew*, hom. 28 (PG 57:453).
36. *City of God* VIII, 14, n. 1 (PL 41:238).
37. Related, ibid.

ond, the position seems impossible because every living body on earth has organs to suit the diverse activities of its soul, and bodies can only be organic if they in themselves can have limit and shape. And the air does not have such a property. And so no ethereal material substance can be living, especially since it could not be distinguished from the surrounding air if it were in itself incapable of limit. Third, since form is not for the sake of matter but rather the converse, the soul is not united to the body because the body is such a body, but rather the body is united to the soul because the body is needed for animal activities, namely, sense perception or other movements. And no movement of any part of the air is needed for generating things, as the movement of heavenly bodies, which bodies some hold to be alive, is necessary. And so a spiritual substance would be united to ethereal matter only in order to move that matter. Therefore, we conclude that a union of spirit with matter in devils would be chiefly for the sake of sense perception, just as in our case. And so also the Platonists held that devils are animals capable of experience in their spirit, and such capacity to experience belongs to the sensory part of the spirit.[38] But there cannot be sense perception without a sense of touch, which is the foundation of all the senses, and so an animal is destroyed when its sense of touch is destroyed. And neither an ethereal nor any simple material substance can be an organ of touch, as the *De anima* proves.[39] And so we conclude that no ethereal material substance can be alive. And so we say that devils do not have bodies joined to them by nature.

Replies to the Objections:

1. Augustine in the cited text and many other places speaks about the bodies of devils as they seemed to some learned persons, that is, the Platonists, as his previously cited authoritative statement makes clear.[40]

2. Experience in the strict sense belongs to the senses. For although the intellect knows both separate forms, as the Platonists held,[41] and material substances, the intellect knows these things by their general nature, not as they exist here and now, which is to have experience. For we also apply the term *experience* to intellectual knowledge, just as we apply the very names of the senses (e.g., *seeing* and *hearing*) to such knowledge. Still, nothing prevents us from saying that Augustine posits experience in devils insofar as he assumes they have bodies and so senses.

3. It is quite likely that Dionysius, who followed the opinion of the Platonists for the most part, agreed with them that devils are animals with sense perception and sense appetites. But we can say that he ascribes anger and desire to devils in a metaphorical sense because of the likeness of their activity. He does not do so as anger and desire signify emotions of the sensory part of the soul belonging to irascible and concupiscible powers, since we also ascribe anger and desire to the holy angels in a metaphorical sense, as Augustine in the *City of God* [42] and Dionysius in his work *On the Celestial Hierarchy* [43]

---

38. Related, ibid., VIII, 16 (PL 41:241).

39. Aristotle, *De anima* III, 12 (434a27–29).

40. In the beginning of the answer.

41. Related by Aristotle, *Metaphysics* I, 6 (987b1–14).

42. *City of God* IX, 5 (PL 41:261).

43. *On the Celestial Hierarchy* 2, n. 4 (PG 3:141D).

make clear. And likewise, we ascribe to devils the power of imagination, which gets its name from vision, as the *De anima*[44] says, just as we ascribe vision to the intellect.

4. Although air is a more excellent material substance than earth, both air and all the other elements are related to complex material substances as the matter of the latter. And so the forms of complex material substances are more excellent than the forms of elements. And the soul, because it is the most excellent form, cannot be the form of ethereal material substances. Rather, the soul can be only the form of complex material substances, in which earth and water are quantitatively more abundant, in order that the mixture have balance.

5. The soul is related to the body in two ways. The soul is related to the body in one way as its form, and then spirits, that is, ethereal material substances, are not a mean between the soul and complex earthly matter. Rather, the soul is directly united to complex matter as its form. In a second way, the soul is related to the living body as the cause of its movement, and ethereal material substances, that is, spirits, in this respect are a mean between the soul and a living body. And because the relation of form is prior to the relation of causing movement, complex earthly matter capable of life is consequently prior to ethereal material substances.

6. If we should assume that heavenly bodies are living, as some hold,[45] it is still not necessary on that account that there be living bodies in the middle atmosphere. For the lowest material substances, which the mixture of elements brings to a mean, have a greater resemblance to heavenly bodies by reason of lacking the contrariety that simple material substances like fire and air (which have very contrary qualities) have.

7. Damascene may have followed Origen in this regard and so believed that both angels and devils have bodies joined to them by nature, by reason of which we call them spirits in comparison with ourselves but corporeal in comparison with God. But we can say that both Damascene and Gregory understood corporeal to mean composite, so that their words mean no more than that angels and devils are simple in comparison with ourselves but composite in comparison with God.

8. The cited definition of devil is presented regarding the opinions of the Platonists.

9. Augustine is also speaking in the cited text regarding the Platonists. And so he said in the same place: "As it seemed to some learned persons."

10. Augustine in the cited text is speaking against the Platonists, who held that divine reverence should be shown to devils because of the eternity of their bodies.[46] And Augustine uses their own position, showing that they are more wretched if they have indestructible bodies, since they are then capable of experiencing pain in their spirit.

11. Augustine in the cited text is speaking against Origen, who held that different spirits received more or less excellent bodies according to their different merits. And devils, whose wickedness is greater, would accordingly have grosser bodies than human beings.

12. The soul has the bodily organs necessary for its natural activities joined to it by nature. But appearing to human beings is not a natural activity of devils, nor is there any

---

44. Aristotle, *De anima* III, 3 (429a3–4).
45. Platonists, as related by Augustine, *City of God* XIII, 16, n. 2 (PL 41:388).
46. Related by Augustine, *City of God* VIII, 16 (PL 41:244).

other natural activity of theirs for which a bodily organ is necessary. And so devils do not need to have bodies joined to them by nature.

13. Many goods are better than fewer, provided that each of them belongs to the same rank. But what has the perfection of its goodness in one good, namely, as God does, is far better than what has its perfection dispersed in different parts. And angels, who are pure spirits by their nature, are accordingly better than human beings composed of body and spirit.

14. Angels and devils, if we should hold them to be immaterial, have no power other than intellect and will. And so Dionysius says in his work *On the Divine Names* that "all their substances, powers, and activities are intellectual."[47] For the powers and activities of everything needs to result from its very nature. But angels are intellectual as to their whole nature, not as to a part of themselves like a human soul. And so angels can have no power or potentiality except one belonging to intellectual cognition or desire. And it is not unfitting that angels move, at least locally, some material substances simply at the command of their will, since we perceive that the human soul moves the body joined to it by intellect and will alone. And the higher an intellectual substance, the more universal the power it has to cause movement. And so an intellectual substance separate from a body can at the command of its will move material substances not joined to the intellectual substance. And the higher the intellectual substance, the more it can do so, to such a degree that people say that the ministry of some angels moves even heavenly bodies.[48] But it belongs to God alone that corporeal matter obey his bidding regarding the reception of forms.

15. Angels do not act directly on material substances distant from them, since angels are active where they are, as Damascene says.[49] But they nonetheless act on distant material substances by using other material substances, whose power is diffused between the angels and the distant substances, and they move the other substances locally simply by the command of their will. Just so, they use the power of material things to produce material effects, as Augustine says in his work *On the Trinity*.[50]

16. Augustine states that opinion tentatively, not categorically, and this is clear from his very mode of expression. For he says in his *Literal Commentary on Genesis*: "It is both most difficult to know, and most laborious to discuss and explain if we should know, how these visions enter the spirit of human beings. We do not know and cannot explain whether the visions are initially formed there, or already formed visions are impressed and perceived by such a conjunction that angels reveal to human beings the angels' own thoughts and the images of material things they preform in their spirit by their knowledge of future events."[51] And the first alternative, namely, that angels form in the imagination of human beings images of the things they reveal, is more probable, and it does not seem probable that angels fashion images in their spirit, or that human spirits perceive such images fashioned in angels.

---

47. *On the Divine Names* 4, n. 1 (PG 3:693B).
48. Cf. St. Thomas himself, *ST* I, q. 110, a. 1, and q. 57, a. 2.
49. *On Orthodox Faith* II, 3 (PG 94:869B).
50. *On the Trinity* III, 8, n. 13 (PL 42:876).
51. *Commentary on the Book of Genesis* XII, 22, n. 48 (PL 34:473).

17. And so also does the foregoing make evident the reply to objection 17.

18. Matter subject to dimensions is the source of numerical distinction regarding things that comprise many individuals of the same species, for such things do not differ in form. But angels differ both specifically and individually, since each angel belongs to a different species, as I have shown elsewhere.[52]

19. Angels are not materially in a place. And so we do not predicate things pertaining to locomotion univocally of angels and material substances.

Replies to the Arguments in the Section On the Contrary:

1. If one were to maintain that devils have ethereal bodies, the answer could be that devils are not subject to their bodies, as we are, but rather have their bodies subject to them, as Augustine says in his *Literal Commentary on Genesis*.[53] And so we can call devils spirits more than we can call ourselves spirits, although devils have bodies joined to them by nature, especially since we call even air itself a spirit.

2. We can say that Dionysius certainly thought that higher angels are immaterial, just as the Platonists held. But he may have thought that devils are among lower angels who have bodies joined to them by nature, not among the higher angels. And so Augustine says in his *Literal Commentary on Genesis* that "some of us do not think that they [the devils] are celestial or supercelestial angels,"[54] and Damascene says that their chief "presided over the terrestrial order."[55]

3. [missing]

4. As air, since it is a material substance, cannot be in the same place with another material substance, nor even confined by locks or doors, since it can escape through the thinnest cracks, so also can we speak of the bodies of devils. We can so speak especially because we do not need to suppose that devils have big bodies joined to them by nature.

Second Article

Are Devils Evil by Their Nature or Their Will?

It seems that devils are evil by their nature, not their will, for the following reasons:

1. Devils, since they are intellectual substances without a body, have only an intellectual appetite, which we call the will. But absolutely speaking, only the good is the object of an intellectual appetite, as the *Metaphysics* says.[56] But no one becomes evil by desiring what is good without qualification. Therefore, devils could not become evil by their will. Therefore, devils are evil by their nature.

2. Nothing unnatural belongs immutably to things, since everything left to itself returns to its nature. But wickedness belongs immutably to devils. Therefore, wickedness belongs to them by nature.

---

52. *ST* I, q. 50, a. 4.
53. Actually, *On the Trinity* III, 1, n. 4 (PL 42:870).
54. *Literal Commentary on Genesis* III, 10, n. 14 (PL 34:285).
55. *On Orthodox Faith* II, 4 (PG 94:873C).
56. Aristotle, *Metaphysics* XII, 7 (1072a27–28).

3. People have said that the devils' will causes such immutability. But a mutable cause cannot produce an immutable effect. And the devils' will is mutable; otherwise, they from being good could not have become evil by their will. Therefore, the devils' immutable wickedness cannot be due to their will. Therefore, it is due to their nature.

4. A power can strive only for its object. For example, the power of sight can see only visible things. But the object of the will is the good as understood. Therefore, the will can strive only for things as understood under the aspect of good. Therefore, either the good is really good, and then the will does not become evil by desiring it, or the good is not really good, and then one's understanding will be false, and one's will cannot be evil. But devils' knowledge is only through understanding, in which there is no falsity. For Augustine says in his *Book of the 83 Questions* that one who understands falsely, understands nothing,[57] and the Philosopher says in the *De anima* that the intellect is always correct, and so it also cannot err regarding first principles, which it understands.[58] Therefore, neither can the devils' will become evil.

5. Our intellect can have falsity only insofar as it composes and divides things in judgments, just as the power of sight can see only visible things, and also insofar as imagination beclouds reason in the course of reasoning. But the intellect of substances without bodies does not understand by composing and dividing things in judgments, nor by reasoning, nor by sense images, which do not exist without a body. Therefore, devils, who are substances without bodies, cannot err regarding the intellect. And so also it seems that their will cannot become evil.

6. The substance and activity of pure intelligences exist beyond time and in the moment of eternity. But such substances are immutable. Therefore, since devils are purely intellectual substances, no activity of their will can change their activity from good to evil.

7. Dionysius says in his work *On the Divine Names* that evil corrupts good.[59] But things having contrariety (namely, elements and composites of elements), not things lacking contrariety (e.g., heavenly bodies), are corrupted. And reason indeed has contrariety, since reason is open to contrary things, but understanding, whose object is one thing, does not. And so understanding is related to reason as the center of a circle is to its circumference, and an instant to the whole of time, as Boethius says in his work *On Consolation*.[60] Therefore, devils, who, like angels, are substances that understand, and not, like human beings, substances that reason, cannot have the evil of voluntary sin.

8. Spiritual substances are more excellent than heavenly bodies. But there can be no error in the motion of heavenly bodies. Therefore, much less can there be error in the voluntary movements of spiritual substances.

9. Human beings can become evil by their will because they can desire things good for them as to their sensory nature but evil for them as to their intellectual nature. But this is not so with devils, since they are not composed of spirit and matter like human beings. Therefore, devils could not become evil by their own will.

---

57. *Book of the 83 Questions*, q. 32 (PL 40:22).
58. *De anima* III, 10 (433a26).
59. *On the Divine Names* 4, n. 20 (PG 3:717B).
60. *On Consolation IV*, prose 6 (PL 63:817A).

10. The *Book of Causes* says that a purely intellectual substance "when it knows its essence knows other things, and knows other things when it knows its essence."[61] Therefore, it knows all things when it knows any one thing. Therefore, regarding desirable objects, a purely intellectual substance could not consider one circumstance by which an object is good, and another circumstance by which an object is evil. But wickedness of the will seems to result from the fact that one considers things as good in one respect and not as absolutely evil. Therefore, it seems that intellectual substances like devils cannot have wickedness of the will.

11. Wickedness of the will corrupts virtue by excess or defect. But there cannot be any excess regarding truth, which is the good that purely intellectual substances desire, since the truer something is, the better it is. And so devils do not have wickedness of the will.

12. If devils became evil by their will, they did so either by a defective will or by a will that is not defective. But we cannot say that their will became evil by a will that is not defective, since such a will is a good tree that cannot bear bad fruit, as Mt. 7:18 says. And if devils become evil by a defective will, the very deficiency of good is an evil, as Dionysius says in his work *On the Divine Names*.[62] And then we will again ask regarding that evil whether a deficient will causes it, and so on endlessly. Therefore, since an infinite regress is impossible, it seems that devils' nature rather than their will is the first cause of their wickedness.

13. Three things, namely, the flesh, the world, and the devil, induce human beings to evil. But these things do not influence the will of devils. Therefore, devils did not become evil by their will.

14. Grace added to nature is more powerful than nature alone. But if grace added to nature does not increase, it decreases, since charity either increases or decreases, as Bernard says.[63] Therefore, if nature alone does not progress, it likewise declines. But the devils' nature could not intrinsically progress. Therefore, devils, necessarily declining, became evil. Therefore, they are evil by their nature, not their will.

15. What things have at the first moment of their creation, they have by their nature. But devils could have been evil at the first moment of their creation. And we perceive this by the fact that physical light and some other created things can have their actuality at the first moment when they begin to exist. Even a child's soul is stained by original sin at the first moment when it is created. Therefore, devils are evil by their nature.

16. God's activity is of two kinds: creation and governance. But it is not contrary to the goodness of governance that something evil is subject to his governance. Therefore, it is not contrary to the goodness of him as creator that he create something evil. And so he could have created evil devils, and so they would be evil by their nature, since what things have at their creation belongs to them by nature.

17. One who has power over a whole also has power over its parts. But God has the power to take away both nature and righteousness from righteous angels by reducing

---

61. *Book of Causes*, comm. 13.
62. *On the Divine Names* 4, n. 24 (PG 3:728A).
63. *On Grace and Free Choice* 9, n. 28 (PL 182:1016C).

them to nothingness. Therefore, he could also from the beginning have deprived angels of righteousness. Therefore, he could have made them evil. And so they would be evil by their nature, since what anything has from God is natural to it.

18. Some human beings have a natural inclination to evil by reason of their bodies. For example, some human beings are angry or sexually lustful by reason of their nature. But some think that devils have bodies joined to them by nature.[64] Therefore, devils could accordingly be evil by nature.

On the Contrary:

1. Dionysius says that "devils are not evil by nature."[65]

2. What things have by nature, they always have. But devils were once good, as Ez. 28:12–13 says: "Full of wisdom, you were in the delights of paradise." Therefore, devils are not evil by nature.

3. A gloss on Ps. 69:5, "I did not pay back what I did not steal," says that the devil wanted to steal divine status.[66] Anselm also says in his work *On the Fall of the Devil* that the devil abandoned righteousness by willing what he ought not have willed.[67] Therefore, the devil is evil by will, not by nature.

Answer:

We call things evil in two ways. Things are evil in one way because they are intrinsically evil (e.g., theft and homicide), and such things are evil in an absolute sense. In a second way we call things evil for particular persons, and nothing prevents such things being good in an absolute sense and evil in some respect. For example, justice, which as such and in an absolute sense is good, turns into an evil for a bandit who is punished to satisfy justice. And we can understand in two ways the statement that things are evil by their nature. We can understand the statement in one way to mean that the things' nature or part of their nature or a property resulting from their nature is evil. We can in a second way call things evil by their nature because they have a natural inclination to evil, as, for example, some human beings are irascible or lustful because of their constitution.

Therefore, nothing prevents something being evil by nature in the first way regarding things to which contrariety belongs by nature. For example, fire in itself is good but is by nature evil for water, since fire destroys water, and vice versa. And wolves are by the same reasoning evil for sheep. But it is impossible that something in this way be by nature evil in itself. For it signifies a contradiction, since we call anything evil because it is deprived of a perfection due it, and a thing is perfect inasmuch as it attains what belongs to its nature. And Dionysius in his work *On the Divine Names* so proves in many ways that devils are not evil by nature.[68]

And if we should in the second way call things evil because they have a natural inclination to evil, it does not even then belong to devils to be evil by nature. For if devils

---

64. Apuleius, *On the God of Socrates*; related by Augustine, *City of God* VIII, 16 (PL 41:241).

65. *On the Divine Names* 4, n. 23 (PG 3:724C).

66. Peter Lombard, *Gloss*, on Ps. 69:4 (PL 191:629C).

67. *On the Fall of the Devil* 3 (PL 158:332A).

68. *On the Divine Names* 4, n. 23 (PG 3:724C).

are intellectual substances without bodies, they can for two reasons have no natural inclination to evil. First, they indeed cannot because desires are inclinations of things that desire, and purely intellectual substances as such have desires regarding good in an absolute sense. And so all their natural inclinations are for good in an absolute sense. And since natures incline to things like themselves, and every being as to its nature is good, as I have just shown, it follows that natural inclinations are only for some good. But insofar as that good may be particular and contrary to good in an absolute sense or even to something else's particular good, there is to that degree a natural inclination for evil in an absolute sense or for something else's evil. For example, the inclination of a desire for the sensibly pleasurable, which is a particular good, if it be immoderate, is contrary to the rational good, which is good in an absolute sense. And so devils, if they are purely intellectual substances, evidently cannot have natural inclinations for evil in an absolute sense. This is so because the inclination of every nature is for something like itself and so for what is befitting and good for it, and something is evil in an absolute sense only if it is evil in itself, as I have just said. And so we conclude that whatever has a natural inclination to evil in an absolute sense is composed of two natures, the lower of which has an inclination toward a particular good befitting the lower nature and contrary to the higher nature by which we consider good in an absolute sense. For example, human beings have a natural inclination for things agreeable to the carnal senses contrary to the rational good. And this is not so regarding devils if they are purely intellectual and simple substances without bodies.

And if devils have bodies joined to them by nature, then they cannot have a natural inclination for evil by reason of their whole nature. First, they indeed cannot because as matter is for the sake of form, the whole matter of a species cannot have a natural contrariety to its formal good, although this perhaps happens in a few instances because of some alteration. And so it is impossible that all devils have an inclination for evil by reason of the nature of their bodies. Second, they cannot because devils are not subject to their bodies, as we are, but have bodies subject to them and change their bodies into any shape they wish, as Augustine says in his *Literal Commentary on Genesis*.[69] And so by reason of their bodies, they could not have any natural inclination that would greatly impede them from good. Therefore, devils are evidently in no way evil by nature. Therefore, we conclude that they are evil by their will.

And it remains for us to consider how this happens. Therefore, we should note that desires are simply inclinations for desirable things. And as natural desires result from natural forms, so sensory or rational, that is, intellectual, desires result from perceived forms, since the only objects of sensory and intellectual desires are goods perceived by the senses or the intellect. Therefore, such desires can be evil because they are not in accord with a higher rule, not because they are not in accord with the perception that gives rise to them. And so we should consider whether a higher rule can direct the perception that gives rise to the inclination of such desires.

For if the perception does not have a higher rule that ought to direct it, then such desires cannot have evil. And this indeed happens in two ways. For the perception of irrational animals does not have a higher rule that ought to direct it, and so their desires

---

69. Actually, *On the Trinity* III, 1, n. 4 (PL 42:870).

cannot have evil, since it is good that sensibly perceived forms induce such animals to desire or avoid things. And so Dionysius says in his work *On the Divine Names* that it is good for dogs to be fierce.[70] Likewise, God's intellect does not have a higher rule that can direct it. Therefore, his desire or will cannot have evil.

But human beings have two modes of perception that a higher rule ought to direct. For reason ought to direct sense perception, and wisdom, or God's law, ought to direct the cognitive activity of reason. Therefore, the desires of human beings can have evil in two ways. They can have evil in one way because reason does not govern sense perception, and Dionysius accordingly says in his work *On the Divine Names* that the evil of human beings consists of being contrary to reason.[71] The desires of human beings can have evil in a second way because wisdom and God's law ought to direct human reason, and Ambrose accordingly says that sin is the transgression of God's law.[72]

And substances without bodies have only one kind of knowledge, namely, intellectual knowledge, which the rule of God's wisdom should direct. And so their will can have evil because it does not follow the ordination of a higher rule, namely, God's wisdom. And devils in this way became evil by their will.

Replies to the Objections:

1. Evil is a privation of form or of due measure and order, as Augustine says in his work *On the Nature of the Good*.[73] And so the will can have evil in two ways. The will can have evil in one way because it strives for what is evil in an absolute sense, something lacking the form of good, as it were. For example, such is the case when one chooses theft or fornication. The will can have evil in a second way when one wills what is good in an absolute sense and as such (e.g., to pray or meditate) but does not strive for it according to the ordination of God's rule. Therefore, we should say that the first evil of the devils' will was not because they willed evil in an absolute sense, but because they willed what is good in an absolute sense and befits them but did not follow the direction of a higher rule, that is, God's wisdom. Just so, Dionysius says in his work *On the Divine Names* that "the evil in devils consists of a turning away," namely, from a higher rule, "and too much of suitable things," namely, in that they, as if ungoverned by a higher rule, willed to obtain a suitable good that exceeded their rank.[74]

2. Things can immutably belong to a thing in two ways. Things can belong immutably in one way as caused positively, and then nothing contrary to the thing's nature can be immutable, since what is contrary to a thing's nature is accidentally related to the thing and so can be absent. Things can belong immutably in a second way as caused privatively, and then nothing prevents something immutably present being contrary to the thing's nature, since a natural cause can be irreparably removed. For example, blindness is contrary to an animal's nature and yet immutably perdures because the animal's sight cannot be restored. Therefore, wickedness irreparably belongs to devils because they are deprived of grace.

---

70. *On the Divine Names* 4, n. 25 (PG 3:728B).
71. Ibid., 4, n. 32 (PG 3:733A).
72. *On Paradise* 8 (PL 14:292D).
73. *On the Nature of the Good* 4 (PL 42:553).
74. *On the Divine Names* 4, n. 23 (PG 3:725B).

3. A mutable cause cannot positively produce an immutable effect. But a mutable cause can do so privatively. For example, one human being's will causes the immutable blindness of another human being.

4. Evil consists both of the privation of form and the privation of due measure and order, as Augustine says in his work *On the Nature of the Good*.[75] And so acts of the will have evil both from their object, which gives the acts their form because one wills evil, and from taking away the due measure or order of the acts themselves, as, for example, if one in the very course of willing good does not observe due measure and order. And such was the sin of devils that made them evil. For they desired a suitable good, not an evil. But they desired it inordinately and immoderately, namely, in that they desired to acquire it by their own power and not by God's grace, and this exceeded the due measure of their status. Just so, Dionysius says in his work *On the Divine Names*: "Evil for devils, therefore, consists of a turning away," namely, inasmuch as their desires turned away from the direction of a higher rule, and "too much of suitable things," namely, inasmuch as they exceeded their due measure in desiring suitable goods.[76] But regarding sin, defect of intellect or reason and defect of will always accompany one another proportionally. And so we do not need to suppose that there was in the devils' first sin such a defect of intellect that they judged falsely (e.g., that evil is good), but that they failed to comprehend the rule governing them and its ordination.

5. Because devils do not use imagination or discursive reasoning, and by other such things, we can hold that they do not err regarding things that belong to natural cognition so as to judge something false to be true. But because they cannot comprehend God because of his infinity, nothing prevents their intellect having failed to comprehend adequately the ordination of God's governance. And this resulted in the sin in their will.

6. Not everything beyond time belongs in the same way to eternity, and so not every such thing has immutability in the same way. For example, God is completely eternal and immutable, but other substances beyond time, each according to its grade of being, partake of eternity and immutability. For we perceive that immutability results from a wholeness. For things receiving something as a part, exchange one part for another, as it were. For example, the matter of elements, since it does not simultaneously receive all material forms or a perfect form that virtually contains in itself all forms (as is evident regarding the matter of heavenly bodies), exchanges one particular form for another. (And this does not happen regarding the matter of heavenly bodies, although their orbits repeat because they have a fixed orbit.) Therefore, regarding its object, the angels' intellect, which understands universal forms themselves as such, indeed has a wholeness that contrasts with our intellect, which gathers universal forms from different kinds of individual things. But in contrast with God's intellect, the angels' intellect has particularity regarding its object. For God's intellect universally comprehends all being and all truth in one object. And so his intellect in its activity is altogether immutable, as it has no need to pass from one thing to another, since it contemplates everything at once in one thing. And the angels' intellect, which contemplates particular things in themselves as particular things, not everything in one, can pass from one thing to another. Still, its activity is

---

75. *On the Nature of the Good* 4 (PL 42:553).
76. *On the Divine Names* 4, n. 23 (PG 3:725B).

immutable in that it has its understanding from the beginning. And we should observe the like regarding the angels' will, whose activity is proportional to their intellect's. And so it is not inconsistent with the angels' nature if their will should change from good to evil.

7. The devils' sin did not result from a defect that would have the nature of contrariety, since they did not approve evil as good or truth as falsity, but only from a defect having the nature of negation, namely, inasmuch as their will did not obey the rule of God's governance. And purely intellectual substances lacking contrariety can indeed have such a defect.

8. Heavenly bodies are subject to the rule of God's governance as acted upon or moved by another, not as if they themselves cause their motions. And if there were to be any defect or deviation from the ordination of God's rule in their motions, this would not be credited as a defect of the ordinance of God, who cannot be deficient. But intellectual and rational natures are subject to God's governance as they direct themselves by God's rule. And so they can have disorder from a defect of theirs without any defect of his rule.

9. The argument of this objection proves that devils could not have sin in such a way that they would desire something evil for them as if it were good, since, because of the simplicity of their nature, something cannot be good for one part of them and not good for another part of them.

10. Purely intelligent beings, when they know their essence or other things, know by the modality of their substance. But the first cause surpasses the modality of an angel's or devil's substance. And so an angel in knowing its essence need not comprehend the entire ordination of God's governance.

11. The argument of this objection also proves that devils did not sin because they desired something that was evil by excess or defect.

12. Devils sinned by a defective will, and the very defect of the will is their sin. Just so, human beings run by their body's movement, and their body's very movement is their running.

13. One of the three things inducing to sin, namely, the devil, induces by way of persuasion, but the other two, namely, the flesh and the world, induce to sin by way of attraction. And although devils did not sin because of another's persuasion, nor because they were attracted by the flesh, which they do not have, nor by the sensibly perceptible things of the world, which they do not need, they sinned because they were attracted by the excellence of their nature. And so Ez. 28:17 says: "You have lost your wisdom in your comeliness."

14. We should not understand that charity always actually diminishes when it does not actually increase. Rather, when charity does not increase in human beings, they are disposed to defects because of the seeds of sins stemming from the corruption of human nature. But this is not so regarding angels.

15. Angels at the first moment of their creation could have an act of the will, but their act at the first moment of their creation could not be the act whereby they became evil, and I shall later show the reason why.[77] Nor is it like the case of the human soul,

---

77. A. 4.

which is stained with original sin at the first moment of its creation, since this stain is not due to the activity of the soul but to the soul's union with the body, and we cannot say this about angels.

16. Everything included in the works of creation comes from God as the cause. And because God does not cause evils, nothing included in the works of creation can be evil. But many things are included in the deeds of God's governance that God only permits and does not cause. And so some evils can be included in his governance.

17. God can withdraw his freely bestowed righteousness from human beings without violating justice even if human beings did not sin, since he out of his generosity freely bestowed righteousness on them beyond what was due human nature. And if he were to withdraw his freely bestowed righteousness in the aforementioned way, they would remain naturally good and not become evil. But natural righteousness results from an intellectual and rational nature, whose intellect is by nature ordained for truth, and whose will is ordained for goodness. And so God cannot withdraw such righteousness from a rational nature as long as that nature abides. But regarding his absolute power, he can reduce a rational nature to nothingness by withdrawing his influx of existence.

18. Even if devils were to be corporeal, they would not have a natural inclination to evil, by reason of the argument mentioned previously.[78]

Third Article

Did the Devil in Sinning Desire Equality with God?

It seems that the devil did not, for the following reasons:

1. Dionysius says in his work *On the Divine Names* that "the evil in devils consists of a turning away."[79] But one who desires equality or like status with another turns toward, not away from, the other. Therefore, the devil did not sin by desiring equality with God.

2. Dionysius in the same place says that the devils' evil consists of "an excess of suitable things," namely, in that they desired to have in a pre-eminent way what befitted them. But having equality with God in no way befitted them. Therefore, they did not desire equality with God.

3. Anselm says in his work *On the Fall of the Devil* that the devil desired what he would have attained had he remained steadfast.[80] But he would never have attained equality with God. Therefore, he did not desire equality with God.

4. People have said that the devil desired equality with God in one respect, namely, to be chieftain of the angels, but not absolutely. But the devil did not sin by desiring what belonged to him by the ordination of nature, but fell from what accords with his nature into what exceeds his nature, as Damascene says.[81] And to be chieftain over all the other

---

78. In the answer.
79. *On the Divine Names* 4, n. 23 (PG 3:725B).
80. *On the Fall of the Devil* 4 (PL 158:332–33).
81. *On Orthodox Faith* II, 4 (PG 94:876A).

angels belonged to him by the ordination of nature, which constituted him more excellent than the other angels, as Gregory says in a homily.[82] Therefore, he did not sin because he desired to be chieftain of the angels.

5. Perhaps someone will say that the devil desired to be chieftain of the angels just like God. But Jn. 5:19 says: "Whatever the Father does, the Son also does," and Augustine proves that the Son is absolutely equal to the Father from the fact that the Son does just as the Father does.[83] Therefore, the devil accordingly would have desired equality with God absolutely.

6. People have likewise said that the devil desired equality with God as regards not being subject to God. But things can exist only by sharing God's existing, which is subsistent existing itself. And everything sharing is subject to what is shared. Therefore, if the devil desired not to be subject to God, then he desired not to exist. And this conclusion is inappropriate, since everything desires to exist.

7. People have said that even impossible things can be the object of the will, as the *Ethics* says,[84] and so angels could have willed to exist without being subject to God, although this is impossible. But although impossible things can be the object of the will, things not understood cannot, since understood goods are the object of the will, as the *De anima* says.[85] And it is incomprehensible that something other than God exist and not be subject to him, since it involves a contradiction. For existing predicated of anything other than God signifies being subject to God by way of participation. Therefore, angels could in no way have desired not to be subject to God.

8. People have said that what implicitly signifies a contradiction sometimes falls within a desire of the will because reason is confused, and so devils because their cognitive power was confused could have desired something signifying a contradiction. But confusion of reason is either a punishment or a moral fault. And neither moral fault nor punishment preceded the first sin of the devil, about which we are presently concerned. Therefore, the devil out of confusion of reason could not have desired anything signifying a contradiction.

9. The devil sinned by free choice, and the act of free choice is choosing. But impossible things are not the object of choosing, although impossible things can be the object of the will, as the *Ethics* says.[86] Therefore, the devil could not have desired not to be subject to God, or equality with God, since this is impossible.

10. Augustine says in his work *On the Nature of the Good*: "Sin is not the desire for evil things but the abandonment of better things."[87] But nothing can be better than being equal to God. Therefore, the devil could not have sinned by seeking equality with God by abandoning something better.

11. As Augustine says in his work *On Christian Doctrine*, "all wickedness consists of enjoying as the end things that should be used as means or using as means things that

82. *On the Gospels* II, hom. 34, n. 7 (PL 76:1250B).
83. *On the Gospel of John*, tr. 20, n. 9 (PL 35:1561).
84. Aristotle, *Ethics* III, 2 (1111b21–22).
85. Aristotle, *De anima* III, 10 (433b11–12).
86. Aristotle, *Ethics* III, 2 (1111b22).
87. *On the Nature of Good* 34 (PL 42:562).

should be enjoyed as the end."[88] But if the devil desired equality with God, he did not desire it as a means, since he could not have related it to anything better. And if he desired equality with God as an end, he did not sin, since he enjoyed as an end what should be. Therefore, he in neither way sinned by desiring equality with God.

12. As the intellect is borne to what is connatural with it, so also is the will. But it is not connatural for the devil to be equal to God. Therefore, he could not have desired it.

13. There is only desire for good. But it would not have been good for the devil to be equal to God, since he would abandon his own nature if he were transformed to the rank of a higher nature. Just so, if a horse were to become a human being, it would not be a horse. Therefore, the devil did not desire equality with God.

14. Isidore says in his work *On the Supreme Good* that the devil did not desire things that belong to God but things that are his own.[89] But equality with God is pre-eminently proper to God. Therefore, the devil did not desire equality with God.

15. As good and evil are contraries, so also are the praiseworthy and the blameworthy. But being unlike God is reprehensible and blameworthy. Therefore, it is praiseworthy to be most like God, and this belongs to the nature of equality. Therefore, angels did not sin by desiring equality with God.

On the Contrary:

1. A gloss on Phil. 2:6, "He [Christ] did not think it robbery to be God's equal," says that the devil usurped for himself equality with God.[90] But Phil. 2:6 is speaking about the equality of the Son with the Father, which is an absolute equality. Therefore, the devil sought absolute equality with God.

2. A gloss on Ps. 69:5, "I did not repay what I did not steal," says that the devil wished to steal divinity and lost happiness.[91] Therefore, he desired equality with God.

3. Is. 14:13 says that Lucifer declared: "I shall ascend to heaven." But we cannot understand this to mean the empyrean heaven, where he was established with the other angels. Therefore, we understand it to mean the heaven of the Holy Trinity. Therefore, Lucifer wished to ascend to equality with God.

4. As we can understand from Augustine in his work *On the Trinity*, the will is moved more than the intellect.[92] And so the soul, which does not know itself perfectly, desires to do so. But an angel's intellect knows that God is infinite. Therefore, still more could an angel's will strive in desire to be equal to God.

5. Things indivisible by nature are sometimes divisible by the will and reason. And so nothing prevents a person desiring something (e.g., to be free of miseries) that results in the person nonexisting, although such a person does not desire not to exist. Therefore, it likewise seems that nothing prevents the devil having desired equality with God although the consequence of this is for the devil himself not to exist.

---

88. Actually, *Book of the 83 Questions*, q. 30 (PL 40:19).
89. *On the Supreme Good* I, 10, n. 16 (PL 83:556C).
90. Peter Lombard, *Gloss*, on Phil. 2:6 (PL 192:233C).
91. Ibid., on Ps. 69:4 (PL 191:629C).
92. *On the Trinity* X, 3 (PL 42:975–76).

6. Augustine says in his work *On Free Choice* that excessive desire predominates in every sin.[93] But the devil's sin was the greatest, since it was the first of its kind. Therefore, it had the most excessive desire. Therefore, the devil desired the greatest good. And such is equality with God.

7. Isidore says in his work *On the Supreme Good* that the devil sinned in that he wanted his power to be preserved by himself and not by God.[94] But preserving creatures and not being preserved by anything higher belongs to God. Therefore, the devil wanted what belongs to God and so to be equal to God.

Answer:
Various authorities seem to incline to the view that the devil sinned by inordinately desiring equality with God, but it cannot be the case that he desired equality with God absolutely.

The reason why is evident, first, indeed, regarding God, to whom it is not only impossible that anything be equal, but such is also contrary to the nature of his essence. For God by his essence is subsistent existing itself. And no two such beings can exist, just as it would be impossible for two intrinsically subsistent separate human forms or whitenesses to exist. And so everything other than God needs to exist as something sharing existence, which cannot be equal to what is by its essence existing itself. Nor could the devil in his status not know this, for it is natural for a purely intelligent being or bodiless intellect to understand its substance. And so the devil by his nature knew that his existing was shared from something higher, and sin indeed had not yet corrupted this knowledge of his. And so we conclude that his intellect could not have understood his equality with God to be within the nature of the possible. And no one strives for what the person understands to be impossible, as the *De caelo et mundo* says.[95] And so the movement of the devil's will could not have inclined to desire equality with God absolutely.

Second, this is clear regarding the very angel who desires. For the will always desires a good for oneself or another. And we say that the devil sinned because he desired equality with God for himself, not for another, for he could without sin have wanted the Son to be equal to the Father. For the Philosopher says in the *Ethics* that everyone seeks good for oneself, and one does not care what would happen to oneself if one were to become the other.[96] And so the devil evidently did not desire something whereby he himself would no longer be the same individual. But he would no longer be the same individual if he were to be equal to God, even if this were possible, since his form would be destroyed if he were to be transformed into the rank of a higher nature. And so we conclude that he could not have desired absolute equality with God. And by like argument, he could not have desired not to be absolutely subject to God, both because this is impossible, and he could not understand it to be possible, as the foregoing makes clear, and because he himself would cease to exist if he were not completely subject to God.

93. *On Free Choice* I, 3, n. 8 (PL 32:1225).
94. *On the Supreme Good* I, 10, n. 2 (PL 83:554A–B).
95. Actually, *Politics* V, 9 (1314a23–24).
96. *Ethics* IX, 4 (1166a19–21).

And his evil could not have consisted of anything else belonging to the order of nature. For only things in which potentiality can be distinguished from actuality, not things that are always actual, can have evil, as the *Metaphysics* says.[97] But all angels were instituted such that they immediately at the moment of their creation had everything proper to their nature, although they had potentiality for supernatural goods that they could obtain through God's grace. And so we conclude that the devil's sin regarded something supernatural, not something belonging to the order of nature. Therefore, the devil's first sin was that, to attain the supernatural happiness consisting of the complete vision of God, he did not elevate himself to God so as to desire with holy angels his ultimate perfection through God's grace. Rather, he wanted to attain his ultimate perfection by the power of his own nature without God bestowing grace, although not without God acting on his nature. And so Augustine in his work *On Free Choice* holds the devil's sin to consist of his pleasure in his own power.[98] And Augustine in his *Commentary on the Book of Genesis* says that "if an angelic substance were to turn to itself, and the angel were to delight in itself more than in the one in whose participation it is happy, it would swell with pride and fall."[99] And because having one's ultimate perfection by the power of one's own nature, not through the favor of something higher, is proper to God, the devil in this regard evidently desired equality with God. And he also desired in this regard not to be subject to God, namely, so as not to need God's grace in addition to the power of his nature. And this agrees with what I said before,[100] that the devil did not sin by desiring an evil but by desiring a good, namely, his ultimate happiness, improperly, that is, not as a happiness obtained through God's grace.

Replies to the Objections:

1. By desiring equality with God, devils indeed turned toward God regarding what they desired, which was in itself good, but they turned away from God regarding the way they desired, namely, in that they thereby turned away from the ordination of the divine rule. Just so, every sinner insofar as the sinner desires a transitory good turns to God, by sharing in whom everything is good, but turns away from God, that is, the ordination of his justice, insofar as the sinner desires such a good inordinately.

2. The devils' evil consisted of "an excess regarding suitable things," namely, insofar as they desired the happiness for which they were made, and that they would have attained if they were to have desired it in the proper way. But they exceeded the measure of right order, as I have said.[101]

3. The latter makes clear the reply to objection 3.

4. The devil sinned because he desired to be chieftain of the angels, not in accord with the ordination of nature but insofar as he wanted to obtain by his own nature the happiness that other angels would obtain through God's grace.

97. *Metaphysics* IX, 9 (1051a4–21).
98. *On Free Choice* III, 25, n. 76 (PL 32:1308).
99. *Commentary on the Book of Genesis* IV, 24, n. 24 (PL 34:313).
100. A. 2, the reply to objection 1.
101. In the answer.

5. In this regard, he also did not desire to preside over lower angels in the same way that God presides, namely, so as to preside as their first cause, as I have said.[102]

6. The argument of this objection is valid with respect to not being absolutely subject to God. And the devil could not have desired such regarding things that belong to the ordination of nature.

7. And we should give a like reply to objection 7.

8. Angels could not have confused knowledge except perhaps after they sinned. But they could have had deficient knowledge regarding supernatural things, as I have said.[103]

9. The will, of which we say impossible things can be the object, is not the complete will striving to obtain something, since no one strives for something the person thinks impossible, as I have said.[104] But such a will is an incomplete will, which we call wishing for what we think impossible, supposing that it were to be possible. And such is the will of turning away and turning toward, of which sin and merit consist.

10. We call sin an abandonment of better things regarding the turning away from God, which formally fulfills the nature of sin. But regarding the devils' sin, we do not consider the turning away from God regarding what they desire. Rather, we consider the turning away regarding the fact that they withdrew from the ordination of God's justice, and they accordingly abandoned better things, namely, in that the rule of God's justice is better than the rule of the angels' will.

11. Whoever desires something for oneself desires it for one's own sake and delights in oneself as the end and uses what one desires as a means. And so devils, desiring equality with God for themselves in the way described,[105] used as means things that should be enjoyed as the end.

12. The sinning angels' will indeed strove for something for which their natures were ordained, although the good surpassed the good of their nature itself, but the way did not befit their nature.

13. The argument of this objection is valid regarding the desire for absolute equality with God.

14. Because the will's movements take their species from their end, we say that one desires things to be one's own who desires things as one's own even if the things should belong to another. And the devil by desiring for himself what belongs to God desired things to be his own in this way.

15. To be like God as befits each thing is praiseworthy. But one who desires likeness to God contrary to the ordination established by him desires wickedly to be like God.

Replies to the Arguments in the Section On the Contrary:

1. It belongs to the excellence of Christ, which the Apostle in the cited text means to commend, that Christ has absolute equality with the Father. And Adam and the devil sinned by desiring equality with God in one respect, not absolutely.

2. And we should give a like reply to the second argument.

---

102. Ibid.
103. Ibid.
104. Ibid.
105. Objection 11.

3. As Augustine says in his *Literal Commentary on Genesis*,[106] some held that the devils who sinned were not in the number of heavenly angels but of those who had charge of the terrestrial order, and so we can understand in a literal sense their ascent to the physical heavens. But if they were in the number of heavenly angels, as is more commonly held,[107] we should say that they wanted to ascend to the heaven of the Holy Trinity by desiring a kind of equality with God, but not an absolute equality, as I have said before.[108]

4. As to its object, the will cannot desire more than the power of understanding understands, since only a good comprehended by the intellect can be an object of the will. But as to intensity, acts of the will can surpass one another, since desire is sometimes more intense than understanding is clear, and sometimes the converse is true. It can also happen that the intellect knows something but does not possess it, and the will can desire it as known. And in this way, because the intellect understands what perfect knowledge is, the will can desire perfect knowledge of the intellect although the intellect does not know itself perfectly, just as, conversely, the intellect can understand what is beyond the power of the will. And so it does not follow that the devil would desire to be something that he could not understand.

5. When one wishes something to be taken away from oneself, one constitutes oneself as the starting point, which does not need to be preserved in the process, and so one can desire not to exist so as to be free of miseries. But when one desires a good for oneself, one constitutes oneself as the end point, and such a terminus needs to be preserved in the process. And so one cannot desire for oneself a good the possession of which would result in the person not existing.

6. The most excessive desire does not need to regard the greatest good but the greatest good among those that can be desired.

7. The devil wanted his power to be preserved with respect to obtaining happiness itself and being preserved in it by his own power, not with respect to everything.

Fourth Article

Did the Devil Sin, or Could He Have Sinned, at the First Moment of His Creation?

It seems that he did or could have, for the following reasons:

1. 1 Jn. 3:8 says that the devil sinned from the beginning. But we cannot understand "from the beginning" to mean when the devil brought death to human beings by tempting Adam, since he himself was evil before that. Therefore, we understand it to mean from the beginning when he himself was created.

2. Jn. 8:44 says that the devil did not stand fast in the truth. But he would have stood fast in the truth if he were not to have sinned at the first moment of his creation. Therefore, it seems that the devil could have sinned at the first moment of his creation.

---

106. *Literal Commentary on Genesis* III, 10, n. 14 (PL 34:285) and XI, 17 and 26 (PL 34:438 and 443).
107. E.g., Alexander of Hales, *Gloss on the Sentences* II, d. 6, n. 3.
108. In the answer.

3. The power the devil had at the first moment of his creation was neither increased nor decreased before he sinned. But he could and did sin after the first moment of his creation. Therefore, he could also have sinned at the first moment of his creation.

4. People have said that if the devil were to have sinned at the first moment of his creation, that sin would be imputed to God, who causes the devil's nature. But God causes an angel's existence as long as the angel exists and not only when he was first created, as Augustine makes evident in his *Literal Commentary on Genesis*.[109] And so Jn. 5:17 says: "My Father and I are active even until now." Therefore, if we should impute to God any sin committed by the devil at the first moment of his creation, then by like reasoning, we would impute to God any sin the devil were to commit at any other moment. And this conclusion is evidently false.

5. Angels' natural power bestowed on them by God is disposed to two things, namely, good and evil. And they would have gone on to do evil only had something determined them to do so. But only their own will, not God, could have determined them to do evil. Therefore, even if angels had sinned at the first moment of their creation, their sin would be imputed to their will, not God.

6. The effects produced by a secondary cause can be deficient without being imputable to the primary cause. For example, we impute lameness to a deformed leg, not to the power to walk. But God is related to angels' activity as the primary cause of the activity. Therefore, if angels were to have sinned at the first moment of their creation, their sin would be imputed to their free choice, not God.

7. Likewise, people have said that if the devil were to have sinned at the first moment of his creation, he could never have been sinless and so would have had evil necessarily and not by free choice, and this is contrary to the nature of sin. But such necessity is only the necessity by which something needs to exist while it exists, and every act of sinning indeed has such necessity. Therefore, if such necessity is contrary to the nature of free choice, then no sin would be the product of free choice. And this conclusion is improper.

8. People have said regarding other sins that a moment when the sinner is not subject to the aforementioned necessity precedes the act of sinning. But no one sins before one causes the act of sinning, and things belonging to the nature of sin coexist with the sin. Therefore, the possibility of sinning or not sinning is not required prior to the act of sinning.

9. The devil's sin consisted of his having desired his happiness in a disordered way. But he could have understood the nature of his happiness at the first moment of his creation. Therefore, he could also have willed his happiness in a disordered way at the first moment of his creation.

10. Any efficient cause not acting out of natural necessity can avoid what it causes. But if the devil were to have sinned at the first moment of his creation, he would not on that account have sinned out of natural necessity. Therefore, he could still have avoided sin, and so nothing seems to prevent the devil having been able to sin at the first moment of his creation.

---

109. *Literal Commentary on Genesis* IV, 12 (PL 34:304–305).

11. If the devil did not sin at the first moment of his creation, something improper seems to result from any perspective. For if the devil did not know about his fall before he sinned, and good angels were sure of their future steadfastness, without which they could not be happy, then God would have differentiated between the latter and the former by revealing to some and not to others what destiny awaited them, without a previous difference of merits. And this conclusion seems improper. And if the devil did foreknow his fall, he had the punishment of sadness before moral fault. And this conclusion also is improper. Therefore, we should not say that the devil did not sin at the first moment of his creation.

12. As Augustine says in his *Literal Commentary on Genesis*, the formlessness of the creatures instituted by God was prior to their formation, described in the deeds of the six days, only in nature and origin, not in temporal duration.[110] But as he himself says afterward, we understand by the separation of light from darkness the separation of good angels from bad angels.[111] Therefore, there were some good and some bad angels immediately at the first moment of the creation of the world.

13. The bad angels turned away from God at the same time that the good angels turned toward him; otherwise, there would be no reason why God would have confirmed the latter and not the former if there would have been no obstacle regarding those not confirmed. But it seems that the good angels at the first moment of their creation turned toward God. For as Augustine says in his *Literal Commentary on Genesis,* we understand "the evening of the first day" to mean the turning of the angels' intellect toward its nature, and we understand "the morning of the following day" to mean the turning of the angels' intellect toward the Word.[112] Therefore, if Augustine thought that all the things related in the deeds of the six days were made at the same time, it seems that the angels turned toward God or away from him by sinning at the same time that they knew themselves at the first moment of their creation.

14. According to Dionysius in his work *On the Divine Names*, angels, unlike us, do not have discursive knowledge, namely, the process of reasoning from first principles to conclusions, but contemplate both principles and conclusions at the same time.[113] But ends are related to means as principles are to conclusions, as the Philosopher says in the *Physics*.[114] Therefore, since the angels' nature is related to God as their end, it seems that they were at the same time moved regarding themselves and God by turning toward or away from him. And so the same conclusion follows as before.

15. If angels at the first moment of their creation were good, they obviously loved God. And they by nature loved themselves. Therefore, either they loved themselves, and God for their sake, and so sinned by delighting in themselves as their end, or they loved themselves for God's sake, which is to turn toward God by the virtue of charity. Therefore, angels would necessarily turn either toward or away from God at the first moment of their creation. And so the same conclusion follows as before.

---

110. Ibid., I, 15, n. 29 (PL 34:257).
111. *City of God* XI, 19 (PL 41:333).
112. *Literal Commentary on Genesis* IV, 22 (PL 34:312).
113. *On the Divine Names* 7, n. 2 (PG 3:868B).
114. *Physics* II, 9 (200a34–b1).

16. God created human beings to compensate for the fall of the angels, as the saints say.[115] Therefore, human beings were not created before the devil fell by sinning. But human beings seem to have been created at the beginning of the creation of the world, according to Augustine, who held that all things were created at the same time.[116] Therefore, the devil also sinned at the first moment of his creation.

17. Spiritual creatures are more powerful than any material creature. But some material creatures (e.g., light and rays of light) have instantaneous movement. Therefore, much more could angels have movements of sin at the first moment of their creation.

18. The more excellent something is, the less idle it is. But the will seems to be more excellent than the intellect is, since the will moves the intellect to its activity. Therefore, since the angels' intellect was not idle at the first moment of its creation, it seems that neither was their will. And so it seems that angels could have by their will sinned at the first moment of their creation.

19. A kind of eternity measures the duration of angels. But we say that the whole of eternity exists at once. Therefore, whenever angels sinned, they sinned at the first moment of their creation.

20. As one sins by free choice, so also does one merit. But one creature, namely, Christ's soul, merits at the first moment of its creation. Therefore, the devil could also have sinned at the first moment of his creation.

21. As angels are creatures of God, so also is the soul. But a child's soul at the first moment of its creation is subject to sin. Therefore, by like reasoning, angels could have been evil at the first moment of their creation.

22. As a creature would dissolve into nothingness were the power of God not to encompass it, as Gregory says,[117] so also would a rational creature fall into sin were grace not to encompass it. Therefore, if an angel did not possess grace at the first moment of its creation, it could not have been without sin. And if it possessed grace and did not use it, it likewise sinned. And if it used grace to turn to God, it was confirmed in good so as also not to be capable of sinning. Therefore, all angels who sinned, did so at the first moment of their creation.

23. A property exists at the same time as the thing to which the property belongs. But sin is a property of the devil, as Jn. 8:44 says: "When he [the devil] speaks lies, he speaks in character." Therefore, the devil sinned at the first moment when he was created.

On the Contrary:

1. Ez. 28:12–13 says to the devil in the person of the king of Tyre: "You were full of wisdom and perfect in beauty, enjoying the pleasures of God's paradise."

2. The *Book of Causes* says: "Between something whose substance and activity exists in the moment of eternity and something whose substance and activity exists in a moment of time, there is something whose substance exists in eternity, and whose activity

---

115. E.g., Augustine, *Enchiridion* 29 (PL 40:246); Gregory, *On the Gospels* II, hom. 34, n. 11 (PL 76:1252B–53C).

116. *Literal Commentary on Genesis* I, 15, n. 29 (PL 34:257).

117. *Morals* XVI, 37, n. 45 (PL 75:1143C).

exists in time."[118] But God's substance and activity exist in eternity, and the substance and activity of material things exist in time. Therefore, angels' substance, which is in between, exists in eternity, and their activity in time. Therefore, angels could not have sinned at the moment of their creation.

3. We call things evil because they cause harm, as Augustine says in his *Enchiridion*.[119] But evil harms because it takes away good, and God made angels good regarding their entire nature. Therefore, since nothing can be at the same time intact and diminished, it seems that angels could not have been evil at the first moment of their creation.

4. Nothing indeliberate can be a sin, at least a mortal sin. But nothing momentary can be deliberate. Therefore, nothing momentary can be a mortal sin. Therefore, it seems impossible for an angel to have become evil by sinning at the first moment of its creation.

Answer:

Augustine deals with this question in his *Literal Commentary on Genesis*[120] and the *City of God*.[121] But in neither work does he reach a definite conclusion on the matter, although he seems in the *Commentary* to incline more to the view that devils sinned at the first moment of their creation, and in the *City of God* more to the view that they did not.

And so some latter-day writers presumed to claim that the devil was evil at the first moment of his creation by the movement of free choice whereby he sinned, not indeed by his nature.[122] But all the masters then teaching at the University of Paris rejected this position.[123] And the authority of the canon of Scripture seems to maintain that angels were once good and did not sin at the first moment of their creation. For example, Is. 14:12 says: "How you, O Lucifer, who rose in the morning, fell." And Ez. 28:13 says: "You enjoyed the pleasures of paradise." But Augustine in his *Literal Commentary on Genesis* explains these texts so as to understand the statements to be about the devil regarding his followers, that is, human beings who fall away from the grace of Christ.[124]

But it is necessary, though difficult, to assign the reason why the devil could not have sinned at the first moment of his creation. For some have assigned the reason for this to the angels' nature established by God.[125] And so they say that the devil at the first moment of his creation was necessarily good as created by God, lest we designate something at once intact and diminished, as was counterargued above.[126] But this argument seems to have no force, since the wickedness of moral fault is not contrary to the goodness of a substance but rather is grounded in the substance as its subject. And so also Augustine says in the *City of God* that those who hold the view that the devil sinned at the first moment of his creation do not agree with the Manicheans, who claim that the devil has an evil nature contrary to God.[127] Nor would it be improper to say that angels as created

---

118. *Book of Causes*, prop. 31.
119. *Enchiridion* 12 (PL 40:237).
120. *Literal Commentary on Genesis* XI, 16 (PL 34:437) and XI, 19–20, nn. 26–27 (PL 34:439–40).
121. *City of God* XI, 13–15 (PL 41:328–31).
122. The first opinion of Peter Lombard, *Sentences* II, d. 3, chap. 4, nn. 2–4).
123. The fifth error condemned at the University of Paris in 1241.
124. *Literal Commentary on Genesis* XI, 24 (PL 34:442).
125. The second opinion of Peter Lombard, *Sentences* II, d. 3, chap. 4, nn. 5–7).
126. Argument 3 of the section *On the Contrary*.
127. *City of God* XI, 13 (PL 41:329).

by God had their nature completely intact from the first moment of their existence but in such a way that the resistance of the angels' will thereupon prevented their nature being intact. Just so, for example, might the rays of the sun be prevented from illumining the air at the very moment of the sun's rising.

And some assign the reason why angels could not have sinned at the first moment of their creation to the fact that deliberation is required regarding every sin.[128] And since deliberation cannot be instantaneous, they hold that the angels' sin could not have been instantaneous. But angels were evil only when they ended up sinning. And so they conclude that angels could not have been evil at the first moment of their creation.

But they are deceived because they judge the angels' intellect by the mode of the human intellect, although the angels' intellect is far different. For the human intellect is discursive. And so as it advances in theoretical knowledge by reasoning deductively about theoretical matters, so also it advances in practical knowledge by reflecting or deliberating about practical matters, since deliberation is an inquiry, as the *Ethics* says.[129] But the angels' intellect understands truth without discursive reasoning and inquiry, as Dionysius says in his work *On the Divine Names*.[130] And so nothing prevents an angel being able to choose at the first moment when it understands truth, and doing so is an act of free choice. Just so, human beings, at the very moment deliberation makes them certain, choose what they are to do. And if they were to be sure about what they should do, they would choose immediately without deliberation, as is evident in the skill of handwriting and the like, in which there is no need of deliberation. Therefore, if angels could understand at the first moment of their existence what they should desire, they could immediately at that very moment choose, since they would not need to deliberate. Therefore, the reason why angels could not have sinned at the first moment of their creation is not because they could not choose at that moment, and choosing is an act of free choice. Therefore, we need to look for the reason elsewhere.

Therefore, we should consider the difference between the motion so measured by time that it causes time (e.g., the first heavenly motion) and the motion measured by time but not causing it (e.g., the movements of animals). And regarding the movements of animals, temporal succession does not correspond to the difference or sameness of moveable objects, since animals may stay put and time march on, for time measures rest as well as motion, as the *Physics* says.[131] But regarding the motion that causes time, the succession of time and the succession of motion accompany one another, since the before and after of motion causes the before and after of time, as the *Physics* says.[132] And so everything we distinguish in such motion exists in different moments of time, and what we do not distinguish in such motion cannot exist in different moments. And so time necessarily ceases at the moment when the heavenly motions cease, as Rev. 10:7 says: "There will be no more time."

128. E.g., Bonaventure, *Commentary on the Sentences* II, d. 3, part 2, a. 1, q. 2.
129. Aristotle, *Ethics* III, 1 (1112a14–15).
130. *On the Divine Names* 7, n. 2 (PG 3:868B).
131. Aristotle, *Physics* VI, 8 (238b23–29).
132. Ibid., IV, 11 (219a14–19).

And we should consider that the angels' thoughts and desires have a temporal succession, as Augustine says in his *Literal Commentary on Genesis* that God moves spiritual creatures through time.[133] For angels do not actually understand everything at once, since angels understand different things by different forms, not everything by one form, and the higher an angel, the more things it naturally knows by fewer forms. And so Dionysius says in his work *On the Celestial Hierarchy* that higher angels have more universal knowledge,[134] and the *Book of Causes* says that higher, purely intelligent beings possess more universal forms, that is, forms that encompass a greater number of knowable things.[135] Just so, we perceive regarding human beings that the more superior a person's intellect, the more things the person can know from fewer principles. But only God knows everything by knowing one thing, namely, his essence.

And so human beings cannot actually understand many things at once, since different forms cannot completely and definitively actualize their intellect, just as different shapes cannot actualize the same material substance. And so also we should say regarding angels that they can know at the same time all the things that they know by one form, and that they can know successively, not simultaneously, all the things that they know by different forms. And the time caused by the heavens' motion, above which are the angels' thoughts and desires, does not measure this succession—and nothing lower measures something higher. Rather, the very thoughts and desires succeeding one another necessarily cause different moments of such time. Therefore, regarding things that an angel cannot understand by one form, the angel necessarily comes to understand them at different moments of its time.

And things above nature belonging to grace, regarding which the angels sinned, as I have maintained,[136] differ more from any things naturally known than any things naturally known differ from one another. And so if an angel cannot by one form and at the same time understand all the things naturally known because of their difference, much less can an angel come at the same time to understand things known by nature and supernatural things, which are freely bestowed. And angels' movements are evidently first to things connatural to them, since they through such movements attain what transcends their nature. And so angels at the first moment of their creation must have turned to natural knowledge of themselves, by which they could not sin, as is clear from what I have said before.[137] But they could later have turned toward or away from what transcends their nature. And so angels at the first moment of their creation were neither in a blessed state by completely turning toward God nor sinners by turning away from him. And so Augustine says in his *Literal Commentary on Genesis* that after the evening of the first day, it becomes morning, when the spiritual light, namely, the angels' nature, after recognizing its nature not to be divine, turns back to praise the light that is God himself, by contemplating the one who fashions it.[138]

133. *Literal Commentary on Genesis* VIII, 20 (PL 34:388).
134. *On the Celestial Hierarchy* 12, n. 2 (PG 3:292C).
135. *Book of Causes*, prop. 10.
136. A. 3.
137. Ibid.
138. *Literal Commentary on Genesis* IV, 22 (PL 34:312).

Replies to the Objections:

1. Augustine in the *City of God* explains the statement, "The devil sins from the beginning," to mean that he persists in sin from its beginning.[139] But some explain "from the beginning" to mean immediately after the beginning.[140]

2. John says that the devil did not stand fast in the truth because he did not persist in it, as Augustine explains in the *City of God*, not because he never stood in it.[141]

3. That the angels could not have sinned at the first moment was neither because of the lack of any power that would have been supplied later, nor because of a perfection that would have been taken away before their sin. Rather, it was because of the ordination of their activity, since they first needed to contemplate what belongs to their nature and later to be moved regarding supernatural things by turning toward or away from God.

4. The activity that something has at the beginning of its existence corresponds to its nature. And so we need to impute such activity to the author of the nature. But angels could later move, rightly or wrongly, from considering natural things to other things, and this should be imputed to the will of angels who sin, not to the author of their nature.

5. The will of rational creatures is predetermined to one thing, and nature moves their will to such things. For example, every human being by nature wills to exist and to live and to be happy. And these are things toward the understanding or willing of which nature first moves rational creatures, since other actions presuppose natural actions. And so if angels were to have sinned at the first moment of their creation, it would seem that this belongs to their nature and so would be in some way imputable to the author of nature.

6. We do not impute deficiencies resulting from primary causes to secondary causes regarding things that secondary causes do not have from primary causes. For example, legs do not have crookedness from the power of locomotion. But the angels' first activity is by their natural powers, which they have from God. And so the argument fails.

7. The argument of this objection proceeded on the assumption that the angels' movement of free choice resulted from consultative deliberation, for one needs to take counsel by deliberating about two alternatives, either one of which one can do in order to choose one of them in the future. But when deliberation does not precede choice, it is not necessary that one have the power to choose or not choose before one chooses. Rather, one is at that very moment freely borne to this or that.

8–9–10. And so we concede objections 8, 9, and 10.

11. As bad angels did not sin at the first moment of their creation, so good angels were not completely happy at the first moment of their creation. And so it was not necessary that the good angels foreknew their future steadfastness, just as the bad angels did not foreknow their fall before they sinned. And because an angel's happiness is chiefly from God, and sin is from a creature's free choice, God could have made angels happy at the first moment of their creation by inducing them to what surpasses nature, since God even caused the very fact that they were at that moment induced to what lay within their natural power. But angels by their own power could have been moved wickedly toward what transcends their nature only after the first moment of their existence.

---

139. *City of God* XI, 15 (PL 41:330).
140. Bonaventure, *Commentary on the Sentences* II, d. 3, part 2, a. 1, q. 2, reply to obj. 1.
141. *City of God* XI, 15 (PL 41:330).

12. We can understand the distinction of light from darkness throughout the whole span of time, which we are now considering, in which we distinguish the good from the wicked, not indeed at the beginning of the world. But such understanding seems to belong to allegory, as Augustine says in the same work.[142] And so he there proposes another explanation, that we understand light to mean the formation of the first creatures, and darkness to mean the formlessness of creatures not yet formed. But he says in the *City of God* that light and darkness signify the distinction between the good angels and the bad angels as God foreknew their distinction.[143] And so he says there: "Only he who could foreknow before they fell those who will fall could have discerned those things."

13. Augustine in his *Literal Commentary on Genesis* leaves in doubt whether angels know at the same time or successively all the deeds related in the six days and so knew day and evening and the next morning at the same time or successively.[144] And whatever the case, it is enough for his meaning that we understand the distinction of days as angels know them and not as days occurring temporally.

14. Angels at the first moment of their creation, when they were moved to understand their own nature, were at the same time moved to know God as the author of their nature, since purely intelligent beings know their cause when they know their essence, as the *Book of Causes* says.[145] But they were not at that moment moved to know God as the author of grace.

15. Loving oneself for the sake of God as the object of supernatural happiness and the author of grace is an act of charity. But loving God above all things and oneself for the sake of God insofar as the natural good of every creature consists of him, by nature befits not only rational creatures but also irrational animals and inanimate material substances insofar as they share natural love of the highest good, as Dionysius says in his work *On the Divine Names*.[146] And angels at the first moment of their creation loved themselves for the sake of God in this way.

16. The argument of this objection fails on three counts. First, it indeed fails because human beings were created chiefly to enjoy God and to complete the universe, even if angels had never fallen, not to compensate for the fall of angels. Second, the argument fails because human beings, at least regarding their body, were in the opinion of Augustine created in the deeds of the six days only virtually, not actually.[147] And according to Augustine, only things that could not exist virtually before they actually existed were created at the beginning of the creation of the world. Third, the argument fails because nothing prevents something being done for the sake of a future end that a human being foreknows. For example, one prepares wood in summer for the cold coming in winter.

17. A spirit's movement of free choice can exist in a moment. But by the argument previously elaborated,[148] a spirit could not have a movement to sin at the first moment of its creation.

---

142. *Literal Commentary on Genesis* I, 17, n. 34 (PL 34:259).
143. *City of God* XI, 19 (PL 41:333).
144. *Literal Commentary on Genesis* IV, 33–35 (PL 34:317ff.).
145. *Book of Causes*, comm. 8.
146. *On the Divine Names* 4, n. 4 (PG 3:700B).
147. *Literal Commentary on Genesis* VI, 15 (PL 34:349).
148. In the answer.

18. Although angels had a movement of the will as well as one of the intellect at the first moment of their creation, it does not follow that they had a movement of the will to sin.

19. A kind of eternity measures angels' existing. But it does not measure angels' actions, and their acts both of the will and the intellect are successive, as is evident from what I have said before.[149]

20. The nature of merit and the nature of sin are different. For merit results from God, who can from the beginning induce creatures to what he has willed, moving the mind of rational creatures. But the very mind of rational creatures, which can move itself only in accord with the requirements of the natural order, moves itself to sin.

21. The soul's union with the tainted body, not its own action, makes it evil at the first moment of its creation. And so the argument regarding angels, who could become evil only through their own actions, is different.

22. The argument of this objection fails in two ways. First, the argument fails because as creatures would dissolve into nothingness were God's power not to sustain them, so also would they fail to be good were God not to sustain them. But it does not follow that they would fall into sin were God not to sustain them through his grace, excepting only the case of a corrupted nature that of itself inclines to evil. Second, the argument fails because the need to keep the commandments does not always bind human beings to use grace, since affirmative precepts do not bind under all circumstances. And so it is not necessarily the case that a person at every moment either merits or sins.

23. John says that the devil characteristically speaks lies because the devil has truth from God and not from himself, and falsity from himself and not from God, not because lying is a natural property of his.

Fifth Article

Can Devils' Free Choice Return to Good
after Their Sin?

It seems that their free choice can, for the following reasons:

1. Dionysius says in his work *On the Divine Names* that the things in devils by nature remain intact after their sin.[150] But devils before their sin could have turned toward good. Therefore, devils could also turn toward good after their sin.

2. Nothing regarding what is contrary to nature remains such permanently, since something contrary to nature is accidental, and accidents can be easily taken away because "accidents are present or absent without destroying their subject."[151] But sin is contrary to the nature of angels, since they fell from what is in accord with their nature to what is contrary to their nature, as Damascene says in his work *On Orthodox Faith*.[152] Therefore, the devils' free choice could not have permanently persisted in evil.

---

149. Ibid.
150. *On the Divine Names* 4, n. 23 (PG 3:725C).
151. Porphyry, "De accidenti," *Isagoge* (Minio-Paluello [Porphyry]:20).
152. *On Orthodox Faith* II, 4 (PG 94: 876A).

3. People have said that it belonged to devils by reason of their condition that they by sinning immediately lost their condition as wayfarers, to which changing from good to evil and the converse belong. But the condition of reward or punishment, which God bestows or inflicts, succeeds the condition of wayfarer. And God cannot cause permanence in sin, since he does not preserve anything of which he is not the author. Therefore, permanence in sin cannot belong to angels by reason of the condition that they now have.

4. Everything that does not belong intrinsically to something needs to belong to it from a cause. But irrevocably sinning does not belong to angels as such, for then such sinning would belong to them by nature, and so they would be evil by nature, which we have disproved.[153] Nor, moreover, does it belong to them from a cause, since it is not from God, or their nature, as I have proved,[154] or even their own will, since inasmuch as a rational creature's will can change, it does not seem that their will can cause irrevocability. Therefore, irrevocably sinning in no way belongs to devils.

5. Augustine says in his work *On True and False Repentance*:[155] "If devils could hope in God and acknowledge their moral fault, they would find in God's kindness what they do not find in themselves," namely, forgiveness of their sin. But devils can hope in God, since hope, like fear, springs from faith, and Jas. 2:19 says that "devils believe and tremble." Therefore, devils can obtain forgiveness of their sin and so not persist irrevocably in their sins.

6. If devils cannot hope for God's mercy, this impossibility of mercy regards either themselves or God. But this does not regard God, since as Augustine says in the same place,[156] every wickedness is shallow in relation to God's mercy. And if we should say that this regards the devils, namely, in that they cannot by their own efforts rise from sin, this would by like reasoning befit everyone who sins mortally, since no one can by one's own efforts abandon sin unless freed by God, and yet not all who sin mortally persist irrevocably in evil. Therefore, devils do not persist irrevocably in evil.

7. It is valid to argue: I can run if I want to; therefore, I can run. But devils can turn to good if they want to, since turning to good consists of the very act of so willing. Therefore, devils can turn to good.

8. If a state of motion be natural, then a state of rest is natural, since something comes to rest in a place by the same nature that moves it to the place. Therefore, by like reasoning, if movement is voluntary, rest is voluntary. But a devil's movement to evil was voluntary. Therefore, his resting in evil is voluntary. Therefore, he does not rest in evil necessarily.

9. According to Chrysostom in his *Commentary on the Gospel of John*, as the light of the sun is related to the air, so the uncreated light is related to spiritual substances.[157] But the purer the air, the more it can receive the light of the sun, and of spiritual substances, angels have a finer nature than human souls do. Therefore, since human souls after sin

---

153. A. 2.
154. Ibid.
155. Augustine (Pseudo), *On True and False Repentance* 5, n. 15 (PL 40:1118).
156. Ibid.
157. Actually, John Scotus, *Homily on the Prologue of St. John's Gospel* (PL 122:290C–D).

can receive the light of grace, it seems much more likely that angels can. Therefore, it seems that angels would not persist irrevocably in evil.

10. What is by nature such is always such. But angels by nature have the capacity to turn to good. Therefore, they always have the capacity to turn to good, as much after sin as before.

11. Devils did not gain any advantage out of their sin. But they were obliged to turn to God before they sinned. Therefore, they were also obliged to turn to God even after they sinned. But no one is obliged to what is impossible. Therefore, devils can turn to God. And so it seems that they do not remain permanently in sin.

12. The lower the nature of an efficient cause, the more it is determined to one thing. For example, heavy and light material substances are more determined to one motion than is reason, which can move to different things. But the soul is by the ordination of nature inferior to the angels. Therefore, since the soul is not so determined to one thing as not to be able to return to good after sin, it seems that much less are the angels.

13. Higher appetites can govern lower appetites, as, for example regarding us, our rational appetite governs our sense appetites, as the *De anima* says.[158] But other appetites, namely, the appetites of God and good angels, are superior to the appetites of devils. Therefore, the appetites of devils, which strive for evil, can be directed to good.

14. By nature, everything turns to what is better. But devils understand that the divine good is better than their own good. Therefore, devils can turn to the divine good. Therefore, devils do not persist irrevocably in turning away from God, which is evil for them.

15. The devils' changed condition does not take away their free choice, which naturally belongs to them. But the capacity to turn to good belongs intrinsically to free choice, since the capacity to sin is not free choice or part of freedom, as Anselm says.[159] Therefore, the devils' changed condition does not take away from them their capacity to turn to good.

16. Devils, before they sinned, could have turned to good. And if they cannot turn to good after they sinned, this results either from a subtraction or an addition. But this does not result from a subtraction, since their natural powers remain intact, just as their other natural goods do, as Dionysius says.[160] And likewise, it does not result from an addition, since things receive additions according to their way of existing. And so since angels' free choice as such can change, it seems that any addition to them belongs to them subject to change. Therefore, devils do not persist irrevocably in evil.

17. The will is proportioned to the intellect, which moves the will. But the angels' intellect does not understand one thing so as not also to be able to understand something else. Therefore, their will does not will one thing so as not also to be able to return to will something else. And so devils do not persist irrevocably in evil.

18. Dionysius says in his work *On the Divine Names* that devils both understand and will good.[161] But only their consent to such a will seems to be required for them to turn to good. Therefore, it seems that they can return to good.

---

158. Aristotle, *De anima* III, 11 (434a12–15).
159. *On Free Choice* 1 (PL 158:490B).
160. *On the Divine Names* 4, n. 23 (PG 3:725C).
161. Ibid.

19. Anselm says that if devils have free choice, they must have it so as to be able either to preserve or to abandon or to recover rectitude.[162] But they do not have free choice so as to be able to preserve rectitude, since they do not have it. Nor do they have free choice so as to be able to abandon rectitude, since this belongs to the capacity to sin, which is not part of freedom. Therefore, we conclude that they have free choice so as to be able to recover rectitude. And so they do not persist irrevocably in evil.

20. Things deformed in the same way can be reformed in the same way. But the devil is deformed in the same way that many human beings, who sin for the same reason, namely, wickedness, are. Therefore, since human beings can be reformed, devils also could be.

21. As the will is disposed to good and evil, so the intellect is disposed to truth and falsity. But there is no intellect that so adheres to falsity that it cannot return to truth. Therefore, the devil's will does not so adhere to evil that it cannot return to good.

On the Contrary:

1. 1 Jn. 3:8 says: "The devil sins from the beginning." And Augustine in the *City of God* explains this to mean that the devil sins forever from the beginning of his sin.[163]

2. Gregory says in his work *Morals*: "The heart of the ancient enemy will be hardened like a stone, since no repentant conversion will soften it."[164]

3. Angels are in between God and human beings. But God has immutable free choice before and after he chooses, and human beings have mutable free choice before and after they choose. Therefore, angels are disposed in a middle way, namely, that they have free choice before but not after they choose, since the contrary is impossible, namely, that they have free choice after but not before they choose. Therefore, angels cannot return to good after they choose to sin.

Answer:

Origen, thinking that the free choice of any creature in any condition can change from evil to good and from good to evil, was mistaken on this question.[165] And so he thought that even devils could at some time by their free choice return to good and by God's mercy obtain forgiveness of their sins. But Augustine says in the *City of God*: "The Church condemned Origen on account of this and other errors, since he lost even the appearance of being merciful by causing the saints real misery, whereby they would suffer punishment for their sins, and false happiness, in which they would not have real and secure (i.e., without fear, certain) joy of eternal good."[166] For Origen by like reasoning held that even good angels and human beings at some time could by their free choice sin and so fall out of the state of blessedness.[167] And this is evidently contrary to the judgment of the Lord, who says: "These [the damned] will go to everlasting punishment, and the just to eternal life."[168]

162. *On Free Choice* 3 (PL 158:494B).
163. *City of God* XI, 15 (PL 41:330).
164. *Morals* XXXIV, 6, n. 11 (PL 76:723D).
165. Related by Augustine, *City of God* XXI, 17 (PL 41:731).
166. Ibid.
167. Related, ibid.
168. Mt. 25:46.

We should note that the error of Origen arose from the fact he failed to consider what belonged to the power of free choice intrinsically, without which it does not exist in any condition. Therefore, we should consider that it belongs to the nature of free choice that it can be for different things. And so things lacking knowledge, whose actions are determined to one thing, do nothing by free choice. And irrational animals indeed do things by choice but not free choice, since nature determines the judgments whereby they seek or avoid things, so that they cannot go counter to them. For example, sheep can flee from wolves only when they see them. But everything possessing intellect and will acts by free choice, namely, as the choice whereby it acts results from intellectual or rational comprehension, and such comprehension is disposed to many things. And so it belongs to the nature of free choice that it can be for different things, as I have said.[169]

And we can consider this difference in three ways. We can consider the difference in one way by the difference of means chosen for the sake of ends. For everything has an end from nature that it seeks by natural necessity, since a nature always strives for one thing. But because many things can be ordained for one end, the appetite of an intellectual or rational nature can strive for different things by choosing means to the end. And thus does God also by nature will his goodness as his end and can only will it. But because different modes of being and ranks of things can be ordained for his goodness, his will is not borne to one of his effects so as not to be able, as such, to be borne to another. And God in this way has free choice. Likewise, angels and human beings have happiness as the end bestowed on them by nature. And so they by nature desire it and cannot will unhappiness, as Augustine says in his work *On the Trinity*.[170] But since different things can be ordained for happiness, the will of both human beings and good or bad angels in choosing means to that end can be borne to different things.

We note a second difference regarding which there can be free choice as the difference between good and evil. But this difference does not intrinsically belong to the power of free choice but is incidentally related to the power inasmuch as natures capable of defect have such free choice. For inasmuch as the will of itself is ordained for good as its proper object, the will can strive for evil only insofar as evil is understood under the aspect of good, and such understanding belongs to a deficiency of the intellect or reason, which causes choice to be free. But it does not belong to the nature of a power to be deficient in its activity. For example, it does not belong to the nature of the power of sight that one see things indistinctly. And so nothing prevents there being a power of free choice that so strives for good that it is in no way capable of striving for evil, whether by nature, as in the case of God, or by the perfection of grace, as in the case of the saints and the holy angels.

And we note a third difference regarding which there can be free choice as the difference of change. And this difference indeed does not consist of the fact that one chooses different things, for God himself also wills that there be different things as befits different times and persons. But changes in free choice consist of the fact that one does not will the same thing and at the same time what the person willed previously, or that one wills what the person previously did not will. And this difference also does not belong intrinsically to the nature of free choice but happens incidentally to the power by reason of the

---

169. In the answer.
170. *On the Trinity* XIII, 3 (PL 42:1018).

condition of a changeable nature. Just so, it does not belong to the nature of the power of sight to see in different ways, but this sometimes happens because of the different disposition of the seer, whose eyes are sometimes clear and sometimes blurred. And likewise, the mutability or diversity of free choice does not belong to its nature but happens to it insofar as it belongs to a nature subject to change. For example, internal and external causes alter our free choice. An internal cause indeed does, either because of reason, as when one knows later what one did not know before, or because of the will itself, as emotions or habits sometimes dispose one to strive for things as suitable that are not suitable in the absence of the emotions or habits. And an external cause alters free choice, as when God by grace changes the will of a human being from evil to good, as Prov. 21:1 says: "The heart of the king is in God's hands, and God will turn it whithersoever he willed."

These two causes cease to act on angels after their first choice. And first, indeed, nature immutably disposes them regarding things that belong to the natural order, for change belongs to things having potentiality, as the *Physics* says.[171] And it belongs to the angels' nature to have actual knowledge of everything they can know naturally, as we by nature have actual knowledge of first principles, from which we by a process of deductive reasoning proceed to acquire knowledge of conclusions. But angels do not have such a process of reasoning, since they intuit in the principles themselves all the conclusions proper to natural knowledge of them. And so as we are permanently disposed regarding knowledge of first principles, so the angels' intellect is permanently disposed regarding everything it knows by nature. And since the will is proportioned to the intellect, it follows that their will is also by nature irrevocable regarding what belongs to the natural order. But it is also true that they have potentiality regarding movements to supernatural things, whether by turning toward them or by turning away from them. And so they can only have the change of moving from the order of their nature to things transcending their nature by turning toward or away from them. But since everything added to something is added to it according to the mode of its nature, it follows that angels persist irrevocably in turning from or toward a supernatural good.

And regarding an external cause, angels are immutable in either good or evil after their first choice, since the condition of wayfarer is ended for them. And so it does not belong to the nature of God's wisdom to infuse more grace to recall them from the evil of their first turning away from him, in which they persist irrevocably. And so, although they choose various things by free choice, they still sin regarding everything they choose, since the force of their first choice abides in their every choice.

Replies to the objections:

1. The devils' natural goods are intact as regards the ordination of nature, but they are corrupt, that is, evil, or diminished in relation to grace or glory.

2. Sin is contrary to nature by reason of the disorder whereby sin has the nature of evil, not by reason of what the one sinning desires. And so nothing prevents the sinner persisting irrevocably in what the sinner desires by sinning.

3. By not imparting his grace, not indeed by causing or preserving their wickedness, God causes the condition whereby devils persist in evil. For we in this way say that

---

171. Aristotle, *Physics* III, 2 (201b31–32).

he hardens some in their sin, as Rom. 9:18 says: "He has mercy on those on whom he wills to have mercy, and he hardens those whom he wills to harden."

4. It belongs to devils to persist irrevocably in evil by reason of two causes, not one. For being in a condition of evil belongs to them by reason of their own will, and adhering irrevocably to the object willed belongs to them by reason of their nature.

5. Properly speaking, the devil cannot acknowledge moral fault in himself, namely, so that he understands and rejects his sin as a culpable evil, since this would belong to a change in free choice. And so he cannot hope for forgiveness by God's mercy from moral fault, as it were.

6. Not only can devils not rise from sin by their own powers, just as human beings cannot, but it also belongs to them by the mode of their nature to adhere irrevocably to what they by their will have chosen. And so their sin is more irremediable than the sins of human beings.

7. When I say, "I can run if I want to," the antecedent is possible, and so the consequent is possible. But when I say, "Devils can return to good if they want to," the antecedent is impossible, as is evident from what I have said.[172] And so the reasoning is different.

8. As the devils' movement of turning away from God was voluntary, so also is their remaining in what they willed voluntary, since they voluntarily persist in evil. And their will abides irrevocably in evil, for the reason already mentioned.[173]

9. The uncreated light illumines spiritual substances in two ways: in one way by natural light, and then good or bad angels are more illumined than human souls are; in a second way by the light of grace, and then bad angels are less capable of such illumination than human souls are, because of the impediment to grace that remains permanently in bad angels, as I have said.[174]

10. By nature, devils' free choice cannot change regarding their natural goods, but their free choice can change only regarding supernatural goods, and devils can turn toward or away from them. And when they have done so, they persist irrevocably in it, as I have said.[175]

11. Drunkards are morally obliged not to sin, not indeed in light of their present condition but in light of the fact that they are the voluntary cause of their drunkenness, by reason of which we impute some moral fault to them for their actions. So also can we understand that devils are morally obliged to turn to God, although this is impossible for them in their present condition, since they arrived at their present condition voluntarily.

12. Lower things are more determined to one thing regarding their object because higher powers extend to more than one thing. But the highest things are more determined to one thing because of their immutability, and the devils' free choice is determined to evil in this way.

13. Only God can move the will, and he could also by his absolute power turn the devils' will to good. But this is not congruent with the devils' nature, as I have said.[176]

---

172. In the answer.
173. Ibid.
174. Ibid.
175. Ibid.
176. Ibid.

And so there is no comparison with sense appetites, which are by their nature subject to change.

14. Devils understand that the divine goodness as the source of natural goodness is better than their own, but not that the divine goodness as the source of supernatural goodness is better than their own, since they still abide in the first wickedness whereby they willed to obtain the highest happiness by their natural powers.

15. By the devils' change of condition, they did not lose free choice so as not to be able to be borne to connatural goods, but they lost the capacity to be borne to the good of grace.

16. The devils' irrevocability in evil, properly speaking, results from their adherence to evil, which has the nature of an addition. And because they adhere to things according to the mode of their nature, it follows that devils adhere to them irrevocably rather than revocably.

17. The devils' will can indeed desire various things, as I have said in the answer. But devils persist irrevocably in evil regarding everything they desire, as is evident from what I have said.[177]

18. The argument of this objection is valid regarding devils' knowledge and willing of natural goods, but we are presently speaking about supernatural good and the evil of moral fault contrary to that good.

19. Devils would have the freedom to preserve rectitude if they were to have it, since, as Anselm says in the cited work, free choice always has the power to preserve rectitude, both when it possesses rectitude and when it does not, just as one has the power to retain money if one were to have money, even if one does not have money.[178]

20. Human beings, although they may sin for the same reason that devils did, they are not completely deformed in like manner. Rather, devils are deformed irrevocably, and human beings revocably, according to what befits their respective natures.

21. As devils persist irrevocably in the evil to which they adhere, so also would they persist in the falsity to which they would assent.

Sixth Article

Is a Devil's Intellect So Darkened after Sin That It Can Err or Be Deceived?

It seems that a devil's intellect is that darkened, for the following reasons:

1. Job 41:23 says of the Leviathan, by which we understand the devil: "It will think the depths come to an end." And Gregory explaining this in his work *Morals* says: "One who thinks that heavenly condemnation regarding punishments will sometime end thinks that the depths come to an end."[179] But this is false. Therefore, the devil has false or erroneous opinions.

---

177. Ibid.
178. *On Free Choice* 12 (PL 158:504A).
179. *Morals* XXXIV, 19, n. 34 (PL 76:737D).

2. Whoever is in doubt can err. But the devil is sometimes in doubt, as is evident by what Mt. 4:33 says: "If you are the Son of God, tell these stones to become loaves of bread." Therefore, the devil can err.

3. People have said that a devil can err regarding supernatural knowledge but not regarding natural knowledge. But Dionysius says in his work *On the Divine Names*: "We affirm that the angelic goods bestowed on them," namely, the devils, "have never been altered and are intact and most splendid, although the devils themselves, blocking their powers to contemplate the good, do not perceive the goods."[180] But those who do not perceive because they block their vision can be deceived or err. Therefore, a devil can err even regarding his natural goods.

4. There can be evil wherever there can be potentiality without actuality, as the Philosopher makes evident in the *Metaphysics*.[181] But the angels' intellect can have potentiality without actuality even regarding their natural knowledge, since they do not actually contemplate at the same time everything to which their natural knowledge extends; otherwise, they would not change over time, as Augustine says in his *Literal Commentary on Genesis*.[182] Therefore, the angels' intellect can have evil. But the intellect's evil is falsity, as the *Ethics* says.[183] Therefore, although the devil has the nature of an angel, nothing prevents his intellect having false opinions.

5. A devil's will can be defective by reason of sin because the will is made out of nothing, as Augustine makes clear in the *City of God*.[184] But the a devil's intellect is likewise made out of nothing. Therefore, by like reasoning, his intellect can be deficient by reason of error.

6. Sin excludes one from happiness. But happiness belongs to the intellect rather than to the will, as Jn. 17:3 says: "This is eternal life, that they know you, the only true God," etc. Therefore, since sin makes a devil's will wicked insofar as it abides forever in sin, much more does sin make his intellect so depraved that it persists forever in error.

7. Anselm in his work *On Truth* proves that there is only one truth, namely, uncreated truth.[185] And Augustine likewise says that everything is perceived in the divine light.[186] But devils are excluded from sharing in God, as 2 Cor. 6:14 says: "What does light have in common with darkness?" Therefore, devils cannot know any truth.

8. On Job 41:33, "He was made to fear no one," Gregory says in his work *Morals* that the devil "turned the desire for pre-eminence into a rigidity of mind so that now due to his hardheartedness, he who sought to be pre-eminent in glory does not think that he has done evil."[187] But he evidently did evil. Therefore, he has a false opinion about his very self.

180. *On the Divine Names* 4, n. 23 (PG 3:725C).
181. *Metaphysics* IX, 9 (1051a19–21).
182. *Literal Commentary on Genesis* VIII, 20 (PL 34:388).
183. Aristotle, *Ethics* VI, 2 (1139a27).
184. *City of God* XII, 8 (PL 41:355).
185. *On Truth* 13 (PL 158:484–86).
186. Augustine (Pseudo), *On Spirit and Soul* 12 (PL 40:788).
187. *Morals* XXXIV, 21, n. 41 (PL 76:741A).

9. One who thinks false what one previously thought true errs in one or the other opinion. But this happens to the devil, since a gloss on Mt. 27:19, "When he [Pilate] was sitting as judge, his wife sent to him," etc., says: "As the devil had first brought death through a woman, so he, at last understanding that he was about to lose his spoils through Christ, now wants to deliver Christ from the hands of the Jews through a woman in order not to lose power over death through Christ's death."[188] And so it seems that he once deemed it expedient that Christ die, when he was working for Christ's death, and it afterward seemed to him that this rule was not expedient for his power. Therefore, it seems that he had a false opinion at one or the other time.

10. Augustine says in his work *On True Religion*: "You should be on your guard against the lower parts of hell," that is, the greater punishments after this life, "where there can be no recollection of truth because there is no rational activity. And there is no rational activity because there is no diffusion of the true light that enlightens every human being that comes into this world."[189] But devils rest in the condition of those lower parts of hell. Therefore, they know no truth, and they have no rational activity.

11. As true knowledge is related to right desire, so false knowledge is related to wicked desire. But there can be right desire only if true knowledge precedes it. Therefore, false knowledge always precedes wicked desire. But devils always have a wicked desire. Therefore, they have false knowledge.

12. A gloss on Lk. 10:30, "After beating the man, they went away, leaving him half dead," says that sin wounds human beings in their natural powers.[190] But grace restores in human beings what sin wounded. Therefore, since grace restores the whole image of God, which includes both the will and the intellect, it seems that a devil's sin wounded his intellect even regarding his natural knowledge. And so it seems that there can be error or deception even in his natural knowledge.

13. Dionysius says in his work *On the Divine Names* that no one perceiving evil does evil.[191] But a devil does evil. Therefore, he is deceived in his perception.

14. Augustine says in his work *On True Religion*: "The devil by loving himself rather than God was unwilling to be subject to God and swelled up with pride and abandoned the supreme being," that is, fell through sin. "And he is something less because he wanted to enjoy something lesser, inasmuch as he wanted to enjoy his own power rather than God's."[192] But because he wickedly clung to his own nature and power and so began to be something less, it seems that he departed from the ordination of his natural powers. Therefore, he can have falsity or deception even regarding his natural knowledge.

15. Gregory says in his *Book of the Pastoral Rule* that what is right seems wicked to a mind filled with rage.[193] But the devil's mind is filled with rage, for Dionysius says in his work *On the Divine Names* that the devil's evil consists of irrational rage.[194] Therefore, the devil thinks that everything right is wicked. And so he is deceived in his opinion.

188. *Ordinary Gloss*, on Mt. 27:19 (PL 107:1131B).
189. *On True Religion* 52 (PL 34:167).
190. The editors of the Leonine text have not found this gloss.
191. *On the Divine Names* 4, n. 19 (PG 3: 716C).
192. *On True Religion* 13 (PL 34:133).
193. *Book of the Pastoral Rule*, part 3, chap. 16 (PL 77:77A).
194. *On the Divine Names* 4, n. 23 (PG 3: 725B).

16. Universal knowledge is a source of deception for us. For example, if we consider the whiteness of lilies, which is common to them and many other things, we are deceived into thinking that being white is identical with being a lily. But angels know by universal forms, and the higher the angel, the more universal the forms it has. Therefore, since Lucifer was the highest of the angels and so has the most universal forms, it seems that he can be deceived.

17. Noncomposite beings turn completely to what they turn toward. Therefore, by like reasoning, they turn completely away from what they turn away from. But a devil is noncomposite by reason of his essence. Therefore, since he has turned away from God, it seems that he has turned completely away from him, namely, both regarding desire and knowledge. Therefore, it seems that his knowledge completely departs from truth, since God is truth.

18. A gloss on 2 Cor. 6:15, "What harmony is there between Christ and Belial?" says that the devil does everything wickedly.[195] But understanding itself is an activity. Therefore, it seems that the devil is wrongly disposed even in his understanding. And so it seems that his intellect has false opinions.

On the Contrary:

1. Dionysius says in his work *On the Divine Names* that angels are pure intellects.[196] But there can be no falsity in pure understanding, even human understanding. Therefore, much less can there be in angels' knowledge. But a devil has the nature of an angel. Therefore, his knowledge has no falsity.

2. Devils, since they are immaterial substances, have only intellectual knowledge. But understanding is always correct, as the Philosopher says in the *De anima*,[197] and Augustine likewise shows in his *Book of the 83 Questions* that no one understands something false.[198] Therefore, it seems that the devils' knowledge cannot be deceived.

3. People have said that the devils' knowledge can be deceived regarding supernatural knowledge, not natural knowledge. But supernatural knowledge is particularly related to God as he surpasses the natural knowledge of creatures. And as the Philosopher proves in the *Metaphysics*, the knowledge of pure substances, who are superior to us, can have no falsity; rather, their knowledge has deficiency only when they do not attain knowledge.[199] Therefore, devils only fail to have supernatural knowledge and cannot have false opinions about it.

4. Everything added to a thing comes to the recipient according to the mode of the recipient's nature, as the *Book of Causes* says.[200] Therefore, if devils cannot err regarding their natural knowledge, it seems that they also cannot err regarding their additional knowledge of supernatural things.

---

195. Peter Lombard, *Gloss*, on 2 Cor. 6:15 (PL 192:49D).
196. *On the Divine Names* 7, n. 2 (PG 3:868B).
197. *De anima* III, 10 (433a26).
198. *Book of the 83 Questions*, q. 32 (PL 40:22).
199. *Metaphysics* IX, 10 (1051b17ff.).
200. *Book of Causes*, props. 10 and 12.

5. People have likewise said that devils can err regarding practical knowledge. But angels' knowledge surpasses all human knowledge, and human beings have a cognitive power that even in sinners does not err, namely, *synderesis*. Therefore, it seems much more likely that the knowledge of sinful angels is without error.

6. Devils sinned by their free choice, which is a capacity of the will and reason. But reason and the will are related to different objects, for the will regards the good, and reason regards truth. But nothing prevents the will of devils being deficient regarding the good without their intellect being deficient regarding truth.

7. Nothing is destroyed or diminished except by its contrary. But sin is not contrary to nature. Therefore, it seems that sin neither destroys nor diminishes natural good. But natural knowledge is not subject to error. Therefore, it seems that neither can a devil err even after he sinned.

8. Gregory says in his *Dialogues* that human souls elevated from the body know truth without error.[201] But angels, even bad angels, are more elevated from bodies than human souls are. Therefore, it seems that much less do bad angels err.

Answer:

False opinions are defective intellectual activities, as monstrous births are defective natural activities, and so also the Philosopher says in the *Ethics* that the intellect's evil is falsity.[202] And defective activity always results from a cause's defect. For example, defects in semen cause monstrous births, as the *Physics* says.[203] And so every false judgment necessarily results from a defective source of knowledge; for example, we often have false opinions due to faulty reasoning. But nothing can be defective regarding that in relation to which it is by its nature always actual, although it can be defective regarding that in relation to which it is potential. For the potential can be subject both to perfection and privation. And actuality is contrary to privation, to which every defect belongs.

And angels by the condition of their nature actually have complete knowledge of everything to which their cognitive power by nature extends, as I have said before.[204] For they immediately perceive conclusions in knowing first principles and do not reason from the principles to the conclusions; otherwise, if they, having actual knowledge of the principles were to know the conclusions potentially, they just like ourselves would need to acquire knowledge of the conclusions by discursive reasoning from the principles. And Dionysius demonstrates the contrary in his work *On the Divine Names*.[205] Therefore, as we cannot have false opinions regarding the first principles that we know by nature, so neither can angels have false opinions regarding whatever things are subject to their natural knowledge. And since devils by sinning did not lose what belongs to their nature, and their natural gifts abide intact and most splendid, as Dionysius says in his work *On the Divine Names*,[206] it follows that devils cannot have false opinions regarding things that belong to their natural knowledge.

201. *Dialogues* IV, 26 (PL 77:357C).
202. *Ethics* VI, 2 (1139a27).
203. Aristotle, *Physics* II, 8 (199b3–7).
204. Aa. 3 and 5.
205. *On the Divine Names* 7, n. 2 (PG 3:868B).
206. Ibid., 4, n. 23 (PG 3:725C).

And although their minds are actual regarding things that they can by nature know, their minds are nonetheless potential regarding things that surpass their natural knowledge, and a higher light needs to enlighten their minds to know such things. For as the higher a causal power, the more things the power can reach to act upon, so a higher cognitive power extends to knowledge of more things. And so a lower intellect, needing to be perfected by a higher intellect, is necessarily potential, as it were, regarding things about which the higher intellect surpasses the lower intellect. Therefore, regarding things belonging to God's knowledge, every angelic intellect, needing a supernatural light, that is, the light of God's grace, to enlighten it, is potential.

And so regarding such supernatural knowledge, every angelic intellect can have a deficiency, but some angelic intellects have deficiency in a different way than others. For good angels can indeed have defective knowledge regarding such things but one of pure negation, as Dionysius says in his work *On Ecclesiastical Hierarchy* that they are freed from their ignorance.[207] And they cannot have the defective knowledge of false opinion, since inasmuch as their will is properly ordered, they do not use their intellect to judge things exceeding their knowledge. But bad angels, because of their disordered and proud will, can also have the defective knowledge of false opinion regarding such things, since they presumptuously use their intellect to judge things exceeding them. And they can have false opinions regarding such things both in theoretical matters, namely, as they rashly rush to false judgments, and in practical matters of desire, as they erroneously judge that things should be desired or done in relation to the aforementioned knowable things.

Replies to the Objections:

1. The permanence of God's condemnation belongs to supernatural knowledge, since the reason for God's judgments surpasses all the natural knowledge of creatures, as Ps. 36:6 says: "Your judgments are a great abyss." And the devil knows the permanence of his punishment. For ignorance of its permanence would lessen his unhappiness, since as the certainty of the permanence of glory relates to an increase of happiness for the blessed, so the certainty of the permanence of unhappiness relates to an increase of unhappiness for the damned. And so we need to say, as Job says, that the devil thinks that the deep will come to an end because, as Gregory explains in the cited text,[208] the devil in this world impresses on the minds of human beings the idea that the punishments of sin come to an end, to induce human beings to have less fear about sinning.

2. This doubt of the devil concerns the mystery of the incarnation, which mystery exceeds the natural knowledge even of the angels.

3. Dionysius does not say that devils do not perceive the natural goods bestowed on them in such a way that they do not perceive them at all; otherwise, they could know nothing, since purely intelligent beings understand all other things by understanding their own essence, as the *Book of Causes* says.[209] Rather, he means that devils, adhering definitively only to their natural goods, do not perceive these goods in relation to supernatural goods, from the contemplation of which they avert their attention.

---

207. *On Ecclesiastical Hierarchy* 6, part 3, n. 6 (PG 3:537B).
208. *Morals* XXXIV, 19, n. 34 (PL 76:737D).
209. *Book of Causes*, comm. 13.

4. We speak of having actual knowledge in two ways: in one way as to actual consideration, and then we do not understand that angels have actual knowledge of all the things to which their natural knowledge extends; in a second way as to habitual knowledge. For we say that a person has potential knowledge in one way before the person learns, namely, when the person does not yet have habitual knowledge, and in another way before the person considers what the person knows habitually, as the *De anima*[210] and the *Physics*[211] say. And angels have actual knowledge in a habitual way regarding all the things they can know naturally. And this suffices to reject contrary falsity, since we do not always actually contemplate first principles. Rather, the habit of first principles suffices to reject every contrary error regarding them.

5. Because something originates out of nothing, it follows that it is mutable in some respect, but it does not need to be mutable in every respect. Heavenly bodies are indeed subject to locomotion but not to substantial change. And likewise, the angels' intellect, because it originates out of nothing, can err regarding supernatural things, although not regarding their natural knowledge, since even the angels' will can err regarding supernatural things, as I have maintained before.[212]

6. Happiness consists of activity of the intellect, to which the vision of God belongs, rather than activity of the will, to which pleasure belongs, since pleasure results from activity as an effect from a cause and is added to it as an extra perfection. And so the Philosopher says in the *Ethics* that pleasure perfects activity as comeliness perfects youth.[213] But desiring one's end and striving for it belong particularly to the will, and sin prevents this. And so sin regards the will rather than the intellect.

7. Devils are excluded from sharing in God's truth and light insofar as these are shared through grace, but not insofar as they are shared through nature.

8. The devil does not think that he has done evil because he does not understand his moral fault as evil and still persists in evil with an obstinate mind. And so this belongs to the falsity of practical knowledge or knowledge related to desire.

9. The effect of Christ's passion belongs to supernatural knowledge, regarding which the devil could err.

10. When Augustine says that there is no recollection of truth in hell, we should not understand this as if the devils should know no truth; otherwise, they would not know that they had committed acts of sin, and so the worm of conscience would be excluded. Rather, we should understand by Augustine's words that devils are not in a condition to acquire knowledge of the truth that would perfect their intellect.

11. A complete and integral cause produces good, but individual defects result in evil, as Dionysius says in his work *On the Divine Names*.[214] And so more things are required for good than for evil. And so it does not follow that there cannot be a wicked will without false knowledge if true knowledge of the intellect is required for rectitude of the will. And we can also say that the will can even be upright when antecedent knowl-

210. Aristotle, *De anima* II, 1 (412a10 and 22).
211. Aristotle, *Physics* VIII, 4 (255a33–34).
212. A. 3.
213. *Ethics* X, 4 (1174b31–33).
214. *On the Divine Names* 4, n. 30 (PG 3:729C).

edge is false. For example, such would be the case if one shows paternal honor to a man whom one falsely thinks to be the person's father. And likewise, a wicked will is always accompanied by some false practical knowledge.

12. Moral fault wounds human beings in their natural powers as to the powers' capacity for supernatural things but not so as to take anything away from their essential nature. And so it follows that a devil's intellect errs only regarding supernatural things.

13. The argument of this objection is valid regarding practical knowledge or knowledge related to desire, whereby one perceiving good chooses evil.

14. The devil, in adhering to love of self rather than love of God, sinned regarding the relation of natural goods to supernatural goods, since he did not relate love of his nature to God. And also in this regard, Augustine says that the devil is something lesser insofar as he is deprived of supernatural existence.

15. Dionysius speaks metaphorically about the devil's rage, and we do not ascribe sound arguments to such figures of speech. But we can also say that even the devil's thinking wrong to be right belongs to practical knowledge.

16. We do not say that angels have universal knowledge because they know only the universal nature of things, in which way our universal knowledge causes deception. Rather, we say that their knowledge is universal insofar as it extends universally to many knowable things, and they have proper and complete knowledge regarding those things.

17. Angels are noncomposite in essence but multiple in power, namely, insofar as their power extends to many things, not indeed by different kinds of powers, as we have sense appetites and an intellectual appetite. For such diversity would be contrary to the simplicity of their essence. Therefore, because of their intellectual appetite, as it can extend to many things, angels can turn away from something in one respect but not in another. And so the devils' will has turned away from God regarding supernatural things but not regarding natural things.

18. The devil does everything evilly regarding what he does by free choice. But properly speaking, his natural actions are good, since those natural actions are from God, who established their nature.

Replies to the Arguments in the Section On the Contrary:

1. Angels have a pure intellect in that they immediately intuit the truth of conclusions in first principles and do not understand truth by reasoning from the principles to conclusions. Just so, they in simple contemplation of subjects immediately contemplate the things proper to the subjects and the things excluded from them, and do not understand by adding predicates to subjects by the way of judgmental composition and separation of our intellect. And the reason for both is the same, because the disposition of a subject is the source of knowing that a predicate belongs to it. And so angels by pure understanding of a subject know that it is or is not such, just as we do by composing and separating subjects and predicates, since nothing prevents understanding the composite through understanding the noncomposite, as the material is known through the immaterial. And so our intellect can have falsity when it composes judgments, as it judges something to be or not to be such. And so a devil's intellect can have falsity, particularly regarding things that transcend his natural knowledge.

2. We say that the intellect is always correct in its understanding, since, as Augustine says in his work *Book of the 83 Questions*,[215] whoever understands something understands that it is as it is. But the power of intellect can err by not understanding the real, as is evidently the case with those who have false opinions.

3. Regarding God's essence itself, devils can have defective knowledge only in not attaining it, as the argument advanced by the objection proves. But regarding the things God does in creatures beyond their nature, the devil's intellect can have the defect of false opinions.

4. The devil's way of understanding is conformed to his substance, but he does not need to have the same power to judge things that transcend his nature as he has to judge things connatural to him. And so although he never has false judgment about things belonging to his natural knowledge, he can nonetheless have false judgment about things that surpass his natural knowledge.

5. *Synderesis* is the cognitive habit of the universal first principles governing human action, which human beings know by nature, just as they know the universal first principles governing theoretical matters. And so we can conclude from this only that devils do not err in their natural knowledge.

6. Good moves the will only insofar as good is understood. And so the will can fail to desire good only if there be an underlying failure to understand regarding particular objects of choice, not indeed regarding universal first principles, which are the objects of *synderesis*.

7. Devils by their sin did not incur falsity as regards their natural knowledge because moral fault is not directly contrary to their nature.

8. Gregory is speaking about the elevation of the soul accomplished by grace, since the light of grace excludes all falsity.

Seventh Article

Do Devils Know Future Things?

It seems that they do, for the following reasons:

1. Augustine says in the *City of God*: "The temporal effects of God's power can be more evident to angelic perceptions, even those of evil spirits, than to the weakness of human beings."[216] But human beings by considering the effects of God's power know many things about future things. For example, doctors know the future state of health of their patients, sailors know when there will be fair weather. Therefore, much more can devils know future things.

2. One can accurately predict the future only if one foreknows it. But devils predict true things about future events, as Augustine says in his work *On the Divination of Devils*.[217] Therefore, devils know future things.

---

215. *Book of the 83 Questions*, q. 32 (PL 40:22).
216. *City of God* IX, 21 (PL 41:274).
217. *On the Divination of Devils* 4 and 5 (PL 40:585–86).

3. If devils are immaterial substances, their substance and activities necessarily transcend time, as the *Book of Causes* says that the substance and activity of pure intelligences transcend time.[218] But the present, past, and future are different periods of time. Therefore, regarding the devils' knowledge, it makes no difference whether things are present, past, or future. But devils can know present and past things. Therefore they can also know future things.

4. People have said that for things to be known, both the knower and the object known need to be present and actual. But God's knowledge is more certain than the devil's. Therefore, if the object known needs to be actually present for the devil's knowledge to be certain, much more is this necessary for God's knowledge. And so neither would God know future things. And this conclusion is inappropriate.

5. All knowledge is according to the mode of the knower. But devils, since they are immaterial substances, have intellectual knowledge and no sense knowledge. Therefore, since the intellect abstracts from the here and now, it seems that it makes no difference regarding devils' knowledge whether things are present, past, or future.

6. Devils evidently know individual things as they exist. But devils do not know them by forms acquired from the things, since this would only be possible by means of sense perception. Therefore, devils know individual things by innate forms. But the devils' mind had innate forms from the beginning of their creation. Therefore, devils knew all future individual things from the beginning of their creation.

7. People have said that for things exceeding angels' natural knowledge, innate forms do not suffice, and infused forms are necessary. But much more is something lesser subject to the knowledge of one to whose knowledge something greater is subject. And immaterial substances, which are much superior to sensibly perceptible substances, are subject to devils' natural knowledge. Therefore, individual sensibly perceptible things do not exceed their knowledge.

8. As ideal natures in God's mind are related to his causing and knowing, so the likenesses of things in angels' minds are related to their knowing. But the ideal natures in God's mind are equally related to causing and knowing past, present, and future things. Therefore, it seems that the forms of things in angels' minds are equally related to present, past, and future things.

9. As God through his Word produced forms in matter, so also he produced forms in the angels' understanding, as Augustine makes clear in his *Literal Commentary on Genesis*.[219] But the forms in corporeal matter are related in the same way to the present, past, and future. Therefore, it seems that the forms in the angels' mind are by like reasoning related in the same way to the present, past, and future. And so it seems that devils can know future things by such forms.

10. Isidore says in his work *On the Supreme Good* that devils are empowered with a triple keenness of wit: partly, indeed, by the fineness of their nature, partly, by their long experience, and partly by the revelations of good spirits.[220] But all these ways can extend to knowledge of future as well as present things. Therefore, devils can know future things.

---

218. *Book of Causes*, comm. 7.
219. *Literal Commentary on Genesis* II, 6, nn. 13 and 14 (PL 34:268) and 8, n. 16 (PL 34:269).
220. *On the Supreme Good* I, 10, n. 17 (PL 83:556C).

11. People have said that devils can know future things that come about necessarily and have necessary causes, but not other future things. But experiential knowledge advances from like things to like things. And of all the things that happen, howsoever contingent they be, some like things occurred in past ages in which devils existed, for Eccl. 1:10 says: "There is nothing new under the sun, since it has already happened in the ages that existed before us." Therefore, devils have knowledge of all future contingent things.

12. Experiential knowledge derives from the senses, for the Philosopher says in the *Metaphysics*: "The senses produce memories, and many memories produce an experiential knowledge."[221] But devils do not have senses. Therefore, they do not have the experiential knowledge to know some future things rather than others.

13. If devils do not know things without necessary causes if the things are future things, and they know such things if they are present things, it seems to follow that their intellect is brought from potentiality to actuality. But this seems impossible, since only something more excellent brings a thing from potentiality to actuality, and we are not to assume that there is any created thing more excellent than the angels' intellect. Therefore, it seems that devils know contingent things without necessary causes even before the things happen.

14. Everything produced by several coordinated and unimpeded causes seems to happen necessarily. But every effect that happens in this world happens by the conjunction of several coordinated and unimpeded causes, since there would be no subsequent effect if the causes were to have been impeded. Therefore, everything in this world happens necessarily, and so it seems that devils know all future things.

15. Fortune and chance regard things that happen infrequently. But if nothing should happen infrequently, nothing will be contingent for the most part, and everything will happen necessarily, since things that happen for the most part differ from things that happen necessarily only in that the former fail to happen in rare cases. Therefore, if nothing happens by fortune and chance, then everything happens necessarily. But the former seems to be true in the opinion of Augustine, who says in his *Book of the 83 Questions* that nothing happens in this world purposelessly, that is, by fortune or chance.[222] Therefore, everything happens necessarily, and so devils know all future things.

16. We trace the causes of all the movements of lower material substances to the movements of heavenly bodies, for Augustine says in his work *On the Trinity* that God governs lower material substances by higher ones.[223] But the movements of higher material substances come about necessarily. Therefore, everything that happens regarding lower material substances comes about necessarily. And so the same conclusion follows as before.

17. People have said that the foregoing argument is valid about purely material movements but not about movements caused by free choice. But the movements of human beings and every animal originate from things newly happening in material things. For example, when the process of digestion is finished, human beings by their

221. *Metaphysics* I, 1 (980b28–981a1).
222. *Book of the 83 Questions*, q. 24 (PL 40:17).
223. *On the Trinity* III, 4, n. 9 (PL 42:873).

own power awaken and get up, as the *Physics* says.[224] Therefore, if the things that happen externally regarding material things are subject to the necessary causality of heavenly bodies, it seems by like reasoning that the things happening by free choice are also.

18. Free choice seems to belong to the will, that is, the rational appetite, and the will's act consists of choosing. But good as the will's proper object moves the will. Therefore, the will is necessarily moved to choose good and avoid evil. Therefore, everything, even the things happening by free choice, come about necessarily. And so it seems to follow that devils can know all future things.

On the Contrary:

1. Damascene says in his work *On Orthodox Faith* that God alone, not human beings or devils, knows future things.[225]

2. Everyone can know better the things that belong to oneself than the things that belong to others. And so 1 Cor. 2:11 says: "No one knows what belongs to a person save the person's spirit within the person." But devils did not foreknow their fall, as Augustine makes clear in his *Literal Commentary on Genesis*.[226] Therefore, much less can devils know other future things.

3. Only truth is the object of knowledge. But future contingent things do not have settled truth, as the Philosopher proves in his work *On Interpretation*.[227] Therefore, devils do not know future things in a settled way.

Answer:

We can know future things in two ways: in one way as they are in their very selves; in a second way as they belong to their causes.

No one but God can indeed know future things in themselves. The reason for this is that future things as such do not yet exist in themselves, and being and truth are convertible. And so since something true is the object of every act of knowledge, no knowledge regarding future things as future can be knowledge of them in their very selves. And since the present, past, and future are different periods of time designating the temporal order, everything that belongs to time in any way is related to future things as future. And so no knowledge subject to the temporal order can be knowledge of future things in themselves. And every knowledge by creatures is such, as I shall explain below. And so no creature can know future things in themselves. And such knowledge is proper to God alone, whose knowledge is so completely beyond the whole temporal order that no part of time is related to his knowledge as past or future. And the whole procession of time and the things transpiring through the whole of time are present to him and conformed to his sight, and his pure vision is at once borne to everything as each thing exists in its own period of time. And we can understand a fitting analogy from spatial relations, since the before and after regarding motion and time result from the before and after regarding quantity, as the *Physics* says.[228] Therefore, God sees as present all things

---

224. Aristotle, *Physics* VIII, 2 (253a18–20).
225. *On Orthodox Faith* II, 4 (PG 94:877A).
226. *Literal Commentary on Genesis* XI, 17 (PL 34:438).
227. *On Interpretation* I, 9 (18a28ff.).
228. Aristotle, *Physics* IV, 11 (219a16–18).

that are related to one another by the relationship of present, past, and future, which none of those whose view falls within the succession of time can. Just so, one positioned on a height sees at the same time everyone passing below but not as before or behind oneself, although the person sees that some below precede others. But one on the path below in the procession of those passing by can see only those preceding or close to the person.

But particular future things can belong to their causes in three ways. Future things can belong to their causes in one way only potentially, namely, in that they can equally exist or not exist, and we call such future things contingent regarding their existence or nonexistence. And some future things belong to their causes both potentially and by reason of their efficient cause that cannot be prevented from producing its effect, and we say that such things happen necessarily. And some future things belong to their causes both potentially and by an efficient cause that can be prevented from producing its effect, and we say that such things happen for the most part. And because everything is known insofar as it is actual and not insofar as it is potential, as the *Metaphysics* says,[229] it follows that things disposed to existing or nonexisting can be foreknown in their causes in a settled way but in disjunction, namely, that they will or will not exist. For they have truth in this way. But human beings can with certainty know in causes things that belong to the causes as proceeding necessarily from them. And devils or angels, who know the power of natural causes better than human beings do, can much more certainly know such things. And things that happen for the most part can be known in their causes with some probability and not complete certainty, but more certainly by good or bad angels than by human beings.

And we should note that knowing a future thing in its cause is simply knowing the present inclination of the cause to produce its effect. And so properly speaking, this is to know the present, not the future. And so knowledge of future things is proper to God, as Is. 41:23 says: "Show us the things to come, and we shall affirm that you are gods."

Replies to the Objections:

1. The argument of this objection is valid regarding future things as known in their causes.

2. Devils sometimes predict true things about the future and sometimes false things. And they predict true things when they foreknow them by the revelations of good spirits that originate from God or in their external causes, whose power they know, or in what causes propose to do, as when they predict the things they themselves are about to do. And they sometimes predict false things wishing to deceive human beings, since the devil is "a liar and the father of lies," as Jn. 8:44 says. And they sometimes predict false things because they themselves are deceived, as when God prevents them from doing what they intend to do, or when something happens by God's power beyond the ordinary course of natural causes, as Augustine says in his work *On the Divination of Devils*.[230]

3. Devils' substance and activities indeed transcend the time that numbers the movements of heavenly bodies, but time is connected with their activity insofar as they do not actually understand everything at the same time. And this time indeed involves change

---

229. Aristotle, *Metaphysics* IX, 9 (1051a29).
230. *On the Divination of Devils* 6, n. 10 (PL 40:587).

in their desires and thoughts about intelligible things. And so Augustine says in his *Literal Commentary on Genesis* that God causes the movements of spiritual creatures through time.[231]

4. There is another argument regarding God, who sees the whole of time as present, since his intellect is completely free from time and so regards the future as existing, and we cannot say this about angels or devils.

5. Every created intellect abstracts from the here and now, but the human intellect does so in a different way than the angelic intellect does. For the human intellect abstracts from the here and now both as to the very things known, since it does not know singulars, which are subject to being here and now, and as to the intelligible forms themselves, which are abstracted from their individuating conditions. But the intellect of good or bad angels abstracts from the here and now as to the intelligible forms themselves, which are immaterial and universal, but not as to the very things known, since the angels' intellect knows both universals and singulars through intelligible forms because of the power of their intellect. And so devils have different knowledge of present and future things.

6. Angels know singulars, when actual, by forms already possessed, not by forms newly acquired, but angels did not know the forms possessed as future things. And the reason why is that an assimilation of the knower and object known produces knowledge. But the intelligible forms in the angelic intellect are directly likenesses regarding specific natures, and angels can know singulars by means of the forms only insofar as singulars partake of a specific nature, which is not the case before singulars actually exist. And so angels immediately know singulars when singulars actually exist. Just so, conversely, it happens with us that our eyes, taking in the form of stone, immediately know the pre-existing stone. For the forms of the angels' intellect exist before things in time, just as the forms of things exist before our sense perceptions of them.

7. Knowing singulars in time as present things is not beyond the power of the angels' intellect, but only knowing singulars as future things is.

8. As Dionysius says in his work *On the Divine Names*, we cannot find an accurate, that is, a perfect, likeness of a creature to God.[232] And so the forms in the angels' intellect, howsoever like the ideal natures of God's intellect, are still unequal to them, namely, to comprise all the things that the ideal natures of God's intellect comprise. And so although the ideal natures of God's intellect, which completely transcend time, are related without distinction to the present, past, and future, it does not follow that the forms of the angels' intellect are disposed in the same way.

9. The forms in things, forms originating from the divine mind, are indeed disposed in the same way regarding specific natures but not regarding individual things' sharing in the natures, since some individual things at times partake of a specific form, and other individual things at other times do. And so also the forms in the angels' intellect in their very selves are always disposed in the same way, but from the alteration in individual natural things it comes about that the individual natural things are sometimes assimilated to the forms in the angels' intellect and sometimes not.

231. *Literal Commentary on Genesis* VIII, 20 (PL 34:388).
232. *On the Divine Names* 2, n. 8 (PG 3:645C).

10. What devils know by the revelations of celestial spirits exceeds their natural power to know, but what they know by the fineness of their nature belongs to their natural knowledge, by which they can foreknow effects in the effects' natural causes. And regarding human acts depending on free choice, which they cannot know from natural causes, devils know many things by experiential knowledge.

11. Future things have indeed transpired in past ages analogously but not analogously in every respect. And future effects may be similar to different past effects in different respects. But the knowledge that comes from the similarities in contingent things has no certitude because of the mutability of matter and constitutes probable knowledge.

12. Experiential knowledge derives from sense perception as the senses know present things. And so we posit experiential knowledge in devils because they know things made present to them in the aforementioned way,[233] things that they had not known before, not because they sensibly perceive anything.

13. The fact that devils do not know something future happens because a future singular does not yet partake of the specific form whose likeness actually pre-exists in the devils' intellect, not because their intellect has potentiality.

14. Proponents of the theory that everything happens necessarily argued in four ways. One way was the way of the Stoics, who imposed necessity on future events by a fixed series of interconnected causes that they called fate,[234] and the argument of this objection inclines to this opinion. But Aristotle answered this opinion in the *Metaphysics*, saying that if we make two suppositions, namely, that everything that happens has a cause, and that we need to posit effects whenever we posit causes, it follows that everything happens necessarily.[235] For the opinion will trace every future effect to either a present or past cause, which, as that from which the effect comes or came about, needs to exist or have existed. Suppose that a person will be killed if the person goes out of the person's home at night, and the person will go out if the person wants to drink, and the person wants to drink if the person is thirsty, and the person will be thirsty if the person should eat salty things, and the person perhaps had eaten or is eating salty things. And then it follows necessarily that the person will be killed. But both of the aforementioned suppositions are false. For it is false that given a cause, even if it be of itself sufficient, that an effect necessarily results, since the cause can be prevented from producing its effect. For example, pouring water on burning wood can prevent fire from burning the wood. Likewise, it is not true that everything that happens has a cause, since some things happen by chance, and what happens by chance has no cause, since what happens by chance is not, properly speaking, being, as Plato said.[236] And so, that a person should be digging a grave has a cause, and also that treasure should have been buried in a place has a cause. But the concurrence of the causes, which is by chance, namely, the concurrence that this person wants to dig a grave in a place where treasure has been buried, has no cause, since it is by chance.

15. Some wanted to impose necessity on future events from divine providence, in which they constituted fate,[237] and it seems that the argument of this objection inclines

---

233. Reply to objection 6.
234. Cf. Nemesius, *On Human Nature* 37 (PG40:752B).
235. *Metaphysics* VI, 3 (1027a29ff.).
236. Related by Aristotle, ibid., VI, 2 (1026b14–15).
237. Stoics, according to Augustine, *City of God* V, 8 (PL 41:148).

to this opinion. For example, Augustine in this manner says that nothing happens in the world purposelessly, since everything is subject to divine providence. But this does not take away the contingency of future events, neither because of the certainty of God's knowledge nor because of the power of his will. And what I have said before makes this evident regarding his knowledge.[238] For God's knowledge is related to future contingent things as our eyes are related to present contingent things, as I have said. And so as we most certainly see that Socrates is sitting when he is sitting, although it be not absolutely necessary on that account that he be sitting, so also the contingency of things is not taken away because God sees everything in itself that happens. And regarding God's will, we should note that God's will universally causes being and every consequence of being, and so both necessity and contingency. And his will is above the ordination of the necessary and the contingent, as it is above the whole of created existing. And so we distinguish the necessity and contingency in things in relation to created causes, which the divine will has ordained in relation to their effects, namely, that there be immutable causes of necessary effects and mutable causes of contingent effects, not by the relationship of things to God's will, which is their universal cause.

16. Some attempted to impose necessity on future events by the power of heavenly bodies, in which they constituted fate.[239] And the argument of this objection proceeds in this way. And the argument indeed fails, first, because not all the causes of future events are subject to the power of heavenly bodies. For example, the intellect, and so the will, which belongs to the power of reason, are not the powers of any bodily organ and so not directly subject to the action of any material power. The argument also fails regarding purely material effects. For the power of heavenly bodies is a natural power, and nature always strives for one thing. And what is by chance is not truly one, as the *Metaphysics* says.[240] And so we can indeed sometimes trace something accidental to an intellectual cause, which can understand something accidental as one thing, but not to a natural cause. And it is evident that many things happen by chance regarding purely material effects. For example, lightning may strike in a grove where there are many trees, and the trees catch fire and burn the whole forest. And so we cannot trace all purely material effects to the power of a heavenly body as their cause. And so not all the material effects of heavenly bodies happen necessarily, since they can be prevented by chance. For example, the Philosopher says in his work *On Divination by Dreams* that many things regarding atmospheric disturbances, signs of which were previously manifest in heavenly bodies, do not happen.[241]

17. External things that induce emotions in the body or sense powers indeed arouse reason and the will to act, but reason and the will retain the power to act or not to act in accord with the movements of such emotions.

18. The argument of this objection touches on the fourth way in which some wanted to impose necessity on human acts.[242] But to refute this, we should consider that good

238. Reply to objection 14.
239. Astrologers, according to Augustine, *City of God* V, 1–7 (PL 41:141–48).
240. Aristotle, *Metaphysics* V, 6 (1015b16ff.).
241. Aristotle, *On Divination by Dreams* 2 (463b23–26).
242. The third error condemned at the University of Paris in 1270.

moves the will as truth moves the intellect. And the intellect necessarily assents to first principles, which are self-evident, and all the things it considers as necessary conclusions from those principles, since the principles cannot be true without the conclusions being true. And likewise, the will necessarily desires the ultimate end, which is to be desired for its own sake, since all human beings necessarily want to be happy, and also the things without which they consider that they cannot be happy. But the will does not necessarily consent to other electible things that it can consider either as belonging to happiness as an aspect of good or as not so impeding that happiness that it would be impossible to be happy without them. Just so, the intellect does not necessarily assent to probable propositions, regarding which it considers that self-evident principles can still be true even if those propositions are denied.

Eighth Article

Do Devils Know Our Interior Thoughts?

It seems that they do, for the following reasons:

1. Gregory says in his work *Morals*: "We cannot perceive others' minds as long as we are in this life, since their minds are enclosed in vessels of clay, not glass vessels."[243] But the density of things of clay cannot prevent the intellectual vision that devils have. Therefore, devils know our interior thoughts.

2. As physical vision is related to physical forms, so spiritual vision is related to spiritual forms. But sensory physical vision can see the physical forms in sensibly perceptible things. Therefore, devils' spiritual vision can perceive the spiritual forms in our souls. But such forms give form to our interior thoughts. Therefore, devils can know the interior thoughts of human beings.

3. People have said that devils can know the interior thoughts in which we employ sense images but not thoughts that consist of pure contemplation. But the Philosopher says in the *De anima* that the soul never understands without a sense image,[244] and a proof of this is the fact that all intellectual activity is prevented when the bodily organ of imagination is destroyed. Therefore, if devils know those thoughts of ours in which we employ sense images, then they know all our thoughts.

4. People have said that we should understand the Philosopher's words about things we know naturally, not about things revealed to us by God. But Dionysius says in his work *On the Celestial Hierarchy* that "the divine rays cannot shine on us unless covered by various sacred veils."[245] And he calls sacred veils sense images.[246] Therefore, we need the images of sensibly perceptible things even regarding things revealed to us by God. And so devils can perceive all our thoughts.

---

243. *Morals* XVIII, 48, n. 78 (PL 76:84B).
244. *De anima* III, 7 (431a16–17).
245. *On the Celestial Hierarchy* 1, n. 2 (PG 3:121B).
246. Ibid., 1, n. 3 (PG 3:124A).

5. Our intellect better knows things by nature less intelligible, since it derives its knowledge from the senses. But this is not true regarding devils. And so they better know things as such more knowable. But the forms in our intellect are actually intelligible and so as such more knowable than the forms in physical things, which are potentially intelligible. Therefore, since devils by their intellect know the forms in material things, much more probably can they know the intelligible forms in our intellect by which we form our thoughts. Therefore, they can perceive our thoughts.

6. The cause of anything being such is more such. But our very intellect is intelligible because of the intelligible forms existing in it, as the Philosopher makes clear in the *De anima*.[247] Therefore, since devils know the very substance of our intellect, much more do they know the intelligible forms in our intellect.

7. Devils know our souls better than we do. But thoughts belong to our soul. Therefore, devils also know our thoughts better than we do.

8. Devils know effects in their causes, as I have said.[248] But they know our soul, both its powers and its habits that cause our thoughts. Therefore, they know our thoughts.

9. No one can truly reveal what one does not know. But as Augustine says in his *Literal Commentary on Genesis*, "The surest signs evidence that devils reveal the thoughts of human beings."[249] Therefore, devils know our thoughts.

10. The assimilation of the knower to the known object produces all knowledge. But sinful thoughts make human beings like devils. Therefore, devils can know such thoughts.

11. Our internal words are more like devils, who are spiritual substances, than are external words, which are material. But devils know the orally expressed external words of human beings. Therefore, much more do they know the internal words belonging to thoughts, as Augustine makes clear in his work *On the Trinity*.[250]

12. Acts are more knowable than habits. But devils know what belongs to the habitual memory of human beings. And as Augustine says in the *City of God*,[251] this is evidenced by an incident in which a philosopher appeared in a dream to someone asleep and answered a question about which the sleeper was in doubt, and a devil seems to have brought this about. Therefore, it seems that devils can much more know the actual thoughts of human beings.

13. The higher a cognitive power, the more power it has to know things. But the devils' cognitive power is higher than that of human beings. Therefore, since human beings can know the thoughts of other human beings by certain physical signs, as Sir. 19:25 says, "We know human beings by their appearance, and wise men by face-to-face encounter," it seems to follow that devils in addition perceive human beings' thoughts in themselves.

14. If devils were to perceive such thoughts only by physical signs and not in themselves, they could not know them at all, since the same physical sign is related to many

247. *De anima* III, 7 (431a 14–15).
248. A. 7.
249. *Literal Commentary on Genesis* XII, 17, n. 34 (PL 34:467).
250. *On the Trinity* XIV, 7, n. 10 (PL 42:1043).
251. *City of God* XVIII, 18, n. 2 (PL 41:575).

things. For example, a flushed face can result from an internal emotion of anger or shame. But it is certain that devils know the thoughts of human beings in some way, as Augustine makes clear in his *Commentary on the Book of Genesis*[252] and his work *On the Divination of Devils*[253] and his *Retractions*.[254] Therefore, they know those thoughts in themselves.

15. Bodily signs are perceptible by the senses. But as Dionysius says in his work *On the Divine Names*, devils do not know intelligible truth by sensibly perceptible things.[255] Therefore, devils know our thoughts in their very selves and not by physical signs.

16. People have said that devils cannot know our interior thoughts in themselves because our will has the power to conceal them. But the will does not conceal them by completely removing them, since one would then have no thoughts. Nor does the will hide them by producing them at a distance, since physical distance does not prevent angels' knowledge. Nor does the will conceal them by interposing something, since nothing else in the soul is hidden from devils. Therefore, the will cannot in any way conceal one's thoughts from devils.

17. As Augustine says in his *Literal Commentary on Genesis*, angels know everything lower than themselves through forms that they receive at their creation.[256] But our thoughts are lower than angels, since our soul is by the ordination of nature inferior to angels. Therefore, devils can know the thoughts of human beings by those innate forms.

On the Contrary:

1. Jer. 17:9–10 says: "The human heart is wicked and inscrutable. Who will know it? I, the Lord, search hearts and test temperaments." Therefore, it belongs to God alone to know the thoughts of human beings. Therefore, devils do not know the thoughts.

2. The Apostle says in 2 Cor. 2:11: No one knows the things within a person except that person's spirit within the person." But thoughts are particularly internal to human beings. Therefore, only the individual human being, not devils, can know the thoughts of that human being.

3. The work *On Church Dogmas* says: "We are certain that the devil does not perceive the interior thoughts of the soul."[257]

Answer:

Augustine say in his *Literal Commentary on Genesis*[258] and the work *On the Divination of Devils*[259] that sure signs evidence that devils know human beings' thoughts in some way. And one may know them in two ways: in one way as one perceives them in themselves; in a second way by certain physical signs.

And the second way is particularly evident when interior thoughts induce human beings to certain emotions. And if human beings have experienced strong emotions, they

---

252. *Literal Commentary on Genesis* XII, 17, n. 34 (PL 34:467).
253. *On the Divination of Devils* 5 (PL 40:586).
254. *Retractions* II, 30 (PL 32:643).
255. *On the Divine Names* 7, n. 2 (PG 3:868B).
256. *Literal Commentary on Genesis* II, 8, n. 16 (PL 34:269).
257. Gennadius, *On Church Dogmas* 81 (PL 58:999A).
258. *Literal Commentary on Genesis* XII, 17, n. 34 (PL 34:467).
259. *On the Divination of Devils* 5 (PL 40:586).

show signs in their external appearance that even the rather dim-witted can apprehend. For example, "Those fearful grow pale, and those ashamed blush," as the Philosopher says in the *Ethics*.[260] And even if an emotion be milder, skilled doctors can detect it from change in the heartbeat that they note by the pulse. And devils can know such external and internal physical signs much more than any human being can, and so it is certain that devils can know some human thoughts in the aforementioned way. And so Augustine says in his work *On the Divination of Devils* that "devils sometimes with complete ease thoroughly understand human dispositions, both those expressed in speech and those conceived in thought, when the soul manifests certain physical signs."[261]

Whether devils can in this way perceive the thoughts in themselves, Augustine leaves unresolved in his work *Retractions*, saying: "Devils evidently gain knowledge of these things through some experience. But human beings can discover only with the greatest difficulty or not at all whether the bodies of those thinking the thoughts reveal certain signs perceptible to devils but hidden from us, or devils know the thoughts by another power, a spiritual power."[262]

Therefore, to study this difficulty, we need to consider that we should pay attention to two things regarding thought, namely, the form itself and use of the form, that is, actual understanding or thinking. For as only in God is there no difference between form and existing itself, so only in him is there no difference between the understood form and understanding itself, that is, being one who understands.

And regarding intelligible forms, we should note that every intellect is related in one way to a higher intellect's forms and in another way to a lower intellect's forms. For a higher intellect's intelligible forms are more universal and so cannot be understood by a lower intellect's intelligible forms. And so a lower intellect cannot completely know a higher intellect's intelligible forms, although a higher intellect can completely know a lower intellect's intelligible forms, as more particular, and can judge regarding them by its own more universal forms. And so inasmuch as the angels' intellect is by the ordination of nature superior to our intellect, good or bad angels can know the forms in our soul.

But regarding our use of the forms, we should note that such use, that is, actual thinking, depends on our will. For we use our habitual forms when we will to do so. And so also the Commentator says in his commentary on the *De anima* that habits are what one uses when one has willed to do so.[263] And the movement of the human will depends on the highest ordination of things, that is, the highest good. And Plato and Aristotle also hold that the highest good is the highest cause,[264] since the will has universal good, not a particular good, as its object, and universal good is rooted in the highest good. And only a higher cause moving someone, and the one moved, not a lower cause, can know what is subject to the ordination of the higher cause. For example, if a citizen is subject to an official as a lower cause and to the king as the highest cause, the official cannot know

---

260. *Ethics* IV, 9 (1128b13–14).
261. *On the Divination of Devils* 5 (PL 40:586).
262. *Retractions* II, 30 (PL 32:643).
263. Averroes, *On Aristotle's On the Soul* III, comm. 18.
264. According to St. Thomas, *Commentary on the Ethics* I, 6 (993b9–10).

what the king has directly ordained regarding the citizen, but only the king and the citizen induced to act by the king's command will know. And so since only God, to whose ordination the movement of the will, and so voluntary thoughts, are directly subject, can move the will internally, neither devils nor anyone else but God and the person willing and thinking can know such thoughts.

Replies to the Objections:

1. Human beings are prevented from knowing the thoughts of others both by the very nature of thoughts, as devils are, and by the very density of clay bodies that bodily senses, on which our knowledge depends, cannot penetrate. And Gregory is speaking in the latter regard.

2. As physical vision can know only the physical forms proportioned to it, not every physical form (e.g., bats cannot see the light of the sun), so also spiritual vision can perceive only the spiritual forms proportioned to it, not every spiritual form. And good or bad angels' spiritual vision can perceive our intellect's spiritual forms, but angels do not on that account perceive how we use the forms in thinking.

3. As long as we are in this life, we always need sense images in using knowledge, no matter how spiritual the knowledge, since we know even God by the sense images of his effects, inasmuch as we know him by negation or causality or excellence, as Dionysius says in his work *On the Divine Names*.[265] But sense images do not need to cause all of our knowledge, for revelation causes some of our knowledge.

4. The foregoing makes clear the reply to objection 4, which is valid regarding the use of knowledge.

5. The argument of this objection proves that devils know our intellect's intelligible forms, but it does not thereby follow that they know our thoughts, by reason of the explanation I have already given.[266]

6. And we should say the like in reply to objection 6. But we could also say in reply to this objection that our intellect is intelligible to ourselves by intelligible forms, namely, insofar as we know the acts of our intellect by reason of their objects, of which intelligible forms are likenesses, and the power by reason of the acts. And this need not be so regarding good or bad angels' intellect.

7. There are two kinds of knowledge of the soul. There is one kind whereby one knows what the soul is, by distinguishing it from all other things, and in this regard, devils, who intuit the soul in its very self, know it better than human beings, who study its nature through its acts, do. And there is another kind of knowledge of the soul whereby one knows that it exists, and in this regard, human beings know their soul by perceiving its existing by its acts, which they experience. And the knowledge whereby we know that we are thinking something belongs to the latter kind of knowledge, but devils know better than human beings what the nature of the human process of thinking is.

8. Although devils know some causes of thoughts, they do not know all of them, since they do not know movements of the will, as I have said.[267]

---

265. *On the Divine Names* 7, n. 3 (PG 3:872A).
266. In the answer.
267. Ibid.

9. Devils reveal the thoughts of human beings insofar as they know the thoughts by physical signs, as I have said.[268]

10. Intentional, not indeed natural, assimilation produces knowledge. For a stone does not belong to the soul in such a way that we by means of it know the external stone, as Empedocles held.[269] Rather, the form of stone belongs to the soul.

11. And we should say the like in reply to objection 11.

12. The soul's habits consist of certain qualities that give it form, and so devils can know the habits better than the soul's thoughts, which are subject to the will. But we cannot conclude from the cited incident that devils know things belonging to human beings' memory, since a devil could have satisfied the doubter by things that the devil himself knew, not because the devil knew that the philosopher knew them. Or the devil could have known by external signs that the philosopher knew them. Or a good angel could have caused the appearance.

13. Devils know a human being's thoughts better than other human beings do because devils perceive the thoughts by more concealed external signs, not because they perceive the thoughts in themselves.

14. Generally speaking, the same physical signs can correspond to many effects, but there are some differences in particular signs that devils can perceive better than human beings can.

15. Angels do not derive from sensibly perceptible things the intelligible truth they know by their nature. But they can surmise about something supernatural from its sensibly perceptible effects (e.g., that a man is God because he raises human beings from the dead) because by perceiving sensible effects by means of the innate forms they possess, angels surmise things exceeding their natural knowledge.

16. In none of those ways does the will conceal a human being's thoughts. Rather, we say that the will conceals them because they are concealed by the very fact that they derive from the will.

17. Augustine meant to speak about lower natures, which angels by their nature know through forms implanted in them, not about voluntary thoughts.

Ninth Article

Can Devils Alter Material Substances by Changing the Substances' Forms?

It seems that devils can, for the following reasons:

1. Augustine says in his *Book of the 83 Questions*: "We reasonably believe that lower powers in the atmosphere also can produce everything visible."[270] But changing the forms of lower material substances takes place visibly, indeed sometimes naturally and some-

---

268. Ibid.
269. Related by Aristotle, *De anima* I, 2 (404b11–15).
270. Actually, Augustine (Pseudo), *Twenty-One Maxims*, maxim 4 (PL 40:726).

times miraculously. Therefore, devils, whom we call the lower powers of the atmosphere, can produce such changes.

2. People have said that devils produce such changes by the power of certain natural causes, not by their own power. But if devils could alter natural material substances only by the power of natural causes, they could produce only changes possible by the power of natural causes. And the power of natural causes cannot transform the human body into the body of a beast, although devils do. And Augustine relates in the *City of God* that Circe by black magic transformed the companions of Ulysses into beasts, and that the Arcadians, while swimming across a pond, were turned into wolves, and that women innkeepers turned men into beasts of burden.[271] Therefore, devils can alter the forms of material substances by other than the power of natural causes.

3. A gloss on Ps. 78:49, "Detachments of bad angels," etc., says that God punishes through the agency of bad angels.[272] But the transformation of human bodies sometimes effects such punishments. For example, we read in Gen. 9:26 that Lot's wife was turned into a pillar of salt. And the companions of Diomedes are said to have been turned into birds, as Augustine relates in the *City of God*.[273] Therefore, it seems that devils can transform material substances.

4. The more actual something is, the more efficacious its causal power, since a thing causes insofar as it is actual. And so fire, since it in comparison to other material substances here below has the most form, has the greatest causal power. But since devils are spiritual substances, they have more form than any material substance, and more actuality. Therefore, they have more causal power than any material substance. Therefore, if the power of some material substances can transform material substances, much more can the power of devils do so.

5. Things having forms sometimes fail to effect the forms' activity because they do not completely receive the forms. Therefore, if forms were separate from matter, they would have all the forms' activity. But since devils signify spiritual and immaterial substances, it follows that they are separate forms. Therefore, they have the power to cause all the activity of their forms, and so, it seems, they can transform material substances.

6. Dionysius says in his work *On the Celestial Hierarchy* that "fiery streams signify heavenly," that is, divine, "harvests providing them [good angels] with plentiful and unfailing abundance and nourishing the life-giving power of generation."[274] But generation is a transformation. Therefore, good angels can transform material substances. Therefore, by like reasoning, devils, who have the same nature as good angels, can.

7. God moves heavenly bodies through the ministry of the angels, and angels cause by their intellect and will. But the will is disposed to different things. Therefore, angels move heavenly bodies in different ways. Therefore, when the movement of heavenly bodies is altered, the transformations of lower material substances, which depend on the movement of those bodies, are altered. Therefore, it seems that angels can transform lower

271. *City of God* XVIII, 17 and 18 (PL 41:573, 574).
272. Peter Lombard, *Gloss*, on Ps. 78:49 (PL 191:740A).
273. *City of God* XVIII, 16 (PL 41:573).
274. *On the Celestial Hierarchy* 15, n. 9 (PG 3:337C).

material substances as they wish. Therefore, by like reasoning, devils, who have the same nature as angels, can.

8. The *Book of Causes* says that the power of pure intelligences is infinite in relation to lower things, although it is finite in relation to what is higher.[275] But all material substances are inferior to pure intelligences. Therefore, pure intelligences can by their infinite power change material substances in whatever way they wish. But we call angels, whether good or bad, pure intelligences. Therefore, devils can transform material substances.

9. Augustine says in his work *On the Trinity* that fire and air and like material substances are subject to devils as much as God allows them to be.[276] But fire and air and like material substances can be subject to transformation. Therefore, devils can transform such material substances.

10. Whoever induces a form transforms. But devils can induce both accidental and substantial forms, for Pharaoh's sorcerers by the power of devils produced frogs.[277] Therefore, it seems that devils can transform material substances.

11. Augustine says in his *Book of the 83 Questions* that the sorcerers worked miracles by private pacts with devils.[278] But material substances are transformed in miracles. Therefore, it seems that devils can transform material substances.

12. Gregory says in a homily that it belongs to angels in the rank of Powers to work miracles,[279] in which, as I have said,[280] material substances are altered. But devils have the same nature as angels. Therefore, it seems that devils can alter material substances.

13. Devils have greater power than human souls do. But the soul's cognitive power transforms corporeal matter, as Avicenna makes clear in the case of bewitching.[281] Therefore, much more can devils transform corporeal matter.

On the Contrary:

1. Augustine says in the *City of God*: "No argument would convince me that the skill or power of devils can transform either the soul or even the body into the features of a beast."[282] But the human body has no less capacity to be acted upon than other material substances do. Therefore, it seems that neither can the skill and power of devils transform other material substances.

2. The Philosopher proves in the *Metaphysics* that the forms in matter come to be from material, not immaterial, forms.[283] And the Commentator comments on the text, saying that immaterial substances cannot transform matter.[284] But devils are immaterial substances. Therefore, it seems that devils cannot transform material substances.

---

275. *Book of Causes*, comm. 16.
276. *On the Trinity* III, 8, n. 13 (PL 42:875).
277. Ex. 8:7.
278. *Book of the 83 Questions*, q. 79, n. 4 (PL 40: 92).
279. *On the Gospels* II, hom. 34, n. 10 (PL 76:1251C).
280. Objection 11.
281. Avicenna, *On the Soul* IV, 4.
282. *City of God* XVIII, 18, n. 2 (PL 41:574–75).
283. *Metaphysics* VII, 8 (1033b19–1034a8).
284. *On Aristotle's Metaphysics* VII, comm. 28.

Answer:

As the Apostle says in Rom. 13:1, "God has ordained the powers of the things he made," and so the good of the universe is an ordered good, as Augustine says in his *Enchiridion*,[285] and as the Philosopher says in the *Metaphysics*.[286] And creatures are subject to this ordination, since God produced them. And God himself, who causes the order, presides over it and is not subject to it. And since each kind of thing has its own activity by reason of its form, we note the ordination of things both by the excellence of their form and as a consequence by their activities and movements, namely, that the higher the form, the higher the activity. And so the highest things move the lowest by means of those in between, as Dionysius says in his work *On the Celestial Hierarchy*,[287] and Augustine also says in his work *On the Trinity*.[288]

And this accords with the necessary proportion between causes and the things they act upon. For although the highest of beings have the most universal powers, the lowest things acted upon are proportioned to receive universal effects by more particular and restricted intermediate powers, not directly. Just so, even the very disposition of material things manifests this, for heavenly bodies cause the begetting of human beings and other perfect animals by means of the particular power in the animals' semen, although only the power of heavenly bodies in the absence of semen begets some animals out of decomposing organic matter. And the latter happens because of the animals' imperfection. For our senses perceive that distant causes produce weak effects, and causes need to be close at hand to produce strong effects. For example, fire can heat things even if they be distant from the fire, but they can be ignited only if they are in contact with the fire. And so one who wants to ignite something at a distance from the fire in a lighted fireplace does so by means of a taper. And heavenly bodies likewise cause the begetting of perfect animals by intermediate proper causes and of imperfect animals directly.

And spiritual substances are by the ordination of nature higher than even heavenly bodies themselves. And so spiritual substances can transform lower material substances only by using material causes proportioned to the effects the spiritual substances want to produce, not by the spiritual substances' own power, as human beings can heat things by using fire.

Replies to the Objections:

1. Devils can produce everything visible in this world by intermediate causes, not by their own power alone, as I have said.[289]

2. Devils use natural causes as instruments to produce certain effects. But the instruments act by the power of the chief cause, not only by their own power. And so the instruments can do some things beyond their power if we consider that power absolutely. For example, saws make beds by the power of a carpenter's skill. And devils can likewise produce certain things beyond the power of natural causes by means of the natural

---

285. *Enchiridion* 11 (PL 40:236).
286. *Metaphysics* XII, 10 (1075a11).
287. *On the Celestial Hierarchy* 4, n. 3 (PG 3:181A).
288. *On the Trinity* III, 4, n. 9 (PL 42:873).
289. In the answer.

causes that they use to produce the effects, but not that the features of the human body be really turned into the features of a beast, since this is contrary to the ordination of nature implanted by God. Rather, imaginary apparitions rather than real things accounted for the aforementioned transformations, as Augustine says in the cited work.[290]

3. God does not always punish through the agency of bad angels. Rather, he sometimes also punishes through the agency of good angels, as is evident in the case of the angel who smote the camp of the Assyrians, as Is. 37:36 relates. But if the turning of Lot's wife into a pillar of salt happened through the agency of devils, they were evidently instruments of God's power regarding that action. And so God's power, not their own, produced such an effect, and God's power can directly produce any effects, whether the highest or the lowest, as he wishes, and is not subject to the ordination of things. And regarding the companions of Diomedes, Augustine does not say that they were turned into birds, but that devils procured birds to substitute for the companions when the latter had drowned,[291] and the birds, some taking the place of others, deceived human beings for a long time.[292] And this indicates that the incident involved more than an imaginary apparition.

4. Spiritual substances, since they are more actual than material substances, have higher and more universal power. And so they can produce the lowest effects only through the agency of intermediate lower causes.

5. The separate form that is pure actuality, namely, God, is not limited to a species or genus but has without limit the whole power of existing, as he himself is existing itself, as Dionysius makes clear in *On the Divine Names*.[293] And so every action is subject to his power. But other separate forms have a limited specific nature, and so not every form can produce any effect. Rather, each produces what is proper to its nature without any impediment from the deficiency of matter. For example, if heat were to be a separate form, no deficiency of matter incompletely partaking of heat (e.g., lukewarm things) would impede the form's capacity to heat. Still, the separate form of heat could not produce the action emanating from whiteness or a different form.

6. The life-giving power of generation about which Dionysius is speaking can also relate to generating intelligible things, as he himself says in his work *On the Divine Names*.[294] He calls angels the fathers of other things, namely, things they purify, illumine, and perfect. But if the life-giving power relates to bodily generation, we should understand that angels have the power to cause generation through intermediate material causes.

7. The argument of this objection fails in three respects. First, indeed, the argument fails because although angels move the heavens, devils, about which we are presently concerned, do not. Second, the argument fails because although angels cause things by their intellect and will, it does not follow that they can cause things in a way different from the way proportioned to their nature. For angels are not identical with their wills,

---

290. *City of God* XVIII, 18, n. 2 (PL 41:575).

291. Ibid., XVIII, 18, n. 3 (PL 41:575–76).

292. Cf. ibid., X, 11, n. 2 (PL 41:290).

293. *On the Divine Names* 5, n. 4 (PG 3:817D).

294. Ibid., 2, n. 8 (PG 3:645C).

as God is. Rather they have wills belonging to a limited nature, and their wills achieve their effects in accord with their nature. But God is identical with his will and can without reservation do everything subject to his will. Third, the argument fails because even if angels were to move the heavens, and some transformations were to result in lower things, they would effect such transformations through intermediate heavenly bodies, not directly.

8. We say that the power of pure intelligences is infinite regarding lower things insofar as lower things cannot lay hold of it, and insofar as it surpasses them, but not in such a way that it can produce every kind of effect in them.

9. Fire and air and like material substances obey angels by the ordination established by God.

10. The Pharaoh's sorcerers produced frogs by using certain natural causes, which Augustine in his work *On the Trinity* calls seminal,[295] as we understand such causes from the hidden purposes of the elements.

11. The signs or miracles that the sorcerers worked by private pacts with devils are not beyond the ordination of natural causes but happen by the power of such causes beyond the understanding and power of human beings. And there are three explanations of this. First, indeed, devils know the power of natural causes better than human beings do. Second, devils can put them together faster. Third, devils' power or skill can extend the reach of the natural causes they use as instruments to produce greater effects than human beings' power or skill can. And so the deeds of devils seem to human beings to be miracles, just as the deeds performed by tricksters seem to the inexperienced to be miracles.

12. The angelic rank of Powers works miracles instrumentally through God's power.

13. In bewitchment, not only cognitive power alters corporeal matter, as Avicenna held. But corporeal matter is altered because spirits are infected with violent emotions of wrath or hatred, as is often the case with witches, and this infection extends even to the eyes, which infect the surrounding air. And the body of an infant because of its tender age receives an infection in the same way that a new mirror is tainted at the glance of a woman who has just menstruated, as the work *On Dreams* says.[296]

Tenth Article

Can Devils Cause the Locomotion of Material Substances?

It seems that devils cannot, for the following reasons:

1. Locomotion is more perfect than every other motion, as the Philosopher says in the *Physics*.[297] But devils cannot transform material substances. Therefore, much less could they cause the locomotion of material substances.

---

295. *On the Trinity* III, 9, n. 17 (PL 42:877).
296. Aristotle, *On Dreams* 2 (459b27–32).
297. *Physics* VIII, 7 (261a13–23).

2. The soul is a spiritual substance just as devils are. But the soul can only cause the locomotion of the body it vivifies. And so a bodily member is rendered immobile if it should become lifeless. But devils do not vivify a body. Therefore, devils cannot cause the locomotion of material substances.

3. Every causal action is through contact, as the work *On Generation and Corruption* says.[298] But it does not seem that there can be any contact between devils and material substances, since they have nothing in common. Therefore, since locomotion is a causal action, it seems that devils cannot cause the locomotion of material substances.

4. If devils could cause the locomotion of material substances, they would be especially able to cause the locomotion of heavenly bodies, which more closely approximate devils in the ordination of nature. But devils cannot cause the locomotion of heavenly bodies, since if they did, inasmuch as causes of motion and things they move exist together, as the *Physics* says,[299] devils would then exist in the heavens, and neither we nor the followers of Plato[300] hold this to be true. Therefore, much less can devils cause the locomotion of other material substances.

5. Higher things move lower things through intermediaries, as I have said.[301] But heavenly bodies, whose movements cause all earthly movements, are in between spiritual substances and lower material substances. Therefore, devils cannot cause the locomotion of lower material substances, since devils cannot cause the locomotion of heavenly bodies.

6. Locomotion causes other movements, as the *Physics* makes clear.[302] Therefore, if devils were able to cause the locomotion of material substances, they would also then be able to cause the forms of material substances. And what I have said before makes clear that this conclusion is false.[303]

7. Movements of nature result from forms tending to fixed places, as is evident in the movements of heavy and light things. But devils cannot imprint forms on corporeal matter, as I have maintained before.[304] Therefore, if devils should cause the locomotion of material substances, such movement would be coercive.

8. The movement of the whole and parts of the whole is the same, as, for example, the movement of the whole earth and particular clods of earth is the same, as the *Physics* says.[305] Therefore, if devils can move one clod of earth, they by like reasoning move the whole earth, and this devils cannot do, since this would be to change the whole order of the universe. Therefore, devils cannot cause the locomotion of any material substance.

298. Aristotle, *On Generation and Corruption* I, 6 (322b22).
299. Aristotle, *Physics* VII, 2 (243a3ff.).
300. Related by Augustine, *City of God* VIII, 14, n. 1 (PL 41:238).
301. A. 9.
302. Aristotle, *Physics* VIII, 7 (260a26ff.).
303. A. 9.
304. Ibid.
305. Aristotle, *Physics* III, 5 (205a11–12).

On the Contrary:

As Augustine says in his work *On the Trinity*, devils put together seminal causes that they use to produce definite effects.[306] But devils could not do this without locomotion. Therefore, they can cause the locomotion of material substances.

Answer:

As I have said before,[307] we need to consider regarding the actions of causal powers the order of things, which we consider both by their natures and by their movements, for even their movements have an order to one another.

And this happens in two ways. It happens in one way by the movements' nature. And locomotion accordingly has a twofold relation to other movements: in one way in that it is the primary movement; in a second way in that it causes the least change respecting moveable objects. For while other movements change things intrinsically (e.g., in quality or quantity or even substantial form), locomotion changes material things only extrinsically, namely, regarding place. And regarding the twofold relation of movements just mentioned, it is proper that spiritual substances move material substances more directly by locomotion than by other movements. First, it is indeed appropriate because prior things bring about subsequent things, and so spiritual substances cause other movements by means of locomotion. Second, it is appropriate because more distant causes can directly produce weak effects, as I have said before,[308] and so spiritual substances, as distant causes, can directly produce the least material change, which locomotion effects, but no greater change, such as the changes belonging to other movements.

In a second way, we consider the order of movements by the order of moveable objects. For example, the movement of the heavens is prior to the movements of material elements. And it accordingly belongs to spiritual substances to move higher material substances, so that the cause of Saturn's orbit cannot move the stellar heavens, nor could that cause move Saturn were Saturn to have many stars, as the *De caelo et mundo* says.[309] Therefore, as higher spiritual substances move higher heavenly bodies, so also lower spiritual substances such as devils can cause the locomotion of lower material substances. Devils can do this whether they have this power by their natural condition or in proportion to their nature (as some say that devils were from the angels God put in charge of the terrestrial order and not from higher ranks of angels).[310] Or this befits devils as punishment for their sin, for which they were cast down from their heavenly thrones into our atmosphere (as Gregory holds that some of the highest angels fell by their sin).[311]

Replies to the Objections:

1. Locomotion is more perfect than other motions because of the perfection of moveable objects, regarding which locomotion itself causes the least change.

---

306. *On the Trinity* III, 8, n. 13 (PL 42:876).
307. A. 9.
308. Ibid.
309. *On Heaven and Earth* II, 12 (292a21–293a11).
310. John Damascene, *On Orthodox Faith* II, 4 (PG 94:874).
311. *On the Gospels* II, hom. 34, n. 7 (PL 76:1250B), and *Morals* XXXII, 23, n. 48 (PL 76:665C).

2. The human soul holds the lowest rank in the order of spiritual substances and so has no power to move material substances, even locally, unless what it animates is related to them.

3. There is only virtual material contact between devils and material substances, and such contact indeed requires a suitable relationship between the cause of movement and the moveable object.

4. Heavenly bodies are beyond the proportional power of devils either because of their natural condition or because of their culpable damnation, as I have said.[312]

5. The natural movements of lower material substances depend on the movements of heavenly bodies and are caused by them. But other causes can produce some movements in lower material substances. For example, human beings themselves can do so by their will, and by like reasoning, devils and angels can do the same. Nonetheless, the disposition of material substances whereby they can receive such movements depends in some respect on heavenly bodies.

6. Heavenly bodies' locomotion but no other movement causes all the other movements that happen naturally. And if devils should by locomotion alter material substances as regards other movements, they do this by the power of the material substances whose locomotion they cause, not by their own power.

7. Nothing prevents us saying that the material substances whose locomotion devils cause are moved coercively, just as material substances are when human beings cause their locomotion in this way.

8. The natural movement of a whole and its parts is the same, but the same power that moves a part does not suffice to move the whole. And so although devils can move a part of the earth, it does not follow that they can move the whole earth, since it is not proportionate to their nature to alter the order of the world's elements.

Eleventh Article

Can Devils Affect the Soul's Cognitive Powers Regarding the Internal or External Senses?

It seems that devils cannot, for the following reasons:

1. Augustine says in his work *On the Trinity* that forms cause both actual and imaginary vision.[313] But forms that belong to an external sense or the power of imagination are more excellent than the material forms of which they are likenesses, as Augustine makes clear in his *Literal Commentary on Genesis*.[314] Therefore, since devils cannot imprint material forms on corporeal matter, as I have shown before,[315] much less does it seem that they can affect the power of an external sense or the imagination to know something.

---

312. In the answer.
313. *On the Trinity* XI, 2–4 (PL 42:985–90).
314. *Literal Commentary on Genesis* XII, 16, n. 33 (PL 34:467).
315. A. 9.

2. Sense perception and imagination are vital activities. But all vital activities derive from the internal source whereby an animal is alive. Therefore, since devils are external causes, it seems that they cannot cause human beings to imagine or perceive anything.

3. People have said that devils affect the external senses and the power of imagination by restoring already existing forms in sentient spirits to bodily organs of the power of imagination or the external senses, not indeed by imprinting new forms. But Augustine says in his work *On the Trinity* that we need to strive to link visible forms to the power of sight in order to see by any act of sight.[316] And striving belongs to appetitive power, which devils cannot affect, since if they could, they would then compel human beings to sin, inasmuch as sin consists of desire. Therefore, devils cannot cause human beings to perceive or image things by restoring forms to bodily organs of the external senses or the power of imagination.

4. As intelligible forms are related to the intellect, so are sense images related to the power of imagination. But intelligible forms are sometimes present in the intellect without the intellect actually understanding them. Therefore, it seems that although devils restore sense images or imaginary forms to the bodily organ of the power of imagination, they do not thereby cause human beings to imagine things.

5. Such forms in sentient spirits are either potential or actual. But they do not seem to be actual, since the forms of known things seem actually to belong to a knower only when the knower actually knows them. And if they are potential, devils could not affect the bodily organs of the power of imagination or the external senses, since only something actual, not anything potential, affects things. Therefore, devils can cause human beings to perceive things by sense perception or imagination by returning sentient spirits to the bodily organs of their external senses or their power of imagination only by first restoring such forms to actuality from potentiality. And it seems that they cannot do this for the same reason they cannot alter corporeal matter to different forms.

6. As Augustine says in his work *On the Trinity*, devils are active in material things through certain natural seminal things, that is, natural causes.[317] But material substances as external objects are the natural causes constituted to affect the external senses and the power of imagination. Therefore, it seems that devils cannot affect the imagination or the external senses of human beings without such material substances as objects.

7. Augustine says in *City of God* that "the sense image of a human being may" by devils' activity "appear to the senses of others as if the human being had the body of an animal."[318] And it seems from this, by like reasoning, that devils can present things to the senses of human beings only by giving the things material form.

8. The senses are passive powers, and proportional causes affect passive things. And there are two causes proportional to the senses: one, indeed, as their source, as it were, namely, the object; the second as something conveying the source, as it were, as a means. But devils, since they are immaterial, cannot be an object of the senses or even

---

316. *On the Trinity* XI, 2–4 (PL 42:985–90).
317. Ibid., III, 8, n. 13 (PL 42:875).
318. *City of God* XVIII, 18, n. 2 (PL 41:575).

a means. Therefore, it seems that devils cannot cause movements of the senses in either way.

9. If devils affect an internal cognitive power, they do this either by presenting themselves as objects to the cognitive power or by affecting the power. But they do not do this by presenting themselves as objects, since if they did, they would need to assume a body. And then they could not internally enter the bodily organ of the power of imagination, since two material substances cannot be at the same time in the same place. Or else they would need to assume a sense image, and they also cannot do this, since sense images have some quantity, and devils completely lack quantity. Likewise, they cannot do this by affecting the cognitive power, since if they did, they would either cause an intrinsic change or a change of situs (i.e., a locomotion). And it seems that they cannot cause an intrinsic change, since active qualities, which they lack, cause every alteration. And it seems for two reasons inappropriate that devils change the situs of the cognitive power. First, it is indeed unsuitable because they could not cause a change of situs of the bodily organ without the subject experiencing pain. Second, it is inappropriate because devils would present to human beings only things the human beings knew, although Augustine says that devils present to human beings both forms the human beings knew and forms they did not.[319] Therefore, it seems that devils can in no way affect the power of imagination or the external senses of human beings.

10. Transforming sense images prevents intelligible knowledge of the truth, as the Philosopher says in the *Physics*.[320] Therefore, if devils could transform a human being's power of imagination, then they could completely prevent all knowledge of truth.

11. Proximate causes need to be joined to the things they affect, since causes of movement and the things they affect exist together, as the *Physics* proves.[321] But devils cannot be joined to the internal power of imagination, for a gloss of Jerome on Hab. 2:20, "The Lord in his holy temple," says that devils cannot be inside idols, and much less inside human bodies, although they produce external effects.[322] Therefore, it seems that they cannot directly affect the power of imagination.

On the Contrary:

1. Augustine says in his *Book of the 83 Questions*: "This evil," namely, the devil, "creeps in by all the approaches of the senses, gives himself shapes, adapts himself to colors, clings to sounds, subjects himself to odors, infuses with tastes."[323] But such things affect the senses. Therefore, it seems that devils can affect human senses.

2. Augustine says in the *City of God* that the transformations of human beings into irrational animals attributed to devils' skill were only apparently, not really, such.[324] But this could not be so if devils were not able to affect human senses. Therefore, devils can affect human senses.

---

319. Augustine (Pseudo), *On Spirit and Soul* 28 (PL 40:799).
320. *Physics* VII, 3 (247b11ff.).
321. Ibid., 2 (243a3ff.).
322. *Interlinear Gloss*, on Hab. 2:20.
323. *Book of the 83 Questions*, q. 12 (PL 40:14).
324. *City of God* XVIII, 18, n. 2 (PL 41:575).

Answer:

Evident signs and experiences make it apparent that devils' activities manifest things sensibly perceptible to human beings. And this indeed happens because devils present external bodies to human senses, both things that pre-exist as formed by nature or things that devils themselves form by natural seminal causes, as is evident from what I have said before.[325] And there is no doubt about this, since the presence of perceptible material substances naturally affects human senses. But devils sometimes cause things that do not subsist in the external world to appear to human beings. And there is doubt about how this can be.

Augustine in his *Literal Commentary on Genesis* touches on this question, proposing three ways, in one or the other of which devils cause unreal things to appear to human beings.[326] He prefaces his discussion by saying that some wanted the human soul in itself to have a power of divination, and this seems to agree with the opinions of the Platonists, who held that the soul has knowledge of every kind of thing by sharing in the Ideas.[327] Augustine then rejects this view by arguing that if human beings were to have divination within their power, they could always divine whenever they wished, and this is obviously false. Therefore, he concludes that human beings need help from something external in order to divine, indeed from a spirit and not from a material substance.

He next asks how spirits help the soul to perceive things: "Does the body possess something so that it allows the soul's attention to be elevated, something whereby the soul comes to a state in which the soul sees in itself meaningful likenesses that were already there but unperceived, just as we have many things in our memory that we are not always recalling? Or are previously nonexistent likenesses produced there?" And he adds a third alternative: "Or are the likenesses in a spirit, where the soul, breaking out and rising, perceives them?"

But the third alternative is completely impossible. For the human soul in the condition of its present life cannot be so elevated as to perceive the very essence of spiritual and immaterial substances, since we in the condition of our present life do not understand without sense images, and we cannot by means of them know what any spiritual substance is. And much less can we perceive the intelligible forms in the mind of spiritual substances, since "no one knows what belongs to a person except the person's spirit within the person."[328] And whatever be the case regarding intellectual knowledge of the human soul, it is certain that the vision of imagination or the external senses can in no way be elevated to perceive immaterial substances and the forms in it, which are only intelligible. Therefore, when Augustine adds that it is doubtful whether the soul perceives in itself or in conjunction with another spirit,[329] we should understand that there is a conjunction because a spiritual substance effects something regarding the soul, not because the soul perceives a spiritual substance. And so we understand the conjunction as a spiritual substance's effect, not as its very substance or the things in it.

---

325. A. 9, a. 10, and objection 6.
326. *Literal Commentary on Genesis* XII, 13, n. 27 (PL 34:464).
327. Related by Aristotle, *Metaphysics* I, 9 (991a8ff.).
328. 1 Cor. 2:11.
329. *Literal Commentary on Genesis* XII, 13, n. 27 (PL 34:464).

Likewise, the second of the three mentioned ways, namely, that previously nonexistent likenesses arise anew in the soul, is impossible. For devils cannot infuse new forms into corporeal matter, as is evident from what I have said before.[330] And so neither can they infuse new forms into the external senses and the power of imagination, in which nothing is received without a bodily organ.

And so there remains the first alternative, namely, that there pre-exists in the body things that changes in the situs of vapors and fluids restore to the sources of the sense organs' acts, so that the soul perceives the things by imaginary vision or external sense perception. For I have said that devils can by their own power cause the locomotion of material substances,[331] and changes in the situs of vapors and fluids even regarding natural activities may result in the power of imagination or the external senses perceiving things. For the Philosopher in his work *On Dreams*, when assigning the causes of apparitions in dreams, says that when animals have been sleeping, most of their blood sinks into the sources of sense perception.[332] And the movements or impressions left by movements of the senses and preserved in sentient spirits sink with the blood and move the sources of sense perception in such a way that certain things seem as if the external things previously experienced were currently affecting the sources. And devils can in this way affect the power of imagination and the external senses, both of those asleep and of those awake.

Replies to the Objections:

1. Devils cannot imprint new forms on the bodily sense organs, but they can somehow translocate forms stored in sense organs, so that those forms cause apparitions.

2. Vital activities, insofar as powers produce them, always result from internal causes. But insofar as objects cause the activities, the activities can result from external causes. For example, visible things cause acts of sight. And devils affect external senses in this way, namely, by presenting objects.

3. Striving is the act of an appetitive power. And there are indeed two kinds of appetite. One kind is a sense appetite, which is indeed the power of a bodily organ. And so material changes can cause such a power's acts. For example, adding or subtracting material things causes a sense appetite to seek or avoid things. And the other appetitive power, namely, the will, is intellectual, and material changes only dispositively affect the will, since it has no bodily organ. But both human beings themselves, insofar as their will moves itself, and God, who acts interiorly, can efficaciously affect the will. And so devils cannot in this regard cause the soul to strive for anything.

4. An intention of the will is required in order that human beings actually contemplate by forms habitually in their intellect, since habits are the means whereby one acts whenever one wants to, as the *De anima* says.[333] And likewise, animals by the striving of their sense appetites may actually imagine things previously stored in their memory, but human beings can also do this by the intention of their intellectual appetite, as the higher appetite moves lower appetites.

---

330. A. 9.
331. A. 10.
332. *On Dreams* 3 (461b11ff.).
333. Actually, Averroes, *On Aristotle's On the Soul* III, comm. 18.

5. Forms already in sense organs are in between complete actuality and pure potentiality, as also are forms habitually in the intellect. And only the striving of appetites restores such forms to complete actuality.

6. Nature constitutes that proper causes affect the sense perception of human beings, as it were, in two ways: in one way by external causes, and movements from things to the soul indeed accomplish this; in a second way by internal causes, and movements from the soul to things indeed accomplish this. And devils can use both kinds of causes to affect the power of imagination and the external senses of human beings.

7. We should not understand the cited words of Augustine to mean that devils supply human beings' very power of imagination or even forms stored in it with materiality, so as to present the forms to the senses of others. Rather, we should understand that devils themselves, who fashion forms in the imagination of particular human beings, either present other like forms externally in a material way to others' senses or produce like forms internally in their senses.

8. Devils affect human beings' power of imagination or external senses insofar as they convey proper objects of the power of imagination or the external senses, not as if they present themselves as means or objects, as I have said.[334]

9. Devils do not affect the external senses or the power of imagination by presenting themselves to the senses or power as objects, as I have shown,[335] but by changing the senses or power. They do not indeed change the senses or power by alteration except as a consequence of locomotion, since they cannot of themselves imprint new forms, as I have said.[336] And they affect the senses or power by translocation or locomotion, by moving vapors and fluids, not indeed by dividing the substance of a bodily organ with a resulting sensation of pain. And regarding the further objection that the consequence of this will be that devils cannot present anything new to human beings, we should say that we can understand "new" in two ways. In one way, we can understand "new" to mean completely new both as such and regarding its sources, and devils cannot in this way present anything new to human beings as to their imagination. For example, devils cannot cause persons born blind to imagine colors or persons born deaf to imagine sounds. In a second way, we call something "new" regarding the form of the whole thing. For example, such would be the case if we should say that it is a new image in the imagination for a person to imagine gold mountains never before seen. But because the person has seen gold and mountains, the person can by a natural movement imagine the image of a gold mountain. And devils can in this way also present new things to human beings' imagination by different compositions of movements and forms, certain seeds, as it were, hidden in sense organs, whose potential devils know.

10. As Augustine says in his work *On the Trinity*,[337] devils can do many things by their natural power that they cannot do because God forbids the things. Therefore, we should say that devils can by their natural power completely prevent human beings' intellectual cognition by disturbing sense images, as is evident in the case of the possessed. But devils are not always allowed to do this.

---

334. In the answer.
335. Ibid.
336. Ibid.
337. *On the Trinity* III, 9, n. 18 (PL 42:878).

11. Because good or bad angels are wherever they are active, as Damascene says,[338] it follows that devils, when they move fluids and vapors in order to present something, are there. And regarding Jerome's assertion that devils are not inside idols, we should not understand this to mean that devils cannot be within a place, since, as spiritual substances, they cannot be prevented from penetrating material substances. Rather, we should understand the statement to mean that devils are not inside idols as souls are in bodies, so that devils and idols do not constitute substantial units, as the Gentiles thought.

Twelfth Article

Can Devils Affect Human Beings' Intellect?

It seems that devils cannot, for the following reasons:

1. The human intellect is comparable to the sun, as Wis. 5:6 says out of the mouth of the wicked: "The sun of understanding has not risen on us." But devils cannot affect the visibility of the sun. Therefore, much less can they affect the human intellect.

2. Only what is potential is subject to change. But the human soul is completely actual regarding intelligible things and even imaginary things. For Augustine says in his *Literal Commentary on Genesis*: "Although we first see a material substance that we did not previously see, and then its image arises in our spirit, by means of which we remember it when it is absent, the very spirit in itself, not the body in the spirit, produces the image."[339] And he says in his work *On the Trinity* that "the soul envelops the images of material substances and seizes the images, when produced, within itself from itself."[340] Therefore, it seems that devils cannot affect the human intellect.

3. The power of imagination more approximates the human intellect than devils do, since the power of imagination is rooted in the same substance of the soul. But the power of imagination cannot affect human beings' intellectual power, since the material does not affect the immaterial. Therefore, it seems that devils cannot affect the human intellect.

4. The intellect is related to intelligible things as matter is to forms, and forms actualize matter just as intelligible things actualize the intellect. But if there be some matter that always has the same form present in it, the matter can never be changed to another form, as is evident in the case of heavenly bodies. But the human intellect has the same intelligible thing always present in it, namely, itself, since it is always intelligible to itself. Therefore, in no way can devils change it to another intelligible thing.

5. Teachers, who bring their pupils' intellect from potentiality to actuality, affect it in the strict sense, as the Philosopher says in the *Physics*.[341] But only God teaches internally, as Augustine says in his work *On the Teacher*.[342] Therefore, it seems that devils cannot affect the intellect internally.

---

338. *On Orthodox Faith* I, 13 (PG 94:852A).
339. *Literal Commentary on Genesis* XII, 16, n. 33 (PL 34:467).
340. *On the Trinity* X, 5 (PL 42:977).
341. *Physics* VIII, 4 (255a33–b5).
342. *On the Teacher* 14, n. 46 (PL 32:1220).

6. Enlightenment affects the intellect. And enlightening the intellect belongs to God, who "enlightens every human being coming into the world," as Jn. 1:9 says. But enlightening the intellect does not belong to devils, since light has no company with darkness, as 2 Cor. 6:14 says. Therefore, it seems that devils do not affect the intellect.

7. Two things, namely, the light of the intellect and intelligible forms, produce intellectual knowledge. But devils cannot move the soul to intellectual knowledge regarding the light of the intellect, since that light pre-exists in human beings by nature. Likewise, devils cannot move the soul to intellectual knowledge regarding intelligible forms, since the forms of the intellect of spiritual substances are more universal and not proportionate to the human intellect. Therefore, in neither way can devils affect the human soul regarding intellectual knowledge.

8. Augustine says in his *Book of the 83 Questions* that those who do not truly understand understand nothing.[343] But it belongs to devils to lead human beings to falsity rather than truth, as Jn. 8:44 says: "When he [the devil] lies, he speaks characteristically." Therefore, it seems that devils cannot affect the human soul regarding intellectual knowledge.

On the Contrary:

1. Augustine says in the *City of God* that a philosopher explained some doctrines of Plato to someone in his dreams, and Augustine attributes this phenomenon to the activity of devils.[344] Therefore, devils can affect the human soul to understand things.

2. Commenting on Job. 37:8, "The beast will enter his cave," Gregory says in his work *Morals* that devils can enter the mind even of the saints but cannot stay there.[345] Therefore, it seems that devils can move the human mind to understand things.

3. Augustine says in the *City of God* that a devil can use a wise man's soul as he wishes.[346] But a wise man's soul is most powerful. Therefore, it seems that devils can much more move other souls to understand things.

4. Augustine says in his *Literal Commentary on Genesis* that as human beings' spirit of imagination is aided to perceive imaginary forms, so also their mind is aided to be able to understand those forms.[347] But devils by aiding human beings' power of imagination cause it to see images. Therefore, devils by aiding the mind cause it to understand things.

Answer:

We should consider two things regarding the activity of devils: first, indeed, what they can do by their natural power; second, how they use their natural power out of the wickedness of their will. Therefore, regarding their natural power, devils can do the same things that good angels can, since both have the same nature. But there is different use of the power according to the goodness or wickedness of the will. For good angels out of the virtue of charity strive to help human beings to attain goodness and complete knowledge of truth, and devils strive to prevent such knowledge and other things good for human beings.

343. *Book of the 83 Questions*, q. 32 (PL 40:22).
344. *City of God* XVIII, 18, n. 2 (PL 41:575).
345. *Morals* XXVII, 26, n. 50 (PL 76:429B).
346. *City of God* XIX, 4, n. 2 (PL 41:628).
347. *Literal Commentary on Genesis* XII, 13, n. 27 (PL 34:464).

And we should note that two things, namely, the light of the intellect and intelligible forms, accomplish the intellectual activity of human beings, but in such a way that the forms cause understanding of things, and the light of the intellect causes judgments about the things understood.

And the human soul has an intellectual light, which is indeed inferior to the angels' intellectual light. And so as the higher powers of material things aid and strengthen lower powers, so the angels' intellectual light can strengthen the light of the human intellect to judge more perfectly. And good angels strive for this, but bad angels do not. And so good angels in this way cause the soul to understand, but devils do not.

And regarding intelligible forms, good or bad angels can affect the human intellect as to understanding things by externally using signs that arouse the intellect to understand things, which even human beings can do, not indeed by infusing forms into the intellect itself. And even more, good or bad angels can somehow internally dispose and arrange forms of the imagination insofar as such dispositions and arrangements are appropriate for apprehending intelligible things. And good angels indeed arrange forms of the imagination for human beings' good. And devils do likewise for their evil. Devils arrange forms of the imagination whether to desire sin, namely, as the things human beings apprehend induce them to pride or some other sin, or to prevent true understanding itself, as things apprehended lead human beings into doubts they do not know how to resolve, and then into error. And so Augustine says in his *Book of the 83 Questions* that "the devil befogs, as it were, all the paths of understanding whereby the mind's rays usually diffuse the light of reason."[348]

Replies to the Objections:

1. The potential intellect of human beings is comparable to air or any diaphanous material capable of being illumined, not to the sun. And Plato, since he held the active intellect to be a separate substance, indeed compares the active intellect to the sun, as Themistius says in his *Commentary on the De anima*.[349] And so also Augustine in his *Soliloquies* compares God to the sun.[350] But Aristotle compares the active intellect to light partaken in a material substance.[351]

2. It is false to say that the soul is completely actual either regarding intelligible things or sensibly perceptible things. For we distinguish two kinds of intellect in the human soul, namely, the active intellect and the potential intellect. And the potential intellect has potentiality for every intelligible thing. And so the Philosopher in the *De anima* compares the potential intellect to a tablet on which nothing has been written.[352]

But the active intellect is indeed an actuality of all intelligible things whereby all things become intelligible. This indeed does not happen in such a way that the active intellect actually includes in itself all intelligible things, just as light, to which the active intellect is comparable, does not actually include in itself all colors. Rather, light makes

---

348. *Book of the 83 Questions*, q. 12 (PL 40:14).
349. *Commentary on the De anima* III (Heinze:103).
350. *Soliloquies* 6, n. 12, and 8 (PL 32:875, 877).
351. *De anima* III, 5 (430a14).
352. Ibid., 4 (429b31–430a2).

all colors actually visible, and the active intellect likewise makes all things actually intelligible. And so material substances and the bodily senses do not cause intelligible forms in the intellect. Rather, the intellect causes the forms by the active intellect and receives the forms in the potential intellect. This is as bodily eyes, if they were to possess light and were to be actually luminous, would make colors actually visible insofar as the eyes were actually luminous, and would receive colors insofar as the eyes were diaphanous and devoid of all color, as is somewhat evident in the case of cats' eyes.

And regarding imaginable things, the power of imagining all things is not completely actual, and sense impressions bring the power into action. For imagination is "a movement caused by the activity of the senses," as the *De anima*[353] says; otherwise, a person born blind could imagine colors. And the action of the sense object on a sense organ causes actual sense perception.

And so Augustine says in his work *On the Trinity* that the external senses receive forms from the material substances they perceive, and the power of memory receives forms from the senses, and the knower's inner vision receives forms from the power of memory.[354] And we should understand his statement in the *Literal Commentary on Genesis*, "The very spirit in itself, not the body in the spirit, produces a material substance's image,"[355] to mean that the material power of external perceptible objects is insufficient to produce perceptible forms as perceived, or imaginary forms as imagined. Rather, the power of the soul produces the forms. But external material substances have the power to affect bodily organs, and this change results in sense perception by the power of the soul. And so Augustine says in his work *On the Trinity*: "We cannot say that visible objects beget sense perception, but they beget forms as their likenesses, which are produced in our sense of sight when we see things."[356] And so also should we understand all similar expressions of Augustine. But we can also understand in another way that the spirit produces imaginary forms in itself, namely, insofar as the spirit begets imaginary forms by combining them in different ways (e.g., the image of a gold mountain, as I have said before).[357]

3. The power of imagination is more one with the human intellect in the subject of both powers. But good or bad angels' intellect is more one with the human intellect regarding the nature of the forms in the respective powers. And so good or bad angels' intellect can affect the human intellect in a way that the power of imagination cannot affect it. And yet the power of imagination somehow affects the potential intellect by the power of the active intellect, not indeed by its own power. For the Philosopher says in the *De anima* that sense images are related to the potential intellect as colors are related to the power of sight.[358] And so as light endows colors with an instrumental power to cause an immaterial change in the power of sight, so also sense images, insofar as they act instrumentally regarding the power of the active intellect, actualize the potential intellect regarding intelligible forms.

353. Ibid., 3 (429a1–2).
354. *On the Trinity* XI, 8, n. 14 (PL 42:995).
355. *Literal Commentary on Genesis* XII, 16, n. 33 (PL 34:467).
356. *On the Trinity* XI, 2, n. 3 (PG 42:986).
357. A. 11, the reply to objection 9.
358. *De anima* III, 7 (431a14–15).

4. There is a difference regarding the angels' intellect and the human intellect. For the angels' intellect is like an actual being within the genus of intelligible things. And so their intellect understands its essence by reason of its very self and understands by reason of its essence everything else it understands. For it is not inappropriate that forms receive other forms, as, for example, surfaces receive colors. And so external things can alter material substances, which always have surfaces, to this or that. But the human soul's potential intellect is like a completely potential being within the genus of intelligible things. And so the soul's potential intellect can understand itself only as intelligible forms actualize it.

5. Only God, who is even the author of the intellect's natural light, teaches human beings by acting internally on their intellect. But angels or devils or human beings can teach by presenting the intellect's object to it, as I have said before.[359]

6. Both the intellect's light and its object can cause its activity, as I have said.[360]

7. Regarding the light of the intellect, good angels can affect the intellect by strengthening the natural light, not indeed by causing it in itself, as I have said.[361] But regarding intelligible forms, both angels and devils can affect the human intellect, not indeed by bringing to the human intellect forms equal to their own forms, but in the way I mentioned before,[362] by composing imaginary forms or even by using external signs. Just so, human beings can make known to others deep intellectual thoughts of theirs by explaining the thoughts as befits the understanding of their audience.

8. Devils strive to lead human beings to lies by means of the very truths devils manifest.

Replies to the Arguments in the Section On the Contrary:
Gregory does not say that devils can enter the mind of human beings substantially. Rather, he says the devils can do so by their effects, namely, insofar as they incite human beings to think about particular things.

Augustine says that devils can use a wise man's soul as they wish, insofar as, God permitting, they sometimes prevent the use of reason in human beings, as is evident in the case of the possessed.

359. In the answer.
360. Ibid.
361. A. 11.
362. Ibid.

Glossary of Terms

The meanings of several key terms used by Aquinas in the *De malo* are explained in the introduction to this book. What follows is a brief account of the meaning of some other terms used in the *De malo* that may puzzle readers unfamiliar with the writings of Aquinas.

Accident (*accidens*): A property or attribute truly ascribable to a substance without being necessary to it for it to exist as what it essentially is. Hence, for example, someone's temperature at some specific time, or someone's particular eye color, would, for Aquinas, be accidents of that person (on the assumption that one can get warmer or cooler without ceasing to be human, and on the assumption that, for example, both blue- and green-eyed people are all human beings). On this account, one and the same substance can acquire and lose various accidents over time. And accidents can exist only in substances and can only truly be ascribed to them (i.e., they have no existence apart from the substances of which they are accidents). *See also* Essence, Potential/Potentiality/Potentially, *and* Substance.

Acquired (*acquisitus*): A term which Aquinas uses to describe that which a created agent can bring about in or for itself by its natural abilities (by virtue of its essence). Aquinas frequently uses the term to describe human dispositions (*habitus*) conceived of as explicable in terms of human choices and activity, as opposed to divine agency *only*. *See also* Essence *and* Infused.

Angel: For Aquinas, an essentially incorporeal creature vastly more intelligent than human beings but in no way equal to God. Aquinas derives his belief in angels chiefly from the Bible. And his view of them owes much to Dionysius the Areopagite. Since he takes them to be non-material, and since he holds that individual members of a genus or species must all be material entities, Aquinas teaches that each angel constitutes a distinct species. On his account, angels differ from each other, not as distinct members of a kind, but as, for example, redness and rectangularity (or felinity and humanity) would differ from each other if they were distinct, existing entities (which Aquinas, by the way, does not think they are). Aquinas's clearest and most sustained discussion of angels is to be found in *Summa theologiae* Ia, 50–64. *See also* Devil, Genus, *and* Species.

Cause (*causa*): What we are seeking to know about whenever we ask "How come?" or "What accounts for this?" or "What explains that?" Much indebted to the teaching found in Aristotle's *Physics*, Aquinas regularly distinguishes between four kinds of causes: efficient, formal, final, and material. We may ask: "What produced or brought X about?" or "What must Y be like if it can manage to account for that?" or "Why (aiming at what) did he do that?" or "What physical properties account for this being the case?" (as, for example, when asking, "Why did the glass shatter when I dropped it, though the wooden bowl did not?"). According to Aquinas, true answers to such questions would put us in touch with, respectively, an efficient cause, a formal cause, a final cause, and a material cause. Causes, for Aquinas, are not always individual entities (in the sense that, for example, particular material objects are). They can be natures, intentions, and physical characteristics. According to Aquinas, God is the cause of all causes and an efficient, formal, and final cause, though not a material one. For the most part, Aquinas thinks of efficient causes as agents that bring about some kind of change. But he denies that God's efficient causality is only a matter of his effecting change (though he thinks that God does this). For he deems God to have produced the world from nothing (*ex nihilo*) and without modifying anything. And (as the *De malo* makes clear), he thinks of God as efficiently causing human actions without acting on people as an external agent bringing about a change in something which exists apart from and independent of the agent in question.

Charity (*caritas*): For Aquinas, the primary theological virtue. It is infused by God, for it is a sharing in the life of love which characterizes the Blessed Trinity. Or, as Aquinas writes in the *Summa theologiae*: "The divine essence itself is charity even as it is wisdom and goodness. Now we are said to be good with the goodness which is God and wise with the wisdom which is God, because the very qualities which make us formally so are participations in the divine goodness and wisdom" (2a2ae, 23,1 ad1). Charity, for Aquinas, is the virtue by which we love God for the sake of God alone. It is also the virtue by which we love things other than God for the sake of the goodness that God is. Aquinas offers a definition of charity in *Summa theologiae* 2a2ae, 24, 1: "Charity is an *amicitia* [friendship] of people for God, founded upon the fellowship of everlasting happiness. Now this fellowship is in respect, not of natural, but of gratuitous gifts. . . . So charity surpasses our natural faculties. Now that which surpasses the faculty of nature cannot be natural or acquired by natural powers since a natural effect does not transcend its cause. Therefore charity can be in us neither naturally, nor through acquisition by the natural powers, but by the infusion of the Holy Spirit, who is the love of the Father and the Son, and the participation of whom in us is created charity." *See also* Acquired *and* Infused.

Concupiscence (*concupiscentia*): The appetite or desire for what is perceived as physically pleasurable in some way (which includes the appetite or desire to avoid what is physically damaging). For Aquinas, it belongs to us as sensual beings. Though he thinks that it can lead us to act badly, he does not conceive of it as a bad thing. Indeed, so he thinks, we would be badly impaired without it. We might, for example, starve to death.

Counsels, Evangelical: *See* Evangelical Counsels.

Devil (*demon*): An angel whose will is set against that of God. An angel who has sinned. Aquinas's teaching on devils is chiefly derived from his reading of Scripture and Patristic authors, together with his own attempts to make sense of the notion of fallen angels. For Aquinas on angelic sin, see *Summa theologiae* Ia, 63 and 64. *See also* Angel.

Essence (*essentia*): That which makes a substance to be the kind of thing it is. For Aquinas, to understand something's essence (not, in his view, an easy thing to do, and impossible for human beings when it comes to the essence of God) is to understand precisely *what it is* by comparison with, and by contrast to, things of *other kinds* (things belonging to a different genus or species). Aquinas repeatedly maintains that the essence of everything other than God can be distinguished from its existence. Much ink has been spilled in trying to explain what Aquinas means by this teaching. All he is basically saying, however, is that everything other than God is what it is by virtue of him, and that God depends on nothing for being what he (changelessly) is. *See also* Form, Genus, Species, *and* Substance.

Evangelical counsels (*consilia evangelica*): Poverty, chastity, and obedience, considered as states of life to which members of religious orders freely commit themselves. Aquinas contrasts them with evangelical *precepts*, and he takes them to be recommended, though not commanded, by Christ. Aquinas explains his distinction between evangelical counsels and precepts in *Summa theologiae* Ia2ae, 108, 4.

Form (*forma*): That by which something is what it is, whether accidentally or essentially. Aquinas distinguishes between accidental forms and substantial forms. He takes an accidental form to be a property or attribute that something has even though it would not cease to be the kind of thing it essentially is without it. He takes a substantial form to be what something has insofar as it has an essence. On his account, therefore, a thing simply ceases to exist as the kind of thing it is if it loses its substantial form. Indeed, for Aquinas, it simply ceases to exist. *See also* Accident, Essence, Matter, *and* Substance.

Formally (*formaliter*): To be contrasted with "materially" (*materialiter*) as a way of understanding ways in which we talk. Consider, for example, the sentence "The dog is dying." And suppose that I use this sentence to assert something true of some particular dog. Aquinas would say that "taken materially," my words "the dog" refer to some particular animal (e.g., Rover). But, so he would add, "is dying" can be "taken formally" to signify a meaning, not an individual or a particular process or a particular state of affairs (on the assumption that none of these can be the meaning of a word). And, with this line of thinking in mind, Aquinas sometimes says that our talk about actions (and, therefore, the actions themselves) can be understood either materially or formally. When doing so, he is, as we might put it, drawing a contrast between (a) what a camera can capture when filming someone's behavior (the person's deed), and (b) what the person's behavior really amounts to when properly reflected on from a moral point of view (the deed as morally good or evil in specific ways). *See also* Materially.

Genus (*genus*): A general term of classification that Aquinas employs in talking about a wide range of things (naturally occurring units in nature, but also, for instance, mathematical figures and human actions) . For Aquinas, members of a genus are all genuinely alike in some important way, though they may differ specifically. *See also* Species

Infused (*infusus*): According to Aquinas, there are dispositions (*habitus*) that people cannot acquire by means of their natural human abilities. These, so he thinks, can be brought about in them only by God. Or, as Aquinas frequently puts it, they must be "infused" by God. For Aquinas, the key Christian virtues of faith, hope, and charity (the "theological virtues") are all infused in those who have them. Aquinas also thinks that God may infuse virtues which can, in principle, be naturally acquired by them. In this context, the distinction between "acquired" and "infused" is a way of distinguishing between nature and grace. *See also* Acquired.

Lending at interest (*usuria/mutare ad usuram*): Aquinas takes usury chiefly to consist in the attempt to charge borrowers for money lent to them. And he believes it to be unjust. Following Aristotle (*Ethics* V, 5. 1133a20), he understands money to be nothing but a means of exchange. And (following thinking codified in Roman law) he says that its *use* cannot be thought of as something separate from *it* (i.e., that money and its use are identical). On this basis, he argues that to charge someone for the use of money (to charge borrowers for the use of money lent to them) is to charge for the same thing twice over (to charge for the money and, additionally, to charge for its use, even though the money and its use are, in fact, identical). Effectively, Aquinas takes usury to be an attempt to charge someone for nothing.

Materially (*materialiter*). To be contrasted with "formally" (*formaliter*) as a way of understanding ways in which we talk. *See also* Formally.

Matter (*materia*). Sometimes Aquinas uses the word "matter" as equivalent to the contemporary English word "stuff" or "material" in sentences like "What stuff is that object made of?" or "Stone is the best material to use for building houses." But he also uses the word to signify that which, if it ceased to exist, might turn something having a nature into something else, as a cow can turn into beef. For Aquinas, matter is what allows us to speak of things' having a capacity for substantial change. It is that factor by which quite distinct individual things are historically connected in a substantial change so that *this* individual is made out of *that* one. Considered as such, matter, for Aquinas, is not intelligible (not something of which we can form a concept to share in talking to others). Rather, it is what we grasp by means of the senses as we recognize that *this* thing (identified by gestures of pointing and the like) is the same as, or derives from, *that* thing (again, identified by gestures of pointing and the like). How do you know that Mary and Jane are two people, not one person? For Aquinas, you cannot explain the difference between Mary and Jane by noting their different accidents (for, so he thinks, two things cannot have different accidents unless they are distinct to begin with). And two things with the same nature can hardly, so Aquinas thinks, be distinguished by talk that refers to their nature (for this is something they share). In the end, so Aquinas thinks, we lay hold of the individuality of things at a sensory level. And he uses the word "matter" to refer to what we lay hold of at this level. *See also* Accident, Form, *and* Substance.

Potential (potentialis)/Potentiality (potentia)/Potentially (potentiā): Terms used by Aquinas when drawing a contrast between how things *are* and how things really (as opposed to logically) *could be*. Something that is actually thus and so might (given its nature and the context in which it finds itself) undergo change and become actually different. For example, a dry towel might become wet. Here Aquinas will say that the towel was once *actually* dry and *potentially* wet, and that it is now *actually* wet and *potentially* dry. Or he will say that the towel, when actually dry, had the *potential* to be wet, or that it was *potentially* wet. In speaking of something's potential or potentiality, Aquinas is sometimes referring to its powers: to what it can do (active power, as in "I can swim") or to what can be done to it (passive power, as in "I can be harmed"). According to Aquinas, potentiality (always contrasted with actuality) is a feature of creaturely existence and in no way belongs to God. For Aquinas, God is wholly immutable (i.e., God cannot in any respect be different what he eternally is).

Purgatory (purgatorium): A state of existence for those who have died free of mortal sin but still attached to sin. A state after death in which people undergo a limited degree of punishment for venial sin. The notion of there being a state between death and beatitude can be found among Christians as early as the time of St Augustine. It was elaborated on by Gregory the Great. Aquinas further develops the notion in the *De malo*.

Soul (anima): For Aquinas, that which makes living things to be *living* things. On his account, therefore, *anything* alive (anything *animate*) has a soul. But different things have different ways of being alive (e.g., what it takes to be a living plant is different from what it takes to be a living sheep). So Aquinas distinguishes between different kinds of soul (different ways of being alive). In the case of people, so he thinks, to be alive is (among other things) to have knowledge and understanding (potentially, if not actually). And, since he holds that knowledge cannot belong to any purely physical object, he argues that the human soul is something immaterial which exists as an individual thing (something "subsistent"). In arguing in this way, Aquinas is not suggesting that people are essentially immaterial substances. He means that to be alive as a human being is not just to be a purely physical object. His views on the human soul lead Aquinas to accept that the souls of the dead continue to exist. But he does not think that these souls ("separated souls," as he calls them) can be strictly identified with the people whose souls they are. On his account, the union of soul and body is, in people, a natural one, so that the separation of soul and body is unnatural for human beings. "My soul," says Aquinas, "is not me" (cf. 15: 17–19 of his commentary on 1 Corinthians). Aquinas concludes that people can really be said to survive death only insofar as their souls are reunited to their bodies (i.e., the notion of resurrection is crucial in his account of human immortality). The main elements of Aquinas's teaching on the human soul can be found in *Summa theologiae* Ia, 75–89.

Species (*species*): A term of classification. Following Aristotle, Aquinas distinguishes between all sorts of things (things in nature, but also, for example, actions) by dividing them into genera and species. On his account, to identify something in terms of its species is to locate it more precisely than by noting the genus to which it belongs. So he thinks that there can be things of different species which all fall within one genus. Readers should realize that, when he discriminates with respect to genus and species, Aquinas does not take himself to be drawing arbitrary distinctions, or to be distinguishing between things merely from the viewpoint of human convenience or convention. He takes himself to be noting genuine similarities and differences which are actually there in the things of which he is speaking. *See also* Genus.

Spiritual apathy (*accidia*): The Latin word *accidia* derives from the Greek word ἀκηδία and is not easily translated into contemporary English, though the word *accidie* existed in old English (one can find it in the writings of Geoffrey Chaucer, for instance). In the Greek translation of the Old Testament (the Septuagint) ἀκηδία occurs several times to mean "negligence" or "indifference." But the word (and translations of it) entered into Christian vocabulary chiefly in monastic circles and in ascetical literature. The word ἀκηδία occurs in the *Praktikos* of Evagrius Ponticus (346–99), where it signifies a malaise affecting monks. In his *Institutes*, John Cassian, using the term *accidia*, reflects what Evagrius says about ἀκηδία and describes it as a matter of sadness, restlessness, spiritual torpor, and sloth (cf. *Institutes* 10. 2). Readers of the *De malo* should get a good sense of what Aquinas understands by *accidia* from the way in which he uses the term. For a succinct account of the meaning of ἀκηδία in Evagrius, see Simon Tugwell, *Ways of Imperfection* (London, 1984), p. 27: "This is a condition in which we cannot settle down to anything; nothing appeals to us, nothing engages our interests. We go wandering round the room, peering out of the window to see whether we are any nearer to supper time. The day seems eighty hours long. And nobody comes to visit us, so we start thinking bitter thoughts about the lack of charity among other people. Then we begin to wonder what the point of it all is anyway; we could perfectly well lead our christian lives elsewhere. Everything that we have to do goes sour on us."

Substance (*substantia*): Aquinas takes a substance to be an individual that exists in its own right and is not just a property or aspect of something (i.e., not an accident). Typical examples of substances, for Aquinas, would be a particular dog or a particular human being. Aquinas believes that some substances can cease to exist because they can turn into different substances—as, so he thinks, happens when, for example, a cow is butchered and becomes a unit of beef. In referring to this kind of change in a substance, Aquinas commonly uses the expression "substantial change." *See also* Accident, Form, *and* Matter.

Synderesis (*synderesis*): The faculty by which people immediately (i.e., not on the basis of inference) recognize the truth of general principles of practical reasoning (e.g., "Good is to be done and evil avoided"). Aquinas thinks of *synderesis* as a disposition (*habitus*). Cf. *De veritate* XVI, 1: "Just as there is a natural disposition of the human mind by which it apprehends the principles of theoretical disciplines, which we call the understanding of principles, so too it has a natural disposition concerned with the basic principles of behaviour. . . . This disposition relates to *synderesis* . . . We may therefore conclude that 'synderesis' either names a natural disposition, without qualification, comparable to the disposition by which theoretical principles are apprehended, or names the potentiality of reason endowed with such a disposition."

Glossary of Authors and Works Cited

Alan of Lille (d. A.D. 1203). Poet, theologian, and preacher who fought against the Catharist heresy.

Alexander of Hales (A.D. c. 1170/1185–1245). A philosopher and theologian whose doctrines influenced St. Bonaventure. A diocesan priest, he became a Franciscan in 1236. The *Summa of Theology* attributed to him is largely the work of his followers.

Ambrose, St. (A.D. c. 339–397). Doctor of the church, bishop of Milan, theologian, famous preacher and upholder of orthodoxy, who helped to introduce Eastern theology to the West and whose writings on Christian ethics were influenced by Cicero. He baptized St. Augustine of Hippo, who greatly respected him.

Anselm, St. (A.D. c. 1033–1109). Doctor of the church, abbot of Bec and archbishop of Canterbury. Much influenced by St. Augustine of Hippo, he was also a philosopher and theologian with a special interest in defending Christian faith by means of reasoning rather than by argument from Scripture.

Apuleius (fl. c. A.D. 155). Latin poet, philosopher, and rhetorician, best known for his romance *The Golden Ass*.

Aristotle (384–322 B.C.). Greek philosopher and natural scientist, student of Plato, tutor to Alexander the Great, founder of the Peripatetic School at Athens and of formal logic, whose works profoundly influenced the philosophy and theology of the medieval schoolmen as well as many Islamic philosophers.

Augustine, St. (A.D. 354–430). Convert to and celebrated father of the Latin church, "Doctor of Grace," teacher of rhetoric whose thinking was influenced by Plato, bishop of Hippo, and strong opponent of Manicheism, Pelagianism, and Donatism. His writings exercised an enormous influence on medieval theology. Aquinas mentions him frequently, but on many major questions (e.g., the source of human knowledge) disagrees with him.

Averroes (Ibn-Rushd, A.D. 1126–1198). Islamic philosopher who strove to integrate Islamic religious tradition and Greek philosophical thought, principally Aristotle's. St. Thomas regarded his commentaries so highly that he designated Averroes "the Commentator."

Avicenna (Ibn-Sina, A.D. 980–1037). Islamic medical doctor, theologian, and philosopher. His writings had a powerful influence on many medieval philosophers and theologians. His thought is strongly Aristotelian, but also, in parts, Neoplatonic.

Basil, St. (c. A.D. 330–379). One of the three Cappadocian Fathers, brother of St. Gregory of Nyssa, bishop of Caesarea, and defender of othodoxy against the Arian emperor Valens. He did much to influence the course of Eastern monasticism.

Bede, St. (A.D. c. 673–735). Doctor of the church, monk, historian, biblical scholar, and teacher whose writings on ecclesiastical history earned him the title "Venerable."

Bernard, St. (A.D. 1090–1153). Abbot of Clairvaux, very influential in ecclesiastical and political affairs, preacher for the Second Crusade, and especially known for a series of sermons on the Song of Songs.

Boethius (A.D. c. 480–c. 524). Philosopher and statesman who was finally imprisoned and executed. He was very influential as a logician. His most famous work, *De consolatione philosophiae*, deals with the themes of providence, evil, and freedom. His writings were an important source for knowledge of Aristotle in the Middle Ages.

Book on Causes. Treatise compiled in Arabic c. A.D. 850, consisting mainly of Proclus's "Elements of Theology" but misidentified in the twelfth century by its Latin translator who thought it a work of Aristotle, to whom therefore many Neoplatonist doctrines were attributed, an error finally detected, by Thomas Aquinas among others, through William of Moerbeke's translation.

Cassian, John (c. A.D. 360–435). Saint of the Eastern church, monk, apparent founder of semi-pelagianism. He is best known for his *Institutes* and *Conferences*, both of which deal with the nature of the monastic life and the notion of monastic perfection.

Chalcidius (A.D. 4th century). Neoplatonist philosopher from whose work on the *Timaeus* medieval writers up to the twelfth century derived knowledge of Plato's philosophy.

Chrysostom. *See* John Chrysostom.

Cicero (106–43 B.C.). Orator, politician, rhetorician, and philosopher of the late Roman Republic who created a Latin philosophical vocabulary and popularized Greek philosophical thought, thus contributing to its interest for thinkers into the Middle Ages.

Clement (Pseudo). Author of many writings falsely attribted to Pope St. Clement I.

Damascene. See John Damascene.

Decretals. Papal letters responding to questions and functioning as laws within the jurisdiction of the pope.

Decretum. A comprehensive and organized compilation of papal decrees, conciliar canons, and decisions by church fathers. Gratian produced it c. A.D. 1140.

Dionysius the Areopagite. Anonymous author of a body of theological writings probably produced c. A.D. 500 in Syria and representing an attempt to synthesize Christian doctrine and Neoplatonic thought. Long erroneously believed to be the disciple of St. Paul mentioned in chapter 17 of the Acts of the Apostles, his work enjoyed a powerful influence on medieval theology. He is much quoted by Thomas Aquinas.

Gennadius (late 5th century A.D.). Semi-Pelagian priest known for his continutation of St. Jerome's catalog "On Famous Men."

Glosses, ordinary and interlinear. Standard medieval commentary on the Bible, composed (early 12th century A.D.) of extracts from the church fathers and in form consisting of both marginal and interlinear glosses.

Gregory I, Pope St. (A.D. c. 540–604). Doctor of the church, Benedictine monk, pope from 590, responsible for establishing the temporal power of the papacy and for the conversion of England. His writings, especially his *Liber Regulae Pastoralis* and his exposition of the book of Job (*Expositio in Librum Job, sive Moralium Libri XXXV*) frequently have a pastoral nature and were influential as sources for moral theology. This accounts for the attention paid to him in Aquinas's *De malo*.

Gregory of Nyssa, St. (A.D. c. 330–c. 395). Theologian, one of the three Cappadocian fathers, brother of St. Basil, bishop of Nyssa, and strong supporter of the Nicene dogma of the Trinity.

Hilary of Poitiers, St. (A.D. c. 315–367). Doctor of the church, bishop of Poitiers, theologian known as the "Athanasius of the West," a convert from Neoplatonism, and defender of orthodoxy against the Arians.

Horace (65–8 B.C.). Latin poet and member of the renowned circle of Augustan poets at Rome.

Hugo of St.-Victor (d. A.D. 1142). Victorine theologian whose biblical commentaries were notable for their new emphasis on the study of Scripture from an historical as well as a literal perspective.

Isidore, St. (A.D. c. 560–636). Doctor of the church, archbishop of Seville, defender of Spain against barbarism and of the church against Arianism, whose encyclopedic writings were later mined by medieval scholars.

Jerome, St. (A.D. c. 342–420). Doctor of the church and propagator of the monastic ideal, fierce opponent of Arianism, Pelagianism, and Origenism, and best known for his Latin translation of the Bible.

John Chrysostom, St. (A.D. c. 347–407). Doctor of the church, Byzantine theologian, bishop of Constantinople, and liturgical reformer who championed literal interpretation of Scripture against allegorical exegesis.

John Damascene, St. (A.D. c. 675–c. 749). Greek theologian and doctor of the church whose writings cover the full range of Christian doctrine and greatly influenced later theologians.

John Scotus Eriugena (9th century A.D.). Irish teacher, theologian, philosopher, and poet who translated the works of Dionysius the Areopagite into Latin. His work, like that of Dionysius, lays special emphasis on the unknowability of God and is therefore a major contribution to apophatic theology (theology stressing the transcendence of God and the limits of the human mind when it comes to understanding the divine nature).

Nemesius (fl. A.D. c. 390). Bishop of Emesa, Christian philosopher who attempted to construct a doctrine of the soul compatible with Platonic thought and who influenced John Damascene, Albert the Great, and Thomas Aquinas (who knew his works mistakenly under the name of John Chrysostom).

Origen (A.D. c. 185–c. 254). Alexandrian theologian, biblical critic, exegete, and founder of a famous school of biblical interpretation in Caesarea, certain aspects of whose doctrine of God were systematized as a line of thought called Origenism, and some of whose works were later condemned as heretical.

Peraldus. See William Peraldus.

Peter Lombard (A.D. c. 1100–1160). Theologian, bishop of Paris, whose *Sentences* was the standard textbook of Catholic theology until superceded by the *Summa theologiae* of Thomas Aquinas.

Porphyry (A.D. 233–c. 301). Greek philosopher, pupil of Plotinus, and important expositor of Neoplatonism.

Prosper of Aquitain, St. (A.D. c. 390–c. 463). Theologian who championed Augustinian doctrines during the semi-Pelagian controversy and whose "Chronicle" is a valuable source for the history of dogma.

Sallust (c. 86–35 B.C.). A Roman historian and literary stylist. He wrote *The Catilinarian War*.

Scotus Eriugena. See John Scotus Eriugena.

Seneca (c. 4 B.C.–A.D. 65). Roman Stoic philosopher and teacher of the emperor Nero, during whose reign he committed suicide.

Simplicius (6th century A.D.). Commentator on Aristotle, whose commentaries include fragments of pre-Socratic philosophers.

Terence (d. 159 B.C.). Roman comedian whose plays closely follow those of the Greek comedian Menander.

Themistius (4th century A.D.). Philosopher and prominent senator at Constantinople, commentator on Aristotle, and writer of orations.

Valerius Maximus (1st century A.D.). Roman historian during the reign of Tiberius whose work exhibits a strong rhetorical and moral emphasis.

William Peraldus (d. c. A.D. 1270). Dominican friar who composed various manuals or textbooks on vices and virtues, mostly intended for use by Dominicans as they engaged in their pastoral work.

Comparable Passages in Other Works of Aquinas

Much that Aquinas says in the *De malo* might be usefully compared with what he says elsewhere, and so here is a list of passages in some of his writings which bear comparison with what he writes in the *De malo*. The list is confined to parallels in the following works only (all of which are available in English translations): *Compendium theologiae*, *De veritate*, *De potentia*, *Sententia libri Ethicorum*, *Summa contra gentiles*, and *Summa theologiae*.

De malo I
Article 1: *Comp* 115; *SG* III, 7; *ST* I, 48,1
Article 2: *Comp* 118; SG III, 11; *ST* I, 48,3
Article 3: *De pot* III, 6; *SG* II, 41; *SG* III, 10; *ST* I, 49,1; *ST* I–II, 75,1
Article 4: *ST* I, 48,5
Article 5: *ST* I, 48,6; *ST* I–II, 19,1

De malo II
Article 1: *ST* I–II, 71, 5–6
Article 2: *ST* I–II, 74,2; *ST* 2a2ae, 10,2
Article 3: *ST* I–II, 20,1
Article 4: *ST* I–II, 18,8–9
Article 5: *ST* I–II, 18,8–9
Article 6: *ST* I–II, 72,9
Article 7: *ST* I–II, 73,7
Article 8: *ST* I–II, 88,5
Article 9: *SG* III, 139; *ST* I–II, 73,2
Article 10: *ST* I–II, 73,4–6; *ST* II–II, 20,3
Article 11: *SG* III, 12; *ST* I, 48,4; *ST* I–II, 85,1
Article 12: *SG* III, 12; *ST* I, 84,4; *ST* I–II, 85,2

De malo III
Article 1: *SG* III, 162; *ST* I, 48,6; *ST* I, 49,2; *ST* I–II, 79,1

Article 2: *ST* I–II, 79,2
Article 3: *ST* I–II, 75,3; *ST* I–II, 80,1 and 3
Article 4: *ST* I–II, 75,3; *ST* I–II, 80,2
Article 5: *ST* I, 114,3; *ST* I–II, 80,4
Article 6: *In Eth* III, 3; *ST* I–II, 76,1
Article 7: *ST* I–II, 74,5; *ST* I–II, 76,2
Article 8: *In Ethic* III, 13; *ST* I–II, 19,6; *ST* I–II, 73,6; *ST* I–II, 76,3–4
Article 9: *In Eth* III, 3; *ST* I–II, 77,2–3
Article 10: *In Eth* V, 13; *ST* I–II, 77,7–8
Article 11: *In Eth* V, 3; *ST* I–II, 73,6; *ST* I–II, 77,6
Article 12: *ST* I–II, 78,1
Article 13: *In Eth* VII, 8; *ST* I–II, 78,4
Article 14: *ST* II–II, 14,1
Article 15: *ST* II–II, 14,3

De malo IV
Article 1: *Comp* 196; *SG* IV, 50–52; *ST* I–II, 81,1
Article 2: *ST* I–II, 82,2–3
Article 3: *ST* I–II, 83,1
Article 4: *De ver* XXV, 6; *ST* I–II, 83,2
Article 5: *De ver* XXV, 6; *ST* I–II, 83,3–4
Article 6: *ST* I–II, 81,3
Article 7: *ST* I–II, 81,4
Article 8: *Comp* 197; *SG* IV, 52; *ST* I–II, 81,2

De malo V
Article 4: *SG* IV, 52; *ST* I–II, 85,1; *ST* II–II, 164,1
Article 5: *ST* I–II, 85,6

De malo VI
De ver XXIV, 1; *ST* I, 83,1; *ST* I–II, 13,6

De malo VII
Article 1: *ST* I–II, 72,5; *ST* I–II, 88,1
Article 2: *ST* II–II, 24,10
Article 3: *ST* I–II, 88,4
Article 4: *ST* I–II, 88,5
Article 5: *De ver* XV, 5; *ST* I–II, 74,9–10
Article 6: *De ver* XXV, 5; *ST* I–II, 74,3–4
Article 7: *ST* I–II, 89,3
Article 8: *ST* I–II, 89,5
Article 9: *ST* I–II, 89,4
Article 10: *ST* I–II, 89,6
Article 12: *ST* III, 87,3

De malo VIII
Article 1: *ST* II–II, 84,3–4
Article 2: *ST* I–II, 84,2; *ST* 2a2ae, 162,2
Article 3: *ST* II–II, 162,3
Article 4: *ST* II–II, 162,4

De malo IX
Article 1: *ST* II–II, 132,1
Article 2: *ST* II–II, 132,3
Article 3: *ST* II–II, 21,4; *ST* II–II, 37,2; *ST* II–II, 132,5

De malo X
Article 1: *ST* II–II, 36,2
Article 2: *ST* II–II, 36,3
Article 3: *ST* II–II, 36,4

De malo XI
Article 1: *ST* II–II, 35,1
Article 2: *ST* II–II, 35,2
Article 3: *ST* II–II, 35,3

Article 4: *ST* II–II, 35,4

De malo XII
Article 1: *ST* II–II, 158,1
Article 2: *ST* II–II, 158,2
Article 3: *ST* II–II, 158,3
Article 4: *ST* I–II, 46,6; *ST* II–II, 158,4
Article 5: *ST* I–II, 84,4; *ST* II–II, 158,6

De malo XIII
Article 1: *ST* II–II, 118,2
Article 2: *ST* II–II, 118,4
Article 3: *ST* II–II, 118,7–8
Article 4: *ST* II–II, 78,1

De malo XIV
Article 1: *ST* II–II, 148,1
Article 2: *ST* II–II, 148,2
Article 3: *ST* II–II, 148,4
Article 4: *ST* II–II, 148,5

De malo XV
Article 1: *ST* II–II, 153,2–3
Article 2: *ST* II–II, 154,2–4
Article 3: *ST* II–II, 154,1 and 6–9
Article 4: *ST* I–II, 84,4; *ST* II–II, 153,4

De malo XVI
Article 1: *SG* II, 91; *De pot* VI, 6
Article 2: *SG* III, 107; *ST* I, 63,1–4
Article 3: *SG* III, 109; *ST* I, 63,3; *ST* II–II, 163,2
Article 4: *ST* I, 63,5
Article 5: *De ver* XXIV, 10; *ST* I, 64,2
Article 6: *SG* III, 108; *ST* I, 58,5
Article 7: *De ver* VIII, 12; *SG* III, 154; *ST* I, 57,3
Article 8: *De ver* VIII, 13; *ST* I, 57,4
Article 9: *De pot* VI, 3; *SG* III, 103; *ST* I, 110,2
Article 10: *De pot* VI, 3; *ST* I, 110,3
Article 11: *ST* Ia, 111,3–4
Article 12: *De ver* XI, 3; *SG* III, 81

Non-Biblical Texts Cited

Alan of Lille [Alanus de Insulis]
Rules on Sacred Theology [Regulae de sacra theologia]

Alexander of Hales [Alexander de Hales]
Glossa on the Sentences
Summa of Theology

Ambrose [Ambrosius]
Commentary on Luke [Super Lucam]
Exposition on Ps. 119 [Expositio in Ps. 118]*
On the Good of Death [De bono mortis]
On Noah and the Ark [De Noe et arca]
On Paradise [De paradiso]
Second Apology of David [Aplogia David altera]

Anselm [Anselmus]
On the Fall of the Devil [De casu diaboli]
On Free Choice [De libero arbitrio]
On the Harmony of Foreknowledge and Predestination [De concordia praescientiae et praedestinationis]
On Truth [De veritate]
On the Virgin Conception [De conceptu virginali]
Why God Became Man [Cur Deus homo]

Apuleius
On the God of Socrates [De Deo Socratis]

Aristotle [Aristoteles]
Categories [Praedicamenta]
Ethics [Ethica Nicomachea]
Eudemian Ethics [Ethica Eudemia]
Metaphysics [Metaphysica]
On Divination by Dreams [De divinatione per somnium]
On Dreams [De insomniis]
On Generation and Corruption [De generatione et corruptione]
On the Generation of Animals [De generatione animalium]
On Heaven and Earth [De caelo et mundo]
On Interpretation [Perihermeneias]
On Sleep and Wakefulness [De somno et vigilia]
On the Soul [De anima]
Physics [Physica]
Politics [Politica]
Posterior Analytics [Analytica posteriora]
Rhetoric [Rhetorica]
Topics [Topica]

Augustine [Augustinus]
Against Faustus [Contra Faustum]
Against Julian [Contra Iulianum]
Against the Letter of the Foundation [Contra Epistolam Fundamenti]
Against Lying [Contra mendacium]
Against Maximinus [Contra Maximinum]
Book of the 83 Questions [Liber 83 quaestionum]
City of God [De civitate Dei]
Confessions [Liber confessionum]
Enchiridion
Expositions on the Psalms [Enarrationes in Psalmos]

* The Latin text follows the Vulgate numbering of the Psalms.

527

Augustine [Augustinus] (*continued*)

Letters [*Epistolae*]

Literal Commentary on Genesis [*De Genesi ad litteram*]

On Christian Doctrine [*De doctrina christiana*]

On Church Customs [*De moribus ecclesiae*]

On the Divination of Devils [*De divinatione daemonum*]

On Faith and Works [*De fide et operibus*]

On Free Choice [*De libero arbitrio*]

On Genesis against the Manicheans [*De Genesi contra Manicheos*]

On the Gospel of John [*In Iohannis Evangelium*]

On Grace and Free Will [*De gratia et libero arbitrio*]

On Holy Virginity [*De sancta virginitate*]

On the Immortality of the Soul [*De immortalitate animae*]

On the Lord's Sermon on the Mount [*De sermone Domini in monte*]

On Lying [*De mendacio*]

On Marital Good [*De bono coniugali*]

On Marriage and Concupiscence [*De nuptiis et concupiscentia*]

On Music [*De musica*]

On Nature and Grace [*De natura et gratia*]

On the Nature of the Good [*De natura boni*]

On the Perfection of Human Justice [*De perfectione iustitiae hominis*]

On Predestination of the Saints [*De praedestinatione sanctorum*]

On the Punishment and Forgiveness of Sins and on the Baptism of Infants [*De peccatorum meritis et remissione et de baptismo parvulorum*]

On the Teacher [*De magistro*]

On the Trinity [*De Trinitate*]

On True Religion [*De vera religione*]

On Two Souls [*De duabus animabus*]

On the Words of the Lord [*De verbis Dominis = sermo 71*]

Retractions [*Retractationes*]

Rule for the Servants of God [*Regula ad servos Dei*]

Sermon on Works of Mercy [*De operibus misericordiae*]

Sermons [*Sermones*]

Soliloquies [*Soliloquia*]

Augustine (Pseudo) [Augustinus (Pseudo)]

Against Five Heresies [*Adversus quinque haereses*]

Book of the 21 Sentences [*Liber 21 sententiarum*]

Hypognosticon

On Spirit and Soul [*De spiritu et anima*]

On True and False Repentence [*De vera et falsa paenitentia*]

Averroes

On Aristotle's Metaphysics [*In Libros Metaphysicorum*]

On Aristotle's On Heaven and Earth [*In De caelo et mundo*]

On Aristotle's On the Soul [*In De anima*]

Avicenna

Metaphysics [*Metaphysica*]

On the Soul [*De anima*]

Basil [Basilius]

Homily on Luke 12:18 [*Hom. in Lucam 12:18*]

Bede [Beda]

Commentary on Acts [*Super Acta*]

Bernard [Bernardus]

On the Degrees of Humility [*De gradibus humilitatis*]

On Grace and Free Choice [*De gratia et libero arbitrio*]

On Precept and Dispensation [*De praecepto et dispenspensatione*]

On the Purification of St. Mary [*In purificatione Sanctae Mariae*]

On Reflection [*De consideratione*]

Sermons on the Liturgical Seasons, sermon 3 on Eastertide [*Sermones de tempore, sermo 3 in tempore resurrectionis*]

Sermons on the Song of Songs [*Sermones in Cantica*]

Boethius

On Consolation [*De consolatione*]

On the Trinity [*De Trinitate*]

Book on Causes [Liber de causis]

Cassian [Cassianus]
Collations [Collationes]
On the Rule of the Cenobites [De institutione
    coenobiorum]

Chalcidius [Calcidius]
Commentary on the Timaeus [Commentarius in
    Timaeum]

Chrysostom
See John Chrysostom

Cicero
On Invention [De inventione]
Tusculan Disputations [Tusculanae
    disputationes]

Clement (Pseudo) [Clemens
    (Pseudo)]
Letter I to James [Epistola I ad Jacobum]

Damascene
See John Damascene

Decretum

Decretals [Decretales]

Dionysius (the Areopagite)
    [Dionysius Pseudo-Areopagita]
On the Celestial Hierarchy [De caelesti
    hierarchia]
On the Divine Names [De divinis nominibus]
On Ecclesiastical Hierarchy [De ecclesiastica
    hierarchia]

Fulgentius
On Faith, to Peter [De fide ad Petrum]
To Monimus [Ad Monimum]

Gennadius
On Church Dogmas [De ecclesiasticis
    dogmatibus]

Glosses
See Lombard

Gloss [interlinear]
See Interlinear Gloss

Gloss [ordinary]
See Ordinary Gloss

Gregory [Gregorius]
Book of the Pastoral Rules [Regulae pastoralis liber]
Commentary on Ezechiel [Super Ezechielem]
Dialogues [Dialogi]
Morals [Moralia]
On the Gospels [In Evangelia]

Gregory of Nyssa [Gregorius Nyssenus]
On Ecclesiastes [In Ecclesiasten]

Horace [Oratius]
Epistles [Epistolae]

Hugo of St.-Victor [Hugo a Sancto
    Victore]
On the Sacraments [De sacramentis]
On the Five Sevens [De quinque septenis]

Interlinear Gloss [Glossa interlinearis]

Isidore [Isidorus]
Etymologies [Etymologiae]
On the Supreme Good [De summo bono]

Isidore (Pseudo) [Isidorus (Pseudo)]
On the Order of Created Beings [De ordine
    creaturarum]

Jerome [Hieronymus]
Against Jovinian [Adversus Iovinianum]
Book of Hebraic Questions on Genesis [Liber
    Hebraearum Questionum in Genesim]
Commentary on Ecclesiastes [Commentarius in
    Ecclesiasten]
Letters [Epistolae]
On Habakkuk [In Habacuc]
On Matthew [In Matthaeum]

John Chrysostom [Iohannes
    Chrysostomus]
On Matthew [In Matthaeum]

John Chrysostom (Pseudo) [Iohannes
    Chrysostomus (Pseudo)]
Unfinished Work on Matthew [Opus
    imperfectum in Matthaeum]

John Damascene [Iohannes
    Damascenus]
On Orthodox Faith [De fide orthodoxa]

Livy [Livius]
*From the Founding of the City [Ab Urbe
    condita]*

Lombard [Lombardus]
Glosses
Sentences

Nemesius
On Human Nature [De natura hominis]

Ordinary Gloss [Glossa ordinaria]

Origen [Origenes]
On First Principles [Peri Archon]

Peraldus
*Summa on Vices and Virtues [Summa de vitiis
    et virtutibus]*

Peter Lombard, see Lombard
Glosses [Glossae]
Sentences [Sententiae]

Porphyry [Porphyrius]
*Introduction [Isagoge]: 'On Accidents' [De
    accidenti]*

Prosper of Aquitaine [Prosper
    Aquitanus]
*Sentences Extracted from Augustine [Sententiae
    ex Augustino delibatae]*

Prosper (Pseudo)
*On the Contemplative Life [De vita
    contemplativa]*

Sallust [Sallustius]
Catilinarian War [Bellum Catilinae]

Scotus Eriugena
*Homily on the Prologue of St. John [Homilia in
    prologium Sancti Johannis]*

Seneca
Moral Letters
*On Remedies for Chance Events [De remediis
    fortuitorum]*

Simplicius
*On the Categories of Aristotle [In
    Praedicamenta Aristotelis]*

Terence [Terentius]
The Eunuch [Eunuchus]

Themistius
*Commentary on the De anima [Commentarium
    In De anima]*

Titus Livy
See Livy

Valerius Maximus
*Extraordinary Deeds and Sayings [Facta et dicta
    mirabilia]*

William Peraldus

Select Bibliography

Bibliographical Works

Bourke, Vernon J. "Thomistic Bibliography: 1920–1940." *The Modern Schoolman* (1921).

Bulletin Thomiste (1940–1965), continued in *Rassegna di Letteratura Tomistica* (1966–).

Ingardia, Richard, ed., *Thomas Aquinas: International Bibliography 1977–1990*. Bowling Green, Ohio, 1993.

Mandonnet, P. and J. Destrez. *Bibliographie Thomiste*. 2nd ed. revised by M.-D. Chenu. Paris, 1960.

Miethe, Terry L., and Vernon J. Bourke. *Thomistic Bibliography, 1940–1978*. Westport, Conn. and London, 1980.

Biographical Works

Ferrua, A., ed. *Thomae Aquinatis vitae fontes praecipuae*. Alba, 1968.

Foster, Kenelm, ed. *The Life of Thomas Aquinas*. London and Baltimore, 1959.

Prümmer, D. and M. H. Laurent, eds. *Fontes Vitae Sancti Thomae Aquinatis*, *Revue Thomiste* (1911–1937).

Torrell, Jean-Pierre. *Saint Thomas Aquinas: The Person and His Work*. Washington, D.C., 1996.

Tugwell, Simon, ed. *Albert and Thomas—Selected Writings*. New York, Mahwah and London, 1988.

Weisheipl, James A., O.P. *Friar Thomas D'Aquino*. Oxford, 1974. Reprint, with corrigenda and addenda, Washington, D.C., 1983.

English Translations of Works by Aquinas Relevant to Reading the *De malo*

Aristotle on Interpretation: Commentary by St. Thomas and Cajetan. Translated by J. Oesterle. Milwaukee, 1962.

A Commentary on Aristotle's De Anima. Translated by Robert Pasnau. New Haven, Conn. and London, 1999.

Commentary on the Metaphysics *of Aristotle*. Translated by John P. Rowan. Chicago, 1964.

Commentary on the Nichomachean Ethics. Translated by C. I. Litzinger. Chicago, 1964.

Disputed Questions on Virtue. Translated by Ralph McInerny. South Bend, Ind., 1999.

Gilby, Thomas, ed. *Summa theologiae*. 61 vols. London and New York, 1964–1981.

The Literal Exposition on Job. Translated by Anthony Damico, with interpretative essay and notes by Martin D. Yaffe. Atlanta, 1989.

On the Power of God. Translated by L. Shapcote. London, 1952.

Questions on the Soul. Translated with an introduction by James H. Robb. Milwaukee, 1984.

St. Thomas Aquinas On Evil. Translated by Jean Oesterle. Notre Dame, Ind., 1995.

Summa contra gentiles. Translated with introduction and notes by Anton C. Pegis et al. New York, 1955–1957.

Summa theologiae. Translated by the Fathers of the English Dominican Province. New York, 1947–1948.

Truth. Translated by R. W. Mulligan, J. V. McGlynn, and R. W. Schmidt. Chicago, 1952–1954.

Some Helpful Selections from Aquinas in English

Baldner, Steven E., and William E. Carroll, eds. *Aquinas on Creation*. Toronto, 1997.

Baumgarth, William P., and Richard J. Regan SJ, eds. *Saint Thomas Aquinas on Law, Morality and Politics*. Indianapolis, 1988.

Bourke, Vernon J., ed. *The Pocket Aquinas*. New York, 1960.

Brown, Stephen F., ed. *Thomas Aquinas: On Faith and Reason*. Indianapolis, 1999.

Hibbs, Thomas S., ed. *Thomas Aquinas: On Human Understanding*. Indianapolis, 1999.

Martin, Christopher, ed. *The Philosophy of Thomas Aquinas*. London, 1988.

McDermott, Timothy, ed. *Thomas Aquinas: Selected Philosophical Writings*. Oxford and New York, 1993.

McInerny, Ralph, ed. *Thomas Aquinas: Selected Philosophical Writings*. Oxford and New York, 1993.

Regan, Richard J., SJ, ed. *Virtue: Way to Happiness: St. Thomas Aquinas*. Scranton, Penn., 1999.

Sigmund, Paul, ed. *Saint Thomas Aquinas on Politics and Ethics*. New York, 1988.

Other Relevant Readings

Aertsen, Jan. "The Convertibility of Being and Good in St. Thomas Aquinas." *New Scholasticism* 59 (1985).

———. *Nature and Creature: Thomas Aquinas's Way of Thought*. Leiden, 1988.

Aillet, Marc. *Lire La Bible avec S. Thomas*. Fribourg, 1993.

Anscombe, G. E. M. *Intention*. Oxford, 1979.

———. "Modern Moral Philosophy." *Philosophy* 33 (1958).

Anscombe, G. E. M., and P. T. Geach. *Three Philosophers*. Oxford, 1961.

Barry, Robert J. *From Metaphysical to Moral Evil: Thomas Aquinas' Theory of Evil and sin in the Disputed Questions De Malo, Questions One to Three*. Ph.D. dissertation, Boston College. Ann Arbor, Mich.: University Microfilms, 1996.

Bazàn, Bernardo C., John W. Wippel, Gérard Fransen, and Danielle Jacquart. *Les Questions Disputées et les Questions Quodlibétiques dans les Facultés de Théologie, de Droit et de Médecine*. Turnhout, 1985.

Blocher, Henri. *Original Sin*. Grand Rapids, Mich. and Cambridge, U.K., 1997.

Bobik, Joseph. *Aquinas on Matter and Form and the Elements*. Notre Dame, Ind., 1998.

Boland, Vivian. *Ideas in God according to Saint Thomas Aquinas*. Leiden, New York, Köln, 1996.

Boyle, Leonard E. *The Setting of the Summa Theologiae of Saint Thomas*. The Etienne Gilson Series, vol. 5, Toronto, 1982.

Bradley, Denis J. M. *Aquinas on the Twofold Human Good: Reason and Human Happiness in Aquinas's Moral Science*. Washington, D.C., 1997.

Brown, Montague. *The Romance of Reason: An Adventure in the Thought of Thomas Aquinas*. Petersham, Mass., 1991.

Burrell, David. *Aquinas, God and Action*. Notre Dame, Ind., 1979.

———. *Knowing the Unknowable God*. Notre Dame, Ind., 1986.

Chenu, M. D. *Towards Understanding Saint Thomas*. Translated by A. M. Landry and D. Hughes. Chicago, 1964.

Chesterton, G. K. *St Thomas Aquinas*. London, 1943.

Cook, Edward. *The Deficient Cause of Moral Evil*. Washington, D.C., 1996.

Copleston, F. C. *Aquinas*. Harmondsworth, 1955.

Corbin, Michel. *Le Chemin de la Théologie chez Thomas D'Aquin*. Paris, 1974.

Davies, Brian. "Classical Theism and the Doctrine of Divine Simplicity." In *Language, Meaning and God*, edited by Brian Davies. London, 1987.

———. *The Thought of Thomas Aquinas*. Oxford, 1992.

———. "Aquinas, God and Being." *The Monist* 80 (1997).

———. "Thomas Aquinas." In *Medieval Philosophy*, edited by John Marenbon. Vol. 3 of the *Routledge History of Philosophy*. London and New York, 1998.

———. "Aquinas on What God is Not." *Revue Internationale de Philosophie* 52 (1998).

DeGandolfi, Maria. "Libertad Necesidad en la *Quaestio Disputata De Malo VI*." *Sapientia* 39 (1984).

De malo: Questions Disputés sur Le Mal. Translated into French by the monks of the Abbey of Fontgombault. Collection Docteur Angélique VIII. Paris, 1992.

Donagan, Alan. *Human Ends and Human Actions: An Exploration in St. Thomas' Treatment*. Milwaukee, 1985.

Dondaine, A. *Secrétaires de saint Thomas*. Rome, 1956.

Dubarle, Andre-Marie. *The Biblical Doctrine of Original Sin*. New York, 1964.

Dubarle, Dominique. *L'Ontologie de Thomas D'Aquin*. Paris, 1996.

Elders Leo J., S.V.D. *The Philosophical Theology of St. Thomas Aquinas*. Leiden, 1990.

Eschmann, Ignatius. *The Ethics of Thomas Aquinas*. Toronto, 1997.

Evans, G. R. *Augustine on Evil*. Cambridge, 1982.

Finnis, John. *Aquinas*. Oxford, 1998.

Foster, Kenelm, OP. Appendices 1 and 2 of vol. 9 of the Blackfriars edition of the *Summa theologiae* (*Angels*).

Gauthier, R. A. *Introduction to Saint Thomas d'Aquin, Somme Contre Les Gentils*. Paris, 1993.

Geach, P. T. *God and the Soul*. Oxford, 1969.

———. *The Virtues*. Cambridge, 1977.

Gilson, Etienne. *The Christian Philosophy of St Thomas Aquinas*. London, 1957.

Glorieux, P. "L'enseignment au Moyan Age. Tèchniques et Méthodes en Usage à la Faculté de Théologie de Paris au XIIe Siècle." *Archives d'Histoire Doctrinale et Littéraire du Moyen Age* 35 (1968).

———. "Les Questions Disputés de Saint Thomas et leur Suite Chronologique." *Récherches de Théologie Ancienne et Médiévale* 4 (1932).

Grabmann, M. *Die Geschichte der Scholastichen Methode*. 2 vols. Fribourg, 1909–1911.

Goris, Harm J. M. J. *Free Creatures of an Eternal God: Thomas Aquinas on God's Infallible Foreknowledge and Irresistible Will*. Leuven, 1996.

Jenkins, John. *Knowledge and Faith in Thomas Aquinas*. Cambridge, 1997.

Jordan, Mark. "The Alleged Aristotelianism of Thomas Aquinas." Toronto, 1992.

Keenan, James F. *Goodness and Rightness in Thomas Aquinas's* Summa Theologiae. Washington, D.C., 1992.

Kenny, Anthony. *Aquinas*. Oxford, 1980.

————, ed. *Aquinas: A Collection of Critical Essays*. London and Melbourne, 1969.

————. *Aquinas on Mind*. London and New York, 1993.

Kors, J. B. *La Justice Primitive et le Peché Original*. Paris, 1922.

Kretzmann, Norman. "Goodness, Knowledge, and Indeterminacy in the Philosophy of St. Thomas Aquinas." *Journal of Philosophy* 80 (1983).

————. *The Metaphysics of Creation: Aquinas's Natural Theology in* Summa Contra Gentiles *II*. Oxford, 1999.

————. *The Metaphysics of Theism: Aquinas's Natural Theology in* Summa Contra Gentiles *I*. Oxford, 1997.

Kretzmann, Norman, and Eleonore Stump, eds. *The Cambridge Companion to Aquinas*. Cambridge, 1993.

Lawn, Brian. *The Rise and Decline of the Scholastic "Quaestio Disputata."* Leiden, 1993.

Le Brun-Gouanvic, Claire. *Ystoria sancti Thorne de Aquino de Guillaume de Tocco (1323)*. Toronto, 1996.

Lottin, O. "Liberté humaine et motion divine." *Recherches de théologie ancienne et médievale* 7 (1935).

————. "Le Libre Arbitre chez saint Thomas." *Revue Thomiste* 12 (1929).

————. "La Preuve de la liberté humaine chez saint Thomas d'Aquin." *Recherches de théologie ancienne et médievale* 23 (1956).

————. *Psychologie et Morale aux XIIe-XIIIe Siècles*. 6 vols. Louvain-Gembloux, 1942–60.

MacDonald, Scott. "Aquinas's libertarian account of free choice." *Revue Internationale de Philosophie* 52 (1998).

MacIntyre, Alasdair. *After Virtue*. Notre Dame, Ind., 1985.

Mandonnet, P. *S. Thomae Aquinatis Quaestiones Disputatae*. Paris, 1925.

Manteau-Bonamy, H. M. *La liberté de l'homme selon Thomas d'Aquin: la datation de la Q. Disp. De Malo*. Paris, 1979.

Maritain, Jacques. *Aquinas on Evil*. Milwaukee, 1942.

Martin, C. F. J. *Thomas Aquinas: God and Explanations*. Edinburgh, 1997.

Maurer, Armand. *Being and Knowing: Studies in Thomas Aquinas and Later Medieval Philosophers*. Toronto, 1990.

McCabe, Herbert, O.P. "Aquinas on Good Sense." *New Blackfriars* 67 (1986).

————. *God Matters*. London, 1987.

McDermott Timothy, ed. *St. Thomas Aquinas, Summa Theologiae: A Concise Translation*. London, 1989.

McGinn, Bernard. "The Development of the Thought of Thomas Aquinas on the Reconciliation of Divine Providence and Contingent Action." *The Thomist* 39 (1975).

McInerny, Ralph. *Ethica Thomistica: The Moral Philosophy of Thomas Aquinas*. Washington, D.C., 1982.

————. *A First Glance at St. Thomas Aquinas: A Handbook for Peeping Thomists*. Notre Dame, Ind. and London, 1990.

————. *St. Thomas Aquinas*. Notre Dame, Ind. and London, 1982.

Montano, Edward J. *The Sin of the Angels: Some Aspects of the Teaching of St. Thomas*. Washington, DC., 1955.

Nolan, Michael. "Aquinas and the Act of Love." *New Blackfriars* 77 (1996).

Noonan, John. *The Scholastic Analysis of Usury*. Cambridge, Massachusetts, 1957.

O'Rourke, Fran. *Pseudo-Dionysius and the Metaphysics of Aquinas*. Leiden, N.Y., Köln, 1992.

Patterson, R. L. *The Conception of God in the Philosophy of Aquinas*. London, 1933.

Person, Per Erik. *Sacra Doctrina: Reason and Revelation in Aquinas*. Oxford, 1970.

Potts, Timothy C. *Conscience in Medieval Philosophy*. Cambridge, 1980.

Rouse, Richard H., and Mary A. Rouse. "The Book Trade at the University of Paris, ca. 1250–ca.1350." In *La Production du Livre Universitaire au Moyen Age*, edited by Louis J. Bataillon, Bertrand G. Guyot, and Richard H. Rouse. Paris, 1988.

Schoot, Henk J. N., ed. *Tibi Soli Peccavi: Thomas Aquinas on Guilt and Forgiveness*. Leuven, 1996.

Stump, Eleonore. "Aquinas's Account of Freedom: Intellect and Will." *The Monist* 80 (1997).

Theron, Stephen. "Esse." *The New Scholasticism* 53 (1979).

———. "Intentionality, Immateriality and Understanding in Aquinas." *The Heythrop Journal* 30 (1989).

Torrell, Jean-Pierre. *Saint Thomas d'Aquin, maître spirituel*. Paris, 1996.

———. *La "Somme" de Saint Thomas*. Paris, 1998.

Vandervelde, G. *Original Sin: Two Major Trends in Contemporary Roman Catholic Reinterpretation*. Amsterdam, 1975.

Velde, Rudi A. te. *Participation and Substantiality in Thomas Aquinas*. Leiden, N.Y., Köln, 1995.

Wadell, Paul J. *The Primacy of Love: An Introduction to the Ethics of Thomas Aquinas*. New York, 1992.

Wawrykow, Joseph P. *God's Grace and Human Action: Merit in the Theology of Thomas Aquinas*. London, 1995.

Weijers, Olga. *La "disputatio" à la Faculté des arts de Paris (1200–1350) Studia Artistarum: Etudes sur la faculténdes arts dans les universités médiévales*. 2. Turnhout, 1995.

Wenzel, S. *The Sin of Sloth: Acedia in Medieval Thought and Literature*. Chapel Hill, 1967.

Westberg, Daniel. *Right Practical Reason: Aristotle, Action, and Prudence in Aquinas*. Oxford, 1994.

White, Victor, O.P. *God the Unknown*. London, 1956.

Wippel, John F. *Metaphysical Themes in Thomas Aquinas*. Washington, D.C., 1984.

———. *The Metaphysical Thought of Thomas Aquinas*. Washington, D.C., 2000.

Index

This Index includes only proper nouns in the answers.